Michael C. Fale

1984

University of St. Francis
GEN 782 M522
Melitz
The opera goers' complete guid   2

3 0301 00024451 3

W9-DAQ-126

Birthday Greeting
from a friend
March 9, 1939
Eleanor

THE OPERA GOERS' COMPLETE GUIDE

THE OPERA GOERS' COMPLETE GUIDE

THE OPERA GOERS' COMPLETE GUIDE

The Opera Goer's
COMPLETE GUIDE

COMPRISING TWO HUNDRED AND SIXTY-EIGHT OPERA
PLOTS WITH MUSICAL NUMBERS AND CASTS

BY

LEO MELITZ

*Director of the Stadt Theatre
at Basel*

TRANSLATED BY RICHARD SALINGER

*Revised and brought up to date after consultation with the
Librarian of the Metropolitan Opera Company*

By LOUISE WALLACE HACKNEY

GARDEN CITY PUBLISHING COMPANY, INC.

Garden City   New York

LIBRARY
College of St. Francis
JOLIET, ILL.

Copyright, 1908, 1911
By DODD, MEAD & COMPANY

Copyright, 1921
By DODD, MEAD & COMPANY, Inc.

Printed in U. S. A.

782
m522
c.2

PUBLISHER'S NOTE

THIS translation of Leo Melitz's well-known work attempts to give to the opera-going public in a short and
convenient form the plots of the more important operas,
with their casts and principal musical numbers. It is not
intended as a serious literary production, but furnishes
in the fewest possible words a comprehension of the opera
texts for quick reference. The work has been adapted
for use in America by the elimination of a few operas
seldom performed here, and the addition of a number of
modern operas in which the American public have perhaps
a greater contemporary interest.

In a supplement to this edition the plots have been
added of a number of operas which are new or have been
newly produced.

109,791

CONTENTS

NOTE.—In this work the operas are arranged alphabetically, according to titles; foreign titles preceded by an article appear under the initial of the article: e. g., *Der Freischultz*, under *D*, *La Gioconda*, under *L*.

vii

CONTENTS

CONTENTS

CONTENTS xi

CONTENTS

CONTENTS

  Merlin   PAGE 264

SAINT SAËNS
  Samson and Delilah   338

SCHENK
  The Village Barber   369

SCHILLINGS
  Fifer's Festival (Pfeifertag)   122
  Ingwilde   150

SMETANA
  The Bartered Bride (Die Verkaufte Braut)   31
  Dalibor   63
  The Kiss   169

SOMMER
  Rübezahl   334

SPINELLI
  A Basso Porto   1

SPOHR
  Jessonda   162

STRAUSS, JOHANN
  Die Fledermaus (The Bat)   85

STRAUSS, RICHARD
  Der Rosencavalier   398
  Elektra   401
  Feuersnoth   118
  Guntram   136
  Salome   337
  The Woman without a Shadow   570

SULLIVAN
  Ivanhoe   159

SWAREGLIA
  Cornelius Schutt   53

CONTENTS

A BASSO PORTO

Lyrical drama in three acts by Niccola Spinelli. Libretto founded upon the work of Goffredo Cognetti by Eugene Checchi.

CAST: Mother Mary—Soprano. Her children Sesella—Soprano, Luigino—Tenor. Ciccillo—Baritone. Pascale, innkeeper—Basso. Pichillo—Tenor. Time, the present. First production, Cologne, 1894.

ACT I. Acquaquilia Street "at the lower harbour." Pichillo, Pascale and Luigino are gambling with other members of the Camorra[1]. Maria attempts to free her son of his passion for gambling but fails. Ciccillo quarrels with his companions, while in another group Maria and Sesella endeavour to pacify the son and brother, who, however, retaliates by deriding his sister for her love for Ciccillo. When the others have departed, Ciccillo detains Sesella and proposes flight. Luigino, who has been listening, attempts to stab Ciccillo, but is prevented by Maria and Sesella. Ciccillo, formerly in love with Maria, determines to revenge himself against her by compelling Sesella to lead a degraded life and by making Luigino a convict. Pascale appears shouting that the Camorra has been betrayed. Ciccillo, who committed this traitorous act through love of power, stands calmly by, but is suspected by Maria.

ACT II. Interior of Pascale's inn. Pichillo and Luigino are singing with a chorus of boon companions, when Ciccillo enters the inn and strikes Luigino in the face. Swearing vengeance Luigino is thrust out by his companions while Ciccillo accuses him of treason. When alone Ciccillo deplores his past life and vows to live for vengeance alone. He again implores Sesella to flee with him, but Maria re-

[1] A secret Italian society.

veals to her his true character and discloses the fact that he is the real traitor. The Camorra meet in council, condemn Ciccillo to death and order Luigino to carry out the sentence.

ACT III.   Street as in Act I.   Maria prays that Luigino may not kill Ciccillo and thus make himself a murderer. When Ciccillo appears she counsels flight.   He, however, has again denounced his comrades to the authorities, and believing them already surrounded by the military, ignores Maria's warning.   As he attempts to call the soldiers to destroy the band, Maria draws a knife and stabs him to the heart.

THE ABDUCTION FROM THE SERAGLIO

Comic Opera in three acts by Mozart.   Libretto by Lentzner.   Adapted by Stephanie.

CAST: Selim Bassa—speaking part.   Konstanze—Soprano.   Blöndchen, her servant—Soprano.   Belmonte—Tenor.   Pedrillo, his servant—Tenor.   Osmin, overseer of the country house of the Bassa—Basso.   Place, the country house of the Bassa.   Time, the sixteenth century.   First produced at the command of Joseph II in 1782 at the National Theatre at Vienna.   This opera is the first real German opera, as former works were mostly imitations and translations of foreign productions.

ACT I.   Belmonte seeks everywhere his betrothed, Konstanze, who with her attendant Blöndchen has fallen into the hands of Selim Bassa.   (Aria: "Here shall I see you, Konstanze, you my hope.")   When Osmin Bassa's servant comes to pluck figs in the garden Belmonte retires.   (Aria: "Who a love has found.")   Belmonte returns to obtain news of his servant, Pedrillo.   (Duet: "Confounded be you and your song.")   Osmin is angry.   ("Such ragamuffins.")   Belmonte hears news of Pedrillo and resolves to abduct Konstanze.   (Aria: "Konstanze, Konstanze, to see

thee again"; chorus: "Sing to the great Bassa.") Selim
presently appears with Konstanze, for whose love he strives
in vain. (Aria of Konstanze: "O forgive! Oh, I loved—")
Upon the recommendation of Pedrillo, the Bassa engages
Belmonte as builder, but Osmin refuses him access to the
palace. (Terzett: "March! March! March!")

ACT II. Blöndchen repulses the rough lovemaking of
Osmin. (Aria: "By tenderness and flattery.") After a
duet ("I go, but counsel thee to avoid the villain Pedrillo"),
Osmin departs. Konstanze greets Blöndchen in distress
(Aria: "Sorrow is my lot"), informing her that Selim demands her love and threatens to use force. (Aria: "This
also will I bear.") When she has gone, Pedrillo comes to
Blöndchen, who is his sweetheart, and informs her that
Belmonte is near and that all is ready for flight. Blöndchen is filled with joy. (Aria: "What happiness, what
delight.") Pedrillo invites Osmin to drink, hoping that
he will become intoxicated. (Aria: "On to the combat"
and duet: "Vivat Bacchus! may Bacchus live!") He succeeds in this plan and gets Osmin out of the way so that
Belmonte again sees his beloved Konstanze. (Quartet,
Belmonte, Konstanze, Pedrillo, Blöndchen: "Oh, Belmonte,
oh my life.")

ACT III.—Belmonte and Pedrillo come to the garden
with ladders. (Aria, Belmonte: "When the tears of joy
do fall"; Romanze, Pedrillo: "Captive in the land of the
Moors.") Belmonte succeeds in abducting Konstanze, but
when Pedrillo is about to escape with Blöndchen, they are
caught by Osmin (Aria: "Ho, how I will triumph"), and
Belmonte and Konstanze are also brought back by the
guard. Selim Bassa, who recognises in Belmonte the son
of an enemy, is about to order their death. (Duet: "Oh
what a fate, oh soul's misery.") His heart, however, is
touched by their sorrow; he forgives, and all are set at
liberty. (Finale: "Never will I thy kindness forget.")

ADRIENNE LECOUVREUR

Lyrical drama in four acts. Music by Francesco Ciléa; text by Scribe and Legouvé.

CAST: Maurice, Count de Saxe—Tenor. Prince de Bouillon—Basso. Abbé de Chazeuil—Tenor. Michonnet, stage manager of the Comédie Française—Baritone. Quinault, actor—Basso. Poisson, actor—Tenor. Jouvenot, actress—Soprano. Dangeville, actress—Mezzo-soprano. Adrienne Lecouvreur, a famous actress—Soprano. Princesse de Bouillon—Mezzo-soprano. Place, Paris. Time, about 1730. First production, Milan, 1902.

ACT I. The foyer of the Comédie Française. A performance of Racine's Bajazet is to be presented, in which two famous actresses, Mlle. Duclos and Adrienne Lecouvreur, are to appear. Michonnet, the stage manager, is hurrying about trying to satisfy everybody. (Michonnet: "Michonnet here, Michonnet there.") The Prince de Bouillon, interested for the moment in La Duclos, arrives with the frivolous Abbé de Chazeuil. Amid compliments and gossip Adrienne appears in costume. She is talking with Michonnet (Adrienne: "The humble handmaid I of glorious art") when Maurice de Saxe enters. Adrienne loves him, believing that he is a poor young officer. (Maurice: "In your sweet, smiling face.") In reality he is the hero of the day in war and love. (Adrienne: "For you and you alone.") She gives him a bunch of violets and hurries away to play her part. The Princess de Bouillon also loves Maurice, and has persuaded La Duclos to make an appointment for her with him at the country villa of the actress. The wording of the note, which is intercepted by the prince, makes it appear to appoint a rendezvous for La Duclos herself with Maurice. The prince is furious. Resealing the letter, he sends it to Maurice, but plans with the abbé to take Adrienne to supper at the villa and entrap the faithless Duclos. (Duet: "What is to be done?") Four members of the company come in gossiping. (Quartet:

"How absurd! How diverting!") The prince departs hastily with the abbé. Michonnet stands in the wings watching Adrienne's performance. (Michonnet: "Good! Splendid!") Maurice sends a message to Adrienne on a scroll used in the play putting off his appointment with her. The four actors return, grumbling volubly. (Quartet: "They are mad!") Adrienne appears, half fainting. She accepts the prince's invitation. He promises her that the famous Count de Saxe will be present at the supper.

Act II. The villa, La Grange Batelière. The princess awaits Maurice in a frenzy of passion. (Princess: "O bitter joy, O torture sweet!") He enters, wearing Adrienne's violets, which provoke the princess's jealousy. Appealing to his ambition, she endeavors fruitlessly to awaken his love (Maurice: "Pity, I implore"), and departs in a jealous rage. The prince and the abbé appear in jesting mood, having observed the sudden departure of a lady. Maurice changes the subject, as Adrienne comes in, joyfully recognising in the great Count de Saxe her adored lover. They are left alone while the others arrange for supper. (Duet, Maurice, Adrienne: "Thou art my conquest, thou my crown.") Michonnet and the abbé appear with the prince's order that no one is to leave the grounds. (Abbé: "This is her bower of love's delight.") The abbé tells Adrienne she is at the villa of La Duclos, and she of course thinks Maurice's appointment was with the actress. Maurice denies it, and implores Adrienne's aid in securing the escape of the fair unknown. Adrienne enters the adjoining room and talks with the princess in the dark. Each avows her love for Maurice. (Duet: "I love him ardently.") The princess flees at the approach of her husband, whom the abbé is trying to convince that La Duclos was not the unknown lady. As they depart arguing, Michonnet enters with a bracelet dropped by a lady who had passed through the garden with Maurice. Adrienne quickly hides the bracelet as the prince enters with his guests for supper.

Act III. The salon of the princess. The abbé is arranging a reception, aided by numerous servants. The princess enters and a rather questionable flirtation ensues (Abbé: "Tell me, the god of love"), which is interrupted by the prince. The princess having asked for face powder, the abbé accidentally gives her a poison, the subtle qualities of which the prince points out. (Prince: "Glittering, light, as snowflake white.") Observing the princess' interest in the methods of using it, the prince hurriedly takes the box to his laboratory. The princess tries to discover from the abbé the name of her rival. Michonnet enters arranging with the prince for a loan to Adrienne on her celebrated diamonds. The guests, who now arrive, are all gossiping about the imprisonment of the Count de Saxe for debt. Adrienne is announced; she wears no jewels. The princess lays a trap for her by saying that Maurice has been wounded in a duel. Adrienne faints. Maurice is announced. Imperturbably he tells of his adventures in Courland. (Maurice: "The Russian, Mentschikoff.") All applaud. (Ballet: "The Judgment of Paris.") The guests are still gossiping. Adrienne shows them the bracelet, and the princess, to divert attention, asks her to recite. She gives a scene from "Phédre," in which she covertly insults the princess. Maurice remains at the palace when Adrienne leaves.

ACT IV. A room in Adrienne's house. Michonnet enters, asking for the actress. (Michonnet: "Peace, weary heart of mine.") Adrienne appears, depressed and sad. She has determined to leave the stage. Michonnet tells her that he, too, loves hopelessly, but that in art lies the remedy for sorrow. Adrienne's fellow-actors bring gifts in honour of her birthday. Michonnet gives her back her diamonds, which he has redeemed. She is deeply touched. All implore her to return to her profession. They divert her with gossip. (Quartet: "Once there was a prince, they say.") The maid brings a casket and a letter from Maurice. Michonnet hurries the comedians off. Adrienne opens the casket, which contains a faded bunch of violets. The princess has impregnated the flowers with poison. (**Adrienne:** "Poor little flowers.") Adrienne is plunged in grief. Michonnet tries to comfort her, confessing that he has written to Maurice to come. Maurice appears, but Adrienne receives him coldly. He tells her he still loves her and asks her to marry him. (Duet: "Ah nobler far than any royal queen.") The poison begins to take effect. Adrienne speaks of the flowers; her mind wanders. Not recognising Maurice, she calls him piteously. Maurice summons assistance. Michonnet rushes in. They try restoratives without avail. Michonnet realises at last that the flowers were poisoned, but Adrienne is past human aid. The four actors enter. She begs all to save her (**Adrienne:** "Save me! I do not want to die"), and falls back dead. The two men are heartbroken. "She is dead," says Michonnet. "Dead," echo the others. But Maurice cries exultantly, "No! Glory cannot die!"

AIDA

Grand opera in four acts by Verdi. Text by Ghislanzoni. CAST: The King of Egypt—Basso. Amneris, his daughter—Mezzo-soprano. Aïda, Ethiopian slave—Soprano. Radames—Tenor. The high priest—Basso. Amonasro, King of Ethiopia—Baritone. The action takes place in Egypt during the reign of the Pharaohs.

Verdi wrote this opera for Ismael Pacha, Khedive of Egypt, and received from him 80,000 francs. First produced at Cairo in 1871.

ACT I. Aïda, the unknown daughter of King Amonasro, lives at Memphis as a slave. Her father has made an incursion into Egypt to deliver her. Aïda loves Radames, a young warrior (Romanza, Radames: "Heavenly Aïda"), but has a dangerous rival in Amneris, the daughter of the king. (Duet, Radames, Amneris: "In thy visage I trace.") Incited by Amneris, the high priest Ramfis (Terzett, Aïda,

Amneris, Radames: "Oh fate o'er Egypt looming") declares that Radames has been selected by Isis to be the leader of the army against Amonasro. (Battle Hymn: "On! Of Nilus' sacred river, guard the shores.") Aïda's heart is torn between her love for her father and for Radames, and she remains at Memphis. (Scene, Aïda: "Return a conqueror.")

Change of scene: Temple of Vulcan. Solemn ceremonies and dance of priestesses. (Chorus of priestesses: "O mighty Ptha.") Installation of Radames to the office of commander-in-chief. (Prayer, Ramfis and chorus: "O mighty one, guard and protect!")

ACT II. Amneris' chamber. Festal dances and music. (Chorus of women: "Our songs his glory praising.") Amneris receives her slave Aïda and cunningly draws from her the avowal of her love for Radames. (Scene and duet, Amneris, Aïda: "The chances of war afflict thy people, poor Aïda;" Aïda: "O love, O joy tormenting.") Change of scene: Radames returns victorious. (Chorus, king and people: "Glory to Egypt, to Isis!") Grand triumphal march, Amonasro appears as a captive; unrecognised except by Aïda. He declares that the Ethiopian king has been slain in battle. (Amonasro: "This my garment has told you already.") The prisoners are released at the request of Radames, and the grateful King of Egypt declares him his successor and the betrothed of his daughter.

ACT III. On the banks of the Nile, near the temple of Isis. (Chorus of priests and priestesses: "O thou who to Osiris art!") Amonasro and Aïda are held as hostages (Aria, Aïda: "Oh, my dear country!") and he forces her to learn from Radames the position of the Egyptian army. (Duet, Aïda, Amonasro: "Once again shalt thou gaze.") Radames only seemingly consents to become the husband of Amneris, and is persuaded through love for Aïda to give her the information required by her father. (Duet, Radames, Aïda: "Again I see thee.") When Amonasro reveals his identity and flies with Aïda, the despairing

Radames allows himself to be taken prisoner. (Terzett, Amonasro, Aïda, Radames: "I am dishonoured.")

Act IV. A hall in the temple of justice. Amneris (Scene, Amneris: "My hated rival has escaped me") desires to save Radames, but he repulses her (Duet, Amneris, Radames: "Now to the hall the priests proceed"), and is condemned to death. The sentence is that he shall be buried alive. (Judgment scene, Amneris, Ramfis and chorus: "Heavenly spirit, descend.") Change of scene: The lower portion of the stage shows the burial place in the temple of Vulcan; the upper portion represents the temple itself. Aïda has come to die with Radames. (Scene and duet, Radames, Aïda: "The fatal stone now closes over me.") They accept their terrible fate (Radames: "To die, so pure and lovely"), while Amneris prays above their tomb in the midst of the priestly ceremonies, and the jubilant dance of the priestesses. (Finale, chorus of priests and priestesses: "Almighty Ptha.")

ALCESTE

Opera in three acts by Gluck. Libretto by Calzabigi.

Cast: Admetos, King of Pharæ—Tenor. Alceste, his wife—Soprano. Evander—Tenor. High priest of Apollo—Basso. Heracles—Basso. Apollo—Baritone. Thanatos, God of Death—Basso. Place, Pharæ, in ancient Greece. Among the many operas upon the subject, that of Gluck, which was first presented at Vienna in 1767, has alone survived. It is founded upon the well-known mythological tale of Alcestes, who suffers death for her husband and is brought back from Hades by Heracles.

Act I. Alceste and the populace are engaged in prayer to Apollo for the dying Admetos. Change of scene: The Temple of Apollo. After the prayers of the priests Alceste presents her petition for her husband's life. The voice of Apollo is heard saying: "Admetos is dedicated to

the Styx unless in his place a victim is found." The crowd
flees in dismay, but Alceste offers her life as a sacrifice.
The priests announce its acceptance by Apollo.

Act II. In the palace. Admetos has recovered and the
people rejoice. The king resolves to die with Alceste.
Heracles, who has come to visit Admetos, arrives and is
informed of Apollo's decree by Evander. He resolves in
defiance of the god to rob him of his prey. Change of
scene: Entrance to Hades. Alceste, who has appeared
to fulfil the sacrifice, is ordered by the Gods of Death to
await the evening, and is joined by Admetos, who wishes
to share her fate. The Gods of Death end the strife of love
and drag Alceste away, whereupon Heracles rushes forward and rescues the wife of his friend, and the peace-
loving Apollo relents and gives his blessing. The people
assemble and the scene ends in general rejoicing.

AMELIA, OR THE MASKED BALL

Opera in three acts by Verdi. Libretto by Piave.

Cast: Count Richard, Governor of Boston—Tenor.
Renato, his secretary—Baritone. Amelia, wife of Renato
—Soprano. Ulrica, fortune teller—Alto. Oscar, page—
Soprano. Silvan, sailor—Baritone. Samuel and Tom,
conspirators—Basso. Place, in and near Boston. Time,
the end of the seventeenth century. First produced at
Rome in 1859. The libretto was originally written by
Scribe for Rossini's "Gustavus III," then composed by
Auber (see "Gustav or the Masked Ball"). At the re-
quest of Verdi the original libretto of Scribe was rewritten
by Piave.

Act I. Officers and citizens in the house of Count Richard express their love for him, while the negro conspirators, Samuel, Tom and their friends, declare their hatred.
Ulrica, a negress, is about to be banished as a witch. Richard loves Amelia, the wife of his secretary. Her husband,

having seen a list of the invited guests, warns the governor of treachery to come, and he resolves to visit Ulrica in disguise. The conspirators, learning of this, determine to take advantage of the opportunity to wreak their vengeance. Change of scene: Ulrica's dwelling. Incantation scene. Amid a crowd of women and children, Richard appears in the disguise of a fisherman and is recognised by Ulrica. When Amelia also arrives the witch dismisses the crowd; Richard overhears that he is beloved by Amelia, who desires forgetfulness from the sorceress. Ulrica tells Amelia to pluck a certain plant at midnight in a lonely place, and she departs. Richard now has his fortune told, and hears that death is his portion and that the man who first presses his hand that day will be the murderer. Renato appears, and extends his hand to Richard. Richard is recognised as the governor and is joyfully greeted by the people.

Act II. Midnight. A deserted spot. Amelia, conquering her fears, approaches; she meets Richard and both declare their love. Renato unexpectedly arrives on the scene to save the governor from the conspirators. He does not recognise his disguised wife, and first having changed cloaks with Richard, promises to escort her to safety. The conspirators are foiled, but in revenge tear the veil from Amelia's face, and Renato, thunderstruck, recognises his wife. Renato's love for the governor turns to hate and he arranges for the conspirators to meet him on the morrow. He keeps his word to the governor and escorts Amelia to the city.

Act III. Renato's chamber. Renato plans to kill his wife, but changes his mind and determines to avenge the insult he has received in the blood of Richard. He promises aid to the conspirators and compels Amelia to take part in the drawing of lots; his name is found on the slip and Amelia suspects his design. Oscar, the page, brings an invitation to the masked ball, which Renato accepts. Change of scene: Masked ball at the palace of the gov-

ernor. Richard resolves to allow Renato and Amelia to
sail for England and thus be true to honour and duty.
Crowd of maskers. The conspirators seek the governor,
but he is warned by Amelia and bids her farewell, renouncing his love for her. He is stabbed by Renato, who has
followed him. Dying, he declares Amelia's innocence and
forgives Renato.

ANDRE CHENIER

Opera in four acts by Umberto Giordano. Libretto by
Luigi Illica.

CAST: André Chenier—Tenor. Charles Gerard—Baritone. Madeleine de Coigny—Soprano. Bersi—Mezzo-soprano. Mme. la Comtesse de Coigny—Soprano. Madelon,
an old woman—Soprano. Mathieu, a *sans culotte*—Baritone. The Abbé—Tenor. A Spy—Tenor. Fouquier-Tin-
ville—Basso. Roucher—Basso. Place, the Château de
Coigny, Paris. Time, the French Revolution. First
production, Milan, 1896.

ACT I. Ball-room at the Château de Coigny. The majordomo and Gerard, with other servants, are preparing for
a ball. A heavy carved sofa is carried in. Gerard apostrophises it. (Gerard: "Thou hast patiently listened.")
As a Revolutionary, he awaits with impatience his escape
from servitude. The countess enters with Madeleine and
her attendant Bersi. (Madeleine: "Now fades the day.")
Madeleine rebels against a life of fashion and longs for
freedom. Madeleine: "As in a vice one struggles gasp-
ing.") The guests arrive, among them the abbé, Fléville,
an author, and André Chenier, a young poet. The abbé
relates the latest news. Fléville exhorts everybody to be
gay (Fléville: "What matters that, my friends"), in spite
of the ominous rumours of uprisings among the people.
To amuse the guests shepherds and shepherdesses enter
singing. (Eclogue: "O gentle nymphs, adieu"; Abbé: "A

hungry fox was sighing.") Madeleine, who is a mere
school-girl, coquettishly asks Chenier to improvise upon
the theme of love, which he willingly does. (Chenier:
"Your scorn has touched me here.") He speaks of the
pride of the rich and its effect upon the poor. All are indignant at his lack of taste, and the countess orders the
musicians to strike up a dance. As the guests choose partners doleful music is heard without, and Gerard appears,
followed by a crowd of ragged men and women. (Chorus:
"Each day, each morrow, brings want and sorrow.") The
countess angrily orders them out. Gerard's father, in the
service of the family for sixty years, intercedes for him.
The servants roughly force the intruders to retire, and
the ball goes on.

ACT II. Paris, 1794. The Café Hottot, near which
stands an altar, with a bust of Marat in place of a holy
image. Chenier sits by himself at one table, Bersi and
the spy at another, while Mathieu and a waiter bustle
about. Bersi asks whether it is true that spies are being
sent through the city. The spy inquires if she fears anything. (Bersi: "Afraid? Not I.") The death wagon rattles by. The spy notes the query in his book with the
opinion that both Bersi and Chenier will bear watching.
Roucher brings André's passport and begs him to leave
Paris. He refuses, saying that he loves an unknown lady,
whom he is to meet that day. (Chenier: "Do you believe in
Fate?") He shows Roucher a letter. (Roucher: "A
truly feminine hand.") The latter begs him to disregard
it. Robespierre passes, followed by the mob. Gerard entering, questions the spy about Madeleine. (Gerard: "Her
eyes are like the sky.") Bersi, returning, goes into the
café with the spy, but presently returns, and mingling
with the crowd addresses Chenier (Chorus of Revolution-
aries: "Let us make merry like Barras"), begging him to
await a lady—whom she calls "Speranza." Darkness
falls—Mathieu brings a lantern—the spy steals along in
the shadows watching. Madeleine comes to meet André.

She throws back her hood when he asks her name. Both he and the spy recognise her; the spy hurries away to report to Gerard. (Madeleine: "In your hour of fame.") She asks André to save her. (Chenier: "Hail! golden hour!") They avow their love and are about to fly when Gerard intercepts them, trying to drag Madeleine away. Roucher interferes and escorts the girl to her home. André and Gerard draw their swords. Gerard, wounded, warns André that he is proscribed, begging him to save Madeleine. Chenier flees, the mob surround the wounded man, vowing vengeance. He pretends his assailant is unknown to him.

ACT III. The Revolutionary Tribunal. Mathieu, a *sans culotte*, addresses the mob (Mathieu: "Dumouriez, the traitor, has betrayed us") when Gerard appears, still suffering from his wound. He makes an eloquent plea to the mob for money. (Gerard: "Citizens, France is weeping tears of blood;" Chorus: "Take them, my earrings.") Old Madelon pushes through the crowd (Madelon: "Make way there! I am old Madelon"), bringing with her a young boy, whom she devotes to the service of France, while the mob sings the Carmagnole. The spy tells Gerard that Chenier has been arrested (Spy: "When lovesick maid complaining"), and that Madeleine is not far away. Gerard is about to denounce Chenier, but cannot do it. The spy urges him on, and he begins to draw up the necessary papers. (Gerard: "Time was when I rejoiced.") He signs them and hands them to the spy as Madeleine appears on the threshold. He tells her André is in prison, and passionately declares his love for her. (Gerard: "Why would I have you here?") Madeleine tries to escape, then turning back offers her honour for André's life. (Madeleine: "Ere death had taken my darling mother.") Documents are brought to Gerard; the mob is heard outside gathering to see the executions. Madeleine's grief moves Gerard; he promises to do what he can. The mob comes into the tribunal. (Chorus of old women: "Mother Cadet! sit by the barrier there.") The judges and the jury arrive, then the prisoners; André is the last to appear. The accusations are read, amid the brutal comments of the mob. Chenier is denounced as a traitor. He denies it, and is called upon to defend himself. (Chenier: "I was a soldier, and faced death in the field.") He speaks with deep feeling. Gerard rushes forward, crying that the indictment is false and inspired by jealous hate. He embraces Chenier, pointing out Madeleine in the crowd. (Gerard: "Our country? Justice, did you dare to say?") The mob cries out, "À la lanterne," and Chenier is led away.

ACT IV. The prison of St. Lazare. Midnight. André is seated, writing. Roucher stands near. The poet reads the verses he has just composed (Chenier: "Like summer day that closes"), and the two friends say farewell. Madeleine enters with Gerard. She offers the gaoler money to substitute her for another woman on the death list, that she may die with André. (Chenier: "From thee, beloved, my restless soul"; Madeleine: "I will not leave thee.") Together they await the gendarmes; together they go to the scaffold.

ÄNNCHEN OF THARAU

Opera in three acts by Heinrich Hofman. Libretto by Feld.

CAST: Simon Dach, professor—Baritone. Neander, pastor of Tharau—Basso. Ännchen, his daughter—Soprano. Gretchen, daughter of the innkeeper—Soprano. Hennewitz, recruiting officer of the Elector—Basso. Yohannes von Berkow—Tenor. Place, in Tharau at the end of the Thirty Years' War. First production, Hamburg, 1878.

ACT I. Simon Dach, the author of the song "Ännchen of Tharau," loves the daughter of the pastor Neander. Just as Simon has proposed for her hand in marriage and has gained the consent of her father the recruiting officers of the Elector of Brandenburg appear under the leadership of Yost von Hennewitz. A lively scene follows. Yohannes von Berkow, student of theology, a native of Tharau, approaches and tells Hennewitz of his love for Ännchen. The dedication of a new church in Tharau, to be presided over by Simon Dach, is being celebrated. During the festival Ännchen gives her consent to the wooing of Simon, but when she sees Yohannes, the friend of her youth, she leaves Simon and joyfully accompanies Yohannes to the dance.

Act II. In the garden of the pastor Ännchen finds she loves Yohannes and is distressed that she has promised to marry Dach. Her friend Gretchen, having found the song composed by Dach, brings it to Ännchen, who believes Yohannes to be the author. The lively Gretchen coquettes with the recruiting officer; when Yohannes arrives Gretchen gives him the poem and he reads it aloud, while Simon listens. An altercation between the two begins. Ännchen is forced to decide which of them she loves. She keeps her word and gives her hand to Simon, but afterward confides her sorrow to Gretchen. Yohannes is about to depart when a deputation from the University of Königsberg announces to Simon Dach his appointment as rector. The young student refuses the proffered hand of friendship offered by Dach, and as Ännchen defends her betrothed from his insults, despairingly throws himself into the arms of the recruiting officers.

Act III. In the house of the pastor. Ännchen, now ill and wretched, resignedly endures the affection of Simon, but begs him to procure the release of Yohannes from the army. Through her fervent pleadings Dach realises that she loves the youth. No longer young, the rector feels that without Ännchen Paradise is lost. He is present at a scene in which Ännchen rejoices with Yohannes, who has rescued her from some rough soldiers, and hearing them declare their mutual affection, he exercises his prerogative as magistrate to obtain the release of Yohannes, and places Ännchen in the arms of her lover.

ANGLA

Opera in one act by Ferd. Hummel. Libretto by Axel Delmar.

CAST: Emperor Charles the Great, disguised as a monk —Basso. Bishop Balduin, his ambassador—Tenor. Widukind, Duke of Saxony—Tenor. Hereford, Priest of Wotan—Baritone. Angla, beloved by Widukind—Soprano. Place, Grove of Wotan. Time, A.D. 800. First production, Berlin, 1893.

Widukind, the heathen Duke of Saxony, opponent of Charles the Great, slumbers in his tent, guarded by Angla. Meanwhile the priest, Hereford, is consulting the oracle of the sacred oak, dedicated to Wotan, which is within the grove. (Chorus: "Wotan, All father, we call"; Hereford: "Sacred voices in the boughs hear I in silvery tones.") The branches of the oak rustle, Widukind hears them in a dream and Angla lulls him to sleep. (Song: "Blooming spring's sweet caress.") The duke awakens, having dreamed of the fall of the holy tree, but hearing the war cry of the Saxons, he arises and endeavours to soothe Angla's alarm. (Widukind: "Dost fear for me, my love"; Angla's answer: "My noble hero, in fear and trembling leave me not alone.") But she has seen tokens of peace in the sky and prays Widukind to forswear Wotan and accept the Christian faith. Widukind fears to lose her through their differing beliefs and falls despairing at her feet. Hereford, to the consternation of the Saxons, foretells disaster from the whispering of the sacred oak, and in the midst of his prophecy, the song of approaching women is heard in the distance. ("Harbingers of peace are we, the women.") The Saxons gaze in mute astonishment. The ambassador of Charles the Great, Bishop Balduin, now approaches with a number of Christian women, accompanied by the emperor, clad in the garb of a simple pilgrim. ("Balduin at the emperor's wise behest is here as his ambassador.")

He offers peace to Widukind, but Hereford reminds him of the massacre which took place by the Aller. ("Will you receive the enemy of your country"; Chorus of Saxons: "Defenceless were ye butchered.") The priest of Wotan demands that the Christian women be offered as a blood sacrifice to Wotan. The emperor interferes, disclosing his rank and offers to die in their stead. As the branches of the oak rustle in the breeze he relates his dream that a beautiful and good woman had grasped his sword and felled the sacred oak, and that he had selected the purest maidens of his realm and journeyed thither with them. Balduin interprets the dream by declaring that the holy woman represented Christianity, and demands of the Saxons that they accept a test. Hereford believes that the hammer of Thor will destroy whoever touches the tree and willingly gives permission; but as the holy tree begins its mysterious whispering the Christian women become frightened and retreat. Hereford is about to triumph, when Angla seizes the sword of the emperor, and fells the tree, calling on the name of the Father, Son and Holy Ghost. The branches fall apart and a cross appears lighted by the rays of the morning sun. Widukind bends low in reverent prayer, and, accompanied by Angla, proceeds to the brook and is baptised by Balduin. (Closing chorus: "The right way have ye chosen.")

DER ARME HEINRICH

Music drama in two acts by Hans Pfitzner. Romance by Grau.

CAST: Heinrich, a German knight—Tenor. Dietrich, one of his men—Baritone. Hilda, Dietrich's wife—Soprano. Agnes, their daughter—Soprano. The physician of Salerno—Basso. Place, Act I, Heinrich's castle in Suabia. Act II, convent at Salerno. Time, 1100.

ACT I. The first act is preceded by a long introduction.

Heinrich, who is very ill, is nursed by Hilda and Agnes. He has sent his servant Dietrich to Salerno to a miracle-working monk. Returning, Dietrich delivers the message of the physician that Heinrich can be cured only through a pure virgin who will give her blood in sacrifice for his sake. ("When she lies naked upon the stone and her heart is cut in two, then will you recover.") Heinrich believes himself lost, but, inspired by God, Agnes resolves to save her dear master and offer her heart's blood to preserve his life.

ACT II. Again a long introduction ushers in the second act. Dietrich and Hilda have accompanied the suffering Heinrich and Agnes to Salerno. As the physician is about to sacrifice Agnes a wonderful change takes place in Heinrich. He, who loves life so well that he would offer up another's life to save his own, refuses to accept it and desires to die that Agnes may live. A storm rages around the convent. Heinrich, with returning strength, tears Agnes from the knife of the physician. He is saved and the monks adore Agnes as a saint.

ARMIDE

Grand opera in five acts by Gluck. Libretto founded upon Tasso's "Jerusalem Saved," by Quinault.

CAST: Armide—Soprano. Phenice and Sidonie, her confidants—Sopranos. Hidroat, King of Damascus—Baritone. Aront, his commander-in-chief—Basso. Rinaldo, commander of the army of Godfrey of Bouillon—Tenor. Artemidor, a knight—Tenor. Ubaldo—Baritone. A Danish knight—Tenor. The Fury of Hate—Alto. Demon as Lucinda—Soprano. Demon as Melissa—Soprano. A Naiad—Soprano. First production, Paris, 1777.

ACT I. The beautiful Armide, who is endowed with magic power, complains to her friends Phenice and Sidonie that Rinaldo, the crusader, has proved insensible to her charms.   As her uncle Hidroat insists that she choose a husband, she declares she will wed the conqueror of Rinaldo.   A grand festival and dance is given to celebrate the victory of Aront, who is expected to return with a band of captive crusaders.   He arrives wounded, for Rinaldo has freed the captives.   The act closes with cries of vengeance from the populace.

ACT II.   A wood.   Rinaldo explains to Artemidor, whom he has freed, that Godfrey de Bouillon is angered with him and that therefore he will go independently on his quest.   Left alone, Rinaldo is dazzled by the magic of Armide, through which a wood is transformed into a garden of wonders.   Armide desires to slay the sleeping Rinaldo, but conquered by the power of love she carries the hero off with her.

ACT III.   Hall in the palace of Armide.   Armide endeavours to conquer her love for Rinaldo, and calls the Fury of Hate to her assistance.   Armide, irresolute, thrusts the Fury away, and becoming angered she declares she will never return.

ACT IV.   The magic wood.   The crusaders have sent Ubaldo and a Danish knight to recall Rinaldo.   Armide tries to prevent their approach, but is overcome by a consecrated sceptre in the hand of Ubaldo.   The images of the loved ones of both knights appear, but this magic also is destroyed by Ubaldo.

ACT V.   Palace of Armide.   Armide and Rinaldo in the power of love.   Ballet.   As Armide, driven by unrest, leaves her lover, the crusaders arrive and bring Rinaldo to a true comprehension of his position.   He recovers his sanity, grasps his sword, bids farewell to Armide and leaves her in despair.   She abjures her magic, the demons destroy the palace and Armide is buried in its ruins.

ARMINIUS

Opera in four acts by Heinrich Hofman. Libretto by Felix Dahn.

CAST: Varus, Roman general—Basso. Fulvia, his daughter—Soprano. Vala and Lucius, his legates—Tenor and Basso. Arminius—Tenor. Segest—Basso. Thusnelda—Soprano. Katwald, friend of Arminius—Baritone. Albrun, a young priestess—Soprano. Germanic princes. Place, Ancient Germany A.D. 9. First production, Dresden, 1877.

ACT I. Camp of the Romans. Varus is seated at the banquet table with Arminius, surrounded by Allemanians and Romans. Arminius tries to lull Varus into security, but is planning to break the yoke of the enemy. He begs his friends to have patience, and to further his design endeavours to gain the friendship of Segest, who favours the Romans, by asking the hand of his daughter Thusnelda in marriage. He succeeds in making peace between the Romans and Allemanians, who threaten to come to blows.

ACT II. Thusnelda's apartments. Thusnelda loves Arminius, upon whom her hopes are centred. She sternly repulses the Roman Vala, whom Segest has chosen for her husband, but allows herself to be carried off by Arminius, who defends her from Segest and Vala.

ACT III. Fulvia's apartments in the Roman castle. Fulvia has induced Arminius to come to her, promising to reveal an important secret. She gives him a love potion, which he drinks, and discloses to him that Varus has determined to destroy the assembled Allemanians at the coming festival. Arminius declares to the astonished Fulvia that he does not love her, but his wife Thusnelda. He then escapes through the window to go to the assistance of his countrymen.

Change of scene: Sacred forest of the Allemanians. Religious festival and dance. The Romans surprise and capture the Allemanians, but Arminius rushes to the rescue and beguiles his enemies into allowing him to guard the prisoners.

ACT IV. A wood. Thusnelda is overpowered by the Romans led by Fulvia and carried off.

Change of scene: A primitive forest of the Weser Mountains. Arminius frees the captives and puts the Roman guard in chains. He discloses his plan for freedom and the Allemanians arm themselves enthusiastically.

Change of scene: The battlefield. Upon Vala's report of the deliverance of the German princes, the Romans under Varus rush to the battle. Fulvia comes to be near Arminius. Varus returns wounded from the field and discovering what Arminius has accomplished commits suicide. Vala drags in the captive Thusnelda and Fulvia, attempting to stab her, is prevented by the appearance of Arminius and Katwald. Fulvia thrusts the dagger into her own heart and the Allemanians rejoice over their recovered freedom.

THE ARMOURER

Comic opera in three acts by Lootzing. Text by the composer.

CAST: Hans Stadinger, armourer and veterinarian—Basso. Marie, his daughter—Soprano. Count von Liebenau—Baritone. Georg, his shield bearer—Tenor. Adelhof, a knight of Suabia—Basso. Irmentraut, Marie's governess—Alto. Brenner, innkeeper—Tenor. Place, Worms. Time, the sixteenth century. First production, Leipsig, 1846.

The Count von Liebenau loves Marie, the daughter of the armourer Stadinger, and as her father is averse to the union, he comes to Worms with his shield bearer Georg, attired as a simple journeyman, wins Marie's affection in this disguise and retains it even after he avows himself a knight. But Stadinger has learned to like Georg and

wishes to have him as a son-in-law. Liebenau now tries to
win favour with the old man, and to further his plan has
Marie abducted by his retainers so that he may, in the person of Konrad, a workman, restore her to her father. This
plan does not succeed, so he leads his army to Worms, and
the councillors of the city, fearing it will be taken, pray
Stadinger to give his daughter to the knight. This he
does, and it is now disclosed that Liebenau and Konrad are
one and the same person. An amusing figure in the opera
is the Suabian knight Adelhof, who always stumbles in at
critical moments to seek Liebenau and is prevented in droll
ways from disclosing the knight's identity. Another
humorous personage is the old maid Irmentraut, who has
no luck in her love affairs. Brenner only plays a sub-
ordinate rôle.

Act I. Work room of Stadinger. (Chorus of journeymen, among them Liebenau and Georg: "Sparkle flame,
glow iron.") Georg reports to the count that his intended
bride, the lady of Katzenstein, has arrived. Liebenau loves
Marie and does not wish to meet her. (Aria of Stadinger:
"Bring quickly hat and cloak.") He orders the journeymen to invite the neighbours and friends to the master's
jubilee the following day. (Georg's aria: "We are born
only once" with the refrain: "One lives only once in this
world.") Aria of Irmentraut, who scorns all men, because they scorn her. ("I am dissatisfied with the world.")
When all have retired, Konrad appears in his true guise
to court Marie. (Finale, Count, Marie, Irmentraut: "In
nightly darkness come I here.") The count is about to declare himself ("Gladly gave I riches and power for your
love"), when Stadinger appears. The latter suspects him
to be the count, but Liebenau outwits him by repairing
hastily to his room and changing back into Konrad's
dress. Marie, alone, gives expression to her love for Konrad. (Aria: "He is so good, so brave and tender.")

Act II. A room in Stadinger's house. Liebenau as
Konrad pretends to be jealous of the count (Duet with

Marie: "You know he loves you"), but is easily consoled by Marie, who repeats his own words: "Gladly give I riches and power for your love." Adelhof arrives seeking the count, sent by the lady of Katzenstein. (Sextet, Marie, Adelhof, Stadinger, the Count, Georg, Irmentraut: "The man seems to be witless.") Adelhof is quickly disposed of, but now Stadinger accosts Georg, whom he desires as a son-in-law. (Duet: "You are an industrious fellow.") Georg makes excuses. (This is sometimes followed by the reappearance of Adelhof: "I must show the people what wisdom I possess.")

Change of scene: The jubilee festival of Stadinger in his vineyard. (Chorus: "How beautiful the spring"; Song of Georg: "Was once a young popinjay," with the refrain of the chorus: "That follows when you travel.") The count now goes to work on his plans of elopement, and, as Konrad, saves his beloved Marie. Stadinger is incensed against the count and determines to send Marie to a convent. (Closing ensemble: "His cheeks are reddened in anger.")

Act III.   Stadinger's room.   (Marie's aria: "We poor, poor girls are so unfortunate.") Stadinger arrives with his people and inquires into the abduction affair, but the more he learns, the more he becomes confused. Adelhof again appears. (Ensemble: "Good that I meet you.") As Liebenau has accomplished nothing he leads his men against the city, to the amusement of Georg, who is anticipating with joy the closing scene. Stadinger left alone thinks of his early youth. (Song: "I also was a youth with curly hair.")

Change of scene: A square in Worms. Liebenau enters with Marie as his bride. (Recognition scene and closing song: "Gladly gave I riches and power.")

A SANTA LUCIA

Melodrama in two acts by Tosca. Libretto founded upon the work of Cognetti by Golisciani.

CAST: Totonno, oyster merchant—Baritone. Ciccillo and Concettina, his children—Tenor and Soprano. Rosella—Mezzo-soprano. Nannina, their little child. Maria—Alto. Tore, police agent—Basso. A fisherman—Tenor. Time, the present. Place, Naples. First production, Berlin, 1892.

ACT I. At Santa Lucia at Naples. Ciccillo, the son of the oyster merchant Totonno, betrothed to Maria, is in love with Rosella, by whom he has a child. Maria is suspicious and plans the death of Rosella. Totonno is apparently averse to the love of his son for Rosella, but is himself infatuated with her, as she resembles her mother, who was his early love. Maria begins a quarrel with Rosella and angers her to such an extent that she draws a knife and is arrested by the police agent Tore, who has been bribed by Maria. Totonno procures her release and takes her to his home, while Ciccillo is absent fulfilling his duties in the navy. Before his departure Ciccillo has sworn to marry Rosella on his return.

ACT II. Same scene. Maria believes that Rosella had had intimate relations with Totonno, which seems the more probable as Totonno makes no secret of his love for Rosella and really intends to marry her. Maria takes advantage of this to enrage Ciccillo, and in his jealous anger he believes her untrue, has a stormy scene with his father and repulses Rosella. When Rosella learns of the dreadful accusation of Ciccillo of her love for both father and son and finds her protestations of innocence doubted, she plunges into the sea. Ciccillo dives after her, but rescues a dying woman, who is only able to whisper the words, "It is not true."

109,791

LIBRARY
College of St. Francis
JOLIET, ILL.

ASSARPAI

Opera in three acts by Ferd. Hummel. Libretto, founded
on one of Wildenbruch's ballads, by Dora Duncker.
CAST: Atahualpa, last king of the Incas. Assarpai, his
daughter. Odahia, her companion. Pizarro, leader of the
Spaniards. Inez, his daughter. Alonzo, Spanish officer.
Pedro, horse boy. Place, Peru. Time, 1533.

ACT I. Valley of Quito. Atahualpa takes leave of his
daughter to fight against the Spaniards. He leaves her in
the care of Odahia, who reveres Assarpai as the saviour
of her life. She is dumb, but expresses by signs that danger is near. Assarpai refuses to believe that any one can
enter the valley until she is suddenly confronted by Alonzo.
Both pause as if turned to stone; Odahia sharply watches
the maiden. Assarpai, who has never been out of the valley, listens with increasing interest to Alonzo's tales of
the sea and of strange lands. Odahia, who tries to separate
them, is sent away at the request of Alonzo. The dumb
girl departs unwillingly and Alonzo is told her story, that
Assarpai had saved her from a burning hut and that she
had lost her speech on that night of horror. During the
recital night has set in, and Alonzo, despite her struggles,
draws Assarpai to his breast and their hearts are united.
After a long embrace they separate.

ACT II. An open country. Tent of Pizarro. It is
night. The crafty Pedro proposes to Pizarro to conquer
the renowned Inca by carrying off his greatest treasure,
his daughter. He has found secret paths which lead into
the valley and proposes to despatch a troop thither under
the leadership of Alonzo. Pizarro, who sees in Alonzo his
future son-in-law, consents, and gives the order. Alonzo,
absorbed in dreams of Assarpai, hardly comprehends the
command; when he realises what is required of him he is
in despair and refuses to obey. Pizarro is astounded at his
conduct and threatens him with imprisonment, but promises

him the hand of his daughter if he obeys. This makes no
impression on Alonzo, and he remains indifferent even after
the mild reproof of Inez. Again commanded by Pizarro
he reluctantly obeys.

Change of scene: The valley of Quito, as in Act I. Assarpai greets the rising sun ("Thee greet I, day") and disappears in the forest. Alonzo, hardly conscious of what he
is doing, with Pedro and the other soldiers creeps through
the forest. His conduct is remarked by his companions,
and when Assarpai is seen on the brow of a hill slowly de-
scending, he becomes incapable of giving orders. Assarpai
is alarmed when she sees the soldiers, but is reassured by
the appearance of Alonzo. Only when she is about to be
bound at the command of Pedro does she realise her peril,
or endeavour to thrust back her captors. She is overpowered, however, and her piteous plea to Alonzo for freedom is denied. Odahia tries fruitlessly to rescue Assarpai,
and Alonzo allows the dumb girl to accompany her friend.

Act III. Camp of the Spaniards by the sea. The field
altar at which the marriage ceremony of Alonzo and Inez
is to take place is prepared, but Pizarro almost regrets
having promised his daughter to the weak Alonzo. He
impatiently awaits Pedro, whom he has sent to make terms
with the Inca. At last he arrives, and reports that the
Inca has refused to surrender even though Pizarro should
carry out his threat to burn Assarpai. The angry Pizarro
has the girl brought before him and a pyre erected. She
proudly approaches Pizarro without replying to his ironi-
cal salutation. Her thoughts are with her father, but
when informed that he has deserted her, she remains apparently unmoved. Pizarro cannot but admire her beauty
and courage and offers to postpone her death if she will try
to influence her father. She refuses his offer and arouses
his anger by her contempt. He leaves her to conduct his
daughter to the altar. At the sight of the sea Assarpai's
memory of the past revives ("From distant shores"), but
she is led away by the watch and tied to the stake. The

bridal procession approaches and the pyre is lighted.
When the despairing Odahia sees Alonzo she thrusts him
forward to behold the scene, and with a shrill scream her
voice returns.   In the confusion which follows Alonzo
rushes into the flames and he and Assarpai find death together.

THE BARBER OF BAGDAD

Comic opera in two acts by Peter Cornelius. Libretto by
the composer.

CAST: The Caliph—Baritone. Baba Mustapha, a cadi—
Tenor. Morgiana, his daughter—Soprano. Bostana, a
relative of the cadi—Mezzo-soprano. Nureddin—Tenor.
Abul Hassan, barber—Basso. The action takes place in
the houses of Nureddin and the cadi at Bagdad. The
opera was first produced at Weimar and was coldly received, but was subsequently a great success.

ACT I. An apartment at the house of Nureddin. Nureddin raves of Morgiana, by whom he hopes to be cured of
his illness. Bostana brings him the happy tidings that
Morgiana will visit him, and he summons the loquacious
barber Abul to improve his appearance. After several in-
termezzos, in which Abul hears of the love of Nureddin for
Morgiana, the barber completes his task but remains, talking continuously. He even proposes to accompany Nureddin to Morgiana, and to be rid of him Nureddin hands him
over to the servants, passing him off as the sick man.

ACT II. An apartment at the house of the cadi. Morgiana is happy at the expected visit to Nureddin, and the
cadi is likewise delighted, as he expets a friend from
Damascus, to whom he has promised the hand of Morgiana.
As the cadi goes to prayer, leaving Morgiana alone, Nureddin arrives, but the happiness of the pair is soon disturbed; first by the song of the barber on the street, then
by the appearance of Bostana, who reports the unlooked-
for return of the cadi. Nureddin hurriedly conceals him-

self in a box. Abul rushes into the room, mistaking the
cries of a beaten slave for the voice of Nureddin. Bostana
tries to have the box removed, but is prevented by the
cadi. The disturbance has caused a crowd to collect and
the caliph is drawn to the spot by the confusion. Abul accuses the cadi of the murder of Nureddin, and when the
caliph has the box opened, the half-suffocated Nureddin
is discovered within. Upon the request of the caliph the
couple are united by the cadi, while the barber, who has
been taken for a madman, is appointed story-teller to the
caliph.

THE BARBER OF SEVILLE

Comic opera in two acts by Rossini. Text founded on
Beaumarchais' comedy by Sterbini.

CAST: Count Almaviva—Tenor. Bartholo, physician—
Basso. Rosina, his ward—Soprano. Basilio—Music
Master—Basso. Marcelline—Soprano. Figaro—Baritone. Fivrillo, servant to the count—Tenor. A notary,
Ambrosio, servant to Bartholo. Place, Seville. Time, the
seventeenth century. Music for this text has been composed by Paesiello, Isonard and Rossini. Though the work
of Paesiello triumphed for a time over that of Rossini, the
latter alone has stood the test of time and is still the main-
stay of the operatic repertoire. First produced at Rome in
1816.

ACT I. Seville. Square before the house of Bartholo.
Almaviva serenades Rosina, whom Bartholo desires to
marry for her fortune. ("See, the morn appears.")
Figaro approaches singing. (Aria: "I am the factotum of
the ladies.") The count, who knows the merry barber,
asks him for assistance in meeting Rosina. (Duet: "The
shine of gold falls upon me.") Figaro advises the count
to disguise himself as a soldier and by feigning drunkenness gain entrance to the house. For this suggestion he
is richly rewarded.

Change of scene: Chamber of Dr. Bartholo. (Rosina's
cavatina: "I ask my timid heart.") Knowing the count
only under the name of Lindoro, she writes to him, and is
leaving the room when Bartholo and Basilio enter. Bartholo suspects the count, and Basilio advises that he be put
out of the way. (Aria: "Calumny is light as air.") When
the two have gone Rosina and Figaro enter. The latter
asks Rosina for a few words for Lindoro, which she has
already written. (Duet· "Is it I that you mean?") Surprised by Bartholo, she manages to fool him, but he is still
suspicious. (Aria: "A doctor, perhaps.") When the
stage is empty, Marcelline tries to pass through the exit,
but is met by the count disguised as an intoxicated soldier.
She rushes to Bartholo for protection, being in fear of the
drunken man. Bartholo endeavours to remove the supposed soldier, but does not succeed. The count manages
to see Rosina, whispers that he is Lindoro, gives her a letter, and she hands the watching Bartholo the list of the
wash. When Basilio, Figaro and Marcelline disappear,
the noise attracts the watch. Bartholo believes that the
count has been arrested, but Almaviva mentions his name
to the officer and is released. Bartholo and Basilio are astounded, and Figaro makes sport of them.

Act II. Almaviva again appears at the house of the
doctor, this time disguised as a tutor, and acting as substitute for the supposedly ailing Basilio, who gives lessons
to Rosina. In order that he may not be alone with Rosina,
the doctor has himself shaved by Figaro. (Quintet:
"What, Basilio! what do I see?") When Basilio suddenly
appears he is bribed by a full purse from Figaro, to play
the part of an invalid. Finally Bartholo detects the trick,
drives everybody out of the room, and rushes to a notary
to draw up the marriage contract between himself and
Rosina. The stage remains empty, while the music describes a thunder storm, then the count and Figaro enter
through a window. When Basilio arrives with the notary,
he is again bribed, and he and Figaro witness the signatures

to a marriage contract between the count and Rosina. The befooled Bartholo is pacified by being allowed to retain Rosina's dowry.

THE BARTERED BRIDE

Comic opera in three acts by Smetana. Text by Sabina.
CAST: Kruschina, peasant—Baritone. Katinka, his wife —Soprano. Maria, their daughter—Soprano. Micha, a landowner—Basso. Agnes, his wife—Mezzo-soprano. Wenzel, their son—Tenor. Hans, Micha's son by a former marriage—Tenor. Kezal, marriage broker—Basso. Springer, manager of a theatrical troupe—Tenor. Esmeralda, dancer—Soprano. Muff, comedian—Tenor. Place, a village in Bohemia. Time, the present. First production, Prague, 1866.

ACT I. Village square and inn. A festival. (Chorus: "See the buds are opening.") Maria loves Hans, but is to marry another, whom Kezal has recommended to her father. (Aria, Maria: "Indeed I will trust thee.") It is Wenzel, son of Micha, a landowner. The mother is on the side of Maria, but Kruschina goes with the marriage broker to interview Micha at the inn. (Terzett, Kruschina, Katinka, Kezal: "All is as good as settled.")

ACT II. Room at the inn. The stuttering Wenzel arrives at the inn (Aria, Wenzel: "Dear son") and meets Maria, who is to him unknown, and who warns him against his bride-to-be. (Duet, Wenzel, Maria: "I also knew a dear sweetheart.") She coquets with him and induces him to promise not to go near Maria. Hans in the meantime has reeived 300 guilders from Kezal, as an inducement to give up Maria, but has accepted the money only on condition that she marry Micha's son. Kezal calls in Kruschina and the peasants and in their presence Hans signs a paper declaring that he has sold his bride. (Hans, Aria: "It must succeed.")

Act III.   The village square as in Act I.   Performance
of the comedians, during which Wenzel is entirely captivated by Esmeralda.   (Wenzel: "Oh, what ails me!").   The
manager induces him to play the part of a bear as a substitute for one of the actors who is intoxicated.   When he
is found by his parents practising a droll dancing part,
he refuses to marry Maria and runs away.   (Quartet:
"This comes like a thunder clap.")   Maria, in tears, enters
with her parents, and as she has heard of the agreement
is quite ready to accept Wenzel.   (Sextet: "Consider a little while, Maria.")   But now Hans is recognised by Micha
as his eldest son, and as Hans knew of the relationship,
from the first he had only been joking about the agreement.
Wenzel, who makes his appearance as a bear (Wenzel:
"Be without fear, all is well"; Terzett: "Blessed be they
who love and trust"), willingly retires and Hans and
Maria, having obtained the consent of their parents (Duet,
Maria and Hans: "My dearest sweetheart"), are married.
(Finale: "Willingly come we!")

THE BEGGAR OF PONT DES ARTS

Lyric opera in three acts and a prelude by Karl von
Kaskel.   Libretto adapted from Hauff's novel by Ludwig.
Cast: Baron von Faldern, a German nobleman—Basso.
Fröben, his university friend—Tenor.   Josepha, a beggar,
afterward wife of Faldern—Soprano.   Don Pedro y Genos,
retired Spanish colonel—Baritone.   Diego, his servant—
Tenor.   Arabella, maid—Soprano.   Place, Paris and Germany.   Time, 1823.
Prologue: Paris, at Pont des Arts.   Josepha stands
shivering and begging at the bridge and sings.   ("Let,
what I suffer.")   As Fröben and Faldern pass by they
give her alms and stand aside to make room for a company
of masqueraders.   (Chorus: "May the storm blow out the
lights.")   When they have departed, the compassionat ᵎ

Fröben again approaches the beggar girl. She tells him of the distress of her mother and herself, but refuses to disclose her residence or show her face. Fröben again gives her money, and she rapidly disappears in order to purchase medicine for her mother. Faldern laughs at his friend and tells him he has been fooled by a loose woman. The departing beggar is molested by several young men. Fröben drives them away, and asks Josepha for her confidence. She relates to him ("In my childhood") that her father has left them to fight for Napoleon in Spain, but has not returned. Meanwhile the mother and child remain in poverty. Fröben, touched by Josepha's grief, draws her to him (Duet: "Oh child, let me in thine eyes"), and prays that she come with him to Germany, the birthplace of her mother. He kisses her, gives her a ring and promises to return at Easter.

Act I. Hotel at Stuttgart. Diego and Arabella love each other. He praises the land of Spain ("There, in the land of the chestnuts") and relates to her the story of Don Pedro, who fought for Napoleon in that country. When he returned after a long illness, he was told that his wife had disappeared with another, taking her child with her. It was supposed that the seducer had fallen at Marengo, and now Don Pedro was seeking through the world for wife and daughter. He had discovered in Stuttgart the picture of a woman who resembled his wife, and carried a copy of it with him wherever he went. As Diego finishes his narration Don Pedro appears, and announces that he will depart for Mayence in an hour. He first receives a visit from Fröben, who believes he has found a clue to the missing ones. He tells Don Pedro of his Paris adventure, but adds that he failed to find the beggar upon his return.

Change of scene: Picture gallery in Stuttgart. Pedro, already known as an eccentric, arrives with Fröben to gaze upon the picture once more. He departs, but Fröben remains, without observing that he has been locked in. He has a vision, in which the persons represented in the pictures step from their frames, and arrange themselves in groups in the chamber. At last, Faldern, who has been seeking his friend, arrives and releases him. He finds Fröben pale and abstracted and determines to take him to his country seat on the Rhine.

ACT II. A park at Faldern's country seat. Fröben believes he has found in the wife of Faldern, Josepha, a resemblance to the beggar of the Pont des Arts. Faldern disclaims this and declares that his wife has no mother, but had a protectress in the Countess Landskrön. Josepha is greatly disturbed by seeing Fröben, particularly when he tells her that in his youth he became enamoured of a picture; she has recognised him at once and is overjoyed at his fidelity. The practical nature of Faldern does not harmonise with the poetic temperament of Fröben, and Josepha is compelled to interfere between them to avoid a conflict. Numerous guests arrive (Chorus: "Good neighbours") and to amuse themselves they begin a play or rhymes; Fröben, being vanquished in the contest, is ordered to sing "What is a kiss?" The song is so suggestive of what has actually occurred that Josepha faints. Faldern gazes suspiciously at Fröben and the guests depart. Josepha recovers and is led into the house by her husband. Later, her face masked, she again enters the dark garden (Song: "Thou ring, that he gave me"), finds Fröben sleeping in the arbour, and places the ring on his finger. He awakes, feigns sleep, and as she bends over him, draws her toward him. She relates that upon the night that they met her mother had died; a Countess Landskrön had saved her from despair; that she had sought Fröben for four years, and finally had resigned herself to become the wife of Faldern. Fröben and Josepha embrace again for the last time (Duet: "The stars are paling"), when Faldern, who has been watching, appears and denounces Josepha. When he hears from Fröben that she was once a beggar girl, he angrily thrusts her from the house. A violent altercation ensues, which leads to a duel; Fröben is wounded and tells Faldern that Don Pedro, who has just arrived upon the scene, is the father of Josepha. Faldern, in great anger, advances to slay him also, but falls on the point of Don Pedro's sword and dies.

ACT III. Terrace at the castle of Countess Landskrön on the Rhine. Don Pedro wishes to return to Spain and declares to Fröben that Josepha can never be his wife. Fröben hopes she will change her mind; Don Pedro does not believe it. (Aria: "Is what I do wrong?") As Josepha appears Fröben retires. (Aria of Josepha: "Without complaint.") The peasants arrive to celebrate the winter festival. (Chorus: "Turn ye around.") After they have departed Fröben and Josepha are left alone to say farewell. (Duet: "Not that which the world builds.") She cannot leave him and throws herself upon his breast. Don Pedro is won over and gives his consent to their union. (Closing Chorus: "Love is over all.")

BELISARIUS

Opera in three acts by Donizetti. Libretto founded upon the drama of Schenk by Cammarano.

CAST: Justinian, Emperor of the East—Basso. Belisarius, his commander-in-chief—Baritone. Antonina, his wife—Soprano. Irene, his daughter—Soprano. Eudoxia, her friend—Soprano. Alamir, prisoner to Belisarius—Tenor. Eutropius, one of the Imperial Guard —Tenor. Eusebius, governor of the prison—Basso. Ottavio, leader of the Alannæ—Tenor. Place, Byzantium and the Hamus mountains. Time, sixth century B.C. First production, Venice, 1836.

ACT I. Hall in the emperor's palace. Irene and the populace greet the victor Belisarius. Antonina hates her husband because Proclus, the slave of Belisarius, has confessed on his deathbed, that upon command of his master he had exposed her son on the shore of the ocean, thus causing his death. The Emperor Justinian greets his commander and grants his prayer for the release of the prisoners. The captive, Alamir, who adores Belisarius, refuses to leave him. (Recitative and duet: "What do I see, does Alamir reject my gift?") The general adopts him in place of his long lost son. Irene congratulates her father, but Antonina has already begun her work of hate, by traducing Belisarius to Justinian, and the innocent man is accused of high treason and thrown into prison on the evidence of his wife.

ACT II. Before the prison. Alamir and his friends lament the fate of Belisarius. His eyes have been put out by his enemies, who have falsely construed and disobeyed the commands of the emperor. Alamir swears vengeance. (Aria: "Tremble, Byzantia, I will repay.") Irene clad as a youth arrives to act as guide to her father, who is about to be released from prison. (Duet: "Oh thou, who in terrible darkness.")

ACT III. In the mountains. As the clang of weapons is heard Irene leads Belisarius to a cave for safety. Alamir now leads the army of the Alannæ against Byzantium to avenge Belisarius. Belisarius confronts him and recognises him as his son through an amulet. At his father's request, the son leaves the ranks of the enemies of Byzantium, and the Alannæ, now under the command of Ottavio, march to Byzantium, having no fear, as the emperor's army is bereft of its leader.

Change of scene: Hall in Byzantium. Antonina, in remorse, tells the emperor that her testimony against Belisarius was false. Irene approaches with news of the victory and informs Antonina that Alamir is her son, and that it was the slave, not Belisarius, who had planned his death. Meanwhile the blind Belisarius has led the Byzantine army and defeated the Alannæ, who had threatened Byzantium, but an arrow has mortally wounded him. He is carried in dying, and the sorrowing emperor promises to be a father to Alamir and Irene.

BENVENUTO CELLINI

Opera in three acts by Berlioz. Libretto by Du Wailly and Barbier.

Cast: Cardinal Salviati—Basso. Balducci, treasurer of the Pope—Basso. Teresa, his daughter—Soprano. Benvenuto Cellini, Florentine goldsmith—Tenor. Ascanio, his apprentice—Mezzo-soprano. Francesco and Bernardino, artists in Cellini's studio—Tenor and Basso. Fieramosca, sculptor to the Pope—Baritone. Pompeo, a bravo—Baritone. Place, Rome, 1532, under Pope Clement VII.

The opera was produced at Paris and London in 1853, and met with little success, but was received at Weimar in 1855 and at Hanover in 1879 with great applause. The opera has scarcely kept its place, but is occasionally produced in prominent cities.

Act I. Hall in the Palazzo Balducci. Cellini wishes to elope with Teresa Balducci, but their conversation is overheard by Fieramosca. As Balducci appears, Cellini manages to escape, while Fieramosca is treated as an intruder.

Act II. A tavern. Cellini receives a sum of money from the Pope to finish his statue of Perseus. As the sum is too small, however, the pupils of Cellini plan revenge against Balducci, the treasurer of the Pope. Cellini has arranged with Teresa to escape in the guise of masqueraders, which Fieramosca, who has again listened, and who hates the goldsmith, determines to prevent.

Change of scene: Crowd of masqueraders at the Colonna square. As Fieramosca and Pompeo arrive in the same costumes as Cellini and his apprentice Ascanio, an altercation takes place. Cellini stabs Pompeo, but escapes, and Fieramosca is arrested instead.

Act III. Before the foundry of Cellini. Cellini appears in a procession of monks, and Balducci tries to force

Teresa to marry Fieramosca. A cardinal endeavours to arrest Cellini on the charge of murder, particularly as the statue of Perseus has not been finished. Cellini thereupon orders that all his works of art shall be melted to form part of the statue. He breaks the plaster cast, and all stand enthralled with the masterpiece. The master is pardoned.

THE BOHEMIAN GIRL

Grand opera in three acts by Michael William Balfe. Libretto by Alfred Bunn.

CAST: Count Arnheim, governor of Presburg—Baritone. Thaddeus, a Polish exile—Tenor. Florestein, nephew of the count—Tenor. Devilshoof, chief of the gipsies—Basso. Captain of the Guard—Basso. An officer—Tenor. Arline—Soprano. Buda, her nurse—Soprano. Queen of the Gipsies—Soprano. Gipsies, huntsmen, guests. Place, Presburg and its environs. Time, the eighteenth century. First production, London, 1843.

ACT I. Scene 1. Count Arnheim's grounds near Presburg. (Chorus of huntsmen: "Up with the banner.") Count Arnheim's retainers are waiting to accompany him to the hunt. He appears with his foppish nephew Florestein, who is afraid of a gun. (Count: "A soldier's life.") He bids farewell to his little daughter Arline, and she goes up a mountain path with Buda, her nurse, and Florestein. Thaddeus, a Polish exile, enters exhausted from pursuit. (Cavatina, Thaddeus: " 'Tis sad to leave our fatherland.") Gipsies appear, headed by Devilshoof. They attempt to rob Thaddeus, but after some parley he decides to join their band. Devilshoof takes everything he has except his commission, but gives him a ragged gipsy dress in return. He mingles with the gipsies just as a troop of soldiers come to apprehend him. (Chorus: "In the gipsies' life you read.") Huntsmen return in excitement; Florestein appears, terrified. (Florestein: "Is no succour near?") Arline has been attacked by a wild animal. Thaddeus rescues her, and the count in gratitude invites him to a feast, during which he refuses to drink to the emperor. He is repudiated by all, but Devilshoof comes to his aid. As a reward for the rescue of Arline the count offers the exile a purse, which he proudly refuses. Thaddeus and Devilshoof are imprisoned, but the latter escaping carries off Arline. He is seen by the count and his guests crossing a frail bridge between two rocks with the child in his arms. He breaks down the bridge and disappears. (Prayer: "Thou who in might supreme.")

Act II. Scene 1. Twelve years later. Street in Presburg. Tent of the queen of the gipsies. Arline sleeps while Thaddeus keeps watch. (Chorus: "Silence! Silence!") Devilshoof enters with a new project to rob Florestein, who is flushed with wine. (Florestein: "Wine, Wine.") They secure his valuables, but the gipsy queen makes them return everything. Florestein is solicitous about a medallion which has disappeared and which is an heirloom of great value. Devilshoof has secreted it. Arline awakens and tells Thaddeus her dream. (Aria: "I dreamt I dwelt in marble halls.") Thaddeus and Arline declare their love. The queen, through jealousy, is angry, but, ridiculed by Devilshoof, joins their hands according to the gipsy rite. (Queen, ballad: "Would I had died ere now.")

Scene 2. Another street. (Arline, song: "Come with the gipsy's bride.")

Scene 3. A fair. Count Arnheim and Florestein appear. Florestein compliments Arline, which amuses her, until he tries to kiss her, and she slaps him vigorously. The queen, recognising him, gives Arline the stolen medallion, so that she will be accused of robbing him. This plan succeeds, but Thaddeus and the gipsies protect Arline. Nevertheless, she and Thaddeus are imprisoned.

Scene 4. Count Arnheim's apartments with a portrait of Arline in her childhood. The count enters sadly, and gazes at the portrait. (Count: "The heart bowed down.")

The captain of the guard reports Arline's capture. She is brought in and pleads her innocence, but in her humiliation is about to stab herself. The count, while stopping her, observes a scar by which he recognises her as his daughter, and Thaddeus, who enters at that moment, as her preserver. (Count: "Mine own, my long lost child.")

Act III. Count's castle. Arline in rich attire is sad and lonely. She looks with longing at her gipsy dress. Devilshoof boldly enters the room and begs her to rejoin the tribe. Thaddeus appears at the window. (Thaddeus: "Then you'll remember me"; Trio: "Through the world wilt thou fly.") The two men hide themselves as the guests enter. The queen of the gipsies suddenly appears and tells the count Thaddeus is concealed in his daughter's room. (Quintet: "To shame and feeling dead.") The count denounces his daughter. (Arline: "See at your feet a suppliant.") Thaddeus comes from his hiding-place, and declares Arline innocent. (Thaddeus: "When the fair land of Poland.") He proclaims his identity as a Polish noble. The count is reassured, but the gipsy queen tries to kill Thaddeus, and Devilshoof, while attempting to snatch the rifle from her hands, accidentally shoots her. The joy of the lovers is too great to be marred, and all ends happily. (Chorus: "Oh, what full delight.")

THE BRONZE HORSE

Fairy opera in three acts. By Auber. Libretto by Scribe.
Cast: Yang-Yang, prince imperial of China—Tenor. Tsing-Tsing, a Mandarin—Baritone. Tao-chin, one of his wives—Soprano. Tschin-Kao, farmer and keeper of tea house—Basso. Peki, his daughter—Mezzo-soprano. Yanko, a young peasant—Tenor. Stella, daughter of the Grand Mogul—Soprano. Heliante, a siren. Place, a Chinese village, the third act partly on the planet Venus. First production, Paris, 1835.

ACT I. The Mandarin Tsing-Tsing has four wives, of whom one, Tao-chin, by virtue of her descent from the emperor, enjoys considerable liberty, but makes life a burden to him. He desires to take a fifth wife, the pretty Peki, daughter of the keeper of the tea house. Peki, however, loves the young peasant Yanko, and is in despair at being compelled to marry the Mandarin. Everything is prepared for the wedding. (Chorus of peasants: "Ring, bells of the pagoda," and Aria of Tsing-Tsing: "Maiden, since first I beheld thee.") Tao-chin approaches to prevent the marriage, then Prince Yang-Yang (Song: "Love and mirth as companions"), who has seen a heavenly picture in his dreams (Aria: "Lulled in soulful dreams"), and expects to find his ideal on the planet Venus. He forces Tsing-Tsing, who has been appointed his tutor by the emperor, to mount a miraculous bronze horse which stands on a pinnacle of rocks above the village, and which quickly carries off in the air any person who seats himself upon it. On this horse the two go forth to seek Yang-Yang's fate.

ACT II. He who is brought back by the bronze horse must not reveal what he has seen, otherwise he will be turned to stone or wood. The tea-house keeper, Tschia-Kao, wishes Peki to marry another rich man (Aria: "Oh daughter, you my pride"), and she is compelled to submit. (Song: "Hear, unmarried.") Yanko, who has also taken a ride on the horse, advises his loved one to don man's attire and to flee with him. Tsing-Tsing returns upon the horse. Weary, he falls asleep and reveals the secret of his journey in his dreams to the listening Peki, whereupon he is changed to wood. He is found in this plight, and Yanko whispers into the ear of Tschia-Kao the cause of the change. He also suffers a like transformation. When Peki, who is now aware of the secret and has already donned male clothes for flight, sees that her lover is bewitched, she resolves to save him, and mounting the bronze horse, rides away in the sight of the astonished people.

Act III.   Fairy landscape on the planet Venus. (Chorus of sirens: "Oh, the groves of Paradise.")   Stella, the daughter of the Grand Mogul, has been transported to Venus because she was too shy when upon the earth.   Now she loves the man of her dreams, the Prince Yang-Yang. He has come to capture her and conquer the fairyland she inhabits, but must remain silent till midnight, a condition to all riders of the bronze horse.   In the duet ("Of what do you complain?") he passionately kisses Stella, is brought back to earth by the bronze horse, and as he also speaks, is changed to wood, like Tschia-Kao and Yanko. All three are erected as pagodas in the temple.   In the meantime, Peki has arrived upon the planet Venus, endures the test, returns to earth with Stella and releases the victims of enchantment.   Tsing-Tsing receives back Tao-chin, the prince marries Stella, and Peki is rewarded by wedding her beloved Yanko.

A CAMP IN SILESIA

Opera in three acts by Meyerbeer.   Text by Rellstab.
Cast: Saldorf, retired captain—Basso.   Thérèse, his niece—Mezzo-soprano.   Vielka—Soprano.   Konrad— Tenor.   Tronk, leader of the Hungarian cavalry—Baritone.   A Hungarian rider—Tenor.   A corporal of grenadiers—Basso.   A corporal of artillery—Baritone.   A huzzar of Ziethen—Tenor.   A Black Huzzar—Basso.   Steffen, an old countryman—Tenor.   Place, Silesia and Sans Souci.   Time, during the seven years' war.   First production, Berlin, 1843.
Act I.   A room in a country house.   Frederick the Great is in danger of being captured by Hungarian huzzars. While Vielka, the adopted daughter of old Saldorf, engages the attention of her countrymen, Konrad exchanges clothes with the king and he escapes.
Act II.   The camp of the Prussians.   Songs, marches

and dances. Upon the report that Saldorf has delivered
the king to the Hungarians, the old captain is in danger
of being put to death, but is saved by the arrival of the
king.

ACT III. In Sans Souci. Leopold, the nephew and
adopted son of old Saldorf, and foster brother of Konrad,
is condemned to death for desertion, but Vielka and Konrad, the saviours of Frederick the Great, obtain his pardon.

(This opera was utilised by Meyerbeer for the Star of the
North.")

CARMEN

Opera in four acts by Bizet. Text by Meilhac and
Halévy, founded on the novel of Prosper Mérimée.

CAST: Zuniga, lieutenant—Basso. José, sergeant—
Tenor. Morales, sergeant—Basso. Escamillo, bull fighter
—Basso. Dancairo and Remendado, smugglers—Tenor
and Baritone. Carmen, Frasquita and Mercedes, gipsies—
Soprano and Mezzo-soprano. Micaëla, a peasant girl—
Soprano. Place, Seville, Spain. Time, the beginning of
the nineteenth century. First production, Paris, 1875.
One of the most popular of the modern operas. The de-
cease of the composer prevented him from witnessing its
success.

The Spanish gipsy Carmen lives only for sensuality.
Love drives her from passion to passion. After she has
loved many, she is attracted by the sergeant Don José, en-
compasses him with her wiles, and leads him to mutiny and
desertion, so that finally nothing remains for him but to
join a band of smugglers of which Carmen is a member.
His fate is endurable as long as he retains the love of Carmen, but when she turns from him he is sunk in the depths
of despair. Called to the death-bed of his mother, on returning he finds his still passionately loved Carmen before
the arena in Seville with the bull fighter Escamillo, to
whom she has promised her love if he is the victor at the

fight. She is approached by José, who asks her to return to him, and when she coldly repulses him and tries to escape to Escamillo he stabs her to the heart.

The sombre action of the opera is enlivened by strong contrasts of light and shade. In the first act: street scene in Seville, march of the watch, the commotion of the cigarette girls and street fight; in the second act: life among the gipsies and dance; in the third act: the picturesque groups of the smugglers; in the fourth act: the procession of bull fighters. The lyric element is represented by the blonde and gentle Micaëla, a youthful companion of José and messenger from his mother. The whole action is quiet, notwithstanding its charming effects and colouring, and is kept together by the originality of the music, which is beautiful and characteristic of the locality in which the scene is laid.

ACT I. A square in Seville with bridge. To the left the guard house, opposite a cigarette factory. Micaëla appears seeking José, but is accosted by the impudent soldiers and retires. José approaches with the guard to relieve Morales. The commanding officer is Lieutenant Zuniga. The workpeople emerge from the factory. Carmen appears, wooed by all, with the exception of José, upon whom she has cast her eyes. (Habanera: "Love is a bird.") Micaëla, who loves José, brings him a letter and greeting from his mother. (Don José: "Tell me what of my mother.") When she has gone, a tumult takes place in the factory and Zuniga arrests Carmen, who has been threatening her companions with a knife. She is placed in charge of José, who is beguiled by the coquette and he allows her to escape. (Seguidilla: "Near to the walls of Seville.")

ACT II. Evening at a smuggler's inn. Song and dance of the gipsies. (Carmen, Frasquita, Mercedes: "The rattling, ringing tambourine.") The bull fighter Escamillo arrives and is boisterously greeted. They sing the Toreador song ("To the fight, torero"). Smuggler quintet of

Dancairo, Remendado, Carmen, Frasquita and Mercedes.
Carmen refuses to accompany them, for she is waiting for
her adored José, who has been arrested on her account and
whose imprisonment has expired.   José arrives and is prevented from rejoining his comrades.   (Canzonetta: "Halt,
who goes there.")   Surprised by Zuniga, he draws his
sword upon his superior officer; the lieutenant is disarmed
by the smugglers and José resolves to fly with Carmen.
(Duet and dance, Carmen, Don José: "I will dance in your
honour.")

ACT III.   A rocky gorge, José arrives with the smugglers (Sextet and chorus: "Listen, comrades"), but Carmen loves him no longer.   Her inconstant heart now
turns to Escamillo.   (Trio, over the cards: "Shuffle, shuffle, cut them, cut them.")   A fight between José and Escamillo is narrowly averted by the smugglers.   (Duet: "I
am Escamillo.")   Micaëla arrives (Aria: "Here is the
smugglers' stronghold") and tells José that his mother is
dying, and with threats to Carmen he leaves the band.

ACT IV.   A square before the arena at Seville.   Festal
procession of the bull fighters.   Carmen promises herself
to Escamillo if he returns victorious.   As she is about entering the arena she is confronted by the pale and despairing José.   (Duet, Carmen, Don José: "Is it thou; it is I.")
For the last time he demands her love and fidelity.   When
she coldly refuses he stabs her to the heart and she expires
at the moment that the victorious Escamillo arrives upon
the scene.

CATARINA CORNARO

Grand opera in four acts by Franz Lachner.   Libretto by
St. Georges and Büssel.

CAST: Jacob of Lusignan, King of Cyprus—Tenor. Andrea Cornaro, Patrician—Baritone.   Onofrio, Member of
the Council of Ten—Basso.   Catarina Cornaro, niece of
Andrea—Soprano.   Marco Onnero, a young patrician—

Tenor.   Spirido and Angelo, bandits—Bassi.   Place, Venice and Cyprus.   Time, 1470.   First production, Munich, 1841.

ACT I.   Hall in the palace of Cornaro.   Catarina is about to be married to Marco Onnero, when Onofrio brings the order of the council that Andrea Cornaro shall give his daughter to the King of Cyprus in marriage in order that Cyprus may be joined to Venice.   Amidst the tumult of the assembled guests the wedding festival is postponed.

ACT II.   Catarina's room in Venice.   The threats of her father induce Catarina to refuse the offer of flight made ¹y her bridegroom, and when Marco is informed of her res-ᴜlution, he believes her to be blinded by the glitter of the crown and vows vengeance against the King of Cyprus.

ACT III.   A hall in the palace of Cornaro.   Marriage and crowning of Catarina.

Change of scene: Square at San Marco.   Marco tries to kill the king on his way to the church.   As he raises the dagger, he recognises in Lusignan his rescuer from the hands of assassins some time before.   He throws away the dagger, flees, and in the general excitement Catarina falls senseless.

ACT IV.   Palace at Cyprus.   Two years have elapsed. The Council of Ten seek the life of the king by poison, in order to take possession of Cyprus through Catarina. Marco arrives as ambassador of the Republic, finds that Catarina still loves him, and as he is aware of the designs of the Venetians, resolves to save the king.   The Venetian party imprison Catarina, but Marco frees the queen, and the dying king declares him protector to the queen and her son before the assembled people.   Catarina remains ruler and Cyprus is lost to Venice.

CAVALLERIA RUSTICANA

Opera in one act by Pietro Mascagni. Libretto adapted from the book of Vergas by Targioni-Torzetti and Menasci.

CAST: Santuzza, a young peasant—Soprano. Turiddu, a young farmer—Tenor. Lucia, his mother—Alto. Alfio, a carter—Baritone. Lola, his wife—Mezzo-soprano. Place, a Sicilian village. Time, the present. First production, Costanzi Theatre, Rome, 1890.

While the curtain is down, Turiddu sings. (Siciliana: "O Lola, lovely as the spring's bright blooms.") The action takes place before the church. Devout pantomime by the church-goers; behind the scene, chorus of peasants. ("Queen of Heaven.") At last Santuzza and Lucia appear from opposite sides of the stage. (Santuzza: "Tell me, mamma Lucia.") Turiddu is the lover of Santuzza and she believes he has discarded her for Lola; she has seen him entering the young woman's house. The carrier Alfio, the husband of Lola, appears with the chorus and also says that he has seen Turiddu, but thinks nothing wrong of it. When Lucia, who has sent her son to Frankofonte for wine, inquires further into the matter, she is asked to be silent by Santuzza. (Romanza: "Well do you know, good mamma.") After the chorus with Alfio has departed, Santuzza recites her wrongs. Turiddu loved Lola, but after his service in the army found her married to Alfio. He then entered into relations with Santuzza, and is now turning back to his former love. The alarmed Lucia enters the church with the peasants. Santuzza awaits Turiddu (Scene: "You, Santuzza"), who, however, treats her coldly and drives her to despair by leaving her and entering the church with Lola. (Duet: "Ah what folly"; Lola: "My king of roses.") "You shall suffer in blood for this," Santuzza exclaims, and discovers to the returning Alfio the unfaithfulness of Lola. (Duet: "God has sent you, neighbour Alfio.") Breathing vengeance, the carrier resolves to kill Turiddu and departs with Santuzza. During the following orchestral music (Intermezzo) the stage remains empty. Turiddu, Lola and the chorus emerge from the church; Turiddu sings a drinking song ("Hail the red wine, richly flowing") and is then challenged by Alfio to a duel with knives after the manner of the Sicilians. Promising to follow Alfio he takes a moving farewell of his mother, and asks her to care for the unhappy Santuzza, whom he has so deeply wronged. After a short pause, Santuzza, followed by a crowd of women, rushes upon the stage, and with the cry of "Turiddu is dead," the opera ends.

THE CHILDREN OF THE PLAINS

Opera in four acts by Rubinstein. Text adapted from Beck's "Yanko" by Mosenthal.

CAST: Count Waldemar, officer—Tenor. Konrad, a German innkeeper on the estate of the count—Baritone. Maria, his daughter—Soprano. Wauja, an hostler—Tenor. Isbrana, a gipsy—Mezzo-soprano. Grigori, Bogdan and Pawel, gipsies—Bassi. Lisa, gipsy—Mezzo-soprano. Place, the plains of the Ukraine. Time, the present. First production, Vienna, 1861.

ACT I. The plains. Bogdan and Pawel plan the death of the innkeeper Konrad and threaten to kill Isbrana, who has been listening, if she reveals their plan. Nevertheless, Isbrana tells her lover, the hostler, Wauja, of the gipsies' designs.

Change of scene: Before the house of Konrad on the heath. The gipsies attack the unguarded house, but when Wauja's horn calls the neighbours, they fly, leaving the house in flames. Wauja saves Maria from death, and as a reward is invited by Konrad to make his home with him.

ACT II. A chamber in Konrad's house. Maria has a lover in a distant country, but to please her father she consents to become the wife of Wauja. Isbrana and the

gipsies arrive to celebrate the wedding of Wauja. Count
Waldemar, the former lover of Maria, also appears. He
distributes money to the people and promises Maria to
send her a message during the evening.

Act III. The same scene. The sun rises. Grigori, a
gipsy, brings a letter from the count to Maria. Isbrana
bribes him to let her read it. Out of compassion for Wauja,
who cannot read, she tells him only a portion of its contents in which the count promises him a horse, but sup-
presses the part in which the count declares he will visit
Maria during Wauja's absence. The meeting takes place,
and Maria is about to elope with the count when Wauja
returns and discovers all. He rushes at Waldemar and slays
him. The neighbours arrive and are about to capture Wauja,
when Isbrana and the gipsies appear and rescue him.

Act IV. Camp of the gipsies. Wauja joins the robber
band of the gipsies, but repulses Isbrana, as he still loves
Maria. The latter and her father are captured; the hostler
plans their escape, but is circumvented. Soldiers arrive
and the gipsies fly. Wauja and Isbrana remain. She endeavours to persuade him to escape, but he refuses. As
the soldiers surround them, she snatches a dagger from
Wauja, stabs herself, and is carried away a prisoner.

CIRCE

Musical tragedy in three acts with the prologue
"Polyphemos" by August Bungert. Text by the composer.

Cast: Gäa, a giant represented by a chorus of bass voices.
Eros—Tenor. Zeus—Basso. Hermes—Tenor. Athene—
Contralto. Polyphemos—Basso. Odysseus—Baritone.
Periander—Baritone. Zurylochos—Baritone. Perimides
—Baritone. Circe—Soprano. The four wells—Soprano
and Alto soli. Helios—Tenor. Teiresias—Basso. Here
—Alto. Poseidon—Basso. The three Fates—Alto soli.

Place, on the island of Äa.   Time, in ancient days.   First production, Dresden, 1898.

PROLOGUE. Scene: A mountain chain, surrounded by the sea and almost hidden by heavy mists. The figure of Gäa appears in giant form. Eros riding upon a lion awakens the earth. The clouds descend showing Olympus, whose gods implore Zeus to save Odysseus. The mists disappear and reveal the cavern of the cyclops Polyphemos at the foot of Mount Ætna. Drunken with wine he snores loudly, but is awakened by Odysseus, who puts out his single eye. (Morning chorus of the Oceanides: "Do you wake, sister?") Polyphemos, now entirely blind, vainly pursues his unknown enemies Odysseus and his companions, who have concealed themselves in the midst of a flock of sheep and easily escape his groping fingers. Only after they have returned to their vessel does Odysseus tell him who they are. Polyphemos curses them and prays to his father Poseidon for vengeance. The Oceanides crying, "Hail, Odysseus!" surround the ship. (Music during change of scene. Periander's song: "Far across the sea.")

ACT I. Coast of the island of Äa. Circe, daughter of Helios, surrounded by her maids, laments her lonely life. Odysseus, led by Hermes, draws near. He receives a potion from the god to render innocuous the magic of Circe, who has changed his companions into swine. Odysseus and Circe fall violently in love with each other. When she finds her magic of no effect upon Odysseus she surrenders herself to him entirely and disenchants his companions. Periander warns Odysseus, but the latter rewards him by wounding him with his lance. Odysseus and Circe celebrate an orgy of love. Gäa appears once more and with their song the act ends.

ACT II. The coast of Äa. The companions of Odysseus, ill of the plague, curse him angrily. The dying Periander sadly recalls his wife to him. Odysseus, stricken with remorse, desires to fly from Circe and helps his companions to build a vessel for that purpose. Helios, the father of

Circe, arrives to kill Odysseus, but Circe begs for mercy
for her lover. The arrows of the sun god have confused
the brain of Odysseus and he can only find relief in the
realm of shadows. Circe lulls him to sleep and makes his
dreams a reality. Musical interlude. Change of scene:
In Hades, where the Styx flows under grottos. Odysseus
sacrifices and calls upon the shade of Teiresias, who foretells his future and that of the Antikleia. He also summons before him Agamemnon, Ajax, and Achilles. The
last two appear bearing Periander and pointing to his
wounds. Overpowered by the thronging shades Odysseus
falls to the ground.

Act III. Olympus. Helios and Poseidon accuse Odysseus to Zeus, but he refuses to listen, for it has long been
determined that Odysseus shall subdue himself. Change of
scene: Palace of Circe. She holds in her arms the slumber-
ing Odysseus, who whispers the name of his wife, Penelope.
Awakening, he demands his freedom of the enchantress.
Circe shows him the lovely sunlit country that surrounds
them, but without avail. She sings and dances for him
("Dost thou love my songs"); she tells him she is soon to
be a mother. Her arts proving useless, she changes the
beautiful landscape into a place of horrors. Odysseus
fights his way out of it and is enthusiastically received by
his friends. Helios once more endeavours to kill him, but
Hermes speedily appears bearing the order of Zeus that
he shall be set free. Odysseus departs, and Circe, receiving
the blessing of Helios, muses upon the future and falls
quietly asleep. The three Fates spin their web. The song
of Gäa ends the drama.

CLEOPATRA

Opera in three acts, with a prologue by August Enna.
Libretto adapted from Rider Haggard by Einar Christian-
sen, German, by Emma Klingenfeld.

CAST: Cleopatra, Queen of Egypt—Soprano. Harmaki, the last of the Pharaohs—Tenor. Sepa, high priest—Baritone. Charmion, his daughter, in the service of Cleopatra—Soprano. Schafra, Egyptian prince—Basso. Iras, slave of Cleopatra—Soprano. Place, Alexandria.

PROLOGUE. Subterranean chamber. The high priest Sepa welcomes Harmaki as the only legitimate King of Egypt, saying that Cleopatra is only a wild shoot from the stem and neglects the native customs in favour of the Greek. Harmaki, he prophesies, shall free the country from her dominion and again make it happy; the latter declares himself ready. At the command of Sepa, a curtain in the rear of the chamber is swept aside, and a throne room becomes visible. (Chorus of Egyptians: "Hathor, holy Hathor.") Sepa reveals his plan to the people; all rejoice and do homage to Harmaki as king, upon which crown, sceptre and scourge are delivered to him as tokens of sovereignty.

ACT I. Garden before the palace of Cleopatra, looking out upon the sea. Charmion, the high priest's daughter, who is one of the conspirators, dreams of her future king. (Aria: "They foam, the holy waves.") Sepa, who enters with Harmaki, approves of her words. (Terzett: "Give strength to us.") When Sepa departs Charmion and Harmaki, who are attracted to each other, form a union against the queen. As the sun goes down (Chorus: "Golden are its rays"), Cleopatra and her attendants appear. Charmion introduces Harmaki as "a soothsayer, star gazer and interpreter of dreams." The queen speaks of a strange dream, which Harmaki interprets by endeavouring to arouse her patriotism. She uses her arts of fascination, and Charmion notes with dismay that Harmaki is unable to withstand her charms. (Ensemble: "Come then, O priest.")

ACT II. The star tower of Harmaki. Harmaki is in love with the queen and prays to Isis to give him strength to resist her. Charmion brings him a list of those condemned

to death by the conspirators. When he finds Cleopatra's
name he trembles, and refuses to stain his hands in her
blood, but Charmion persuades him that it is his duty to
stab the queen the next night, when she is to visit him
alone under cover of the festival. When Cleopatra comes
to him late at night Charmion hides behind a curtain and
realises bitterly that Cleopatra's fascination for Harmaki
is as strong as ever. The queen bids him come the following night to foretell her future from the stars. When
Cleopatra has departed, Charmion chides him severely and
he confesses that he loves her. Charmion departs in
despair.

ACT III. A hall in the palace of Cleopatra. A ballet
ends the festival, and Cleopatra calls upon Harmaki to explain the chart of the stars. He stands behind her, dagger in hand, but his courage fails him, and he cannot kill
her. His strange behaviour arouses the attention of Cleopatra; she sings to him. (Song: "I sing for you.") She
caresses him, and at last he succumbs to her arts and sinks
into her arms. She suddenly snatches from him the concealed dagger and tauntingly casts him from her. As he
attempts to kill her Sepa and the other conspirators are
brought in manacled and bitterly reproach Harmaki for be-
traying them and his country. Cleopatra contemptuously
throws the dagger at his feet and orders the prisoners removed. Charmion courageously delivers herself as a prisoner, declaring herself to be guilty of treason to the queen.
Harmaki, in despair, drives the dagger through his heart,
and Charmion, horror stricken, falls dead at his side.

CORNELIUS SCHUTT

Opera in three acts, by Swareglia. Libretto by Illica.
CAST: Cornelius Schutt, painter—Tenor. Franz Hals,
painter—Basso. Craesbecke, painter—Baritone. Elizabeth

von Thourenhoudt—Soprano. Gertrud—Mezzo-soprano.
Kettel, Elizabeth's old nurse—Alto. Place, Antwerp.
Time, 1630. First production, Prague, 1893.

ACT I. Square before an inn at Antwerp. Drinking
bout of painters. They wonder at the absence of Cornelius
Schutt, whose whereabouts is unknown even to his betrothed, Gertrud. Cornelius appears unexpectedly but in
a strange mood. He takes an evening stroll and sees Elizabeth, who is accompanied by her nurse Kettel. His friend
Craesbecke engages the nurse in conversation while
Cornelius pays court to Elizabeth, making little progress
in his suit, however. When Elizabeth appears later on
the balcony of her house she confesses her love to
Cornelius, and they fly together.

ACT II. Country house. After Cornelius has resided
here two years with Elizabeth his desire for work returns
and he wishes to see the world. In the motley masquerade
of the Kirmess, Kettel arrives with money to purchase a
picture from Cornelius. His friends, however, have followed the old woman and have discovered his hiding-place.
They induce Cornelius to join them once more, leaving
Elizabeth behind.

ACT III. The stage setting represents the naves of a
Carmelite church. One part is occupied by the studio of
Cornelius; he sits before his canvas but cannot work. Gertrud, to whom he has returned, cannot dispel his gloomy
thoughts, and he falls into deep melancholy. Even his
friends Craesbecke and Franz Hals cannot rouse him, so
they leave him to himself. Elizabeth, who has become a
nun, is seen in the adjoining nave. The painter hears her
voice in prayer, rushes toward her and again awakens her
love by a recital of his misfortunes. When the voices of
the other nuns are heard, Elizabeth tears herself from
him, realising that she is now dead to him forever. He
hastily rushes to the easel, sketches a Madonna, which
bears the likeness of Elizabeth, falls to the ground, and
when his friends arrive, has breathed his last.

COSI FAN TUTTE

(Or "La scuola degli amanti," "The School of Lovers," also known under the German title "So machen es alle.")

Comic opera in two acts by Mozart. Libretto by da Ponte.

CAST: Fiordiligi—Soprano. Dorabella, her sister—Soprano. Ferrando, officer—Tenor. Guglielmo, officer—Baritone. Alfonso, bachelor—Basso. Despina, maid—Soprano. Place, Naples. Time, the eighteenth century.

This opera was written and composed at the suggestion of the Emperor Joseph II, and was first produced at Vienna in 1790. It is founded upon an actual occurrence. The libretto is of rather a doubtful character and has often been improved and altered.

ACT I. Don Alfonso lays a wager with the officers Fernando and Guglielmo, by which they are to test the fidelity of their brides, Fiordiligi and Dorabella, for the space of a day. The officers seemingly bid farewell to them, but return disguised as rich Albanians. They are unrecognised and make love to each other's wives. The maid Despina tries to induce her mistresses to give ear to the rich strangers, but the sisters remain steadfast. Alfonso, who does not wish to lose his wager, bribes Despina, and when the Albanians seemingly take poison before the eyes of the ladies, the maid appears disguised as a physician, and saves their lives by pretended magnetism.

ACT II. Persuaded by Despina, Dorabella is the first of the two to listen to the pleadings of the disguised Guglielmo, to whom she gives the picture of her betrothed Fernando. Fernando wins Fiordiligi. Despina, at the suggestion of Alfonso, now disguises herself as a notary and brings the marriage contracts. At this moment news arrives of the return of the officers. The cowering Albanians, who have been hidden by the sisters, escape in order to reappear in their true characters. They unmask Despina, show the faithless brides their marriage contracts, and finally reveal themselves, but at the critical moment Alfonso, who has won the bet, explains all and brings about a reconciliation.

THE CRICKET ON THE HEARTH

Opera in three parts by Karl Goldmark. Text by Willner, founded upon Dickens's tale.

Cast: John—Baritone. Dot, his wife—Soprano. May —Soprano. Edward Plummer—Tenor. Tackleton— Basso. The cricket—Soprano. Place, a village in England. Time, the beginning of the nineteenth century. First production, Berlin, 1896.

Part I. A room in John's house. After the prologue of an invisible chorus of elves the cricket relates that it is the guardian spirit of the house. (Song: "I am the cricket.") Dot tells it she has a sweet secret which it must not reveal. She hopes soon to have a child. May laments her fate as a jilted bride, who is to marry old Tackleton, a rich toy-maker, on the morrow. John returns home accompanied by May's lover Edward, disguised as an old sailor, who distributes letters to the villagers. (Song: "Home, sweet home.")

Part II. A garden. May and Tackleton take supper together and John manages to make him jealous of the mysterious stranger. (Quintet: "My heart beats.") Edward has made himself known to Dot and John endeavours to overhear their conversation, but is prevented by Dot in a merry scene. He is jealous, and wishes to kill himself and the stranger, but the cricket lulls him to sleep and in dreams shows him his future as a happy father.

Part III. John's dwelling. May, touched by Edward's song ("Hulla, list to the song of the sea"), resolves to be true to him. They are reunited (Duet: "Oh speak, my adored one") and drive away in Tackleton's carriage to be married, while the latter is detained by the villagers. John and Dot are reconciled when she tells him her secret, and the concluding tableau represents four happy people and a scene of domestic peace.

CRISPINO E LA COMARE

(The Cobbler and the Fairy)

Opéra bouffe in three acts by Luigi and Federigo Ricci. Libretto by Piave.

CAST: Crispino Taccheto, a cobbler—Baritone. Annetta, his wife, a ballad singer—Soprano. Count del Fiore—Tenor. Fabrizio, a physician—Basso. Mirabolano, an apothecary—Tenor. Don Asdrubale, a miser—Basso. Bortolo, a mason. La Comare, a fairy—Mezzo-soprano. Scene, Venice. Time, the seventeenth century. First production, Venice, 1850.

ACT I. Crispino, a poor cobbler and his wife Annetta are always unhappy and in debt. No one wants Crispino's shoes, or Annetta's songs, and they are about to be dispossessed by their landlord, Don Asdrubale, an old miser, who is slily making love to Annetta. Crispino sits on a bench patching shoes, across the street the apothecary's apprentices are mixing drugs (Chorus: "Beat, beat, pound, pound"), and Don Asdrubale and the count are drinking coffee at the café. The count is in love with the miser's ward, and the latter is withholding his consent, and Lisette's dowry. (Count: "Lovely as an angel art thou.") Crispino to drive away the blues builds castles in the air. (Crispino: "Once on a time a humble cobbler.") Annetta enters, vending her ballads. (Canzonet, Annetta: "Pretty stories, fine to read.") Every one refuses to buy and Don Asdrubale once more demands the rent. (Quintet and chorus: "Pay what you owe.") Crispino, almost mad, rushes away. Don Asdrubale detains Annetta, who finally runs off after her husband. Fabrizio and the Don consult about Lisette's illness, which the latter says is due to an absurd love affair. (Fabrizio: "I'm something of a philosopher.") Crispino, meanwhile, has reached a deserted spot, and resolves to end his life. He beholds a well and is about to drown himself therein, when a fairy suddenly rises from its depths. He tells her his story, and promising to aid him, she gives him money. She tells him that through her he will become a famous doctor, and that whenever she does not appear beside the patient a cure will be performed. Crispino can hardly believe his ears, but the money is real at all events and he quickly takes it home to Annetta. On the way he meets her and they rejoice together. (Duet: "Yes indeed, O husband mine.")

Act II. Crispino and Annetta are greatly elated. Crispino nails a doctor's sign to his door, while Annetta capers about (Annetta: "No longer am I poor Annetta") planning the fine dresses she is going to wear. All the neighbours come to look at the placard. The apothecary is by turns furious and contemptuous. Presently Bortolo, a mason, is brought in, badly hurt. The doctors give him up, but Crispino's prescription cures him immediately. (Duet, Annetta, Crispino: "Many kisses, dearest fairy.") Every one is mystified (Chorus: "Long live Crispino the cobbler"), for the doctors are forced to admit that the cure was genuine.

Act III. The count tries to bargain with Fabrizio to take a letter to Lisette. (Duet: "Quick, quick, to work.") The apothecary Mirabolano is jealous of Crispino, who has acquired the pompous airs of most beggars on horseback, and refuses to fill his prescriptions. Fabrizio makes peace between them. Annetta entertains her friends and tells them how cross and unkind Crispino has become. She sings a ballad. ("Dearest Pietro, here is a cake.") Crispino enters, angrily driving away the guests. Opening the door, he is confronted by the fairy, whom he impudently berates. Reproaching him, she gives him a blow on the arm, and they disappear beneath the earth. They are now

in a subterranean cavern, where the fairy shows him figures of Time and Judgment, and a row of candles, some
burning brightly, some dimly, which represent human lives.
Crispino's candle is almost extinguished and the fairy informs him that he will soon die, but Annetta will live long
and happily on his money. Looking at the fairy in alarm
Crispino sees that she has the face of a skull. She commands him to make a will; having finished his bequests he
attempts to depart. The fairy tells him he must stay
where he is. He falls on his knees, and asks to see his wife
and children once more. (Crispino: "Dear fairy, not much
do I ask.") The fairy forgives him and disappears. In a
mirror he sees Annetta and the children praying for him.
He becomes unconscious, and awakens to find himself at
home surrounded by his family and friends. (Annetta:
"Ne'er have I known so joyous a moment.")

THE CROWN DIAMONDS

Comic opera in three acts by Auber. Text by Scribe and
St. Georges.

CAST: Bazaro, Count of Campo-Major, minister and member of the regency—Basso. Diana, his daughter—Soprano. Don Enriquez de Sandoval, his nephew—Tenor.
Don Sebastian d'Aveyro, officer—Tenor. Rebolledo, a
counterfeiter—Basso. Theophila, his niece—Mezzo-soprano. Munholz and Barbarigo, counterfeiters—Tenor
and Basso. Place, the mountains of Estramaduro, the castle of Campo-Major in Coimbra and the palace of the king
at Lisbon. Time, 1777. First production, Paris, 1841.

ACT I. A gorge in the mountains of Estremadura. Don
Enriquez has lost his way, but finds the adventure interest-
ing. (Song: "Roll on, roll on.") He discovers a gang
of counterfeiters. They are about to kill him but are prevented by Theophila, niece of Rebolledo. She knows Don
Enriquez, for she herself is in reality the Queen of Portu-

gal, who has sought out the counterfeiters to substitute false gems for the crown diamonds for the benefit of the treasury. The counterfeiters obey her. Enriquez believes the false diamonds to be genuine, and thinks they have been stolen. Threatened by soldiers, the band, with the aid of the passport of Enriquez, attempt to reach the border. But it is too late. The soldiers arrive, and on the advice of Theophila the counterfeiters throw the diamonds into a coffin and prepare to pass the soldiers disguised as pilgrims. (Chorus: "Unto the hermit of the chapel.")

Act II. Castle of Coimbra. During the six years' absence of Don Enriquez his friend Don Sebastian has gained the heart of Enriquez's bride Diana. The latter arriving, meets Theophila and Rebolledo, whose carriage has broken down on the road. The news is brought from Lisbon that the crown diamonds have been stolen; a certain Theophila is suspected. From the description Diana recognises the pseudo-robber Theophila, but Enriquez, who loves Theophila, persuades Diana to be silent and in requital releases his rights to her hand.

Act III. The palace of Lisbon. The initiated learn that Theophila is the queen who has sold the genuine crown diamonds to save the state from ruin. She is asked by the council to choose a husband. She refuses the Infante of Spain and selects the happy Enriquez as her bridegroom. Diana, now free, marries her faithful lover Sebastian.

CZAR AND ZIMMERMANN

(Czar and Carpenter)

Comic opera in three acts by Lortzing. Libretto by the composer.

Cast: Peter I, Czar of Russia, under the name of Peter Michaelow, a journeyman carpenter—Baritone. Peter Iwanow, a young Russian, journeyman carpenter—Tenor.

Van Bett, Burgomaster of Sardam—Basso. Marie, his
niece—Soprano. General Lefort, Russian ambassador—
Basso. Lord Syndham, English ambassador—Basso. Mar-
quis of Chateauneuf, French ambassador—Tenor. Widow
Brown—Alto. An officer. Place, Sardam. Time, 1698.
First production, Leipsic, 1837.

Two Russian journeymen carpenters are residing in Sardam, Czar Peter, under the name of Peter Michaelow, and
his friend the deserter, Peter Iwanow. The news circulates
in Sardam that the Czar is living there *incognito,* and the
ambassadors of foreign powers begin to seek him in order
to enter into favourable treaties. The French Marquis de
Chateauneuf is successful and comes to an agreement with
Peter and Lefort while the wise Burgomaster van Bett and
the English ambassador take Peter Iwanow for the Czar
and are not convinced by his denial. The Englishman even
gives Iwanow a passport, which he delivers to the real
Peter. The czar receives notice of the revolt of the Strelitz
and is compelled to leave for Russia at once. He pardons
his friend Iwanow and unites him with Marie, whom he
loves.

Act I. The carpenter's workshop on the wharf in Sardam. (Chorus of carpenters and song of the czar: "Comrades, grasp the axe.") Iwanow is jealous of Chateaueuf,
who is pursuing Marie, but she soothes him. (Aria:
"Jealousy is a plague.") The burgomaster, who considers
himself a very wise man, but is in reality so stupid that he
cannot even understand the orders to search for a certain
Peter, now appears. (Aria: "O sancta Justitia, I will go
mad"; with the popular strophe: "I am wise, and me no
one deceives.") He orders the bell to be rung to call together the carpenters, but can learn nothing from them,
although he suspects Iwanow. (Duet, Burgomaster,
Iwanow: "Can I trust their words.") Chateauneuf discovers the czar, who cautions him to be silent (Finale: "The
people gather to the festival"), and the czar appoints a
place of meeting with the ambassador.

Act II.   The garden of an inn. (Wedding chorus: "Long live joy," and romance of Chateauneuf: "Farewell, my girl of Flanders.") The guests retire, and at opposite tables are seated the burgomaster, Lord Syndham and Iwanow, while Chateauneuf and Lefort are seated with the czar. (Sextet: "The work that we begin.") The ambassadors have disguised themselves in order that they may not be detected either by the real or presumable czar. Marie returns with guests and sings the bridal song. ("Lovely blushes tinge my cheeks.") The joy of the feast, however, is disturbed by an officer who brings an order to the burgomaster to stop the secret enlistment of soldiers in the city. Van Bett, who is drunk, wants to arrest everybody, including himself, in order to detect the guilty Peter. All are asked to give their names, but the czar refuses to do so. (Finale: "For some time have I seen strange faces.")

Act III.   A hall in the court-house. Van Bett is practising a cantata dedicated to Iwanow, whom he still believes to be the czar ("Hail the day on which you appeared"), but has great difficulty in drumming it into the heads of the stupid singers. When the czar arrives he is believed to be a criminal by Van Bett, the latter departs with the chorus, and after Peter has cheered up Marie he remains alone. (Song: "Once played I with sceptre, with crown and with star.") After his departure Marie arrives with Iwanow and makes fun of him as the false czar. (Duet: "May a lonely maid dare.") The czar joins Iwanow and is enraged at the news that the harbour is closed, but Iwanow gives him the passport which he has received from the English ambassador. Peter hastens away, and when Van Bett arrives to sing the cantata for Iwanow, the curtain in the background is pulled aside and the vessel of the czar is seen sailing away. Iwanow is appointed imperial superintendent and receives permission to marry Marie.

DALIBOR

Opera in three acts by Friedrich Smetana. Libretto by Joseph Wenzig. German by Max Kalbeck.

CAST: Wladislaw, King of Bohemia. Dalibor, Captain of the guard. Budiwoj, a judge. Benesch, jailer. Veit, Dalibor's esquire. Milada, sister of the Burgrave, who has been killed by Dalibor. Yutta, an orphan. Place, Prague. Time, the fifteenth century. First production, Prague, 1868.

ACT I. Court of the castle at Prague. Yutta and chorus of the populace praise the valour of Dalibor, although he is that day to be judged by the king as an insurgent. (Aria: "He feels compassion.") The girl hopes to save him. The king and his followers approach, he takes the judicial seat, and commands Milada to narrate how Dalibor had at night suddenly attacked her brother's castle and slain him. (Aria: "It was late.") Dalibor is brought in. Milada is astonished at his manly beauty. He defends his course sturdily (Aria: "Nothing will I deny"), saying that the burgrave had captured his best friend Zdenko, who was a singer and a hero, and cruelly murdered him. In answer to an offer of ransom, the burgrave had sent Zdenko's head to Dalibor in derision. For this Dalibor had sworn vengeance and had kept his oath. Milada is filled with compassion and admires Dalibor's bravery in answering the king so fearlessly. He does not fear death, but is condemned by the judges to imprisonment for life and is led away by the guard. Milada asks for his pardon in vain, and Yutta, who soon observes that she loves Dalibor, unites with her to effect his release.

ACT II. Street in Prague. The song of the esquires in the inn is heard. ("A real soldier.") Yutta awaits her lover Veit, Dalibor's esquire (Duet: "Oh so long it is"), and talks over her plans with him. Milada has already appeared in male costume at the castle and fooled Benesch.

the jailer, so that she has been engaged as his helper. Veit communicates with the faithful esquires, and they hope to succeed in effecting Dalibor's release.

Change of scene. An open hall at the castle. Budiwoj fears an attempt of Dalibor's friends to free him and cautions Benesch to be doubly watchful. (Aria of Benesch: "Between these dark walls.") Milada (in male costume) has prepared a goodly meal for the jailer, but the compassionate old man desires to take a violin to Dalibor, who has asked for one. He allows Milada to take it. (Aria of Milada: "Then it is true.")

Change of scene. The dark dungeon. Dalibor sees in his dreams his friend Zdenko, who is playing on the violin. (Aria: "Vanished art thou.") Milada brings the violin, discloses her identity (Aria: "Moved by compassion"), and tells him of her plans for his escape. (Love duet: "My lovely dream.")

Act III. Hall in the palace of the king. Budiwoj reports that the people are restless and that strange soldiers have come to free Dalibor. The jailer Benesch is compelled to tell of Milada's unsuccessful attempt to release him: she had suddenly disappeared after opening the doors of the prison, but fortunately he had been in time to frustrate her design. (Aria: "You see, my lord.") The king directs that Dalibor shall die that very day (Aria: "Yes, the snake of revolt") ; he orders him to be brought in chains before him and announces his resolution. Dalibor remains calm (Aria: "Why do I tarry?") and is taken back to prison.

Change of scene: Square before the castle. It is night. Milada in the garb of a soldier approaches with friends of Dalibor, and listens for the tones of his violin, believing him to be free. As she hears nothing, she becomes alarmed, and when the bell for the condemned is heard, understands the reason. She demands of her followers to free Dalibor by force. ("Then take to arms.") They advance to the charge, and after terrific fighting, return with Dalibor, who is carrying the mortally wounded Milada. With the song, "Where am I," and a last loving "Dalibor"! she dies in his arms. (Final chorus: "From earth's depth.")

THE DAMNATION OF FAUST

Legend in four parts by Hector Berlioz.

CAST: Margaret—Soprano. Faust—Tenor. Mephistopheles—Baritone or Basso. Brander—Basso. Place, a German village. First production, Paris, 1846, in concert form; complete, Manchester, 1880.

PART I. Faust, a learned philosopher, wanders in the fields at sunrise meditating upon Nature. (Faust: "Now ancient winter hath made place for spring.") He observes a crowd of peasants who dance and sing, jesting rudely. The Hungarian troops approach to martial music. Great excitement prevails among the peasants. Faust alone remains cold and unmoved. (Chorus: "The shepherd early dons his best"; Hungarian March.)

PART II. Faust in his study deplores his unhappy lot. Neither in nature, nor in books, nor in old memories has he found solace. He decides to take poison, but as he raises the cup to drink the strains of an Easter hymn turn his thoughts toward good. (Chorus: "Christ is risen!") Even then the fiend Mephistopheles is at his elbow, tempting him with promises of earthly joys. He succumbs and goes forth with the fiend in search of pleasure. They enter a wine cellar in which a number of boon companions are carousing. (Chorus: "Fill up again with good red wine"; Brander: "Master Rat lived in the cellar.") Mephistopheles joins them, but Faust is disgusted by their uproarious ribaldry. (Mephistopheles: "Once a king be it noted.") Led by Mephistopheles to a garden on the banks of the Elbe, he falls asleep amid the music of a chorus of sylphs (Chorus: "Dream, Dream"), and dreams of Margaret, a fair unknown peasant girl. As the sylphs dance about him (Ballet of sylphs), he awakens, still thinking of Margaret and desiring to find her. A troop of soldiers march by, returning from war and eager for pleasure (Chorus: "Towns with their battlements.") They are joined by a band of students, who proclaim in song the joys of wine and love. (Chorus: "Gaudeamus igitur.")

PART III. Distant drums and trumpets sound the retreat. Faust impatiently awaits Margaret in her dwelling. Mephistopheles warns him of her coming, and he conceals himself in her room. (Faust: "O welcome, gentle twilight.") Margaret enters musing upon a strange dream of an unknown lover. She braids her hair, singing dreamily of the faithful King of Thule. (Ballad, Margaret: "There dwelt a king in Thule.") Mephistopheles invokes the powers of evil and begins a mocking serenade (Mephistopheles: "Dear Katherine, why, to the door of thy lover"), while in the garden without the will-o'-the-wisps dance. Faust appears before Margaret, who is startled, but in an ardent love scene they declare their mutual passion, and Margaret at last is persuaded to give herself to her lover. The entrance of Mephistopheles, to tell them that the villagers are coming to warn Margaret's mother of her danger, terrifies the bewildered girl. She and Faust part reluctantly, while Mephistopheles exults over the enslavement of his victim. The villagers approach muttering threats, as Mephistopheles forces Faust to depart. (Trio and chorus: "Angel of light.")

PART IV. Margaret, heavy-hearted, sits alone, thinking of her lover who comes not. Soldiers march by singing of the glories of war.

Faust alone in his study has found solace in Nature (Faust: "Majestic spirit, calm and resistless"), but Mephistopheles disturbs him with the news that Margaret is in prison, condemned to death for the murder of her mother, Martha, to whom the fiend had given too powerful

a sleeping potion. Faust signs a paper which he believes
will free Margaret, but which really gives over h's own
soul to perdition. Faust and the fiend then set forth on
a wild ride through the darkness. As they gallop along
they hear women and children praying. Strange shapes
close around them presaging death. The horses tremble
and snort with fear. Faust imagines that it rains blood.
Everywhere he sees horrible visions, and at last he is
hurled into the abyss to which the fiend has craftily led him and is forever lost. The Prince of Darkness appears attended by infernal spirits, who exult over
his downfall. (Chorus of Infernal Spirits.)

With a change of scene a celestial chorus is heard and the
spirit of Margaret saved by faith and repentance is received into heaven. With her apotheosis the drama ends.

DAS NACHTLAGER VON GRANADA

(The night camp at Granada)

Romantic opera in two acts by Konradin Kreutzer. Text
by Karl von Braun.

CAST: Gabriele—Soprano. Gomez, a young shepherd—
Tenor. A huntsman—Baritone. Ambrosio, an old
shepherd, uncle of Gabriele—Basso. Vasco and Pedro,
shepherds—Tenor and Basso. Count Otto, a German
knight—Baritone. Place, Spain. Time, the sixteenth century. First production, Vienna, 1834.

ACT I. A shepherd's village in the mountains. Gabriele
laments that her dove has been seized by an eagle. ("All
has been taken from me.") Gomez loves her but cannot
marry her, as her uncle Ambrosio intends to marry her to
Vasco. Gomez determines to ask the aid of the Prince
Regent, who is hunting near. (Duet: "Sorrowing I tend
my sheep.") He hurries away, and a huntsman brings
Gabriele's dove, which he has taken from the eagle. She

asks him who he may be. (Romance of the huntsman: "I am a huntsman in the service of the regent.") She tells him of Gomez and he promises to assist her. As he is kissing her to seal his promise, the shepherds Ambrosio, Vasco and Pedro enter. (Quintet: "Away! how dare you.") The huntsman asks for shelter and offers to pay so lavishly that the cupidity of the shepherds is aroused, and urged on by Vasco's jealousy, they resolve to murder the stranger in the night. The other shepherds descend into the valley and greet him, and for his entertainment Gabriele sings the romance of the Moorish castle. ("Who stands despairing at the window bars.") Gabriele becomes suspicious of the three shepherds as they lead the huntsman to his quarters. (Chorus and ensemble: "The chimes of night are heard.")

Act II. A mountainous, rocky country. (Recitative and aria, Gomez: "To whom may this steed belong?") A company of huntsmen inquire for the stranger and Gomez directs them to the Moorish castle. (The beginning of the second act is generally omitted.)

Change of scene: A Moorish castle in ruins. The huntsman is ushered into a room by the shepherds. (Scene: "The night is fine"; and aria: "Surely this is an adventure.") They leave him, and he falls asleep, but Gabriele comes to awaken him (Romance: "The mist surrounds us"), and warn him against the shepherds. Finding that his gun has been rendered useless, to defend himself he grasps his sword as Pedro, Vasco and Ambrosio creep forward in the darkness. (Quartet: "Now, out with the sword.") He cries out to the villains that he is the Prince Regent, and Ambrosio, fearing punishment, attacks him, but is wounded. Gabriele comes to his assistance, but the huntsman winds his horn and his companions hasten to his aid. Gabriele is now informed that the stranger is the Prince Regent, and he rewards her fidelity by uniting her to Gomez.

THE DAUGHTER OF THE REGIMENT

Comic opera in two acts by Donizetti. Text from the French of St. Georges and Bayard by Gollmick. First production, Paris, 1840.

CAST: The Marchioness of Maggiorivoglio—Soprano. Sulpice, sergeant—Basso. Tonio, a young Swiss—Tenor. Marie, a vivandière—Soprano. The Duchess of Craquitorpi—Soprano. Hortensio, master of ceremonies—Basso. A corporal—Basso. A notary—Speaking part. A servant—Speaking part. Place, near Bologna and at the castle of the marchioness. (In the original the soldiers are Austrians, but on the stage are Frenchmen.)

Marie, having been found on the battlefield as a baby by the soldiers of the second regiment, is adopted by them and follows her "fathers" as vivandière. Her life is saved by the young Swiss Tonio. She loves him, and as she has sworn only to belong to a member of the regiment, he enlists. She is separated from her lover, however, as she is recognised as her niece by the marchioness from letters which the honest sergeant Sulpice has saved. Marie bids farewell to her beloved regiment and to her lover and follows her relative. The second act takes place at the castle of the marchioness. Marie's only pleasure, notwithstanding her riches, is conversing with old Sulpice, who has become an invalid and is living at the castle. She is to marry the son of the duchess of Craquitorpi and is almost reconciled to her fate when she hears martial music. Her old regiment arrives and with it Tonio as an officer. She throws all her finery into a heap, joyfully hails the troops and rushes into Tonio's arms. The duchess indignantly retires, and when the marchioness, who loves Marie as a daughter, gives her consent, amid universal rejoicing she is married to Tonio.

ACT I. Chorus and ensemble. (Duet between Sulpice and Marie: "Ha, it is she, the thunder, the joy"; Marie's song: "On the field of honour." Ensemble.) Tonio is to be shot as a spy, but is rescued by Marie. who declares that he has saved her life. (Marie's song of the regiment: "Does the world not know, does the world not say"; Love duet: "You love me"; Finale, chorus of soldiers; Tonio's song of the recruit: "I join your flag"; Marie's farewell: "Farewell, dear brothers.")

Act II. (Scene: "The young day arises"; Marie's aria of joy at the appearance of her old regiment: "Hail to thee, my country"; Terzett between her, Sulpice and Tonio: "At last we are united.") Finale: Marie tells the story of her life, the marchioness gives her consent and unites her with Tonio. (Final chorus: "Hail to thee, O my country.")

THE DEMON

Fantastic opera in three acts by Anton Rubinstein. Libretto adapted from the poem of Lermontoff by Wiskowatoff.

Cast: Prince Gudal—Basso. Tamara, his daughter—Soprano. Prince of Sinodal, her betrothed—Tenor. Tamara's nurse—Alto. An old servant of the Prince of Sinodal. The Demon—Basso. An Angel—Soprano. Place, in the Caucasus. Produced in Russian at St. Petersburg in 1875; in German at Hamburg, 1880.

Act I. Storm in a wild country. The angel tells the demon that he may gain heaven through love, but is answered with derision. The supernatural powers disappear and the storm ends. Tamara appears with her maidens; to her alone is the demon visible, who plants restless thoughts in her brain.

Change of scene: Mountains. The Prince of Sinodal is on the way to his bride Tamara. As he sleeps, Tartars persuaded by the demon fall upon and kill the prince.

Act II. Hall of the palace of Gudal. The marriage feast is prepared, when the sad news of the death of the prince is brought. The demon again tries to ensnare Tamara, but she demands to be allowed to enter a convent. The old Prince Gudal resolves to take vengeance for the murder of the prince.

Act III. The convent. Again the demon approaches his victim, but is driven away by the angel.

Change of scene: The convent cell of Tamara. The demon again appears, asking for her love, and Tamara can no longer withstand him. As she receives his kiss, she sinks dying to the ground. The demon believes he has triumphed, but is driven to flight by the angels, who carry Tamara to heaven.

DER BÄRENHÄUTER

Opera in three acts by Arnold Mendelssohn. Libretto by Herman Wette.

Cast: Ruppert, a rustic—Tenor. Frieder, innkeeper and village magistrate—Basso. Anna, his daughter—Soprano. Yunker Kunz von Knaufen—Baritone. Satan—Basso. Frau Hellya, his grandmother—Contralto. Place, a village in lower Germany; hell. Time, the Middle Ages.

Act I. Ruppert woos Anna. (Duet: "Hardly has the cock crowed.") The girl refuses mockingly. He fears that her father will sell her to Kunz von Knaufen, and both make merry over the old and vain Yunker. Believing that Anna loves him, Ruppert breaks out in the ecstatic song ("Hurrah, she loves me"), but is roughly treated by the Yunker and the guests accompanying him, and by Anna's father, who resents being addressed as father-in-law. As Anna refuses to take his side, Ruppert flies in such a rage that Frieder, with curses, drives him from the house. While still angry he meets Satan and agrees to his proposal to serve one year in hell, after which Satan will help him to vengeance. He must likewise swear never to wash, to let his hair, beard and nails grow, and not to change his clothes. Only the kiss of a pure maiden can free him from his compact with Satan. Despite the warnings of the good spirits he consents, after Satan has shown him the image of Anna in the arms of the Yunker. The imps wrap him in the skin of a bear and lay his clothes at the side of the brook so that Anna will think he has drowned himself. Amid thunder and lightning he and Satan descend into hell.

ACT II. Hell's kitchen with large kettles under which fire is lighted. Ruppert, now a dirty frowsy bear, places wood under the fire and performs other menial tasks (Song: "In his workshop"), the hell maidens warn him against Frau Hellya, and she forbids him to sing. He is tired of his life in hell and wishes to return to earth; she laughs at him: he is unaware of his uncouth appearance and Frau Hellya informs him that Anna would flee at his approach. Finally she shows him Anna's picture, which only strengthens his resolve to return. (Infernal ballet with chorus.) Ruppert declares to Satan that the compact is fulfilled and asks for his reward: the promised power to obtain vengeance against his enemies. Satan laughs at him and tells him that to achieve this he must himself become a devil; but shows him Frieder and the Yunker, who have since died and are forgotten, in the torments of hell. Deeply agitated, he regrets having turned from God and asks for mercy; he desires to do penance for his sins, refuses all further reward and resolves to obtain a kiss of a pure maiden and secure his release. At last Satan shows him his image in the mirror and he sinks horror-stricken to the ground.

ACT III. At the brookside. The people of the village celebrate the harvest festival. (Chorus: "The seeds, they fall.") Ruppert, followed by Satan, joins them; all flee in terror. Satan, believing that no maiden can be found to free Ruppert, derides him, and expresses a parting hope soon to see him back in hell. Left alone, Ruppert in despair throws himself to the ground, when the song of the good

spirits is again heard ("Do not fly to distant lands"), and
he folds his hands in prayer. As Anna approaches, pale
and distressed, Ruppert hides in the reeds. She is seeking
death and is singing a farewell song ("Summer has
passed"), when she hears her name called. She recognises
Ruppert's voice and confesses that she has never forgotten
him—but thinks she only hears his spirit voice. Ruppert
tells her how he has suffered, and in despair she determines
to plunge into the water. He confronts her joyfully, and
she is about to throw herself into his arms when Satan
throws the full light of the moon upon him. As she falls
senseless, Satan carries him back to hell.

Change of scene: In hell. Ruppert asleep, watched by
evil spirits, who deride his plight, while the good spirits
from the height endeavour to console him with cheering
words. The voice of Anna is heard without, praying to
God that Ruppert may emerge victorious from the conflict.
Hellya, in the guise of a demon woman, tries to drive her
away; at her behest the demons disappear, the clock strikes
twelve, darkness sets in. Hellya calls upon Satan and is
changed to a magnificently beautiful woman, so that Ruppert awaking is dazzled by her splendour. She tries with
every art to entwine him in her net and with Satan's aid
win him to hell for all time. ("Come, dearest, come.")
Ruppert almost yields. Strengthened by the songs of the
good spirits he resists. ("My soul rests in God.") The
portals of hell open and in beauteous splendour Anna appears. She approaches him rapidly, kisses him with closed
eyes on the mouth, whereupon the ugly husk falls from him
and she leads him forth through the ranks of the staring
demons, while hell sinks from beneath their feet. At the
village brook the lovers are once more united, and to the
chime of bells and the song of the good spirits they proceed to the church.

DER BÄRENHÄUTER

Opera in three acts by Siegfried Wagner. Libretto by the composer.

CAST: Hans Kraft—Tenor. Melchior Fröhlich—Basso. His daughters, Lena—Soprano; Gunda—Soprano, Luisel —Soprano. Pastor Wippenbeck—Baritone. Nikolaus Spitz—Tenor. Anna—Mezzo-soprano. Colonel Muffel— Basso. Kaspar Wild—Basso. The Stranger—Baritone. The Devil—Basso buffo. Place, in Bayreuth. Time, the Thirty Years' War. First produced at Munich, 1899.

ACT I. Hans Kraft, returned from the war, finds his mother dead, and is refused shelter by the peasants. He attempts to enforce his demands, but the devil, who has been listening, laughs at him and offers him the position of stoker in hell. He is to serve for one year and receive all the gold he wishes, but should a soul escape he must suffer the penalty imposed by Satan. After a short interval for reflection he takes the oath and they descend to hell. The devil points out the field of his labours and leaves him. As Hans stirs the fire a "stranger" appears and induces him to cast dice. They dice for souls and Hans loses them all. Before departing the stranger promises to assist Hans with word and deed when his punishment has ended. Amid terrific thunder the devil appears to find all the souls gone. Hans is punished severely by being changed to a blackamoor and compelled to wander the earth in that shape. He can only be released when he finds a maiden who will love him and remain true to him for three years. At the devil's command a number of demons disfigure Hans.

ACT II. Hans, by reason of his appearance, is taken for the devil by the peasants until they see that he has no cloven foot. The devil has given him a bag from which flows untold gold. He is very liberal with his money, and pays the tavern score of the burgomaster, who in return promises him the hand of his daughter. During the night the innkeeper attempts to steal the money bag, but a number of demons emerge from it, and he flees shrieking. Hans laughingly comes to his assistance. The next morning the burgomaster arrives with his daughters, but the two oldest make game of Hans and deride him with mocking song. Luisel, the youngest, notices the tears in his eyes and takes pity upon him. She divides his ring into two pieces and ties one piece around her neck, giving Hans the other. If she wears it three years and it is still bright Hans will be released. Hans again warns her, but she remains firm. The innkeeper has summoned assistance and the peasants advance threateningly toward Hans. Moved by the prayers of Luisel they allow him to depart.

Act III. Scene 1. Three years have elapsed. The imps endeavour to change Hans back to his former shape. He awakens to find the glittering ring in his hands. Since he has been saved, the devil must grant him three wishes, but he is moderate in his demands.

Scene 2. At the rising of the curtain Hans and the stranger are seen walking together. Following the advice of the stranger Hans becomes the saviour of Plassenberg by delivering it from the power of Wallenstein. As he approaches a victorious triumphal motif announces his coming. He finds Luisel faithful and waiting for him. Unrecognised he approaches her; when she learns of his identity she falls joyfully into his arms and they are betrothed. The peasants recognise him with joy, and a merry chorus ends the scene.

DER EVANGELIMANN
(The Evangelist)

Musical drama in two acts by Wilhelm Kienzl. Libretto by the composer, adapted from the work of Dr. Meiszner.

CAST: Friedrich Engel—Basso. Martha, his niece—Soprano. Magdalena, her friend—Alto. Yohannes Freudhofer, teacher at St. Othmar—Baritone. Matthias Freudhofer, his brother, clerk at the convent—Tenor. Zitterbart—Tenor buffo. Schnappauf—Basso buffo. Aibler—Basso. His wife—Mezzo-soprano. Frau Huber—Soprano. Hans—Tenor. Time, in the nineteenth century. Place, convent of the Benedictines at St. Othmar, Vienna. First production, Berlin, 1895.

ACT I. Courtyard of the convent at St. Othmar. Yohannes informs Engel that Martha loves Matthias, the clerk of the convent. Engel orders him to leave the convent at once. The citizens amuse themselves playing ten pins. Matthias asks Magdalena to procure him an interview with Martha, to bid her a last farewell. Yohannes, who is also in love with Martha, overhears the conversation and plots the ruin of the lovers. Fire breaks out while they are taking leave of each other in the arbour at night. Matthias, who helps to fight the flames, is arrested as the incendiary.

ACT II. Vienna, thirty years later. Part I. A courtyard. Matthias arrives as Evangelimann and meets Magdalena, who is nursing Yohannes, who is seriously ill. They recognise each other, and he tells her that he has served a twenty-year sentence for incendiarism, and when released heard that Martha had drowned herself. He had turned Evangelimann for that reason, and owing to the fact that he had not been proved innocent of the crime.

PART II. A day later; living-room of Yohannes. Hearing the voice of Matthias, he asks that he be brought to his bedside. He does not recognise him, and in his dying confession acknowledges that he was the real incendiary. Matthias recognises Yohannes as his brother and pardons him. Yohannes dies.

DER FREISCHÜTZ

Opera in three acts by Carl Maria von Weber. **Libretto** by Friedrich Kind.

CAST: Ottokar, Duke of Bohemia—Baritone. Kuno, head ranger—Basso. Agatha, a young relative—Soprano. Caspar and Max, rangers—Basso and Tenor. Samiel, the black ranger—Speaking part. A hermit—Basso. Kilian, a rich peasant—Tenor. A bridesmaid—Soprano. Time, immediately following the Thirty Years' War. First performance, Berlin, 1821.

The young ranger Max loves Agatha and is to become the successor to Kuno, the head ranger. A test of skill in marksmanship is requisite, the trial to be held the following day. A preliminary scene, not usually represented on the boards, of the consecration of the bridal wreath consists of a dialogue between Agatha and the hermit.

ACT I. The target shooting. Max has failed in the test, and the young peasant Kilian is proclaimed "King of marksmen." (Chorus: "Victory, long live the master"; and the good-naturedly mocking song of Kilian: "Let him gaze on me as king.") As Max has had ill-luck for several days he easily falls under the influence of Caspar, who also loves Agatha, and persuades Max to cast some magic bullets to be used in the contest. Caspar, whose soul on the morrow is to be forfeited to the devil, by the sacrifice of Max, hopes to obtain three more years of grace. (Trio, Kuno, Caspar, Max and chorus: "O the sun, fearsomely it rises.") Left alone, Max, at the thought of losing Agatha through failure at the shooting contest, sinks into deep melancholy. (Aria: "Through woods and fields.") Caspar with weird incantations tries to imbue him with courage. (Song: "Here in this vale of tears.") He hands him his gun loaded with one of the magic bullets, and to his own astonishment Max kills an eagle soaring at a great height. He resolves to go with Caspar at midnight to the terrible wolf's gorge to cast the magic bullets in order

to win the prize. Caspar, left alone, triumphs. (Aria:
"Silence, let no one him warn.")

ACT II. Agatha's chamber. Agatha is filled with sad
forebodings. She sings of her meeting with a hermit in the
forest, who told her that in some danger which menaced her,
she would be protected by her bridal wreath. At the moment when Max shoots the magic bullet, the picture of
Agatha's ancestor hanging against the wall falls to the
floor, slightly wounding her. The lively Ännchen replaces
it. (Duet: "Rogue, hold fast, I will teach you.") Agatha
is still more disturbed, but Ännchen endeavours to cheer
her with jests. (Arietta: "Comes a pretty boy this path.")
Agatha left alone awaits Max with the news of his success, which she decides to interpret as a favourable omen.
(Recitative: "My eyelids droop in slumber"; Prayer:
"Low, low, sacred words"; Scene: "All have long since
gone to rest"; and Aria: "All my pulses beat.") Max arrives; he acknowledges that he has not been the victor, but
explains that he has killed a deer, which he will bring this
evening from the wolf's gorge. Notwithstanding the
prayers of Agatha and Ännchen, Max departs. (Trio:
"What, oh horror! there in the wolf's gorge?")

Change of scene: The wolf's gorge at night. Caspar
calls upon the black ranger for assistance, and prepares
the casting of the magic bullets. Max arrives and is
warned by the spirit of his mother to abandon the project.
Samiel conjures up the shape of Agatha, representing
her as drowning herself in despair at Max's ill success,
whereupon he plunges into the gorge and with demoniacal
noise the casting of the bullets is begun.

ACT III. Agatha's chamber. Agatha in prayer. (Aria:
"Through clouds obscure still shines the sun in radiant
sky.") Her doubts have returned, owing to a dream of
ill omen, but Ännchen again cheers her with laughter and
song. (Romance and aria, subsequently added by Weber:
"My deceased cousin had a dream.") The bridesmaids arrive with the bridal wreath. (Song: "We wind round thee

the bridal wreath.")   When Ännchen opens the box, however, she finds within a funeral wreath, which still further increases Agatha's misgivings. She is somewhat comforted by the memory of the hermit's promise that she shall be protected by her bridal wreath.

Change of scene: Meeting of the marksmen.

Max has discharged six of his bullets successfully and Caspar is triumphant, knowing that the course of the seventh will be guided by the Evil One.

Change of scene: The prize shooting.

Duke Ottokar awaits Max at his tent.   (Chorus of foresters: "What excels the pleasures of the chase.")   Max is now to shoot a dove.   As he takes aim, Samiel, the black huntsman, appears to guide the bullet, and causes Max to fire at Agatha, who is apparently wounded.   (Finale: "See, oh see, he shoots his bride.")   Her bridal wreath turns the bullet aside and she revives.   Caspar, seeing a holy hermit by her side, realises that he has failed.   Samiel grasps him instead of Max, whereupon Caspar expires with a curse upon his lips.   Duke Ottokar orders the corpse to be thrown into the wolf's gorge, receives the explanation of Max, and touched by his repentance and the prayers of the hermit ("Who puts on him this dreadful ban"), inflicts upon him but a slight penalty.   A year of trial is imposed, the prize shooting abolished and a promise given that at the expiration of the time of probation the duke himself will place the hand of Agatha in that of Max.

DER KOBOLD

In three acts by Siegfried Wagner.

CAST: Gertrud, innkeeper in the village. Verena, her daughter. Old Eckhart. Trutz, Fink, Kümmel, Friedrich, strolling singers and actors. The count. The countess. Jeannette, maid. Jean, Knorz, servants. Käte, wife of Trutz. Seelchen, a hobgoblin. Hobgoblins, people, guests.

Time, beginning of the nineteenth century. First production, Hamburg, 1904.

ACT I. Scene concealed by fog. Verena asleep at a table in the open. The hobgoblin Seelchen whispers into her ear that she must set him at liberty. He lays upon the table a magic stone. Verena finds the talisman and attaches it to a chain which she has received from her lover, the actor Friedrich. She exhibits it in her delight, and the love-lorn countess desires to possess it. When Verena refuses to give it up, it is taken from her by her mother, who gives it to the countess and is lavishly rewarded. The countess, who is in love with Friedrich, a strolling singer, is happy in his society, as her husband has invited him to a festival at the castle. Verena is not invited, and is consoled for the neglect by her father's friend old Eckhart.

ACT II. Park of the castle. Verena, who follows Friedrich, meets him at the festival, but is coldly received and neglected by him. When the lascivious count annoys her with his attentions she stabs him with a dagger and is brought by honest Trutz to old Eckhart for protection. In the meantime the countess attempts to captivate Friedrich; as he is trying to restrain the coquettish dame he breaks Verena's chain, to which the countess has attached the magic stone, and takes possession of it. The countess cries for help and accuses Friedrich of theft. The count, seriously wounded, is brought in, and to shield himself accuses Trutz of the attempted murder. Trutz and Friedrich escape, the stone is thrown into the sea and the hobgoblin again recovers his property.

ACT III. A wood in sunlight. Eckhart accompanies the exhausted Verena. The servants who are looking for Trutz and Friedrich are persuaded to take the wrong path, and Verena resolves to release the hobgoblin by the sacrifice of her own life. Eckhart explains to her that the hobgoblins are the souls of unborn children.

Change of scene: A moonlight night. The interior of a barn, in which the strolling players have found refuge.

When Trutz and Friedrich quarrel over Verena they are attacked by the servants of the count. Verena receives the dagger intended for Friedrich, dies and by her death the hobgoblin Seelchen is free.

DER WILDSCHÜTZ

(The Poacher)

Comic opera in three acts by Lortzing. Libretto adapted from Kotzebue's comedy, "The Roebuck," by the composer.

CAST: Count of Eberbach—Baritone. The Countess, his wife—Soprano. Baron Kronthal, her brother—Tenor. Baroness Freimann, a young widow, sister of the count— Soprano. Nanette, her maid—Mezzo-soprano. Baculus, schoolmaster—Basso. Gretchen, his bride—Soprano. Pankratius, steward—Baritone. Place, the castle and adjoining village. Time, 1803. First production, Leipsic, 1842.

In order to comprehend the action it is necessary to know that the Baroness Freimann does not recognise her brother, the Count Eberbach, and likewise Baron Kronthal is not acquainted with his sister, the countess, as they have been separated for a considerable time.

ACT I. The village green, schoolhouse and the house of Gretchen. (Chorus: "As merry and lively as to-day.") Baculus is about to celebrate his marriage with Gretchen. (Song: "A B C D bachelorhood is painful.") A letter from the count arrives dismissing the school-teacher. He had shot a deer for consumption at the feast, had killed it in the dark, and the news coming to the ears of the count caused his dismissal. Baculus would like to send Gretchen to the castle to obtain the count's forgiveness; but as the count's amatory nature is known he cannot make up his mind to do so. (Duet: "In this desperate case nothing will

do but to ask.") But help is near. The somewhat emanci-
pated Baroness Freimann appears in the dress of a student
accompanied by her maid, Nanette, as her servant. (Aria
of the baroness: "Upon life's billows.") When she hears
the cause of the trouble she offers to go with Baculus to
the castle in the dress of Gretchen. (Quartet: "What
think you, dear friend?") The baroness departs to assume her disguise, and the count, who has been hunting,
arrives in the village accompanied by his brother-in-law,
Baron Kronthal, who is playing the rôle of Master of
Horse unknown to his sister. (Hunting song: "See the
merry huntsmen.") When the baroness steps forward
dressed in the costume of a handsome peasant girl she immediately attracts the attention of the gentlemen. (Finale:
"Let us go home," with the song of the baroness: "I am a
simple child from the country.") The count invites her
and the rest of the company to a feast at the castle on the
morrow.

ACT II. A hall of the castle with a billiard table. The
countess is in the adjoining room and is reading aloud a
tragedy of Sophocles, and the servants are seated on the
stage listening. (Chorus: "Do not talk! Pay attention!")
When Pankratius dismisses the people Baculus enters. The
steward gives him a book of Sophocles, and with its assistance he hopes to win over the countess. She arrives
with the baron, and has not yet recognised him as her
brother. He jestingly declares his love. (Duet: "I will
remain and see you always.") Baculus arrives to plead
with the countess, but is ordered out by the count, when
the baroness, dressed as Gretchen, arrives and informs him
that she is the bride of the schoolmaster. ("What do I
see, out of my sight.") Both the count and the baron now
attempt to remain alone with the supposed peasant girl,
and the baron is successful, as Baculus falls asleep. He
asks her to leave the schoolmaster for him. (Duet: "Your
wife? My dear wife.") The count now also approaches
with plans of conquest, and in order to engage the baron

plays a game of billiards with him. Baculus awakes and
sings a melody from the song book in his pocket. The
count, while playing, puts out the lights; when both gentlemen try to grasp the girl, the countess, attracted by
the noise, enters. She takes the peasant girl to her room,
to the alarm of the schoolmaster, who thinks the baroness
is a student. (Quintet: "I have number one.") The
baron, however, is seriously in love and offers the schoolmaster five thousand dollars to cede his rights, to which
he agrees. (Aria of Baculus: "Five thousand dollars! Am
I awake or asleep?")

ACT III. The castle park. The count appears. ("How
sweetly shines the sun of May"; Aria: "Gaiety and joy.")
The young peasant girls congratulate the count on the
festival. He thanks them by dancing with them, but they
are driven to flight by the arrival of the countess. Baculus
arrives and brings the baron his purchased bride; but as
it is the real Gretchen, the baron demands the other one,
whom, however, the schoolmaster thinks is a man. (Terzett: "Now, dear Gretchen, confess freely and without
shame.") When the baron hears the truth he chides the
baroness, who discloses herself. She is interrupted by the
countess, who leads Gretchen away, of which the count
takes advantage to kiss the baroness, which she allows him
to do, as he is her brother. She then discloses her identity,
whereupon the count and the countess, who also ascertains
that the supposed master of horse is her brother, designate
her affection as the "Voice of Nature." At the close Baculus
and all the school children appear and sing in praise of the
count. As it is ascertained that the supposed Roebuck was
a donkey belonging to the schoolmaster, which had strayed
in the dark, Baculus is reinstated and is now enabled to
marry his Gretchen, and the baron weds the baroness.

THE DEVIL'S PORTION

(Carlo Broschi)

Comic opera in three acts by Auber.   Text by Scribe.

CAST: Ferdinand VI of Spain—Baritone.   Maria Theresia, his wife—Soprano.   Rafael d'Estuniga—Tenor. Gil Vargas, his steward—Basso.   Carlo Broschi—Soprano. Casilda, his sister—Soprano.   Grand Inquisitor—Basso. Place, near Madrid and Aranjuez.   Time, 1763.   First production, Paris, 1843.

The king is melancholy and is kept in this state of mind by the Grand Inquisitor, who desires to separate him from his wife, who is of more liberal opinions.   Ferdinand is willing, as he loves Casilda, but she escapes him and he believes her dead.   The queen receives unexpected assistance in her efforts to amuse the king through Casilda's brother, the singer Carlo Broschi, who enlivens the king's mood by his songs, and who succeeds in thwarting the plans of the Grand Inquisitor.   He also ascertains that young Rafael loves his sister Casilda, and that it is his intention to form a compact with the devil in order to attain a position at court.   Carlo introduces himself to Rafael as the devil, agrees to share with him and procures for him the position of colonel.   The king attaches Rafael to his person, believing him to be the husband of Casilda, whom Ferdinand had supposed to be dead.   The timorous Rafael reveals the entire plot to the king, and the Grand Inquisitor seems about to gain the victory, when Carlo explains that he has only acted in this manner to disclose the wiles of the king's enemies.   Ferdinand gives him credence and Rafael, who in the meantime has inherited a large fortune, is now united by the king to Casilda.

ACT I.   A wood with convent and inn.   (Aria of Rafael: "I see her before me"; Recitative and aria of Carlo: "Without a friend on this wide earth"; Romance of Casilda: "Mute and mild"; Duet, Casilda, Carlo: "Oh, my friend, my only support!" Carlo's romance: "Close thine eyes, my lovely child," and scene betweeen the king, queen and Carlo; Hunter's chorus: "The pleasure of the chase"; Recitative and incantation aria of Rafael: "Asmodeus, spirit of the deep, appear." Scene between Carlo and Rafael.)

Act II.   Chamber in the palace in Madrid.   (Chorus, scene and song of Carlo: "Signora amalata, me voilà, I am here"; Scene, chorus and song of Rafael: "What is the use of wisdom and genius"; Quartet, Casilda, king, queen and Carlo: "Pale fear makes me tremble"; Duet, Casilda, Rafael: "What will he say to me"; Finale, ensemble: "Almighty love, protect me.")

Act III.   A chamber in the garden.   (Carlo's aria: "My true messenger"; "Oh let me not be afraid"; Duet, Casilda, Rafael: "As if the devil were near"; Finale, ensemble: "It is too rash"; Closing chorus: "Sweet fortune, descend on us.")

DIE FLEDERMAUS

(The Bat)

Comic opera in three acts by Johann Strauss.   Text by Haffner (from the French; but the action in general preceding the second act is the same as the comedy of Benedix, "The Prison").

Cast: Rosalinde—Soprano.   Adèle—Mezzo-soprano. Eisenstein—Tenor.   Alfred—Tenor.   Dr. Blind—Tenor. Falke—Baritone.   Frank—Basso.   First production, Vienna, 1874.

The Baron von Eisenstein has been committed to prison for eight days for insulting an official, partly through the inefficiency of his attorney, the stuttering Dr. Blind, and is to begin his imprisonment this day.   His friend, Notary Falke, however, persuades him to postpone it until the morrow and to accompany him to a ball at the resi-

dence of Prince Orlofsky, where he will meet the handsome
ladies of the opera ballet.   Falke had been at a masked
ball the previous winter, costumed as a bat, and had been
compelled by Eisenstein to walk to his home in broad day-
light to the joy and amusement of the populace.   He hopes
to find an opportunity for vengeance at the coming ball.
Eisenstein accepts the invitation, and telling his wife he is
going to prison, and taking a mournful farewell of her
and the maid Adèle, hastens with Falke to the ball.   After
his departure Rosalinde, his wife, is visited by a former
admirer, the singing teacher, Alfred, whose behaviour is
rather free.   The night has set in and Frank, the governor
of the prison, has come to take Eisenstein to jail.   He finds
Alfred taking his ease attired in a smoking jacket, and he,
in order not to compromise Rosalinde, moved by her
prayers, is induced to represent himself as Eisenstein and
to accompany Frank.   Falke, who has received *plein pou-
voir* from Prince Orlofsky, has also invited the governor
of the prison, Frank, the maid Adèle, and to complete the
joke, Rosalinde, to be his guests at the ball.   The latter, in
order to observe her husband, appears masked.   She is introduced by Falke as an Hungarian countess, and succeeds
during an amorous tête-à-tête in abstracting from the pockets of her husband his valuable watch, to use in the future as a *corpus delicti*.   Frank has paid court to Adèle,
and the next morning they all find themselves in prison,
when the confusion increases, for Falke has introduced
Eisenstein as Marquis Renard, Frank as Chevalier Chagrin
and Adèle as an actress.   It is still further increased by
the jailer, Frosch, who has profited by the absence of the
prison director to become gloriously drunk.   Adèle arrives
to obtain the assistance of the Chevalier Chagrin, Eisenstein to begin his prison term, Alfred wants to get out of
jail, Rosalinde to commence action for divorce, and Frank
is still intoxicated.   Frosch locks up Adèle and her companion, and the height of the tumult has been reached
when Falke arrives with all the guests of the ball and de-

clares the whole as an act of vengeance for the "Fledermaus." Everything is amicably arranged, but Eisenstein
is compelled to serve his full term in jail.

Act I. Apartments of Eisenstein. Alfred serenades his
former sweetheart. ("Dove, that has escaped.") Adèle
has received the invitation to the ball ("My sister Ida
writes to me"), and asks for leave of absence. Eisenstein
comes to Rosalinde in altercation with his attorney.
(Terzett: "Well, with such an attorney.") Falke brings
the invitation to the ball. (Duet: "Come with me to the
souper.") Eisenstein's farewell to Rosalinde and Adèle.
(Terzett with the refrain: "Oh dear, oh dear, how sorry
I am.") Alfred arrives. (Finale, drinking song: "Happy
is he who forgets"; Rosalinde's defence when Frank arrives: "In tête-à-tête with me so late," and Frank's invitation: "My beautiful, large bird-cage.")

Act II. Summer house in the villa Orlofsky. (Chorus:
"A souper is before us.") Departure of the chorus, introduction of Eisenstein and song of the prince. ("I love
to invite my friends.") Eisenstein meets Adèle. (Ensemble and song of Adèle: "My dear marquis.") Falke leaves
Rosalinde to Eisenstein. (Watch duet: "My eyes will soon
be dim.") The company approaches, Rosalinde is introduced as an Hungarian. (Czardas: "Sounds from home"
and finale. Drinking song: "In the fire stream of
the grape"; canon: "Brothers, brothers and sisters";
Ballet; waltz finale, "Ha, what joy, what a night of delight.")

Act III. Office of the governor at the prison. Appearance of Frank. (Melodrama; Couplet of Adèle: "I am
an innocent from the country"; Terzett between Rosalinde,
Eisenstein, Alfred: "A strange adventure"; and finale,
"Oh bat, oh bat, at last let thy victim escape.")

DIE MEISTERSINGER

Opera in three acts by Wagner. Text by the composer.
CAST: Hans Sachs, cobbler—Baritone. Walther von Stolzing, a young knight—Tenor. Veit Pogner, goldsmith—
Basso. Eva, his daughter—Soprano. Magdalena, her
nurse—Alto. Beckmesser—Basso buffo. Kothner, baker
—Basso. David, apprentice of Sachs—Tenor. A night
watchman—Baritone. Eight other master singers—
Tenori and Bassi. Place, Nuremberg. Time, the sixteenth century. First performance, Munich, 1868.

ACT I. The interior of St. Catharine's Church. Walther
von Stolzing, a young knight, sees Eva in the church and
asks her whether she is already a bride. Eva takes a fancy
to the knight, and her nurse, Magdalena, explains that
Eva's father, the goldsmith and master singer Veit Pogner, will give her hand in marriage to the victor at the
prize singing on St. John's day. Magdalena induces her
lover, the apprentice David, to instruct the knight what
steps he must take in order to participate in the singing.
David, who has come to that part of the church with the
other apprentices to take part in the free singing (*Freeing*), in his inexperience gives the knight some very curious
and conflicting advice. But love triumphs, and notwithstanding these strange instructions Walther makes appli-
cation to the assembled mastersingers to take part in the
competition. Pogner announces his intention as to Eva
to the assembled singers. He pays no heed to the advice
of Sachs to give the people a voice in the matter, but leaves
the decisions to the guild. Pogner designates Walther
von Stolzing as one of the wooers of Eva, which displeases
Beckmesser, the "writer," and Wächter, the "marker," who
are rivals for her hand. Upon being questioned as to his
teachers, the knight mentions the Minnesinger, Walther
von der Vogelweide as his instructor in poetry and the
birds of the woods as his teachers in singing. As the masters agree to admit Walther, Pogner takes his station be-

hind a curtain, and Walther begins his song. Beckmesser maliciously notes one error after another, so that the decision of the guild is: "Badly sung and spoken."

Act II. Street between Pogner's house and the corner house, in which Hans Sachs has his workshop. Magdalena is informed by David of Walther's failure, and in her disappointment forgets her usual custom of sharing the contents of her basket with David, which arouses the derision of the apprentices. Pogner arrives with Eva, but the latter is afraid to inquire for Walther. Hans Sachs, upon whom Walther's song has made a deep impression, takes a seat with his tools before the door of his house to work in the pleasant evening upon a pair of shoes for Beckmesser. Eva, who has always been his pet, questions him, and he adroitly ascertains that she loves the knight. When Walther appears she impulsively rushes toward him, and after some talk promises to fly with him immediately. As they are about to leave, Hans Sachs, apparently without design, illumines the street with his lantern and defeats their purpose. The loving couple retreat to the shadow of Pogner's house just as Beckmesser appears with a lute to serenade Eva. Sachs interrupts Beckmesser by his loud hammering and finally agrees to allow the writer to sing, while he himself marks each error by a thump upon the shoe. Beckmesser begins, but makes so many errors that from the repeated knocks Sachs finishes the shoe. The neighbours are attracted by the noise; David appears with a stick and belabours Beckmesser, whom he takes for a rival for the favour of Magdalena. The other apprentices take advantage of the opportunity to inaugurate a general scrimmage. In the confusion Walther endeavours to escape with Eva, but Sachs, discovering them, drags Walther into his workshop, while Eva runs to her home. Quiet is restored, the street is empty, the moon rises, and the night watchman, who is supposed to keep order, but who has been sound asleep during the disturbance, calls out the hour in a droning voice.

Act III.   A room in the house of Sachs.   The master
sits studying in his arm-chair.   He is in good humor and
forgives the repentant David for having started the disturbance on the street.   David congratulates the master
upon his saint's day (Johannes).   Walther, who has spent
the night with Sachs, relates an agreeable dream, and upon
Sachs's suggestion frames it in verse, in order to produce a
new prize song.   Walther sings two bars of his song, and
Sachs, satisfied, writes them down.   The knight departs to
compose another bar and to dress for the festival.   Beckmesser, thoroughly beaten, finds the two verses in the hand-
writing of Sachs and places them in his pocket.   He shows
them to the master as an evidence of his pretensions to the
hand of Eva, and Sachs allows him to carry off the incom-
plete song.   Eva arrives with the excuse of an order for a
pair of shoes, and when Walther, finely attired, sees her,
he improvises the third verse of his song.   The enchanted
Sachs calls Magdalena and David, boxes the apprentice's
ears in his joy, thereby advancing him to journeyman and
names the prize song "The lay of morning's dream."

Change of scene: The feast of St. John in the meadow
near Pegnitz.   Procession of the guilds, young girls from
Fürth and entrance of the mastersingers.   Hans Sachs
is applauded by the people, who love him; he thanks them,
and the singing begins.   The apprentices improvise a
stage of sod for the singers and Beckmesser begins by
singing the two verses of Walther's song, but so clumsily
that he is well laughed at.   When he angrily points out
Hans Sachs as the author of the composition the latter
denies it and asks Walther to sing.   Walther ascends the
sod platform and sings the prize song amid general enthusiasm.   The mastersingers wish to make him a member
of their guild on the spot, but he courteously declines the
honour, saying that he is entirely satisfied with the hand
of Eva.   Sachs closes the contest by praising German
poetry and song.   "Do not despise the masters," he wisely
advises, to which the people give ready assent.

DINORAH

Comic opera in three acts by Meyerbeer. Libretto by
Barbier and Carré.

CAST: Hoël, a goatherd—Basso. Corentin, bagpiper—
Tenor. Dinorah—Soprano. Huntsman—Basso. A har-
vester—Tenor. First shepherd boy—Soprano. Second
shepherd boy—Mezzo-soprano. Place, Bretagne. First
production, Paris, 1859.

The farm of Dinorah's father has been totally destroyed
by a thunderstorm on the day she was to be married to
the goatherd, Hoël. The village magician, Tonik, tells
the shepherd of a lost treasure which can be recovered on
condition of living one year in a lonesome glen. He, however, who first touches the treasure must die. Hoël disappears for a year, taking with him the coward Corentin,
whom he hopes to persuade to touch the treasure first.
Hoël encounters Dinorah, who, believing herself discarded
by him, has become insane and now roams with her goats
upon the mountains. During a storm the dam bursts, and
the girl having been swept away by the flood, on being
saved recovers her sanity. Hoël relinquishes his search
for the treasure and remains with Dinorah. The story is
preceded by an introduction, which forms the groundwork
of the libretto.

ACT I. Chorus during the overture. Near the hut of
Corentin. Dinorah with her goat crosses the stage. (Duet
with Corentin: "Blow, blow lively.") Hoël seeks out
Corentin and resolves to make use of him to secure the
treasure. (Aria: "Mighty abyss of magic.") Corentin
departs with Hoël.

ACT II. A wood by moonlight. Dinorah's shadow
dance.

Change of scene: A rocky gorge with a dam. Thunder.
The dam breaks, causing a flood. Hoël is making his way
to the glen with Corentin, who, hearing from Dinorah
that he who first touches the treasure must die, refuses to

follow the shepherd. Corentin proposes that the insane Dinorah, whom Hoël does not recognise as his bride, shall be sent to touch the treasure. When Dinorah, pursuing her goat, falls into the flood, she is recognised by Hoël, and he hastens to the rescue.

Act III. The country. Idyllic scene of herdsmen, mowers and huntsmen. Hoël brings Dinorah (Romance: "You are avenged by my remorse.") As the girl awakens she recovers her reason. The chanting of the pilgrims is heard. Hoël determines to cease hunting for the treasure, and proceeds with Dinorah to the altar to be married.

DJAMILEH

Comic opera in one act by Bizet. Libretto by Gallet.

Cast: Harun, a rich young Turk—Tenor. Splendiano, his tutor—Basso. Djamileh, his slave—Mezzo-soprano. A dancer. A slave dealer. Place, the palace of Harun in Cairo. First production, Paris, 1872.

Djamileh is the slave of Harun, a young and rich but blasé Turk, who is insensible to the charms of woman. (Aria: "To name you the wife who fascinates me.") Although Splendiano himself loves Djamileh, he has a suspicion that the slave is friendly to her master; and it is true that she is violently in love with Harun. Nevertheless, the tutor concocts a plan to gain possession of Djamileh. Harun only retains his slaves for a short while, when he showers presents upon them, sends them away and purchases others. A slave dealer appears, and Djamileh prays that as she is free he sell her again to Harun. Splendiano, in order not to lose Djamileh, prevails upon the slave dealer to agree to this. The love-breathing dance of an Almée excites Harun and his friends, who have spent the evening in feasting and dicing. Harun sends Splendiano away to join the gamblers. Alone at night he receives the new slave, who approaches veiled. As she attracts him strongly he uncovers her face, and is so enraptured that his love is again enkindled, and he draws her to his heart.

DOCTOR AND APOTHECARY

Opera in two acts by Dittersdorf. Libretto by Stephanie. CAST: Dr. Krautmann—Basso. Gotthold, his son— Tenor. Stöszel, apothecary—Basso. Claudia, his wife— Soprano. Leonore, her daughter—Soprano. Rosalie, Stöszel's niece—Soprano. Sichel, surgeon—Tenor. Sturmwald, retired captain—Tenor. Gallus, servant— Tenor. Place, a small town. Time, the eighteenth century.

This light opera and farce ("The Village Barber") is occasionally produced at the present time on the German stage. "Doctor and Apothecary" was first produced at Vienna in 1786.

Apothecary Stöszel and Dr. Krautmann are deadly foes, but their children are in love with each other. Leonore is destined to marry the retired Captain Sturmwald, but refuses to leave Gotthold, whose elopement with her has been frustrated. Gotthold plays all sorts of tricks on the captain, but wins Leonore's mother to his cause. She pacifies the apothecary Stöszel, and through the efforts of the lovers the friendship of the older men is renewed. Another pair of lovers in the opera are the surgeon Sichel and Rosalie, the niece of Stöszel, who also attain their wishes.

ACT I. Quintet, Stöszel, Claudia, Sturmwald, Leonore, Rosalie: "Oh, how wonderful, how refreshing"; Aria of Leonore: "How can joy yet remain in my heart?" Sextet, Claudia, Stöszel, Sturmwald: "First we must know," in which Claudia makes extravagant demands on the captain for her dowry; Gotthold's aria: "When do you cease, beloved pain?" Duet: Sichel and Gotthold seek to remove

Stöszel from the house in order to elope with the girls.
Stöszel's aria: "Galenus and Hippocrates"; Sturmwald's
aria: "Wine is a *specificum*."

Change of scene: A room in Stöszel's house. (Romance
by Rosalie and Leonore: "Two maidens sat many a night";
Finale: "Who takes time to think when wrecked.") The
two young lovers come to carry off the girls but are driven
away by Claudia. When Stöszel corners them in their hiding-place in the laboratory, they take advantage of his
slumber to take off his wooden leg, remove his weapons and
escape.

ACT II. A street. (Dr. Krautmann's aria: "A doctor
is, upon my honour"; Duet, Gallus and Krautmann:
"Damned be the method.")

Change of scene: A room in Stöszel's house. (Aria by
Stöszel: "Sooner shall she not be wedded"; Gotthold's aria:
"True love will hope"; Sextet: "What conduct is that?")
Sichel and Gotthold come disguised as the captain and the
notary to obtain the signatures to the marriage contracts,
but when Stöszel finds the real captain in the laboratory,
the young people run away, but have succeeded in gaining
Claudia as a friend. (Leonore's aria: "Contentment is
more than a crown"; Sturmwald's aria: "Thus we treat
the soldiers.")

Change of scene: A street. (Strife duet between doctor
and apothecary: "You are a charlatan.")

Change of scene: The garden. (Rosalie's aria: "To each
one fortune is due"; Duet, Gotthold and Leonore: "Never
will I so far forget myself"; Finale: "Ha, powder and
cannon.") The two couples want to escape; Stöszel demands the arrest of the young people, but as Claudia takes
their part and Krautmann is inclined for peace, Stöszel
finally gives his consent to both marriages, and is reconciled with his old friend.

DON GIOVANNI

(Or "The Marble Guest")

Opera in two acts by Mozart.   Libretto by Da Ponte.

CAST: Don Giovanni—Baritone.   The Comthur.   Donna Anna, his daughter—Soprano.   Don Octavio, her betrothed—Tenor.   Donna Elvira—Soprano.   Leporello, servant to Don Juan—Basso.   Masetto, a peasant—Basso. Zerline, his betrothed—Soprano.   Place, Seville.   Time, the seventeenth century.

There are a great many operas upon the subject of Don Juan and his amours, but Mozart's master work is unapproachable.   It was first produced at Prague in 1787. Originally music and dialogue were heard alternately, but at present the secco-recitatives composed by Mozart are mostly in use.

ACT I.   The garden of the Comthur.   Leporello is keeping watch before the house into which Don Giovanni has crept in order to seduce Donna Anna, the betrothed of Octavio.   (Aria: "No rest night or day.")   Donna Anna appears with Don Giovanni, she wishes to know who he is and cries for help; but when the governor appears, he is stabbed by Don Giovanni, who escapes unrecognised. ("Yes, I endangered my life.")   Anna stands aghast and Octavio swears vengeance.   (Recitative: "What terrible sight before mine eyes"; Duet: "Away, away from my sight.")

Change of scene: A public square before the palace of Don Giovanni.   Giovanni and Leporello arrive.   (Recitative: "Now then, declare yourself.")   Elvira, whom he has seduced, appears.   Don Giovanni does not recognise her and tries to make her acquaintance.   (Sextet: "Where will I discover him?" Recitative: "What now? Heavens, what do I see?")   As Don Giovanni realises who is before him, he shoves Leporello to the front and hurries away. Leporello endeavours to console Elvira by unrolling a list of Don Giovanni's amours. (Aria: "Dearest Donna, this little register.") Elvira vows vengeance. (Recitative: "In what darkness of sorrow," and Aria: "The ungrateful one leaves me.") When she has departed, a marriage procession with Masetto and Zerline comes upon the scene. (Duet and chorus: "Dear sisters, born to love.") Don Giovanni sees Zerline, who pleases him, and he attempts to remove the jealous Masetto. (Recitative: "Oh, see, Leporello, the pretty young people"; Aria of Masetto: "Have I comprehended? Yes, dear sir.") Don Giovanni and Zerline are soon alone; he immediately begins his seductive arts. (Recitative: "At last we are released," and Duet: "Give me your hand, my life.") Elvira joins them, but Don Giovanni answers her reproaches by declaring to Octavio and Anna that both Zerline and Elvira are insane. (Recitative: "Away from her, seducer"; Aria of Elvira: "Lost one, hear him not"; Recitative, Octavio and Anna: "Oh, Don Giovanni"; Quartet, Elvira, Octavio, Anna, Don Giovanni: "Flee the hypocrite's smooth tongue.") Anna believes she has recognised in Don Giovanni the murderer of her father, and Octavio determines to observe his friend. (Recitative: "What a misfortune, horrible"; Aria: "You know the traitor, he threatened me with disgrace.") Leporello informs Don Giovanni that all the guests of the peasant wedding are in the house, that he had found occupation for Masetto, but that the return of Zerline has spoiled all. Elvira he had locked in an empty room. The careless Don Giovanni is extremely gay. (Champagne aria: "When the champagne drives the blood coursing.") He hurries to the palace. Zerline follows the jealous Masetto and tries to pacify him. (Recitative and aria: "Be not angry, dear boy.") Don Giovanni leads both to the bridal chamber, which has been gaily decorated, and Leporello also invites three maskers, Elvira, Octavio and Anna. (Sextet: "Here clasp we our hands in covenant.")

Change of scene: Ball room, quadrille, waltz, minuet.

("Come ye maidens to pleasure born.") Don Giovanni leads Zerline away, while Leporello engages Masetto's attention. When Zerline's cry for help is heard, Don Giovanni plays a comedy by rushing upon Leporello with drawn sword and accusing him of the seduction of Zerline. When he is not believed, and they attack him, he fights his way through the crowd.

Act II. Before Elvira's house. Don Giovanni pacifies Leporello and exchanges cloak and hat with him. (Duet: "Be content, be true to me.") Leporello is compelled to deliver a message to Elvira. (Terzett, Elvira, Leporello, Don Giovanni: "Oh hearts, cease to beat.") In the meanwhile, Don Giovanni serenades the maid. ("Hear the music of the zither.") Surprised by Masetto and his friends, the false Leporello escapes and thrashes Zerline's bridegroom. (Recitative and aria: "You go in that direction.") Zerline arrives and cheers Masetto. (Aria: "If you are good, if you are you.")

Change of scene: Elvira's room. It is dark. To Elvira come Octavio, Anna, Masetto and Zerline, who unmask the pseudo-Don Giovanni. Their suspicion is strengthened more and more that the real Don Giovanni is the murderer of the governor. (Sextet: "In the evening's quiet shadow.") Octavio alone. (Aria: "Tears dried by friendship.")

Change of scene: A graveyard with the statue of the governor. Leporello tells Don Giovanni what has occurred. The voice of the statue commands the libertine to be silent; upon the command of Don Giovanni, Leporello reads the inscription upon the statue's base: "Vengeance here awaits my murderer." The servant trembles, but the unabashed Don Giovanni mockingly invites the statue to dine with him at the evening meal. (Duet: "The governor on horseback.") The statue nods its head and answers, "Yes."

Change of scene: The room of Donna Anna. Octavio taxes her with cruelty for postponing the wedding. (Recitative: "I cruel! Oh, my love"; Aria: "You are dear to me beyond all.")

Change of scene: Room of Don Giovanni. (Finale: "Merry be my evening meal.") Elvira appears, hoping to move Don Giovanni to repentance. ("The might of love has led me to you.") As Elvira departs in despair, the statue of the Comthur approaches with heavy tread; it also exhorts the careless villain without avail and then sinks into the ground. Hell fire surrounds Don Giovanni, and he is carried below. A concluding chorus of the entire cast of the opera is generally omitted.

DONNA DIANA

Opera in three acts by Hofmann. Libretto by Wittkowsky.

CAST: Don Diego, reigning Count of Barcelona—Basso. Donna Diana, his daughter—Soprano. Donna Fenisa, his niece—Mezzo-soprano. Floretta, Diana's youthful companion—Soprano. Don Cæsar, prince of Urgel—Tenor. Don Gaston, count of Foir—Baritone. Perin, secretary—Basso. Place, Barcelona. First production, Berlin, 1886. The libretto is adapted from the comedy of Moreto "El desden con el desden."

ACT I. A hall in the palace. Cæsar has been victorious in the lists, but is unhappy, as he hopelessly loves the fair Diana. Perin counsels him to conquer the proud fair one with pride. Diego, Diana's father, arrives with Gaston and expresses his regret that no one can gain the love of his daughter.

Change of scene: Diana's room. Forced by Don Diego, Diana is compelled to receive Gaston and Cæsar as guests. She invites the knights to the coming festivities, and is astonished at Cæsar's seeming coldness.

ACT II. A garden. Masked ball. The guests pair off by choosing colours. Fenisa wins Gaston and Diana accompanies Cæsar. She desires to have him present at the feast in order to have an opportunity of refusing him, but advised by Perin, he is on his guard. She endeavours to gain his love and exercises all her arts of fascination, but proving unsuccessful, becomes angry and plans revenge. Perin expresses his joy.

ACT III. Gaston serenades Fenisa, with whom he has fallen in love, but Cæsar remains silent. Diana endeavours to bring him to terms, and informs him that she loves Gaston. Cæsar, however, is forewarned by Perin, who is the confidante of Diana, and he defeats her plan by declaring that he loves Fenisa. In the meanwhile, the hearts of Fenisa and Gaston and of Perin and Floretta have become united. Diana in tears confides to Fenisa that she loves Cæsar. Fenisa beckons to him to approach and the conquered Diana falls into his arms.

DON PASQUALE

Comic opera in three acts by Donizetti. Libretto adapted from the older Italian opera, "Ser Marc' Antonio," by Camerano.

CAST: Don Pasquale, an old bachelor—Basso. Dr. Malatesta, physician—Baritone. Ernesto, nephew of Don Pasquale—Tenor. Norina, a young widow—Soprano. A notary—Basso. Place, Rome. First production, Paris, 1843.

Don Pasquale refuses his sanction to the marriage of his nephew Ernesto with Norina, a lovely widow. The old man himself desires to wed, and his physician, Dr. Malatesta, proposes his sister, Sofronia, as the bride. The Don accepts, and Norina disguises herself as the doctor's sister, and the marriage contract is signed before a supposed notary. Norina now behaves like one possessed of the devil, and makes life so miserable for the old man that he is delighted when he discovers that he has been duped.

He relinquishes his desire for marriage and consents to the union of his nephew with Norina.

Act I.   Introduction between Don Pasquale and the doctor. (Romance of Malatesta: "Oh, like an angel of beauty"; Cavatina, Pasquale: "Oh, how I feel the glow of fire in my heart"; Duet between Ernesto and Pasquale: "How? You will? Marry me.")

Change of scene: Norina's cavatina: "Ah, beneath all eyes"; Duet between Norina and the doctor: "See, I am ready with love to surround him."

Act II.   Ernesto alone; then Pasquale, Norina, doctor. (Terzett: "Take courage"; Finale: "On one side," etc.)

Act III.   Chorus: "Bring the jewels at once"; Duet between Pasquale and Norina: "Dear wife, may I ask"; Duet between Pasquale and the doctor: "Softly in the dark."

Change of scene: Ernesto's serenade: "As Luna laughs in the fragrant night"; Duet between Ernesto and Norina "Do I read in your looks?" Finale: "Heaven, what do you say? This is Norina."

DON QUIXOTE

Musical tragi-comedy in three acts by Wilhelm Kienzl. Libretto by the composer.

Cast: The Duke—Tenor. The Duchess—Soprano. Don Clavijo—Basso. Alonzo Quixano (called Don Quixote de la Mancha)—Baritone. Mercedes, his niece—Mezzo-soprano. Sancho Panza—Tenor buffo. Carrasco—Baritone. Tirante—Basso buffo. Maritones, his daughter—Soprano. Aldonza—Alto. A messenger—Basso. Scullery boy—Soprano. A girl in the service of the duchess, Frasquita—Soprano. Rosita—Soprano. Marieta—Alto. Juanita—Alto. Place, La Mancha, Spain. Time, the sixteenth century. First production, Berlin, 1898.

Act I.   Apartment of Don Quixote. He is seated sleep-

ing in an arm-chair. In the background appear in striking
tableaux the personages of his dreams.

First: "Don Quixote in combat with a knight"; second,
"The twelve champions at the round table of King
Arthur"; third, "Dulcinea of Tobosa placing the laurel
wreath on the brow of the kneeling Don Quixote." Mercedes, who awakens her uncle, Don Quixote, notices from
his confused talk that he has lost his senses, and in this
state he imagines that as a roaming knight he must go
forth to seek adventures.

Change of scene: An open inn. Don Quixote believes the
inn to be a castle and desires to have knighthood conferred
upon him by the owner. Carrasco, the innkeeper, knows
him and narrates to the others the story of his madness,
and they enter into the joke. Carrasco tells of the giant
Mambrin, who has wronged the Princess Micomicona, and
asks Don Quixote to deliver her. With many fantastic
ceremonies Don Quixote is knighted by Tirante. A love
adventure with Maritones, whom he imagines to be a princess, has a sorry ending. He takes the peasant Sancho
Panza as his esquire.

The duke and his court come to the inn and apparently
listen with great interest to the adventures of Don Quixote.
When he is asked to pay the score, he takes to flight, and
Sancho Panza is soundly thrashed by the innkeeper in consequence.

Act II. Before the duke's palace. The duke has invited
Don Quixote to the court and all prepare to be amused by
his imaginary adventures. After the feasting, Don Clavijo,
attired as a woman, throws himself at Don Quixote's feet
and prays him to conquer the giant Malambruno, who has
transformed him and many others by his magic arts. To
reach the giant, they compel Don Quixote and Sancho
Panza to bestride a wooden horse. After teasing them in
many ways, fireworks are exploded at the back of the horse,
which tears it to pieces and throws both riders to the ground.
In the meanwhile, Don Clavijo has arranged a masquerade,

and Don Quixote rides contentedly away assured that another magician has already conquered the giant.

Act III.   A road in a romantic country.   Mercedes has disguised herself as Dulcinea and Carrasco is attired as "the Knight of the White Moon."   Mercedes has promised Carrasco to listen to his suit if he is successful in inducing Don Quixote to return home.   Sancho Panza arrives first, pursued by an armed mob.   Dreadfully beaten, he sinks to the ground.   Don Quixote finds him in this condition, and now fights with the "Knight of the White Moon," who is the victor and compels him to accompany him, as a condition of submission.

Change of scene: Don Quixote's room.   Don Quixote makes his will and throws the tales of chivalry which have led to his delusions into the fire.   He suddenly falls to the ground and expires.   Mercedes, Carrasco and Sancho Panza stand around him weeping.

THE EAGLE'S EYRY

Opera in three acts by Franz Glaeser.   Libretto by Von Holtei.

Cast: Father Renner, innkeeper—Basso.   Veronica, his wife—Mezzo-soprano.   Anton, their son—Tenor.   Marie, their foster daughter—Soprano.   Rose—Soprano.   Richard, forester—Baritone.   Cassian and Lazarus, smugglers —Tenor and Basso.   Place, in the Silesian mountains. Time, 1830.   First production at Berlin in 1833 at the old Koenigstadt Theatre.

Act I.   Scene in the Silesian mountains.   Rose is on the stage; Renner, Veronica, Marie and Anton approach, and after a prayer of thanksgiving depart, leaving Rose alone. (Aria: "Though the heart is desolate.")   Cassian appears. (Song: "Life shall be crowned with boughs of spring.") He attacks Rose, and Anton, hearing her screams, returns to protect her, though opposed by his mother, who separates them.   She has heard that her husband has also be-

friended the girl, and that he is not averse to her marriage
with Anton.   Veronica desires that her foster daughter
Marie and the forester Richard shall become man and wife.
Richard appears.   (Aria: "Oh, that the rocks in deep
abyss.")   The following scene discloses that Richard and
Rose are in intimate relationship.   Peasants arrive for a
feast.   (Chorus: "We greet again this day.")   While the
crowd is merry Rose is recognised as a girl who some time
before had fled from home disgraced.

Act II.   Rose confesses to the good-hearted Renner that
she is the wife of Richard and has concealed her child in
the forest.   She gives expression to her grief.   (Aria:
"Where the meadows' green bands twixt clefts do lie.")
Renner promises protection, and in the scene which follows
Rose refuses Anton's love and sends him to Marie, who loves
him.   This pleases Renner, as he is unwilling that Veronica's desire to betroth Marie to the forester shall be grati-
fied.   Renner and the smugglers carouse.   (Trio: "The
bottle at hand, now choose with sense.")   Veronica approaches and Renner persuades her to adopt his plans.
The stage is deserted.   An eagle rises into the air, a child
in its talons.   All rush out in consternation.   (Chorus:
"The eagle, he is carrying off a child"; Rose: "God
in Heaven, 'tis my child.")   After a short pause all hasten
to the rescue.

Act III.   The pinnacle of the rocks with eagle's eyry.
Richard appears.   (Aria: "And darker yet the clouds do
gather.")   Rose is seen near at hand, and tells Richard
what has occurred.   He tries to shoot the eagle, rescue
the child and thus obtain Rose's forgiveness; but his hand
trembles, his eyes waver, he cannot aim.   The thunder
rolls and the lightning strikes a tree, which falls and forms
a bridge to the eagle's nest.   Rose crosses it despite the
threatening bird, which is shot by Richard.   "Victory,"
cries Rose, "my child is saved."   Amid the joyful shouts
of the crowd, who have climbed the rocks to meet them,
Rose and Richard are reconciled.

ERNANI

(First produced under the title "Il Proseritto.")

Opera in four acts by Verdi. Libretto adapted from Victor Hugo's drama by Piave.

CAST: Don Carlos, King of Spain—Baritone. Don Ruy Gomez, grandee of Spain—Basso. Elvira, his niece and affianced—Soprano. Johanna, her nurse—Mezzo-soprano. Ernani, a bandit—Tenor. Don Riccardo, armour bearer to the king—Tenor. Iago, armour bearer to Don Ruy Gomez—Basso. Place, in Aragon, Aix la Chapelle and Saragassa. Time, 1519. First production, Venice, 1844.

ACT I. Mountains of Aragon. The bandits demand the reason for Ernani's gloom. (Chorus of bandits: "To you we drink"; and "Ernani, so gloomy? Why, oh strong one, does care sit on your brow?") Ernani replies (Recitative: "Thanks, dear friends"; Cavatina: "As the flower turns to the sun") that he loves Elvira, who is to be led unwillingly to the altar by old Gomez de Silva. He asks the bandits to abduct her.

Change of scene: Elvira's apartment. (Scene: "Now sinks the sun and Silva does not return"; Cavatina: "Ernani, Ernani, save me.") Silva's wedding presents are brought in, for which Elvira makes acknowledgment. King Carlos, poorly attired, enters, but is recognised by Elvira and his love repulsed. As he attempts to use force, she grasps a dagger, but Ernani suddenly arriving, interferes. (Terzett: "A friend comes quickly to your aid.") Carlos recognises in Ernani the leader of the bandits, and he in turn expresses his hate for the king, who has robbed him of his lands. As he invites the king to fight, Silva appears. (Finale: "Dreadful sight"; Cavatina of Silva: "Unfortunate one, could you deem—!") Ernani offers to fight them both when Riccardo approaches and recognises the king. Ernani whispers to Elvira to prepare for flight.

ACT II. A hall in Silva's palace. Ernani comes thither

disguised as a pilgrim. (Terzett, Silva, Ernani, Elvira: "The pilgrim may appear.") He alleges that he is pursued and is seeking safety, which is granted him by Silva. A scene between Ernani and Elvira follows. The latter believes Ernani dead and intends to kill herself at the altar. (Duet: "Ha, false one, you hypocrite.") Ernani reveals his identity; Silva surprises them. (Terzett: "Shameless ones, ye shall rue it.") He keeps his word to Ernani and saves him from the king, but only postpones his personal vengeance. Carlos arrives and wishes to know why the castle is barred. Silva refuses to surrender Ernani. (Carlos's aria: "Let us see, thou prater of virtue.") Don Carlos's men do not find the hiding-place of the bandit; Silva keeps his word, even when the king secures Elvira as a hostage. He releases Ernani, and then challenges him to a duel. Ernani refuses to fight with his saviour, but unites with Silva in his plans to free Elvira from the king. Ernani swears to appear at the summons of Silva, wherever he may be at that time.

Act III. In the burial vault of Charles the Great at Aix la Chapelle. Carlos visits the grave of the emperor. (Cavatina: "Ye golden dreams of youth.") Standing behind the vault, he overhears the conversation of the conspirators; Silva and Ernani are among them, and the latter resolves to murder Carlos. The conspiracy is foiled by the appearance of Carlos's attendants upon the scene. The king commands that all the noblemen be executed. Ernani then steps forward, declaring that he also must die. He announces himself as Don Juan of Aragon, who has been proscribed. Elvira begs mercy for her lover, and Carlos, whose mood has changed, forgives them both and places Elvira's hand in that of Ernani.

Act IV. Castle of Ernani. Elvira and Ernani have just been married, when, in consternation, Ernani hears a bugle call. Silva arrives and silently hands Ernani a dagger. Ernani keeps his oath and stabs himself to the heart. (Terzett: "Cease, oh music, put out the lights.")

EUGEN ONEGIN

Lyric opera in three acts by Peter Tschaikowsky. Libretto adapted from Puschkin's tale. German by Bernhard.

CAST: Larina, a landowner—Mezzo-soprano. Tatjana—Soprano, and Olga, her daughter—Alto. Filipjewna, nurse—Mezzo-soprano. Eugen Onegin—Baritone. Lenski—Tenor. Prince Gremin—Baritone. A captain—Basso. Saretzki—Basso. Triquet, a Frenchman—Tenor. Place, Russia. Time, about 1815. First production, St. Petersburg, 1877.

ACT I. A garden. Frau Larina is preserving fruit and listens to the song of her daughters. (Duet: "Have you been listening.") It has been familiar to her since youth, when she loved a careless officer, but was compelled to marry an unloved husband. She has gradually accustomed herself to her fate, however, and has found happiness in the love of a good man. The peasants bring in the harvest wreath. (Chorus: "My feet find nothing more," and "Through the fields runs a brook.") Tatjana grows pensive with the music, while the lively Olga prefers to dance. (Aria: "With silent melancholy.") All are astonished at the pallor of Tatjana, and believe she is affected by the contents of a book she is reading. Lenski arrives in a wagon accompanied by his neighbour Onegin. It soon appears that Tatjana loves Onegin (Quartet: "What I hoped for has come"), while Lenski is attracted to Olga. The latter soon comes to an agreement, while Onegin remains stiffly polite to Tatjana.

Change of scene: Tatjana's room. She is about to retire and begs the nurse Filipjewna to tell her stories. While listening she tries to conceal her emotion. At last she confesses to the old nurse that she is in love, and sends her away. Instead of sleeping, she writes letters, but tears them up when written. At last she finishes one and seals it. She remains at the window the rest of the night, and when

Filipjewna arrives in the morning, she sends the letter secretly to Onegin.

Change of scene: The garden. A number of maids gather berries and sing. ("Come, girls, all in a heap.") Tatjana arrives running in excitement and throws herself on the sward followed by Onegin, who has received her letter. He explains to her coldly that he honours the candour of her confession, but cannot fulfil her hopes, as he is a profligate and not suited to the marriage state. A maiden's love is only phantasy, and she must overcome it. Deeply hurt, Tatjana departs.

ACT II. A room in Larina's house, filled with a merry crowd. Lenski dances with Olga, Onegin with Tatjana. They are compelled to endure the tattling of the older dames. Notwithstanding the protest of Lenski, Onegin asks Olga to dance. (Chorus: "Here's to joy.") Lenski is angry with Olga, because she is flirting with Onegin, and becomes so jealous that the girl, to punish him, says that she will dance the quadrille with Onegin. Before it begins the Frenchman Triquet sings a song of doubtful character to the praise of Tatjana, which is received with applause. ("A cette fête conviés.") Onegin dances with Olga, the captain with Tatjana, and Lenski stands moodily apart. When Onegin asks him what is wrong, he answers angrily; a quarrel ensues, and the dance is interrupted. Amid general consternation Lenski asks his friend to fight a duel. (Finale: "Here in this house the hours have flown.")

Change of scene: A mill. It is early in the morning. Lenski and his second, Saretzki, are impatiently awaiting their opponents. (Lenski's aria: "Where have you disappeared.") At last Onegin arrives, accompanied only by his servant, who is to act as second. While he arranges with Saretski, the erstwhile friends regret ("My enemy") that they are now enemies. Lenski falls dead, struck by the bullet of Onegin, and overwhelmed with grief, Onegin falls upon the body of his friend.

ACT III. Six years later. Hall in the palace of Princess

Gremina (Tatjana). Onegin is among her guests. He has found no peace, and is constantly troubled with pangs of conscience. (Aria: "Alas, no oblivion.") He learns that the princess is Tatjana, and she is profoundly agitated when she meets him. The prince tells Onegin that he loves his wife passionately (Aria: "Every one knows love on earth") and introduces him to her. She addresses a few indifferent words to him, and is led away by her husband. Onegin gazes after her. (Aria: "Is this then really Tatjana?") He feels that he loves her, laments his former conduct and resolves to gain her affection.

Change of scene: Reception room in the palace of the prince. Tatjana has received a message from Onegin that he will visit her. She still loves him, but she wishes to retain her peace of mind, and when he appears she reminds him with deep emotion of the conversation in the garden. She has pardoned him and acknowledges that he had acted rightly, but declares it to be his duty to leave and never return. Notwithstanding his outbreak of passion, she remains firm and leaves him. Completely cast down, he stands silent, and then rushes away in despair.

EURYANTHE

Romantic opera in three acts by Carl Maria von Weber. Libretto founded on an old French tradition by Helmine von Chézy.

CAST: Louis VI—Basso. Adolar, Count of Nevers— Tenor. Euryanthe of Savoy, his bride—Soprano. Lysiart, Count of Forest—Baritone. Eglantine von Puiset, the captive daughter of a mutineer—Mezzo-soprano. Place, Castle Preméry and Burg of Nevers. Time, 1110. First production, Vienna, 1821.

Adolar von Nevers is affianced to Euryanthe of Savoy. His betrothed resides at Castle Nevers, where Eglantine, the daughter of a mutineer, has also found refuge. Eglan-

tine loves Adolar, who repulses her, and Lysiart loves
Euryanthe without avail.

Act I.   A hall in the king's palace.   (Chorus: "Hail to
peace—hail to women.")   The king informs Adolar that he
wishes Euryanthe to appear at court, and demands a song
in her praise.   (Adolar's cavatina: "Under blooming al-
mond trees.")   All sing in praise of Euryanthe except
Lysiart; he questions the fidelity of women, and professes
to be able to win the love of Euryanthe with ease.   Adolar
stakes his life and all he possesses upon the fidelity of
Euryanthe.   Lysiart accepts the challenge and the stakes.
The king attempts to dissuade them from their foolish
wager, but in vain.

Change of scene: The palace garden of Nevers.   Euryanthe alone.   (Aria: "Bells in the dale.")   Eglantine
joins her.   (Cavatina: "Oh my sorrow is unmeasured.")
Euryanthe confides in Eglantine and tells her Adolar's secret.   Emma, his sister, had lost her affianced in battle,
and in despair had drunk poison from a ring.   Her spirit
could find no rest in the grave until the tears of an innocent in deep distress had been shed upon the ring which
caused her death.   Euryanthe regrets having broken her
oath of silence, but Eglantine first soothes her and then
triumphs over her.   (Recitative and aria: "Deluded one,
who believes in my love," "He could for her me despise.")
She enters into a compact with the approaching Lysiart.

Act II.   The same garden.   Lysiart despairs of winning
the love of Euryanthe.   (Recitative: "Where can I hide?
Where find peace"; Aria: "I vow myself to powers of
vengeance, they lead me to dark deeds.")   Eglantine has
stolen Emma's ring from the vault, and Lysiart takes it to
show as an evidence of Euryanthe's unfaithfulness.   (Duet:
"Come then to avenge.")

Change of scene: Same scene as Act I.   Adolar enters.
(Cavatina of Adolar: "Zephyrs wave me peace.")   Euryanthe joins him.   (Duet: "Take my soul.")   Lysiart
now appears, declares himself victor in the wager before

the assembled court and presents the ring. Adolar loses his lands and determines to travel to a distant country where he is not known. Euryanthe accompanies him as his wife.

Act III. A wood. Adolar and Euryanthe. (Recitative: "Here do you dwell"; Duet: "How I love you! You were my richest prize.") Adolar is about to kill Euryanthe, when a large snake menaces his life. Euryanthe tries to save Adolar by throwing herself in its path. (Aria: "Protecting angel's choir.") After Adolar has killed the snake, he repents of his desire to kill Euryanthe, but leaves her. (Cavatina of Euryanthe: "Now am I forlorn.") The king arrives with hunters. (Chorus: "The vales are in mist, the heights glow.") He finds Euryanthe in the forest. (Duet: "Leave me here in peace.") She narrates to the king the treachery of Eglantine, and proclaims her own innocence. The king takes her with him. (Aria and chorus: "To him, to him, oh tarry not.")

Change of scene: Garden of the castle of Nevers. (Adolar's cavatina: "Truth no longer on earth prevails.") Eglantine appears with Lysiart in bridal procession, but becomes insane, and in the act of revealing everything is slain by Lysiart. Adolar is about to be manacled, but is released by the king, who orders the execution of Lysiart, and re-establishes Adolar in his possessions. Euryanthe and her lover are wedded and the soul of the unhappy Emma is now at rest, for the tears of an innocent have bedewed the ring that caused her death. (All cry: "Hail to Adolar, hail Euryanthe.")

FALSTAFF

Opera in three acts by Verdi. Adapted from Shakespeare's play by Boito.

Cast: Sir John Falstaff—Baritone. Ford—Baritone. Alice, his wife—Soprano. Nanette, her daughter—Soprano. Fenton—Tenor. Dr. Caius—Tenor. Bardolph and Pistol, servants of Falstaff—Tenor and Basso. Mistress Quickly—Alto. Mistress Page—Soprano. Place, Windsor. Time, the fifteenth century. First production, Milan, 1893.

ACT I. A room at the Garter Inn. Falstaff is surrounded by his friends Bardolph, Pistol and the innkeeper, when Dr. Caius arrives and insults him, but the excited doctor is soon ejected. Falstaff hands a letter to his servants and another to the page, for delivery to Mistress Ford and to Mistress Page, and then angrily dismisses them.

Change of scene: Ford's garden. Alice and Meg have received the letters of Falstaff, both of like contents. They exchange them, and in conjunction with Mistress Quickly resolve to punish the knight. Not only the women, but the men, Ford, Fenton, Dr. Caius, and Bardolph and Pistol, who have been maltreated by their master, are athirst for vengeance. A love duet between Fenton and Nanette follows; the women return home and through Mistress Quickly invite Falstaff to an interview. The men also arrive upon the scene, and Bardolph and Pistol are persuaded to introduce Ford to Falstaff under an assumed name.

ACT II. Same room as in Act I. Bardolph and Pistol announce to their master the arrival of Dame Quickly, who delivers the invitation. Ford is now introduced as Signor Fortuna, who offers money to the fat knight to intercede for him with Mistress Ford. Falstaff agrees with pleasure, and while he is absent, attiring himself in splendid array, Ford is consumed with jealousy.

Change of scene: A room in Ford's house. Mistress Quickly announces the coming of Falstaff and Mistress Ford has a large wash basket placed in readiness. When Falstaff arrives, Mistress Quickly reports the arrival of Mistress Page, and the knight is compelled to conceal himself behind a screen. When the angry Ford with his friends appear to capture Falstaff, the latter hides in the clothes basket. In the meanwhile, a love scene between Fenton and

Nanette takes place behind the screen, and the men returning, hear the sound of a kiss; they think to entrap Falstaff, but find Fenton, who is ordered to leave the room by
Ford.   When the men again proceed with the search, the
women order the wash basket to be thrown into the ditch,
where Falstaff is compelled to endure the jeers of the crowd.

Act III.   Before the inn.   Falstaff again receives an
invitation through Dame Quickly, which is overheard by
the men.   After Falstaff has promised to go to Herne's
Oak, the place of meeting, he enters the house with Dame
Quickly, and the men concoct a plan for his punishment.
Dr. Caius is promised the hand of Nanette, and is also to
appear disguised as Nanette at the appointed place.   The
plot is overheard by Dame Quickly.

Change of scene: At Herne's Oak in Windsor Park.   A
moonlight night.   The women disguise Fenton as a monk,
and arrange that he shall spoil the plans of Dr. Caius.
Falstaff's love scene with Mistress Ford is interrupted by
the announcement that the Wild Huntsman is approaching,
and the men disguised as elves and fairies thrash Falstaff
soundly.   When their vengeance is satisfied, Dr. Caius finds
that he has captured Bardolph instead of Nanette in the
garb of a fairy queen, but Fenton and Nanette, with the
consent of Ford, are joined in wedlock.

FAUST

Opera in five acts by Charles Gounod.   Words by Barbier
and Carré, founded upon Goethe's tragedy.

Cast: Faust—Tenor.   Mephistopheles—Basso.   Valentin
—Baritone.   Brander—Baritone.   Siebel—Soprano.   Marguerite—Soprano.   Martha—Alto.

Of the many Faust operas, the one composed by Spohr
was formerly frequently produced, but has disappeared
from the stage since the advent of Gounod's composition.
First production, Paris, 1859.

Act I. Faust's study. He is about to take poison, as he despairs of completely solving the secrets of science. Hearing the Easter carols, he resolves to continue living, but calls on Satan, who shows him a vision of Marguerite, whereupon Faust sells Satan his soul, and is transformed into a handsome youth.

Act II. Before the city gate. Festival of the citizens. Students sing. Valentin arrives and gazes upon his sister's picture. (Aria: "Oh, holy emblem.") Siebel promises to protect Valentin's sister while the soldier is in the field. Mephistopheles mingles with the crowd of students and sings ("Yes, gold rules the world"); he then tells fortunes, predicts Brander's early death, and prophecies to Siebel that never again will he carry a bouquet to Marguerite, as all the flowers he touches will fade. Hearing the name of his sister, Valentin approaches, and with his friends rushes upon the jeering Mephistopheles. The fiend draws a magic circle around him, which protects him from their weapons; but when the retreating men thrust their crossed sword hilts in his face, he cowers in fear. The people return and dance. Faust offers his arm as escort to the blushing Marguerite, but is refused. The dance continues.

Act III. Marguerite's garden. Siebel binds a bouquet for Marguerite, but the flowers fade. (Ariette: "Flowers, dear, speak for me.") He dips his hands in holy water, and through this expedient now successfully fulfils his task, laying his offering at Marguerite's door. During this scene, Faust and Mephistopheles appear, and Satan departs to select a more valuable gift for Marguerite than a bouquet. Faust alone. (Cavatina: "Greeting, oh holy spot.") Mephisto brings a casket of jewels, places it at the door and departs with Faust. Marguerite sits pensively at the spinning wheel. (Ballad: "There was a king in Thule.") Discovering the casket she is blinded by its contents, and in delight adorns herself with the jewels. (Aria: "Oh, what joy, to see myself so prettily adorned.") Martha appears, then Faust with

Mephisto. Satan leads Martha away. Faust declares his love to Marguerite. (Quartet: "Let me, I adjure you.") Marguerite loses her heart to her persistent lover, and night having set in, recalls Faust, who is about to depart.

ACT IV. A street. The soldiers return from the war. Valentin is welcomed by Siebel and enters his house. The soldiers accompanied by the people seek their quarters. Mephisto arrives with Faust at dusk, and scoffingly serenades Marguerite. Valentin rushes out of the house and is stabbed by Faust in the duel which ensues. The people assemble in excitement. Marguerite sorrowfully bends over the dying Valentin, who curses her as a wanton.

Change of scene: The church. Satan punishes the guilty Marguerite by awakening her conscience, and avoided by the citizens, she falls in a swoon.

ACT V. The Walpurgis revel. Mephisto transports Faust from the dreary scene to the bacchanal revels of the Walpurgis night, but when Marguerite's image appears, Faust orders Satan to convey him to his beloved.

Change of scene: Marguerite in prison. She has become insane, but recognises Faust, who, desiring to save her, once again recalls the scenes of their love and joy. She finally repulses him and submits to the judgment of God. Faust flees with Satan, Marguerite dies, and the angels bear her to heaven.

FEDORA

A lyric drama in three acts by Umberto Giordano and Victorien Sardou.

CAST: Princess Fedora Romazov—Soprano. Countess Olga Sukarev—Soprano. Count Loris Ispanov—Tenor. De Siriex, diplomat—Baritone. Dmitri, a groom—Contralto. A Savoyard—Contralto. Desiré, a maid—Soprano. Cyril, a coachman—Baritone. Borov, a doctor—Baritone. Grech, a police officer—Basso. Baron Rouvel

—Baritone. Place, St. Petersburg and Paris. Time, the
present. First production, Milan, 1898.

ACT I.   St. Petersburg, at the house of Count Vladimir
Andrejevich. His servants are playing dominoes and discussing the approaching marriage of their master, a handsome, dissolute nobleman. Fedora Romazov, his betrothed,
arrives unexpectedly in evening dress. She is ushered into
a sitting room to await the count's return. Seeing his
photograph, she kisses it rapturously (Fedora: "O eyes,
clear with truth"), unaware that he is deceiving her. The
sound of sleigh-bells is heard without and the count is
brought in mortally wounded. Doctors and a priest are
quickly summoned. The servants are questioned and it
develops that a certain Count Ispanov was probably the
assassin. De Siriex, a diplomat, and Grech, a police officer,
plan an investigation. Fedora is agonised (Fedora:
"Speak, courage, speak"), and determines to devote her
life to vengeance. The crime is believed to have been inspired by the Nihilists.

ACT II.   Paris. A reception at Fedora's house. Countess
Olga Sukarev, an accomplished coquette, is entertaining a
crowd of distinguished men. Fedora enters with Ispanov,
whom she is purposely fascinating, in order to gain her
revenge. De Siriex, joining them, is introduced to Ispanov.
Dr. Borov warns the latter against Fedora. Olga is flirting with Baron Rouvel. (Olga: "I'm a caprice swift and
light.") Fedora explains to De Siriex her plan concerning Ispanov, whom, however, she cannot force herself to
hate. De Siriex, between amusement and disgust at Olga's
coquetries, wittily describes the typical Russian woman.
(De Siriex: "The Russian woman is a woman twice over.")
She retorts with a description of the typical *boulevardier*.
(Olga: "Like bubbling wine is your true Parisian.") All
applaud, laughing. Fedora continues to fascinate Loris
Ispanov. (Loris: "My love must make you love me.")
She tells him she is no longer an exile and is about to return
to Russia. He declares that having committed a crime.

he cannot follow. She draws from him subtly the confession that he is the murderer of Vladimir. De Siriex brings news of a Nihilist plot against the czar, which breaks up the reception. Loris promises to return to Fedora later. She betrays him to Grech, and it is arranged that he shall be arrested before he leaves the house. Fedora learns from Loris that he killed Vladimir for seducing his wife. He shows her letters which prove his story. She realises she loves him (Loris: "Behold! I weep, but not for mine own grief") and that he will lose his life through her if he leaves the house. She therefore detains him there.

Act III. Fedora's villa in Oberland. She and Loris are as happy in their love as two children. Fedora sits in a swing; Loris swings her. A mountain lad is heard singing. ("Spring is come, the birds are trilling.") Olga joins them in a pensive mood, weary of rural life. (Olga: "Still the same old green, still the same old blue!") Seeing their joyousness she changes her tune. (Olga: "While love allures, while passion guides.") Loris goes off to post some letters. De Siriex appears in bicycling dress, and challanges Olga to a ride. He tells her teasingly that her latest admirer was a detective. She pretends to faint (De Siriex: "Never mind, fair lady"), but, quickly recovering, runs off to dress, pouting prettily. De Siriex, growing serious, tells Fedora that Ispanov's brother has been killed (De Siriex: "The grim old tiger, having lost his cub") for complicity in a Nihilist plot, and that the shock caused the death of their aged mother. Fedora is overwhelmed, crying out: " 'Twas all my fault!" Olga returns, departing with De Siriex. Fedora faces her problem alone, listening dully to the Angelus, and the song of the little boy. (Fedora: "O God of justice.") Loris enters, with dispatches containing the news. (Loris: "O my dear mother.") He observes Fedora's changed demeanour, and anxiously questions her. She tries to keep him from opening the letter from Borov, which tells him that a woman spy caused the death of his brother. Loris breaks down and sobs. Fedora is almost mad. She makes excuses for the spy, imploring pardon for her. Borov arrives in a carriage. Fedora detains Loris, but finding it useless, pours some poison contained in a cross she wears into a cup of tea, which she drinks. Borov entering tries to save her. Olga and De Siriex appear laughing, but are quickly silenced, for Fedora is dying. (Fedora: "Darkness is falling, life is far away.") Loris, in anguish, forgives her, and embracing him, she falls lifeless, while far away echoes the voice of the little lad: "My mountain maid comes nevermore!"

FERAMORS

Opera in three acts by Anton Rubinstein. Text adapted from Thomas Moores's "Lalla Rookh" by Rodenberg.

CAST: Lalla Rookh, princess of Hindostan—Soprano. Hafisa, her friend—Alto. Feramors, a singer—Tenor. Fadladin, grand vizier of Hindostan—Basso. Chosru, ambassador of the King of Bokhara—Baritone. Place, valley of Cashmere. First performance, Dresden, 1863.

ACT I. The King of Bokhara is the intended husband of Lalla Rookh. The arrangements for the wedding feast have been made by the grand vizier. The princess arrives with her friend Hafisa to greet Chosru, the ambassador of the king, but she is sad, as she loves Feramors, the singer. Solemn reception. (Ballet: "Dance of lights of the brides of Cashmere.") Grand final scene in which Chosru and Hafisa find they love each other. The call to prayer is heard from the minaret, and Feramors' ballad ("The moonlight dreams on Persia's sea") causes Lalla Rookh to avow her love for him.

ACT II. Fadladin woos Hafisa in vain. She leads the old man aside to give Feramors and Lalla Rookh an opportunity to declare their love. The grand vizier, returning and discovering Feramors, treats him as an intruder, and his life is in danger from the assembled crowd. Chosru's interference saves Feramors from death, but does not prevent his imprisonment.

ACT III.   Feramors escapes and Lalla Rookh is compelled to adorn herself for her marriage with the king.   When he appears, to the surprise and joy of Lalla Rookh, she beholds the singer Feramors, who has taken this method to test the heart of his bride.

FEUERSNOTH

(Lack of fire)

A song poem by Von Wolzogen.   Music by Richard Strauss.

CAST: Gundelfingen, the castellan.   Sentlinger, the burgomaster.   Diemut, his daughter.   Three playmates.   Kunrad, the leveller.   Yörg Pöschel, Hamerlein, Kasel, Gilgenstock, Tulbeck, Aspack, citizens.   Ursula, Walpurg, wives, etc., of citizens.   Children, servants.

The action takes place in Munich on Sonnenwendtag (the day of the turning of the sun) in remote times.   First production, Weimar, 1902.

On the occasion of the holiday (Sonnenwendtag) a number of children are engaged in collecting chips for the Sonnenwend fire.   (Chorus: "Give us some wood.")   They obtain from the burgomaster a basket filled with wood for the purpose, and his daughter Diemut distributes candy among them.   (Diemut: "There are some sweetmeats.")   The children then knock at the door of the little house opposite, out of which steps the mysterious Kunrad.   (Chorus of children: "In Munich stands a new built house.")   In honour of the occasion, he allows the children to use all the wood of the house.   Kunrad and Diemut stand opposite each other in the crowd and they fall in love.   Kunrad takes the liberty of kissing the damsel, whereupon she is ashamed and angry, and enters the house.   (Kunrad: "Sonnenwend, Sonnenwend, rings in my ears!")   At night, when the candles are lighted, and the Sonnenwend fire is blazing at the gates (Chorus: "Hurrah! the pretty fire!"), Kunrad stands under the balcony of Diemut and asks to be admitted. Diemut allows him to step into the basket, pulls him up half way, and leaves him dangling as punishment for his impertinence. (Burgomaster: "Me-ow! Meow! What's afoot?") When Kunrad understands her object, he becomes enraged and curses the city and the citizens who have assembled to deride him. He calls in the aid of magic. (Kunrad: "Help, O master.") Feuersnoth takes place, that is, all the light in the city is extinguished and darkness and cold is its fate in the future. "Icy cold surround you in endless night, because you the power of song have derided," sings Kunrad, and "All warmth comes from woman, all light comes from love—from the body of a maiden alone can you again receive your warmth." He swings himself to the windowsill. Diemut, whose love has conquered her pride, is at the window, and she draws Kunrad into her chamber. When, after a short time all fires are again lighted, the citizens know that the maiden body of Diemut has conquered the magic. In his scene in the basket, Kunrad sings of Reichart the Wagner (Richard Wagner), who has been driven from the city by contemptible tricks. This gives the opera a strongly satirical flavour, which is emphasised by the use of themes from "The Flying Dutchman" and from Strauss's own opera, "Guntram."

FIDELIO

Opera in two acts by Beethoven. Text from the French of Bouilly by Sonnleithner.

CAST: Don Fernando, minister—Baritone. Don Pizarro, governor of the States prison—Baritone. Florestan, a prisoner—Tenor. Léonore, his wife, under the name of Fidelio—Soprano. Rocko, keeper—Basso. Marzelline, his daughter—Soprano. Jaquino, gatekeeper—Tenor. A captain.

Place, a Spanish States prison in the vicinity of Seville. First production, Vienna, 1805. The opera at first contained three acts, afterward condensed to two by Breuning, at which time Beethoven wrote a new overture (Léonore III). In this form the opera was produced in 1806 under the title "Léonore," but was again revised by Treitschke in 1814. This representation, under the original title "Fidelio," was preceded by the well-known Fidelio overture, the fourth written by the composer for the opera.

Don Florestan, a courtier of noble character and a favourite of the king, determines to thwart the traitorous designs of Don Pizarro, who thereby becomes his bitter enemy. Florestan mysteriously disappears, and all search is fruitless. Léonore, his faithful wife, suspects that Pizarro has captured him, and, disguised as a youth under the name of Fidelio, she enters the service of Rocko, the jailor of the States prison, of which Pizarro is the governor. To her horror she finds that she is not mistaken. She runs great risk of discovery, as the daughter of Rocko falls in love with the supposed youth, and Rocko, with whom she has also found favour, desires to unite them. Léonore is enabled to visit the underground dungeons and finds her husband. The cruel Pizarro has condemned him to death by famine, but determines to hasten his end, as the powerful minister, Don Fernando, a friend of Florestan, is coming to inspect the prison. Rocko and Fidelio are compelled to dig a grave, as Pizarro intends to murder Florestan before the minister arrives. Léonore succeeds in saving her husband with the aid of Don Fernando, who arrives opportunely. The villain Pizarro receives his well-deserved punishment.

Act I. Courtyard of the prison. (Duet between Jaquino and Marzelline: "Now, darling, we are alone.") Jaquino is ready to marry Marzelline, but she loves the new assistant, Fidelio. Fidelio is in reality Léonore disguised as a youth. Her husband, Florestan, has disappeared. She suspects Pizarro and believes that Florestan is in the prison. Having gained the confidence of Rocko, she hopes to find her husband. Marzelline desires to win Fidelio's love. (Aria: "Would I were wed to thee.") Rocko is willing (Quartet, Marzelline, Léonore, Rocko, Jaquino: "I feel so strange"; Rocko's aria counselling thrift: "Has one not also gold besides"). Léonore agrees to everything in order to be allowed to visit the prison, which, however, requires the consent of the governor. (Terzett: "Good, son, good, always have courage.") Pizarro appears, filled with anxiety, as he has imprisoned Florestan from motives of personal vengeance; and to prevent discovery of this he determines that Florestan must die before the minister's inspection. As Rocko refuses to murder the dying man, he is ordered to uncover an old well in which the prisoner is to be buried. Pizarro himself resolves to do the deed. (Aria of Pizarro: "Ha, what a moment! My vengeance will I cool"; Duet: "Now old man, be quick.") Léonore has been listening and is in despair. (Aria: "Wicked one, whither do you go?") Rocko allows the prisoners to breathe the air at the request of Léonore, who wishes to see her husband. (Finale, chorus of prisoners: "Oh, what joy, in heaven's fresh air.") She cannot find Florestan, but accompanies Rocko to the underground cells, and helps him dig the grave. Pizarro returns and orders the prisoners back to their cells. (Second chorus of prisoners: "Farewell, warm sunlight.")

ACT II. The dark dungeon of Florestan. (Aria: "God, how dark, this dreadful quiet.") He sinks to the ground from weakness, when Rocko and Léonore arrive. (Melodrama: "How cold in this dark dungeon.") Léonore recognises him, but dares not speak and helps to dig the grave. (Duet: "Be brisk and dig cheerily.") Florestan revives and Léonore gives him bread. (Terzett: "May a better world reward you.") Pizarro descends to the dungeon, and is about to stab Florestan, when Léonore throws herself before her husband, and crying, "First kill his wife," points a pistol at Pizarro. This saves her husband, for trumpet calls, heralding the appearance of the minister, are heard, and Pizarro hurries away. (Quartet: "He shall die, but first know who crushes his false heart.") In the following duet ("Oh! endless joy"), Florestan and Léonore express their happiness.

Change of scene: Courtyard of the castle. Fernando announces the king's pardon. (Chorus: "Hail to the day, hail to the hour.") Léonore takes the chains from her husband, he is free, and Pizarro is arrested. (Fernando: "You freed him from the grave," and closing chorus: "He who a lovely wife has won.")

THE FIFERS' FESTIVAL

Comic opera in three acts by Max Schillings. Text by Ferdinand Count Sporck.

CAST: Schmasmann of Rapoltstein, king of the fifers of Alsace—Basso. Herzland, his daughter—Soprano. Ruhmland, his son—Baritone. Velten Stacter, a fifer—Tenor. Alheit, his sister—Soprano. Jockel—Tenor. Weihdampf —Tenor. Surgand—Baritone. Henselin—Basso. Fifers, Jost and Jorg, fifer apprentices—Soprano and Alto. Loder, innkeeper—Basso. Place, Rapportsweiler in Alsace. Time, end of the fifth century.

ACT I. Garden before the city gates. Jost and Jorg march around the town playing upon the fife, and drumming to invite all to Fifers' day. Jockel and three other fifers, who compose the fifer council, appear, and, with the usual ceremonies, Surgand relates the legend of Herr Egenalf of Rapoltstein, to whom is due the elevation of the fifers' guild to its high estate. The crafty council is concerned for its re-election. Old Jockel is sure of victory, but the others fear that Velten Stacter and his friend Rasbert (which name Ruhmland, who has fallen out with his father, has adopted) may be elected, as they are in high favour. Weihdampf has told the knight that Velten is secretly in

love with Herzland, and that he had to leave Rapoltstein's
house in order to obtain information of the coming judgment. The procession of fifers approaches (Chorus: "Hail
a thousand times") and is received by Rapoltstein and his
daughter. Herzland seeks to take advantage of the good
humour of her father by pleading for his discarded son and
her lover Velten, but is rudely repulsed. Alheit tells Herzland that Velten and Ruhmland, of whom the sister has but
a dim recollection, are to arrive that day, and confesses
that she loves Ruhmland. When she has thus prepared
Herzland she calls the young men, who have been hiding
in the neighbourhood. (Quartet: "It must be she!") They
seek some plan of softening the anger of their father, and
Velten, who is convinced that one is only appreciated after
death, resolves to spread the news of his death. Rapoltstein approaches and greets Velten coldly; he does not recognise his son. He has been told that old Jockel is a villain
and ought no longer remain sub-king of the fifers. The
procession approaches and greets Rapoltstein, sings of his
ancestors, but arouses the anger of the knight by compli-
mentary allusions to his son. When Velten in his song
("When from Adam's young lips") clearly intimates his
love for Herzland, he refuses the two friends the customary
drink of honour and angrily departs. (Ensemble: "The
crafty beaver.")

Act II. Inn of the fifers. Girls are decorating the inn
for Fifers' day. (Chorus: "In the fall on ladies' day.")
Velten appears. ("The crazy lot of a fifer.") A thunder
storm. The lovers resolve to take advantage of it to serve
their purpose. The knight remains stubborn; the merry
Alheit persuades him to the curious project of marrying
his daughter to Velten on his death-bed. The Fifers' day
begins, and Jockel describes the condition of the guild under his administration in the rosiest colours, but Ruhmland
and Velten contradict him, and Jockel's accounts are found
in bad shape. A general tumult ensues; the innkeeper
rushes in and reports that the creek has overflowed its

banks, has carried away the bridge, and that the house is in danger. There is no outlet; Velten steps through the window, and Ruhmland cries out that his friend has been struck by lightning. Masses of water rush in and all is in confusion.

Act III. ' Courtyard of the castle. Velten lies "dead" on a bier, the conspirators laugh, drink and make merry; Rapoltstein, who has always liked the merry Velten, is in deep distress. Herzland, in bridal dress, comes with her friends and demands that her father keep his word and marry her to Velten. This is done, and when Velten is asked to say yes, he jumps joyfully from the bier and rushes into Herzland's arms. Rapoltstein submits to the inevitable, forgives his son and unites him with Alheit. The council of fifers is deposed and Velten is elected king.

FLAUTO SOLO

Musical comedy in one act by Eugen d'Albert. Text by Hans von Wolzogen.

Cast: Prince Eberhard. Prince Ferdinand, his son. Maestro Emanuele, conductor of orchestra. Musjö Pepusch, German conductor of orchestra. Signora Peppina, a singer. Guests of the prince, musicians, servants, an aide-de-camp. Place, a German principality. Time, eighteenth century. First production, Prague, 1905.

The German capellmeister Pepusch has written the celebrated swine canon for six Bassoons at the request of the stout soldier, Prince Eberhard. Prince Ferdinand, his son, who is enthusiastically devoted to Italian music and art, and his teacher on the flute, the intriguing Italian Emanuele make sport of the German music. Eberhard goes on a journey, and Ferdinand takes advantage of this to inaugurate a night festival. He has invited a critic from Vienna, and the singer Peppina, who is to sing a new aria of Emanuele. Emanuele has slandered Pepusch to the prince, and Ferdinand compels the German master to be present at the festival and to produce the swine canon with his bassoons in order that he may be derided by the guests, who are accustomed only to hear elegant Italian music. The singer Peppina, however, has learned to love the honest Pepusch as a man, and respect him as an artist, and desires to save him from annoyance. He, however, a thorough master of his art, confounds his enemies by arranging the aria of Emanuele, which Peppina sang for him for the flute and includes it in the canon. Eberhard, who has unexpectedly returned, having been informed by Peppina of what has taken place, appears at the festival, and at his command Ferdinand is compelled to play the Flauto Solo part in the canon himself. In doing so Ferdinand learns to respect the artistic ability of the German master, who has heretofore been set aside. The prince is also pleased by the musical ability of his son and reaches the conclusion that "A boy who can manage his instrument so well will also succeed in learning the art of playing upon the princely flute and managing his subjects." The affair, therefore, is pleasantly concluded. As a reward Pepusch is given the hand of Peppina, and the lovely singer, who declares herself a countrywoman of the prince, concludes with the words: "Germany, Tyrol, each has its art, long live music, which has united us all."

THE FLYING DUTCHMAN

Dramatic opera in three acts by Richard Wagner. Text by the composer.

CAST: Daland, a Norwegian sea-captain—Basso. Senta, his daughter—Soprano. Erik, a huntsman—Tenor. Mary, Senta's nurse—Alto. Daland's steersman—Tenor. The Flying Dutchman—Baritone. Place, on the coast of Norway. First production, Dresden, 1843. In this opera Wagner, for the first time, departed from the usual opera form of arias, duets, etc., and created the uninterrupted melody and the Leitmotif, which here appears in the first bars of Senta's ballad in the second act.

ACT I. On his homeward journey, the sea-captain Daland is compelled by stormy weather to seek a port of refuge. He leaves the helmsman on watch and he and the sailors retire. (Song of the helmsman: "With tempest and storm on distant seas.") The helmsman falls asleep. A ghostly vessel appearing astern is dashed against Daland's vessel by the sea and the grappling irons hold the two ships together. Invisible hands furl the sails. A man of pale aspect, dressed in black, his face framed by a thick black beard, steps ashore. He laments his fate. (Aria: "The time has come and seven years have again elapsed.") Having broken his troth, he is compelled to roam the sea without rest. At the end of every seven years the angry waves cast him upon the shore; if he can find a wife who will be true to him forever he will be released. Daland meets him. He offers him treasure, and when he hears that Daland has an unmarried daughter, he asks for her as his wife. Tempted by gold Daland consents, and favoured by the south wind joyfully acclaimed by Daland's men (repetition of the song of the helmsman and chorus), both vessels set sail.

ACT II. Girls are singing and spinning in Daland's house. (Spinning chorus: "Spin, spin, fair maiden.") Senta dreamily gazes upon the picture of the Flying Dutchman, whom she desires to save. Against the will of her nurse she sings the story of the Dutchman (Ballad with the Leitmotiv), and declares she will save him by her fidelity. Erik arrives and hears her; the girls depart, and the huntsman, who loves the maiden, warns her, telling her of his dream, in which Daland returned with a mysterious stranger, who carried her off to sea. She listens with delight, and Erik leaves her in despair. Daland arrives with the stranger; he and Senta stand gazing at each other in silence. Daland is scarcely noticed by his daughter, even when he presents his guest as her betrothed. In the fol-

lowing duet, which closes the act, Senta swears to be true
till death.

Act III.   Later in the evening the crew of Daland invite the men on the strange vessel to join in the festivities, but in vain.   The girls retire in wonder; ghostly
forms appear at work upon the vessel of the Flying Dutchman, and Daland's men retreat in fear.   Senta arrives, followed by Erik, who reproves her for her desertion, as she
had formerly loved him and vowed constancy.   When the
stranger, who has been listening, hears these words, he is
overwhelmed with despair, as now he is forever lost.   He
summons his men, tells Senta of the curse, and to the consternation of Daland and his crew declares that he is the
"Flying Dutchman."   Hardly has he left the shore when
Senta plunges into the sea, faithful unto death.   This is
his salvation.   The spectral ship disappears, and Senta
and the Dutchman are seen ascending to heaven.

THE FORCED MARRIAGE

Comic opera in three acts by Humperdinck.   Text freely
adapted from a comedy by Dumas.

Cast: King Philip V—Baritone.   Robert of Montfort—
Tenor.   Emil Duval—Baritone.   Hedwig of Merian—Soprano.   Louise Mauclair—Soprano.   Loscouse, governor
of the Bastille—Basso.   Marquis d'Estrée—Speaking
part.   Abbess—Mezzo-soprano.   Chamberlain—Tenor.
Housekeeper—Mezzo-soprano.   Two maids—Sopranos.
Ladies, pupils, officers, the guard, servants, guests, etc.
Place, Paris and Madrid at the beginning of the eighteenth century.   First production, Berlin, 1905.

Act I.   Park of St. Cyr with nunnery.   Count Montfort, the friend of the future King of Spain, the Duke of
Anjou, enters the park to meet Hedwig of Merian.   He
induces his friend Duval, who is about to marry an unloved but noble dame, to occupy the attention of Hedwig's

friend, Louise, so that he can remain undisturbed. All four are captured by the watch and taken to the Bastille.

Aᴄᴛ II.   Prison cell of the Bastille. Madame de Maintenon has induced the king to issue an order, confining Montfort and Duval on bread and water until they have re-established the honour of the ladies by marrying them. Thus forced, they consent.

Change of scene: An elegant chamber in the palace of the count.   Montfort and Duval believe that the ladies have conceived between themselves the plan for the marriage, and in order to escape the raillery of their friends, they desert their wives and depart for Spain, where Montfort's friend, the Duke of Anjou, has in the meanwhile ascended the throne as Philip V. Hedwig, who dearly loves Montfort, is in deep distress. The merry Louise, however, bids them a cheery farewell.

Aᴄᴛ III.   Ball-room in the king's palace at Madrid. Duval fears the anger of his father, and Montfort's property has been confiscated. Madrid proving tedious, the two men long for home, Paris and their wives. Hedwig and Louise have followed their husbands, and Montfort is informed by Louise that Hedwig is innocent of the supposed deception, because she herself told Madame de Maintenon about the adventure in the park. As Montfort really loves his wife, he is content and resolves to save Hedwig from the advances of the king, who has fallen in love with her. Philip forgives his friend, and when Duval is informed that he has been created a baron through the influence of Louise, he is also satisfied, and the reunited couples return to France in perfect happiness.

FORTUNE

Musical fairy tale in one act by Rudolph Baron Prochazka. Text by Dr. Theodor Kirchner.

Cᴀsᴛ: Winfried. Hermit. Knight. Merchant. Soldier. Poet. Fortune. A hermit's cell in a lonely forest,

Winfried is saying his morning prayers ("The quiet wood awakes"), when Fortune approaches and asks for shelter. Imagining he is encompassed by the devil's wiles he refuses; she discloses her identity and declares that she is the most unhappy being on earth, since all pursue her in wild chase and rob her of peace. Her pursuers appear, and Winfried sends her to his cell advising her to don a monk's attire for concealment. The crowd approaches, and each tells Winfried what he demands of Fortune. When the Poet declares that Fortune means renunciation, the hermit directs him to her cell, saying he will find it there. All enter, but are disappointed to see only a monk and threaten Winfried. He apologises and declares he is mistaken; that Fortune, as they describe her, has passed that way and entered the forest. They all hurry away. (Chorus: "Let us leave all.") When they have gone Fortune shyly appears, thanks him for his aid, and asks to remain with him, as the world will only misuse her. He consents and she causes flowers to appear, the birds begin to sing. (Duet: "Youth comes again.") For the first time Fortune is happy in not being compelled to confer happiness. Winfried is astounded at her joy, and she inquires what his desires are. He tells her he wants nothing, and rejects her proposals to make him young and wise.

When he finally wishes to be free of all the ills of life, Fortune is terrified, but desires to grant his request. She informs him that in order that she may do so he must first kiss her. He fears that she wishes to stir him to sinful pleasure; praying for strength to resist (Duet: "I fly to thee"), he prepares to escape to the silent forest, where he can find peace once more. Fortune complains that she cannot benefit man either as pursuer or pursued. The brook, the wind and other voices of the forest console her with low melodies and she falls asleep. For the first time she is happy. (Chorus: "Now let us be silent.") The hermit, deep in thought, returns; he has not found the sought-for peace. He is tempted to kiss the sleeping Fortune—it is no sin to be happy. (Song: "The forest around us.") The thorns try to prevent him, but he tears himself away and kisses her—and at that moment he falls to earth dead, freed of all earthly ills. Fortune awakes and gazes upon him, but he has found happiness, and Fortune must again endure the pursuit of mankind. She slowly vanishes; roses fall on Winfried's body. (Closing chorus of spirits of the air: "Freed, freed of life's ills.")

FRA DIAVOLO
(Or The Inn of Terracina)

Comic opera in three acts by Auber.   Text by Scribe.

CAST: Fra Diavolo, under the name of the Marquis of San Marco—Tenor.   Lord Cockburn, a travelling Englishman—Basso.   Pamela, his wife—Mezzo-soprano. Lorenzo, Roman officer of dragoons—Tenor.   Matteo, innkeeper—Basso.   Zerline, his daughter—Soprano. Giacomo and Beppo, bandits—Basso and Tenor.   Francesco.   A miller.   Place, a village near Terracina.   First production, Paris, 1830.

Fra Diavolo is a celebrated bandit chief, who carries on his operations in numerous disguises.   The Roman government has sent dragoons to capture him and offered a reward of 10,000 piastres.   The officer in command, Lorenzo, loves Zerline, who is to be married to a rich peasant.

ACT I.   Matteo's inn.   Chorus of Roman dragoons and scene, in which Lorenzo proclaims the reward for the capture of the brigand.   Lord Cockburn and his wife Pamela rush in and declare they have been robbed.   Lorenzo and his soldiers depart to capture the robbers.   Lord Cockburn is jealous of his wife and accuses her of receiving the attentions of their travelling companion, the Marquis of San Marco.   (Duet: "I should like to see you admired, my lady.")   The marquis, who is no other than Fra Diavolo, arrives and is welcomed by Matteo and Zerline. (Quintet: "See, a carriage has come.") He dines at his ease at the inn and allows Zerline to relate the exploits of the celebrated brigand. (Romance: "On yonder rock reclining.") He impudently again pays court to Pamela and abstracts from her a medallion surrounded by jewels. Lorenzo now returns; he has killed most of the band and recovered the Englishman's property, and has received the reward of 10,000 piastres. He now hopes to win Zerline. (Finale: "Here, I hear the marchers coming.")

Act II. Zerline's sleeping chamber, adjoining that of the English couple. Zerline conducts Lord and Lady Cockburn to their apartments and expresses her joy at her coming union with Lorenzo. (Aria: "What luck, I breathe again"; Terzett: "Dear wife, let us go to rest.") Diavolo's companions, Giacomo and Beppo, have arrived in the meantime, and by singing an air known to them he gives them the signal and they enter the window. (Barcarole: "The little one.") All three conceal themselves in a niche and observe Zerline preparing for bed. (Cavatina: "Yes, tomorrow, to-morrow, what joy"; Quartet scene: "What a pretty child"; Zerline's aria: "For such a country maid.") When Zerline has fallen asleep, the bandits again proceed to rob Lord and Lady Cockburn. A noise is heard, Lorenzo arrives with the dragoons, the awakened couple and Zerline appear, and Diavolo as the marquis covers the retreat of the two bandits. The presence of the marquis awakens the jealousy of Lord Cockburn and Lorenzo. The latter challenges him to a duel at the Black Rock, in which Diavolo hopes to be the victor. (Finale: "Would it not be well to see whence comes this alarm.")

Act III. In the forest. Diavolo arrives in bandit dress and awaits Lorenzo. (Aria: "My friend I hear.") The marriage procession of Zerline and the peasant Francisco approaches. Giacomo and Beppo, who are with the crowd, are recognised and arrested by Lorenzo. The young captain hopes to catch the chief of the brigands, but laments

the loss of Zerline. (Aria: "Forever will I think of thee.")
The well-guarded brigands, Giacomo and Beppo, are compelled to lure Diavolo into a trap and he is shot. (Finale:
"Away, away, to new strife.")   Lady Cockburn recognises with dismay in the brigand her former admirer, and
the happy Lorenzo wins his Zerline.

THE GARDENER

(Also known under the name of "The Gardener from
Love")
Opera in three acts by Mozart. Text by Calzabigi,
adapted by Coltellini.
CAST: Don Anchises, podesta—Tenor.   Arminda, his
niece—Soprano.   Count Belfiore—Tenor.   Marchesa
Violante—Soprano.   Roberto,   her   servant—Basso.
Ramiro, Arminda's former lover—Soprano.   Sergetta,
Arminda's maid—Soprano.   First production, Munich,
1775.
The jealous Count Belfiore has wounded his affianced, the
Marchese Violante, and, thinking he has killed her, flees.
After a time he is betrothed to Arminda, the niece of the
podesta of Lagonero.   Violante and her servant Roberto
enter the service of the podesta, both as gardeners, under
the names respectively of Sandrina and Nardo.   The
podesta falls in love with Sandrina, Arminda with Nardo,
Roberto with Sergetta.   Belfiore recognises Violante, but
she denies her identity.   The podesta receives a letter nam-
ing Belfiore as the murderer of Violante, and she gives her
proper name, but tells Belfiore that she had used her resemblance to the deceased to save him.   In the end she forgives her lover, and thus frees Arminda, who marries Don
Ramiro.   Roberto and Sergetta are also wedded; only the
podesta is left to his own devices.

THE GOLDEN CROSS

(Das goldene kreuz)

Opera in two acts by Ignaz Brüll.   Text by Mosenthal.
CAST: Gontran de l'Ancre, a young nobleman—Tenor.
Colas, innkeeper—Baritone.   Christina, his sister—Soprano.   Therèse, his bride—Soprano.   Bombardon, sergeant—Basso.   Place, a village near Melun.   Time, 1812 and 1815.   First production, Berlin, 1875.

ACT I.   Before the inn of Colas.   Therèse is to be married to Colas, and the young girls bring her rosemary bouquets adorned with ribbons.   Their joy is interrupted, however, as Colas has been conscripted for the army. Christine, Colas's sister, in vain offers her golden cross, and promises to marry the man who will take the place of her brother and bring the cross back to her.   A young nobleman, Gontran de l'Ancre, has seen Christine and fallen in love with her.   He is alone in the world, having no kindred, so he takes the golden cross and departs with Sergeant Bombardon and the recruits.   Gontran bids farewell to Christine, who feels her heart stirred with emotion.

ACT II.   The same scene.   Colas has taken up arms when the enemy invaded the country and returns wounded. Another wounded man is in the house, who is loved and tended by Christine.   It is the unknown Gontran, who, however, has lost the token for whose return Christine is waiting.   Bombardon returns an invalid from Russia.   He has found the cross, and although Christine is distressed, she resolves to keep her word.   Bombardon recognises Gontran, whom he has believed to be dead, gives him the cross, and he and Christine find happiness.

(SCENES FROM) GOTZ VON BERLICHINGEN

Opera in five acts (nine scenes) by Karl Goldmark. Text freely adapted from Goethe by Willner.

CAST: Götz. Elizabeth. Maria. Karl. George. Bishop. Weislingen. Franz. Adelheid. A maid. Selbitz. Lerse. Sikkingen. Metzler. Sievers. Members of counoil. Judges of the Fehme. Pages. Courtiers. Servants. At- tendants. Working men. Merchants. Peasants. The people. First production, Pesth, 1902.

ACT I. A hall in Götz's house. Several scenes are here combined: Weislingen's betrothal with Maria, George's song of the child who caught a bird, Selbitz's appearance without his shirt after the dicing, the feast of Götz with his friends, the invitation to Heilbronn, and the announcement of Franz of the presence of the beautiful Adelheid at the court of the Bishop of Bamberg.

ACT II. Scene 1: The council chamber of Heilbronn The councillors of Heilbronn attempt to force Götz to swear eternal peace. He refuses, and the citizens try to take him prisoner, but he is rescued in the nick of time by the Knight Sikkingen. Scene 2: At the court of the Bishop of Bamberg. Weislingen is enmeshed in the net of Adelheid, who desires to use him to her profit. She has also captivated the young fiery Franz. George, who has been sent by Götz as a messenger, is derided by the pages of the bishop, is disowned by Weislingen, and the bishop, who is an enemy of Götz, performs the marriage ceremony between Weislingen and Adelheid.

ACT III. Scene 1: An opening in the wood. Götz sets upon some Heilbronn merchants and hears of Weislingen's desertion and the breaking of his oath. Scene 2: Imperial Court at Augsburg. Weislingen's heart is filled with re- morse at his treachery, particularly as Adelheid is unfaith- ful to him, not alone with Franz, but also with the son of the emperor, Karl. When he attempts to force her to leave

the court and follow him to his castle, she induces Franz
to poison him.

ACT IV. The country and revolt of the peasants. Götz
is forced to assume the leadership.

ACT V. Scene 1: Park of the castle of Weislingen.
The judges of the Fehme assemble and condemn Adelheid to
death. Scene 2: Sleeping apartment in the castle of
Adelheid. Adelheid has this whole scene alone. She is
disturbed by Weislingen's death; she yearns for the absent
Franz, and as she gazes from the window perceives the
judges of the Fehme approaching, and knows that her end
is at hand. Scene 3: Götz in prison. Elizabeth and
Lerse stand at his side and he dies in their arms.

GRINGOIRE

Opera in one act by Ignaz Brüll. Text adapted from the
play of Banville by Victor Leon.

CAST: Louis XI—Baritone. Olivier, his barber—Tenor.
Simon Fourniez, merchant—Basso. Loyse, his daughter
—Soprano. Nicole, his sister—Alto. Pierre Gringoire,
a street singer—Baritone. Place, the house of Fourniez in
Tours. Time, 1496. First production, Munich, 1892.

Olivier reports to Fourniez that the king, who is hunting
in the neighbourhood, is coming to his house as a guest.
Fourniez is overjoyed at this distinction, particularly as
the favourite Olivier desires to marry his daughter Loyse.
Loyse, however, will have nothing to do with him. When
the king arrives Fourniez seeks his good offices in behalf
of Loyse. The street singer Gringoire, who is hated by
Olivier for having ridiculed him in his poems, is before the
door, and the king bids him enter. Louis, prejudiced
against the singer by his favourite, demands that Gringoire, who is half-starved and does not know the king, shall
earn his meal by a song. He sings a song of derision
against the king, and then ascertains before whom he

stands. He gives himself up for lost. But things do not turn out as the cunning Olivier intends, for Louis recognises the genius of Gringoire, and when he discovers the mutual love of Loyse and the singer he unites them in marriage.

GUNTRAM
(Not classified)

Opera in three acts by Richard Strauss. Text by the composer.

CAST: The old duke—Basso. Freihild, his daughter—Soprano. Duke Robert, her husband—Baritone. Guntram and Friedhold, minstrels—Tenor and Basso. Jester to the duke—Tenor. An old woman—Alto. An old man—Tenor. Two young men—Bassi. Three subjects—Bassi. Place, a German duchy. Time, thirteenth century. First production, Weimar, 1894.

Guntram and Friedhold are members of the Holy Society of Peace, to which they have vowed fidelity and obedience. The old duke has delivered his daughter and relinquished his lands to the Duke Robert, who oppresses the people to such an extent that they are compelled to revolt. They are defeated by Robert, and their lot is only made the harder. Many of the serfs and poor people take to flight. Freihild, the daughter of the old duke, has been heretofore their good angel, but even she has been so maltreated by the cruel husband whom she was forced to marry that she voluntarily seeks death in the sea. Freihild leads thither young Guntram to begin his work of peace. Guntram feeds and comforts the poor fugitives, prevents Freihild from seeking death, attempts to soften the heart of the old duke by his song and to awaken the conscience of Robert. His love for Freihild awakens. When Robert rushes upon him with his sword he kills the duke in self-defence. He is thrown into prison by order of the old duke, and is to be executed with tortures; but before meeting his end he desires to pacify the people, who have again revolted. Freihild induces the faithful jester to aid her in freeing Guntram. She opens the prison cell, avows her passionate love for Guntram, and wishes to fly with him. Friedhold approaches and demands that Guntram stand trial before the Holy Tribunal for his bloody deed. Guntram refuses to marry Freihild. She thinks she has won him, but when the news of the death of the old duke and his defeat in battle arrives and the people proclaim their beloved Freihild as ruler, Guntram recognises her exalted mission as leader of her people and nobly relinquishes his love. He departs.

Act I. Forest and sea. Appearance of Guntram, Friedhold and people. (Guntram: "Here, good people, take your ease.") They tell their sad story. ("Bitter poverty, hunger—desolation.") Friedhold tells him his goal is near and departs. Guntram remains behind and seeks excuses for his action. ("Never prayed for—secretly longed for.") The great scene with Freihild follows, in which he saves her from death and obtains mercy from the duke for the imprisoned fugitives. He accompanies the duke to the palace.

Act II. Festival at the court of the duke. The jester is charitable to the poor and awakens the anger of Robert. Song of the minstrels. ("Hail to the ruler"), turned into ridicule by the jester. Secret revolt of the vassals of Robert. Guntram's great song of peace. ("I see peace.") Robert rushes upon Guntram, the serfs protect him, and a messenger brings news of a new revolt. (Ensemble: "War, war, oh duke.") Guntram advises peace and when Robert is about to kill him as a traitor, he stabs his assailant. The old duke wins over the vassals, has Guntram thrown into prison and rushes to the combat. Freihild loves Guntram, and resolves to save him and fly with him.

Act III. Prison in the burg. Song of the monks. ("Et lux perpetua luceat ei.") Guntram now regrets his deed. He does not conceal from himself that his guilt has been influenced by his love of Freihild. He renounces his love and departs.

GUSTAV, OR THE MASKED BALL

Opera in five acts by Auber.   Text by Scribe.

CAST: Gustav III, King of Sweden—Tenor.   Ankarström, his confidant—Baritone.   Amalie, wife of Ankarström—Soprano.   Count Horn and Count Ribbing, conspirators—Tenor and Basso.   The minister of war—
Basso.   The minister of justice—Basso.   A chamberlain,
Oskar, page to the king—Soprano.   Arverson, a fortune
teller—Mezzo-soprano.   Christian, an old sailor—Tenor,
Roslin, a sculptor.   Sergell, a painter.   Place, Stockholm,
Time, 1792.   First production, Paris, 1833.

The action is exactly the same as in Amelia, or the Masked
Ball by Verdi (see that opera), with the difference that
the librettist has changed the historical text to a popular
one.   Gustav loves the wife of Ankarström, and thereby
makes him his enemy.   He joins the conspirators and kills
the king at a masked ball.   (In 1861 at Paris the text of
this opera underwent a further change.   The scene was
transferred to Naples, Gustav was appointed Duke of
Olivarez, in deference to the singer Mario, whose audience
evinced hostility to the Swedish text.)

GWENDOLINE

Opera in two acts by Chabrier.   Text by Catulle Mendés.
CAST: Gwendoline.   Harald.   Armel.   Aella.   Erik.
Place, the hills on the coast of Great Britain.   Time, the
eighth century.   First production, Paris, 1893.

ACT I.   A valley near the sea coast.   Harald, a Danish
sea king, lands and besieges the venerable Saxon Armel
and his people.   Armel is to be executed for defiantly refusing to give up his treasure.   Harald, who has never
seen a woman before, sees the beautiful blonde Gwendoline,
daughter of Armel.   His heart awakens, his wildness vanishes, and notwithstanding the warning of the Danes he
succumbs to the power of love and asks her to be his wife.

Armel gives his consent, and tells the Saxons that he will murder the weaponless Danes at the marriage feast.

ACT II. Bridal chamber. Armel gives his daughter a dagger and whispers to her to kill Harald in the night. But Gwendoline loves Harald and wishes to save him. When the cry for help of the defenceless Danes is heard she gives her lover the dagger and follows him. Change of scene: The sea. The Saxons slay the Danes, and when Harald appears he is killed by Armel. Gwendoline seizes the dagger, and, stabbing herself to the heart, dies with her lover. Armel is overwhelmed with despair. The burning vessels of the Danes add horror to the scene.

Songs. Act I: Chorus and scene between Armel and Gwendoline; Chorus and legend of Gwendoline: "They are cruel, strong, like raging beasts"; Appearance of the Danes and sword song of Harald: "Our good sword strikes like the lightning's bolt"; Harald and Gwendoline (*a*), scene: "Come here!" (*b*) Gwendoline's song: "Tell, dear maid, what do you here?" (*c*) Duet: "Spin, spin, blonde maiden"; Ensemble, Harald, Gwendoline, Armel, chorus of Saxons and Danes: "Harald, be warned."

Act II. Scene and chorus: "Oh see the bride in marriage dress"; Duet, Harald, Gwendoline: "Gwendoline, oh Gwendoline." The cry for help of the Danes is heard during the love duet.

Change of scene: Chorus: "Saxons, arise! punish the robbers"; Duet, Harald, Gwendoline: "United in death, as in life"; Finale: "Wotan opens for you his halls."

HAMLET

Opera in five acts by Ambroise Thomas. Text adapted from Shakespeare by Barbier and Carré.

CAST: Hamlet—Baritone. The ghost of Hamlet's father —Basso. Claudius, King of Denmark—Baritone. Polonius, chancellor—Baritone. Läertes, his son—Tenor. Marcellus and Horatio, officers and friends of Hamlet.

Gertrud, Hamlet's mother, Queen of Denmark—Soprano. Ophelia, daughter of Polonius—Soprano. Place, Helsingfors. First production, Paris, 1868.

Act I. Hall in the palace. The king and Gertrud celebrate their marriage. Love scene between Ophelia and Hamlet, who desires to leave the country, as he is overwhelmed with grief at the conduct of his mother, who, only two months after the death of his father, had married again. Laërtes, who is going to foreign parts, confides Ophelia to Hamlet. Horatio relates the appearance of the ghost of the deceased king.

Change of scene: Rampart of the castle. Night. Hamlet and his friends await the ghost. He appears and tells Hamlet of his murder by Claudius and Gertrud, and demands vengeance.

Act II. The garden. Hamlet, in despair at the distress of Ophelia, feigns melancholy, and asks that a play be produced by a strolling company.

Change of scene: The festal chamber. Hamlet has arranged a play in which the action reproduces the murder of his father, and feigning madness accuses the king of the deed.

Act III. Chamber of the queen. Hamlet overhears a conversation between the king and Polonius, in which he discovers that Polonius, the father of Ophelia, is also guilty. The queen offers him Ophelia as a bride, but he repulses her, and discloses his knowledge of his father's murder to his mother.

Act IV. Ophelia's death by drowning. She has gone mad through despair.

Act V. The church yard. Hamlet, pursued by the vengeance of the king, meets Laërtes, who calls him to account for his breach of faith to his sister. The approaching funeral procession of Ophelia prevents a quarrel, and Hamlet resolves to commit suicide at the bier of Ophelia. When the ghost again appears he arises and stabs the king. The people elevate Hamlet to the throne.

HÄNSEL UND GRETEL

Fairy opera in three acts by Engelbert Humperdinck. Text by Adelheid Wette.

CAST: Peter, broom-maker—Baritone. Gertrud, his wife—Mezzo-soprano. Hänsel and Gretel, their children —Mezzo-soprano and Soprano. The Crunch Witch— Mezzo-soprano. The Sand Man—Soprano. Dew man-nikins—Sopranos. The fourteen angels. Children. First production, Munich, 1893.

ACT I. At home. A poverty-stricken room in which the children Hänsel and Gretel are working. Hänsel is making brooms and Gretel knitting stockings. They try to forget their hunger in song. (Gretel: "Suse, dear Suse, what rattles in the straw"; Hänsel: "Eia, popeia, what poverty.") They wish their mother were at home, for they are very hungry. For weeks they have had nothing but dry crusts. But when Gretel tells Hänsel that the neighbour's wife had presented their mother with a vessel of milk to make rice pudding, he jumps for joy, drops his work and dances around with Gretel, who is more than willing. ("Little brother, come dance with me.") They tease and play, when the mother suddenly enters. She is very angry that the work has not been completed. ("Do you call that work? to yell and sing.") In looking for the stick to chastise the children, she upsets the pot of milk, and cries at the loss of her supper. Angrily she sends the children into the woods to pick strawberries and threat-ens: "If you bring not the basket back to the full, I will whip you and your hair pull." The children creep fear-fully from the house, and she sinks upon the chair ex-hausted; the father arrives in good spirits. He has been drinking, having sold all his brooms at a good price, and brings a basket full of food. (Song: "Oh, we poor, poor people.") He asks after the children, and she tells him of the broken pot and of sending them to Ilsenstein in the woods to pick strawberries. When the father hears this he is in despair, for at Ilsenstein lives the bad crunch witch, who lures the children with her magic cakes, then puts them into the oven, where they are baked into Leb-kuchen (a favourite German cake), which she then de-vours. ("A witch of hoary age roams in the forest.") The parents quickly leave the house to seek the children.

ACT II.   In the wood.   In the background the Ilsenstein thickly surrounded by pines.   While Hänsel is seeking for strawberries Gretel binds a wreath.   ("A little man is in the wood.")   Hänsel merrily arrives with the filled basket, but when the cuckoo calls, they play cuckoo with the berries, and as he continues to call they devour the whole of them.   Now they are afraid, and as it is getting dark, Hänsel cannot find the way.   They see all kinds of spectres, are scared at the echo of their own voices, and draw close together when the mist rises.   In vain do they call for their parents.   Out of the mist appears a little grey man, the sandman ("Little sandman and I-st!"), who throws sand in their eyes, whereupon they fall asleep under a pine tree after praying.   ("When at night I go to sleep, fourteen angels watch do keep.")   From the mist a shining ladder is seen, with angels ascending to heaven, and surrounding the children in accordance with their prayer.

ACT III.   The crunch witch's hut.   The same scene, but the angels have disappeared and the mist conceals the background.   The dream man comes and awakens the chil-dren.   They tell each other of the angels they have seen in their dreams.   As they turn around, the mist has vanished and they see the little crunch witch's hut on the Ilsenstein. On the left is a bake oven, on the right a cage, connected with the house by a hedge of gingerbread men.   Attracted by the smell they begin to nibble at the hut.   A voice is heard: "Nibble, nibble, who nibbles at my hut?"   But they are not disturbed and answer: "The wind, the wind, that heavenly child."   Unperceived, the witch approaches, captures Hänsel, locks him into the cage and sends

Gretel into the house to fetch almonds and raisins with which to fatten Hänsel. In glee the witch looks into her oven, snatches her witch broom, and with the prospect of a good meal in sight dances around. ("Hurr, hopp, hopp, hopp, gallop, gallop.") Hänsel, who feigns to be asleep, watches her and warns the returning Gretel. ("Sister dear, be careful.") When the witch asks Gretel to look into the oven she acts clumsily and asks the witch to show her how it is done; when the witch bends over to peer into the oven, Hänsel rushes out of the cage, he and Gretel shove the witch in, and she is consumed. All the children who have been turned into ginger-bread figures are released. (Chorus of gingerbread children: "Thanks, thanks, forever and ever.") The parents arrive, and the witch is taken out from the ruins of the oven in the shape of a large piece of gingerbread. ("Father, children, look at the miracle"; Final Chorus: "When misery is at its lowest ebb, God, the Lord, stretches forth His hand.") The opera closes with the merry dances of the children.

HANS HEILING

Romantic opera in three acts and an introduction by Heinrich Marschner. Text by Eduard Devrient.

Cast of the introduction: The queen of the spirits of the earth—Soprano. Her son—Baritone.

Cast of the opera: The queen of the spirits of the earth—Soprano. Hans Heiling—Baritone. Anna, his bride—Soprano. Gertrud, her mother—Alto. Konrad, huntsman to the burgrave—Tenor. Stephan and Nikolaus, peasants—Basso and Tenor. Place, the Hartz Mountains. Time, the sixteenth century. First production, Hanover, 1833.

Introduction. The subterranean abode of the spirits of the earth. (Chorus: "Labour without rest.") The queen's son, by his love for a daughter of earth, is driven

to its surface, having rejected all warnings and prayers.
(Duet: "Enough: end your unceasing labours.") The
queen resolves to use her power to win him back.

Act I. After the overture (which follows the introduction), Hans Heiling (the son of the spirit queen) is seen
to emerge from a subterranean passage. He is now a human being, living in a human habitation, and hails with
delight his beloved Anna, who comes to him with her mother
Gertrud. ("Welcome to this spot.") Anna finds a book
of magic, which Hans brought with him, and at her request he throws it into the fire. (Terzett: "Ha, what
signs! so sparkling and beautiful.") He has now sacrificed for Anna all that once gave him power as a spirit;
his happiness rests now only in her love. (Aria: "The day
when you pledged your faith to me.") To please Anna
he agrees to accompany her to a country festival. (Terzett: "Very well! Let us go.")

Change of scene: Festival of peasants. (Chorus: "Ju-
cheisa! to-day spare not the gold"; Song of Konrad: "A
lovely coy maiden.") As Anna and Konrad hurry to the
dance (Finale: "How my heart jumps for joy") Heiling
is troubled and fears to lose her love.

Act II. The wood. Anna loves Konrad. (Recitative:
"Woe is me, to what have I come"; Aria: "Once my heart
was at peace.") The queen of the spirits of the earth
appears with her following, and terrifies Anna by telling
her who Heiling really is. (Ensemble: "From the abyss,
from the depths of the earth.") Konrad finds Anna unconscious from fright, and when she recovers they confess
their love. (Recitative: "Through the green wood";
Duet: "Ha, these words renew my life.")

Change of scene: Gertrud in her room. (Song: "The
night upon the heath.") Konrad comes with Anna and
asks her mother for her hand, as she looks with abhorrence
on her former bridegroom, whom she now knows to be a
spirit of the earth. (Finale: "You hear it, his name alone
is terrible to her.") When Heiling arrives with the bridal

jewels and Anna repulses him, declaring her knowledge of
his origin, Heiling stabs his rival Konrad to the heart, and
flees.

Act III.   A rocky gorge.   Heiling calls upon the spirits
of the earth, and they inform him that Konrad is not dead.
When he attempts to force the spirits to obey him they
remind him that he has voluntarily surrendered his power
over them.   In despair he realises that both his happiness
on earth and his power as a spirit have departed, but the
spirits promise him vengeance if he will return to them
and renounce Anna forever.

Change of scene: Konrad is about to celebrate his marriage, and the peasants join in the festival (Stephan's
song: "A huntsman would marry"; Duet between Konrad
and Anna: "Now you are mine.")   As is the custom the
peasants play blindman's-buff, and during the game Anna,
blindfolded, catches Heiling, who has mysteriously appeared.   When he is about to avenge himself, Konrad and
the peasants come to her rescue.   Heiling calls on the
spirits, but, besought by his mother, he gives up his vengeance, and resolving that no mortal eye shall again behold him, he sinks beneath the earth.

THE HERMIT'S BELL
(Les Dragons de Villars)

Opera in three acts by Maillart.   Text by Common and
Lockroy.

Cast: Thibaut, a rich farmer—Tenor.   Georgette, his
wife—Soprano.   Bélamy, officer of dragoons—Baritone.
Sylvain, Thibaut's servant—Tenor.   Rose Friquet, a poor
peasant girl—Soprano.   A fugitive—Basso.   Place, a
French village in the mountains.   Time, 1704.   First production, Paris, 1856.

Act I.   Thibaut's farm.   He announces the approach of
a regiment of dragoons: the women conceal themselves, and

his wife hides herself in the stable. When the dragoons under the command of Bélamy arrive, Thibaut assures him that all the women have fled. Rose Friquet approaches with mules, which the farmhand Sylvain had lost in the forest. She knows that Sylvain has befriended the fugitives, persecuted for the sake of religion, whom the soldiers pursue. Rose confronts Bélamy and reveals the hiding-place of the women. Bélamy has been told of a wondrous bell in the chapel of the hermit, which is rung whenever a woman becomes unfaithful, and he induces Georgette to lead him thither; Rose overhears this and informs Sylvain that his departure is a favourable opportunity for the rescue of his friends.

Act II. The hermit's chapel in the forest. Rose shows Sylvain the only unguarded path, and his heart begins to turn to the girl, who heretofore has been universally despised. Thibaut suspects Bélamy and his wife, but Rose manages to get rid of him, and concealing herself in the chapel, twice rings the bell when the dragoon attempts to kiss Georgette. The superstitious farmer's wife runs away, and Bélamy allays the distrust of Thibaut. The tired Rose falls asleep, Bélamy returns to investigate, and is a secret witness to the escape of the fugitives.

Act III. Before the house of Thibaut. Sylvain is about to marry Rose, when Thibaut accuses her of treachery. Sylvain believes him and is in despair. Rose, unconscious of the accusation, arrives to be married, but is treated with scorn by Sylvain. He attempts to strike her, when she produces proof of the safety of the fugitives. Bélamy is about to order the execution of Sylvain, when Rose threatens to accuse him to the authorities for allowing the fugitives to escape during his interview with Georgette. Bélamy quickly releases Sylvain and he marries Rose.

THE HUGUENOTS

Opera in five acts by Meyerbeer. Text by Scribe and Deschamps.

CAST: Marguerite de Valois—Soprano. St. Bris, Catholic nobleman—Basso. Valentine, his daughter—Soprano. Raoul de Nangis, Protestant nobleman—Tenor. Marcel, his servant—Basso. Urbain, page—Soprano. Count de Nevers—Baritone. Bois Rosé, Protestant soldier—Tenor. Cossé, Tananneo and Thoret, Catholic noblemen. Petz, Méru and Maurevert—Small parts. A night watchman. Place, in Paris and Touraine. Time, 1572. First production, Paris, 1836.

The night of St. Bartholomew is the subject of this opera. Peace ostensibly exists between the Catholics and Huguenots, but the Catholic party, with St. Bris at its head, is determined to destroy the Huguenots, while Marguerite and the noble De Nevers are for permanent amity.

ACT I. De Nevers's chamber. The assembled Catholic noblemen entertain the Protestant Raoul at a banquet. (Raoul's aria: "To find myself at such a place.") When in the course of the carouse each guest is asked to name his adored one, and Raoul is requested to be the first, he declares that he loves an unknown, whom he had once freed from molestation. (Romance: "Her cheeks.") When his servant, Marcel, a rough but honest soldier, appears, the latter warns him of danger, by singing Luther's hymn: "The Lord is our refuge." Marcel refuses to drink, but sings by request and in scorn: "The convents are burning." De Nevers, the host, leaves the room to receive a lady, whom his friends believe to be his mistress; Raoul, gazing through the window, recognises his unknown, and from this moment thinks of her only with contempt. But it is Valentine, who sincerely loves Raoul and who came to De Nevers to ask that he release her from her promise to marry him, to which he sorrowfully agrees. A page, Urbain, brings Raoul an anonymous note, and requests him to follow with his eyes bandaged, to meet a lady. (Urbain: "A lovely, noble lady.")

ACT II. Garden of Queen Marguerite, wherein she is walking with her ladies. (Aria: "A happy country.") She and her followers are enthusiastic for peace (Terzett of ladies: "Dissension depart"), and she receives Valentine, for whom she has selected another nobleman to be her husband. It is Raoul to whom Marguerite now speaks. (Duet: "Who are you?") When the ladies and gentlemen return, he recognises the queen, to whom he pays homage. She announces that she will unite Raoul with Valentine as a sign of peace, and demands that they bury all animosity. (Ensemble: "Sweet amity, protect us.") When St. Bris introduces his daughter Valentine, who Raoul considers to be the mistress of Count de Nevers, the young Protestant nobleman refuses the alliance with scorn, and only the command of the queen prevents the shedding of blood.

ACT III. Catholics and Protestants are drinking before an inn at Paris. (Song of the Huguenots, Bois Rosé and his comrades: "He took the sword in his right hand.") A band of gipsies prevents a fight and they dance. Valentine, commanded by St. Bris, is betrothed to De Nevers, and he is plotting vengeance against Raoul, when he receives a challenge from Raoul, through Marcel, which is accepted by the nobleman Maurevert in his stead. Valentine has overheard the conversation in a nearby chapel and wishes to save Raoul from certain death. In the following magnificent duet she induces Marcel to see that Raoul does not come unattended to the duel. A septet of men precedes the affair. The clash of swords attracts the adherents of both parties; Marguerite, who is passing, compels the combatants to cease. Valentine confirms Marcel's statement that Raoul's life is in danger, and he realises that he has falsely accused her.

ACT IV. Chamber of De Nevers. Valentine has become the wife of De Nevers, but loves only Raoul. (Romance:

"He alone fills my heart.") When Raoul appears to bid her farewell she conceals him behind a curtain from the assembling Catholics, and he overhears that all the Huguenots are to be murdered that night. The noble De Nevers, who refuses to take part in the plot, is removed by St. Bris. The celebrated blessing of the swords follows: ("Holy be our vengeance.") When the Catholics have left the room Raoul seeks to escape in order to warn his brethren, but is restrained by Valentine. (Duet: "To save all am I chosen.") For a while he is detained by his love, but when he hears the signal for the attack upon the Huguenots, he leaps through the window, leaving Valentine in a swoon.

ACT V. (In many theatres only the last scene of this act is presented, as the opera is very long. The original text has three scenes.)

Chamber in the Hotel de Nesle. The leaders of the Huguenots are assembled. Raoul enters and relates the terrors of St. Bartholomew's night. He reports the death of the Huguenot leader, Admiral Coligny, as its first victim. All arm themselves.

Change of scene: The churchyard. Valentine finds Raoul with Marcel. De Nevers, who has escaped, is dead; she accepts Raoul's faith, and Marcel unites them in marriage and blesses them. The Huguenot women are concealed in a neighbouring church: the Catholics enter, and a terrible scene of carnage ensues. Raoul is separated from Valentine in the combat.

Change of scene: Quay of Paris. Raoul arrives mortally wounded: Valentine and Marcel support him. St. Bris enters, the soldiers fire a volley, and Raoul and Valentine are united in death.

INDRA

Opera in three acts by Flotow. Text by Putlitz.

CAST: Don Sebastian, King of Portugal—Tenor. Don Luiz Camoëns—Baritone. Pedro, officer—Tenor. The king's confessor—Basso. Fernand, companion to the king

—Basso. José, innkeeper—Tenor. Zigaretta, his wife—
Soprano. Kudru, East Indian juggler—Mezzo-soprano.
Indra, her slave—Soprano. Place, Lisbon and Lofala in
East Africa. Time, 1751. First production, Vienna,
1852.

Act I. Harbour of Lofala. Indra, with a band of jugglers, is performing. She sings a composition by Camoëns,
who is present as a soldier, and who falls in love with her.
Pedro, the officer, is jealous, and sends the soldier Camoëns
away. His comrades collect money that he may purchase
his freedom from the service, but Camoëns uses the money
to free Indra from her mistress, Kudru, and flies with her,
accompanied by the gay José, who has deserted his wife
Zigaretta at Lisbon.

Act II. The harbour at Lisbon. King Sebastian, being
wounded in battle, is brought to Camoëns and healed by
Indra. When Pedro sees Indra once more, he endeavours
to take from her Camoëns's poem, "The Lusiade," but the
king interferes and saves his preserver.

Act III. José's room. He does not escape his fate, as
Zigaretta has followed him disguised as a sailor. The king
meets Indra, from whom he has received the poem, and asks
the name of the author. Indra refuses to tell him, but
when Camoëns is brought in by Pedro as a deserter, she
divulges his name. The king releases Camoëns and places
the faithful Indra, whose love he himself had tried to gain,
in the arms of her lover.

INGWILDE

Opera in three acts by Max Schillings. Text by Ferdinand
Count Sporck.

Cast: The Thorstein sons: Klaufe—Baritone. Bran—
Tenor. Siwart—Tenor. Gorm—Basso. Ortolf—Baritone. Gandulf—Basso. Ingwilde, his daughter—Soprano. Gest, his foster-son—Tenor. Place, Norway.

Time, the days of the Vikings.   First production, Karlsrühe, 1894.

ACT I. An apartment in the castle of Gladgard. Gandulf and Ingwilde see in a dream the battle of vengeance with the Thorstein sons. Gest explains the dream. Gandulf laments the death of his four sons, and Gest swears fidelity to him in their place. Ortolf, the herald of the Thorstein sons, arrives, mockingly attired in the dress of a clown, to announce hostilities. A short love scene follows between Gest and Ingwilde.

Change of scene: The open meadow. The battle begins and gradually nears the wood. Ingwilde gazes from the windows of the castle. Unseen by the combatants, Klaufe crosses the water to abduct Ingwilde. She sees him coming and sets fire to the castle. Klaufe enters the burning castle and captures the maiden. The battle approaches nearer, Gest frees Ingwilde, and strikes Klaufe to the earth. Siwart demands Ingwilde as his by blood right. Chance is to decide to which brother she belongs. To save herself, she takes a dreadful oath that she will belong only to the dead. Klaufe revives, having only been stunned, and bound by her oath, Ingwilde must follow him. Both sides swear vengeance till death.

ACT II. Chamber in the castle of the Thorstein sons. The Skald Bran has sung the praises of Ingwilde at the marriage feast. She replies that she will obey the custom, but will not consummate the union. The men go hunting. When alone with Klaufe, Ingwilde persuades him to go with her to Gandulf to make peace, afterward she will give him her love. The torch of Bran shall show the way. Bran, remaining alone, dreamily sings ("A star arose"); but soon he becomes suspicious of Ingwilde's mildness. The torch is extinguished. Klaufe's ghost returning announces his death and stirs Bran to vengeance. The mild youth becomes a warrior, and whets his axe with wild song. ("So, so, inanimate stone.") The brothers enter, bringing Klaufe's corpse, but consider his death atoned for by the

death of Gandulf.   Bran divides Klaufe's treasure, making
no claim for himself, but swears vengeance.

Act III.   On the shore near Castle Gladgard.   Ingwilde,
tortured by remorse for her treachery, is engaged in loving
converse with Gest.   She continually sees Klaufe's spirit,
and begs Gest to take her to distant lands.   He promises,
when Bran arrives to take vengeance upon Gest.   He kills
Gest, who tries to protect Ingwilde.   Bran, confused by
the sight of Ingwilde, falters in his design to kill her.
Klaufe's spirit speaks to him in vain.   Ingwilde endeavours
to kill Bran, but cannot force herself to the deed.   Only
when the burning death boat of Klaufe appears on the
waves do they realise their coming fate.   They both seek
death in the sea.   The terrified warriors see a boat gliding
toward the vessel of the dead.   It contains Ingwilde and
Bran, who go on board of the spirit ship of Klaufe, which
sinks into the waves.   A song is heard from the deep.
("You daring heroes.")   The warriors on the shore fall on
their knees in prayer.

THE INQUISITIVE WOMEN

Musical comedy in three acts after Goldoni by Sugana.
Music by Wolf-Ferrari.

Cast: Ottavio, a rich Venetian citizen.   Beatrice, his wife:
Rosaura, his daughter.   Florindo.   Pantalove.   Lelio.   Le-
andro.   Colombina, maid.   Eleonora, wife of Lelio.   Arlechino, servant.   Several friends of Pantalove's.   Servants.   Populace, etc.   Place, Venice in the middle of the
eighteenth century.   First production, Munich, 1903.

Act I.   A room in the club house, over whose door is
written: "Women are excluded."   A number of married
men are making merry at a feast, well knowing that their
wives and daughters are curious to discover what takes
place within the walls of the club.   To-day Pantalove is
the host, and he orders his rogue of a servant, Arlechino—

who poses as a woman hater—although he loves Colombina, to prepare the feast.

Change of scene: A chamber in the house of Ottavio. Beatrice, Rosaura and Eleonora believe that dreadful orgies are carried on at the club, and are strengthened in their belief by the tales of Colombina. They endeavour to extract information from Arlechino and Ottavio, but in vain. Rosaura tries to gain her ends with her lover Florindo by swooning and jealousy, and at last Colombina, by a stratagem, obtains the password, "Amicizia," from Florindo.

Act II. A room in the house of Lelio. Eleonora discovers from a letter in her husband's pocket that new keys have been made for the club. When Ottavio and his family arrive on a visit all the women endeavour to obtain the keys from the men. Again Colombina's cunning triumphs, and she secures the keys. The women now resolve to gain entrance to the club; only Rosaura, as a young girl, is left at home, but she appeals to Florindo, who, being lovesick, is persuaded to deliver his key to her.

Act III. A street near the club house. The women arrive singly, but manage so clumsily that they cannot enter the club. They capture Arlechino, and take his key by force.

Change of scene: Festival hall in the club, separated from the anteroom by a door of thick glass. The women assure themselves that the men are enjoying themselves harmlessly at the meal, and when they are discovered, they are forgiven, and all join in a merry dance.

IPHIGENIA IN AULIS

Lyric tragedy in three acts by Gluck. Text by Du Rollet. CAST: Agamemnon—Baritone. Clytemnestra, his wife—Mezzo-soprano. Iphigenia, their daughter—Soprano. Achilles—Tenor. Patroclos—Basso. Calchas, high

priest—Basso. Arkas, captain of the guard of Agamemnon—Tenor. Artemis (Diana)—Soprano. Place, Aulis.
First production, Paris, 1774.

Act I. Camp of the Greeks. (Aria of Agamemnon: "O
Artemis, angry one! in vain this dreadful sacrifice.") The
king has angered the goddess, and she revenges herself by
preventing the departure of the Greek fleet for Troy by
contrary winds. In order to appease her wrath, Agamemnon offers his daughter Iphigenia in sacrifice. Calchas tells
the Greeks of the demands of the goddess. ("The goddess
wills that I enlighten you.") He insists that Agamemnon
shall comply. (Duet: "You see how the army is disturbed.") Clytemnestra and Iphigenia arrive at the camp
unexpectedly, and Calchas declares this to be a sign from
the goddess. The arrival of the women is celebrated with
dances and music. Clytemnestra relates that Achilles, the
bridegroom-to-be of Iphigenia, has become unfaithful.
(Duet: "Achilles, by you be hated"; Aria of Clytemnestra:
"Arm yourself with angry courage.") Iphigenia cannot
believe it. (Aria: "My heart is inexperienced.") Achilles,
ignorant of all, joins her; when she accuses him of infidelity,
he denies it and reaffirms his love. (Duet: "Is it a dream
which deludes me?")

Act II. Palace of Agamemnon. Iphigenia is again in
doubt as to her father's intention, but Clytemnestra brings
joyful news. (Duet: "Soon, daughter, Hymen will make
thee happy.") Achilles celebrates his love for Iphigenia
with song and dances. He is about to lead her to the altar,
when Arkas proclaims that Agamemnon is waiting to sacrifice her. Clytemnestra asks Achilles to save the maiden.
(Aria: "Condemned to death by her cruel father"; Terzett,
Achilles, Clytemnestra and Iphigenia: "Princess, be comforted.") Achilles threatens Agamemnon. (Duet: "He
comes! Gods, assuage the anger of my heart.") Angered,
the king commands the sacrifice to proceed. (Recitative:
"My command obey"; Aria: "Dear to thy father's heart.")

Act III. A tent. Arkas guards Iphigenia, and the

Greeks clamour for the sacrifice. Achilles arrives to attempt the escape of Iphigenia. (Duet: "Loved one, follow me!") The daughter of Agamemnon, however, wishes to save Achilles from disgrace, and resolves to die. (Aria of Achilles: "Well then! go and obey, cruel one!") The Greeks arrive to take away Iphigenia. (Aria of Clytemnestra: "Cast, Zeus, thy bolts.")

Change of scene: Altar of Artemis on the shore of the sea. As Achilles is about to save Iphigenia by force of arms the goddess appears, declares herself appeased, and Achilles clasps his bride in his arms before his departure for Troy. (This ending does not agree with the myth. According to it Iphigenia is saved by Artemis [Diana], but, unknown to the Greeks, is brought to Tauris, where she is installed as priestess of the temple.)

IPHIGENIA IN TAURIS

Opera in four acts by Gluck. Text from the French of Guichard by Sander.

CAST: Iphigenia, high priestess of Diana—Soprano. Orestes—Baritone. Pylades—Tenor. Thoas, King of Scythia—Basso. Diana—Soprano. First and second priestess. A Scythian. A servant of the temple. Place, Tauris. First production, Paris, 1779.

Through the curious ending of "Iphigenia in Aulis" (which see above) this opera is not produced as a continuation of the other, which it is in action. Clytemnestra has slain Agamemnon after his return from Troy, and is murdered by her son Orestes in consequence. Pursued by the Eumenides, the matricide consults the oracle of Apollo, and is promised safety if he delivers his sister out of Tauris. As he knows nothing of the deliverance of Iphigenia by Diana (Artemis), he thinks he is commanded to carry off the statue of Diana (Apollo's sister). He hurries with his friend Pylades to Tauris, but finds and recognises his own sister Iphigenia, and returns with her to Greece, relieved from the vengeance of the Eumenides.

ACT I.   Temple of Diana.   Iphigenia attempts to change the customs of the temple of the goddess, by which heretofore all strangers have been offered in sacrifice.   She has dreamed of Orestes, and longs for her brother; her present situation is hateful to her, and she prays to Diana for relief.   (Aria: "Oh, thou, who once did save me.")   Thoas, king of Scythia, frightened by dreams, brings new sacrifices to Diana.   (Aria: "Grave fears.")   The Scythians conduct to the temple Orestes and Pylades, whom they have taken prisoners, and Thoas orders their death.

ACT II.   The interior of the temple.   (Aria of Orestes: "You, who persecute me"; Aria of Pylades: "Only one wish.")   Pylades is taken away, but Orestes remains; the Eumenides appear at the entrance and torture him.   When Iphigenia arrives, and ascertains his name and the dreadful events that have taken place in her father's house, she is utterly cast down.   (Aria: "O let me weep.")

ACT III.   Chamber of Iphigenia.   (Aria: "Ever will I remember him.")   When Orestes and Pylades are brought in, Iphigenia declares that she will save one of them, and chooses Orestes.   When she has gone Pylades expresses his joy at his friends' deliverance, but Orestes refuses the sacrifice.   (Duet: "And you tell me that you love me.")   When Iphigenia returns Orestes declares that she must save Pylades or he will kill himself.   Thus forced, the priestess yields and sends a letter by Pylades to her sister, Electra.   Pylades resolves in his turn to save Orestes.

ACT IV.   The hall of sacrifice.   Iphigenia, shuddering at the coming sacrifice, announces to Orestes that she is his sister, but Thoas, when informed of Pylades's escape, angrily demands Orestes's death.   Pylades arrives with an armed band, and a conflict ensues.   During the fray Diana appears, and drives off the Scythians, whose worship she refuses.   Driven by gentle winds, Iphigenia, the Greeks and the priestesses leave the inhospitable shores of Tauris.

IRIS

Opera in three acts by Pietro Mascagni. Text by Luigi Illica.

CAST: Cieco, a blind man—Basso. Iris, his daughter—Soprano. Osaka, a rich youth—Tenor. Kyoto, keeper of the Yoshiwara—Baritone. A geisha—Soprano. A peddler—Tenor. A rag-picker—Tenor.

The action takes place in Japan. The opera was first produced at the Teatro Costanzi, Rome, in 1898.

ACT I. In the dawn, the Voice of the Sun is heard proclaiming himself God. (Chorus: "I am I! I am Life!") Iris, the fair daughter of Cieco, a blind man, is in her garden, playing with her doll. (Iris: "Silence, O flowers, my little doll is sick.") Reverently she salutes the Rising Sun. Cieco calls from within. (Duet, Cieco, Iris: "Pure and sweet, gay and bright, life goes on.") Osaka, a rich young libertine, won by the maiden's beauty, conspires with Kyoto, a procurer, to secure her for himself. Seeing her guilelessness, the two men arrange a puppet show to gain her attention. (Cieco: "That play is all a lie!") Iris runs out of the garden to look at it, and while intent upon the dancing of the geishas, is surrounded and carried off. Her father calls her repeatedly until the neighbours tell him she has gone to the Yoshiwara, a place of evil resort. Believing that she went willingly, Cieco breaks into tears and curses. (Cieco: "Oh, beloved home.")

ACT II. Iris lies asleep on a bed in the Yoshiwara, surrounded by geishas playing and singing softly. Osaka enters, asking for Iris. Kyoto cunningly inflames the youth's desire for her by praise of her beauty. He demands rich gifts of Osaka, and the two men retire to complete their bargain. Iris awakens. Wondering at her rich surroundings, she imagines herself in Paradise. (Iris: "Always visions! visions and visions!") She examines her apparel, and everything in the room, then to amuse herself takes a brush and idly paints a flower, which turns into a

snake. Osaka enters with magnificent gifts. He makes
ardent love to Iris, who is alarmed and resists him. (Osaka:
"Ah! your hair so long and thick.") To divert him she
speaks of her home and her garden. (Iris: "Once, when
I was little.") He answers cynically, and, at last wearied
by her innocence, calls Kyoto to take her away. (Iris: "I
want my garden.") Kyoto orders the geisha women to
robe her in transparent garments, and displays her beauty
upon the gallery of the house to a gaping crowd below.
(Chorus: "O wonder of wonders.") Osaka enters again,
offering to buy Iris from Kyoto at his own price. (Osaka:
"Iris! 'Tis I!") Cieco appears in the crowd, calling Iris,
who answers him. The people, now threatening, lead Cieco
to the window, while Kyoto proclaims loudly that the girl
is his through purchase from her father. Cieco draws near,
and with bitter curses throws mud upon Iris in token of
contempt. Maddened, the girl hurls herself from the window into the mouth of a sewer below, and perishes.

Act III. Rag-pickers, exploring the sewer with long
hooks in hope of gain, find little of value until they secure
the body of Iris. They quarrel over her rich dress and
tear it off. The body seems to move, and they run away in
terror. Iris, almost motionless, is half-way between life
and death. In this strange state she sees before her the
egos of Osaka, Kyoto and Cieco, plaintively justifying
their existence. Iris bemoans her own sad destiny, asking
why—why? (Iris: "The little world of my cottage, why
destroy?") The Rising Sun caresses her with his rays.
She salutes her one helper, the God of Day. The flowers
opening in the warm sunlight surround the body of Iris,
uplifting it toward the sun. She becomes one with the
flowers, and as the scene ends the Voice of the Sun is raised
in exultation. (Chorus: "I am I! I am Life.")

IVANHOE

Romantic opera in four acts by Arthur Sullivan. Text
from Scott's novel by Julian Sturgis. German by Witt-
man.

CAST: Richard Lion Heart, King of England. Prince
John, his brother. Cedric, a noble Saxon. Wilfred of
Ivanhoe, his son. Lady Rowena, his ward. De Beaumanoir,
grand master. De Bois Gilbert, commander of the Knights
Templars. De Bracy, Norman knight. Brother Tuck, a
hermit. Locksley, leader of the outlaws. Isaac of York,
a Jew. Rebecca, his daughter. Ulrica. Wamba, a fool.
Oswald, chamberlain of Cedric. Place, England. Time,
end of the twelfth century. First production, London,
1891.

ACT I. A chamber in the castle of Cedric. Cedric, a
Saxon prince, laments the fate of England under the rule
of the Normans. He has quarrelled with his son, Ivanhoe,
for daring to raise his eyes to Lady Rowena, who is of
kingly Saxon blood. With the cry of "All hail," he and
his retainers sit down to a feast. Isaac of York, a Jew, asks
for refuge for the night, also Bois Gilbert and De Bracy,
who as Normans are but coldly received by the Saxons.
The Templar praises Rowena's beauty and regrets that
she is not present. She appears covered with a veil. The
knights tell of the Crusades, and Cedric is pleased to hear
that the Saxon knights have behaved with valour. A pilgrim, who has also claimed hospitality, and who is none
other than Ivanhoe, also relates his adventures, but does not
mention the name of the victorious knight in the lists who
had overthrown Bois Gilbert. But the latter mentions
the name himself, Wilfred of Ivanhoe, and is sorry that
he cannot obtain satisfaction. The pilgrim assures him
that Ivanhoe would willingly meet him, which the knight
doubts. Rowena takes the part of the absent one; Cedric
ends the feast and all go to rest. De Bracy asks the help of
the Templar to abduct Rowena.

Change of scene: Rowena's apartment.   Rowena is alone. (Song: "O moon, thy light like silver.")   Her women lead the pilgrim to her, for she wishes to receive news of Ivanhoe; she plainly shows that she loves him, and Ivanhoe leaves her with renewed hope.   He warns Isaac of the plot of the Templars to capture him for ransom and promises protection to the Jew if he will procure him arms and armour for the tourney.

Change of scene: Before the lists in Ashby.   The people acclaim the "black knight," who is King Richard, and has been the victor on the preceding day.   The hermit Tuck teases him with rough play, and the king threatens to visit and chastise him in his cell.   Tuck laughs at him.   To insult the Saxons, Prince John attempts to seat the Jew Isaac among them, but Rebecca asks him to desist.   A messenger brings a letter with the news that Richard is free and in England; John is troubled and suspicious that h's brother may be the black knight.   In the meantime Boïs Gilbert has been overcome by Ivanhoe, and the latter doffs his helmet to receive the reward from Rowena.   Amid general rejoicing he is recognised, but Cedric turns from him in anger.

Act II.   The hermitage in the wood.   King Richard has sought the coarse but honest Tuck, who feigns to live only on bread and water, but finally produces delicacies and wine.   They eat and drink and resolve to fight it out another time.   The king sings for his host ("What care I for glory and gold"), and Tuck likewise trolls a merry lay. ("The wind blows cold upon the sea.")   Locksley and other outlaws appear and ask aid for Cedric and Rowena, who have been captured and taken to Castle Torquilstone, the home of the Templar.   Ivanhoe lies wounded in the same castle, and is nursed by Isaac and Rebecca. With the outlaws King Richard departs from the wood.

Change of scene: Before the castle.   Cedric accuses De Bracy of having taken part in the assault upon the castle.

He denies the charge and warns Cedric that the mention of Ivanhoe's name as that of the wounded man would cause his death. If Rebecca will become the Templar's bride, he will spare the wounded knight. Rebecca, to save Ivanhoe, is willing; but Cedric refuses to allow this, saying that his son is dead to him. The Templar leaves the castle; he loves the beautiful Rebecca, and desires to possess her. (Song: "I was the cold one.")

A room in the turret of the castle. The insane Ulrica sings a wild song. ("Grind the axes.") She warns the despairing Rebecca of her coming fate. Ulrica's father was slain in the same chamber, and she herself has been the victim of the Templar's lust. Rebecca begs her to save her, but she repulses the Jewess. (Rebecca's prayer: "God of Israel, come.") She offers her jewels to the Templar for her freedom; he refuses and exults in his power. In her despair, she attempts to leap from the window, when a trumpet blast announces the approach of enemies, and the Templar departs.

ACT III. A chamber at Torquilstone. Ivanhoe lies on a bed of sickness. (Song: "Softly, with winged feet.") Rebecca and Ulrica enter; Ivanhoe is asleep. Ulrica, who knows Rebecca loves the knight, tells her to nurse him, and she will light her marriage torch. Rebecca, alone with the sleeping Ivanhoe, realises that she loves him. ("Yes, she spoke truth.") The sounds of combat awaken Ivanhoe. Rebecca, looking from the window, reports its progress. The outlaws, the black knight at the head, are storming the outer court when flames appear; Ulrica has set fire to the castle. The Templar rushes in, bearing Rebecca away, and Ivanhoe is saved by the king from the burning building. Ulrica finds death in the flames.

ACT IV. The saved assemble in the wood of Torquilstone. The black knight, now known as the king, induces Cedric to forgive his son and to allow him to marry Rowena. Isaac comes forward and asks aid for Rebecca, who has been dragged to the house of the order of Templars and accused

of witchcraft by the Templar. Ivanhoe, although not fully
recovered, accompanies Isaac to rescue her.

Change of scene: In the tower of the Templars. (Chorus
of Templars: "Fremuere, principes.") The grand master
announces that the convicted Jewess has demanded a champion. As no one appears she is about to be taken to the
stake, notwithstanding the protest of the Templar, who desires to save her for himself. At the last moment Ivanhoe
appears as Rebecca's champion and slays Bois Gilbert in
combat. The king abolishes the order of the Templars,
and orders the flag of England to be displayed on the ramparts. (Closing chorus: "O love, which rules us all.")

JESSONDA

Opera in three acts by Spohr. Text by Gehe.

CAST: Jessonda, widow of the Rajah—Soprano. Amazili,
her sister—Soprano. Dandau, high priest of Brahma—
Basso. Nadori, Brahmin—Tenor. Tristan d'Acunha,
Portuguese general—Basso. An East Indian officer—Baritone. Place, Goa. Time, the sixteenth century. First
production, Cassel, 1823.

The Portuguese officer, Tristan d'Acunha, many years ago
had loved Jessonda, but she was compelled to marry a
rajah.

ACT I. Interior of a pagoda. The old rajah is dead,
and Dandau, the high priest, orders Nadori to inform Jessonda that she must ascend the funeral pyre with the
corpse. (Chorus: "Cold and stark, but majestic"; Recitative: "Nadori! You have failed"; Duet: "From the holy
walls of this temple.") An officer comes to announce that
a celebrated general has taken command of the Portuguese,
and that the city is to be stormed. Dandau replies that he
relies upon Brahma for protection. (Aria and chorus:
"The glow of morning and night.")

Change of scene: Apartment of Jessonda. She knows she

must die, and her sister Amazili speaks to her of her former
lover. She laments that she has not again seen him. (Aria:
"Know'st thou silent anguish?") Nadori arrives to carry
out the orders of Dandau; when he sees Amazili, he is enraptured by her beauty, having never before seen a woman.
("Yes, that—that is woman's beauty.")

Act II. The Portuguese camp. (Chorus: "No music on
this earth.") Festivities in honour of Tristan. He remembers his love. (Aria: "Conquered by war-like dreams.")
Tristan has allowed the Brahmin women to use the holy
well, near the camp for bathing. The Portuguese leave the
camp. Jessonda arrives with Amazili. (Duet: "For him
whom I loved.") Nadori has followed them; through love
for the sister he resolves to save Jessonda. (Aria: "Let
roses crown my happiness.") He confesses his love to
Amazili, and she acknowledges that she returns it. (Duet:
"Thou lovely girl, wilt thou hate me"; Aria: "O strange
emotions, which glow in me.") When Jessonda returns
from the bath she beholds Tristan, and gladly rejoins her
lover. Dandau arrives, to whom Tristan has pledged his
word, and with bleeding heart he sees Jessonda led away to
her death.

Act III. A truce has been declared, and Tristan is helpless, when Lopez reports that Dandau has broken his peace
compact. Tristan, supported by Nadori, rushes to arms.
(Terzett: "Up! let the flag wave.")

Change of scene: In Goa. A tempest. Jessonda appears
dressed for the sacrifice, and implores protection at the
statue of Brahma. (Aria: "Ye Gods, gaze upon me.")
Amazili approaches and reports Tristan near. Dandau,
to prevent his victim from falling into the hands of the
Portuguese, attempts to murder Jessonda, but Tristan arrives in time to fold his love to his heart, while Amazili flies
to Nadori. Tristan then returns with Jessonda, Nadori
and Amazili to his home. ("Come to my fatherland.")

THE JEWESS

Opera in five acts by Halévy.   Text by Scribe.

CAST: Sigismund, King of Germany—Silent.   Brogny, President of the council of Constanz—Basso.   Leopold, Prince of the realm—Tenor.   Eudoxia, his betrothed, niece of king—Soprano.   Eleazar, a Jewish goldsmith—Tenor. Recha, his daughter—Soprano.   Rugierro, chief bailiff of Constanz—Baritone.   Albert, officer of bowmen.   Place, Constanz.   Time, 1414.   First production, Paris, 1835.

ACT I.   Before the cathedral of Constanz; the emperor orders a festival in honour of the victory of his son Leopold.   Rugierro arrests the Jew Eleazar, because he is at work on the Sabbath day.   Cardinal Brogny emerges from the cathedral and recognises Eleazar, whom he had known in Rome before he had taken holy orders, and was still a husband and father.   His family is now dead.   Eleazar curses the cardinal, for it was by his orders that his sons had been burned at the stake.   The cardinal answers mildly and frees him.   (Cavatina and chorus: "When hate and vengeance forever.")   Eleazar still thinks only of revenge. When the street is empty of people, Prince Leopold appears dressed in plain attire.   He loves Eleazar's daughter Recha, and has entered her house as a coreligionist.   (Aria: "Far from thee, loved one.")   Recha approaches Samuel (his assumed name), believing he has returned from a journey; she expects him at her father's house in the evening. The festival begins.   Ballet.   Eleazar and Recha mix with the crowd, and ascend the steps of the church for a better view.   The incensed people are about to throw them into the sea, but they are rescued by Leopold.   The scene closes with the march of the imperial procession.

ACT II.   A room in Eleazar's house.   Eleazar, Recha, Leopold and the Jewish servants are at table.   (Prayer: "Visit us, O God of our fathers.")   A knock at the door interrupts the meal.   Everything is put out of sight, and Eleazar admits the princess Eudoxia.   Leopold tries to conceal himself from his affianced bride, who has come to order gems from the Jew. (Terzett: "They say you possess jewels.") Eleazar escorts her to the door, and Recha demands an explanation from Leopold. He promises to return in the night and tell all. (Recha, Romance: "How my heart beats.") When the father has retired, Leopold returns. (Duet: "When my heart I gave to thee.") He tells her he is a Christian, but she is ready to fly with him, when they are discovered by Eleazar. (Terzett: "Where do you go?") When he hears that Leopold is not a Jew he attempts to kill him, but is prevented by Recha. Eleazar relents, and is willing that his daughter should marry Leopold, but the prince is in fear of his father. He departs, Eleazar curses him, and Recha falls unconscious.

Act III. Feast in the hall. The emperor and his guests at the table. Song and ballet. The foreground is occupied by the people, among them Eleazar and Recha. Eudoxia declares her willingness to marry Leopold, when Recha steps forward and accuses the prince of treachery and of being in love with a Jewess. When the excitement has subsided, Eleazar asks the nobles to sentence Leopold. The cardinal curses the Jews, excommunicates the prince, and he, Eleazar and Recha are cast into prison.

Act IV. A chamber in the Court of Justice. Eudoxia has Recha brought before her, and pleads with her to save Leopold's life by declaring him innocent. (Duet: "You alone can save him.") Recha, who still loves Leopold, consents. The gentle cardinal tries to save Eleazar, by asking him to become a Christian, but he is determined to die a devout Jew, and threatens before his death to take vengeance. He reminds the cardinal of the day when he had lost his wife and children by fire; tells him he had saved his daughter, who is still alive, but refuses to state her dwelling-place. The cardinal departs in despair. Eleazar alone; he loves Recha as his own child, but she is the daughter of the cardinal. He asks Heaven for aid, and deliberates whether he shall sacrifice her. (Aria: "God direct my acts.")

Act V.   Street in Constanz.   Recha is to be thrown into a boiling cauldron, which is exhibited on the stage.   The people are assembled.   March and procession of the cardinal and his suite with Eleazar and Recha.   The death warrant is read.   The two Jews must die, but Leopold's sentence has been changed to banishment by Recha's statement of his innocence.   Eleazar hesitates and again asks Recha whether she is willing to live as a Christian, but she wishes to die with him as a Jewess.   They are led to their death, and as Recha is thrown into the cauldron, Eleazar calls aloud to the cardinal, "Behold your child."

JOHN OF PARIS

Comic opera in two acts by Boieldieu.   Text by St. Just.
Cast: The Princess of Navarre—Soprano.   The chief seneschal of the princess—Baritone.   John of Paris—Tenor.   Olivier—Soprano.   Pedrigo, innkeeper—Basso. Lorezza, his daughter—Mezzo-soprano.   Place, an inn in the Pyrenees.   Time, the seventeenth century.   First production, Paris, 1812.

The dauphin, as John of Paris, is on a journey to meet his bride, the princess of Navarre, whom he finds at an inn in the Pyrenees.   His unceremonious invitation to the princess to sup with him arouses the horror of the seneschal, but she enters into the fun, which ends, however, in her falling in love with him.

Act I.   Before the inn.   Everything is in readiness to receive the princess.   (Chorus and scene: "Do not delay, do your duty.")   Olivier arrives and demands a room for John.   (Terzett: "Welcome, host"; Aria of Olivier: "When my master travels.")   John appears.   (Aria and chorus: "Friends, make yourself at home"; Duet between John and Olivier: "To love honour above everything.")   The seneschal of the princess in great dignity orders a meal. (Aria: "All must obey me.")   John declares he is master

of the house. (Quartet: "John, Seneschal, Pedrigo and
Lorezza: "How dare you.") The princess arrives and immediately awakens John's admiration. (Aria of the princess: "What pleasure to travel.") She recognises John as
the prince, resolves to circumvent him, and accepts his invitation to dinner.

ACT II. The same scene. (John's aria: "The pride of
knighthood.") Olivier sings a romance, and John and the
princess the concluding stanzas. ("The troubador, proud
of love's bands," with the refrain of the chorus: "When
castanets clash.") The prince reveals his name and station (Duet: "The husband of my choice"), and he and the
princess confess their love for each other. (Closing chorus:
"To beauty, honour and glory.")

THE JUGGLER OF OUR LADY

Miracle play in three acts. Text by Léna. Music by
Massenet.

CAST: Jean, a juggler—Tenor. Boniface, the cook—
Baritone. The Prior—Basso. The Poet, a monk—Tenor.
The Painter, a monk—Baritone. The Musician, a monk—
Baritone. The Sculptor, a monk—Basso. Two angels—So-
prano and Mezzo-soprano. Apparition of the Virgin.
Monks, cavaliers, townspeople, angel voices. Place, Cluny.
Time, the fourteenth century. First production, Paris,
1903.

ACT I. Marketplace in Cluny. A market day on the
first of May. (Chorus: "Let us dance.") The juggler
Jean wanders hungry and miserable through the country-
side, but rejoices in his freedom. It does not satisfy his
wants, however, and he is unsuccessful in gaining the attention of the people, who deride his performance. (Jean:
"Give place to the king of jugglers"; Chorus: "Gentle king,
choose thy queen.") They care nothing for his globes, his
hoops, his old songs and dances. They do applaud a ribald

song (Jean: "Alleluia to wine"), and although in his heart Jean is a good Christian, his stomach remains egotistical, and he sings a parody on the Mass. The prior appears (Prior: "Hence, infamous band"), the crowd disperses, leaving Jean to his fate. The juggler is about to be excommunicated for his blasphemy, when he confesses his guilt, and is received among the monks. (Prior: "He weeps! he shall be pardoned.") Hunger overcomes him, and he relinquishes his freedom, sorely tempted by the rich food of the abbey. (Jean: "O Liberty, it is thou!" Boniface: "For the Blessed Virgin.")

Act II.   Study at the abbey. Musicians, poets, painters and sculptors labour for the feast of the Holy Mother (Chorus: "Ave rosa, speciosa"), but Jean takes no part. (Jean: "Each one in this holy house.") Alas! he knows no Latin. Brother Boniface, the cook, consoles him (Boniface: "Ah, envy them not"; "The Virgin with the Infant Jesus"), and Jean resolves to serve the Holy Mother in his own way. (Jean: "Oh, Virgin, Mother of Love.")

Act III.   Chapel of the abbey, in which stands the image of the Blessed Virgin. Jean slowly approaches. He puts off his monastic garb, and appears in his juggler's dress. He offers to Mary the only gift he possesses, his songs and dances. In his ecstasy, he does not notice the entrance of the monks (Chorus of monks: "Ave cœleste Lilium"), and dances on unheeding. (Jean: "Adorable mother of Jesus.") The prior in horror is about to throw himself upon Jean, when the Holy Mother interferes; a miracle takes place, for the image raises its hands, and places them in benediction upon the head of the juggler. (Angel chorus: "Hosanna!") The monks now acclaim him a saint, and as they sing, led by Boniface, "Sancta Maria, ora pro nobis," Jean declares in softly childish tones, "Oh, dear, I understand Latin now!" Overcome with joy, at the favour of the Holy Mother, the juggler sinks to the ground, and dies. (Jean: "Radiant vision.")

THE KISS

Opera in two acts by Friedrich Smetana.   Text by Kras-
nohorska.   German by Ludwig Hartmann.

CAST: Fedor Zarkow, a countryman.   Marinka, his daughter.   Hanno, a young widower.   Janusch, his brother-in-
law.   Brigitta, an old relative of Marinka.   Clara, servant
with Zarkow.   Steffan, leader of the smugglers.   A frontier
guard.   Place, the Bohemia mountains near the frontier.
Time, the present.   First production, Prague, 1876.

ACT I.   A peasant's room in Zarkow's house.   Brigitta
hastily calls Marinka to enter as Hanno has appeared as
a suitor for her hand.   He had formerly rejected her for
a richer girl, but being now a widower wishes to right the
wrong.   Marinka is delighted, and does not heed the warnings of her father.   They all busy themselves in dressing
suitably for Hanno's reception, and, according to custom,
Marinka leaves the room.   Janusch does the wooing for
his timorous friend Hanno (Aria: "Hanno approaches as
a suitor"), and as the father is willing, if Marinka does
not refuse, the compact is made.   (Aria, Hanno: "Father,
I thank thee.")   The father thinks the couple are ill-mated,
as they are both obstinate.   (Aria: "Hard is thy head.")
Hanno promises never to quarrel with his wife, and Marinka
is brought in.   (Duet: "Joined forever.")   But when
Hanno tries to kiss her, she thrusts him violently away, and
thus proves her father's prediction true.   Hanno is overwhelmed with advice as to the means of overcoming her obstinacy.   (Ensemble: "I see into her heart.")   Hanno and
Marinka are now left alone and are as loving as if nothing
had occurred.   She strews sand around the cradle of his
child, brought in by Brigitta and Clara, that the footsteps
of its dead mother may be seen when she visits it (Aria:
"The sun sank") and promises to be a good mother to the
little one; only Hanno must not kiss her; she thinks the
deceased wife would not approve of it until after the ceremony.   Hanno is angry (Aria: "I will not wait"), and tries

to force her, but does not succeed. (Duet: "Then go.")
He threatens to seek another. The father scolds them
both roundly (Aria: "It has come, as I said"); Hanno
angrily leaves the house. Marinka is sunk in thought
("Where does he go?"), but remains obdurate when
Brigitta criticises her conduct. Brigitta advises her to
leave the house and join the smugglers (Aria: "Then listen
to good advice"); Marinka refuses, and sings a lullaby to
the child. ("Sleep, my child.") She falls asleep herself;
Clara enters frightened, for Hanno is approaching with
girls and musicians to make sport of Marinka. (Song:
"Play for the dance.") Marinka awakens, and conscious
of the disgrace, and seeing Hanno kissing another girl
(Song: "Pretty girls are everywhere"), she packs up her
clothes and joins the smugglers. (Ensemble: "Shame on
you.")

ACT II. A dense wood. Steffan, rifle in hand, is on
guard ("Be careful and watchful"), and issues his orders
to the smugglers. (Chorus: "Free is our way.") Hanno,
who feels he has done wrong, arrives and seeks Marinka.
(Aria: "The stars would I ask.") Janusch consoles him.
Hanno is willing to acknowledge his wrong before the whole
village if Marinka will return. The smugglers have overheard the conversation, but do not interfere. They are
waiting for Brigitta, who appears with Marinka. The latter is excited and frightened. (Aria: "Oh, hear the
groans.") They are pleasantly greeted by the smugglers,
and Steffan, who ascertains that Marinka still loves Hanno,
resolves to smooth matters. (Terzett: "Scold my follies.")
Marinka still refuses to kiss Hanno. The women who have
been left alone are to remove a basket of fruit, at whose
bottom is smuggled goods. They are surprised by one of
the frontier guards, and Brigitta's presence of mind alone
saves the inexperienced and trembling Marinka from arrest.
Brigitta again endeavours to persuade Marinka to give
way. (Duet: "Roses and thorns are always together.")
Marinka hesitates.

Change of scene: At the edge of the woods near Brigitta's hut. Clara reports that Steffan's intercession has been successful with Hanno. (Song: "Let thy song be heard!") Brigitta is not at home. The repentant Hanno arrives with father Steffan and Janusch to ask Marinka's forgiveness. (Song: "Well then, but a sermon.") At last she comes with Brigitta, rushes into Hanno's arms and wants to kiss him, but now *he* refuses. (Ensemble: "What? again you will.") But he is not in earnest; and Marinka kisses him heartily. (Closing chorus: "Now follows the union.")

LA BELLE HÉLÈNE

Burlesque opera in three acts by Jacques Offenbach. Text by Meilhac and Halévy.

CAST: Menelaus, Agamemnon, Achilles, Ajax I, Ajax II, Greek princes. Helena, wife of Menelaus. Clytemnestra, wife of Agamemnon. Prince Orestes. Pylades, his friend. Calchas, high priest of Jupiter. Philocomus, his assistant. Eutycles, his locksmith. Laëna, Parthenis, pretty maidens of Sparta. Paris, Prince of Troy. The old servant of Helena. Place, Sparta and the shores of the sea. First production, Paris, 1864.

Paris, son of Priam, arrives with a missive from the goddess Venus to the high priest Calchas, commanding him to procure for Paris the love of Helena, promised him by Venus when he awarded the prize of beauty to her and refused it to Juno and Minerva.

Paris disguises himself as a shepherd, and wins three prizes at the competition of the stupid and weak Greek princes, whereupon he reveals his identity. All the world had known that he had awarded the apple to Venus, and Helena recognises him as her destiny. The Trojan prince is crowned victor by Helena, to the disgust of the rough Achilles, and the two giants Ajax I and Ajax II. Paris is invited to a banquet by the timid Menelaus, husband of

Helena. Paris has bribed Calchas to have Philocomus rattle the thunder gong and to prophesy that Menelaus must at once proceed to Crete, in order to save the nation.

After parodies on the life of the Greek court, in which the honest Calchas appears as a gambling cheat, Paris comes to Helena at night. Although she knows her fate, she seemingly resists him, and he uses strategy. He departs, but returns when she has fallen asleep. He tells Helena that what will now occur is only a dream, and she is content to risk all with this understanding at this moment. Menelaus unexpectedly returns. Helena has hardly time to clothe herself, and Paris departs in haste, but, returning in the guise of a priest of Venus, carries Helena away. Menelaus is enraged, Achilles angry, but Calchas smiles contentedly, for he has made a good profit out of the transaction. Agamemnon shrugs his shoulders and resignedly exclaims: "Well, nothing remains but to mobilise the army and prepare for the ten-year Trojan war."

LA BOHÈME

Lyric opera in four acts by Ruggiero Leoncavallo. Libretto by the composer. German by Ludwig Hartmann. CAST: Marcel—Tenor. Rudolph—Baritone. Schaunard —Baritone. Gustav Collin—Baritone. Barbemache— Basso buffo. Count Paul—Baritone. Gaudenzio—Tenor. Durand—Tenor. A gentleman on the first floor—Tenor. An idler of the street—Tenor. Musette—Mezzo-soprano. Mimi—Soprano. Euphemia—Mezzo-soprano. Place, Paris. Time, one year from Christmas, 1837 to Christmas, 1838. First production, Milan, 1897.

ACT I. At the Café Momus. The innkeeper Gaudenzio tries in vain to eject the Bohemians, who never pay, and are always in mischief. During the conversation another piece of horseplay on their part is discovered. They sit down to dine, while Musette gaily sings. (Canzonette:

"Mimi is the name of my sweet blonde.") Naturally when they are asked to pay the score, they have no money. A comic fight ensues between them and the innkeeper, who has called his servants to assist him. It is ended by Barbemache, who offers to pay the bill.

Act II. In the court of Musette's house. Musette's lover has left her and refuses to pay her debts any longer. In consequence, her furniture is levied upon and carried down to the courtyard. When this has been done, she returns home; she expects guests and cannot entertain them in any other way than by receiving them in the courtyard. Here the Bohemians, who arrive in large numbers, celebrate joyously. In vain the neighbours awakened from sleep protest, and the scene ends in a general fight between the two factions.

Act III. Garret room of Marcel. Musette, who can no longer bear the sufferings of hunger and want, desires to leave him. Mimi, during the festival in the courtyard, has allowed herself to be carried off by Count Paul, but actuated by love for Rudolf, returns. Musette begs her to go with her, but in vain. Marcel and Rudolf in anger compel both to leave the apartment.

Act IV. Garret room of Rudolf. Mimi returns to Rudolf in a dying condition. Musette, who accidentally meets her there, sacrifices her jewels to procure fuel to warm the room for Mimi. As the Christmas chimes are heard, Mimi expires.

LA BOHÈME

Scenes from Henry Murger's "Vie de Bohème," in four acts, by Giacomo Puccini. Libretto by Giacosa and Illica. German by Ludwig Hartmann.

Cast: Rudolf—Tenor. Schaunard—Baritone. Marcel —Baritone. Collin—Basso. Bernard—Basso. Mimi— Soprano. Musette—Soprano. Parpignol—Tenor. Al-

cindor—Basso. Sergeant of the toll watch—Basso. Place,
Paris. Time, about 1830. First production, Turin, 1896.

Act I. Garret. Marcel is painting while Rudolf gazes
out of the window. As they have no fire, they use the
manuscript of Rudolf's drama for fuel. Collin enters
shivering; he is followed by three young fellows with
victuals, wood and cigars. Schaunard, who follows, explains the source of his riches. Nobody listens, but they
fall ravenously upon the food, which is removed by Schaunard, leaving only the wine. While they drink, Bernard,
the landlord, arrives to collect the rent from Marcel. They
flatter him and give him wine. In his drunkenness, he recites his amorous adventures, but when he also declares
he is married, they thrust him from the room in comic
moral indignation. The rent money is divided for a
carousal in the Quartier Latin. The other Bohemians go
out, but Rudolf remains alone in order to work. Some one
knocks, and Mimi, whose candle has been snuffed out, asks
Rudolf to light it. She departs, but returns in a few minutes, saying she has forgotten her key. Both candles are
extinguished; they stumble in the dark, and Rudolf finds
the key, which he pockets. They relate the story of their
varied experiences in the two arias. ("Who am I? Then
hear"; and "They call me merely Mimi.") The waiting
friends call Rudolf impatiently. He wishes to remain at
home with Mimi (Rudolf: "Your tiny hand is frozen"),
but she decides to accompany him. Departing they sing
of their love. (Duet, Rudolf, Mimi: "Love alone.")

Act II. Quartier Latin. A great crowd on the street,
sellers praise their wares. (Chorus: "Come buy my
oranges."). The friends repair to a café. While they
eat, Musette, formerly beloved of Rudolf, arrives with
her rich admirer Alcindor. She tries to attract Rudolf's
attention (Song, Musette: "As through the streets I wander"), and succeeds after many efforts. She feigns to be
suffering from a tight shoe, and to get rid of him, sends
Alcindor to the shoemaker. (Duet, Marcel, Musette:

"Break it, tear it, I can't bear it.") During the ensemble, Musette and Marcel fall into each other's arms. The friends wish to pay the bill, but to their consternation find Schaunard's riches gone. Musette has the entire bill charged to Alcindor. The police appear, and they rush in all directions. Marcel and Collin carry Musette out on their arms amid the applause of the spectators. When all have gone, Alcindor arrives with the shoe seeking Musette. The waiter hands him the bill, and horror-stricken at the amount he sinks upon a chair.

ACT III. At the toll gate. (Chorus: "Pass the glass! Let each toast his lass!") Clothing peddlers come to the city. Mimi, coughing violently, wishes to speak to Marcel, who resides in a little tavern near the barrier where he paints signs for the innkeeper. She tells him of her hard life with Rudolf, who has abandoned her that night. (Mimi: "O good Marcel.") Marcel tells her that Rudolf is sleeping at the inn. He has just awakened and is seeking Marcel. Mimi conceals herself. Rudolf speaks of her deadly illness. (Rudolf: "Love in my heart was dying.") Marcel, out of charity for Mimi, endeavours to silence him, but she has already heard all. She is discovered by her coughing. Marcel joins Musette, Rudolf and Mimi are about to separate, but are finally reconciled. (Duet: "Adieu, glad awakenings.") Musette approaches with Marcel, who is jealous. They depart after a fierce quarrel. (Duet, Musette, Marcel: "You were laughing, you were flirting.")

ACT IV. Garret room. Marcel and Rudolf are seemingly at work. (Duet: "Ah Mimi, ah Musette.") Schaunard and Collin arrive with the dinner. They parody a plentiful banquet, dance and sing. (Quartet: "Now take your partners.") Musette and the suffering Mimi appear; all assist the dying girl. Mimi and Rudolf, left alone, recall their past happiness. (Duet, Mimi, Rudolf: "Have they left us?") The others return, and while Musette prays aloud, Mimi dies. (Prayer, Musette: "O virgin, save.")

LA DAME BLANCHE

(The White Lady)

Comic opera in three acts by Boieldieu. Text by Scribe.

CAST: Gaveston, in charge of the castle of the former Count of Avenell—Basso. Anna, his ward—Soprano. George, a young English officer—Tenor. Dickson, farmer—Tenor. Jenny, his wife—Soprano. Margaret, housekeeper at the castle—Alto. Mac Irton, justice of the peace—Basso. Place, Scotland. Time, 1759. First production, Paris, 1825.

The young officer, George Brown, arrives in time to become godfather to the child of farmer Dickson, who has been left in the lurch by the friend selected for this honour. Dickson is of a very timorous nature; he has once received assistance in the shape of banknotes from the spectral white lady of the castle, and promised her his services in return. He receives a mysterious letter, inviting him to come to the castle in the evening. George offers to go in his place. Notwithstanding the distrustful behaviour of Gaveston, the housekeeper Margaret allows George to enter the castle, and assigns him a room. A lady in white appears, who in the darkness addresses him as Dickson, and asks him to outbid the other bidders at the sale of the castle, which is to be held in the morning, to prevent it from falling into the hands of Gaveston, and to retain it for the heir of the Count Avenell, who has disappeared. The spectre is really Anna, Gaveston's ward, who is in possession of the fortune of the count, and is keeping it for the heir. She is frightened when she finds a stranger in the castle, but recognises in George the brave young officer she had once tended when he was wounded. She promises to meet him the next day if he will carry out the undertaking intended for Dickson. George agrees, and the sale takes place. The farmers of the neighbourhood have combined to prevent the castle from falling into the hands of

Gaveston, as was Anna's intention, and bid until they can no longer compete with Gaveston. He is certain of having succeeded in securing the property, when George appears, and bids so high that Gaveston can hold out no longer and is wild with anger. . The castle is sold to the lieutenant, but Anna, who whispered to him to bid, promises to bring the money the following day. Everything is made plain. Anna brings the money, and George, who is recognised as Julius of Avenell, the rightful heir, marries Anna, and she explains that she and the white lady are one and the same.

ACT I.   Before Dickson's house with a view of the castle in the distance. (Chorus of mountaineers, who are coming to the christening: "Let the music play.") Dickson announces that the festival must be postponed, as the judge who was to be godfather has not arrived. (Entrance of George and aria: "Oh what joy to be a soldier.") His amiable manners encourage Jenny, Dickson's wife, to ask him to be godfather to the child, to which he consents. (Terzett with chorus: "I see my little wife approach.") Every one drinks, and Jenny narrates the tale of the white lady. (Ballet and chorus: "Observe the castle with its turrets.") Dickson and the other farmers retire and talk of the auction sale of the castle to be held next day. George remains with Jenny. (Duet: "He goes and leaves us alone?") When Dickson returns he timorously narrates his experience with the white lady, and George promises to go to meet her in his place. (Terzett and finale: "I cannot understand it.")

ACT II.   Gothic room in the castle. (Aria of Margaret: "Spin, poor Margaret.") When Gaveston and Anna enter the entrance bell rings. (Terzett: "Hark, they ring the bell at the gate.") Anna departs, and Margaret, having admitted George, assigns him a room for the night. He makes himself comfortable in an armchair and calls for the white lady. (Cavatina: "Come, gracious lady.") Anna appears as the white lady. (Duet: "This castle belongs to

Count Avenell of right.")   Day breaks.   The auction begins and Gaveston is defeated by George.

Act III.   Hall with portraits of ancestors.   Anna expresses her joy at the success of her plan.   (Aria: "My feet tread on air.")   The people congratulate George, who gazes around the hall, and is beset with dim memories of the past.   Anna has fallen in love with George, and recognises in him the rightful heir, and one far above her in station.   Old Margaret also recognises him.   (Duet, Anna, Margaret: "My dear young lady, much news have I to relate.")   The hour of payment arrives, and with it the white lady, visible to all, who delivers to George his property and declares him to be Julius of Avenell, the rightful heir. Angrily Gaveston tears the veil from the white lady's face, and Anna stands before him.   His game is lost, he leaves the castle, and Julius and Anna are happily united.

LA FAVORITA

Opera in four acts by Donizetti.   Libretto by Scribe.

Cast: Alfonso XI, King of Castile—Baritone.   Leonore de Guzman—Mezzo-soprano.   Fernando—Tenor.   Balthasar, Prior of the Monastery of St. Jacob—Basso.   Don Gasparo, officer of the king—Tenor.   Inez, confidante to Leonore—Soprano.   Place, Castile.   Time, 1340.   First production, Paris, 1840.

Fernando, a novice in the monastery of San Iago de Compostella, is destined to become the successor of the prior. He had seen and loved Leonore, who is unknown to him. Finding his love returned, he leaves the monastery.   Ignorant that Leonore is the mistress of the king, he is made an officer through her influence, distinguishes himself for bravery in the wars against the Moors, and saves the life of the king.   Alfonso is compelled by the pope to discard Leonore, and gives her to Fernando as his wife.   Leonore intends to disclose all to Fernando before their marriage, but her message goes astray, and he only discovers subsequently that his wife has been the king's favourite. He bids farewell to love, breaks his sword before the king, and returns to the monastery.

ACT I. Chorus of monks and scene between Balthasar and Fernando. (Fernando's romance: "A woman, beautiful, whom I never saw"; Duet: "You, my son, my only hope.") Scene between Fernando, Inez and Leonore. (Duet: "My loved one, God sends you"; Fernando's aria: "Yes, to new life feel I uplifted.")

ACT II. In the palace of the king. Scene between Alfonso and Gasparo, then Leonore, then Balthasar, who brings the threat of the ban of the pope.

ACT III. The same. Fernando and Alfonso, then Leonore. (Terzett: "Fernando? before him covered with shame.") Leonore alone. (Aria: "Oh, my Fernando, for you would I give all treasures of the world"; Chorus: "See the chapel lightened by shining rays"; Finale: "Brightest fortune smiles on me this day.")

ACT IV. In the monastery. Fernando comes to Balthasar. ("When once I left thee for world's alarms.") Leonore seeks Fernando, but in spite of her pleading he takes the vows.

LA DOLORES

Lyrical drama by Tómas Breton. Libretto by the composer.

CAST: Dolores—Soprano. Gaspara, an innkeeper—Mezzo-soprano. Lazaro, her son—Tenor. Celemino—Tenor. Melchior, a barber—Baritone. Patrizio—Baritone. Rojas, a sergeant—Basso. A muleteer—Tenor. Place, Calatayud, Spain. Time, the present. First production, Madrid, 1895.

ACT I. Market place in Calatayud. Venders selling their produce, women washing clothes, workmen, townspeople. (Chorus of workers: "Rub! rub! it's a feast day to-morrow.") Patrizio and Celemino are seated at a table before the inn kept by Gaspara, talking of Dolores, a beautiful wild creature employed as servant there. (Muleteer's song: "The heart has but two strings.") Patrizio, who has money, wishes to marry her; Celemino discourages him. A troop of soldiers enter, preceded by a crowd of small boys imitating the fife and drum. (Chorus: "Plan, rataplan.") They stand at attention, while Rojas, the sergeant, enters pompously, ironically cheered by the crowd. (Rojas: "I am a valiant soldier.") Celemino and Patrizio ask him to drink with them. Dolores brings in wine, mocking both Rojas and Patrizio for making love to her (Terzett: "He who my honour means to buy"), ending by sitting at the table and drinking with them. Celemino departs. (Dolores, Patrizio, Rojas: "Ha! ha! ha! here's to luck.") Lazaro, son of Gaspara, who is being educated for the priesthood, comes in, looking sadly at Dolores, whom he secretly loves. He gives her a message from his mother, and Dolores answers gently. Melchior, a barber, enters. When the others depart Dolores tells him she hears rumours of his marriage. "True rumours, for once," replies Melchior. Dolores flies into a frenzy of rage. "Give up this marriage, cursed of God," she cries repeatedly, "Restore to me my honour." Melchior laughs scornfully. Dolores curses him. (Dolores: "Cursed be the hour in which thou wast born.") Melchior replies: "I was born cruel and I will bring you to my feet." Patrizio now enters with a merry company, the chorus of the Rondalla, who are imitating various musical instruments. They dance the *Jota*, the national dance of Aragon, in which the principal guests in turn improvise couplets in tune to the music. Melchior, being called upon, jeeringly sings: "If you should go to Calatayud, ask for the lovely Dolores, who grants her favours to all." Dolores is beside herself with rage.

ACT II. The courtyard of the inn. Gaspara enters with her son Lazaro, to whom she speaks of his coming ordination. She goes out and Lazaro sings of his hopeless love for Dolores. ("O God, what shall I do?" Madrigal: "A holy ardent love.") Patrizio, Rojas and Celemino appear, the former quarrelsome through drink and weary of the boastful sergeant. Rojas explains in a spirited song how easily he can win the bull fight. (Rojas: "While the music goes faster and faster.") Melchior enters, boasting that he is the lover of Dolores. She, appearing with a guitar, tries to drown his words, growing more and more excited. Warning her, he goes out with the others, who presently return, making the sign of the cross. They tell Dolores what he has said. She laughs loudly, denying it, but Melchior is to come to her room that night. Lazaro enters when the others depart, and declares his love for Dolores. She is at first incredulous, having looked upon him as a boy. "Can the night go to the day?" she cries, and Lazaro replies: "For a year your dear image has been in my heart." He clasps her in his arms in an ecstasy of joy. The people, headed by Celemino, enter with rude jests. Lazaro angrily strikes Celemino. The bull fight is about to begin; the people are hurrying to the arena. (Chorus: "Huzza! hear the tumult.") Patrizio and Celemino describe the scene. Rojas is getting the worst of it, and Lazaro, seeing that his life is in danger, leaps into the arena and kills the bull. The populace applaud. Dolores promises Lazaro her love.

Act III. A room in the inn. Lazaro is chanting the Litany, while the people kneel in prayer. Gaspara bids her son good-night; Dolores whispers to him that he must not come to her room that evening. Celemino, taking him aside, informs him of Melchior's boasts about Dolores, but Lazaro will not listen. Dolores asks Rojas and Patrizio to come to her room at ten o'clock. She fears Melchior, and does not know whether he will come or what he intends to do. She first tells Gaspara that Lazaro loves her. The mother is horrified—"What, a priest? Sacrilege!" Dolores goes to her chamber. Melchior soon appears, and in a

terrible scene he insults and tortures the now desperate
girl. Just as she is at the end of her strength, Lazaro
bursts into the room almost distraught. He attacks Melchior, and in the struggle the two men fall through the
window. Lazaro has declared that he will kill Dolores also.
He returns, covered with blood, and is barely inside the
room when loud knocks are heard. Dolores refuses to unlock the door, and it is broken down. Celemino, Patrizio,
Rojas and Gaspara rush in followed by a curious crowd.
"What is it, what has happened?" they ask. Dolores says
bravely: "Melchior insulted me and I have killed him."
"No," cries Lazaro, "I was the matador. She was an impure woman, and he a vile wretch who made her so. He is
dead by my hand."

L'AFRICAINE

Grand opera in five acts by Meyerbeer. Libretto by Scribe.
CAST: Don Pedro, Councillor to the King of Portugal—
Basso. Don Diego, admiral—Basso. Inez, his daughter—
Soprano. Vasco de Gama, officer—Tenor. Don Alvar—
Tenor. Grand Inquisitor—Basso. Nelusko—Baritone.
Selika—Soprano. Chief priest of Brahma—Basso. Scene
of action: Act I. The council chamber at Lisbon. Act II.
Prison at Lisbon. Act III. On board the admiral's ship.
Act IV and V. India. The opera was written in 1860, but
only produced at Paris in 1865, one year after the death
of the composer.

ACT I. Inez loves Vasco de Gama, but is about to be
married to Don Pedro. Her lover is at sea with Bartholome
Diaz, endeavouring to discover the route to India. As she
is lamenting his absence (Romance: "Adieu, dear Tagus"),
Diego and Pedro appear. The latter tells Inez of the death
of Vasco. (Terzett: "Oh, childhood's love.") Meanwhile,
the council is in session deliberating about the fate of
Diaz. He, however, has perished, and the only survivor
of the expedition is Vasco de Gama, who, in proof of the

existence of the discovered country, brings with him as
slaves Nelusko and Selika. Vasco asks the council for a
new ship, but is refused through the influence of Don
Pedro. Becoming enraged, he is cast into prison. Don
Pedro discovers Vasco's charts, and determines to make use
of them.

Act II. Vasco lies asleep in prison; Selika, who loves
him, guards his slumbers. (Aria: "In my lap rest thy
weary head.") She saves him from the rage and jealousy
of Nelusko (Nelusko: "Daughter of kings"), who attempts
his murder. A duet follows, in which Selika discloses to
Vasco the route to her home. (Duet: "In vain their powerless fury.") Inez, arriving with Don Pedro, announces
Vasco's release, which she has accomplished by marrying
his rival. Vasco presents Selika to Inez as a wedding gift.
Don Pedro has been appointed commander of a new expedition, and engages Nelusko as steersman.

Act III. Nelusko stands at the helm of the admiral's
ship, now commanded by Don Pedro; Don Alvar warns
the latter against Nelusko, but fails to shake Don Pedro's
confidence. Nelusko expresses his delight in a song.
("Adamastor, the king of the waves.") Vasco follows Don
Pedro in another ship, and approaches in a boat to give
warning, but is put into irons by Don Pedro. The ship is
attacked by the Indians, and all on board are killed or imprisoned with the exception of Vasco, who is saved by
Selika, the queen of the tribe.

Act IV. Grand festival of the Indians with ballet.
Selika is compelled by the chief priest of Brahma to swear
destruction to all strangers, but saves Vasco, who is enchanted with the beauty of the land. (Aria, Vasco: "Oh
wonderful country"), by declaring him to be her husband.
Vasco, touched by the self-sacrifice of Selika, who now proposes his secret departure, resolves to remain. Weak
of character, however, upon hearing the voice of Inez,
who is being borne to execution, he leaves Selika once
more.

ACT V. Selika magnanimously frees Vasco and Inez. She directs Nelusko to escort them to a vessel, and they set sail for Portugal. When she knows that they are safely on board Selika lies down beneath the Manzanillo tree, having eaten of its poisonous flowers, and expires, attended by the faithful Nelusko. (Finale: "What wondrous music.")

LA GIOCONDA

Opera in four acts by Ponchielli. Libretto by Tobia Garrio (Arrigo Boito).

CAST: La Gioconda, a ballad singer—Soprano. La Cieca, her blind mother—Contralto. Alvise Badoëro, inquisitor—Basso. Laura, his wife—Mezzo-soprano. Enzo Grimaldo, a Genoese noble—Tenor. Barnaba, a spy—Baritone. Zuane, a boatman—Basso. Isepo, a letter-writer—Tenor. A pilot—Basso. Monks, senators, sailors, ladies, masqueraders, populace. Scene, Venice. Time, the seventeenth century. First production, Milan, 1876.

ACT I. The Lion's Mouth. Grand court of the ducal palace at Venice. Festival; crowd in holiday attire, some masked. Barnaba, a spy of the Inquisition, gloats over the secrets he has learned and schemes to accomplish the ruin of Gioconda, a ballad singer, who presently enters with her blind mother. (Terzett, Barnaba, Gioconda, La Cieca: "Daughter, by thee my faltering steps"; Recitative: "Erelong the vesper chimes"; Gioconda: "Go, I despise thee!") A regatta has taken place; the winner is carried in on the shoulders of the people. Gioconda having slipped away, Barnaba declares that Zuane, the defeated boatman, who stands gloomily apart, is the victim of La Cieca's witchcraft. The people rush at her, crying: "Kill the witch!" Gioconda returns with Enzo, whom she had been seeking. They are attempting to rescue La Cieca, when Laura enters, masked. Through an appeal to her the blind woman is released (La Cieca: "Thanks to thee, angelic voice"), and in gratitude gives her a rosary. Laura learns that Enzo, whom she loves, and to whom she was once affianced, is now betrothed to Gioconda; but Barnaba, observing Enzo's infatuation for Laura, proposes to him a meeting with her on board Enzo's ship, during her husband's absence. (Duet, Enzo, Barnaba: "Ah, with what joy my heart is filled.") Barnaba, leaving Enzo, orders Isepo, a letter-writer, to send word to Laura's husband that she is about to elope with Enzo. Gioconda, heart-broken, overhears them. (Barnaba: "O mighty monument.") A crowd appears singing and dancing the Furlana. Strains of religious music sound from the church. (Chorus of prayer: "*Angele dei.*")

ACT II. The Rosary. On board Enzo's ship, the *Hecate*, at night. (Marinesca: "Heave—ho, heave—ho, look to the rudder.") Barnaba rejoices over his success. Enzo comes from below to take his watch. (Enzo: "Heaven and ocean!") Laura draws near in a boat. (Duet: "Who comes?") Love scene, after which Enzo goes below, while Laura kneels before the Virgin's shrine. (Laura: "Star of the Mariner.") Gioconda, who has hidden herself on the ship, comes forward, masked, and as Laura prays for a blessing, says violently, "A curse, rather." (Duet: "Who art thou?" Gioconda: "In my grasp now I hold thee.") Gioconda tries to stab Laura, first informing her that her husband is approaching by sea. Laura calls on the Virgin, holding up La Cieca's rosary. Gioconda recognises it, and resolves to save her. Enzo returns seeking Laura, who is now on board Gioconda's boat. The latter tells him she has fled, conscience-stricken, and that Barnaba has betrayed them. (Finale, Gioconda, Enzo: "I've saved her.") Sailors rush about in excitement, while Enzo sets fire to the ship. All escape by taking to the boats.

ACT III. House of Gold. Alvise, Laura's husband, determines her fate—death by poison. (Alvise: "Yes, to die

is her doom!") When she appears in ball dress, he denounces her, declaring that she must die. (Duet: "To die,
to die.") Lifting a curtain, he points to a funeral bier.
(Chorus, behind scenes: "Our gay songs are ending.") He
gives her a phial of poison, and departs. Gioconda, entering, substitutes for the phial a narcotic, which Laura
drinks. Gioconda, pouring the poison into the empty
phial, takes to flight. When Alvise returns he sees Laura
lying apparently dead. The guests enter. Alvise greets
them ceremoniously in the room adjoining the death chamber. Gioconda enters unnoticed. (Chorus: "House of
Gold"; Recitative, Alvise: "Thanks let me offer"; Dance of
the Hours; Scene and finale, Gioconda, Barnaba, La Cieca,
Chorus: "Come! On!") La Cieca tells the guests that
Laura is dead. Amid general excitement Enzo enters. He
informs the guests of Alvise's former treachery in taking
Laura, then his betrothed, from him. Alvise draws aside
the curtain, and the guests in horror behold Laura pale
and lifeless.

ACT IV. The Orfano canal. Gioconda alone in a deserted house. Two men carry in the unconscious Laura,
refusing the money which Gioconda offers them. (Gioconda: "No one has seen you?") She asks their aid in
finding her mother, who has strangely disappeared. When
they depart, she determines to take poison. (Gioconda:
"Yes, suicide, the sole resource now left me.") She is
tempted to kill Laura first, but resists. Enzo, entering,
finds her in tears. She tells him Laura has been removed
from the tomb. To her joy, he is about to kill her, when
Laura feebly calls, and he hastens to her side. Gioconda
veils her face from their rapture. (Terzett: "The poison·
meant for Laura.") She helps them to escape in a boat,
and bids them farewell. She returns to the dark, empty
house to end her life (Gioconda: "Now I can die"), but
her enemy Barnaba comes to claim her. She stands before the mirror, adorning herself, and singing a gay little
song. Suddenly she stabs herself. Barnaba, in rage,

shrieks into her dying ears that he has strangled her mother. Even this cruel satisfaction is denied him, for Gioconda is dead. With a furious curse, he rushes out of the house.

LAKME

Opera in three acts by Delibes. Text by Goudinet and Grille.

CAST: Gerald and Frederick, officers of the English army in India—Tenor and Baritone. Nilakantha, a Brahmin —Basso. Lakme, his daughter—Soprano. Mallika, her companion—Contralto. Hadji, servant—Tenor. Ellen and Rose, daughters of the Viceroy—Soprani. Miss Benson, their governess—Contralto. Place, an English possession in India. Time, the present. First production, Paris, 1883.

ACT I. Hindoo temple in a sacred grove. (Chorus of Hindoos: "May our prayers ascend!") Lakme, with her slave Mallika, goes into the jungle to gather flowers for the altar. (Duet: " 'Neath the dome.") Gerald, a young officer, enters with his friend Frederick. They are accompanied by the two daughters of the viceroy and their governess (Quintet: "If a maiden's young and charming"), who wander about the grove curiously examining everything they see. Gerald remains alone to make a sketch. (Gerald: "Vagrant fancies, ye shall not deceive me.") Lakme returns in a boat (Lakme: "In the jungle, ever would I roam"); she sees Gerald (Lakme: "Whence come you?") and they fall in love with each other. They are interrupted by the entrance of Nilakantha, who has a fanatical hatred of foreigners. Gerald departs, followed by the threats of the priest.

ACT II. A market place. (Chorus: "Come, before the noon bell ringeth.") Dance of the Bayadères. At the command of her father (Nilakantha: "Lakme, some grief your glance is veiling"), who is in the crowd disguised as a beggar, Lakme sings (Lakme: "Where goes the maiden straying") to an accompaniment of bells. Nilakantha hopes that Gerald will be attracted by her voice. (Nilakantha: " 'Mid the songs of mirth and pleasure.") Gerald at last appears (Gerald: "Lakme, I see but thee!") and is stabbed by the priest. (Chorus of Hindoos: "Dourga, hear our prayer!") He is left for dead, but Lakme, still finding signs of life, has him carried away by her servant, Hadji.

Act III.   A hut in the jungle. Lakme has nursed Gerald back to life (Lakme: " 'Neath the starry heavens"), when he hears in the distance the voices of soldiers, and the music of the regimental band. Frederick appears during Lakme's absence to seek a cooling draught for her lover, and reminds him of his duty. (Gerald: "Lakme, ah come.") Lakme returns, and seeing that Gerald desires to go, poisons herself with the juice of a flower, and dies (Lakme: "Love, thou hast given me beauteous dreams") as the soldiers approach. (Chorus of soldiers: "Be ready; be steady.")

LA MUETTE DE PORTICI

(Masaniello)

Opera in five acts by Auber.   Text by Scribe.

Cast: Alfonso, Count of Arcos, son of the Viceroy of Naples—Tenor. Elvira, his betrothed—Soprano. Lorenzo, Alfonso's confidant—Tenor. Masaniello, Neapolitan fisherman—Tenor. Fenella, his sister, a mute—Dramatic rôle. Selva, captain of the Spanish guard—Basso. Borella, Pietro and Morena, friends of Masaniello—Tenori and Basso. A court lady—Contralto. Place, Naples and Portici. Time, 1647. First production, Paris, 1828.

Masaniello's sister Fenella, a mute, has been outraged and then imprisoned by Alfonso, son of the viceroy. She escapes, and Masaniello, who can no longer endure the viceroy's oppression of his people, leads an insurrection against him. When Selva, the captain of the guard, attempts to arrest Fenella once more, Masaniello stabs him and gives his followers the signal for revolt. Alfonso and Elvira, his betrothed, who have fled, seek refuge in Masaniello's hut. Not knowing them, he promises them shelter and keeps his word, even when he ascertains their identity. He is offered the crown of Naples and accepts it, but is given poison by his former friend, Pietro, through jealousy, and becomes insane. Alfonso returns with an increased force to overcome the rebellion. Masaniello once more leads the people against him, and falls in battle. Upon the news of the death of Masaniello, Fenella plunges into the sea and is drowned.

Act I. Before a chapel in Naples. (Chorus, and aria of Alfonso: "O thou, destined to grief.") Lorenzo, Alfonso's friend and confidant, seeks Fenella, who has escaped, but cannot find her. Alfonso loves her fervently, although she is dumb, and he is betrothed to Elvira. (Elvira's aria: "The glamour of joy.") Fenella flies to Elvira for refuge, telling her by means of signs that her love had been unhappy, and that Selva, captain of the guard, had thrown her into prison, whence she had escaped. Elvira promises protection. Alfonso and Elvira celebrate their marriage, Fenella recognises in the bridegroom her lover, points him out to Elvira as her seducer, and then disappears.

Act II. By the seashore. (Chorus of fishermen: "Up, friends, the morn appears"; Masaniello, barcarole: "See, the morn in brilliance.") Pietro, who has also been seeking Fenella, approaches. (Duet: "Rather death than a shameful life.") Fenella suddenly appears, falls into Masaniello's arms and confesses her shame. Frenzied, he calls his companions to arms.

Act III. Market place at Naples. (Chorus: "Come, old, young, large and small"; Ballet: "Tarantelle.") Selva attempts to arrest Fenella once more and is slain by

Masaniello.   (Chorus, prayer: "Heavenly Father, have mercy.")

ACT IV. Hut of Masaniello. (Recitative, aria and scene of Masaniello: "Oh day of horrors.") He watches the slumber of his exhausted sister. (Lullaby: "Oh sweet slumber!") Pietro reports that the people are thirsting for the blood of Alfonso. He departs, and Alfonso and Elvira come to ask shelter of Fenella. She wishes to save her lover, but declares that her rival shall die. (Cavatina of Elvira: "Oh, spare my life.") Fenella relents, and asks Masaniello to protect both. He entertains them hospitably. The magistrates approach surrounded by the people and bring Masaniello the golden key of the city. Pietro recognises Alfonso. Masaniello, learning his identity, is enraged, but bound by his promise, saves him from the people's wrath. (Terzett and chorus: "You gave your word.") Masaniello accepts the crown of Naples and leaves the hut.

ACT V. Hall in the palace with distant view of Vesuvius. (Pietro and chorus, barcarole: "See, see, upon wild waves.") Borella reports the approach of Alfonso and his army; the people have faith in Masaniello, but he has become insane through poison given to him by the jealous Pietro. When he hears the name of Alfonso he calls his followers to arms and hastens to battle. Alfonso is victorious, Masaniello falls, and Fenella, ascending the terrace overlooking the bay, plunges into the sea and is drowned.

LA SERVA PADRONA

(The Maid as Mistress)

Comic opera in two acts by Pergolesi. Text by Nelli.
CAST: Pandolfo—Baritone. Serpina—Soprano. Scapin, silent. Produced at Naples, 1731, and in Paris, 1752, in Italian; in Paris, 1754, in French (La servante maitresse).

This work is the first genuine comic opera (opera-bouffe). There are only three characters in the cast.

The bachelor, Pandolfo, and Serpina, his maidservant, live amicably in the same house, but he does not think of marriage. Serpina has designs upon him, however, and determines to awaken his jealousy. She induces the servant Scapin to dress as a sailor who has come to sue for her hand, and when Pandolfo begins to fear that the supposed captain will take Serpina away from him, he marries her himself, and in this way the maid becomes the mistress.

LA SONNAMBULA

Opera in three acts by Bellini. Libretto by Romani.

Cast: Rodolfo—Baritone. Thérèse, wife of the miller—Soprano. Amina, an orphan, adopted by Thérèse—Soprano—Elvino, a well-to-do landholder—Tenor. Lisa, an innkeeper—Alto. Alexis, a peasant—Basso. A notary. Scene: A village in Switzerland. Period, the nineteenth century. First production, Milan, 1831.

Act I. A square in the village. (Chorus: "Cheers for Amina.") Friends congratulate Amina, who is about to marry Elvino. This grieves Lisa, who loves him, and for his sake has rejected Alexis, a young peasant. The people praise Amina. (Chorus: "Helvetia's finest flower is the lovely Amina.") Amina thanks the villagers for their kindness, especially her adopted mother, Thérèse. (Aria: "Let thy dear hand rest in mine.") Amina also wishes Lisa and Alexis to be as happy as she is, but Lisa is not responsive. Elvino enters and greets Amina affectionately. (Duet: "Take now the ring of fidelity.") A stranger approaches (Aria: "Once more my home I behold"), who gazes ardently at Amina in admiration of her beauty. He announces to the people that Rodolfo, the owner of the castle, still lives, and they tell him in return that a spectre appears there, and is seen nightly by the light of the misty moon. The stranger himself is Count Rodolfo, and when he pays court to Amina's beauty the jealousy of Elvino is aroused. (Duet: "I envy those amorous toyings.")

Act II. (Sometimes produced as the second scene of Act I.) Room at the inn. Rodolfo jokes with Lisa, who greets him as the count. A noise is heard, and Lisa hurries away. Amina enters Rodolfo's room, walking in her sleep. Believing that she is in her own home, she begins to disrobe. Lisa watches her, and actuated by jealousy, calls in Elvino and the neighbours. The sleeping Amina, discreetly left alone by Rodolfo, awakens to meet the eyes of Elvino, who, considering her faithless, thrusts her from him. No one believes in her innocence and the poor girl is heart-broken.

Act III. In the forest. The peasants are on their way to the castle to greet the count. (Chorus: "In the forest's cooling shade.") Amina meets Elvino, but is again repulsed by him. He declares their union dissolved, tearing from her hand the betrothal ring.

Change of scene: Fields with mill and a bridge. Alexis again courts Lisa, who refuses him, being informed by her friends that Elvino intends to make her his bride. Elvino approaches and corroborates the news to the great joy of Lisa. Count Rodolfo draws near, and explains the presence of Amina in his room by declaring her to be a somnambulist. Elvino refuses to believe it, but when Thérèse produces Lisa's handkerchief, thoughtlessly left in Rodolfo's room, he turns his back on her also. As Rodolfo is again declaring Amina innocent, to the astonishment of all, she herself appears, walking in her sleep over a bridge that shakes under her weight. (Amina: "The bells announce the wedding hour.") Elvino realises his mistake, and prompted by Rodolfo, softly approaches her. He places the ring on her finger, and she awakens to find herself in his arms. (Aria: "No words can tell the bliss I feel.")

LA TOSCA

Opera in three acts by Puccini. Text based on Sardou's drama by Illica and Giacosa.

CAST: Floria Tosca, a singer—Soprano. Mario Cavaradossi, a painter—Tenor. Baron Scarpia, chief of police—Baritone. Cesare Angelotti—Basso. A sacristan—Baritone. Spoletta, police agent—Tenor. A gaoler—Basso. A shepherd boy—Contralto. Scene, Rome. Time, about 1800. First production, Rome, 1900.

ACT I. Angelotti, an escaped political offender, seeks refuge in the church of Sant' Andrea alla Valle. Here his sister, the Marchesa Attavanti, while praying for his release, has unconsciously served as a model to the painter Cavaradossi for his picture of the Magdalen. As a sacristan enters followed by Cavaradossi, Angelotti conceals himself, but when the painter is alone once more, the two men talk together until they are interrupted by Tosca, a singer, beloved by Cavaradossi. She jealously imagines an intrigue with a woman, her fears being apparently confirmed by the picture. (Tosca: "Our soft nest, hidden amid the trees.") Appointing a meeting with her lover she departs. (Duet: "What eyes are like thine eyes, my queen.") Angelotti reappears, and his escape in woman's dress is planned. A cannon shot from the fortress warns him to flee. The sacristan returns surrounded by a laughing crowd of choir boys and acolytes. (Sacristan and chorus: "Quick! into the sacristy.") Scarpia, chief of police, in search of the escaped prisoner, finds the fan of the Marchesa, and the painter's basket emptied of food and wine. He is suspicious, and when Tosca returns, also suspicious, he watches her from behind a pillar. He arouses her jealousy by producing the fan, and she departs in anger. Ordering his agent to follow her, he passionately avows his love for the singer, then kneels devoutly in prayer. (Scarpia: "Twofold is the goal I aim at"; Chorus: "Rise to the heavens.")

Act II.   In the Farnese palace, Scarpia awaits Tosca's
arrival for supper.   Cynically he sings of amorous pleasure.   Spoletta, his agent, enters with Cavaradossi in cus-
tody, Angelotti having eluded him.   Scarpia closely questions the painter without result, and sends him to the torture chamber.   When Tosca appears (Scarpia: "Now, let
us talk of pure friendship") Scarpia describes to her in
detail her lover's anguish under torture.   She can hear
his groans, but is powerless to help him.   At last, utterly
prostrated, she divulges Angelotti's hiding-place.   The
painter is brought out, and in his pain and humiliation denounces Tosca for her betrayal of the secret.   Distant
drums announce the probable victory of Bonaparte over
Scarpia's forces.   Cavaradossi, exulting, is dragged away
to prison.   Tosca tries to follow him, but Scarpia holds
her back.   (Scarpia: "Venal, my enemies call me.")   He
avows his passion for her and demands her virtue as the
price of her lover's freedom.   During the struggle drums
are heard.   Tosca repulses Scarpia again and again
(Tosca: "Love and music have I lived for"; Scarpia: "Too
lovely art thou"), but finally pretends to yield.   Scarpia
then gives orders for a mock execution of Cavaradossi, and
Tosca also exacts a safe-conduct for herself and the painter
to leave the country.   She waits until he writes it, then,
having secured a knife from the table, stabs him as he advances to embrace her.   Having piously composed the body
for burial, she departs to the sound of drums in the distance.

Act III.   Cavaradossi in prison at dawn awaits his execution.   (Cavaradossi: "The heavens blaze with stars.")
Musing sadly on Tosca's beauty and their love, he writes
her a farewell letter.   She enters with the safe-conduct and
tells him her news (Tosca: "He asked thy life or my love"),
explaining the need for a mock execution.   He agrees to
this and they part happily.   (Cavaradossi: "O soft
hands"; Duet: "The time is short.")   But it happens that
the execution is real.   Cavaradossi lies dead, while Tosca

playfully compliments his marvellous acting. As she realises the truth Spoletta enters with soldiers, denouncing her as a murderess. He comes forward to take Tosca prisoner, but she forcibly thrusts him back, and leaping from the castle parapet is dashed to pieces.

LA TRAVIATA

(Violetta)

Opera in four acts by Verdi. Text by Piave, founded upon the novel by Dumas fils "La dame aux Camelias."

CAST: Violetta Valery—Soprano. Flora Beloix—Soprano. Annina, servant—Mezzo-soprano. Alfred Germont—Tenor. Germont ainé, his father—Baritone. Gaston de Létorières—Tenor. Baron Douphal—Baritone. Marquis d'Orbigny—Baritone. Dr. Grenvil—Basso. Joseph, servant. Place, Paris and vicinity. Time, about 1700. First production, Venice, 1853.

The frail Violetta Valery forms the acquaintance of Alfred Germont, and for love of him abandons her questionable life. They lead an idyllic existence in the country, until during Alfred's absence his father comes to Violetta and tells her that the future of Alfred and the fortunes of his sister have been destroyed by his connection with her. With growing remorse she listens to the pathetic words of old Germont, and through his influence leaves her lover, giving as explanation a desire for her old gay existence. In order to drown her grief, she plunges more wildly than ever into dissipation, and when met by Alfred at an entertainment is insulted by him. Violetta's admirer, Baron Douphal, challenges Alfred, and Violetta, already far from strong, is made seriously ill by the excitement. Old Germont, moved by compassion, and realising that Violetta's love is sincere, gives his consent to the union of the lovers. Alfred hastens to her side, understanding at last that Violetta had sacrificed herself for his sake, comes to beg her forgiveness, and she dies in his arms.

Act I.   Chamber of Violetta.   Ensemble of the guests. (Drinking song, Alfred and Violetta: "Who merrily enjoys this life"; Alfred's confession of love: "A year ago— so lovely, so charming"; Chorus: "Soon shines the light of day"; Scene and aria of Violetta: "Strange, very strange," and " 'Tis he, his handsome face.")

Act II.   Chamber in a country house.   (Alfred's scene: "Far from thee"; Aria: "Her eyes' magic charm"; Scene and duet, Violetta, Germont's father: "Mademoiselle Valery?" and "God gave me a daughter"; Scene, Violetta, Alfred: "What are you doing?" Scene of Alfred and aria of Germont: "In Provence, by the sea.")

Act III.   (Sometimes played as second scene of Act II.) At Flora's house.   (Scene and masked gipsy chorus: "We are gipsy girls"; Chorus of bull-fighters: "From the circus at Madrid.")   Scene, Violetta and Alfred, and challenge of Douphal.   Scene between Violetta, Germont and Alfred. (Violetta: "Alfred, you know not my love.")

Act IV.   Bedchamber of Violetta.   Scene between Violetta, Annina and physician.   Violetta reads the letter of Germont giving his consent to her union with Alfred. ("Farewell! past days of joy"; Scene and duet, Violetta, Alfred: "Oh, you my life, you my highest joy"; Aria, Violetta: "O great God"; Finale, Germont, Violetta, Alfred, with Violetta's death.)

LA VIE PARISIENNE

(Life in Paris)

Operetta in four acts by Jacques Offenbach. Text by Meilhac and Halévy.

Cast: Baron and Baroness von Gondermark. Baron von Gardefen. Baroness von Quimper. Bobinet, nephew of Baroness von Quimper. A rich Brazilian. Jean Frick,

shoemaker. Gabrielle, glovemaker. Metella, a demi-mondaine. Josef, servant of Gardefen. Urbain, Prosper, Clara, Pauline, servants of Baroness von Quimper, etc. Place, Paris. Time, the present. First production, Paris, 1866.
The Baron von Gardefen is bored. While lounging about he sees at the railway station the Baron von Gondermark and his wife, who are paying their first visit to Paris. The baroness pleases him, so he introduces himself as an employé of the Grand Hotel, and leads them to his own dwelling, where he induces the shoemaker, Jean Frick, and the glovemaker, Gabrielle, and their friends to represent the guests at the table d'hôte. Gondermark, who is impatient to plunge into the pleasures of the city, has been recommended to the elegant and beautiful *demi-mondaine* Metella by his friend, the Baron Frescata; but Gardefen, who desires to have the baroness to himself for the evening, has his friend Bobinet invite the stumbling block of a husband out to supper. Bobinet hurriedly arranges an evening festival, with the aid of the servants of his absent aunt, and pretends to Gondermark that he is in the midst of the *élite* of French society. The lovely girls charm the old countryman, he is perfectly happy, and ends by joining in a can can, which reaches extreme limits. During the absence of the husband Gardefen makes violent love to the baroness, but the latter is rescued by Bobinet's aunt, Baroness von Quimper. The would-be betrayer escapes, but the returning Gondermark is received by the valorous aunt with the fire shovel.

A brilliant ball, in which the entire cast appears, concludes the performance.

LE CID

Opera in three acts by Cornelius. Libretto by the composer.
CAST: Fernando, King of Castile—Tenor. Calvo, bishop —Basso. Chimène, Countess of Lozan—Soprano. Ruy

Diaz, Count of Bavar, called Cid Campeador—Baritone. Alvar Fannez—Tenor. Herald—Basso. Place, Burgos, Spain. Time, 1064. First production, Weimar, 1865.

ACT I. At the court of the king. Chimène accuses Ruy Diaz, to whom she is betrothed, of the murder of her father, and demands justice of the king. Diaz, who has been joyfully acclaimed by the people, defends himself for killing the count by declaring that he was slain in lawful combat for assailing the honour of Diaz, but to satisfy the daughter, he agrees to abide by the ordeal of combat. He throws down his gauntlet, which is lifted up by Alvar as the champion of Chimène. Bishop Calvo interferes, and persuaded by him, Diaz places his sword in the hands of Chimène. News arrives of a terrible assault by the Moors; it is believed that only Diaz as leader can save the day, as he is trusted by the people, and his love for his country prevails. Chimène hands the sword to the king, who delivers it to the young hero.

ACT II. The palace of Lozan. Chimène, her heart torn between vengeance and her awakening love for Diaz, dismisses her knight Alvar. When Diaz appears to bid her farewell before going into battle, her feelings of vengeance are overcome by love, and she bids him depart with her blessing.

ACT III. Before the gate of Burgos. Diaz has been successful in repulsing the Moors, and the people sing praises of his victory. Captive Moors acclaim the victor as Lord (Cid). When Diaz himself fails to appear, and Alvar lays the sword of the Cid at the feet of Chimène, reduced to despair, she openly avows her love. The Cid is not dead, however, and Alvar has merely come to announce his coming. Embraced by the king, and with the arms of Chimène around him, the hero receives his reward.

LE CID

Opera in four acts by Massenet. Text by D'Ennery, Gallet and Blau.

CAST: Chimène—Soprano. Count de Gormas, her father —Baritone. Roderigo (the Cid)—Tenor. Don Diego— his father—Basso. The King—Baritone. The Infanta— Soprano. Moorish envoy—Basso. Don Arias—Tenor. Don Alonzo—Basso. St. James—Baritone. Scene, Burgos, Spain. Time, the twelfth century. First production, Paris, 1885.

ACT I. Burgos. A salon at the house of the Count de Gormas. Don Arias tells the assembled friends of the count that the king will that day confer knighthood upon Don Roderigo, and that Count de Gormas will probably be appointed governor to the Infanta of Spain. Chimène, daughter of the count, enters, and her father informs her that he desires to arrange a marriage for her with Don Roderigo, son of his old friend Don Diego. Chimène cannot conceal her joy, for she already loves Roderigo. Left alone, she gives expression to her love. (Chimène: "Love! Love! I can show my love to the world.") The infanta enters sad and depressed. Chimène discovers that she, too, loves Roderigo. (Duet, Chimène, Infanta: "Leave the doubt in my soul.")

Change of scene: A gallery leading to the cathedral. (Chorus: "Blessed be the name of the Lord.") The king enters with his suite. Don Diego bows low before him. Roderigo passes along the gallery on his way to receive knighthood. The king confers this honour upon him. (Chorus: "May St. James and God your Father receive you as knight.") Roderigo replies in an impassioned apostrophe to his sword (Roderigo: "O noble gleaming blade"), and takes his vows. (Roderigo: "To St. James of Compostella have I pledged my faith.") He remains in ecstasy for a time, then, half-unconsciously, addresses his sword once more. The priests and people echo his words in a magnificent chorus. Roderigo repairs to the chapel according to custom, and the king, turning to Don Diego, appoints him governor, to the great chagrin of Count de Gormas and his friends. The count reproaches the king, who coldly departs in anger. De Gormas, now infuriated, denounces Don Diego, who has advanced to take his hand with a proposal of marriage for Roderigo with Chimène. (Don Diego: "To the honour which his majesty has done me add another.") The count laughs ironically, growing more and more insulting until at last he strikes the aged warrior. Don Diego draws his sword, which De Gormas wrests from him, departing with his friends, who jeer at the feeble old man. (Don Diego: "O rage, despair, O baneful feebleness.") Hearing his son's voice within the chapel, he determines in his humiliation to avoid him, then decides that it is Roderigo's duty to avenge his father's wrongs. Roderigo enters, Don Diego tells his story. The young knight is overcome, for De Gormas is the father of Chimène. (Don Diego: "He it was who struck me.") Chimène comes from the church looking earnestly at her lover. (Chimène, Roderigo: "O vows of love, eternal faithfulness.") She passes by. Roderigo is in despair, but swears to avenge his father.

Act II. A street in Burgos. (Roderigo: "Pierced to the heart's core"; "O God, this unaccustomed grief.") Roderigo comes forward and challenges the count, who has just entered. The count ridicules his youth, but is forced to draw his sword. (Roderigo, De Gormas: "Know'st thou Don Diego?") They fight, and De Gormas is mortally wounded. His friends rush in; Don Diego thanks his son for avenging him. Chimène appears, pale and dismayed. A requiem sounds from within. She demands the name of the murderer. All are silent, but she challenges every one present in turn. Roderigo's pallor shows her that he is the man she seeks. (Chimène: "No oblivion, no pardon"; Requiem: "*Requiem dona ei sempiternam Domine.*") Change of scene: the square at Burgos. Gay scene with dancing crowd. (Chorus: "Blest day of plenty.") The infanta enters, going about from group to group. (Infanta: "More torment, more sorrow.") Popular dances of the different provinces. The king arrives with his suite. Chimène appears and throws herself at his feet demanding justice. (Chimène: "Neither pity nor pardon.") Don Diego tells what occurred, but Chimène remains unmoved. (Chorus: "No! honour forbids!") The people take different sides, and in a scene of great excitement an envoy comes from the Moorish leader Boabdil, offering battle to Spain. The king takes up the challenge, but a leader must be found. Roderigo offers himself. The king accepts him. (Chorus: "On to the fray, Roderigo.")

Act III. Chimène's chamber at night. She sits alone in a despairing attitude. (Chimène: "Weep, O mine eyes!") Roderigo enters to bid her farewell. (Duet: "O days of first love.") Chimène is deeply moved by his words, but suddenly remembering her father's death recoils from him in horror. Roderigo gloomily speaks of death, but Chimène arouses him to action by a spirited description of the coming fight. Roderigo, overwhelmed by her apparent forgiveness, tells her he will return a conqueror. (Roderigo: "To arms, Navarrais, Moors, and Castilians.") Change of scene: The Spanish camp. Soldiers carousing. Prisoners in chains. (Chorus: "Let us live without fear or remorse.") Roderigo upbraids the men for their lethargy, when a Moorish army surrounds them. He calls them to arms. Many of them refuse to fight, but a faithful band stand by their leader, who keeps watch all night. Change of scene: Roderigo's tent. He is alone, on guard. (Roderigo: "O Sovereign, Father, Judge, always veiled, always at hand.") He submits himself to the will of God. A vision of St. James announces a coming victory. He arouses his comrades. (Roderigo: "O noble gleaming blade.")

Act IV. Granada. Hall in the palace. Roderigo's cowardly companions have returned with news of his death.

(Don Diego: "He has nobly done what honour counselled.") Unable to confront the father's trust in his son,
they retire confused. Chimène and the infanta hear the
sorrowful tidings. (Chimène, Don Diego, Infanta: "O
heart twice broken.") Chimène openly declares her love.
(Chimène: "Yes, I loved him still.") The king appears on
the threshold. "Why do you weep," he asks, "when all are
filled with joy?" Roderigo, he tells them, is not dead, but
is returning victorious. Change of scene: The palace court.
Soldiers march by. (Chorus: "Glory to him whom the
Moorish kings have acclaimed their lord.") The Moorish
kings are led in chains in the triumphal procession. Roderigo enters, and kneels before the king. (Roderigo: "O
king, from thy hand did I take this sword.") The king
offers him any reward he desires, but he asks only for the
forgiveness of Chimène. Amid the plaudits of the people
she places her hand in his. (Chorus: "Glory to the Cid, the
conqueror.")

L'ÉCLAIR

Comic opera in three acts by Halévy. Libretto adapted
from the French by Fredericke Elmenreich.

Cast: Madame Darbel, a young widow—Soprano. Henrietta, her sister—Soprano. George, their cousin—Tenor.
Lionel, officer—Tenor. Place, a plantation near Boston.
Time, 1797. First production, Paris, 1835. This opera
has no chorus.

Act I. A room in the country house of Henrietta. She
loves the country, but the lively Madame Darbel only finds
pleasure in the crowds of the city. Their cousin George arrives from England, and informs them that they and he
have inherited the wealth of an uncle, with the sole condition that George shall marry in twenty-one days either one
of his cousins. (Aria and terzett: "I come from England's
shores.") The ladies excuse themselves and George is left

alone. He falls asleep and is awakened by a terrific thunder storm. Henrietta enters the house with Lionel, whom she has just saved from drowning. His boat was struck by lightning, and he has become blind.

Act II. Aria by Madame Darbel. ("Yes, I have just arrived.") She is welcomed by her relatives. Lionel enters; thinking he is alone, he laments his fate. (Quartet: "Be quiet, be still, he appears.") Henrietta, who has learned to love him, approaches. (Duet: "Oh, how my heart is filled with joy.") The time arrives when the physician is to operate on the patient. Lionel is cured, but when he regains his sight, to the distress of Henrietta he believes Madame Darbel to be his rescuer.

Act III. Lionel has discovered his mistake. (Aria: "When still the night with covered veil.") Henrietta, who has fled to Boston, returns with the belief that Lionel and her sister are betrothed. Joy reigns when the misunderstanding is cleared up, and Henrietta and Lionel are joined in marriage, while Madame Darbel willingly gives her hand to her cousin.

LE DOMINO NOIR
(The Black Domino)

Opera in three acts by Auber. Text by Scribe.

Cast: Lord Elfort—Baritone. Count Juliano—Tenor. Horatio of Massarena—Tenor. Gil Perez, bailiff of the royal nunnery—Basso. Angela—Mezzo-soprano. Brigitta —Soprano. Claudia, Juliano's housekeeper—Alto. Ursula, a nun—Soprano. Gertrude, doorkeeper. Place, Madrid. First production, Paris, 1837.

A year previous to the period of the opera Angela, the abbess of the royal convent, has met and loved Horatio at a masked ball. She again visits a similar ball with Brigitta in the hope of meeting Horatio, which hope is fulfilled. Engaged in loving conversation, the hour for returning has passed, and Angela enters the house of Count Juliano, a friend of Horatio, where she is introduced by the house-keeper Claudia as her niece. When Gil Perez, the bailiff of the convent, comes upon a visit to Claudia, Angela frightens him with her mask, takes his keys and thus obtains entrance to the convent. Horatio, who comes to the convent to obtain dispensation from the abbess from a forced marriage, recognises Angela. She is released from her vows by the queen and Horatio marries her.

ACT I. Antechamber of the ballroom. (Terzett, Angela, Brigitta, Horatio: "Is everything prepared?" Romance of Angela: "A fairy"; Duet, Horatio, Angela: "Break this silence at last.")

ACT II. In the house of Count Juliano. (Claudia's arietta: "Much trouble and profit"; Ensemble: "Awake who loves and lives"; Angela's Aragonese song: "To see him daily"; Scene, Juliano, Horatio, Angela, Claudia, Chorus: "Impossible! it cannot be she!" Finale, Gil Perez: "To-day we receive, the Lord be thanked"; Angela: "Ha, dastard! You dare to approach me!" Claudia, Horatio, Juliano, Elfort and cavaliers: "Quiet and low!")

ACT III. The reception room at the convent. (Arietta of Brigitta: "Instead of wise, tedious lectures"; Recitative and aria of Angela: "Oh this night, in which I waked"; Cavatina: "Night of destiny, flames which I kindled"; Ensemble of nuns; Aria and prayer of Horatio: "Sweet strains"; Finale, Angela and ladies: "Dear sisters, hear what the queen has ordered.")

L'ELISIR D'AMORE

(The Love Potion)

Comic opera in two acts by Donizetti. Text from the Italian of Romani by Ott.

CAST: Adina, a rich young landowner—Soprano. Nemorino, a young peasant—Tenor. Belcore, sergeant—Baritone. Dulcamara, a travelling quack—Basso. Gi-

anettina, a peasant—Soprano. A notary. A Moor in the
service of Dulcamara. Place, a village in Italy. First production, Milan, 1832. The same libretto, French by Scribe,
is the subject of the opera "Le Philtre," by Auber. Paris,
1831.

ACT I. Nemorino loves Adina, who does not believe that
love can be faithful. (Chorus of peasant women: "Before
the sun's rays"; Cavatina of Nemorino: "What loveliness
and grace"; Cavatina of Adina: "Nothing has been so
bizarre.") Adina also repulses the advances of the sergeant Belcore, who is more persistent than Nemorino.
(Cavatina of Belcore: "Like the handsome youth Paris.")
Nemorino cannot leave Adina. (Duet: "Ask the winds of
spring.") The quack Dulcamara enters the village. (Cavatina: "Hear and be astounded, you peasants.") He sells
a love potion, in reality a bottle of wine, which Nemorino
purchases. (Duet: "Take courage!") The young peasant drinks the contents of the bottle, and in his drunkenness treats Adina so coldly that she determines to win him
in spite. (Duet: "Tra la, not yet can I discover.") She
seemingly gives her consent to Belcore's suit (Terzett:
"Now must it be speedily done"), and the peasants rejoice
at the prospect of the feast.

ACT II. The wedding feast is held, but Adina refuses to
sign the marriage contract. Dulcamara sings a barcarole.
("Dear child, you are beautiful and I am rich.") The despairing Nemorino allows Belcore to enlist him in the army.
(Duet: "Twenty ducats? in shining gold?") The maidens
of the village arrive, bringing the news that Nemorino's
rich uncle is dead and has made him sole heir. (Chorus of
girls: "Can it be possible?") They all try to capture him,
and he believes the love potion is taking effect. (Quartet,
Nemorino, Adina, Dulcamara, Gianettina and chorus: "The
dose has done me good.") Dulcamara likewise offers his
love potion to Adina, but she refuses it, thinking she has
lost Nemorino forever. (Duet: "Oh, how cruel, this warm
love.") Nemorino (Romance: "Out of my heart") still

loves her.   Adina purchases his release from the army,
which proves her love, and they embrace.   Belcore resigns
his pretensions to Adina's hand, and Dulcamara, who pretends to attribute the happy result to the efficacy of his
love potion, does a good business in the village.

LE ROI DE LAHORE

Opera in four acts by Massenet.   Text by Gallet.
CAST: Alim, King of Lahore—Tenor.   Scindia, his minister—Baritone.   Timur, a priest—Basso.   Indra—Basso.
Sita—Soprano.   Kaled, confidant of the king—Mezzo-soprano.   Place, India.   Time, the eleventh century during
the incursion of the Mohammedans.   First production,
Paris, 1877.

The king of Lahore loves Sita, the niece of the high
priest Timur.   His rival, Scindia, reports the visits of a
lover to the temple, and Sita is condemned to death.   The
king now declares that he himself had visited Sita, and desires to make her his wife.   The Sultan Mahmud makes an
incursion into the country, and Scindia, having slain King
Alim in battle, ascends the throne.   The God Indra hears
Alim's prayers and allows him once more to visit the earth.
Sita is about to become the wife of Scindia, when Alim
appears in the guise of a beggar, and is recognised by her.
As Scindia attempts to carry Sita away from the temple,
she kills herself, and she and Alim are united by Indra after
death.

ACT I.   Before the temple of Indra.   Scindia asks Timur
for the hand of Sita, and when refused, he brings an
accusation against her virtue.   Sita is condemned to
death.

Change of scene: The interior of the temple.   Alim declares that he has visited Sita in the temple, and asks her
hand in marriage.

ACT II.   Alim's camp.   Alim is defeated by Mahmud and

dies. Scindia takes possession of the throne and carries
Sita away.

Act III. Indra's paradise. Ballet. Indra accedes to
Alim's prayer to return to earth and Sita once more on
condition that Sita's death shall forfeit his own life.

Act IV. Before the palace of Lahore. Scindia has defeated the Mohammedans and is about to marry Sita.
When Alim appears and claims Sita, Scindia has him arrested as a madman, but the priests protect him.

Change of scene: The interior of the temple. Scindia attempts with violence to remove Sita from the temple, but
she grasps Alim's dagger and stabs herself, according to
Indra's mandate. Alim dies with her. Apotheosis: Alim
and Sita are united in the paradise of Indra.

LE ROI L'A DIT!

Comic opera in three acts by Leo Delibes. Text by Goudinet.

Cast: Marquis of Moncontour—Basso. The Marquise—
Mezzo-soprano. Baron of Merlussac—Basso. Gautran,
minister of finance—Basso. Marquise de Flarambel—Soprano. Marquise de Bluette—Contralto. Javotte, maid—
Soprano. Mitou, professor of dancing—Tenor. Benoit,
a peasant—Tenor. Pacome, servant—Tenor. The four
daughters of the Marquis of Montcontour—Soprani.
Place, Versailles. Time, 1688. First production, Paris,
1873.

The favourite parrot of Madame de Maintenon has disappeared, and the Marquis of Montcontour has the luck to
capture it. Presented to Louis XIV he becomes confused,
and in answer to the king's question, says he has a son.
The king orders him to bring him to court. What is he
to do? He has only four daughters! But the king has
said it, and he must procure a son. Fortunately he finds a
bright peasant boy, Benoit, whom he adopts. The youth

readily assumes the manners of a gentleman, plays many pranks, lives the life of a grand seigneur, sets fire to the convent in which reside the four daughters of the marquis, and even has the effrontery to ask for the hand of one of them in marriage. Finally he fights a duel and is wounded. The marquis hurriedly takes advantage of this accident to proclaim him dead, and the king consoles him for his loss by creating him a duke. Benoit recovers speedily from his wound, and having fallen in love with the maid Javotte, he contents himself with marrying her.

LES CONTES D'HOFFMANN

Fantastic opera in three acts, a prologue and a closing scene, by Jacques Offenbach. Text by Jules Barbier.

CAST: The Poet Hoffmann. Olympia, Giulietta, Antonie, Stella, his mistresses. Lindorf, Coppelius, Dapertutto, Dr. Mirakel, his opponents. Luther, innkeeper. Nathanael, Hermann, students. Andreas, servant to Stella. Schlemihl, Giulietta's admirer. Spalanzani, an apothecary. Councillor Krespel, father of Antonie. The voice of the deceased mother of Antonie. Cochenilla. Pitichinaccio. Franz, servant to Krespel. Students, etc. The tales of the German author E. T. A. Hoffmann, translated into French, have been received with much favour; particularly those in the style of Callot of ghostly, mysterious or enigmatical character. This induced Barbier to write the text of this opera for Offenbach. The first production took place at Paris in 1880.

The action is as follows: The rich Lindorf loves the singer Stella. Hoffmann formerly had a love affair with the artist at Milan, and when she sees the young poet again at Nuremberg, her tenderness for him revives, and she writes to him appointing a meeting. Lindorf bribes Andreas, Stella's servant, obtains the letter, and resolves to make the poet drunk and then show him in that condition to Stella to disgust her with him. The action of the introduction shows Hoffmann in the midst of his friends, young students, at the inn of Luther. (Chorus of students: "Drig! Drig! Drig! Master Luther!" Hoffmann: "An ugly hump served him for stomach.") The same building contains the theatre in which Stella is to sing the rôle of Donna Anna in Mozart's "Don Giovanni." (Hoffmann: "She had a lovely face"; Chorus: "Luther is a splendid fellow.") Between the acts. Lindorf succeeds, Hoffmann is drunk and relates to his friends the story of his three love adventures with the automaton Olympia, the Venetian courtesan Giulietta and the singer Antonie. Each of these adventures takes up one act. The closing scene again shows Luther's inn, where Lindorf has brought Stella to witness the degradation of Hoffmann and thus win her for himself.

ACT I. Hoffmann falls in love with the beautiful Olympia. (Hoffmann: " 'Tis she! she sleeps.") Spalanzani, a mechanical genius, with the help of Coppelius, has constructed an automaton, which he exhibits to an astounded public as his daughter. Hoffmann is enraptured and desires to possess her, so Coppelius suggests that he write her an impassioned love letter. (Coppelius: "A doll with china eyes.") A meeting is appointed, but Olympia does not seem responsive. (Olympia: "The birds in the trees"; Hoffmann: "Sweet avowal.") Coppelius, having discovered that Spalanzani is cheating him, in revenge informs Hoffmann that he is about to marry a mechanical figure. (Chorus: "She dances in time.")

ACT II. The courtesan Giulietta is entertaining her admirers at Venice. (Duet, Giulietta, Dapertutto: "Fair night, O night of love"; Bacchic song: "Love, tender and dreamy"; Chorus: "Those who weep may go to the devil.") The favoured one is Schlemihl, the well-known character of Chamisso, who casts no shadow. Hoffmann is madly in love with the voluptuous woman. Hoffmann: "The sky lends thee its splendour"). Dapertutto, his enemy, who already owns Schlemihl's shadow, with the help of Giulietta, who is in his power, also acquires that of Hoffmann. (Dapertutto: "Turn here, turn there, thus one catches larks.") The courtesan beguiles the lovelorn poet, and he barters his shadow for her love. Giulietta, however, cruelly breaks her word (Giulietta: "Unlucky one, you did not know"), and leaves him in the hands of his enemies. (Chorus: "Fair night, O night of love!")

ACT III. The wife of Krespel during her life was a famous singer. Too great devotion to her art occasioned an illness, and the mysterious Dr. Mirakel caused her death with his strange mixtures instead of curing her. The daughter of Krespel, Antonie, inherits her mother's talent and devotion to music, but her father, who sees her slowly fading, forbids her to sing. Hoffmann forms her acquaintance. (Antonie: "Remembrance far too sweet.") They love, but Krespel is prejudiced against Hoffmann, for he too is fond of music, and may influence her to continue her studies. (Duet, Hoffmann, Antonie: " 'Tis a song of love.") Against the will of Krespel, Dr. Mirakel obtains entrance to their apartments. A quarrel ensues (Krespel, Mirakel: "Why, yes, I hear"), and by hellish arts the doctor causes the apparition of Antonie's dead mother to materialise and ask her to sing. (Antonie: "Ah, what is this voice"; Mirakel: "You will sing no more.") She does so, and falls dead. Krespel has lost his daughter and Hoffmann his bride, but Dr. Mirakel triumphs. In Coppelius, Dapertutto and Dr. Mirakel, as in Lindorf, we see Hoffmann's enemy, who by various and mysterious methods always takes from him the maiden he loves. He is really a fiend in different guises. Stella is reproduced in Olympia, Giulietta and Antoine, so that these four characters, and those of Hoffmann's enemies, are all impersonated by one male and one female singer. The character of Hoffmann, of course, is the same throughout.

In the epilogue Hoffmann is intoxicated and sings a

ribald song. (Hoffmann: "The last verse of the song is
for her.") He is left alone with his bottle. (Hoffmann:
"You are all that I have to embrace.")

LES PÊCHEURS DES PERLES
(The Pearl Fishers)

Opera in three acts by Bizet. Text by Carré and Cormon.
CAST: Leila, a priestess—Soprano. Nadir, a pearl-fisher
—Tenor. Zurga, a chief—Baritone. Nourabad, high
priest—Basso. Priests, priestesses, pearl-fishers, women,
etc. Scene, Ceylon. Time, barbaric period. First production, Paris, 1863.

ACT I. Shore of the island of Ceylon. A few scattered
huts and palm trees; in the distance an ancient pagoda.
The people are assembled for a ceremonial dance and festival. (Chorus: "On the strand.") Zurga announces that a
chief must be selected. They name Zurga himself with ac-
clamations. Nadir appears after a long absence in the
forest. (Nadir: "Plains and forests.") Zurga welcomes
him to a home with the tribe, and the dance continues, followed by an incantation to drive away evil spirits. Nadir
and Zurga hold converse together, renewing their friendship of former days. Nadir reminds his friend of a visit
to the temple, the calling to prayer by the Brahmins, the
kneeling crowd, and the sudden appearance of a woman
beautiful as a goddess, who passed through the throng and
vanished. Zurga and Nadir both fell in love with her, and
quarrelled for this reason. As Nadir ends his tale a boat
draws near, and Zurga relates how each year on a certain
day a woman comes to pray on the rocks above the village.
No one dares approach her, or look upon her face, but her
prayers protect and help the tribe. Leila, closely veiled,
steps from the boat, followed by Nourabad, the high priest.
The people await her in awe. (Chorus: "Deign to accept
our gifts.") They ask her intercession with the spirits

of the deep.   Adjured by Zurga, she promises to remain
veiled, to pray for the tribe night and day, to invoke good
and drive away evil, to be pure in word and deed.   Zurga,
in his turn, swears that if she keeps her oath, she will receive a pearl of great price, but if she breaks it, death
will be her lot.   Nadir, who has watched the ceremony with
deep interest, advances toward Leila, exclaiming, "How
hapless is her fate!"   She starts, and Nourabad, observing
this, tells her that even now, if she desires it, she may re-
voke her vows.   She adheres to her purpose, however, and
solemnly repeats the oath.   (Chorus: "Brahma, divine
Brahma, may thy hand protect us.")   Leila proceeds to
the temple with Nourabad; the people return to the shore.
Zurga approaches Nadir, who stands gazing after Leila.
She looks back.   Zurga grasps Nadir's hand, and slowly
follows the pearl-fishers.   The sun sets.   Nadir, alone, confesses that he has discovered the identity of the apparition in the temple, and following her, has heard her voice.
He determines to tell Zurga.   (Romance, Nadir: "Once
more I think I hear.")   Throwing himself on the ground,
he sleeps.   The returning priests build a fire on the rocks.
(Leila and chorus: "O Brahma, god, O sovereign master!"
Aria, Leila: "In the cloudless sky sown with stars.")   Nadir
awakens, recognising her voice.   He calls softly, and she
subtly answers in her song.   Under cover of the growing
darkness he hastens to her side.

ACT II.   Ruins of a temple.   A terrace looking upon
the sea.   (Chorus: "Darkness falls from the heavens.")
Nourabad advances toward Leila and tells her her solitary
watch will now begin.   She is trembling and fearful, but
he assures her that if she has kept her vow she need not
fear.   She tells him that once as a child she had saved a
fugitive from pursuit, and that she still possesses a chain
which he gave her in gratitude.   Nourabad departs and the
vigil begins.   (Leila: "I tremble, I fear.")   She hears the
cries of wild beasts in the jungle, and in the distance, gradually coming nearer, Nadir's song.   (Nadir: "O my beloved,

a hidden flower art thou!") Leila joins in his song (Duet: "By this narrow path"), and Nadir passionately declares his love. As they embrace, in ecstasy, Nourabad, who has been secretly watching them, calls on the people (Chorus: "What voice calls us?"), telling them that the priestess is false to her vow. He points to Nadir, who stands before Leila, protecting her. The pearl-fishers advance, threatening him with their knives, and demanding his punishment by death (Chorus: "No! Death! Death!"), but Zurga impulsively steps forward and commands them to depart. As Nourabad tears off Leila's veil, Zurga recognises her. A storm arises in fury. The people kneel in prayer. (Chorus: "Brahma, divine Brahma.") Nadir is carried off, and the priests lead Leila away. Change of scene: A tent by the sea. Zurga stands gloomily in the doorway (Recitative: "The storm is calmed"), suffering deep remorse for having condemned Nadir to death. (Zurga: "O Nadir, when I gave thee over to death.") He sinks on the ground in despair. Leila is brought in by two pearl-fishers, who threaten her with knives. Kneeling before Zurga (Leila: "I tremble, I falter"), she implores him to grant her Nadir's life. Zurga declares his love for her and his jealousy of Nadir. She curses him. Nourabad enters to announce the coming sacrifice. Leila gives Zurga the chain she received from the fugitive and asks him to send it to her mother. The people enter and begin a barbaric dance. (Chorus: "When the sun shall pour his flame.") Leila returns conducted by Nourabad, and gazes steadily at her lover, who is in chains. (Nourabad: "O sombre gods.") A light is seen in the sky. The people hail the dawn and advance, holding their knives aloft to strike. Zurga enters, carrying a battle axe. He intercepts them, pointing to their camp, which is in flames. (Zurga: "No, 'twas not the dawn.") Terror-stricken the people hasten away to extinguish the flames and save their families. Zurga exultantly declares that he is the incendiary. With his battle axe he breaks Nadir's shackles, and the lovers embrace. Nourabad, having heard all, departs to inform the people. (Terzett: "O holy light.") They return, but Zurga, having planned the escape of the lovers, now prevents the people from reaching them, until at last he is struck down by a knife thrust. Nadir and Leila appear on a rock far above. Zurga encourages them to proceed, by calling to them; but falls back dead just as they disappear. (Terzett, Leila, Nadir, Zurga: "No more fear, but sweet embraces.")

LE VILLI

(The Witch Dancers)

An opera in two acts by Giacomo Puccini. Text by Ferdinando Fontana.

CAST: William Wulf—Baritone. Anna, his daughter— Soprano. Robert—Tenor. Mountaineers, witches, forest spirits. Scene, the Black Forest. Time, the present. First production, Milan, 1884.

ACT I. A forest scene in summer. Robert, a young peasant, has fallen heir to the property of a relative in Mayence. But before he goes to claim his fortune, he and Anna announce their betrothal at a parting feast. (Chorus: "Long live the happy pair.") The guests join in a dance, and Anna's old father trips a lively measure with the rest. (Chorus: "Here we go, turn and whirl.") Anna is about to place some flowers in Robert's travelling bag (Anna: "Were I but you, little flowers!"), and Robert seeing the tears in her eyes begs for a smile. (Anna: "Vainly I try my grief to hide.") She tells him she dreamed he had forsaken her, and he laughs at her fears. (Robert: "My angel, why should you doubt my love"; Anna: "Thy soft, sweet words drive sorrow from my breast.") Robert's friends come to tell him it is time to depart (Chorus: "Quick! Quick! Forward!"), and he bids Anna a loving farewell. All kneel in prayer. (Chorus: "Angel of God, whose wings now stir the air.")

ACT II. The same forest scene in winter. Once in Mayence, amid gay scenes, with plenty of money, Robert forgets his betrothed and devotes himself to pleasure. Anna waits for him in vain, and at last dies of grief. Her friends assemble for her funeral. (Chorus: "Like a broken lily.") The people of the Black Forest believe that if a maiden is deserted by her lover the Villi, or witch dancers, lie in wait for him in the forest and carry him away to their domain. They dance around him and oblige him to dance with them, whirling and turning this way and that until he falls dead of fatigue. Robert returns to his home a broken man. His money is gone and the evil woman upon whom he has spent it has left him. He struggles through the cold and snow, while the witches dance madly before him, and strange lights dazzle his eyes. William sits before his cottage mourning for his lost daughter. (William: "It cannot be his guilt will go unscathed.") Rising, he goes into the cottage. Robert crosses a bridge close by. (Chorus: "He comes.") He is overcome with terror and dread. (Robert: "Here stands the cottage.") He attempts to knock, but is unable to do so. He sinks to his knees in abject terror and prays. (Robert: "O great God.") Strange voices sound in his ears. A funeral chant is heard within the cottage. He curses the influence that caused him to forget his love for Anna, and as he speaks, she appears on the bridge. At first he believes her to be alive, but starts back in horror when he finds it is an apparition. She comes slowly forward (Anna: "Do you remember what you said among the flowers?") and denounces him for his betrayal. He stands as if spellbound, and the witch-dancers whirl around the pair more and more swiftly, until at last they are carried off in the air. (Chorus of witch-dancers: "Whirl and turn, turn and whirl! Now you are ours.") Robert, for a moment eluding them, tries to enter the cottage, but the dread spirits pursue him mercilessly. Turning back he finds Anna in his path. She grasps his arm and around him whirl the dancers faster and faster. With a last appeal to Anna he falls dead. Anna vanishes followed by the chorus chanting a derisive "Hosanna!"

LES TROYENS
(The Trojans)

By Hector Berlioz. Text by the composer.

PART I

THE CONQUEST OF TROY

Opera in three acts.

CAST: Priam—Basso.   Hecuba—Alto.   Cassandra— Mezzo-soprano.   Polyxena—Chorus part.   Hector's spirit —Basso.   Andromache — silent.   Astyanax — silent. Æneas—Tenor. Ascanius—Soprano. Pantheus—Basso. Choroëbus—Baritone. Place, before and in Troy. First production, Paris, 1863.

ACT I. The deserted camp of the Greeks before Troy. The Trojans plunder the camp and gaze with much interest upon the mysterious wooden horse which they find there. The prophetess Cassandra predicts misfortune, and in vain endeavours to persuade her betrothed Choroëbus to save himself.

ACT II. Before Troy. The Trojans are engaged in sports, and when the tidings of the death of Laöcoön are brought, they resolve to bring the wooden horse into Troy, to conciliate Pallas, who has been insulted by Laöcoön. Cassandra again warns the Trojans of impending evil.

ACT III. Tent of Æneas. The spirit of Hector announces to Æneas the doom of Troy, and directs him to repair to Italy and found a new kingdom there. Pantheus and Choroëbus report the appearance of the Greeks, who have been brought into Troy by the Trojans—concealed in the wooden horse, and who are devastating the city. Æneas takes his place at the head of the Trojan forces.

Change of scene: The sanctuary of Vesta in the palace of King Priam. Cassandra announces to the priestesses the death of Choroëbus and the retreat of Æneas. When the Greeks enter the sanctuary, Cassandra and the vestals choose death rather than bondage.

PART II

THE TROJANS IN CARTHAGE

Opera in five acts.

Cast: Dido—Soprano. Anna—Alto. Æneas—Tenor. Ascanius—Soprano. Pantheus—Basso. Narbal—Basso. Jarbas—Tenor. Hylas—Tenor. Place, Carthage. First production, Paris, 1863.

Act I. A chamber in Dido's palace at Carthage. The Numidian King Jarbas is about to force Dido to marry him, when Æneas and the survivors of Troy come to ask for shelter. Hospitably received, Æneas calls upon his companions to save Dido, as Jarbas is approaching with an army.

Act II. The victorious Æneas returns, and is received in state by Dido. He tells the story of Troy and wins Dido's love. Mercury warns him and calls him back to Italy.

Act III. Hall of pillars in the palace. Narbal, who knows of Æneas's intention to found a state in Italy, does not believe that he will remain in Carthage as the husband of Dido. He expresses this opinion to Æneas and determines to warn Dido.

Change of scene: An ancient forest near Carthage. Dido and Æneas take shelter from a storm in a grotto, where, in a panoramic scene, they see the spirits of the woods.

Act IV. The seashore, with the camp of the Trojans and their vessels in the harbour. Warned by the spirits of the slain Trojans, Æneas resolves to conquer his passionate love for Dido and to proceed to Italy. In vain Dido endeavours to detain him, and when she finally leaves him in despair he goes on board his vessel.

ACT V. A chamber in the palace of Dido. Dido sends messengers to Æneas to delay his departure. When she hears he has left the harbour, she resolves to die, and orders her servants to erect a funeral pyre.

Change of scene: Terrace by the sea and funeral pyre. Dido curses Æneas and mounts the pyre. She announces prophetically that from her ashes shall arise an avenger (Hannibal). She then stabs herself with the sword of Æneas. Dying, she beholds in a vision the Roman Capitol with the inscription "Roma."

L'ÉTOILE DU NORD

(The Star of the North)

Comic opera in three acts by Meyerbeer. Text by Scribe.

CAST: Peter Michaeloff, carpenter—Baritone. George Skawronsky, cabinet maker—Tenor. Katharine, his sister —Soprano. Prascovia, his bride—Soprano. Danilowitsch, confectioner—Tenor. Gritzenko, corporal—Basso. Reynolds, innkeeper—Basso. General Tschermeteff. Colonel Kermeloff. Natalia and Eskimona, vivandières—Soprano and Mezzo-soprano. Ismailoff, a Cossack. Place, Wiborg, the Russian camp and palace of the Czar at St. Petersburg. Time, the eighteenth century. First production, Paris, 1854. The major portion of the music of the opera is taken from "The Camp in Silesia" (see this opera).

ACT I. A village near Wiborg. The Czar Peter, disguised as a carpenter, forms the acquaintance of Katharine, who is planning to don masculine attire and enter the army in place of her brother George. He falls deeply in love with her.

ACT II. The Russian camp. Military evolutions and

songs. Katharine, now a recruit, reports a conspiracy against the czar, which he subdues.

Act III. The palace of the czar. Peter, amid all his splendour, longs for Katharine, whom he believes to be dead. She is alive, but is considered insane. Peter sends for her, but in order to awaken her memory has the garden laid out in imitation of the village of Wiborg. When she sees Peter in his disguise as a carpenter she rushes joyfully to his arms. He informs her that he is the czar, and by marrying him the village maiden becomes czarina.

A LIFE FOR THE CZAR

Opera in five acts by Glinka. Text by Baron von Rosen.
Cast: Ivan Susannin, a peasant in the village of Domnin —Basso. Antonida, his daughter—Soprano. Sobinjin, her bridegroom—Tenor. Wauja, an orphan boy, adopted by Susannin—Contralto. A Polish commander—Baritone. Place, Domnin, Moscow, and the camp of the Poles. Time, 1613. First production, St. Petersburg, 1836.

Act I. The village of Domnin. (Introduction: "The storm rages wildly.") Sobinjin brings the news of the defeat of the Poles, and woos Antonida. (Cavatina, Antonida: "All day long"; Scene and chorus, Susannin: "This is no time to dream.") She loves him, but refuses to be his wife until the country has been pacified by the election of a new czar. The election has already taken place, however, and the landowner, Romanow, has been selected. Thus nothing stands in the way of the marriage. (Finale: "Blissful farewells.")

Act II. The camp of the Poles. (Chorus of soldiers: "God of War!" Festival; Ballet.) Upon the news of the defeat of the Poles and the election of Romanow, the army advances upon the monastery in which Romanow is living. (Recitative: "Whence comest thou?")

Act III. Susannin's hut. (Duet, Sobinjin, Antonida:

"The bird's real mother"; Chorus of men: "We go to work.") The Poles endeavour to force Susannin to lead them to the czar, but the latter resolves to save him. (Quartet, Susannin, Sobinjin, Antonida, Wauja: "You, dear children.") His foster son, Wauja, seemingly allows the Poles to bribe him to betray the czar. (Finale, duet, Sobinjin, Antonida: "How—what do I hear?")

Act IV. Before the monastery. Wauja has ridden his horse to death, in an effort to save the czar. (Aria, Wauja: "Death in the field.")

Change of scene: A wood. Susannin is compelled to lead the Poles through the snow. (Aria, Sobinjin: "Brothers in the storm.") They suspect him of having led them astray, and he resolves to die for the czar.

Act V. Before the Kremlin in Moscow. (Scene and chorus: "Russia, holy fatherland.") The czar enters Moscow; he and the people honour Antonida, Sobinjin and Wauja, but grieve over Susannin, who has given his life for the czar. (Finale: "Hail to Russia's czar!")

LILI-TSEE

Japanese fairy tale in one act by Franz Curti. Text by Wolfgang Kirchbach.

Cast: Kiki-Thum, a runner. Lili-Tsee, his young wife. Ming-Ming, priest of Buddha. Lady Whirlbottle, a travelling English lady. Taime, friend of Lili-Tsee. An official. Place, a Japanese industrial village.

Street, showing craftsmen at work. Kiki-Thum, to the accompaniment of the zither, sings in praise of his wife. ("Lili-Tsee, dear dove.") She listens, flattered, but coquettishly tells him he is only deceiving her. To tease her, he sings the praises of her friend Taime and arouses her jealousy. Taime, however, is delighted. (Terzett: "What? what does he say?") Lili-Tsee reproaches her, and while they quarrel (Duet: "Let Buddha") Lady Whirlbottle, who has been listening, appears and advises them to look into the mirror to determine which is the prettier. As neither has ever seen a mirror before, she wishes to give them her own, but cannot find it. (Aria: "How can I comb my hair.") All three go to look for it. When they have gone Kiki-Thum appears. (Song: "In Europe's distant lands.") He finds the mirror on the ground, gazes into it and thinks he sees the image of his father as he had known him in his youth. He takes the mirror (Aria: "Do I look on thee?"), and, entering the house, conceals it in a flower vase. Lili-Tsee arrives with Ming-Ming, who makes love to her, and tells her that her husband is unfaithful. Kiki-Thum returns to see if the mirror is still there. His behaviour arouses the suspicion of his wife, and when the sly priest Ming-Ming uses every argument to gain her love, she promises consent if he will reveal to her the name of her rival. Kiki-Thum again arrives, dragging the carriage of a high official. Ming-Ming thinks it prudent to disappear, and Kiki-Thum, still finding the mirror in its place, departs with the carriage. Lili-Tsee examines the vase and finds the mirror. She gazes into it, and, believing she sees the image of her rival, prays to the gods for vengeance. (Aria: "O Buddha.") She again demands the name of her rival from Ming-Ming. He promises to tell her in a secluded nook of the temple garden. (Duet: "But secretly.") Kiki-Thum returns and caresses his wife; she accuses him of infidelity and shows him the mirror with the supposed figure of her rival. (Ensemble: "She, yes she.") He asserts repeatedly that it is the image of his father. The sound of the quarrel attracts the neighbours. Lili-Tsee takes the mirror from her husband, and relates her distress to Lady Whirlbottle, who is delighted to recover her property. Lili-Tsee demands that Ming-Ming declare before every one that the mirror shows the picture of Kiki-Thum, but upon gazing into it he can see only a devout priest and wishes to hang it on the temple walls. Lady Whirlbottle demands her property, and allows several of the neighbours to look into it at the same time. As they see each other's faces the puzzle is solved. (Quartet: "They are both here.") Ming-Ming's hypocrisy is unmasked, and he is driven away in disgrace.

LINDA DI CHAMOUNIX

Opera in three acts by Donizetti. Text from the Italian of Rossi by Proch.

CAST: The Marquis of Boisfleury—Baritone. Arthur de Sirval, his nephew—Tenor. The parish priest—Basso. Antonio, a farmer—Basso. Martha, his wife—Mezzo-soprano. Linda, their daughter—Soprano. Pierotto, a poor Savoyard—Alto. The bailiff of the Marquis—Tenor. Place, Chamounix and Paris. Time, 1760. First production, Vienna, 1842.

ACT I. Antonio's farm at Chamounix. The fate of Antonio's family hangs in the balance, through the expiration of a lease. The marquis arrives, promises to renew the lease and asks to see Linda. She loves Arthur, whom she supposes to be a painter. Pierotto arrives with a crowd of Savoyards, and at the request of Linda sings. ("From the mother went a daughter into foreign climes.") Arthur joins Linda. (Duet: "As I, dear one, gazed upon you.") The worthy priest of the parish warns the father of Linda that the intentions of the marquis toward her are not honourable, and Antonio resolves to send her to Paris with the Savoyards to save her from disgrace. A prayer in which all take part closes the act.

ACT II. Linda's room at Paris handsomely furnished. She has had no news from her parents for three months, when she hears Pierotto singing in the street, and calls to him. He is astounded at the magnificence of her apartments. Arthur, to whom she is to be married, has furnished the rooms, and she now knows him to be the son of the countess of Sirval. After Pierotto's departure the marquis arrives, and offers her wealth to be his mistress. She refuses, and is in dread lest Arthur may find him in her apartments. Arthur arrives, and to her grief tells her that his mother wishes to force him to marry another. A beggar enters, in whom she does not at first recognise her father, and to whom she gives alms. Her father, believing her to be an abandoned woman, throws the money at her feet and bitterly curses her. When, in addition, Pierotto reports that a marriage is taking place at the house of the countess, Linda becomes insane through grief.

Act III. In Chamounix. The Savoyards return. The insane Linda follows at a distance, led by the faithful Pierotto. Arthur, who has overcome all obstacles, brings to Linda's parents the deed of their home, and finds Linda in a deplorable condition. She does not know him until he reminds her of his love, when she sinks to the ground, and recovering from her swoon is again in possession of her senses. The happy parents and Arthur embrace Linda, and all are made happy.

LOBETANZ

Opera in three acts by Ludwig Thuille. Text by Otto Julius Bierbaum.

Cast: Lobetanz—Tenor. The Princess—Mezzo-soprano. The King—Basso. The forester—Speaking part. The hangman—Speaking part. The judge—Speaking part. Place, Germany. Time, in the Middle Ages.

Act I. A garden in spring. A number of young girls strew roses and sing. (Chorus: "A wreath is twined.") Lobetanz, a strolling musician, appears on the wall and listens. He jumps into the garden and joins the merry maidens. They tell him that to-day is the festival of "song day." He wishes to depart with his violin, as he is poorly clad. The girls detain him (Song: "In the palace, where reigns our king"), and tell him of the sudden illness of the beautiful young princess; no doctor can cure her, and the king has organised a "singing day," hoping that she may be cured by hearing new songs and poems. Many poets are to compete. The maidens ask Lobetanz to stay and promise to cover the rents in his clothes with roses. The king and the pale princess approach, accompanied by their attendants, and by poets bearing their harps. At the king's request the princess greets the guests ("Pure white on all boughs"), and the prize singing begins. A quarrel ensues between the poets, as each claims precedence, when suddenly from the arbour in which Lobetanz is concealed, a lovely violin melody is heard. The princess commands that the unknown player shall sing, and his song ("Shall I sing to thee?") affects her in such a degree that she becomes unconscious. A general tumult follows, Lobetanz is accused of magic, but escapes, and the princess recovers.

Act II. In the wood. Lobetanz has sought out the old forester and gained his good will by his music. (Song: "Spring, thy wonders.") He falls asleep in the linden tree, in which is the princess' favourite seat, and dreams that a raven has stolen his cap. He tells the forester, who replies that the raven has flown in the direction of the gallows. Lobetanz laughs and continues to dream. He thinks of his mother (Song: "Blue as the waters of the sea"), when the princess approaches, sunk in thoughts of the unknown musician. Their hearts are united. (Duet: "The world sinks.") The princess, now well again, laughs at Lobetanz's merry song. (Lobetanz: "Sit in the saddle and ride!") They are interrupted by the king, who comes upon them with his huntsmen, and Lobetanz is arrested. When he is sentenced to die as a magician, the princess again becomes ill.

Act III. In the prison. Prisoners are lying shackled in the straw, among them two wretched women. Lobetanz, his violin slung over his shoulder, sits in deep thought. They make game of him for having raised his eyes to a princess. (Song: "You are a young lad.") When he rises and sings the gruesome song of death (Lobetanz: "Unwind the clock, friend Satan") the prisoners join in and accompany the song with pantomimes of death. An old prisoner represents "Friend Death." The headsman appears and leads Lobetanz away.

Change of scene: A hill with the gibbet. The people come from all directions to attend the execution. A young lad sings. (Song: "Before the sun dispels the mist.") The headsman approaches, and declares that Lobetanz must die for exercising witchcraft upon the princess; his blood is to release her from the magic. A bier, upon which the lifeless body of the princess is lying, is brought in and Lobetanz is allowed to speak for the last time. He asks leave to play upon his violin once again, and as the first tones are heard the cheeks of the princess become flushed with life and health. The king declares that Lobetanz shall be as a son to him, if the princess recovers. At the strains of the song (Lobetanz: "Dost thou remember when the birds sang to us") the princess arises and gazes lovingly at the musician. He plays a dance melody ("The wind drives the leaves") and all begin to dance, even the king, his daughter and the headsman. The raven drops the stolen cap on the gibbet, which all declare is the sign of a marriage, and the opera ends in universal rejoicing.

LOHENGRIN

Romantic opera in three acts by Richard Wagner. Text by the composer.

CAST: Henry I, King of Germany—Basso. Elsa of Brabant—Soprano. Friedrich Telramund, a nobleman of Brabant—Baritone. Ortrud, his wife—Mezzo-soprano. Herald—Baritone. Place, on the Scheld. Time, the tenth century. First production, Weimar, 1850.

ACT I. King Henry is living in Brabant and assembles

the German tribes to expel the Hungarians from his domin-
ions. Count Telramund acts as regent for Duke Gottfried of Brabant, who is a minor, and brother to Elsa. Gottfried has mysteriously disappeared, and incited by Ortrud
Telramund accuses Elsa of her brother's murder. He also
demands the dukedom. Elsa appears, surrounded by her
attendants. Knowing herself innocent, she declares that
she is willing to submit to the judgment of God and the
ordeal of combat. She chooses as her champion a knight
she has beheld in her dreams. (Narrative: "Alone in dark
days.") She sinks to her knees and prays God to send her
relief. Telramund, at the behest of the king, accepts the
gage of battle. The Herald at first calls in vain upon the
unknown knight, but when he calls the second time a miracle takes place. A boat appears on the river, drawn by a
swan. In it is a knight in shining armour, he lands, dismisses the swan, respectfully greets the king and asks Elsa
if she will have him as her champion. Elsa kneels to him
and places her honour in his keeping. He makes but one
condition. Never shall she ask him who he is or from
whence he comes. Elsa agrees to this, prayers are said,
and the place of combat is prepared. Telramund is conquered. The victor grants him his life, and taking Elsa
by the hand, declares her innocence, and asks her hand in
marriage.

Act II. The courtyard and cathedral. It is night. Telramund and Ortrud, who have been banished, appear in
wretched garments. Ortrud endeavours to reanimate Telramund's courage. She is a heathen, the daughter of Rad-
bod, the duke of Frisia, and deals in magic. She schemes
to induce Elsa to ask Lohengrin the forbidden questions.
When Elsa appears on the balcony in the light of the
morning, she sees Ortrud and pities her. Telramund unobserved retires into the shadow of a house. The populace
assembles and the Herald announces that the king has made
Lohengrin Duke of Brabant, which title he refuses and
wishes to be known only as "Guardian of Brabant." As the

king, Lohengrin, Elsa and her attendants are about to
enter the church, Ortrud, clad in magnificent attire, appears and accuses Lohengrin of being a magician, whose
name Elsa herself does not know. Telramund also appears and claims to have been vanished by fraud, as he
does not know the name of his opponent. Lohengrin refuses to reveal his identity, saying that one only has the
right to know his origin. To Elsa alone will he answer.
Elsa assures him of her confidence, and they enter the
church.

ACT III. The bridal chamber. Elsa and Lohengrin are
ushered in with bridal music. They express their love for
each other, but Ortrud's words are impressed upon Elsa,
and, despite Lohengrin's warning, she asks the fatal question. Telramund rushes in to attack the knight, but is
slain by Lohengrin, who sorrowfully turns to Elsa, and
asks her to follow him to the king, to whom he will now
reveal the mystery.

Change of scene: On the banks of the Scheld, as in Act I.
The troops arrive equipped for war. Telramund's corpse
is brought in, and Lohengrin defends his act. One thing
remains, he must now disclose his identity to the king and
Elsa. He tells the story of the Holy Grail, and reveals
himself as Lohengrin, knight of the Holy Grail, and son
of King Parsifal. The time for his return has arrived,
he has only tarried to prove Elsa's innocence. As he sadly
bids farewell to his beloved bride, the swan reappears.
Lohengrin prays that Elsa may recover her lost brother,
and lo! the swan dives into the river and appears again
in the form of Gottfried, Elsa's brother, who had been
turned into a swan by Ortrud's magic arts. A dove descends from heaven, and taking the place of the swan
leads Lohengrin in his boat back to the castle of the Holy
Grail.

LOUISE

A musical romance in four acts and five scenes by Gustave
Charpentier.   Libretto by the composer.

Cast: Louise—Soprano.   Her mother—Contralto.   Her
father—Baritone.   Julian—Tenor.   Irma—Contralto.
An errand girl—Mezzo-soprano.   The King of the Fools
—Baritone.   Several small singing parts. Peddlers, housekeepers, working people, grisettes, Bohemians, street boys,
etc.   Scene, Paris.   Time, the present.   First production,
Paris, 1900.

Act I.   A garret room in a tenement in Paris, one evening in spring.   Louise, a young sewing-girl, filled with
sentiment and romance, has hurried from her work to a
rendezvous with her lover Julian, who has a studio hard
by.   Louise's mother hates Julian for being an artist.
"Shiftless lot," she declares.   "Who will set the pot a-boil-
ing?"   To be sure Julian sings a charming love song as
he stands opposite to Louise's window.   (Julian: "O loving
heart! O heart all mine.")   The lovers plan to overcome
opposition; Julian's letter to her father will surely win
him over.   The door opens softly behind Louise.   Her
mother stands listening on the threshold smiling maliciously as the young pair talk of her with little respect.
Suddenly she catches Louise by the arm, and drags her
away, berating Julian for his impudence. He laughs mockingly, and she, retaliating, mimics him to Louise, who is
furious.   "'My Louise!' What would your father say to
that?   He who thinks you such a pattern."   Louise defends
Julian.   "Why shouldn't I marry him?" she cries.   "You
will drive me to something worse!"   Heavy footsteps are
heard without; the father enters wearily.   "Is the soup
ready?" he asks, and the two women prepare for supper.
Louise sets the table; the mother is busy in the kitchen.
The father reads Julian's letter, and glances at Louise, who
hangs her head.   He holds out his arms and they embrace.
The mother brings in the soup, grumbling about her hus-

band's hard work, with sly thrusts at the idleness of young
artists. The father, genial and content, refuses to quarrel.
Why should he, when he has a home and a pipe? The
mother, still nagging, asks about the letter. They discuss the match, and the mother hotly accuses Julian of
mysterious wrong-doing. Louise defies her; they quarrel,
and the mother in a passion leaves the room. Louise now
pleads with her father, who replies by speaking of Julian's
wild life, his lack of money or settled business. The mother
returning mimics the lovers. Louise, affectionately embracing her father, says she will do her best to forget
Julian. Choked with sobs, she reads aloud from the paper
that "Paris is very gay."

Act II. Montmartre—the hill in the background. It is
early morning. Venders, rag-pickers and scavengers go
about their work. A few night wanderers straggle in;
street cries begin to sound. Housekeepers pass by to market. A man in evening clothes hums a song, ogling the
girls ("Fate's full of spite"), while an old rag-picker declares that he carried off his daughter. Old men and women
make rude jests on love and spring; one, a street sweeper,
brags of her former conquests. A gamin laughs at her,
and is chased away by the police. Julian and his Bohemian
friends appear with an air of mystery, planning to run
away with Louise. Servants shake rugs from the windows. (Chorus of Bohemians: "Bohemia's sons are we.")
They depart amid the laughter of the crowd. Julian walks
up and down impatiently. Street venders cry their wares,
workwomen go by to work, an errand girl makes a face
at Julian, Louise and her mother appear. Julian hides.
Louise enters the house she works in, and her mother, looking about suspiciously, returns home. Julian hurries after
Louise, brings her back, tells her his plans. She will not
commit herself and goes to work, fearing she will be late.
Julian, in despair, stands irresolute; then disappears.

Change of scene: The workroom. Girls sewing at tables,
one draping a skirt on a form, several running machines.

while an errand girl picks up pins from the floor. Louise
sits apart, very silent. All sing (Chorus: "La! la! la!
la!"); gossip goes round. As the room grows noisy the
forewoman claps her hands for silence. The other girls
look curiously at Louise, and the errand girl jokes broadly
about her altered looks. Irma suggests that she is in love,
which Louise indignantly denies. (Gertrude and Camille:
"He looks at us, we blush"; Irma: "When I walk down
the street.") All laugh and applaud (Irma: "A voice of
mystery, breathing of joy") as Irma sings of the call of
the great city. The forewoman raps for order, and in the
street Julian is heard singing. (Julian: "In the far off
city.") The girls wave at him, throwing kisses. As he
continues for several verses, begging Louise to come to
him, they grow weary and hisses are heard. Some girls
pretend to faint, and the errand girl throws the cuttings
out upon Julian's head. A band is heard outside, diverting
their attention. Louise, pretending that she is ill, leaves
the workroom, and joining Julian, goes off with him.

Act III. A tiny house and garden on the hill of Montmartre. Night is falling; the city lights twinkle in the
distance. Julian and Louise are in the garden; he reads,
while she watches him lovingly. (Louise: "Life is sweet,
indeed.") She speaks of her parents and of her sordid
home with self-pity. Julian, scorning the wisdom of experience, claims the right of freedom for all. (Julian:
"All who live have a right to freedom.") Louise thinks
of her father, but Julian diverts her by pointing out the
lights of the city. The lovers break into a panegyric of
Paris. (Duet: "Paris, thou city of strength and light.")
Fireworks are seen in the distance. Louise and Julian are
in an ecstasy of love. (Duet: "A woman with heart
aflame.") They embrace rapturously, and turn toward
the house. As they disappear a bohemian enters. He
calls softly and another joins him. They decorate the
house with streamers and lanterns. (Distant chorus:
"Feast, sweet ladies.") A curious crowd gathers at the

gate. Grisettes and bohemians arrive in procession, dancing the *farandole*, and capering about. (General chorus: "O happy day, O day of love.") The lovers emerge. A bohemian calls on all to admire Louise ("Good friends! Good friends!"), who, he announces, is to be crowned the Muse of Montmartre. The King of the Fools makes an extravagant address. ("By Mercury am I requested.") Dancing girls come from the crowd, as their leader, circling about, takes roses from the guests in turn, presenting them to Louise in a bouquet, while the grisettes invest her with an embroidered shawl as a symbol of royalty. All kneel before her in mock homage. Louise gives Julian a rose from her bouquet. (Chorus: "Amorous beauty, thy song of pleasure.") The lovers stand happily side by side, their arms around each other. In the midst of this gay scene the mother of Louise appears like a forlorn ghost. She advances slowly and sadly, and at the sight of her face the joyous crowd seems to melt away. The bohemians alone remain near Julian; the grisettes minister to Louise, who has fainted with fright. Julian stands before her as if to protect her from some mysterious enemy. She rises, half-dazed, throws herself into his arms, then in terror and shame enters the house. Julian defiantly bars the threshold, but the mother continues to advance uncertainly, as if in the dark. "I am not here to quarrel," she says in a voice choked with unshed tears. "But Louise's father is dying, and only her return can save him." She speaks of their sadness since Louise left them, the suspense, the dread, the final despair. She appeals to Julian to let her daughter come back. "We have loved her longer than you have," she says piteously. As she speaks a ragman passes along the street dolefully singing. ("A father seeks his daughter, all he had—that's why!") The lovers look at him with pity, and Julian relinquishes Louise on condition that she will be allowed to return. They embrace fervently; Louise comes back more than once, then throwing a last impassioned kiss, disappears.

ACT III. Garret room of Act I. The house of Julian is torn down. It is a summer night. The father sits by the table; the mother toils in the kitchen, and Louise sews swiftly in her bedroom beside a lamp. The mother brings in some soup, pointing to the fine view of the city they now have. The old workman is terribly broken. Gone is his genial content of other days; he now takes a gloomy view of life, talking of the toilers' burdens and the ingratitude of children, until Louise bursts into tears. Her mother calls her, and she rises sullenly, passing her father without a glance. The mother declares she shall never return to Julian, to a life of "misery set to tunes." Louise, growing defiant, is ordered off to bed. She coldly kisses her father good-night, but he holds out his arms, speaking to her tenderly. He takes her on his knee, singing a homely lullaby, as if to a child. (Father: "If the little child is good.") They talk earnestly, Louise pleading for freedom, the father explaining what the life she desires will lead to. The mother interferes, and Louise reminds her of her promise to Julian. The father makes a last appeal to Louise as his dear little girl, once more taking her on his knee. She is defiant and he grows harsh. As he threatens her, she loses command of herself (Louise: "Every one has the right to be free"; the father: " 'Tis not thy real self that speaks"), and grows more and more excited. "Paris, Paris, Paris," she cries in exaltation. They try to silence her, but she is now beside herself. "Oh my beloved, come," she says passionately. "I am a woman with heart on fire for you." She tries to go out. The father stops her, and she dances about as if possessed. (Louise: "La! la! la!") She calls, almost screaming for Julian, and her father, tempted at first to strike her, throws open the door and bids her "Begone!" Louise hesitates a moment, and the mother vainly endeavours to restrain the father's rage. He rushes forward as if to push Louise out of the room, and with a terrified scream she flies down the stairs. The city lights go out—Louise is gone forever. Coming to himself, the father runs to the stairhead, calling, "Louise! Louise!" while the mother goes to the window. Returning, the old workman, overcome by weakness and grief, sways as if he would fall. A sound is heard without. He listens, thinking Louise has come back, then shaking his fist toward the town, exclaims with rage and despair, "Oh, Paris!"

LUCIA DI LAMMERMOOR

Opera in three acts by Donizetti. Text from Scott's novel, "The Bride of Lammermoor," by Kammerano.

CAST: Lord Henry Ashton—Baritone. Lucia di Lammermoor, his sister—Soprano. Edgar of Ravenswood—Tenor. Lord Arthur Bucklaw—Tenor. Raymond—Basso. Gilbert—Tenor. Alice, Lucia's confidante—Soprano. Place, Scotland. Time, 1700. First production, Naples, 1835.

Edgar and Lucia love each other, although their families are at enmity. When Lucia's brother, Henry Ashton, the head of the family, ascertains the state of affairs, he endeavours by a forged letter to prove Edgar unfaithful, and informs Lucia that only by a marriage with Lord Arthur can the ruin of their house be averted. Lucia yields to pressure, but when Edgar returns, curses her for her unfaithfulness, tears the ring from her finger and treads it under foot, she becomes insane. She slays Arthur in the bridal chamber and dies in anguish. When Edgar learns of Lucia's death and of her innocence, he kills himself upon her grave.

ACT I. A grove near a Scottish castle. Ashton has discovered the love of Lucia for Edgar, and declares that only a marriage with Arthur can save the fortunes of the house. (Aria, Lucia: "In this grove.") Lucia meets Edgar (Duet: "Forgive, Lucia, that I in this hour"), and they bid each other farewell.

Act II.   A chamber in the castle.   Ashton makes preparations for the wedding of Lucia and Arthur.   (Duet:
"Dear sister, come hither.")   Raymond, Lucia's teacher,
persuades her to give her consent.   (Aria: "Oh heaven,
they me persuade.")   Edgar rushes in to stop the marriage
preparations, but is overpowered.   He curses Lucia for her
faithlessness.

Act III.   A room in the castle of Edgar.   Ashton and
Edgar arrange a duel.

Change of scene: A chamber in Ashton's castle.   The
marriage has just taken place, when Raymond announces
that Lucia has slain her bridegroom.   Lucia appears, insane.   (Aria: "Sweet tones! I heard his voice.")

Change of scene: The graveyard.   Edgar awaits his enemy.   (Aria: "Graves of my ancestors.")   He has heard
that Lucia has become insane and is dying, and that she
asks only for him.   The bell for the dead is tolled.   Lucia
is gone, and Edgar stabs himself.

LUCREZIA BORGIA

Opera in three acts by Donizetti.   Text from Victor
Hugo's drama by Romani.

Cast: Don Alfonso, Duke of Ferrara—Baritone.   Lucrezia Borgia, his wife—Soprano.   Gennaro—Tenor.
Orsino—Alto.   Liveretto—Tenor.   Petrucci—Basso.
Vitelozzi—Basso.   Gazella—Tenor.   Young Venetian
noblemen in attendance on the ambassador to Ferraro.
Rustighello, servant of the duke—Tenor.   Gubetta, servant of the duchess—Basso.   Place, Venice and Ferrara.
Time, the sixteenth century.   First production, Milan,
1834.

Gennaro, a young officer, is unaware that he is the natural
son of Lucrezia Borgia.   His existence is equally unknown
to Lucrezia's husband, the duke of Ferrara.   Desirous
of seeing her son, she seeks him in Venice.   Gennaro is told

by his friends that Lucrezia is a monster of wickedness, and
he turns from her in horror. He insults the duke of Ferrara by defacing the shield of Lucrezia. The duke has
overheard part of the conversation between Lucrezia and
Gennaro in Venice, and taking him for her lover, determines
to have him poisoned by a goblet of wine. Lucrezia saves
him by an antidote. The Princess Negroni arranges a
feast in Ferrara for Gennaro and his friends. Lucrezia,
who desires to be avenged on the Venetians, has procured
poisoned wine for the occasion. When all have drunk, she
appears, to gloat over her deed and to her horror sees
Gennaro, whom she believed to be in Venice. She again
tries to counteract the poison, but as there is not a sufficient quantity of the antidote to save all the guests, Gennaro, who has learned with horror that Lucrezia is his
mother, refuses to drink, and dies with his friends. Lucrezia falls beside him, crying that the judgment of heaven
is upon her.

Act I. In Venice. An open hall. Gennaro's friends
praise Venice and speak of their journey to Ferrara in the
train of the ambassador. Orsini warns them against the
Borgias. ("Alone after the wild battle.") The assemblage disperses and Gennaro falls asleep. Lucrezia approaches. (Romance: "Softly in slumber.") Her husband, Alfonso, listens; Gennaro awakes (Duet: "What do
I see") ; Gennaro's friends reappear, call Lucrezia by name
and reproach her with her crimes.

Act II. Before the palace in Ferrara. Alfonso has
seen Gennaro among the Venetians and plans vengeance.
(Cavatina: "The joy of vengeance.") His friends appear, they tell of the invitation to the feast of the Princess
Negroni. Gennaro defaces the shield of the Borgias, and
is arrested.

Change of scene: Lucrezia does not know who perpe-
trated the outrage, and demands a speedy vengeance. To
her amazement she recognises Gennaro as the prisoner.
She prays Alfonso to pardon him, but he refuses, only al-

lowing her to choose the form of Gennaro's death, whether by poison or by the sword. Lucrezia chooses poison, and fills a goblet of wine for her son. Jeering, the duke pretends to give him his freedom, but offers him the wine to drink. Lucrezia saves him by an antidote.

Act III. A street. Gennaro follows his friends to the feast of the Princess Negroni. (Duet between Orsino and Gennaro: "Hear me, then, Orsino, decide.")

Change of scene: Hall of the princess. Feast. (Drinking song of Orsino: "To live merrily.") Suddenly the lights are extinguished; Lucrezia appears and informs the guests that they have taken poison. She has selected five victims, and shows them their coffins; to her dismay, a sixth is present—her son Gennaro. When the latter hears there is not sufficient of the antidote she offers him to save all, he refuses to take it. He is about to slay Lucrezia, when she exclaims, "You are a Borgia, and my son." Again she begs him to take the saving draught, but hearing the death cries of his friends he determines to die with them. Lucrezia, believing that the judgment of heaven is upon her, falls at his side.

THE MACCABEES

Opera in three acts by Rubinstein. Text adapted from the drama of Otto Ludwig by Mosenthal.

Cast: Antiochus, King of Syria—Basso. Cleopatra, his daughter—Soprano. Georgias, leader of the army—Baritone. Leah—Alto. Judah—Baritone. Eleazar—Tenor. Naomi, Judah's wife—Soprano. Joarim—Mezzo-soprano. Benjamin, her son—Soprano. Boas, father of Naomi—Basso. Yoyakim, a priest—Basso. Simei—Baritone. Amri—Tenor. Place, the mountainous city of Modim, in and near Jerusalem. Time, 160 A.D. First production, Berlin, 1875.

Act I. In Modim, before the house of Leah. Eleazar,

son of Leah, is in ill-humor, being jealous of his brother
Judah, the lion-hearted hero.   Leah loves Eleazar better
than any of her sons, and consoles him with the prospect
of attaining the office of high priest, and perhaps the
crown.   Judah is estranged from his mother, for he has
taken to wife Naomi, who is a member of a hated tribe.
Nevertheless, when Judah presents Naomi to Leah, she
gives them her blessing.   Upon the death of the high
priest, Eleazar takes his place, and as he is about to go
to Jerusalem news is brought of the approach of the Syrians.   They arrive under the leadership of Georgias, erect
a statue of Pallas and compel the Jews to do homage to it.
Judah slays Boas, the father of his wife, for complying
with this order, and throws down the image of Pallas.   En-
couraged by his valour the Jews put the Syrians to flight.

Act II.   The valley of Emmaus.   In the midst of the
conflict, Judah is compelled to cease fighting, as the priest,
Yoyakim, commands the army to celebrate the Sabbath.
Judah protests in vain.   The Jews obey the priest, are
attacked by the Syrians and slain.   Judah escapes with
difficulty.

Change of scene: Chamber of Cleopatra.   The cowardly
Eleazar, who has taken the Greek name of Phaon, is passionately in love with Cleopatra and prays to the heathen gods.

Change of scene: In Modim.   Leah's adherents have been
victorious, but are cast down by the news of the defeat of
Judah.   The victors approach, their leader is Phaon, the
son of Leah.   The people, incensed against Leah, fasten
her to a tree, and her younger sons, Joarim and Benjamin,
are sent to the enemy as hostages.   Naomi rescues Leah,
and they go to seek her sons.

Act III.   Judah rouses the people in Jerusalem, and, informed by Naomi of what has taken place, advances with
a new army against the Syrians.

Change of scene: Tent of the King Antiochus.   Dreams
and ill-news trouble the heart of the king.   When Leah
arrives to ask pardon for her sons, he commands her to

pray to the gods or suffer death by fire. Eleazar joins his brothers, who will not deny Jehovah, and all three die the death of martyrs before the eyes of their mother. Antiochus becomes insane and Leah dies of grief just as the victorious Judah enters the camp and is proclaimed by the people King of Israel.

MADAM BUTTERFLY

A Japanese tragedy in two acts by Puccini. Founded on the book by John Luther Long and the drama by David Belasco. Text by Illica and Giacosa.

CAST: Madam Butterfly (Cho-Cho-San)—Soprano. Suzuki, a servant—Mezzo-soprano. Kate Pinkerton—Mezzo-soprano. Lieutenant Pinkerton, U. S. N.—Tenor. Sharpless, U. S. Consul—Tenor. Goro, a marriage broker—Tenor. Prince Yamadori—Baritone. The Bonze—Basso. Scene, Nagasaki, Japan. Time, the present. First production, Milan, 1904.

ACT I. Lieutenant Pinkerton, U. S. N., and Cho-Cho-San, or Madam Butterfly, a Japanese girl, are about to enter into a Japanese marriage. Goro, a marriage broker, has arranged the match, and has rented a little house on the hillside for them to live in. The American consul, Sharpless, a kind-hearted man, begs Pinkerton to forego this plan, because the girl believes the marriage to be binding. The lieutenant laughs at him, and the bride appears with her friends, joyous and smiling. Sharpless finds that to show her trust in Pinkerton she has renounced the faith of her ancestors so that she can never return to her own people. (Butterfly: "Hear what I would tell you.") The marriage contract is signed and the guests are drinking a toast to the young couple, when the bonze, a religious fanatic, uncle of Cho-Cho-San, enters, uttering imprecations against her for renouncing her faith, and induces her relatives to abandon her. Pinkerton, annoyed, hurries the

guests off, and they depart in anger. With loving words
he consoles the weeping bride, and the two begin their
new life happily. (Duet, Pinkerton, Butterfly: "Just like
a little squirrel"; Butterfly: "But now, beloved, you are
the world"; "Ah! night of rapture.")

Act II. Part I: Three years later. Pinkerton is absent
in America, having promised to return "When the robins
nest again." Suzuki, Madam Butterfly's faithful servant,
rightly suspects that this means never, but is upbraided for
want of faith by her trusting mistress. (Butterfly:
"Weeping? and why?") Sharpless has been deputed by
Pinkerton in a letter to tell Butterfly that the lieutenant
has married an American wife. Seeing her wonderful
faith, the consul cannot bear to destroy it. Butterfly is so
wild with delight at the sight of her lover's letter that she
is unable to comprehend its contents. She believes Pinkerton is coming back, and in her joy refuses to listen to
Yamadori, a rich suitor brought by Goro, saying that she
is already a wife. Goro tries to explain, but she declares
proudly, "That may be Japanese custom, but *I* am an
American." Sharpless cannot move her, and at last, as if
to settle all doubt, she proudly shows him her fair-haired
child, saying, "Can my husband forget this?" The consul
departs sadly, just as the guns salute the newly arrived
man-of-war, the *Abraham Lincoln*, Pinkerton's ship.
Butterfly and Suzuki, in wild excitement, deck the house
with flowers, and array themselves and the child in gala
dress. All three peer through the *shoji* to watch for
Pinkerton's coming. As the night passes, Suzuki and the
child fall asleep, but Butterfly, alert and sleepless, never
stirs.

Part II. At dawn poor little Butterfly is still watching.
Suzuki awakens and brings the baby to her. (Butterfly:
"Sweet, thou art sleeping.") She persuades Butterfly to
rest. Pinkerton and Sharpless arrive and tell Suzuki the
sad truth, but the lieutenant is deeply moved (Pinkerton:
"Oh, the bitter fragrance of these flowers!"), and cannot

remain. Suzuki, at first violently angry, is finally persuaded to listen as Sharpless tells her that Mrs. Pinkerton will care for the child if Butterfly will give him up. Butterfly appears, radiant, expecting to see Pinkerton, but is confronted instead by his wife. She receives the truth with pathetic calmness, politely congratulates the new wife, and asks her to tell her husband that in half an hour he may have the child, and that she herself will "find peace." Then having bowed her visitors out, she is left alone to face her sorrowful fate. At the appointed time Pinkerton and Sharpless return to find Madam Butterfly dead by her own hand (Finale, Butterfly: "You, O beloved idol!") after having bidden farewell to her little child. She had used as a weapon her father's sword, with the inscription: "To die with honour, when one can no longer live with honour."

THE MAGIC FLUTE

Opera in two acts by Mozart. Libretto by Schickaneder. CAST: Sarastro—Basso. Tamino—Tenor. Speaker—Basso. Two priests—Bassi. The Queen of the Night—Soprano. Pamina, her daughter—Soprano. Three ladies—Soprani and Alto. Three boys—Soprani and Alto. Papageno—Basso. Papagena—Soprano. Monostatos, a Moor—Tenor. First production, Vienna, 1791.

Sarastro, the wise priest of Isis, has taken Pamina to the temple for the humane purpose of releasing her from the influence of her mother, the Queen of the Night. The queen induces the young Prince Tamino to go in search of her daughter and free her from the power of Sarastro; Tamino accomplishes his end, but becomes the friend of Sarastro, whose mildness and wisdom he has learned to admire. The prince and Pamina are united.

ACT I. A wood. Tamino, who is lost in the forest, is pursued by a serpent. ("Help! Help! or I am lost.") He faints from fatigue and three attendants of the queen, in black robes, appear and kill the serpent with their lances. ("Die, monster, through our might.") They all fall in love with the prince and each plans to possess him. Tamino recovers, and sees before him Papageno, arrayed entirely in the plumage of birds. (Humorous aria, Papageno: "I am the bird catcher.") This strange being explains to Tamino that the Queen of the Night is near and boasts that he himself has killed the serpent, but the three attendants punish his lie by placing a padlock over his mouth. They show to the prince a miniature of a young maiden, upon which he gazes in ecstasy. (Aria: "This picture is wondrously beautiful.") The Queen of the Night now appears, demanding that Tamino shall free her daughter, the original of the picture, from the hands of Sarastro. (Recitative and aria: "To misfortune am I born.") The attendants give Tamino a magic flute, remove the padlock from Papageno and present him with a chime of bells. Papageno accompanies Tamino, and they set forth, guided by three boys. They escape all danger by the use of the magic instruments. (Quintet.)

Change of scene (this scene forms Act II when the opera is divided into three acts): A room in Sarastro's palace. Pamina is dragged in by the Moor Monostatos, who is persecuting her. Papageno arrives and announces to her that her mother has sent Tamino to her aid. Monostatos is terrified by Papageno's strange appearance and takes to flight. (Duet, Monostatos, Pamina: "Dear dove, enter"; Appearance of Papageno and duet with Pamina: "Men who love feel.")

Change of scene: Grove and entrance to the temples. The three boys lead in the prince. ("This road leads to your destination.") As Tamino reaches the temple he is denied entrance at two of the doors, but at the third a priest appears, who reveals to him the noble character of Sarastro. ("Where will you go, rash stranger?") When Papageno appears with Pamina all three are about to escape, but are

prevented by Monostatos. ("Ha, I have caught you.")
Sarastro enters. (Chorus: "Long live Sarastro.")
Pamina falls at his feet and confesses that she was trying
to escape because the Moor had demanded her love. Sarastro receives her kindly and tells her that he will not force
her inclinations, but cannot give her freedom. He punishes the Moor for his insolence and leads Tamino and
Papageno into the temple of Ordeal.

Act II. Grove of palms. The council of priests determine that Tamino shall possess Pamina if he succeeds in
passing through the ordeal, as they do not wish to return
her to her mother, who has already infected the people
with superstition. (Aria and chorus: "O Isis and Osiris.")

Change of scene: The courtyard of the temple of Ordeal.
The first test is that Tamino and Papageno shall remain
silent under temptation. (Duet, Speaker and Priest: "Beware of the wiles of women.") The three ladies appear,
and tempt them to speak. (Quintet: "How? You at this
place of terror?") Tamino and Papageno remain firm.

Change of scene: A garden. Pamina asleep. Monostatos
approaches and gazes upon her with rapture. (Aria: "All
feel the joys of love.") When the Queen of the Night
appears and gives Pamina a dagger with which to kill
Sarastro (Aria: "The vengeance of Hell is in my heart"),
Monostatos retires and listens. He tries to force Pamina's
love by using the secret, but is prevented by Sarastro, who
allays Pamina's alarm. (Aria: "In these holy halls.")

Change of scene: A hall in the temple of Ordeal. Tamino
and Papageno must again suffer the test of silence.
Papageno can no longer hold his tongue, but Tamino remains firm, even when Pamina speaks to him, and as he
refuses to answer believes he loves her no longer. (Aria,
Pamina: "Ah, all is lost.")

Change of scene (sometimes used as Act III): The
pyramids. (Chorus: "O Isis and Osiris, what joy.") Sarastro parts Pamina and Tamino. (Terzett: "Shall I, dearest, see thee no more?") Papageno also desires to have

a little wife. (Aria: "A little wife does Papageno wish.")
At the first ordeal, an old woman had appeared to him
and declared herself his bride. She now again appears and
changes herself into the young and pretty Papagena.

Change of scene: An open country. The three boys prevent Pamina from committing suicide because she believes
Tamino to be faithless. ("Soon the morning sun appears.") Papageno also wishes to take his life, but dances
merrily when the boys advise him to use his magic bells to
summon the image of Papagena. (Duet: "Pa-pa-geno!
Pa-pa-pagena!")

Change of scene: Rocks with water and a cavern of fire.
Men in armor lead in Tamino. ("He who wanders this
road of difficulty.") Pamina arrives and is overcome with
joy to find Tamino, who is now allowed to speak to her.
Both pass unscathed through the final ordeal of fire and
water with the help of the magic flute. The scene now
changes to the entrance of the chief temple, where Sarastro
bids the young lovers welcome and unites them. (A scene in
which the traitorous Monostatos appears with the Queen of
the Night and her ladies to destroy the temple is frequently
omitted.)

MANON

Opera in five acts by Massenet. Text by Meilhac and
Gille.

CAST: Chevalier des Grieux—Tenor. Count des Grieux,
his father—Basso. Lescaut, Manon's cousin, one of the
Royal Guard—Baritone. Guillot Morfontain, a roué—
Basso. De Brétigny, a nobleman—Baritone. Manon—
Soprano. Poussette, Rosette and Javotte, actresses—Soprani and Contralto. Place, Amiens, Paris, Havre. Time,
1721. First production, Paris, 1884.

ACT I. An inn at Amiens. (Chorus: "The clock now
strikes the hour.") Guillot Morfontain, minister of
finance, is entertaining a lively party of friends, when

Manon Lescaut steps from the coach. She is young, gay and fond of pleasure, so much so that her parents have destined her for a convent. (Manon: "My brain is in a whirl.") Her cousin Lescaut, who is escorting her, leaves her for an hour at the card-table. (Lescaut: "Now look me straight in the eyes.") Morfontain, observing her charming youthfulness, plans to abduct her, and offers her a seat in his carriage. The Chevalier des Grieux is also attracted, although he is about to take holy orders. (Des Grieux: "What is your name, I wonder?") He makes such excellent use of his time that when Morfontain's carriage arrives the adventurous Manon suggests that they go away in it. The postilion whips up his horses, and they are off to Paris to the dismay of Morfontain and Lescaut.

ACT II. Manon lives quietly at the house of Des Grieux, who loves her devotedly, and is vainly trying to make his father consent to a marriage. Manon, gay and inconsequent, flirts with everybody, and when Lescaut arrives with De Brétigny, a rich nobleman, she wins the latter's heart. (Quartet, Manon, Lescaut, De Brétigny, Des Grieux: "Dear chevalier, they frighten me.") He warns her that Des Grieux's father intends to take him away that night. Manon is appalled, realising her own weakness in resisting temptation. When Des Grieux goes to post his letter, she decides that she will give him up. (Manon: "What voice is this that seems to call me hence.") He returns, and they sit down to their evening meal. (Des Grieux: "As in a dream I see.") A knock is heard. Des Grieux goes out and is forcibly carried away in a coach.

ACT III. A promenade in Paris. It is a fête day. A group of actresses surround Lescaut (Poussette, Javotte: "What a delightful walk"), who jests with them. (Lescaut: "O Rosalind.") De Brétigny and Guillot are talking of Manon, who presently appears gaily singing. (Manon: "With me all roads lead to a throne.") She extols youth and love. (Manon: "Shall we not follow young

love where he leads us.") The Count des Grieux enters and
tells De Brétigny his son has entered a monastery to prepare for the priesthood, owing to Manon's faithlessness.
Manon approaches, sending De Brétigny in search of a
bracelet. She inquires for her former lover, asking plaintively whether she is forgotten. The count answers with
gentle raillery (The count: "This then is all you would
know?"), telling her laughingly that the wise forget when
remembrance hurts. Change of scene: The seminary at
St. Sulpice. Manon visits Des Grieux there, and hears
him praised by a number of noble visitors. (Chorus of
women: "How eloquent he is!") The count enters with his
son (The count: "Why not marry some fair young girl?"),
suggesting a suitable marriage rather than the priesthood.
He departs, and Des Grieux thinks sadly of Manon (Des
Grieux: "Leave me, fair vision"), who appears before him.
(Duet: "Wicked and cruel was I.") He reproaches her,
saying his love for her is dead. Manon is incredulous.
(Manon: "Can we not bring it to life?") She refuses to
leave him, and at last, won by her pleading, he departs
with her.

Act IV. A gambling house in Paris. Des Grieux, in
order to satisfy Manon's demands for money, has become a
gambler. (Chorus of gamblers: "Some imprudent players
trust too much to luck.") Entering into a game, he wins
large sums. (Des Grieux: "Manon! mysterious siren.")
Manon is delighted. (Manon: "The chink of gold, soft
laughter, these I love.") The stakes are raised higher and
higher, and at last Guillot accuses Des Grieux of cheating.
The police appear and he and Manon are arrested. This
is Guillot's revenge. (Duet, Manon, Des Grieux: "O sorrow! no more thou'lt be near me.")

Act V. (Usually played as second scene of Act IV.)
A road near Havre. Manon is to be deported. Lescaut
and Des Grieux determine to rescue her. Soldiers' voices
are heard far off. (Soldiers: "Tell us, captain gay.")
They come into view escorting a group of unfortunate

women; among whom is Manon, worn out with grief and fatigue. She joyfully salutes Des Grieux (Manon: "Dear love of mine"), and asks pardon for her wickedness, speaking of the past with tears. At last, overcome with sudden weakness, she falls into Des Grieux's arms, and dies. (Manon: "Ah! I shall ne'er forget those days of joy.")

MANON LESCAUT

Lyric drama in four acts by Puccini. Text founded on Prévost's "Manon Lescaut."

CAST: Manon Lescaut—Soprano. Lescaut, her brother, sergeant in the king's guard—Baritone. Chevalier des Grieux—Tenor. Geronte de Ravoir, treasurer general— Basso. Edmund, a student—Tenor. An innkeeper— Basso. A singer—Mezzo-soprano. A dancing master— Tenor. A sergeant of archers—Basso. A sea-captain— Basso. Time, the eighteenth century. Place, Amiens, Paris, Havre, New Orleans. First production, Milan, 1893.

ACT I. Before an inn. Crowd strolling about; men drinking and gaming. Students waiting for the girls to come from work. (Madrigal, Edmund: "Hail! lovely night," with mocking chorus: "Ha! ha! ha!") Edmund sings of youthful pleasure. ("Youth is ours.") The girls appear. Des Grieux enters, but is melancholy and does not join the other students. (Des Grieux: "No, away, you tempting fair ones!") They joke with him. (Chorus: "Dance, revel's wild enjoyment.") Manon and Lescaut descend from the coach. Des Grieux is enchanted with Manon. ("Never did I behold so fair a maiden.") He approaches her when Lescaut enters the inn, and she promises to meet him later. The students laugh, pointing at them merrily. Lescaut returns with Geronte, who also is captivated by Manon, saying she will only be wasted upon a convent. He plans to carry her off, while Lescaut is engaged at cards, but Edmund, overhearing, suggests to Des

Grieux to go off with Manon himself in the old roué's post-chaise. Manon appears (Manon: "Behold me!"), coquets with Des Grieux, and they fly together. Geronte and Lescaut arrive on the scene as they disappear, and Lescaut proposes that they follow post haste to Paris. (Chorus: "Fragrant breezes lightly wafting.")

Act II. Paris; room in Geronte's house, where Manon is installed as his mistress, having left Des Grieux when his money gave out. The hairdresser has come, and while he is arranging her hair she talks with Lescaut, who congratulates her. (Lescaut: "A modest little cottage.") Manon is sad and her thoughts turn to Des Grieux. Geronte is too old and wicked, he bores her. Singers enter to amuse her. (Madrigal: "Speed we o'er the mountain's fastness.") Geronte brings a dancing master; he and his friends kiss Manon's hand. All dance a minuet, (Manon, Geronte and chorus: "All the golden praise you murmur."); when the men go to stroll along the boulevards, Des Grieux suddenly appears. (Manon: "You love me then no more?" Duet: " 'Tis love's own magic spell.") As they renew their vows, Geronte returns unexpectedly. He salutes them ironically, reminding Manon of his many favours to her. She replies that by looking in his mirror he will see that she cannot love him. Bowing low he leaves them. The lovers rejoice in their freedom, but Manon half regrets her jewels and pretty frocks. (Des Grieux: "Ah, Manon, you betray me!") Lescaut enters in breathless haste, making signs that they must depart immediately. Manon snatches up her jewels, and they go to the door. It is locked by Geronte's order. A squad of soldiers appear, to arrest Manon, who, in trying to escape, drops the jewels at Geronte's feet. She is dragged off, and Des Grieux is not permitted to follow her. Intermezzo.

Act III. Havre. A square near the harbour. Manon is in prison. Lescaut and Des Grieux linger near. By talking to her through the bars, they learn that she is to be deported to America. (Des Grieux: " 'Tis dawn!").

Vainly they attempt a rescue. The guard appears, escorting a group of women, who are going on the same ship as Manon. She walks among them, pale and sad. (Chorus: "Indeed she is lovely.") The crowd make brutal comments. Des Grieux, going to Manon's side, is roughly pushed away by the sergeant, but the captain of the ship, seeing his intense grief, allows him to board the ship. (Des Grieux: "Madness seizes me.")

Act IV. A plain near New Orleans. Manon and Des Grieux appear, half-dead with fatigue. (Des Grieux: "Fear not to lean on me.") They do not know where to go for shelter. (Duet: "Most cruel fate.") Des Grieux is alarmed by Manon's appearance and goes to look for water for her. Manon thinks he has left her forever. (Manon: "Alone, forsaken.") He returns, frantically calling her, but she is beyond human aid and dies in his arms.

MANRU

Opera in three acts by Paderewski. Text by Nossig.

Cast: Manru, a gipsy—Tenor. Ulana, a maiden of Galicia—Soprano. Hedwig, her mother—Mezzo-soprano. Asa, a gipsy girl—Soprano. Urok, a dwarf—Baritone. Oros, a gipsy chief—Basso. Jagu, a gipsy fiddler—Basso. Scene, among the Tatra Mountains, Hungary. Time, the early nineteenth century. First production, Dresden, 1901.

Act I. Village in the Tatra Mountains. Hedwig and the village maidens are gathered together. (Hedwig and chorus: "From on high darts a hawk.") They sing of the pleasures of the dance, and Hedwig tells them that her daughter Ulana has married the gipsy Manru against her parents' will. Urok, the dwarf, entering, pleads for Ulana, whom he loves. The maidens make sport of him, dancing around him gaily. Ulana appears. She is sad, believing her husband no longer loves her. (Duet, Ulana,

Urok: "Alas! alas! what suffering dire.") She knocks at her mother's door, and is driven away. Hedwig soon relents. (Ulana: "Lonely and sad.") Urok informs them that it is said that gipsies become inconstant under the full moon. Hedwig again drives her daughter away, since she refuses to leave Manru. (Ulana: "He alone is my delight.") Ulana asks Urok, who is believed to be a sorcerer, for a love potion to give to her husband. Manru returns calling for Ulana, and carries her off, followed by Hedwig's imprecations.

Act II. Manru's hut. He is restless and uneasy. (Manru: "She sits within.") Almost beside himself, he sings wildly of freedom. Ulana, who has borne him a child, is singing it to sleep. (Lullaby, Ulana: "Sleep, precious one.") Manru cannot bear to hear her. (Manru: "Who can feel joy in such a life?") Urok appears, greeting them; jokingly he informs Manru that a rope will do for him. Gipsy music is heard in the distance. Manru disappears in the forest, returning with old Jagu, the fiddler, who tells him that now is his chance to become chief of the tribe, since Asa, its queen, loves him and awaits him with longing. Jagu departs without Manru and Ulana's well-meant efforts to soothe her husband only irritate him. (Manru: "I ramble not, I'm drawn afield.") Urok cunningly increases his restlessness by picturing gipsy scenes. Ulana gives Manru the love potion. (Manru, Ulana: "A torrent through my veins is coursing.") He becomes quieter, and his love for his wife is renewed as of old. (Duet: "As the balmy breezes.")

Act III. A lake. (Manru: "Air! Air! I stifle.") Manru again hungers for the forest, and at last worn out by his struggles to resist its call falls asleep. (Gipsy chorus: "Like the restless billows curling.") The gipsy band come to the spot where he lies and recognise him. Asa wishes to carry him off with them, but Oros, the chief, is unwilling. (Oros and chorus: "No! he is a traitor to his tribe.") The gipsies curse him, but Asa takes him in her arms and tries to lure him back to his old life. (Duet: "No! No! my wound you ne'er can heal.") She dances a wild gipsy dance, and he succumbs. Oros, in anger, throws down his staff of office and departs. (Asa and chorus: "Now all is done!") Urok, arriving opportunely, reminds Manru of his home. (Manru: "My wife, my son.") He stands irresolute. Ulana is heard calling, but Manru does not heed her, and turns again to Asa. In despair, Ulana throws herself into the lake. (Ulana: "O God, forgive him!") Oros, returning, hurls Manru after her, and the voice of Urok the dwarf echoes among the mountains as he gloats over Manru's death.

MARA

Opera in one act by Ferdinand Hummel. Text by Delmar. CAST: Eddin, a Circassian—Tenor. Mara, his wife— Soprano. Dmitri, their child—Soprano. Djul, Mara's brother—Baritone. Place, the Caucasus, plateau of the Elbrus. Time, the present. First production, Berlin, 1893.

During the overture the sound of a shot is heard. Upon the rise of the curtain a valley is seen; in the rear rocks and a gorge, in the foreground Eddin's hut, opposite a hollow tree, whose opening is covered with ivy. Mara awaits Eddin, whom she has married against the will of her tribe, who are his enemies. She has heard the shot, and is frightened. Dmitri, her son, runs in, and much relieved, she plays "cuckoo" with him, and, singing him to sleep ("Slowly, slowly bends the rose"), carries him into the hut. Eddin appears, greatly excited, with his gun discharged and still smoking. When he loads it again, Mara knows that it was his shot which frightened her. He tells her he has killed a pursuer. The avengers are near, and he hastily conceals himself in the hollow tree to escape them. Mara's brother arrives with a band of Circassians

to avenge the death of her father, who came to collect
tribute, and whom Eddin has shot. Mara refuses to surrender Eddin, and Djul threatens to kill her child. When
the Circassians are about to seize the child Eddin comes
forth from the tree and surrenders. ("No one shall enter
the holy ground.") He bids his wife a sad farewell, and
asks to be shot. "No!" exclaims Djul; "from the rock
upon which he shot my father shall he be hurled to the valley." Eddin pleads, "Not living, never living," but he is
led away while Mara kneels in prayer and makes a resolve
that he shall find death from her own hand. Eddin is now
seen upon the rock. As he bids her farewell, Mara grasps
the gun, and crying, "The Holy Mary bless you!" shoots
him through the heart. She sinks to the ground in an
agony of grief, and buries her face in her hands. The little Dmitri comes from the hut, takes her hands from her
face and cries innocently, "Cuckoo!" As he dries her
eyes with his skirt the curtain descends.

THE MARRIAGE OF FIGARO

Comic opera in four acts by Mozart. Words by Da Ponte,
founded upon Beaumarchais's comedy.

CAST: Count Almaviva—Baritone. The countess, his
wife—Soprano. Figaro, valet to the count—Basso.
Susanna, his bride—Soprano. Cherubino, page to the
count—Soprano. Marzelline, housekeeper—Alto. Bartholo, physician—Basso. Basilio, music master—Tenor.
Don Guzman, judge—Tenor. Antonio, Susan's uncle, gardener—Basso. Barbarina, his daughter—Soprano. First
production, Vienna, 1786.

The action in this opera is the direct continuation of the
"Barber of Seville." Rosina is now the Countess Almaviva;
her husband, however, is not a pattern of virtue, but is
seeking the love of Antonio's daughter, Barbarina. When
he detects the rivalry of the forward page, Cherubino, he

tries to get rid of him by procuring for him an officer's
commission. Figaro has entered the service of the count
and is making preparations for his nuptials with Rosina's
ward, Susanna.

Act I. A room in the palace. Figaro is measuring the
space for the placing of the furniture. Susanna is trying
on a hat before the mirror.[1] (Duet: "Five, ten, twenty,
thirty.") They talk of the future. (Duet: "Should the
countess ring for you at night.") Susanna is annoyed by
the gallantry of Almaviva, but is reassured by Figaro.
(Aria: "Should the little count dare to dance.")   Dr.
Bartholo arrives, and is engaged by Marzelline, the housekeeper, as counsel, for she intends to bring suit against
Figaro, who had previously promised her marriage to can-
cel a debt. (Bartholo's aria: "Sweet revenge, you give
great joy"; Duet between Marzelline and Susanna: "Forward, I pray, thou model of beauty.") Cherubino arrives
and asks Susanna's aid with the count, as he does not wish
to go away. (Aria: "New joys, new pains.") When the
count and Basilio appear, he hides himself, and Susanna
feigns a swoon; in the confusion, Cherubino jumps upon
a chair and covers himself with a woman's dress. (Terzett:
"What do I hear? Go at once and drive the imp away.")
The count discovers him, and he is only saved from punishment by the entrance of the peasants. (Chorus.) Cherubino is compelled to depart, and Figaro gives him good advice. (Aria: "There forget low-voiced prayers, sweet
alarms.")

Act II. Room of the countess. The countess laments
her husband's infidelity. (Aria: "Holy source of my desires.") Susanna admits Cherubino, and they proceed to
attire him in women's clothes in order that he may attend
the wedding. (Aria of Cherubino: "Ye, who know the desires of my heart.") They dress his hair. (Susanna's
aria: "Come nearer, kneel before me.") The count arriv-

[1] At the present day, following the French original more closely, the
bridal wreath is substituted for the hat.

ing, Cherubino flies into the next room, into which the count wishes to enter, having heard some one moving about. The countess pretends it is only Susanna, and the count, locking all the doors, leaves with the countess to find some way of getting into the room. (Terzett: "Now, then, will it soon be done?" Duet: "Dear countess, may I ask.") Susanna frees Cherubino, who jumps from the window, and she enters the room from which he has escaped. The count and countess return. He thinks Cherubino has hidden himself, but finds to his astonishment only Susanna. (Finale: "Come out, young miscreant.") In the meantime, Figaro, who fears the gallantries of the count, attempts to prevent him from appearing at his wedding by an anonymous letter, but interrogated by the countess confesses that he has written it. When Antonio, the gardener, brings in a letter, which he says has been dropped by a man who escaped through the window, Figaro pretends that he has been with Susanna. The document, however, proves to be Cherubino's appointment as an officer, and Figaro gets out of this scrape also by presenting it to the count for the purpose of affixing his seal, which was missing. Marzelline, Bartholo and Basilio now appear, and the former brings her charge against Figaro. The wedding is postponed in order that the count may investigate.

Act III. The festal chamber. The count is confused by the preceding occurrences, and at the request of the countess, Susanna agrees to meet him in the garden. She first changes clothes with the countess. (Duet: "Long have I languished.") Susanna whispers to Figaro that success is now certain and his suit is won. The count is angry. (Aria: "Shall I have my happiness?") The court scene follows (Sextet, Almaviva, Figaro, Don Guzman, Bartholo, the countess and Susanna: "Behold your father"), in which it appears that Figaro is the natural son of Marzelline and Bartholo, so he cannot possibly marry the housekeeper. The countess is left alone (Recitative and aria: "And Susanna comes not"), when the maid arrives and reports everything favourable. The countess dictates a love letter for Susanna to send. (Duet: "Now shall I?") The count is to return the pin which fastens the letter, in token that he has received it. A chorus of young peasants, among them Cherubino, serenades the countess. ("Countess, the roses.") The count arrives with Antonio, and, discovering the page, is enraged, but is appeased by Susanna's letter. He tears his finger with the pin, which annoys him once more. (March and finale: "Let us march in order.") The act closes with an invitation to the evening's feast. (Chorus: "Faithful lovers with wreaths bedecked.")

ACT IV. In the garden (sometimes preceded by a scene in the corridor). Following the directions in the letter, the count has sent Barbarina with the pin, but she has lost it. (Aria: "Unfortunate little pin.") Figaro learns its significance from Barbarina. (Recitative and aria: "All is well, the hour is near.") Actuated by jealousy, he induces Bartholo and Marzelline to come to the garden also and be present at the interview between the count and Susanna. Marzelline informs Susanna of this plan. (Aria: "The hour approaches" and "Tarry not, dear love.") The countess arrives in Susanna's dress; Cherubino seeks to kiss the supposed Susanna, but is prevented by the interference of the count, who aims a blow at Cherubino, which is received, however, by the ever-present Figaro. The count is pursuing the supposed Susanna, who eludes him, when the real Susanna arrives in the countess' clothes. Figaro tells her of the count's intentions, but recognises his bride. He enters into the comedy by paying deference to her as the countess, and again has his ears soundly boxed. They make peace, however, and he continues to play his rôle. As the count appears, he declares his love and sinks on his knees at her feet. The count calls for his people and for arms. Lights appear and universal recognition takes place to the confusion of the count, who has no excuses to make. (Finale: "Still, be still, I will approach.")

MARTHA

Opera in four acts by Von Flotow. Text from the French by Friedrich.

CAST: Lady Harriet Durham, maid of honour to the queen—Soprano. Nancy, her confidante—Mezzo-soprano. Lord Tristan, her cousin—Basso. Lionel—Tenor. Plunkett, a rich country gentleman—Basso. The judge of Richmond—Basso. Three maids and three servants of the lady—small vocal parts. Place, the castle of Lady Harriet, near Richmond. Time, in the reign of Queen Anne. First production, Vienna, 1847.

For a diversion, Lady Harriet forces her stiff English cousin Tristan to accompany her and her maid Nancy to the market of maids in Richmond, and they disguise themselves as servants. Here they meet the rich farmer Plunkett and his foster-brother Lionel, whose birth is unknown, but who possesses a ring by which he hopes to be recognised. Harriet and Nancy take service under the names of Martha and Julia, but as they accept money on account of their wages the fun changes to earnest and the judges force them to follow the farmers. An amusing scene takes place in the second act, when Martha and Julia try in vain to spin, and are instructed by the men. The susceptible Lionel falls deeply in love with Martha, and when at his request she sings for him he declares his love. Although Martha also admires Lionel, she does not intend to carry the joke to this extent, and admonished by Tristan, she and Julia escape during the night. Plunkett discovers Julia in the guise of a huntress, but is driven away by her and her companions. Lionel preserves a rose which he has received from Martha, but when he sees her as a lady of the court and she disowns him and declares him to be insane, he tries to tear his love from his heart. He is recognised by the ring on his finger as the son of a man of high position and is reinstated in his possessions. Harriet is overjoyed, for she loves him, and is now willing to marry him. But Lionel in his turn repulses her for having played with him so cruelly. After Plunkett and Nancy have come to an agreement, they desire to assist their friends also to obtain happiness. Harriet and Nancy again attire themselves as servants, seek Lionel at the market of Richmond, where they had first seen him, and Lionel, touched by the submission of Harriet, discovers that she loves him truly, and they are united.

ACT I. Chamber of Lady Harriet. Chorus and scene. (Duet, Nancy and Harriet: "From the noble cavaliers"; Scene and terzett, Nancy, Harriet, Tristan: "Dear lady and cousin," with the chorus of maids behind the scene: "Well then, young blood, over sticks and stones.")

Change of scene: The market of maids at Richmond. Chorus and march of the maids. (Scene and duet between Lionel and Plunkett: "Yes, since early childhood"; Finale: "The market begins, the bell rings.")

ACT II. A room at Plunkett's farm. (Scene, Lionel, Plunkett, Harriet, Nancy: "Come nearer, bashful maidens," and spinning quartet: "Merrily turn the wheel"; Scene, Lionel with Harriet and popular song: "The last rose of summer"; Finale: "Only wait, for that you shall suffer"; with a terzett, Tristan, Harriet, Nancy: "Let us fly from here.") (This generally concludes the second act, although in the original the scene in which Plunkett and Lionel prepare to follow the maids is added.)

ACT III. The wood and inn. (Plunkett's song and chorus: "Let me ask you, can you tell me"; Chorus of huntresses and song of Nancy: "Huntress, thou sly one," with the accompanying ensemble: "Lightning, the wild hunt"; Scene and aria of Lionel: "O so gentle, O so faithful"; Finale: "The mistress takes her rest," with the grand ensemble: "May heaven forgive you.")

ACT IV. The chamber at the farm as before. (Aria of Harriet: "To reconcile the dear one"; Duet between Harriet and Lionel: "Spring has come, the roses bloom.")

Change of scene: The market of maids at Richmond.
(Finale: "Here the booths, there the inn," with the closing
song: "Spring is here.")

MASON AND LOCKSMITH

Comic opera in three acts by Auber.   Text by Scribe and
Delavigne.

CAST: Colonel Leon of Merinville—Tenor.   Emma, a
Greek—Soprano.   Roger, a mason—Tenor.   Baptiste, a
locksmith—Basso.   Henriette, his sister—Soprano.   Zobeide, Irma's playmate—Soprano.   Madame Bertrand—
Mezzo-soprano.   Usbeck and Ricca, Turkish slaves in the
following of the ambassador—Basso and Tenor.   Place,
the suburbs of St. Antoine at Paris.   Time, 1788.   First
production, Paris, 1825.

ACT I.   Before an inn.   Roger and Henriette are celebrating their marriage.   (Song, Roger: "Up, mechanics, to-
day is Sunday," with the refrain: "Now courage, do not
despair.")   The envious Madame Bertrand cannot understand where Roger has obtained the money for the marriage.   ("He went forth from my house much poorer than
a church mouse.")   Roger has received the money from
the young officer Leon, whose life he has saved.   Leon arrives and is received by Roger with joy.   (Quartet, Leon,
Roger, Baptiste, Bertrand: "Do I see aright, noble sir";
Love duet between Roger and Henriette: "I must go, for
I am expected.")   Two unknown men appear and are looking for a mason (Finale: "Be silent, some one is coming")
and ask Roger to go with them.   Roger refuses ("No, to-
day I cannot accompany you"), but they force him to
follow.   ("O God, I cannot resist.")

ACT II.   Chamber of the Turkish ambassador.   (Chorus
with Irma and Zobeide; Song of Irma: "Before beautiful
Zelmire.")   Left alone Irma expresses her longing for her
beloved Leon.   (Aria: "Everywhere upon my way.")   The

unknown men of the first act, Usbeck and Ricca, lead in
Roger and Baptiste, both of whom have been forced to accompany them, and they put them to work.   Roger is
forced to prepare the stone and wall up a door, and
Baptiste to forge chains.   (Duet: "No rest.")   They are
then led away by slaves.   Leon arrives to elope with Irma.
(Aria: "Soon I will see her"; Duet with Irma: "Come let
us hasten away.")   They are discovered by Ricca and
Usbeck, who put them in chains and compel Roger to imprison them.   The mason recognises his benefactor Leon,
and plans to save him, and singing while he works: "Have
courage, do not despair," he tries to cheer his friend.

ACT III.   Same scene as Act I.   Henriette is anxious
about Roger.   (Aria: "I think of my marriage only with
despair.")   She gets into a quarrel with Madame Bertrand.
(Quarrel duet with chorus: "Is it permitted, young woman,
to ask.")   Roger, led by slaves, returns and plans the deliverance of Leon and Irma.   (Aria: "God, what is to be
done?")   As his eyes have been bound he does not know
the house in which he has been confined, but when Madame
Bertrand accuses him of having entered the house of the
Turkish ambassador, he sees light, rushes away and has
the prisoners released by the authorities.   His friends come
to thank him, and all is made clear.   (Finale: "Noise and
bustle in the quarter"; closing chorus: "Now courage,
never despair.")

THE MEDICI

Opera in four acts by Leoncavallo.   Text by the composer.
CAST: Lorenzo de Medici—Baritone.   Giuliano de Medici
—Tenor.   Gimbattista da Montesecco, papal captain—
Basso.   Francesco Pazzi—Basso.   Bernardo Bandini—
Tenor.   Archbishop Salviati—Basso.   Poliziano—Bari-
tone.   Simonetta Catanei—Soprano.   Fioretta de Gori—
Soprano.   The mother of Simonetta—Alto.   Place,
Florence.   Time, period between 1471 and 1478.

"The Medici" is the first part of the epic poem in the form of an historic trilogy, "Crepusculum," of which the other parts, "Girolamo Savonarola" and "Cesare Borgia" are to follow.

Act I. The first act forms the idyllic portion of the opera and recites the first meeting of Giuliano and Simonetta. Lorenzo and his guests, among whom are Poliziano and Montesecco, are resting from the hunt. Lorenzo speaks of poetry and love, and is pleased with the praise accorded him by the celebrated poet Poliziano. Simonetta appears with her friend Fioretta. While the latter is gazing at the hunt she remains behind. Simonetta is ill, death is near, but she yearns for life and enjoyment. Montesecco discovers her and tries to snatch a kiss, but is prevented by the approach of Giuliano. They love each other and arrange a meeting for the next day. Fioretta, returning, is suspicious of what has taken place, for she herself loves Giuliano. Montesecco has been listening and believes Giuliano to be the lover of Simonetta.

Act II. Santa Trinita in Florence. Night. Francesco Pazzi, Archbishop Salviati, Bandini and Montesecco conspire against the life of the Medici with the connivance of the pope. Both brothers are to be murdered at a feast, as the pope fears the growing power of the family who are about to ascend the throne of Florence. For the present Lorenzo poses as a poet and singer. Simonetta is in the crowd, which applauds his efforts; she is asked to sing. She consents, becomes more and more excited, and falls to the ground with a hemorrhage. She is taken away, the crowd departs, and no one remains but Giuliano and Fioretta. He asks her to bring him news of Simonetta, and ascertains that she also loves him.

Act III. The Pontevecchio, with the houses of Simonetta, Montesecco and Fioretta. The latter is open to the public and Fioretta's room is visible. She returns from the bedside of Simonetta, and accuses herself of having deceived her friend. The conspirators appear in the dark street. Their plan has miscarried, as only Lorenzo appeared at the banquet. Now both are to be slain in the church. Simonetta overhears the conversation. At the same time Giuliano has entered Fioretta's house observed by Montesecco; he asks after Simonetta, but when Fioretta tells him that he is the father of her child he is touched with remorse. Simonetta admits to Montesecco that she intends to thwart the murder of the Medici. He hopes to induce her to change her mind through jealousy, and leads her to the door of Fioretta, where she sees her beloved in the arms of her friend. She rushes in and Montesecco, with drawn dagger, lingers at the door ready to murder Giuliano, should she reveal the plot. The dying Simonetta can just whisper: "The Medici—murder—to-morrow—I—" when she expires.

ACT IV.   The interior of the church of Santa Regarata. During the *Credo* the conspirators assemble and incite the people to rebellion. When the *Sanctus* begins Francesco Pazzi stabs Giuliano, who falls at the feet of Fioretta. Lorenzo is saved by Poliziano in the sacristy, but rushes out and wins back the people by reminding them of the deeds of his ancestors. The people angrily rush after the escaping murderers. Giuliano dies, declaring Fioretta to be his bride, and commends her to the care of his brother. Lorenzo takes Fioretta to his heart as a sister, and, rising to his full height, he exclaims to the receding crowd: "They smooth my path to the throne. Be ye my avengers, O people! I still rule!"

MEFISTOFELE

Opera of four acts, a prologue and an epilogue by Boïto. Text by the composer.

CAST: Faust—Tenor.   Mefistofele—Baritone.   Wagner, a student—Basso.   Pantalis—Tenor.   Helen of Troy—Soprano.   Marguerite—Soprano.   Martha—Contralto.

Scene, Acts I, II, III, Frankfort.   Act IV, Greece.   First production, Milan, 1868.

The prologue is not unlike that of Gounod's "Faust." After a chorus of the heavenly hosts, Mefistofele appears, and is commanded to go upon earth to tempt the philosopher Faust, who is too confident of his own wisdom. The cherubim prostrate themselves before the Most High, and the voices of repentant sinners are heard in prayer. Angelic voices swell the chorus, which is full of beauty and strength.

Act I. Frankfort. A day of festivity. Bells are ringing in merry chorus. Soldiers, students and peasants mingle in the crowd, cheering as the elector appears. The peasants take partners for the dance (Chorus, waltz: "Ohé! Ohé!") and Faust enters with Wagner, a student. They observe in the crowd a friar, clad in a grey robe, and strangely sinister in appearance. Wherever they go they find him at Faust's elbow, and the latter finally declares that it must be the devil. To escape the man, Faust returns to his study, but Mefistofele, for the friar is none other, stands in a dark corner awaiting him. Faust apostrophises Nature (Faust: "Fields and meadows"), and soothed by pastoral musings, opens his Bible. The fiend, with a loud scream, shows himself, but recovering, answers Faust's questions as to his identity and his business there, by proclaiming himself as the Evil One. (Mefistofele: "I am the spirit of evil.") His grey robe falls from him, and he appears richly dressed, and ready to do Faust's bidding, in exchange for his soul. He carries the philosopher away on his cloak.

Act II. A garden. Faust and Marguerite walk arm in arm, while Mefistofele makes violent love to Martha, Marguerite's mother, who is greatly flattered. The lovers wander off under the trees, and forget time and space, until Mefistofele reminds Faust that they must leave. (Quartet: "Farewell, I must depart.") Change of scene: The Brocken; witches' Sabbath. The witches dance and sing in weird revelry; they make incantations, bringing before

Faust a realistic picture of Marguerite's sorrowful fate. Mefistofele receives from them a crystal ball, which he balances on his hand, saying: "Behold the earth." The witches disappear amid diabolic music.

ACT III. A prison. Marguerite has been convicted of killing her child, and is about to be executed. She becomes insane, calling upon God for pardon. Faust appears to take her away, but she scarcely understands his words. (Duet, Faust, Marguerite: "Far, far away.") The day breaks, and Mefistofele summons Faust to depart, just as Marguerite falls back dead. Angelic voices chant of pardon and peace.

ACT IV. The banks of a river in Greece. Here Faust and Mefistofele meet Pantalis and Helen of Troy, to whom Faust makes ardent love. (Duet: "The changing moon.") Helen dramatically describes the fall of Troy, and the tragic events to which it gave rise. Change of scene: Epilogue. Faust is in his study considering his past life, which he regrets bitterly. Mefistofele, appearing once more, offers to transport him in his cloak anywhere he desires to go. Faust refuses to accompany him, and angel voices are heard as in the prologue and Act III. Baffled, the fiend surrounds Faust with voluptuous women, who tempt him with every art in their power. Once more the philosopher opens his Bible, and therein reads that the vilest sinner if repentant can be saved. He prays fervently for protection from evil, and dies. Roses cover his body in token of the forgiveness of heaven. Mefistofele vanishes, utterly discomfited, and in a magnificent finale angelic voices proclaim that the powers of evil are vanquished and Faust is pardoned.

MERLIN

Opera in three acts by Karl Goldmark. Text by Lipiner. CAST: Artus, king of Britain—Baritone. Ginevra, his wife—silent. Modred, his nephew—Tenor. Gawein—

Baritone. Launcelot—Baritone. Merlin—Tenor. Led-
wyr—Baritone. Knights of the Round Table. Viviane—
Soprano. The fairy Morgana—Alto. The demon—
Basso. Place, Wales. Time, the sixth century. First
production, Vienna, 1886.

ACT I. Before the castle of Arthur, near the city of
Caerleon. Merlin is the offspring of the prince of darkness
and a pure maiden. He is a wizard of power as long as
he withstands the love of woman. When Merlin forces the
demon to assist the Christian Arthur against the heathen
Saxons, he obeys with reluctance, and informed by the
fairy Morgana of the limitations of Merlin's power, he
determines to create a beautiful woman to enthrall the
senses of the wizard. Her name is Viviane, and when Merlin falls in love with her the magic harp is silent.

ACT II. Merlin's magic garden. King Arthur, who has
come to advise with the wizard, bids him farewell. When
Launcelot, the nephew of the king, accuses Modred of being a traitor, Merlin, who through his magic arts has always been enabled to recognise the truth of all things, can
see no fault in him, and Arthur continues his journey. The
demon now brings Viviane to the garden. She tempts Merlin, and at last grasps his veil and throws it into the air,
which causes lovely spirits to appear for play. Merlin
avows his love for Viviane, and warns her not to touch
the veil, for had she wound it around his head, the garden
would have been turned into a desert. Merlin hears of the
treachery of Modred, who has proclaimed himself king.
Modred a traitor? Then Merlin's magic must have departed, since it has played him false. Knowing that his
love for Viviane has caused his loss, he thrusts her away.
In anger she throws the veil around his head, and the garden changes to a rocky waste, wherein Merlin finds himself
bound in fiery chains.

ACT III. Same scene at end of Act II. The fairy Morgana appears to the repentant Viviane and announces that
only a love stronger than death can release Merlin. The

chained magician sees the battle between Arthur's forces and the Saxons under Modred going against the king. In vain he tries to burst his bonds, and finally in despair promises the demon his soul, and is released.

Change of scene: The restored magic garden of Merlin. Merlin gains the victory for Arthur, but is brought in dying. When the demon comes to receive his soul, Viviane, out of love for Merlin, dies with him, and, according to the prediction of the fairy, his soul is saved.

MERLIN

Opera in three acts by Rüfer. Text by Hoffmann.

CAST: Merlin—Tenor. The devil—Basso. Viviane—Soprano. King Arthur—Baritone. Ginevra, his wife—Mezzo-soprano. Gawein—Basso. Aleard—Tenor. Place, the land of phantasy and Arthur's court. Time, the sixth century. First production, Berlin, 1887.

ACT I. A wood. The devil endows his son Merlin with magic power and sends him to King Arthur.

Change of scene: A mythical valley. Here Merlin discovers Viviane and gains her love. Departing, he promises to reappear in three days.

ACT II. The court of Arthur. Merlin arrives at the court and helps Arthur to reach the Holy Grail by lending him his magic steed, which he asserts will bring him to the desired goal. Merlin himself hurries back to Viviane.

Change of scene: A fantastic landscape. Merlin, by his magic, surrounds Viviane with splendour. He points out to her a spring, which by ceasing to flow would signify his death. He also tells her that by wishing she can summon the storm wind to carry her to him wherever he happens to be.

ACT III. The desert. Merlin meets Arthur, who has been carried thither by the magic steed. When the tired king falls asleep the devil shows his son the Holy Grail, and demands that he desecrate the sacred blood. Restrained by a choir of angels Merlin hesitates. Viviane, meanwhile, having seen the waters of the well disappear, has been brought to the desert by the storm wind. Happy in her love Merlin refuses to perform the sacrilegious act, and he and Viviane are slain by the fiend.

THE MERRY WIVES OF WINDSOR

Comic opera in three acts by Otto Nicolai. Text from Shakespeare's comedy by Mosenthal.

CAST: Sir John Falstaff—Basso. Fluth—Baritone. His wife—Soprano. Rich—Baritone. His wife—Mezzo-soprano. Anna, their daughter—Soprano. Fenton— Tenor. Younker Spärlich—Tenor. Dr. Caius—Basso. Place, Windsor. Time, the seventeenth century. First production, Berlin, 1849.

ACT I. A courtyard with the houses of Fluth and Rich. Both Mrs. Fluth and Mrs. Rich have received love letters from Falstaff, which they exchange, and find the contents identical. (Duet: "This is really too bad.") They resolve to be avenged. Fluth and Rich arrive with Dr. Caius and Spärlich. The latter is rich, but foolish, and is to become the husband of Anna. Dr. Caius is also a wooer. Anna's favourite, however, is young Fenton, who has been rejected by her father. (Duet: "If your soul has ever felt.")

Change of scene: A room at Fluth's house. Mrs. Fluth prepares to receive Falstaff, and rehearses a scene in which a large armchair represents the fat knight. (Aria: "Mirth and jollity are the spice of life.") Mrs. Rich appears and hides, while Mrs. Fluth receives Falstaff. The ladies have agreed that the interview is to be interrupted by Mrs. Rich, who announces Mr. Fluth and his friends. Falstaff runs behind the screen, is put into a wash basket by the women, covered with old clothes, and thus escapes the raging husband.

ACT II.   At the inn of the Garter.   Falstaff receives a note to meet Mrs. Fluth.   He carouses with his friends, receives a visit from Fluth, who introduces himself under the name of Bach, and asks Falstaff to woo Mrs. Fluth for him.   He gives the knight money, and Falstaff consents, telling Fluth he had already received an invitation to an interview.   (Duet: "What joy.")

Change of scene: Rich's garden.   Fenton drives away Dr. Caius and Spärlich and meets Anna, who acknowledges her love.

Change of scene: Fluth's room as before.   Falstaff is again discovered by Fluth, and escapes to an adjoining room, where Mrs. Rich dresses him in women's clothes. Fluth reproaches his wife for unfaithfulness.   Falstaff escapes, happy but badly beaten, as they take him for an old and hated fortune teller.

Change of scene: Herne's oak in the woods.   Falstaff as Herne, the huntsman, is teased and pommelled by elves and spirits, after which they disclose to him how he has been fooled by all.   Fenton and Anna take advantage of this opportunity to be secretly married, and Dr. Caius and Younker Spärlich are left out in the cold.

ACT III.   Rich's room.   The women have told their husbands of their pranks, and the four combine to have additional sport with Falstaff.   Upon this occasion Rich desires to complete the union of Anna with Spärlich.   Mrs. Rich intends her for Dr. Caius, while Anna herself plans to obtain her beloved Fenton.   (Aria: "I will come to thee, my loved one.")

MIGNON

Opera in three acts by Thomas.   Text from Goëthe's "Wilhelm Meister," by Barbier and Carré.

CAST: Wilhelm Meister—Tenor.   Friedrich—Tenor. Philine—Soprano.   Laërtes—Baritone.   Lothario—Basso.

Mignon—Mezzo-soprano. Jarno—Basso. Place, a small city; a castle in Italy. Time, the eighteenth century. First production, Paris, 1866.

ACT I. The courtyard of an inn. Wilhelm Meister appears just as the gipsy Jarno is about to force Mignon to dance by means of a whip. Wilhelm protects the girl, and after he has purchased her from the gipsies, she accompanies him in the dress of a boy. In the meantime Meister meets the actor Laërtes, in whose company is the coquettish Philine. Laërtes warns Wilhelm of her inconstancy. The young Baron Friedrich is foolishly enamoured of Philine, but cannot prevent Meister from following her when the company receives an invitation from his uncle.

ACT II. An apartment in the castle of Friedrich's uncle. Accompanied by Mignon, Wilhelm visits Philine, and is compelled to bear her ridicule on account of the "boy." When Mignon is alone, she dons Philine's clothes, to be once more attired as a girl, but is discovered by Wilhelm, who leaves her in distress.

Change of scene: The castle park. Mignon meets the insane old singer Lothario, and, impelled by jealousy, calls down the wrath of heaven upon the house. During a garden festival in honour of Philine, Lothario sets fire to the castle, and Mignon is with difficulty saved by Wilhelm.

ACT III. A chamber in the Italian castle of Cipriani. Wilhelm and Lothario have brought the ailing Mignon thither, for Wilhelm, having perceived her love, his own is awakened. The insane Lothario is found to be the marquis of Cipriani, who, as a strolling singer, has been seeking his daughter Sperata, long ago stolen by gipsies, and now discovers her in Mignon. The poor girl finds love and happiness in the arms of her father and Wilhelm.

MONTECCHI E CAPULETTI

(Romeo and Juliet)

Opera in four acts by Bellini.   Text by Romani.

Cast: Capellio, head of the Capuletti—Basso.   Giulietta, his daughter—Soprano.   Romeo, head of the Montecchi—Alto.   Tebaldo—Tenor.   Lorenzo, physician—Baritone.   Place, Verona.   Time, the thirteenth century.   First production, Venice, 1830.

Act I.   Courtyard in the house of Capellio.   Romeo desires to end the strife between the houses of Capuletti and Montecchi, and sends a propitiatory message to Capellio. But as Romeo has slain his son, Capellio refuses to consider it until he has avenged his death.   Tebaldo, the betrothed of his daughter Giulietta, is selected as the instrument of vengeance.

Change of scene: Giulietta's room.   Romeo, who has been his own messenger to Capellio, visits Giulietta, for secret love has united them.

Act II.   A hall at Capellio's house.   Romeo arrives with his adherents to prevent the marriage of Giulietta and Tebaldo, and fly with his beloved.   It is reported that Romeo has been killed in the fray which ensues.

Act III.   A room at Capellio's house.   Giulietta is informed by Lorenzo that Romeo and his followers have not been slain, but that he has been defeated and has fled.   In order to escape the marriage with Tebaldo, she obtains a sleeping potion from a friendly physician and is supposedly dead.   Even Romeo, who has secretly entered the house, believes the sorrowful news.

Act IV.   The cemetery vault.   Romeo takes poison at the bier of Giulietta and dies in the arms of the awakened girl, who immediately stabs herself to the heart.   The contending parties rush into the vault and stand aghast at the mournful spectacle.

MOZART AND SCHICKANEDER

(The Theatrical Manager)

Vocal comedy in one act with music by Mozart.

CAST: Schickaneder (Frank)—Basso. Philip—Speaking part. Mozart (Vogelsang)—Tenor. Lange (Herz)—' Soprano. Uhlich (Silberklang)—Soprano. A messenger. First production, Schönbrunn, 1786.

This work is a Pasticcio (Pasty), i. e., an opera, the music of which has been collated from older operas. The names in the original are not the same and Mozart wrote only one overture and one terzett for it. In the adaptation by Louis Schneider and W. Taubert (1861), which is now in common use, all the songs are by Mozart. In the original ("The Theatrical Manager"), which was written at the request of the Emperor Joseph II, the manager, Frank, is seeking members for his company and tries their voices. The action introduces Schickaneder and Mozart, while the latter is composing "The Magic Flute."

Songs: Song of Schickaneder: "If the verses only sound well," with the refrain, "The world must be deceived, therefore it is deceived"; Aria of Uhlich: "Dearest youth, with delight I accept your love"; Mozart's song: "When my image from your blue eyes doth look"; Song of Uhlich: "Men seek to taste"; Terzett, Lange, Mozart, Schickaneder: "Dear Mandel, where is your band?" Aria of Lange: "Soon comes the hour of parting"; Terzett, Uhlich, Lange, Mozart: "I am the primo singer"; closing song: "Artists must always strive."

NERO

Opera in four acts by Rubinstein. Text from the French by Barbier.

CAST: Nero Claudius, emperor—Tenor. Julius Vindex, prince of Aquitania—Baritone. Tigellinus, prefect of the

Pretorians—Baritone. Balbillus, astrologer—Basso. Saccus, poet—Tenor. Severus, high priest—Basso. Terpanter and Kitharist, freed men of Agrippina—Tenori. Poppæa Sabina—Soprano. Epicharis, a freed woman—Alto. Chrysa, her daughter—Soprano. Agrippina, Nero's mother—Alto. Lupus, a boy—Soprano. Piso Rubus, Sporus and Messala, conspirators—small vocal parts. Place, Rome. Time, 59-68 A. D. First production, Hamburg, 1879.

ACT I. Atrium, near Epicharis. The Gallic Prince Vindex tries to protect Chrysa, who is pursued by Nero. As the emperor persists in his pursuit of her, her mother, Epicharis, gives her a potion which apparently kills her, and Vindex is arrested.

ACT II. At the request of Poppæa, his mistress, the emperor slays his wife Octavia. Agrippina, the emperor's mother, sends Poppæa jewels to win her favour, among them a bracelet containing Chrysa's picture, which Poppæa wears. When Nero learns that Chrysa is not dead, but has been spirited away, he orders the execution of Epicharis and Vindex. Poppæa pleads for mercy, and, observing on her arm the bracelet containing Chrysa's picture, the emperor's rage abates and he grants her request.

ACT III. Apartment of Epicharis. Nero's mother, Agrippina, had taken Chrysa away, but Vindex has freed her. He and the maiden confess their mutual love, and Chrysa tells Vindex that she is a Christian. When Nero arrives Poppæa protects Chrysa. Suddenly the cry is heard, "Rome is burning!" Nero receives this news with a scornful laugh, for he himself is the instigator of the fire and intends to accuse the Christians of the crime.

Change of scene: In Rome. The people become incensed against the Christians and slay Chrysa.

ACT IV. A street in Rome. Conspiracy of Tigellinus and Balbillus against Nero. The people learn that Nero has fled, and cry for vengeance.

Change of scene: Mausoleum of Augustus. Nero appears,

driven insane by his excesses and haunted by his numerous victims. Restored to reason by Saccus, he flees.

Change of scene: The Campagna. Vindex and his army approach Rome. Discovered by his enemies, Nero, who is too cowardly to commit suicide, is stabbed to death by Saccus.

NORMA

Opera in two acts by Bellini. Text by Romani.

CAST: Sever, Roman proconsul in Gaul—Tenor. Orovist, chief of the Druids—Basso. Norma, his daughter, an astrologer—Soprano. Adalgisa, priestess in the grove of the Irmin statue—Alto. Klotilda, Norma's friend—Soprano. Flavius, Sever's companion—Tenor. Children of Norma and Sever. Place, Gaul, the holy grove and Irmin's temple. First production, Milan, 1832.

ACT I. The grove. A secret love unites the seeress Norma with Sever, the Roman proconsul, by whom she has borne two children. Sever had loved the priestess Adalgisa before he knew Norma, but has not seen her for some time. When he finds her in the temple of Irmin his love for her returns, and they resolve to fly together. Adalgisa innocently tells Norma of her love, and the seeress curses Sever for his treachery.

ACT II. Norma's apartment. She is about to kill her children, but through maternal pity finally confides them to the care of Adalgisa. When Sever comes to take Adalgisa from the temple, Norma denounces him and he is seized by the Druids, after having refused to give up Adalgisa. Norma proclaims herself equally guilty with him. The funeral pyre is lighted, and ascending it, Norma dies with her lover.

Songs, Act I. Orovist and chorus: "Ascend the hill, Druids"; Scene and cavatina, Sever: "With Adalgisa stood I at Rome's altar"; Chorus: "Norma appears"; Scene and cavatina of Norma: "Chaste goddess, in the silver light";

Scene and duet, Sever and Adalgisa: "Go and sacrifice to false gods"; Recitative, duet and terzett, Norma, Adalgisa, Klotilda, and Sever: "Go and conceal them both," "Here he robbed me of peace," "Norma, not in this hour."

Act II. Scene of Norma: "Both asleep, they see not the steel that pierces them"; Recitative and duet between Norma and Adalgisa: "O Adalgisa, hear my prayers," "See, oh Norma, O have pity."

Change of scene: The temple. Norma, Klotilda, chorus: "He returns!" Battle song of the Gauls: "Fight! fight!" Recitative and duet between Sever and Norma: "Now are you in my hands"; Finale: "A new sacrifice I offer to your rage."

THE NUREMBERG DOLL

Comic opera in one act by Adam. Text by De Leuven and Beauglan.

Cast: Cornelius, dealer in toys—Basso. Benjamin, his son—Tenor. Heinrich, his nephew—Baritone. Berta—Soprano. Place, the toyshop of Cornelius. Time, the nineteenth century. First production, Paris, 1852.

Cornelius has fashioned a life-size doll and exists in the illusion that it will become alive and be the bride of his son. While he is absent at a festival with Benjamin, Heinrich has a rendezvous with his beloved Berta. They are surprised by the returning couple; Berta hastily conceals herself in the doll's cabinet and puts on its clothes. She is dragged forth by Cornelius, who is convinced that the period for the coming to life of the figure has arrived. To his joy the doll seems to be alive, but Berta, as the doll, behaves so wildly that Cornelius is glad when it again becomes apparently lifeless. The crafty Heinrich advises him to have nothing more to do with it. Berta quickly places the doll back in position, and it is destroyed by Cornelius, who now believes it to be a work of the devil. Heinrich is rewarded for his warning advice to Cornelius with the hand of Berta.

OBERON, KING OF THE FAIRIES

Opera in three acts by Carl Maria von Weber. Text from Wieland's poems by Planché. German by Hell.

CAST: Oberon—Tenor. Titania—silent. Puck—Alto. Droll—Speaking part. Huon of Bordeaux—Tenor. Scherasmin, his shield bearer—Baritone. Harun al Raschid —Speaking part. Rezia, his daughter—Soprano. Fatima, her slave—Soprano. Namuna, Prince Babekan; Emir Almansor, Roschana, his wife; Nadine, their slave, and Abdallah, a pirate—Speaking parts. Mermaids—Soprani. First production, London, 1826.

This opera originally contained an unusual number of speaking parts, which caused Franz Wüllner to change the entire dialogue into recitative; from which the following new singing parts originated: Harun al Raschid—Baritone. Droll—Alto. Babekan—Tenor. Almansor—Baritone. Roschana—Alto. Abdallah—Basso. The Emperor Charles—Basso.

ACT I. Oberon's palace. (Chorus of elves: "Light as fairy feet.") Puck tells of a quarrel between Oberon and Titania and the oath of the king of the elves, only to be reconciled when they should find a loving couple, whose fidelity would withstand calamity and death. Oberon soon laments his oath and gives aid to the knight Huon of Bordeaux, who has slain a relative of the Emperor Charles in self-defence, and is to be pardoned upon condition that he repair to Bagdad, slay the man sitting at the left of the caliph and kiss the Princess Rezia as his bride. Oberon shows Rezia to Huon in a vision, she also sees him in a dream, and Oberon enkindles love in their hearts. He gives Huon a magic horn, whose subdued tones protect him from danger, while, if loudly blown, the sound brings the king of the elves himself to his assistance. Oberon also gives Huon's shield bearer an empty goblet, which has the quality of being refilled when touched by the lips. He then transports Huon and Scherasmin to Bagdad with his magic wand.   (Aria, Huon: "Bred to the camp from early youth.")

Change of scene: In the harem at Bagdad. Rezia is to marry Prince Babekan. (Aria: "Yes, O lord! my life, my salvation.") Fatima, her slave, reports Huon's arrival at Bagdad.

Act II.   Hall in the palace of the caliph. Chorus and recitative.   Huon forces his way into the hall, slaps Prince Babekan, who is sitting at the left hand of the caliph, and kisses Rezia as his bride. The magic power of the horn enables him to escape.

Change of scene: Garden of the palace. Scherasmin finds Fatima and woos her. (Aria, Fatima: "Arabia's desolate child.")   Huon arrives with Rezia and Oberon. The latter, after warning them all against unfaithfulness, brings them back safely to the harbour of Askalon. (Quartet: "On the blue sea.")

Change of scene: A rocky cavern on a desolate island. To test their fidelity Puck orders the spirits (Puck: "Spirits of the air, the earth and sea") to wreck the vessel of Huon and Rezia. Huon carries Rezia ashore and goes to seek assistance. Left alone Rezia sees a vessel and signals to it. (Aria: "Ocean, thou mighty monster.")   The vessel is manned by pirates, who carry her away. The spirits convey Huon to Tunis, the home of the robbers. Change of scene and song of the mermaids. ("How delightful the waves.")   Oberon and Puck assemble the spirits for a dance by moonlight.

Act III.   Garden of the Emir at Tunis. Fatima is here as a slave. (Aria: "Arabia, my country.")   Scherasmin, who has also been rescued from the water, joins her. (Duet: "On the banks of the Garonne.")   They meet Huon, and telling him that Rezia is a slave, advise him to rescue her in the guise of a gardener. (Terzett: "I must myself disguise.")

Change of scene: Hall in the palace of the Emir. (Cavatina, Rezia: "Grieve, my heart.")   Almansor pleads for her

love, but is repulsed.   He treats Roschana, a former
favourite, with coldness, and she swears vengeance.   She
orders Huon to appear before her.   He believes that he
is to meet Rezia.   ("I rejoice in new hopes.")   When he
sees that it is Roschana who wishes to ascend the throne
with him if he will slay Almansor, he recoils in dismay,
and, being surprised by the Emir, is led away to death.

Change of scene: Before the palace.   Rezia and Huon
are to be burned alive, when Scherasmin finds the lost horn,
and, blowing a loud blast on it, summons Oberon.   As the
lovers have released him from his oath by their fidelity, and
he has become reconciled to Titania, Huon, Rezia, Scherasmin and Fatima are carried to Aix la Chapelle, where they
are received and honoured by the Emperor Charles.

ODYSSEUS' RETURN

Musical tragedy in a prologue and three acts by August
Bungert.   Text by the composer.

CAST: Odysseus—Baritone.   Penelope, his wife—Alto.
Telemachus, her son—Tenor.   Laertes, father of Odysseus
—Basso.   Hyperion—Tenor.   Antinous—Tenor.   Euril-
ochos—Baritone.   Mentor—Basso.   Eumaos—Basso.
Theoklymenos—Basso.   Phemios—High baritone.   Medon
—Baritone.   Leiodes—Baritone.   Athene—Alto.   Eury-
kleia—Mezzo-soprano.   Despoina—Mezzo-soprano.   Mel-
antho—Mezzo-soprano.   Place, palace of Odysseus.   Time,
ten years after the end of the Trojan War.   First production, Dresden, 1896.

Prologue.   The shore of Ithaca.   Athene passes, singing.
The wooers of Penelope conspire against the life of Telemachus, and are joined by Hyperion.   Telemachus boards a
vessel to seek his father Odysseus.

ACT I.   A grotto.   Odysseus awakens, but does not recognise his fatherland.   Athene comes to his aid by dis-
solving the mist, and he joyfully greets his home.   **He**

recognises old Eumaos and clothes himself in the dress of a beggar, which Athene has left for him. He sees with despair the changes that have taken place during his absence. He pretends to be a messenger from Odysseus, and Eumaos promises to lead him to Penelope. The ships of Telemachus and those of the wooers of Penelope approach, and Odysseus hastens to the assistance of Telemachus, who is hard pressed by his enemies. Laertes foretells the return of his son.

Act II. A garden near the sea. Chorus of maidens and wooers. Change of scene: A chamber in Odysseus's palace. Penelope is weaving her web. She grieves over her sad fate and prays for the return of her husband. She greets Hyperion as the friend of her son, but to her dismay discovers that he also loves her. The impatient wooers now insist upon an answer, and Penelope promises to arrange a contest and give her hand to the victor.

Act III. The courtyard of Odysseus's palace. Penelope appears at the combat and brings with her the bow of Odysseus. Telemachus tries to bend it in vain; none of the wooers succeed in the attempt. Odysseus, who has revealed his identity to his son, asks for the bow and bends it with ease. A combat between Odysseus and the wooers ensues, in which Odysseus obtains the victory. The rejoicing Penelope rushes to his arms.

ORESTES

A trilogy adapted from the "Oresteia" of Æschylus by Felix Weingartner.

PART I.   AGAMEMNON

Cast: Agamemnon, king of Argos. Clytemnestra, his wife. Ægisthos, cousin of Agamemnon. Cassandra, daughter of Priam, king of Troy. A watchman. A messenger. Chorus of sages. People, etc. Place, the royal castle of Argos.

Fire signals on the hills announce the fall of Troy. Agamemnon returns victorious after a ten years' absence and brings a prize in the person of Cassandra, daughter of the king of Troy. His wife, Clytemnestra, receives him with hypocritical rejoicing, though she bears him unchanging hate for the sacrifice of her daughter, Iphigenia. She leads the king to the bath; Cassandra is to follow them into the castle, but the seeress shudderingly recoils from its gates. She announces to the sages that Clytemnestra is about to slay Agamemnon, afterward turning upon her. Her hearers do not believe this prophecy, but hardly has she entered the castle when the king's death cry is heard. Clytemnestra returns, proclaiming that she has slain her husband and Cassandra, his mistress. Ægisthos protects the queen from the fury of the people, and together they ascend the throne.

PART II.   THE SACRIFICE

CAST: Clytemnestra. Ægisthos. Orestes, son of Agamemnon and Clytemnestra. Electra, his sister. Kilissa, the old nurse of Orestes, housekeeper. Pylades, son of Strophios, king of Phocis, silent. Chorus of maidens.

Orestes, having been brought up far from home, at Phocis, by Strophios, king of Phocis, has grown to manhood and visits his friend Pylades at Argos. Clytemnestra has brought up her daughter, Electra, as a servant. The first scene shows the grave of Agamemnon, which Electra has been sent to visit by the queen. Orestes meets her there and swears vengeance for his father's murder. The scene changes to the king's castle, where Clytemnestra has been disturbed by a dreadful dream. Orestes, appearing as a stranger, first meets Ægisthos, whom he slays. He then discloses his identity to his mother, draws his sword and drives her into the palace, where he kills her also, notwithstanding her prayers. The goddesses of vengeance appear, under whose sway the matricide now falls. Upon the advice of the servants Orestes flies to Delphi, to receive the oracular sentence of Apollo.

PART III.   THE ERINNYES

Cast: The Goddess Athene. Orestes. The venerable seeress of Apollo. The spirits of Agamemnon and Clytemnestra. The spirit of Cassandra. Chorus of the Erinnyes. People. Place, the oracle of Delphi. Hades. The vicinity of Athens.

Pursued by the furies, Orestes flies for aid to the temple of Apollo at Delphi. Upon the advice of the prophetess he descends to Hades, but the vengeful spirit of Clytemnestra leads the Erinnyes to him. He seeks aid from the shade of Agamemnon, and the spirit of Cassandra brings him a holy olive branch and leads him to Athens to secure protection from the goddess of the city. Notwithstanding the vengeful opposition of the Furies, the cause of Orestes is brought before the highest authority of the country, the counsel of the Areopagus, and by the aid of the goddess he is declared innocent of the death of his mother, but is commanded to free his sister, Iphigenia, who resides at Tauris. The Erinnyes, now the Eumenides, accept this decree, and thus ends the long list of crimes of the house of Tantalus, the ancestors of the family of Orestes. It is prophesied that the laurels of victory will never crown his brow, but he will rule over his people to a good old age, beloved and respected.

ORPHEUS AND EURYDICE

Opera in four acts by Glück. Text by Calzabigi. German by Sander.

Cast: Orpheus—Alto. Eurydice—Soprano. Amor—Soprano. First production, Vienna, 1762.

Act I. At the tomb of Eurydice. Orpheus and his

friends in grief mourn for her. (Chorus, scene and aria:
"Thou, whom I passionately loved"; Scene: "Eurydice,
dear shade"; Aria: "Bereft of all joy"; Recitative: "Eurydice, where'er I roam"; Aria: "Lost to me forever.")
Orpheus prays the gods to restore his wife and is ready
to descend to Acheron's shores to regain her. (Recitative: "Gods! cruel gods, gods of death!") Amor appears.
(Recitative: "Confide in Amor.") He tells Orpheus that
Zeus has taken pity on him and that he may descend to
Hades, to touch the heart of Pluto and of Minos by his
song. But he must not turn his head to look at Eurydice
until he has left the shores of the Styx. If he does, Death
will hold her forever. (Amor's aria: "Fulfil with joy the
will of the gods.") Orpheus implores the aid of the gods.
("What did he say, heard I aright?")

Act II. Tartarus. Scene and chorus of the Furies.
Ballet of Furies. Orpheus appears at the entrance of
Hades (Chorus: "Who is the mortal?") and is accosted by
the Furies and the shades of the departed. Orpheus asks
for mercy. ("Oh, take pity.") The chorus replies: "Sacrilegious mortal, what brought you here?" and Orpheus
gives vent to his grief. (Aria: "A thousand griefs, threatening shades.") The shades are mollified by his sweet
singing. (Chorus: "By what magic?") Orpheus sings
again (Aria: "Gods of death, have pity"), and they allow him to enter Hades.

Act III. The happy valley. Dance. Orpheus arrives.
(Recitative: "What pure light.") He inquires for Eury-
dice. The chorus of happy ones console him. ("Sweet
singer, you are welcome.") They bring his wife (Chorus:
"Who would not remain"), and, averting his head, he takes
Eurydice by the hand, and leaves the happy valley.

Act IV. A wood. Orpheus leads Eurydice from a cave.
(Orpheus: "Hurry, follow my footsteps.") He has relinquished her hand and begs her to follow swiftly. She implores him for one look of love, and when he refuses, in
despair wishes for death (Duet: "Come, oh come! with thy

shades"), believing that Orpheus no longer loves her.
(Aria: "What dreadful anguish.") He can resist no
longer, and, forgetting Amor's warning, turns to gaze
upon her. Eurydice dies once more. Orpheus is in despair.
("Woe is me, it is done"; Aria: "I have lost her.") Not
for the second time he declares shall she pursue her sad
path alone, he will die with her. Amor approaches. (Amor:
"Stop, what will you?") Believing that Orpheus has suffered enough, the god of love again restores Eurydice to
life and leads her back to earth.

Change of scene: Before Amor's temple. (Finale, Terzett, Orpheus, Eurydice, Amor and chorus: "Triumph is
thine, Amor.")

ORPHEUS IN HADES

(Orphée aux Enfers)

Burlesque opera in two acts by Jacques Offenbach. Text
by Meilhac and Halévy.

CAST: Jupiter, Juno, Diana, Venus, Cupid, Mars, Mercury, Pluto and other gods. Orpheus, teacher of music
at the conservatory of Thebes. Eurydice, his wife. Popular Opinion. John Styx (the shade of the Prince of Arcady in Hades). Chorus of gods and goddesses of Olympus and of Hades. Bacchantes. Place, Act I, near Thebes
and Olympus. Act II, chamber of Pluto and festal hall
in Hades. First production, Paris, 1858.

Orpheus lives unhappily with Eurydice. While he pursues the beautiful shepherdess, Chloe, his wife loves the
shepherd, Aristeus, who is really Pluto. While she is
gathering flowers in the meadows (Aria, Eurydice: "She
whose heart dreams") Orpheus appears, takes her for
Chloe, and each discovers the falsity of the other. Eurydice flies with Aristeus, and Orpheus, overjoyed, dances and
sings with pleasure at getting rid of her. But, alas! Popular Opinion, to whom he is subject as a teacher of music

and professor at the conservatory of Thebes, forces him to proceed to Olympus and implore Jupiter to restore his wife. After an interval of idyllic peace, broken by the sound of Diana's horn (Diana: "When Dian comes into the plain"), there has been a revolt in Olympus. The gods refuse to receive Nectar and Ambrosia any longer, and demand more substantial fare. Together they grumble and gossip like mortals. Venus, aided by Cupid, makes mischief as usual. Jupiter quarrels with Pluto, and the latter takes advantage of the opportunity to inaugurate a rebellion. Orpheus and Popular Opinion are announced at this moment. Orpheus accuses Pluto before Jupiter of having abducted Eurydice, which he denies, and Jupiter and all the gods of Olympus determine to accompany Orpheus and Public Opinion in their investigation of the charge. Pluto, in the meantime, has concealed Eurydice in Hades in a secret chamber with only one attendant, the idiotic John Styx (Styx: "When I was king"), once prince of Arcady, who has been instructed to guard her carefully. Jupiter craftily enters the chamber in the guise of a fly, and Eurydice, hoping to get away, promises him her love and is transformed into a Bacchante. (Song, Eurydice: "Pretty fly, with gilded wing.") Pluto is compelled to return Eurydice to her husband, while Jupiter plans to retain her. Orpheus is only to receive her, if, on the way from Hades to the upper world, he can reach the Styx without turning his head to look at his wife. He is about to succeed, when Jupiter causes the lightning to flash before him, and the terrified Orpheus looks back. Jupiter triumphs, for he has won Eurydice. (Chorus: "Long live wine!") In the future she will belong neither to her husband nor to Pluto, but as a Bacchante will be subject only to him. (Eurydice: "Bacchus has appeared to me.") Pluto is angry, Popular Opinion is sad, but Orpheus returns to his home in delight.

OTHELLO, THE MOOR OF VENICE

Opera in three acts by Rossini. Text from the Italian by Grünbaum.

CAST: The Doge of Venice—Basso. Roderigo, his son—Tenor. Othello—Tenor. Brabantio—Basso. Desdemona, his daughter—Soprano. Iago and Lucio, Othello's friends—Baritone and Tenor. Emilia, confidante of Desdemona—Alto. Place, Venice. Time, the fifteenth century. First production, Naples, 1816.

ACT I. The market place at Venice. The senate and people of Rome greet the victorious Othello, returned from Cyprus, and his prayer to be received as a son of the Republic is granted by the Doge. Roderigo knows that Othello loves Desdemona and fears to lose her, as she has been promised him by her father, Brabantio; but Iago, Othello's false friend, informs him that he knows of a way to estrange Desdemona from Othello. (Chorus of the people: "Hail, Othello! hail to the conqueror"; Recitative and aria, Othello: "Thanks and sweet love"; Recitative and duet between Iago and Roderigo: "Up! take courage!")

Change of scene: Chamber of Brabantio. Desdemona is secretly married to Othello; a letter written by her has been found by Brabantio, who thinks it addressed to Roderigo. This letter is in the possession of Iago, and he proposes to use it as a weapon against the lovers. Brabantio and his guests are about to celebrate the marriage of Desdemona and Roderigo, when Othello interrupts the ceremony by declaring that he himself possesses the heart of the bride. (Recitative and duet, Desdemona and Emilia: "Oh let me see clearly"; Scene with Iago, Roderigo, Brabantio and Desdemona, Finale: "Sweet love, come.")

ACT II. Chamber of Desdemona. Scene between Desdemona and Roderigo, in which she confesses that Othello is her husband. (Aria, Roderigo: "Love's despair.") Desdemona resolves to go to Othello.

Change of scene: Othello's garden. Iago arouses the

jealousy of the Moor by giving him the letter, and he challenges Roderigo, repulsing his wife, who has hastened to
meet him (Scene and duet between Othello and Iago: "My
shame must I behold"; the same, with Roderigo, Terzett:
"Come, follow me! you shall pay for this disgrace with your
life"; Finale, Desdemona, Brabantio, and mixed chorus:
"What news do you bring?")

Act III. Desdemona's chamber. Oppressed by gloomy
thoughts, she allows her friend Emilia to depart, and retires; Othello entering awakens her, and murders her in
the fury of his passion of jealousy. The news is brought
that Roderigo, whom he believes he has slain, still lives,
but that Iago is dead, and confessed his treachery on his
death-bed. When Brabantio arrives to make peace, Othello
shows him his murdered daughter and stabs himself to the
heart. (Scene between Desdemona and Emilia and aria:
"In the shade of the willow"; Recitative, Othello: "It is
finished"; Scene and duet, Othello and Desdemona: "No
threats will move me"; Finale: "Roderigo is saved.")

OTHELLO

Opera in four acts by Verdi. Text from Shakespeare by
Boito.

Cast: Othello—Tenor. Iago—Baritone. Cassius—
Tenor. Roderigo, a noble Venetian—Tenor. Lodovico—
Basso. Montano—Basso. Desdemona—Soprano. Emilia,
Iago's wife—Mezzo-soprano. Place, Cyprus. Time,
the fifteenth century. First production, Milan, 1887.

Act I. Before the palace. Othello, joyfully acclaimed
by the people, lands in Cyprus. Iago, who hates Cassius,
Othello's lieutenant, because he has been preferred by
Othello, and also dislikes the Moor, at first incites Roderigo
to gain Desdemona's love, then induces Cassius to drink
heavily. The latter, excited by wine, draws his sword
against Montano, and is punished by being banished by
Othello. Othello takes his wife Desdemona to the palace.

ACT II.   A room in the palace.   The scene closely follows Shakespeare.   Iago first advises Cassius to ask Desdemona to intercede for him, thus bringing about his reinstatement; then he arouses the jealousy of the Moor against his lieutenant.   Iago takes from his wife Emilia a handkerchief, which Desdemona has lost, to use as an evidence of her infidelity.   Othello and he together swear to be revenged upon Cassius.

ACT III.   A room in the palace.   Iago brings Cassius to the palace, while Desdemona is interceding for him with Othello.   Iago leads in Cassius, after Othello has left the apartment, and arranges the conversation in such a way that the listening Othello becomes furiously jealous.   He manages to slip Desdemona's handkerchief into Cassius's hands, then he takes it from him before the eyes of Othello, and gives it to the Moor after Cassius's departure.   Othello is now convinced of Desdemona's guilt.   When a Venetian delegation announces his degradation from office he beats Desdemona and faints from anger, which arouses the malicious laughter of Iago.

ACT IV.   The bedchamber of Desdemona.   Awaiting death, Desdemona bids Emilia leave her, and retires. Othello steps to her bedside, awakens her, again becomes furious, and kills her, not with poison, as the villain Iago has counselled, but by throttling her with his own hands. Emilia rushes in, witnesses the dreadful deed, and reveals Iago's treachery, explaining that he has received the handkerchief from her.   When the noblemen, aroused by the tumult, enter the chamber, Othello slays himself beside the corpse of Desdemona.

PAGLIACCI

Known also under the name of "The Clown" (Bajazzi). Opera in two acts and a prologue by Leoncavallo.   The libretto, by the composer, is founded upon an actual occurrence.

CAST: Canio, chief of a village comedy troupe (Clown)—
Tenor. Nedda, his wife (Columbine)—Soprano. Tonio
(Taddeo)—Baritone. Beppo (Harlequin)—Tenor. (The
alternate names are those of the cast in the second act of
the representation.) Silvio, a young peasant—Tenor.
Place, near Montalto, in Calabria, August 15, 1865. First
production, Milan, 1892.

ACT I. Near the village. The curtain ascends during
the overture, and from behind a second curtain Tonio appears as Prologue. (Tonio: "A word allow me!") He
explains the character of the performance in a serious manner as an actual occurrence, and the performance begins.
The primitive theatre of the village comedians is erected
and the actors parade in fantastic costumes to the great
delight of the villagers. (Chorus: "This way they come,
with fife and drum.") Tonio, who resides in the village,
offers his hand to assist Nedda in alighting, but is assaulted
by Canio, who boxes his ears, swearing vengeance. The
peasants ask the actors to drink with them. Canio and
Beppo accept, while Tonio remains with Nedda. Amid the
good-natured raillery of the villagers Canio declares solemnly that as clown he will take part in any joke, but
will resent any insult to his honour as a husband. The
angelus is heard. (Chorus: "Ding-dong! The shadows
fall!") He plainly evinces his fiery temperament. (Canio:
"Such a game is hardly worth the playing.") Nedda, who
is untrue to her husband, trembles at the words of Canio
(Nedda: "How fierce he looked"), and, to conceal her fears,
sings. (Nedda: "As the songbirds soar.") The ugly
Tonio remains and becomes offensive in his attentions to
Nedda, whereupon she strikes him with a whip, which drives
him to frenzy. (Tonio: "I know you hate me.") He departs, swearing revenge. Silvio approaches Nedda; they
love each other (Silvio: "Why hast thou taught me?"),
and Silvio wins Nedda through the ardour of his love and
induces her to fly with him at night. Tonio, who has been
listening to their conversation, calls Canio and Beppo, and,

with great difficulty, Silvio escapes, unrecognised by the pursuing clown. Returning, Canio, dagger in hand, demands from Nedda the name of her lover. Tonio whispers that the lover will surely attend the performance and will then be detected. Canio in despair prepares for the performance. (Canio: "To jest with my heart maddened with sorrow.")

Act II. The comedy begins before the assembled crowd. Columbine, represented by Nedda, collects the money, and warns Silvio, who is present. The play begins. (Harlequin: "O Columbine.") Canio stumbles confusedly through his part, and again demands from Nedda the name of her seducer. When she replies lightly, hoping to disarm him (Nedda: "I never knew you were so witty"), he seizes a knife from the table, and stabs Nedda, who tries to escape in the crowd. As Silvio comes to her aid, Canio recognises him, and plunges the knife in his heart. (Canio: "No Punchinello am I—but a man!") All are filled with horror and dismay, and stand irresolute, not knowing what to do. Tonio, coming forward, gravely dismisses the audience, saying with grim cynicism, "The comedy is played."

PARSIFAL

By Richard Wagner.

Cast: Amfortas—Baritone. Titurel—Basso. Gurnemanz—Basso. Parsifal—Tenor. Klingsor—Baritone. Kundry—Mezzo-soprano. Place, country and castle of Montsalvat and Klingsor's magic palace. First production, Bayreuth, 1882.

This opera is founded on Wolfram von Eschenbach's Epos "Parsifal" (1204). Herzeleide, of the royal house of the guardians of the Holy Grail, has brought up her son Parsifal in a lonely forest, to prevent him from following in the footsteps of his father, Gamuret, who had departed in quest of heroic adventure and died an early death. Ignorant of the world Parsifal grows up a "guile-less fool." One day he sees by accident a company of knights, his love of adventure is roused, and he begs his mother to allow him to depart.

ACT I.   An opening in the forest near Montsalvat, the castle of the Grail, which is situated upon an inaccessible mountain. Amfortas has been appointed by his venerable father, Titurel, keeper of the Grail. Contrary to his solemn obligation to refrain from the love of woman, Amfortas has succumbed to the seductive arts of Kundry, and has been wounded by the enchanter Klingsor with his own lance, which fell from his hand and was grasped by Klingsor. The lance of Amfortas is the one with which Longinus pierced the side of Christ on the cross, and which was saved by Joseph, together with the Grail—the vessel which caught the blood of the Redeemer. Amfortas, mortally wounded, suffers agony, but cannot die nor be healed until a "guileless fool, by compassion wise," brings back the lance and touches with it the wound. Kundry is in the power of the enchanter Klingsor, but is also the messenger of the Grail. She is the woman who scorned Christ on the cross, and now, longing for release, and alternating between good and evil, is condemned to wander the earth forever. She brings Gurnemanz a healing potion, as Amfortas is being carried to be bathed in the sea. Gurnemanz in a long recitative relates how Klingsor, refused by Titurel as one of the knights of the Holy Grail, had created a magic garden, and peopled it with beautiful maidens, destined to seduce the knights of the Grail. Parsifal enters the precincts of the castle of the Grail, wounds a swan with his arrow and is brought before Gurnemanz. He excuses his fault as one of ignorance, and Gurnemanz recognises in him the "guileless fool" who alone can heal Amfortas. Kundry informs him of Parsifal's descent, and when the wounded king returns to the castle, the youth is brought before him. While he and Parsifal ascend the heights to the castle, the scene gradually changes, so that they always remain visible until the castle appears. At the end of their wandering the scene changes to a hall within the castle. The knights of the Grail enter, the wounded Amfortas is carried in, and is compelled, against his will, to display the miracle of the Grail, the sight of which will keep him alive against his will. Parsifal is astounded at the miracle, but forgets to utter the question which would release Amfortas, and when he confesses to Gurnemanz that he comprehends nothing of what he has seen, he is roughly ejected from the castle.

Act II. The dungeon beneath an open turret, in which are displayed Klingsor's implements of magic. When Parsifal approaches Klingsor, who recognises his danger, he compels Kundry to attempt to seduce him. The magician has aroused Parsifal's fighting spirit by sending against him knights, whom he conquers, and he now enters the magic turret. Klingsor and the turret suddenly vanish, and in their place appears a wonderful garden peopled with fairy flower girls. They surround Parsifal, who resists them, but is almost vanquished by the beautiful Kundry, who touches his heart by announcing to him the death of his beloved mother. When he kisses Kundry the "guileless fool" is awakened, and he now understands why Amfortas suffers and how he can be relieved. When Kundry tells him of her sin against the Lord he turns away from her in horror. In vain Klingsor comes to the rescue, for when he throws the holy lance, taken from Amfortas, at Parsifal, it remains suspended above his head. Parsifal seizes the lance, making the sign of the cross, and Klingsor and his magic forces disappear. Kundry bitterly curses Parsifal, predicting that he will seek the Grail in vain, but Parsifal replies that she now knows where to seek him and that she will soon be released.

Act III. A wood in the glory of spring, flowers, a well and the hut of a hermit. Parsifal, after wandering for years, has learned wisdom, and journeys once more toward the castle of the Grail. Gurnemanz lives in the wood, be-

low the castle, and having found Kundry, just awakened
from a long magic sleep, takes her as his servant. Gurnemanz, like the other knights, has grown old, for Amfortas has not exhibited the youth-giving Grail since Parsifal's departure. When he sees the holy lance in Parsifal's
hand, he recognises with enthusiasm the "guileless fool."
It is Good Friday; Kundry, who only utters the word
"serve," washes Parsifal's feet, that he may enter the castle
clean and pure, while Gurnemanz annoints his hair.
("Good Friday spell.") Parsifal releases Kundry by bap-
tising her as a Christian. All three proceed to the castle
in the same manner as in Act I. (Change of landscape.)
The knights of the Holy Grail have assembled to bury the
aged Titurel, and Amfortas, himself about to die once
again, prepares to exhibit the Grail. Remembering that
this act will again prolong his sorrowful life, he shows his
wounds to the knights and implores them to slay him. But
Parsifal, entering, seizes the holy lance and heals the king's
wound by touching it with the point. He proclaims himself the king of the Grail, which he reverently holds aloft.
The repentant Kundry, dying, falls to the ground, and
for one moment Titurel comes to life. As Parsifal raises
his hands in benediction, Amfortas, Gurnemanz and the
other knights acclaim him as the new king of the Grail.

PAUL AND VIRGINIA

A romantic opera in three acts by Massé. Text by Barbier and Carré.

CAST: Paul—Tenor. St. Croix, a planter—Baritone.
Domingues, a slave—Baritone. M. de la Bourdonnais,
governor—Basso. Virginia—Soprano. Meala, a slave—
Contralto. Mme. de la Tour, Virginia's mother—Mezzo-
soprano. Marguerite, Paul's mother—Mezzo-soprano.
Zambra, a negro—Mezzo-soprano. Scene, the Isle of
France. Time, the eighteenth century. First production,
Paris, 1876.

Act I. Marguerite's cottage. She and Mme. de la Tour are discussing their children, Paul and Virginia, who have always been like brother and sister (Duet: "Thus, their day of childish friendship"), but are now unconsciously drifting into a deeper feeling. Marguerite talks of sending Paul to India for a time. Domingues, a trusted slave, starts up, protesting. (Domingues: "Let him not go, my dear young master.") Laughter and shouts are heard when a ship from France is sighted; Mme. de la Tour hurries off, thinking it may bear news of the forgiveness of a wealthy aunt. (Chorus: "A ship! a ship!") Domingues talks of Paul and Virginia, wondering what changes the money will cause, and, as a storm arises, goes to seek the young people, who presently enter, laughing, shielded from the storm by a great banana leaf, held above their heads. (Duet: "O joy! O delight!") Virginia seats herself; Paul throws himself on a rug at her feet. (Paul: "What is the spell"; Virginia, "Asketh thou why?") As they innocently sing of their love and innocent pleasures, Meala enters, footsore and weary. She is wounded by the lash of a whip. Virginia gives her food (Terzett: "God himself has led you to our dwelling"); they cannot keep an escaped slave, so Virginia offers to intercede for her with the planter. (Trio: "If God grants an inspiration.") Change of scene: Plantation of St. Croix. (Chorus of slaves: "The air vibrates like flame"; Zambra: "O thou poor slave, thy sorrows none can heal.") St. Croix appears, followed by two huge negroes with whips. He kicks and cuffs the slaves, and orders bloodhounds set on Meala's track. She enters with Paul and Virginia. Virginia sweetly asks his forgiveness for the slave ("Oh grant this boon"), kneeling at his feet. (Chorus: "How sweet her voice"; Trio: "When through heaven's will.") St. Croix, moved by her girlish beauty, grants what she asks, with a mental reservation. They turn to depart. St. Croix asks them to stay and rest after their long walk. The negroes sing, dance and play for their amusement. (Chorus: " 'Tis

our master's pleasure," with a weird refrain, "Bamboula!
Bamboula," during which the singers strike cocoanuts together with a startling effect.) Meala now sings alone, and
in her song warns Paul that Virginia will be in danger
if she stays (Meala with chorus: "Through the deep lush
grasses!"), as St. Croix is drinking heavily. They hurry
away. St. Croix in a rage turns on Meala and orders her
to be lashed while she can stand. He drinks himself into a
stupor. (Chorus of slaves: "Heaven grant us freedom.")
Meala screams wildly, and St. Croix, rousing himself,
orders the slaves to sing louder to drown her voice.
Entr'acte. In the forest.

Act II. House of Mme. de la Tour. Virginia is arrayed in festival attire and decked with jewels. Domingues
sits on the floor, weaving a mat. Virginia's mother hands
her a mirror. Domingues, shaking his head, declares that
the gold will bring sorrow. Virginia is to go to France,
and she is overcome with grief (Romance: "Through the
forest at night"), because she now realises her love for
Paul. Domingues advises her in a song not to go.
(Domingues: "Through the clear air, the bird doth fly.")
Paul is at the door. He enters, but does not recognise the
grand young lady before him as Virginia. She remains
silent as he reproaches her, then hurries away. Marguerite,
calling Paul, tells him that there is a stain upon his birth.
(Paul: "Can I forgive?") They decide to depart forever.
Meala warns them of the coming of St. Croix, who now
appears. (Duet: "At his sneering disdain.") Virginia,
entering, buys Meala from him with some of the gold.
(Duet, Paul, Virginia: "Since from us thou wilt fly.")
Meala warns Paul to keep watch, or St. Croix will carry
Virginia off. Change of scene: A fountain beneath the
trees; sea in the distance. (Chorus: "Hoy-o! Hoy-o!")
Virginia enters, singing a joyous song (Virginia: "Ye far
off winds that murmur low"), then falls asleep, while Meala
hums a lullaby. ("Softly sleep.") She sees in a vision
the planter's house in flames. The governor brings an

order from the king for Virginia's deportation. They waken her, and she is swiftly carried to the ship.

Act III. The seashore. Paul, now melancholy, stands looking out to sea. (Recitative: "Wearily time with sighs beguiling"; Song: "In vain on this shore.") He is half-crazed by grief. His mother is in despair. Paul receives a letter, in which Virginia tells of her loneliness and love for him. (Paul: "O my beloved, even now I hear.") He sees in a vision a ballroom, with Virginia dancing a minuet, amid splendid surroundings. Her harp is brought in; she sings and her voice is wafted to her lover. (Virginia: "On spirit wings.") He sings in unison with her, begging her to sing once more. Their voices seem to mingle regardless of intervening space. St. Croix appears in the room beside her; she repulses him, and refuses his hand. Paul is entranced, and tells Domingues what he has seen. A ship is seen on the horizon approaching the island. A storm arises, causing it to be wrecked. Paul hears Virginia calling him, and at last her body is washed up upon the shore at his feet. (Chorus: "O hapless fate!")

PELLÉAS AND MÉLISANDE

A lyric drama in five acts by Maurice Maeterlinck. Music by Claude Debussy.

Cast: Arkël, the aged king of Allemonde—Basso. Genevieve, the wife of his son—Soprano. Golaud, her eldest son—Baritone. Pelléas, the younger son—Tenor. Mélisande, a mysterious visitant, wife of Golaud—Soprano. Yniold, son of Golaud through a former marriage—Soprano. A physician. Servants, blind beggars, etc.

Act I. A forest. Mélisande, a pale, mysterious creature with long golden hair, sits pensively by a well. Golaud, who is a mighty hunter, is lost in the forest. He hears the sound of crying and approaches curiously, asking Mélisande why she weeps. She runs away terrified, begging him not to touch her. He gently questions her, talking as if to a child, but she can only give him vague replies. She has been wronged she says, but will not tell by whom, and has worn a crown, which is now at the bottom of the well. She will throw herself after it, if he tries to recover it. Asking his name, she tells him she is sure he must be quite old for his hair and beard are beginning to turn gray. Observing her wide open eyes, he inquires how old she is. She does not reply and he suggests that she allow him to take her to some shelter, which she is persuaded to do. They wander off through the forest, scarcely knowing whither to turn their steps.

Act II. A hall in the castle. Genevieve is reading to the blind old king a letter from Golaud, which he has written to his brother Pelléas. It tells of his marriage to a maiden he found wandering in the forest. He asks Pelléas to intercede for him with his mother and Arkël, since they had wished him to marry instead the Princess Ursula. A light in the tower is to be the signal of forgiveness. Arkël quietly accepts the situation, with the philosophy of age, for, as Genevieve says, Golaud has always been thoughtful and prudent, and devoted to his little son. Pelléas enters, a youth of passionate, emotional nature, just now in deep grief over the approaching death of his friend, Marcellus. Arkël reminds him that his own father is at the point of death upstairs, and he must remain at the castle. Genevieve tells him to hang the light out for Golaud. Change of scene: A terrace in front of the castle. Genevieve and Mélisande walk together. The young bride is impressed by the gloom of the castle, and the great trees surrounding it. Pelléas enters, they talk together of ships and the sea. Mélisande is sorry when he speaks of departing the next day.

Act II. A fountain in the grounds. Pelléas and Mélisande are seated on its rim, idly talking. It is a sultry day. She looks into the fountain's clear depths, then tries to dip her hands into it. As she reaches down her hair falls about her like a cloud. Pelléas questions her about her meeting with Golaud. She takes off her marriage ring and tosses it in the air, catching it in her hand. At last she throws it too high, and it splashes into the water. She is disturbed and asks Pelléas what she shall say to Golaud. He replies, "The truth, the truth." Change of scene: A bedroom in the castle. Golaud has been thrown from his horse and hurt. Mélisande anxiously ministers to him. Tears come into her eyes, and to his questions she replies that she is unhappy. "Is it Pelléas?" he asks. "No, no," she says, "but I feel that I am going to die. Golaud attributes her fears to the gloom of the castle, and tells her that she need not mind Pelléas, who has always been different from others. Taking her hands in his, he misses the ring, and Mélisande, with the instinct to avoid the truth that characterises timorous, sensitive natures, says she dropped it in a cave by the sea while trying to escape from the tide. Golaud tells her she will have to go there at once to find it, and to take Pelléas with her, since it is dark. Change of scene. A grotto. Pelléas enters with Mélisande, talking very rapidly to cloak his emotion. Mélisande only answers in monosyllables. The sound of the waves is heard, and a moonbeam penetrating the dark cavern falls upon three old blind beggars, who have taken refuge there. Mélisande screams with fright, and Pelléas leads her out of the cavern.

Act III. A turret in the castle, surrounded by a well-worn path. It is night. Mélisande is combing her long hair at the window, crooning a strange song. (Mélisande: "To the foot of the tower my tresses flow down.") Pelléas hails her gaily, saying that he thought her hair was a great light. She leans out to speak to him and her hair brushes against his cheek. He tells her he is to depart the next day, and asks if he may kiss her hand. As she reaches far out, her masses of hair stream down suddenly, covering Pelléas like a mantle. (Pelléas: "Oh! Oh, your hair, your beautiful hair!") Deep emotion seizes him, and he caresses her beautiful tresses, holding them in his hands and kissing

them passionately, declaring the while that she is now his
prisoner and his kisses are going to her along her hair.
They are frightened by a sudden flight of doves around
the tower. Mélisande is troubled, and begs Pelléas to let
her go, or the doves will never return. Golaud enters, suspicious, upbraiding them for their folly. "You are such
babes," he cries, and departs with his brother. Change of
scene: Vaults under the castle. Golaud and Pelléas ex-
plore them. Golaud asks if his brother has been there
before. He leads him to a chasm in the cold dank vault,
and stands behind him sorely tempted to push him in.
Pelléas gives a hoarse cry and shakes off his grasp. They
depart without saying a word.

Change of scene: A terrace. The brothers emerge from
the vault; Pelléas greatly overcome, and glad to be in the
light and air again. Golaud warns him about Mélisande,
who, he says, is about to become a mother. Change of
scene: Before the castle. Golaud questions little Yniold
about Pelléas and Mélisande, and the child's artless answers only inflame his jealousy. Yniold cries out that his
father is hurting him, and is promised a bow and arrow as
a peace offering. Golaud still continues his jealous queries:
"Does Pelléas kiss your little mother?" he asks, and when
answered in the affirmative, he is filled with rage and
despair. At last he holds Yniold up to the window to spy
upon them, but they are sitting quietly looking at each
other. The child is frightened.

Act III. A room in the castle. Pelléas and Mélisande
enter from different doors. Pelléas tells of his father, who
is better, but has counselled him to go away. With the
prescience of those who are near death he has seen that his
son is not going to live much longer. Pelléas and Mélisande arrange to meet for a last farewell. They go out.
Arkël returns with Mélisande. He, too, has a premonition
of doom, and tells the girl that being so young she should
have joy instead of grief, and that she must awaken joy
in the hearts of others. He kisses her tenderly as Golaud

enters. There is blood on his forehead from the branches in the garden. Mélisande advances to wipe it off, but he turns on her savagely. He asks abruptly for his sword, and asks Mélisande why she trembles so. Taking her roughly by the arm, he demands of Arkël what he sees in her eyes? The old man replies slowly: "A great innocence only." Golaud bursts into a torrent of words. (Golaud: "Innocence? More than that.") He seizes Mélisande in frantic excitement, wildly talking to her of mysterious doubts, forcing her to her knees, and dragging her about by her long hair, with which he makes motions as if about to strangle her. Arkël, at first strangely passive, interferes. Golaud calms himself, speaking in a choked voice. (Golaud: "Do as you wish!") He flings open the door and departs. Change of scene: A terrace in twilight. Yniold struggling to lift a great stone. Sheep heard bleating in the dusk. Change of scene: A fountain. Pelléas enters, musing sadly about Mélisande, who appears presently, very quiet and gentle. She is breathless from her encounter with Golaud, but is no longer timorous and fearful. Pelléas suddenly kisses her and they pour out their love without reserve. (Pelléas: "Your voice sounds like the sea in springtime.") Mélisande says very simply that she has no other thought but Pelléas. Visions pass before her, and a grating sound is heard as the castle gates are barred by the castellan. Pelléas embraces her with suppressed passion, and they talk happily until Mélisande sees that Golaud is watching. Pelléas tells her to go, but it is too late. They bid each other a desperate farewell, knowing that their doom is at hand. Golaud, raining blows upon Pelléas with his sword, kills him. Mélisande, her tremors returning, flies, pursued by Golaud.

ACT V. A bedroom in the castle. Mélisande lies in bed pale and wan. Arkël sits quietly beside her. The physician attends her. Golaud is suffering horribly, believing that he is the cause of her illness. Mélisande awakens, asking to have the window opened—the one looking upon the sea. She speaks as if with the voice of a spirit. Golaud is brought to the bedside, and they are left alone. He asks her forgiveness, and she grants it listlessly as if she were troubled by so many words. Even then he cannot resist asking her if she loved Pelléas. "Yes," she says simply. "Is he here?" Golaud presses the question, and she is manifestly disturbed like a child that wishes to go to sleep, and is asked if it has been good that day. Arkël and the doctor enter and she turns with relief to the old man, who understands her so well. He shows her her child and Mélisande feebly says: "I am so sorry for her." The serving women enter, feeling that her death is at hand. Mélisande weeps. Golaud speaks to her, but Arkël hushes him, since a soul is about to depart. The serving women kneel in prayer. Mélisande's spirit has fled, and the old king, with a sacrificial gesture, raises the child from the cradle and leaves the room, followed silently by Golaud and the physician. "A life is ended, a life begins," he says solemnly.

PHILÉMON ET BAUCIS

Opera in two acts by Gounod. Text by Barbier and Carré. CAST: Philémon, an old peasant—Tenor. Baucis, his wife—Soprano. Jupiter—Baritone. Vulcan—Basso. Time, mythical period. Place, Phrygia. First production, Paris, 1860.

ACT I. Philémon and Baucis, two old peasants, are seated before their cottage at eventide. (Duet: "It is the hour of rest.") They are happy and contented with their lot and with each other. There is a strange stirring in the air, as if something unusual were about to happen. Bacchanalian chorus: "Daughters of Athor, mad bacchantes.") A storm arises, and amid thunder and lightning Jupiter and Vulcan visit the earth to punish the impious Phrygians for sacrilege. They arrive soaked with rain at the cottage and ask shelter for the night. (Jupiter:

"Strangers are we in this country.") Philémon receives
them hospitably, lighting a fire to dry their wet garments.
(Philémon: "Look! the flame has caught; the wood is
smoking.") Jupiter, in lightsome mood, jests with the
morose Vulcan, whose grievance is the indiscretion of
Venus. (Duet: " 'Mid the crashing sounds of hammers";
Jupiter: "Eh? What? Because Mercury fell in love?")
Baucis, left alone, meditates on her life with Philémon, and
their happiness in spite of trials, but, womanlike, deplores
her vanished youth and beauty. (Baucis: "Ah, were I
beautiful once more!") The two gods take their places at
the table. (Quartet: "Be seated at the table. Accept our
humble cheer.") Jupiter continues to jest with Vulcan,
and finding no water in the pitcher, commands Baucis
nevertheless to keep on pouring, and to her wonder, wine
flows from the spout. The gods warn the couple of coming trouble in Phrygia, promising immunity to them.
They may sleep in peace and will be protected. (Quartet:
"A sombre veil extends its shade.") Philémon and Baucis,
quietly reclining, lose consciousness of their surroundings
in slumber.

Act II. Intermezzo. Hunting call far off: "E-vo-hé!
E-vo-hé!") Baucis awakens with thoughts of vanished
youth in her heart. (Baucis: "Philémon would love me
ever.") To her surprise she sees beside her a handsome
youth, who still sleeps. (Baucis: "Memories steal o'er me.")
She recognises that it is Philémon, as he used to be, and
finds that she, too, is young and fair, for their guests have
given them back their youth. She awakens Philémon.
He is confused and does not know her. (Baucis: "Ungrateful one, my heart all filled with love.") Jupiter is delighted with his work, and, ever susceptible, woos Baucis
himself. (Jupiter: "Venus herself is not more fair.") His
advances are so pronounced that Baucis flees from him in
terror, hiding in the woods. (Baucis: "O laughing Nature! O fragrant gardens.") When Jupiter pursues her,
she kneels before him in supplication. (Jupiter: "Do not

kneel, fair mortal.") He asks for her love, and offers her riches and dazzling honours. (Duet: "O Philémon! Think not that I forget.") Though greatly flattered, she reminds him that he is transgressing the laws of hospitality, but they finally compromise upon a kiss. Philémon, finding out what is going on, becomes jealous, quarrelling with his once adored wife. Vulcan now takes a hand in the matter, and adjures them to live in peace; at their age they should be ashamed to quarrel so fiercely. Philémon is greatly upset, but Baucis, still elated by Jupiter's preference, replies that there is surely no harm in being attractive. Vulcan cynically declares that all women are false—Venus certainly is. Philémon sharply responds that he has no desire to copy the morals of the gods in Olympus. Vulcan becomes decidedly unpopular, and a lively discussion ensues. (Terzett: "Live the gods like us, or no.") Baucis at last decides that though her grey hairs and wrinkles were hateful, she would gladly have them back again, for peace sake. (Baucis: " 'Neath the weight of age our loving hearts.") Jupiter is too gallant to make her old again, but promises to leave her alone in future. The opera ends with a joyous quartet. (Quartet: "O happiness enchanting.")

THE PIPE OF DESIRE

An opera by Frederick S. Converse. Text by George Edward Barton.

CAST: Iolan, a peasant—Tenor. Naoia—Soprano. The Old One—Basso. Chorus of elves.

The opera opens with the song of the elves at their work in the forest, by command of the Old One, their king. The peasant Iolan, who formerly lived in the valley, but left it for a wider field, returns in high feather at his success, singing joyously as he anticipates the realisation of all his hopes. He is about to claim Naoia, to whom he is betrothed, as his bride. The elves stop their work to salute him, and when reproached by the Old One, claim a holiday in honour of spring's first day. Iolan, mounting the rocks, asks them all to the wedding feast, and they accept. The Old One, however, sits silent and grim, and when Iolan hears that he is their king, he mocks at him, saying, "What, that old fellow?" The elves hasten to inform him that the Old One possesses the wonderful Pipe of Desire, through which he can rule the world if he so desires. Iolan is incredulous at first, and the elves coax their king to play upon the pipe for him, which he does against his will, as its strains bring only sorrow to any mortal who listens to them. (Dance of Spring.) The dance is a marvellous one, but does not impress the self-confident peasant, who declares that the elves were not obliged to dance, but desired to do so, to avoid honest toil. The elves, now angry, demand that the pipe shall be played for Iolan alone. As they have said, he finds himself compelled to dance willy nilly. Furious with rage, he takes hold of the pipe, and swears that he will make the Old One cut capers now at will. The most horrible discords come from the pipe until he plays a love tune and calls Naoia to come to him. He sees before him a vision of domestic contentment, after the struggle he has had to win his way. The pipe gives forth no sound, and the Old One tells him it is because he has made a selfish use of it. He himself takes the pipe, and as he plays on it strange things happen. Iolan beholds before him the cottage of his betrothed, who lies dangerously ill. She has heard his call, and in her delirium rises from her bed, and goes barefoot into the forest. She raves as she sees him, but knows that it is he, and speaks of their marriage as if it had already occurred. At last, overcome by excitement and fever, she falls dead at his feet. Iolan is distraught. He flings his money into the bushes, curses the cruel God, who has thus wronged him, and behaves like a madman, until the Old One brings him to himself by reminding him that his own folly, not God's decree, had brought these things about. Iolan now begins to feel sorry,

and the elves, who are more sympathetic than these **wood**
creatures usually are, ask the Old One to play upon the
pipe again. Softly he begins the song of autumn, following it by the song of winter. Iolan loses his self-confidence
and youthful vigour, and feels himself attacked by the
chill of age and approaching death. "Not my will, but
God's," he reflects, for he has learned his lesson. Looking
upward to the heavens he sees Naoia on the rocks above him,
stretching out her arms in greeting. With a joyous shout,
he bounds up the path to meet her, and hand in hand they
begin their life together.

PIQUE-DAME

(The Queen of Spades)

Opera in three acts by Peter Tschaikowsky. Text from
Pushkin's novel by Tschaikowsky. German by Bernhard.
CAST: Hermann—Tenor. Count Tomsky—Baritone.
Prince Jeletsky—Baritone. Czekalinsky—Tenor. Ssurin
—Basso. Tschaplitzky—Tenor. Narumoff—Basso. Mas-
ter of ceremonies—Tenor. Countess—Mezzo-soprano.
Lisa, her granddaughter—Soprano. Pauline, her friend
—Alto. Governess—Mezzo-soprano. Mascha, servant—
Soprano. Place, St. Petersburg. Time, end of the eigh-
teenth century. First production, St. Petersburg, 1890.

ACT I. A large summer garden. A number of men,
women and children are walking about singing and laughing. Several officers, among them Czekalinsky, Ssurin,
Tomsky and Hermann, are talking of the previous night
passed in gambling and of Hermann, who was conspicuous
at the table by his pale face and gloomy manner. Hermann confesses to his friend Tomsky that he is in love, but
is too poor to marry the noble lady of his choice, whom
indeed he hardly knows, though he fears he will die if he cannot win her. The two friends meet Prince Jeletsky, and
congratulate him on his betrothal to Lisa, and Hermann

discovers to his distress that she is the lady whom he adores.
(Quintet: "I am in despair.") He has attracted the attention of the old countess and her grandchild, however,
by his pale and gloomy countenance, and the fair Lisa has
become deeply interested in him. Tomsky relates the history of the countess. When a young girl she was a desperate gambler and had lost all her money in Paris. A
certain count, whose advances she had formerly repulsed,
promised, for an interview, to name the three winning cards;
after long wavering she sold herself to him and ac-
cumulated a fortune. She had revealed the names of the
cards to two persons, her future husband and a lover, but
a spirit appeared to her and announced that she would die
if another lover should appear, and should force her to
reveal the secret. Since that time she had been universally
known as Pique-Dame (the queen of spades). The listeners
agree that the old mummy of a countess is undoubtedly
safe from any new love affair, and laughingly invite Hermann to secure a knowledge of the winning cards.

Change of scene: Lisa's room. The young girl and Pauline and her friends amuse themselves with songs and dancing. (Duet: "Already night.") Lisa sings a sad song
("Yet untouched by grief"), but the other maidens merrily
answer with a popular Russian melody. ("Now, little
Marianne.") The governess sends them all home. Lisa,
having retired to rest, cannot sleep; she thinks she loves
her intended husband, yet she cannot forget the face of
Hermann. (Aria: "The flood of tears.") Hermann appears upon the balcony; and Lisa flees in alarm, for he
threatens to shoot himself. She returns, and, weeping, listens to his protestations of love. Hearing voices, the
countess appears and Hermann conceals himself; she is
angry that Lisa is still awake and orders her to retire. Hermann is thinking of the three cards, and when the old
woman has gone renews his wooing and Lisa yields.

Act II. Masked ball at a stately mansion. (Chorus of
guests: "Laughing and toying.") The young officers are

astonished at Hermann's altered demeanour. The prince is annoyed by Lisa's coldness and swears that he loves her. (Aria: "I love you.") Hermann has received a note, saying that Lisa must see him at once. (Interlude: "The sincere shepherdess." Chloe refuses the rich Plutos and accepts the poor but loved Daphnis.) Hermann cannot rid himself of the thought of the three cards. He meets Lisa; she gives him the key of the garden, and directs him to pass through the chamber of her grandmother, who is absent.

Change of scene: Bedroom of the countess. Hermann enters through a secret door and gazes upon the picture of the countess, whose fate is bound up in his own. He hears footsteps and conceals himself behind a curtain; the countess and several servants approach; she enters the adjoining room and returns in her night dress. She seats herself in an armchair and muses upon the past. (Song: "Je crains de lui parler le nuit," from Grétry's opera, "Richard the Lion Heart.") As she is about to fall asleep Hermann stands before her and pleads with her to tell him the secret of the three winning cards. She refuses and he threatens her with a pistol. She dies of fright, but the secret is buried with her. Lisa rushes in, and when in his confusion Hermann tells her of the cards, she is incensed that he has deceived her, and orders him off as a murderer.

Act III. Hermann's room in the barracks. Lisa has relented and asked him to meet her at the quay at midnight. A funeral procession passes, the old countess is carried to her grave. Her spirit appears to Hermann and commands him to marry Lisa and to place his money upon the cards: "three, seven and ace." Half insane, he repeats their names.

Change of scene: At night on the canal. Lisa awaits Hermann. (Aria: "I will succumb to grief.") The clocks strike the midnight hour and he rushes to her arms. (Duet: "Now we are united forever.") They determine to fly, but first Lisa follows her lover to the gambling rooms, where he hopes to win the gold. Frightened, she listens to his insane ramblings; he laughs, throws her from him and rushes away. In despair she throws herself into the water.

Change of scene: The gambling house. (Chorus: "Let us enjoy life.") The prince is here for the first time; he says he has been unlucky in love and hopes to win. Tomsky sings a merry song ("If girls had wings"), then follows a gambling melody in chorus. ("Whether it snows or rains.") Hermann enters; the prince asks Tomsky to be his second. All are astonished at his appearance, but he declares that he will play. He places 30,000 rubles on the tray and wins; his comrades expect a misfortune. He again wins on the seven; he endeavours to dispel the ominous silence by a song. ("Life is like gambling.") No one will play with him any longer, only the prince expresses his willingness; Hermann is uneasy. When he uncovers the ace, the spirit of the countess appears; now totally insane he draws his dagger and stabs himself to the heart; dying he asks the forgiveness of the prince.

THE POLISH JEW

Opera in two acts by Karl Weis. Text from Erckmann-Chatrian by Victor Léon and Richard Batka.

Cast of the action: Hans Mathis, burgomaster and innkeeper—Baritone. Katharina, his wife—Mezzo-soprano. Annette, their daughter—Soprano. Christian Brehm, officer of gendarmes—Tenor. Dr. Frank, notary. Schmitt, forester. A Polish Jew. Niklas, servant. Night watchman, peasants, musicians, etc.

Cast of the dream: The presiding judge (Forester Schmitt). The actuary (Notary Frank). An associate (night watchman). An apparition. Niklas. Mathis. Katharina. Annette. Brehm. A hangman and assistants. Gendarmes, etc. Place, an Alsatian village in the winter of 1833. First production, Prague, 1901.

The rich burgomaster Mathis is about to marry his beloved daughter Annette to an officer of gendarmes, Christian Brehm. Forester Schmitt relates a tale to the bridal
couple, of a severe winter, the winter of the Pole. The
name originated in the following manner: Some fifteen
years ago the inn was filled with guests, while a storm
howled without. Suddenly the bells of a sleigh were heard
and a Polish Jew entered, asking for shelter, which was
granted. The next day the stranger proceeded on his journey. Soon afterward his horse was found running loose,
and on the road was a blood-stained cap; the Pole had undoubtedly been murdered, but notwithstanding all efforts,
neither his body nor any trace of the murderer was ever
discovered. The unknown murderer is Mathis, who was at
that time in need of money, and founded his riches upon
the gold thus obtained. No one suspects him, as he is universally loved and respected for his charity and cheerful
demeanour. But his conscience troubles him, and this evening, at the betrothal of his daughter, with the circumstances precisely the same, a snow storm and the sound of
bells and the entrance of a Polish Jew into the inn, he falls
unconscious to the ground. He is put to bed and has a
strange dream, which is represented on the stage. He
imagines that he stands before the judge, and at first denies
his crime, but subsequently confesses and is condemned to
death. When he is grasped by the headsman, he cries out
in despair and awakens. He is found dead in his bed in the
morning.

THE POSTILION OF LONGJUMEAU

Comic opera in three acts by Adolphe Adam. Text by
De Leuven and Brunswick.

Cast of the first act: Chapelou, postilion—Tenor. Bijou,
wheelwright—Basso. Marquis de Corcy—Basso. Madelaine, hostess—Soprano. Place, the village of Long-

jumeau. Time, 1756. Cast of the second and third acts:
Saint Phar (Chapelou)—Tenor. Alcindor (Bijou)—
Basso. De Corcy—Basso. Bourdon—Basso. Madame de
Latour (Madelaine)—Soprano. Rosa, her maid. Place,
country house of Madame de Latour, near Fontainebleau.
Time, 1766. First production, Paris, 1836.

Act I. In the village of Longjumeau. The postilion
Chapelou, who possesses a fine voice, is celebrating his marriage with Madelaine, when the Marquis de Corcy appears.
A wheel of his carriage is broken, and the smith, Bijou,
who is envious of Chapelou, hastens to repair it, in order
to disturb the feast, since Chapelou, as postilion, is compelled to drive. De Corcy, the manager of the royal amuse-
ments, who is on a voyage of discovery for a new tenor,
hears Chapelou sing, and makes him such a brilliant offer,
that he leaves Madelaine and accompanies the marquis.
(Scene, chorus, Chapelou, Madelaine: "Prosperous and
happy be this hour"; Madelaine's song: "Dear husband, believe me"; Duet: "That is wonderful"; Ensemble: "A
happy pair"; Rondo of Chapelou—song of the postilion:
"Friends, hear the story"; Terzett and finale, marquis,
Chapelou, Bijou: "Do not turn away your luck"; Madelaine, Bijou and chorus: "Come, sweetheart.")

Act II. A chamber in the garden. Chapelou has become a great singer under the name of St. Phar. Bijou has
also followed him, but remains a member of the chorus.
Madelaine, who has been living with her aunt, returns as a
rich heiress and wins St. Phar's love as Madame de Latour.
He has become a great admirer of the fair sex and promises her marriage, but as he cannot keep his word, on account of his previous marriage with Madelaine, he induces
the opera singer Bourdon to array himself in the garb of
a priest, in order in this way to enjoy the love of Madame
de Latour. The Marquis de Corcy, who has suffered severely from the caprice of St. Phar, also woos Madelaine.
She has become aware of the trick and engages a real priest.
(Aria of Madelaine: "I will see him again"; Chorus and

ensemble of the royal singers: "Oh, what misery"; Romance
of St. Phar: "From early dawn"; Aria of Alcindor
(Bijou): "By the chorus of our stage"; Duet, St. Phar
and Madame de Latour: "Oh most beautiful of women";
Chorus and finale: "My wishes are fulfilled.")

ACT III. An apartment in the country house. The marquis discloses the cheat of St. Phar, and when he and his
associates have been duly frightened, Madelaine reveals her
identity to the happy Chapelou. (Chorus and scene: "O
what joy"; Aria of St. Phar: "I am now one of the aris-
tocracy"; Terzett, St. Phar, Alcindor, Bourdon: "Hanged!
hanged!" Duet, Madame de Latour and St. Phar: "You
see me in anguish"; Finale: "Quick, in the name of the
king.")

THE PRISONER OF WAR

Opera in two acts by Karl Goldmark. Text by Emil
Schlicht.

CAST: Achilles—Baritone. Agamemnon—Basso. Priam—
Basso. Automedon—Tenor. Idaeus—Tenor. Thetis—
Mezzo-soprano. Briseis—Soprano. Place, the Greek
camp before Troy. Time, toward the end of the Trojan
war. First production, Vienna, 1899.

ACT I. In the tent of Achilles. The Greek hero grieves
deeply over the death of Patroclus, whose funeral urn he
has just buried. He swears vengeance against his enemies,
and encourages his men to victory. Left alone he again
laments his loss. ("Gone from my sight.") Thetis, his
mother, and the Nereids approach on the sea and endeavour
to appease his wrath. Briseis, sent by Agamemnon to
Achilles, covers Hector's dishonoured corpse with earth.
Asked by Achilles the reason for this action, she answers
that she has been requested to do so by the spirit of
Patroclus. Dismissed by Achilles, she departs and prays
to Aphrodite that she may win the heart of Achilles, whom
she secretly loves.

Act II. The same scene. Achilles, disturbed by visions, receives a soothing drink from Briseis. He asks for music, and she sings of his own life, devoid of love. (Briseis: "In the roaring forest.") Priam and Idaeus appear, led by Hermes. Priam exercises all his powers of persuasion to move the heart of Achilles, in order to obtain from him the body of Hector. Only when Briseis calls to Achilles, "Take from Patroclus the other burden," does he relent. Priam thanks Briseis, and a truce of twelve days is granted by Achilles for the funeral ceremonies. Briseis, set at liberty by Achilles, comes to bid him farewell before going on board of the king's ship. Achilles realises that he loves her. After a grand duet between them the slaves open the doors of the tent and the waiting warriors cry: "To the battle! to victory!"

THE PROPHET
(Le Prophète)

Opera in five acts by Meyerbeer. Text by Scribe.

Cast: John of Leyden—Tenor. Fides, his mother—Alto. Bersa, his bride—Soprano. Jonas, Matthiesen and Zacharias, Anabaptists—Tenor and Basso. Count Oberthal—Baritone. Place, Holland, in and near Munster. Time, 1536. First production, Paris, 1849.

Act I. A scene in Dordrecht, Holland. Berta wishes to be married to John, but they require first the consent of Count Oberthal, her liege lord. The Anabaptists, led by Jonas, Matthiesen and Zacharias, are inciting the people to revolt, and the count has repulsed their attack on his castle. He listens to the petition of Berta and Fides, but refuses to grant it. Berta's beauty finds favour with him, and he drags the two women by force to his castle. The Anabaptists return and continue to incite the people to rebellion.

Act II. Inn of John of Leyden. The Anabaptists, who come to the inn, attempt to induce John to accompany them to Munster. They have discovered in him a striking resemblance to the picture of King David in Munster, and desire to make use of it for their purposes. John is a visionary, well suited for a religious leader. He has a dream, which the three men interpret according to their own interests, but his love for Berta keeps him at home. But now Berta suddenly returns, having escaped from the castle. Oberthal follows her with an armed force and gives John the choice of surrendering Berta, or having his mother put to death. John, in despair, gives up Berta and receives the blessing of his mother. The Anabaptists promise him revenge, and he accompanies them.

ACT III. Camp of the Anabaptists before Munster. Ballet and ice carnival.

Change of scene: A tent. Oberthal has been taken prisoner and the Anabaptists decree his death. John has resolved to leave the Anabaptists, whose cruelties he abhors, and being told by Oberthal that Berta has escaped and is living in Munster, he is about to set the count free, when he receives intelligence of a revolt of his men.

Change of scene: The camp. John quells the revolt and compels the obedience of his followers.

ACT IV. Square of the City Hall at Munster. John has now conquered Munster and governs it as prophet, feared and cursed by the people. Fides has become a beggar in the city, where Berta, clad as a pilgrim, finds her, and being convinced that the prophet has slain John she determines to avenge him.

Change of scene: Before the cathedral. In solemn procession John and his followers enter the church, and the prophet is crowned with great pomp. When his coronation is proclaimed Fides recognises her son and makes her way to his side. He longs to press her to his heart, but is compelled by his position to disown her. When the people are about to slay him if she persists in her statement, she declares that she is mistaken and is led away in chains.

ACT V. A chamber in the palace of John at Munster.

The three Anabaptists, Jonas, Matthiesen and Zacharias, are willing to betray John to gain the pardon of the emperor. He visits Fides in the dungeon and beseeches her forgiveness. Berta, bent on revenge, appears at the palace. She now learns that John is the hated prophet; in vain he asks her pardon. She stabs herself in his presence, cursing him with her last breath. John discovers the treachery of the Anabaptist leaders and resolves to punish them.

Change of scene: A banqueting hall in the palace. Bacchanalian scene and ballet. The Anabaptists surround Johann, who is singing a drinking song, when Oberthal appears with the imperial troops to arrest him. The prophet is prepared, however. Unobserved, he signals—and smoke pours into the hall. Loud explosions follow, and the hall is soon in flames. John, who has filled the palace with powder, sets fire to it and with a dreadful crash the walls fall upon the crowd. The prophet dies with Fides, who has joined him, and in their dying hour gives him her forgiveness.

THE QUEEN OF SHEBA

Opera in four acts by Karl von Goldmark. Text by Mosenthal.

CAST: King Solomon—Baritone. Baal Hanan, overseer of the palace—Baritone. Assad—Tenor. High priest—Basso. Sulamith, his daughter—Soprano. The queen of Sheba—Mezzo-soprano. Astaroth, her slave—Soprano. Place, Jerusalem and the desert. First production, Vienna, 1875.

ACT I. Palace of Solomon. Sulamith, daughter of the high priest, is to be married to Assad, a young courtier, who has been sent to receive the queen of Sheba, the guest of King Solomon. Assad repulses his bride, and the king demands the reason. The youth has not seen the face of the queen, for she will unveil only when she comes before King Solomon, but, as he believes, he has surprised one of her companions while bathing in a stream, has fallen in love with her and his love is returned. The queen of Sheba enters and is magnificently entertained. When Assad sees her face he falls to the earth, for she is the lady of the bath. He approaches the queen, but she draws away from him and declares that she does not know him. Assad loses his senses.

Act II. The garden. Moonlight. The queen loves Assad and seeks him secretly, assures him of her love, and departs. As the guards appear they find Assad drunken with love and take him for a madman. Change of scene: The temple. During the solemn ceremonies Sulamith, according to custom, sacrifices doves; she is to be married to Assad that day. When Assad, led by Solomon, enters the temple he rushes toward the queen, but is again repudiated by her. Driven to madness the youth curses God, and is handed over to justice. When the queen intervenes in his favour, Solomon begins to understand the situation and orders Assad to be led away.

Act III. The festival chamber. Ballet. The queen demands Assad from the king, and when he refuses, she departs, uttering threats. Solomon soothes the grief of Sulamith and prophesies peace and happiness.

Act IV. The desert. Assad, wandering in the desert, is found by the returning queen. She again attempts to beguile him, but he curses her and she departs in anger. A storm rages in the desert, during which Sulamith appears to the despairing Assad; she forgives him and he dies in her arms.

THE RATCATCHER OF HAMELIN

Opera in five acts by Neszler. Text by Hofmann.

Cast: Gruwelholt, burgomaster—Basso. Tunneborne, bailiff—Basso. Rhynperg, canon—Basso. Ethelerus, writer to the council—Tenor. Heribert, son of the bailiff, architect—Tenor. Hunold Singuf—Baritone. Wulf, the

smith—Baritone. Regina, daughter of the burgomaster
—Soprano. Dorothea, her cousin—Alto. Gertrud, a
fisher girl—Soprano. Place, in or near Hamelin. Time,
1284. First production, Leipsic, 1879.

ACT I. The council chamber. There is a plague of rats
in the town, and Hunold Singuf undertakes to get rid of
them. He does not disclose his identity, and his proposi-
tion is accepted.

Change of scene: Garden of the burgomaster. Heribert
has returned from a journey and greets Regina as his
bride.

ACT II. An inn. Hunold entertains the guests with song.
When the smith, Wulf, and his bride, Gertrud, enter, the
latter gazes upon Hunold with astonishment and rushes to
his arms, for he is the embodiment of her dreams.

Change of scene: The river and fisherman's hut. Wulf
tries to regain Gertrud's love, but in vain.

ACT III. The cellar of the council chamber. Humorous
scene between Ethelerus, Rhynperg and Hunold. The latter is a favourite with the women, and Rhynperg wagers
that he cannot obtain a kiss from Gertrud.

Change of scene: A street on the banks of the Weser.
Wulf is furious over the loss of Gertrud. Hunold having
caused the rats and mice to drown themselves in the river,
had then met Wulf and wounded him in a fight.

ACT IV. Chamber of the council. Hunold asks for his
100 marks, according to agreement, but is refused, for
the reason that the burgomaster's house still holds the
king of the rats. When he offers to relinquish his
claim for a kiss from Regina, he is indignantly ordered
out.

Change of scene: The market place and statue of Roland.
Despite the warning voice of the statue, Hunold resolves
to obtain the kiss by magic.

Change of scene: Festal chamber of the council. Hunold enters as a singer and exercises his power upon Regina,
who jumps from her chair and kisses him. Hunold is ar-

rested and imprisoned. His trial is to be held the following day.

ACT V. Bridge over the Weser. After a scene in which Gertrud laments the lost love of Hunold, he is convicted of sorcery and ordered to be burned at the stake. Gertrud saves him by choosing him for her husband. Hunold swears to keep the peace and to live for Gertrud alone, but she refuses to believe him and throws herself into the Weser. Hunold swears vengeance against the town, and while the citizens are at church, he lures all the children of the city with his fife and leads them into the magic mountain, which closes after them.

REGINA; OR, THE MARAUDERS

Romantic opera in three acts by Albert Lortzing. Text by Adolf L'Arronge.

CAST: Jobst Zadeck, steward—Basso. Regina, his daughter—Soprano. Reinhard, bailiff—Tenor. Wolfram, forester—Baritone. Steffen Balder—Tenor, Lise—Soprano, both in Zadeck's service. Barbara, Steffen's mother—Mezzo-soprano. Ruprecht, a vagabond—Basso. Place, a valley in Silesia. Time, end of August, 1813.

ACT I. Before the castle. The field hands, who have not been paid for some time, refuse to work any longer; Steffen tries in vain to pacify them. Reinhard, the bailiff, arrives and reminds them of the kindness of their master. (Aria: "Think of your master.") He succeeds in persuading them to return to work. Regina, who has heard all, thanks him and complains that Wolfram, the forester, pursues her with his love. Reinhard longs to protect her, but he is poor, and fears that her parents will think him presumptuous in asking for her as his bride. He determines, however, to try his fate, and if unsuccessful to go to the war. (Duet: "My loving heart beats.") Zadeck brings news of a victory of the Prussians; he is satisfied with Reinhard's ability and industry and blesses the lovers. (Quintet: "O day of joy.") Wolfram, overhearing this, complains that he who once saved Zadeck's life has received no reward. He swears he will be avenged and compel Regina to be his. (Aria: "Brought up in poverty.") The countrymen have received their wages, and arrange a dance, when Steffen reports a number of suspicious characters in the wood. The marauders appear and demand money. Wolfram exercises his authority over them, and tells Zadeck he will again save him if he will bestow on him the hand of his daughter. (Ensemble: "Despair and fright.") When Zadeck refuses, the marauders set fire to the castle. Reinhard is wounded, and Wolfram carries off Regina.

Act II. A peasant's hut, separated into two parts by a wall. Barbara sings ("At early morn"); Wolfram enters and orders Barbara to attend upon Regina. He refuses to listen to her prayers (Aria: "Brought up by a loving mother"), and after threatening her with violence, unless she will give up Reinhard, he departs. The marauders have now become intoxicated and retire to the house. (Chorus: "The devil can endure this no longer.") Steffen fills their glasses anew (Song: "What is the best in this world"), and when they have rushed out in search of new excitement leaves the house with the women.

Act III. In the open country. A company of volunteers approach. (Chorus: "Sound, songs of joy.") Zadeck is seeking his daughter and Reinhard asks the soldiers to assist him in punishing the robbers. Steffen rushes in and reports that Regina has again been taken from him by Wolfram and carried to a lonely castle. They follow him in haste.

Change of scene: The ruins of a castle. Wolfram curses the marauders for allowing Steffen to escape. Ruprecht reports that Reinhard and a band of armed men are approaching. Regina is joyful, but Wolfram informs her that he has placed powder in the castle, which he would explode to prevent her from falling into the hands of her friends. The fight draws near, Regina is alone. (Aria: "The deciding moment approaches.") Thinking the robbers have been victorious, she seizes a torch to set fire to the powder, when she thinks she hears Reinhard's voice. Wolfram returns defeated, and hurries to the turret. Regina seizes his gun and shoots him, and hearing the noise, soldiers come from all directions. They find in the turret the silver which had been taken from the castle, and deliver it to Zadeck. The Silesian army passes returning from war. (Closing chorus: "Hail to our chief!")

RIENZI

Opera in five acts by Wagner. Text from Bulwer's novel by the composer.

CAST: Cola Rienzi, papal notary—Tenor. Irene, his sister—Soprano. Steffano Colonna—Basso. Adriano, his son—Mezzo-soprano. Paolo Orsini—Basso. Raimondo, papal legate—Basso. Baroncello—Tenor. Cecco—Basso. A messenger—Soprano. Place, Rome. Time, the fourteenth century. First production, Dresden, 1842.

ACT I. A street with house of Rienzi. Rienzi, a papal notary, rescues his sister Irene from the Orsini, and confides her to the protection of Adriano Colonna, who loves her. Rienzi resolves to give peace to Rome and refuses to accept the crown, but is willing to lead the people in their revolt against the nobles.

ACT II. A chamber in the Capitol. Rienzi, who is now in full power, proclaims peace, receives foreign ambassadors and entertains his guests royally. The defeated nobles come to kneel in submission to him. Adriano succeeds in circumventing a conspiracy of the nobles, but Rienzi is only saved from the dagger of Orsini by a shirt of mail. Rienzi condemns his enemy to death, but later pardons him at the request of Adriano and Irene on condition that the nobles will take an oath of fealty.

Act III. The nobles have fled to raise a new revolt against Rienzi, thus breaking their oath, but he conquers them in a bloody battle, in which Colonna, Adriano's father, loses his life. This event estranges Adriano from Rienzi, and the former also accuses him of having separated him from Irene.

Act IV. A street. The pope and the emperor of Germany have combined against Rienzi; Adriano incites the people against him to avenge his father's death. Once again Rienzi appears in all his power, but when about to proceed to high mass at the Lateran Church is confronted by the legate with the ban of the church. Adriano endeavours to gain the consent of Irene to fly with him, but she refuses.

Act V. A hall in the Capitol. Adriano wishes to save Irene, but she refuses to follow him, and determines to cast in her lot with her brother.

Change of scene: Before the capitol. Rienzi kneels in prayer. Against his will Irene remains with him. The people rush forward with torches, bent on Rienzi's destruction, and when he appears on a balcony to speak to them they set fire to the Capitol. To complete their work they hurl stones at Rienzi and Irene. Adriano bravely enters the Capitol to save Irene from the flames, but the building collapses and all three perish in the ruins.

RIGOLETTO

Opera in four acts by Verdi. Text adapted from Victor Hugo's "Le roi s'amuse" by Piave.

Cast: The prince of Mantua—Tenor. Rigoletto, his court jester—Baritone. Gilda, Rigoletto's daughter—Soprano. Count of Monterone—Basso. Count of Ceprano—Baritone. The countess, his wife—Soprano. Marullo,

cavalier—Baritone.   Borsa, a courtier—Tenor.   Sparafucile, a bravo—Basso.   Maddalena, his sister—Mezzo-
soprano.   Giovanna, Maddalena's companion—Alto.   An
officer—Basso.   A page—Mezzo-soprano.   Place, Mantua
and vicinity.   Time, the sixteenth century.   First production, Venice, 1851.

ACT I.   A room in the palace.   The king has seen an
unknown beauty in the church and desires to possess her.
He also pays court to the Countess Ceprano.   (Ballad: "I
love beauty.")   Rigoletto, the humpbacked jester of the
prince, mocks the husbands of the ladies to whom the prince
is paying attention, and advises the prince to get rid of
them by prison or death.   The noblemen resolve to take
vengeance on Rigoletto, especially Count Monterone, whose
daughter the prince had dishonoured.   Monterone curses
the prince and Rigoletto.

ACT II.   (Or, if the opera is produced in three acts,
change of scene of the first act.)   A street; half of the
stage, divided by a wall, is occupied by the courtyard of
Rigoletto's house.   Thinking of the curse, the jester approaches and is accosted by the bandit Sparafucile, who
offers his services.   (Duet: "The old man cursed me.")
Rigoletto opens a door in the wall and visits his daughter
Gilda, whom he is concealing from the prince.   (Scene: "We
are alike."   Duet: "My father! when I see thee.")   She
does not know her father's occupation, and as he has forbidden her to appear in public, she has been nowhere except
to church.   When Rigoletto has gone the prince enters,
whom Gilda only knows as a student she had met at the
church.   (Duet: "My heart calls, I love him.")   He calls
himself Gualtier Maldé.   Later, the hostile noblemen seeing her at the wall, believe her to be the mistress of the
jester.   They abduct her, and when Rigoletto arrives they
inform him they have abducted the Countess Ceprano, and
with this idea he assists them in their arrangements.   Too
late Rigoletto realises that he has been duped, and shudderingly thinks of the curse.

Act III (or Act II). The prince hears that Gilda has been abducted. (Aria: "I see her tears.") The noblemen inform him that they have captured Rigoletto's mistress, and by their description he recognises Gilda. She is in the palace, and he hastens to see her. The noblemen now make sport of Rigoletto. He tries to find Gilda by singing, and as he fears she may fall into the hands of the prince, at last acknowledges that she is his daughter. (Rigoletto: "Yes, my daughter!") Gilda begs her father to send the people away, and acknowledges to him her shame, of which the prince was guilty. (Finale: "Speak, we are alone.") The act ends with Rigoletto's oath of vengeance against his master.

Act IV. A street. The half of the stage shows the house of Sparafucile, with two rooms, one above the other, open to the view of the audience. Rigoletto enters with Gilda, who still loves the prince. Rigoletto shows her the prince in the house of the bandit amusing himself with Sparafucile's sister Maddalena. (Canzone: "Oh, how deceitful are women's hearts.") Rigoletto bargains with the bandit, who is ready to murder his guest, whom he does not know, for money. (Quartet: "As a dancer you appear.") Rigoletto orders his daughter to put on man's attire and go to Verona, whither he will follow later. Gilda goes, but fears an attack upon the prince. Rigoletto offers the bandit 20 scudi for the death of the prince. As a thunderstorm is approaching, the prince determines to remain in the house, and Sparafucile assigns to him the ground floor as sleeping quarters. Gilda returns disguised as a man and hears the bandit promise Maddalena, who begs the life of the prince, that if by midnight another can be found to take the prince's place he will spare his life. Gilda resolves to sacrifice herself for the prince and enters the house. When Rigoletto arrives with the money he receives from the bandit a corpse wrapped in a bag and rejoices in his triumph. He is about to cast the sack into the river, weighting it with stones, when he hears the voice of the prince singing as he leaves the house. Bewildered, he opens the wrappings, and to his despair discovers the corpse of his daughter, who for a moment revives and declares she is glad to die for her beloved. As she breathes her last, Rigoletto exclaims in horror, "The old man's curse is fulfilled."

THE RING OF THE NIBELUNG

An operatic representation in three days and an introduction by Richard Wagner.

THE INTRODUCTION: THE RHEINGOLD

CAST: Wotan—Baritone. Donner—Basso. Fröh— Tenor. Loge—Tenor. Alberich—Baritone. Mime—Tenor. Fricka—Soprano. Woglinde—Soprano. Wellgunde— Soprano. Flosshilde—Alto. First production, Munich, 1869.

The three Rhine daughters, Woglinde, Wellgunde and Flosshilde, are engaged in play at the bottom of the Rhine. As they swim about, to them comes the dwarf Alberich, a Nibelung (inhabitant of the under world, Niflheim), who tries to catch one of them, but is laughed at by the three maidens. The sun shines into the water and illumines the Rheingold, guarded by the Rhine daughters, and, despite the warning of their father, they relate to Alberich that "he who can fashion a ring from the Rheingold and possess it will own the world and all its mighty power." As they do not consider Alberich dangerous, they confess "that only he who cares nought for the power of love can obtain the magic power to convert the gold into a ring." But the daughters of the Rhine have underestimated Alberich's cunning. Mightier than love, which he now curses, is his desire for riches and power. He snatches the gold from the Rhine daughters and, laughing derisively, disappears within the depths. In an open change of scene

(in fact, the entire representation should be in one scene),
the stage shows a broad country, with Walhalla, the home
of the gods, built by the giants, in the background. Wotan
and Fricka are sleeping. Fricka awakes, sees the completed structure, and arouses Wotan. The gods realise
sorrowfully that the giants will receive as their reward the
goddess Freya, whose apples confer everlasting youth.
When the giants Fafner and Fasolt demand their pay,
Donner and Fröh attempt to protect Freya. Loge appears
and tells of the ring which Alberich has fashioned from the
Rheingold. Both Wotan and the giants are seized with a
desire to possess it. Fafner and Fasolt take Freya away
by force, but agree to release her if Wotan will produce the
gold by nightfall. The departure of Freya causes the
gods to lose their youth, and Wotan determines to obtain
the ring. Alberich having subjugated in Niflheim all the
Nibelungs by the power of the ring, drives them to slavish
tasks in order to accumulate treasure. His brother, the
smith Mime, has fashioned for him a magic helmet, which
has the power of making its bearer invisible and to change
him into any other form he desires. When Loge guides
Wotan to the regions beneath the earth, the gods obtain
from Alberich the secret of the helmet, and Loge outwits
the suspicious Nibelung by expressing doubt of its power.
Alberich changes himself before the eyes of the gods first
into a dragon, then into a toad, which Wotan quickly
crushes with his foot, while Loge grasps the helmet. Alberich is carried by the two gods to the upper world, and they
refuse to release him until he has delivered to the gods the
treasure of the Nibelungs as well as the helmet and ring.
When Alberich sees that his ring is stolen he becomes
frantic and curses it and declares it will bring death to him
who wears it. When the giants return, the gold and helmet
are piled up for them in a heap, but Wotan refuses to give
up the ring. Erda arises from the depths of the earth to
warn Wotan against the ring and predicts the destruction
of the gods. Wotan, awakening from his trance, throws

the ring to the giants, and thereby Freya is released. The curse of Alberich strikes the next wearer of the ring, the giant Fasolt, at once, for he is killed in a quarrel with Fafner. Disturbed by the prophecy of Erda, Wotan resolves to descend to the Wala, to conquer her by the magic of love, and obtain the secret of the Götterdämmerung. Before doing so he leads the gods to Walhalla upon the rainbow, which Donner has constructed as a bridge. During their journey the complaining song of the Rhine maidens is heard from the depths of the river.

THE FIRST DAY: THE WALKÜRE

CAST: Siegmund—Tenor. Hunding—Basso. Wotan—Baritone. Sieglinde—Soprano. Brünhilde—Mezzo-soprano. Fricka—Mezzo-soprano. The Walküre. First production, Munich, 1870.

Wotan has ascertained from Erda that the gods will perish if Alberich again obtains the ring. The Walküre are the offspring of the love of Wotan and Erda. They are the shield maidens of the god, who lead the heroes to Walhalla to battle for the future power of the world. Wotan, in order to secure the ring, which he cannot take from the giants without breaking his word, descends to earth and founds the family of Wälsungs, predestined to produce the hero who will accomplish his purpose.

ACT I. Hunding's hut. In the centre is a mighty ash tree, which has grown through the roof. A weaponless, exhausted man rushes into the hut and sinks upon the hearth, which is an asylum even for an arch enemy. Sieglinde, Hunding's wife, tends the stranger while her husband is absent, and when he returns prepares the evening meal. Hunding asks the stranger's name, and he replies "Wehwalt"; he is a Wälsung and is pursued because he has slain a man whose wife he had protected. Hunding recognises him as his enemy, but allows him refuge for the night. Sieglinde is much interested in the stranger, and when she has given her husband a sleeping draught she returns to the hearth and shows Siegmund, whose origin she suspects, a sword sticking in the mighty tree, which a one-eyed wanderer (Wotan) had thrust there at her marriage feast. She tells him the sword will be the property of the man who succeeds in withdrawing it from its place. The handle of the sword glows with magic light. The stranger rushes forward and pulls it forth, and Sieglinde recognises in him the valiant hero, who can be no other than her brother Siegmund. In suddenly awakened love they rush into each other's arms and fly into the forest.

ACT II. A wild forest. Wotan calls his favourite Walküre Brünhilde and commands her to protect the Wälsung in the coming fight between Hunding and Siegmund. In the meanwhile Fricka approaches her husband, and as protectress of marriage, asks for Siegmund's punishment for having joined in love with his sister Sieglinde. Wotan's words and warnings are in vain; he must do as Fricka bids. He recalls Brünhilde and tells her to take the strength from Siegmund's sword and give the victory to Hunding. Brünhilde knows that her orders are against the real wishes of Wotan and takes the part of Siegmund, but Wotan himself interferes, protecting Hunding, and the sword is split in two parts, broken on the projecting spear of the god. Siegmund is slain by Hunding, but Sieglinde, who has borne a son to her lover, is saved by Brünhilde, and the latter is pursued by the wrath of Wotan after he has in turn killed Hunding.

ACT III. The rock of the Walküre, where they greet each other tumultuously. Brünhilde brings Sieglinde and claims protection from the sisters. But nothing can save her from the anger of Wotan. After she has predicted the birth of a son to Sieglinde and sent her to the forest, where she will be secure from her father's wrath, she quietly awaits the god. He deprives her of her godhead and causes her to fall into a magic sleep. It is decreed by Wotan that she shall belong to him who shall awaken her with a kiss. Moved by the pleading of his favourite child, and remembering that she had only fulfilled his secret wish, Wotan causes flames to surround the peak of the mountain, so that only a fearless knight can penetrate them and awaken her to life.

SECOND DAY: SIEGFRIED

Cast: Siegfried—Tenor. Mime—Tenor. The Wanderer —Baritone. Alberich—Baritone. Fafner—Basso. Erda —Alto. Brünhilde—Mezzo-soprano. The bird—Soprano.

Sieglinde had given birth to Siegfried in the wood where the dragon Fafner lay concealed, and at her death had delivered her son and the broken pieces of the sword to the smith Mime, who found her dying in the forest. Mime is a coward and is terrified at the enormous strength of his foster son.

Act I. Mime's smithy, a cavern in the forest. Mime, who is a clever smith, tries in vain to join the pieces of the sword, called Notung, for he hopes Siegfried may slay with the weapon the fierce dragon Fafner, who is guarding the treasure received from Wotan. Siegfried returns from the forest and frightens the cowardly Nibelung with a captured bear, whom he allows to escape. The young hero easily breaks a new sword that Mime has fashioned for him and begins to ask questions about his origin. Mime refuses to answer, but when Siegfried grasps him angrily by the throat he tells him of Siegmund and Sieglinde and shows him the broken sword of the Wälsung. Mime tries in vain to mend it, when Wotan, in the garb of a wanderer, approaches and asks for shelter, seating himself at the hearth. He wagers with Mime that he can answer three questions satisfactorily, the stake to be Mime's head, and then Wotan also requires an answer to three questions or he himself must pay the forfeit. The smith answers two questions correctly, but the third, "Who will be able to join the broken sword?" he cannot solve. Wotan tells him that he who had never known fear would accomplish it and also obtain the head of Mime. Siegfried returns, goes to work at the forge, joins the broken parts and produces a magnificent sword. The timorous Mime now sets Siegfried upon Fafner in order that he may learn fear and lose his power. He brews a sleeping potion to give to Siegfried when he is exhausted from his combat with Fafner, and intends to slay him and obtain the treasure.

ACT II. The cavern. Alberich is waiting outside the cavern to slay the hero who shall overcome Fafner, for he longs to obtain possession of the ring. Wotan announces to him the approach of Siegfried. Alberich demands the ring from Fafner in exchange for his life, but is refused. Siegfried appears guarded by Mime and slays the dragon with Notung. His finger is covered with the dragon's blood, and when he accidentally touches his lips with it he is able to understand the language of the birds, and on the advice of one of them and to the despair of Alberich takes possession of the magic helmet and the ring. By the magic power of the dragon's blood Siegfried is enabled to read the mind of Mime and slays him without compunction. He again hears the voice of the bird, who sings of the beautiful maiden on the Valkyr's rock, who can only be awakened by a fearless hero. Led by the bird, Siegfried proceeds on his way to Brünhilde.

ACT III. A wild, rocky scene. Wotan calls to Erda to arise from the earth, and informs her that he does not fear the twilight of the gods, as he himself wishes it to arrive. He declares he will leave to Siegfried the ring of Alberich, and he and Brünhilde shall possess the earth. He confronts the approaching Siegfried, who splinters the spear of Wotan with his sword Notung. The flames which surround Brünhilde reach Siegfried, but he springs through them without fear.

Change of scene: The rock of Brünhilde. Siegfried awakes Brünhilde with a kiss. With a magnificent love duet this part of the trilogy ends.

THIRD DAY: THE TWILIGHT OF THE GODS

(GÖTTERDÄMMERUNG)

CAST: Siegfried—Tenor. Gunther—Baritone. Hagen—Basso. Brünhilde—Mezzo-soprano. Gutrune—Soprano. Waltraute—Mezzo-soprano. Alberich—Baritone. Woglinde—Soprano. Wellgunde—Soprano. Flosshilde—Alto. The Norns. Chorus of men and women. First production, Bayreuth, 1876.

Introduction. The Norns seated under the world ash, Ygdrasil, spinning the thread of fate, foresee the destruction of Valhalla and the approaching sorrow of the gods. Suddenly the thread breaks, and the three sisters in fear seek Erda for protection. Wotan has ordered that the world ash shall be felled to make him a spear in place of that which Siegfried had destroyed. Loge is to set fire to Valhalla when God and the world have been freed from the curse of the ring and the Rheingold is again in possession of the Rhine daughters. Wotan is seated in Valhalla awaiting the end. Siegfried comes from the forest with Brünhilde. She has instructed him in the wisdom of the gods, but he longs to try his strength among men. He gives her the ring of the Nibelungs as a love token and she presents him with her Valkyrie steed Grane, that he may go forth into the earth and perform deeds of valour. Lovingly they bid each other farewell, each promising fidelity.

ACT I. Hall of the Gibichungs on the Rhine. (With some modifications, the action of the Nibelungen song follows to the death of Siegfried, while the preceding action, taken from old northern legends, has been brought by Wagner into co-relation. Gutrune is Kriemhild and Hagen is here the son of Alberich, who has conquered Gunther's mother by force, and in hate produced a son to be the avenger who shall slay Siegfried and obtain from him the ring.) Hagen, endowed with secret knowledge, tells Gunther of the beautiful Brünhilde and Gutrune of the youthful Siegfried. The young hero arrives on the back of Grane in a boat, and having landed, is greeted by Hagen and hospitably entertained. Hagen brews a potion to produce oblivion, which is given to Siegfried by Gutrune. After drinking it he has no recollection of Brünhilde and woos Gutrune. He drinks blood brotherhood with Gunther and joins him in the adventure to win Brünhilde.

Change of scene: The rock of Brünhilde. Waltraute, a Valkyrie, has come secretly to Brünhilde to tell her of the unexpressed wish of Wotan to return the ring to the Rhine maidens, but Brünhilde retains it as Siegfried's love token. Siegfried now appears in the guise of Gunther, by the magic of the helmet. He takes the ring from her hand and leads her away.

ACT II. On the banks of the Rhine before the hall of the Gibichungs. Night. Alberich demands that Hagen keep the ring from the Rhine maidens. At the approach of day Siegfried announces the arrival of Gunther and Brünhilde. Now for the first time in the course of the action the chorus of men and women come upon the scene to receive the bridal pair. When Brünhilde, in astonishment and grief, sees her beloved Siegfried united to Gutrune, and the ring upon his finger, she accuses him of having betrayed Gunther, who has been united to her. Filled with a frenzy of jealousy, she unites with Hagen to murder Siegfried and also wins over to her side the hesitating Gunther.

ACT III. A forest and valley on the Rhine. Siegfried has been hunting and arrives at the river, where he meets the complaining Rhine maidens. When they vainly ask him for the ring, they predict his approaching death. Hagen, who arrives with Gunther and his followers, at the banquet hands Siegfried a goblet of wine, and after drinking it his memory returns. He now relates to his companions his deeds, how the voice of the bird had brought him to Brünhilde and of their mutual love in the forest. When Hagen calls to him scornfully, "Do you understand also the language of the raven?" he turns to answer and is stabbed in the back by Hagen's spear.   Siegfried dies, his last moments filled with thoughts of Brünhilde.   His companions lay him upon a shield and with solemn death music bring him to Gutrune.

Change of scene: Hall of the Gibichungs.   Gutrune with cries of anguish rushes to the body of Siegfried and hears from Gunther that Hagen has slain her husband and now demands the ring.   Gunther refuses to deliver it to him, and when Hagen attempts to take it by force, the hand of the corpse is raised threateningly.   Siegfried's body is laid upon the funeral pyre, to which Brünhilde applies the torch, after having taken the ring from Siegfried's finger.   When the flames arise, she mounts her horse Grane and ascends the burning pyre.   The Rhine rises above the flames, the Rhine daughters grasp the ring, and when Hagen tries to obtain it, they drag the son of Alberich down to the depths of the river.   At this moment a great light appears in the distance; it is the conflagration of Walhalla, and denotes the "twilight of the gods"—the destruction of Walhalla.

ROBERT THE DEVIL

Opera in five acts by Meyerbeer.   Text by Scribe and Delavigne.

CAST: King of Sicily—Basso.   Isabella, Princess of Sicily—Soprano.   Robert, banished Duke of Normandy— Tenor.   Bertram, his friend—Basso.   Alberti, a knight— Baritone.   Raimbaud, a peasant of Normandy—Tenor. Alice, a peasant girl from Normandy—Soprano.   An armourer, a master of ceremonies, Helène, abbess of the spirit nuns, a dancer.   Place, Palermo.   Time, the thirteenth century.   First production, Paris, 1831.

An offspring of Satan has formed a union with the Duchess of Normandy, and Robert is their son.   The evil traits inherited from his father have caused his banishment. He wanders through the country and at the time of the action is in Sicily, where he is wooing the Princess Isabella. He is ignorant of his parentage on his father's side, and under the guise of Bertram his diabolical father accompanies him as a friend, in order to lead him into temptation and gain his soul for hell. Robert loses his money at play, and Bertram persuades him to rob a church and to take a twig from the grave of St. Rosalie, by its influence forcing Isabella to marry him. Her love and prayers, however, prevail and he throws the twig away. He now falls into the hands of the Sicilian knights, but Bertram frees him and acknowledges that he is his father. His love for his mother and Isabella gains the victory over the wiles of Bertram, and the latter returns alone to the infernal regions, while Robert is united to Isabella.

ACT I. Camp near Palermo. Robert, Bertram, Alberti and other knights are holding a feast. Raimbaud comes from Normandy, disguised as a pilgrim minstrel. (Ballad: "Once ruled in Normandy.") He narrates the story of the union of the duchess with a demon. Robert has Raimbaud arrested, but frees him when he hears that Alice, the Norman's bride, has come to him with a message. Alice is brought in, and Robert recognises in her his foster sister; she brings him the last will of his mother. (Romance: "Go, she said, do not tarry.") Robert is not to read the will until he has proved his worth. Alice offers to carry a message to Isabella, and prays that she may be united to Raimbaud. Bertram arrives and induces Robert to gamble. (Sicilienne: "Now, fortune, smile on me," with the refrain, "Gold is but a chimera.") Robert loses all, even his weapons and horse.

ACT II. A chamber in the palace. Isabella (scene and cavatina: "How hateful to me all this splendour"). Alice brings Robert's letter and Isabella sends him the money for new weapons and armour, that he may appear for her in the lists and be victorious. Bertram foils this proceeding by luring Robert away.

ACT III. A wild, rocky scene. Raimbaud awaits Alice, but meets Bertram, who dazzles him with gold. (Duet:

"Oh, what generosity.") In triumph Bertram descends to hell. Alice, seeking Raimbaud (Scene and romance: "Ere I left Normandy"), hears the voices of the demons, who call loudly for Robert. She gazes into the abyss with horror. Bertram arises from hell, and seeing Alice, threatens her with his vengeance if she reveals what she has seen. As Robert approaches (Terzett: "Moments of dread") Alice hurries away in fright and Bertram induces Robert to purloin a twig from the grave of St. Rosalie.

Change of scene: Convent and graveyard with tombstones of nuns. Bertram commands the dead nuns to arise from their graves that they may induce Robert to break off the twig. Robert approaches hesitatingly, the nuns throw off their grave clothes and appear as beautiful maidens. They dance around him seductively and persuade him to accomplish the deed.

Act IV. A hall in the palace. Robert, with the aid of the magic twig, compels the knights and ladies at the palace to fall asleep. (Cavatina: "How beautiful.") He makes himself invisible, and entering Isabella's room, awakens her. She asks him for mercy. (Cavatina: "Robert, my beloved"; Aria of mercy.) Touched by her pleading, he throws away the magic wand, and when he is attacked by the knights, who have recovered from the spell, is saved by Bertram.

Act V. Entrance to the cathedral of Palermo. It is a consecrated spot, and for that reason Robert has come thither and has brought with him the trembling Bertram, who shrinks from entering the place. Bertram endeavours to gain Robert's soul for the underworld, but under the sway of the solemn music in the cathedral, he abjures Bertram and denounces him as an enemy. Bertram immediately acknowledges him to be Robert's father. Robert, strongly affected, is about to follow him once more when Alice informs him that Isabella is waiting in the cathedral to become his bride. (Terzett: "What shall I do?") Robert finally agrees to sign the contract by which he forfeits his soul when Alice hands him his mother's will. Robert is still hesitating when the hour of midnight strikes. The time granted to Bertram to win his soul has expired. As he sinks into the earth the doors of the church open. Robert is united in marriage to Isabella and Raimbaud to Alice.

ROLAND OF BERLIN

Text (adapted from the work of Alexis) and music by Leoncavallo. German by Droescher.

CAST: Prince Friedrich—Basso. Burgomaster Rathenow —Baritone. Elsbeth, his daughter—Soprano. Gertrud, his sister—Alto. Henning Moller—Tenor. Councillors: Wintz—Baritone. Schum—Basso. Ryke—Basso. Bergholz—Tenor. Eva, Melchior, Schum's children—Soprano and Tenor. Blankenfelde, Burgomaster of Cologne— Basso. Peddler Makensprung—Basso. Baruch, a Jew— Tenor. Conrad von Knipprode—Baritone. Barber Felbirt—Basso. The clown—Tenor. Servant of Rathenow. The town crier. Cavaliers. Councillors. A captain. Citizens. Salome, a Jewish girl. The hangman. Servants. Doorkeepers. Masqueraders. Soldiers. Place, Berlin, 1442. First production, Berlin, 1904.

ACT I. A square beside the long bridge. A beautiful day in February. An animated scene in front of the state house, in the street, in the barber shop of Felbirt and in the inn. The statue of Roland of Berlin stands near the church. The citizens of Berlin are enraged with the councillors for their injustice. The peddler Makensprung has been robbed and no effort is being made to discover the robber, and there is no security in the city for life or limb. The people joyfully accept the offer of the young weaver Henning, who has been standing near the church, to find and punish the robbers. The prince, who resides at Spandau, is in the crowd in disguise and witnesses a masquerade which lampoons the council. He also sees the honest Henning

save the burgomaster Rathenow from danger, although
the council owes him 20,000 groschen, which it is unwilling
to pay. Henning has been brought up with Rathenow's
daughter Elsbeth and loves her. The prince praises Henning and predicts that he will become a knight. Henning
recognises the prince and enables him to escape.

Act II. . A chamber in Rathenow's house. The burgomaster becomes bondsman to Henning for the return of the
20,000 groschen, and as the council will not agree to pay
it, offers the Jew Baruch his family jewels to obtain the
sum. Henning overhears a conversation between Schum
and Rathenow, in which they agree that Schum's son Melchior shall marry Elsbeth at a festival on the following
day. In a pretty scene Henning is assured by Elsbeth of
her love and fidelity.

Act III. The principal hall of the council. Festival.
Henning appears as a wandering minstrel at the masquerade, but Elsbeth recognises him. A quarrel ensues
between the citizens of Cologne and Berlin at the feast.
Elsbeth is robbed of the family jewels. The drunken Schum
insults Elsbeth by declaring her to be the mistress of Henning, and Rathenow and his daughter leave the hall.

Act IV. Same room as in Act II. Henning brings
Elsbeth the lost jewels and declares his love for her.
Although she loves him in return, she does not wish to marry
him, as she is the daughter of a patrician and he is of humble
birth. The burgomaster declares to Henning, "Not until
Roland steps from his pedestal shall my daughter be yours."
Henning rushes away in despair and meets the friendly
prince, who with his forces is marching against the city.

Change of scene: Street and square as in Act I. The
prince demands admittance to the city. When Rathenow
hesitates, Henning grasps an axe and breaks down the
gates; the prince orders the statue of Roland to be thrown
from its pedestal, and confirms Rathenow as burgomaster.
When he is about to reward the valiant Henning he is
brought in a corpse, having been slain in the tumult.

ROMEO AND JULIET

Opera in five acts by Gounod. Text by Barbier and Carré.
CAST: Prince of Verona—Basso. Count of Paris, his
relative—Baritone. Count Capulet—Basso. Juliet, his
daughter—Soprano. Gertrude, her nurse—Alto. Tybalt,
Capulet's nephew—Tenor. Romeo, a Montague—Tenor.
Mercutio—Baritone. Benvolio—Tenor. Stefano, Romeo's
page—Soprano. Gregorio, Capulet's servant—Baritone.
Friar Lawrence—Basso. Place, Verona. Time, the fourteenth century. First production, Paris, 1867. A musical
prologue, which shows the cast in tableaux, opens the opera.

ACT I. Chamber at the Capulets'. A masquerade.
Romeo and his friends have appeared in the house of their
enemy; he sees Juliet and they fall madly in love without
knowing each other's identity. Tybalt recognises Romeo
and the Capulets attack him, but he is protected by his
host.

ACT II. A pavilion in Capulet's garden. Love scene
between Romeo and Juliet, interrupted by the servants, who
are seeking Romeo's page, but resumed to the end of the act.

ACT III. Lorenzo's cell. Secret marriage of the lovers
by Lorenzo, who believes their union will bring about peace
between their houses.

Change of scene: A street with Capulet's house. Mercutio's combat with Tybalt. Mercutio's death. Romeo
avenges his friend, kills Tybalt and is banished by the
prince.

ACT IV. Juliet's chamber. Romeo has come to Juliet to
celebrate his bridal night. When he has gone, Capulet
announces to his daughter that she is to marry the Count
of Paris. Juliet receives a potion from Lorenzo which is
to give her the semblance of death.

ACT V. The family vault of the Capulets. Romeo believes Juliet dead and takes poison at her bier; Juliet
awakens, and when he dies in her arms, stabs herself to the
heart.

THE ROSE FROM THE GARDEN OF LOVE

A lyric opera in two acts, a prologue and conclusion by Hans Pfitzner. Text by James Bruno.

CAST: The star maiden with the child of the sun, gods and goddesses from the garden of love. Siegnot. The master of arms. The master of song. The keeper of the gates of winter. Minneleide. Schwarzhilde. Rotelse. The moorman. The wanderer of the night. Noblemen, moormen, woodnymphs, giants, dwarfs. Place, in and near the garden of love. First production, Elberfield, 1901.

The action begins with an allegory, the scene of which is the garden of love. There children are decking themselves with flowers for a festival. The master of arms and the master of song arrive. They arrange a procession, in which the keeper of the winter gate takes his place as leader. The procession advances to the temple of the maidens of the stars, to whom the keeper delivers his sword. She presents it to the nobleman Siegnot, who joyfully proceeds to the gates of spring. With the opening of the gates bloom and growth appear; all nature awakens.

ACT I. Bearing the rose of the maiden of the star, Siegnot keeps watch at the gate of the garden of love. Before him lies an ancient forest, within whose depths live the clumsy moorman and the summer nymph Minneleide. The nymph's beauty enchants Siegnot. He desires to lead her to the garden of love and delivers to her his sword and keeper's crown. But as Minneleide does not wish to surrender her power for love, the garden is closed to them. The hateful night wanderer is in power and captures Minneleide. His dwarfs sorely wound Siegnot, and only through the care of the moormen is his life saved.

ACT II. With the crown given her by Siegnot, Minneleide has also received the magic rose. She holds this as her talisman. The wounded Siegnot is carried by the moormen to the under world to the cavern of the night wanderer. He desires to free Minneleide. The prince of hate declares in scorn that when Minneleide of her own will shall give up her power and forego the beauty of the woods, she and Siegnot shall be free; otherwise, she shall be subject to the lust of the night wanderer and Siegnot shall die. For a moment Minneleide hesitates, but Siegnot, in returning strength, grasps the supporting columns of the cavern, throwing them to the ground and buries himself and the people of the night in the ruins. Minneleide and her nymphs are saved by the power of the wondrous rose.

Conclusion: Minneleide brings the corpse of Siegnot to the gates of the garden of love, where the keeper of the winter gate is again on guard. The woodnymph voluntarily resigns her power and suffers death. She can now be freed from the powers of evil. The maiden of the stars approaches, carrying the sun child, and brings Siegnot and Minneleide back to life and love.

RÜBEZAHL AND THE BAGPIPER OF MEISSE

Drama in four acts by Eberhard König. Music by Hans Sommer.

CAST: Rübezahl. Buko, bailiff of Neisse. Gertrud, his foster child. Brigitte, maid. The servant of Buko. The guard. Wido, a young painter. Bernhard Kraft. Kettner, coppersmith. Stäblein, clerk. The sexton. Citizens, people, etc. Time, the early middle ages. Place, Neisse. First production, Brunswick, 1904.

ACT I. Wido's studio. Buko, the bailiff, rules tyrannically over Neisse. The painter Wido is the leader of the citizens who wish to free the city. He loves Gertrud, the lovely daughter of the bailiff, so his heart and duty are in conflict. In his distress he calls on the spirit of the mountains. Rübezahl approaches in the garb of a piper, and after testing him, promises assistance, smilingly reminding Vido that the affair may turn out differently from mortal expectations. Rübezahl will be aided by his magic bag-

pipes, at whose tones men and women alike are compelled
to dance. "Only he who is pure and true can defy the
power of the pipes."

Act II.   Square before the state house.   The excited
people are joined by Wido and the sturdy mountaineers
(Rübezahl's creatures).   The mountain spirit sits contentedly among them smoking his pipe.   He makes fun of
Wido and advises him to let things take their course.   Wido
attacks Buko's house, but protects Gertrud.   The mob are
beginning to turn against their leader, when Rübezahl plays
on his bagpipes and all dance and follow the piper.   Only
Gertrud and Wido are unaffected by the music, and they
realise the good intentions of the mountain spirit.

Act III.   At the council chamber Rübezahl cautions
Buko to be careful what he does.   He declares Wido to be
his son and asks for him the hand of Gertrud in marriage.
Buko is enraged and has Rübezahl put in irons.   The spirit
laughingly allows the jailers to lead him away, and Gertrud,
who comes to defend Wido, is thrust from the house.   Servants report that Rübezahl has been found dead in prison.
Buko plans to have Wido burnt as a magician.

Act IV.   Graveyard by moonlight.   At the grave of the
bagpiper Buko meets Wido.   The inconstant citizens have
declared for the bailiff and Wido is to be burnt at the stake.
Gertrud pleads in vain for her lover, but Rübezahl once
again intervenes.   The conscience-stricken Buko sinks to
the ground in terror when Rübezahl suddenly arises from
the grave.   The mountain spirit appoints a new bailiff for
the town, the lovers are united and the beneficent Rübezahl
returns to his mountain home.

THE RUBY

Musical fairy tale in two acts adapted from the tale of
Hebbel by Eugen d'Albert.

Cast: The caliph.   The vizier.   The cadi.   Asaf, a youth.
Hakam, his comrade.   Irad, an old man.   Rustan, execu-

tioner. Soliman, a jeweller. Bedura. Place, Bagdad. First production, Carlsrühe, 1893.

ACT I. A prominent street in Bagdad. The poor fisherman's son, Asaf, enters with his friend Hakam, whom he leaves when he finds him to be a thief. Asaf has had a dream, in which honour and glory have been predicted for him. The vizier approaches and announces that the caliph had promised the crown to him who will discover and bring back the Princess Bedura, who has mysteriously disappeared. When the people have gone, the jeweller Soliman shows young Asaf his treasures, and he, charmed by a ruby, takes it, and refuses to give it up, even when the cadi and the executioner have him arrested and order his execution. As he is about to be led away to the scaffold an old man, Irad, suddenly appears, and taking Asaf by the hand, sinks with him into the earth, to the astonishment of the people.

ACT II. A subterranean passage. Fantastic decorations. Irad and Asaf are talking together. The old man informs the youth that the Princess Bedura will appear to him if he kisses the ruby, which is still in his possession, three times. Irad disappears, but Asaf does as he is bidden and beholds the Princess Bedura. She tells him that a magician whose love she had repulsed imprisoned her within the ruby. She returns the love which Asaf already feels for her and declares that he can save her, but that she cannot reveal the way, which he must find for himself. Bedura is again imprisoned in the stone, and Asaf with his ruby finds himself upon the earth near Bagdad. His former friend Hakam sees him, but when he tries to grasp the ring Asaf violently resists. Their struggle attracts the attention of the cadi and the executioner, who carry Asaf before the caliph, who is holding a court of justice.

Change of scene: Garden of the caliph on the Tigris. Asaf is sentenced to die, but is first ordered to deliver up the ring. He refuses and throws the ruby into the river. Bedura appears, and embracing her happy father praises

Asaf as her preserver, for the throwing away of the ring had broken the spell. The caliph remembers his promise, and as Bedura confesses her love for Asaf, he unites them, and the fisherman's son, conducted by the sage Irad, ascends the throne as the new caliph.

SALOME

Drama in one act adapted from Oscar Wilde's romance. Music by Richard Strauss.

CAST: Herod—Tenor. Herodias—Mezzo-soprano. Salome—Soprano. Yochanaän—Baritone. Narraboth—Tenor. A page of Herodias—Alto. Five Jews—four Tenors, one Basso. Two Nazarenes—Tenor and Basso. Two soldiers—Bassi. A Cappadocian—Basso. A slave. Place, terrace of the palace of Herod. Time, A.D. 30 First production, Dresden, 1905.

Salome lives at the sensual and cruel court of her stepfather, Herod. She is still a maiden, but imbued with unholy passion, and she longs to touch the ivory-tinted skin and the glorious hair, and to kiss the red lips of the Prophet Yochanaän. Herod has thrown the latter into a cistern near the palace, and Salome orders him to be brought before her. The young Syrian commander, Narraboth, is insanely in love with Salome, and against the orders of the king, obeys her commands. When he finds she has discarded him for the prophet, he slays himself before her eyes. Salome scarcely observes his death, but revels in the thought of kissing the lips of the prophet. When Yochanaän repulses the sinful daughter of Babylon and returns to his prison, she becomes half insane in her passion. She takes advantage of the desires of Herod, who wishes to see her dance, to extort from him a promise of reward, which he gives without conditions. Scantily clad, she dances alluringly before him, and then immediately demands the head of the prophet

Yochanaän, the Baptist. Herod fears to slay the prophet of God lest the people be incited to revolt, and offers his treasures and half his kingdom if Salome will withdraw her demand. She refuses, saying that she has his binding promise, and once more demands the head of the Baptist. Herod angrily gives the order for his execution. The executioner descends into the cistern, and throws out the bloody head. When Salome triumphantly grasps it and kisses the pallid lips over and over again, Herod is filled with disgust and terror and orders her to be slain. The infuriated soldiers crush her with their shields.

SAMSON AND DELILAH

Opera in three acts by Camille St. Saëns. Text by Ferdinand Lemaire. German by Richard Pohl.

Cast : Delilah—Mezzo-soprano. Samson—Tenor. High priest of Dagon—Baritone. Abimelech, satrap of Gaza—Basso. An old Hebrew—Basso. Messenger of the Philistines—Tenor. Place, Gaza in Palestine. Time, 1150 b.c. First production, Weimar, 1877.

Act I. The city of Gaza. The Israelites pray for relief from the oppression of the Philistines. (Chorus: "God of Israel.") Samson tries to comfort them by predicting an early victory over their enemies. Abimelech, satrap of Gaza, mocks them and tells them their God is weak and cannot save them. Samson, filled with the hope of victory, sings a song of triumph (Aria: "You know not the God of our fathers"), which uplifts the Hebrews and causes Abimelech to cower in fear. The satrap attempts to repress the revolt of the Israelites with violence, but is slain by Samson, whom Abimelech's attendants fear to arrest. Samson hastens away to complete his victory, and a messenger reports to the high priest that the Israelites are everywhere in full rebellion. (Aria of the high priest: "Curses on him.") The Philistines fly, the victorious Israelites intone a hymn of praise. (Chorus of old men: "Praise the Lord.") Delilah, the woman of Sorak, and her maids greet the victor (Chorus: "In spring's full bloom"), and Samson tries in vain to withstand her charms. (Terzett: "Greetings to thee.") A dance of the women and Delilah's song, "The sun smiled," completes the downfall of the hero, who can resist no longer.

Act II. House of Delilah in the valley of Sorak. Delilah, richly attired, awaits Samson. (Aria: "Samson! this night will bring him.") The high priest commands her to deliver the hero to the Philistines; she herself has sworn to be avenged upon him, as he had deserted her once before, and her love is now only hypocrisy. (Duet: "I will cool my hate.") Samson appears, his heart filled with doubts and remorse, and even her bewitching song (Delilah: "See, my heart opens at thy voice") cannot tear from him the secret of his strength. But he succumbs at last to Delilah's anger and scorn, and, telling her his strength is in his hair, follows her to her chamber. Delilah, lulling him to sleep, cuts off his hair, which causes his strength to depart. She calls in the Philistines, who are waiting without, and Samson is overpowered and blinded.

Act III. Prison in Gaza. The blind Samson is in prison, weak and filled with remorse. ("Oh see my pain, Lord!") The reproaches of his countrymen penetrate his cell and increase his agony. He is dragged out by the Philistines to be shown as a captive in their triumphal procession.

Change of scene: The interior of the temple of Dagon. (Chorus: "The sun arises"; ballet.) Samson, led in by a boy, is ordered by the high priest to sing in praise of Delilah. He is filled with the memory of bygone days. ("I offer you my hand in greeting.") He prays to the Lord to give him his strength and vision once more; the Philistines overwhelm him with malice and mockery. The festival of victory begins (Duet and chorus: "Dagon, to thee, thanks!"); the tumult increases and one libation after the other is poured in honour of the god. Samson prays to the Lord once more, and, grasping with all his former strength the two marble pillars of the temple, bends them, and with his enemies finds death in the ruins.

SILVANA

Opera in four acts by Weber. The original text, "The Wood Maiden," by Hiemer, adapted by Pasqué, and music added by Langer.

CAST: The legend—Speaking part. The Count of the Rhine—Baritone. Count Gerold, his son—Tenor. Silvana —Soprano. Ratto, the charcoal burner—Basso. Dryada, wood nymph—Alto. Guntram, vassal of the count—Baritone. The abbot of St. Goar. A turnkey. Place, the castles Sternberg and Liebenstein and vicinity. First production of "The Wood Maidens," Frankfurt A.M. 1810; of "Silvana," Hamburg, 1885.

ACT I. On the banks of the Rhine. Legend tells the story. The count of the Rhine has slain his brother through jealousy, and believes that his nephew is also dead. The child is alive, however, and has been brought up by the charcoal burner Ratto, under the protection of the nymph Dryada. The count regrets his act. His son Gerold is roaming through the forest in which Silvana is living. Legend and his group of listeners disappear and the action continues in the forest, where Gerold first beholds Silvana. They love each other, and Gerold leads Silvana to the castle.

ACT II. At Sternberg. The old count is informed of the approaching marriage of Gerold and Silvana. The latter discovers her protectress, the nymph, who remains near her as a wandering minstrel.

Change of scene: In the village on the Rhine. Festival. The minstrel enrages the count by a recital of his deeds, and is protected by Silvana. Gerold's jealousy is aroused. Ratto is recognised as Silvana's father, and the count orders father, daughter and singer to be thrown into the dungeon of the castle.

ACT III. The turret. The count endeavours to compel Silvana to release Gerold, but she refuses. She falls asleep, and the nymph changes the prison into a fairy wood and shows to Silvana a happy future in her dreams.

ACT IV. A chamber at Sternberg. Gerold in vain defends Silvana from his father's wrath. She is about to be led away to death, when Dryada appears, and reveals the maiden's identity as the niece of the count. The count, overcome with gratitude, embraces the lovers, and joyfully sanctions their union.

THE SUNKEN BELL

Musical drama in five acts by Heinrich Zoellner. Text by the composer, founded upon the fairy drama of Gerhart Hauptmann.

CAST: Heinrich, a bell founder—Baritone. Magda, his wife—Soprano. Their children—Mezzo-soprani. The parish priest—Tenor. The schoolmaster—Basso. The barber—Basso—Baritone. Wittichen, an old woman— Alto. Rautendelein—Soprano. The Nickelman—Basso. Waldschratt—Tenor buffo. Place, the Hartz Mountains.

ACT I. A meadow in the hills. Rautendelein sits on the edge of a well, from which the Nickelman emerges. Waldschratt appears and narrates that he has thrown the bell, which should have been hung in the new chapel, into the abyss. Heinrich arrives and falls in a faint from exhaustion. Old Wittichen finds him and summons Rautendelein. Heinrich awakes and falls in love with her. When the priest, schoolmaster and barber offer to assist the bell founder to find his way, she draws round him a magic circle, and he is then carried to the valley. Dance of the elves. Rautendelein refuses the offers of the Nickelman and flies to the homes of men.

Act II.   Old German interior; house of the bell founder. The barber and schoolmaster carry him in on a litter. When he recovers consciousness he expresses his discontent with his former life.   Magda leaves in order to bring a wonder-working woman.   Rautendelein enters, and by her magic restores Heinrich to life and hope.   He falls in love with her.

Act III.   A deserted glass furnace in the mountains. Nickelman laments that Rautendelein has bestowed her love upon a human being.   The priest endeavours to persuade Heinrich, who is living with Rautendelein in the mountains, to return to his wife and children, but he refuses.

Act IV.   The same scene.   Heinrich is working in his new workshop with six dwarfs.   He falls asleep, and is troubled by his conscience in his dreams.   Rautendelein consoles him.   Chorus of elves.   The inhabitants of Heinrich's village approach to stone the miscreant, but are put to flight.   He thinks he sees his two children, who are carrying in a pitcher, the tears shed by his dead wife.   Overcome with remorse Heinrich leaves Rautendelein and returns to the home of human beings.

Act V.   Same scene as Act I.   Rautendelein has given herself to the Nickelman.   Heinrich, who sees his completed work go up in flames, tries to ascend the mountain. He loses the way and sinks exhausted at the edge of the well.   Once again he holds Rautendelein in his arms, then dies.

THE TAMING OF THE SHREW

Comic opera in four acts by Goetz.   Adapted from Shakespeare by Widmann.

Cast: Baptista, a rich nobleman of Padua—Basso. Catharine and Bianca, his daughters—Soprani.   Hortensio and Lucentio, Bianca's suitors—Baritone and Tenor. Petruchio, a nobleman of Verona—Baritone.   Place, Padua and Verona.   First production, Mannheim, 1874.

Act I.   Street in Padua and house of Baptista. Catharine, the daughter of the nobleman Baptista, is known to be of an obstinate, quarrelsome disposition. She is just giving an evidence of it by driving her servants from the house, and they take refuge in the street, where they interrupt the serenade ("Sound, sweet tones") with which Lucentio is saluting his beloved Bianca. After Baptista has calmed the tumult, Lucentio continues his song and the old popinjay Hortensio also arrives to serenade Bianca. The two admirers quarrel until they are separated by Baptista, who declares that the marriage of Bianca will be impossible until Catharine is first wedded. Notwithstanding, the rivals determine to enter the house in disguise in order to gain Bianca's love. They depart to make preparations and meet Petruchio, who arrives from Verona. They relate to him the facts about Catharine and her temper, which interest him strongly, and he resolves to make her his wife, saying that she is created for him. (Song: "She is a wife for such a man.")

Act II.   A room in the house of Baptista. Petruchio is introduced by Baptista, and is a witness to Catharine's strife and violence as she scolds the servants and makes game of her sister and of old Hortensio, who wishes to give her a music lesson, and whose lute she breaks upon his head. (Catharine: "I'll give myself to nobody.") In vain Petruchio's father warns him, but he persists in his determination to marry Catharine. He is received by her with mockery and scorn, but as he remains calm and accepts all her objections as if she agreed with him, and takes her bitterness as amiability, she is driven to distraction, but feels that he is her master. Although she refuses her consent, Petruchio informs his father and Hortensio and Lucentio that Catharine is fully in accord with him, and that the marriage will be celebrated without delay. (Petruchio: "All is well.")

Act III.   A chamber in Baptista's house. The preparations for the marriage feast are discontinued, as the bridegroom does not appear. Lucentio and Hortensio take advantage of this interlude to woo Bianca. The old man is obliged to give way, for Bianca surrenders to Lucentio, who has quoted a portion of Virgil to make a declaration of love. Petruchio appears. He is dressed in ordinary clothes, but insists that the ceremonies proceed forthwith. He orders preparations for their departure to be made immediately after the marriage and remains firm, though Catharine first begs and then commands him to desist from his folly. As she refuses to follow him willingly, he uses compulsion.

Act IV. Petruchio's room. Petruchio arrives with the half-famished Catharine, has a sumptuous meal set before her, but immediately throws it out of the window, declaring it not fit to eat. A change in Catharine's character now takes place, obstinacy turns to humility, contradiction to love. After a by-play with the dressmaker, in which Catharine admires her costume, upon which the woman is thrown out of doors by Petruchio, she declares herself submissive to his will and acknowledges her love. Petruchio joyfully receives his guests, and to the astonishment of Baptista, Hortensio and the united Lucentio and Bianca, they find Catharine a most modest and beautiful wife, who even admonishes her sister to duty and obedience.

TANNHÄUSER AND THE SINGERS' CONTEST AT THE WARTBURG

Opera in three acts by Wagner. Text by the composer.

Cast: Herrmann, landgrave of Thuringia—Basso. Tannhäuser—Tenor. Wolfram von Eschenbach—Baritone. Walter von der Vogelweide—Tenor. Biterolf—Basso. Heinrich the writer—Tenor. Reimar von Zweter—Basso. Elizabeth, niece of the landgrave—Soprano. Venus—Soprano. A young shepherd—Soprano. Place, Thuringia and the Wartburg. Time, the thirteenth century.

The poet composer characterises this work not as an opera, but as "action." First production, Dresden, 1845.

ACT I. The Venusberg (the Hörselberg of "Frau Holda" in Thüringia, in the vicinity of Eisenach.) Tannhäuser is held there a willing captive through his love for Venus. The goddess has won the dreaming Tannhäuser by her fascinations. His head is pillowed in her lap. (Ballet scene; bacchanalian music.) Tannhäuser's desires are satiated, and he longs for freedom, spring and the sound of church bells. Once again he grasps his harp and pays homage to the goddess in a passionate song of love, which he ends with an earnest plea to be allowed to depart. When Venus again tries to charm him he declares: "My salvation rests in Mary, the mother of God." These words break the unholy spell. Venus and her attendants disappear, and he suddenly finds himself just below the Wartburg. It is springtime; a young shepherd sits upon a rock and pipes an ode to spring; pilgrims in procession pass Tannhäuser as he stands motionless, and stricken with remorse he sobbingly sinks to his knees. Thus he is found by the landgrave and his companions in the chase, Wolfram, Walter, Biterolf, Reimar and Heinrich. They joyfully welcome the sorely missed singer, who has fled from them because he was unsuccessful in the prize singing. He refuses to join them, but when Wolfram informs him that his song had gained for him the heart of Elizabeth, he follows the landgrave and the singers to the Wartburg.

ACT II. Hall of the Wartburg. Elizabeth has been living retired from the world since Tannhäuser's disappearance. When she hears of his return she joyfully agrees to be present at a prize contest of song, and enters the hall. Wolfram leads Tannhäuser to her; he loves her, but dares not tell her the evil he has done. The landgrave and Elizabeth receive the guests who assemble for the contest, the noblemen of the neighbourhood, who appear in rich attire. (March and chorus.) The landgrave announces the subject of the day to be "Love's Awakening." Elizabeth is to grant a wish to the victor whatever it may be. Wolfram begins; he declares that love is like a pure stream, which should never be troubled. Tannhäuser replies hotly that he finds the highest love only in the pleasure of the senses. The other singer upholds Wolfram. Tannhäuser replies to each separately, and at last in growing excitement he answers Wolfram with a love song to Venus, and declares that if the knights wish to know love as it is they should repair to the Venusberg. The women, with the exception of Elizabeth, leave the hall in horror, and the knights draw swords upon Tannhäuser. Elizabeth protects him, and since he expresses his penitence, the landgrave allows him to join a band of pilgrims bound for Rome, where he may perhaps obtain forgiveness from the pope.

ACT III. The valley of the Wartburg. An autumn scene. Orchestral music describes the pilgrimage of Tannhäuser. Elizabeth, accompanied by Wolfram, falls on her knees in prayer. She asks the returning pilgrims for news of Tannhäuser, but in vain. Once again she prays earnestly and returns broken-hearted to the Wartburg. Wolfram, who loves her with faithful devotion, has a presentiment of her death. (Wolfram: "Song to the evening star.") He sees before him a tottering pilgrim in torn garments. It is Tannhäuser, who in despair is seeking the path to the Venusberg. The pope has not forgiven him, but has cursed him irrevocably; he, therefore, calls for Venus, who appears and bids him welcome to her cavern. Wolfram points upward to a funeral procession, which now slowly descends the hill, carrying on a bier the corpse of Elizabeth. Tannhäuser throws himself upon the body, and dies with the words, "Holy Elizabeth, pray for me" upon his lips. The younger pilgrims enter and announce that the staff of Tannhäuser, which the pope had ordered to be erected as a token of his damnation, had sprouted with young leaves in sign of the forgiveness of God. (In 1875 Wagner made some changes in this opera, and in this form it was first produced at Vienna in November, 1875.)

THE TEMPLAR AND THE JEWESS

Opera in three acts by Marschner.   Text founded on Walter Scott's romance "Ivanhoe," by Wohlbrück.

CAST: Cedric, a Saxon knight—Basso. Wilfrid of Ivanhoe, his son—Tenor. Rowena, his ward—Soprano. Beaumanoir, grand master of the Templars—Basso. Brian de Bois Guilbert, templar—Baritone. Maurice de Bracy—Tenor. Albert Malvoisin—Baritone. The black knight—Basso. Locksley, chief of the outlaws—Tenor. Wamba, Cedric's servant—Tenor. Oswald, Cedric's steward. Robert, shield bearer of Bois Guilbert. Elgitha, Rowena's maid. Friar Tuck, hermit—Basso. Isaac of York, a Jew. Rebecca, his daughter—Soprano. Place, county of York in England. Time, 1194. First production, Leipsic, 1829.

ACT I. A wild country. De Bracy and his companions are encamped, awaiting the passing of Rowena and her train, upon which they plan an attack. They fall in with De Bois Guilbert, who desires to obtain possession of the person of Rebecca, daughter of Isaac of York. The two bands of conspirators unite. Cedric, the Saxon, returns from the lists, where Wilfrid, his banished son, has carried off the prize. Cedric is an adherent of Lord Athelstane, to whom, in his opinion, the crown belongs in the absence of Richard at the crusades, and intends that Rowena, who is of the blood of the old Saxon kings, shall be his wife. Wilfrid loves Rowena, and has been banished in consequence, although she returns his love and hates Athelstane. Cedric is attended by Wamba, a jester. (Wamba's aria: "The world is round.") The Jew Isaac and his daughter Rebecca, bringing with them Wilfrid, who has been wounded in the lists and is unconscious, join the following of Cedric, after Rebecca has disclosed to Rowena the name of the wounded man.

Change of scene: The hermits' hut of Friar Tuck. An unknown knight asks for shelter, and is furnished with wine and food. (Tuck's song: "The barefoot monk his cell doth leave, ora pro nobis.") Locksley reports that a band of robbers have carried off Cedric, Athelstane and Rowena to the castle of De Bracy. Tuck and the knight accompany Locksley to free them.

Change of scene: A chamber in De Bracy's castle. Rebecca is in the power of De Bois Guilbert, who avows his love, but is repulsed. The war cry of the Saxons is heard and De Bois Guilbert rushes out to meet them in battle. Ivanhoe arises from his couch, but is restrained by Rebecca. (Duet: "Dear maiden.") Ivanhoe discovers that she is a Jewess, but vows eternal gratitude.

Change of scene: Courtyard of the burning castle. The Saxons have conquered. Ivanhoe has escaped, but Rebecca is still in the burning building. Brian de Bois Guilbert carries her out by force.

ACT II. A wood. Cedric returns home. Rebecca's father enters with Friar Tuck. The unknown knight sends the Jew to the castle of the Templars to find his daughter. After a song and chorus, Ivanhoe appears, and greeting the unknown knight as Richard the Lionhearted, reports the approach of his army. Locksley and the other outlaws do homage to the king, who pardons them. (Aria of Ivanhoe: "To the king power and glory.")

Change of scene: Chamber in præceptorium of the Templars. Isaac has petitioned the grand master for Rebecca's release, but she is accused of being a witch and is condemned by the order. Guilbert's love for Rebecca has turned to wild passion. (Scene: "Do you refuse me?" Recitative and aria.)

Change of scene: The lists of the Templars. De Bois Guilbert is chosen champion for the Templars and Rebecca is given till the following day to procure a defender.

ACT III. In Cedric's castle. King Richard reconciles Cedric and his son and unites Ivanhoe to Rowena. (Chorus: "Let merry dances"; Ivanhoe's song: "Who is the knight so highly honoured!" Rowena: "The fatherland, severed by hate.") Isaac reports the action of the Templars and the young knight departs to save his benefactress. (Wamba's song: "How fine to be a king!")

Change of scene: Rebecca's prison cell. (Prayer, Rebecca: "Lord, from deep distress!") De Bois Guilbert wishes to save her, but she refuses. (Duet: "Woe is me! 'tis you.")

Change of scene: The lists. Ivanhoe arrives at the last moment and conquers De Bois Guilbert. The king enters and frees Rebecca. He punishes the Templars, declaring that he alone is king and that he is and has ever been an enemy of injustice. (Closing chorus: "Let all rejoice.")

THAÏS

A lyric opera in three acts by Massenet. Text by Gallet. CAST: Athanaël, a monk of the Cenobite Order—Baritone. Nicias, a young Sybarite—Tenor. Palemon, an old monk —Basso. Thaïs, a courtesan—Soprano. Albine, an abbess —Mezzo-soprano. Crobyle and Myrtale, slaves—Soprani. La Charmeuse, a dancer. Monks, philosophers, nuns, populace. Scene, Thebes and the Theban desert, Egypt. Period, Greek occupation. First production, Paris, 1894.

ACT I. Cenobite dwellings beside the Nile, at even. The monks partake of a rude meal under the direction of Palemon. Athanaël, an eloquent young monk, has gone to Alexandria to denounce the luxury and license of the Greeks. As they speak of his mission he returns, weary and discouraged, having found Alexandria under the rule of Thaïs, a beautiful courtesan, over whom every one in the city has gone mad. The monks separate, each making his own prayer. Athanaël commends his soul to God and falls asleep. In a dream he sees Thaïs, half clad, posing before the people as Aphrodite. The crowd applaud, acclaiming her. Athanaël awakens. (Athanaël: "Oh, shame! Oh, madness! Oh, eternal gloom!") Palemon rebukes him, and he departs once more on his mission.

Change of scene: Alexandria. House of Nicias. Athanaël enters, asking to see Nicias. At first refused, he
assumes a commanding posture. (Athanaël, alone: "O
dreadful city of doom.") Nicias appears, supported by
women slaves. He hastens to greet Athanaël, who questions him about Thaïs. Somewhat ruefully the youth declares that her extravagance has ruined him, but for the
moment he possesses her. Athanaël very seriously announces his intention of reclaiming her. Nicias laughs in-
ordinately at this, but invites Athanaël to a supper at which
she will be present. The slaves array the monk in gorgeous
apparel, admiring his fine eyes and athletic figure. They
hide his ragged robes under a magnificent embroidered garment, while Nicias looks on, smiling. Shouts and cheering
are heard in the distance, and Thaïs enters, surrounded by
an adoring crowd. Athanaël stands a little apart, and his
unusual appearance draws the attention of the courtesan.
She asks his name and his business. Nicias jestingly tells
her that he has come for her. "Bringing love?" she demands, mockingly. Athanaël comes forward to explain
his mission, but she will not listen. She tries to allure him
with her charms. (Thaïs: "Why art thou so hard, so un-
yielding?") Athanaël denounces her, and is silenced by the
crowd. But when Thaïs prepares to pose as in his dream,
he flees, horror-stricken.

Act II. In the house of Thaïs. Accompanied by her
friends, she enters, listless, dispirited and fatigued, and retires to her apartment to array herself anew. (Thaïs: "Alone
at last.") She apostrophises her own beauty, gazing into
a mirror with delight. Athanaël stands at the door, regarding her. He prays silently for her (Athanaël: "Thaïs, I
love thee"), and tells her he loves her with the love of the
spirit. She listens idly, then pours into an incense burner
some grains of incense. Athanaël is troubled, but prays
that he may withstand her. She murmurs a soft incantation to Venus. (Thaïs: "Venus, enchantress, queen.")
Athanaël commands her to rise and follow him. The voice

of Nicias is heard far off calling her. Thaïs makes a
gesture of disgust. Athanaël goes out, saying he will wait
for her until day. Thaïs, alone, falls into a reverie.

Change of scene: Before the house of Thaïs. It is still
night, and moonlight floods the square. Athanaël lies
asleep on the stone pavement. Nicias and his friends are
feasting. Thaïs slowly appears, bearing a lamp. She tells
the monk she has chosen his way, and will go whither he
leads her. He tells her she must leave all behind, and she
asks if she may take the image of Eros, which stands
before her door (Thaïs: "This little ivory image"), given
to her by Nicias. Athanaël throws the image on the pavement, where it falls in fragments. Thaïs enters the house
with him. Nicias and his friends appear, flushed with wine,
and call for dances to amuse them. La Charmeuse appears,
and Crobyle and Myrtale sing to the accompaniment of
zithers. (Duet: "She whose light steps turn hither.")
Athanaël is seen on the threshold of the house of Thaïs
bearing a smoking torch. The revellers are amazed. Thaïs
follows him, clad in a simple robe of wool. Flames burst
from the house behind her. Her slaves follow her wistfully.
Nicias tries to detain her, but she follows Athanaël, amid
the execrations of the crowd, whom Nicias appeases by
throwing gold among them.

Act III. An oasis in the desert. Thaïs and Athanaël
appear, the former overcome with fatigue. Athanaël
harshly urges her onward, but seeing her prostration, relents and, kneeling, kisses her feet, with tears. He points
to the convent, then goes to the well for water. (Thaïs,
alone: "O holy messenger.") The voices of the nuns are
heard. (Chorus: "Pater noster, qui es in cœlis.") Athanaël
confides Thaïs to the care of the holy abbess. She bids him
farewell forever, and he stands silent, watching her out of
sight.

Change of scene: The Cenobite dwellings. A storm is
coming up. The sky is black and threatening. Athanaël
appears among the monks with sunken eyes and pale aspect.

They greet him with veneration. He confesses to Palemon
that since he reclaimed Thaïs he has been haunted by impure visions of beautiful women. (Athanaël: "Stay by my
side.") Palemon talks with him gently, admonishing him to
beware of the world and its people, then, departing, leaves
him to his prayers. A vision of Thaïs, seductively beautiful, comes before the unhappy monk. She smiles alluringly.
Athanaël calls her name in an agony of passion. The
vision disappears, and he beholds the monastery. Voices
chant the passing of Thaïs. This vision also leaves him,
and overcome, he rushes into the desert, where a storm is
fiercely raging. (Athanaël: "Thaïs must die.")

Act IV. The garden of the monastery. Thaïs lies dying
under a fig tree while the white nuns kneel around her.
Albine is looking at her with pity. (Albine: "God calls her,
and a shroud will veil her soon.") The nuns pray fervently.
Athanaël enters the garden, asking for Thaïs. The nuns
separate and he beholds her. He kneels by her side. She
opens her eyes, recognising him. She is an ecstasy, reminding him of her conversion. Athanaël's thoughts, however, are centred on earthly passion. Thaïs, rising to her
feet, points to the sky, where she sees angels approaching
to carry her away. (Thaïs: "Heaven opens its gates. Angelic forms I see.") Athanaël, torn with passion, tries to
divert her thoughts to human emotions. (Athanaël: "Come!
Mine art thou!") But with eyes uplifted, she calls on God,
and falls dead at his feet. Athanaël, with a loud and bitter
cry of anguish, sinks to the ground beside her.

THAT WAS I

Village idyll in one act by Batka. Music by Leo Blech.
Cast: Farmer Paul. Martha. Laborer. Peter. Cousin
Röschen. The neighbour. Place, a German village, about
1830. First production, Dresden, 1902.

Röschen loves Peter, whose father, Farmer Paul, with-

holds his consent. He himself flirts with the pretty girl,
helps her to water the flowers, snatches a kiss, places a
bouquet at her bosom, and rides her in a wheelbarrow. His
female neighbour is gazing on the scene with interest,
and because she is envious, having herself an eye on the
farmer, she circulates the news. Paul and Röschen, however, have noticed her, and plan to anticipate her malice.
Paul introduces his wife and Röschen her Peter into the
situation. Paul kisses his wife and Peter kisses Röschen.
Paul waters the flowers with Martha; Röschen does the
same with Peter, and the pinning on of the bouquets and
the wheelbarrow-riding go merrily forward. When the
neighbour attempts to calumniate Röschen, the farmer's
wife replies, "That was I," and when the farmer is accused,
Peter says, "That was I." The loud protestations of the
woman are of no avail; every one laughs at her, and the
farmer, in high good humour, unites Peter and Röschen.

THE THREE PINTOS

Comic opera in three acts, unfinished, by Carl Maria von
Weber, libretto by Hell. New adaptation of the text by
Karl von Weber, with addition of the missing music from
motives of C. M. von Weber by Gustav Mahler.

CAST: Don Pantaleone and Don Gomez, noblemen of
Madrid—Baritone. Clarissa, daughter of Pantaleone—
Soprano. Laura, her maid—Mezzo-soprano. Don Gaston
Viratos, student—Tenor. Ambrosio, servant—Baritone.
Don Pinto, a country gentleman—Basso. The village inn-
keeper—Basso. Inez, his daughter—Soprano. Place, a
village inn between Madrid and Salamanca.

ACT I. The veranda of the village inn. The somewhat
uncouth country gentleman, Pinto de Fonsera, is on the
way to Don Pantaleone at Madrid with a letter of recommendation, through which he expects to take home Clarissa
as his bride. On the journey he meets the student, Gaston

Viratos, who, aided by his servant, Ambrosio, gives him directions as to his behavior. The young student finally resolves to go to Madrid himself in place of Pinto, and taking from him while asleep the letter of recommendation, proceeds on his journey.

ACT II. Apartment of Pantaleone. Clarissa loves Don Gomez, and is therefore distressed when her father announces that she is to marry Pinto, whose arrival is expected at any moment. Gomez, Clarissa and Laura, the sly maid, conspire to defeat this plan, but are driven away by Pantaleone.

ACT III. Another room in the house of Pantaleone. Gaston, with his servant, Ambrosio, arrives and introduces himself as the expected Pinto. Informed of the situation, he gives the letter to Gomez, who now also appears as Pinto. While his arrival is being celebrated, the real Pinto appears, causing much merriment by his clumsiness, but proving to be a coward when attacked by Gaston. Pantaleone is informed of the true state of affairs, pardons the lovers and gives his consent to their marriage.

TIEFLAND

Music drama, in three acts and a prologue, adapted from the work of Guimera by Lothar. Music by Eugen d'Albert.

CAST: Sebastiano, a rich landowner. Tommaso, an old man. Moruccio, Martha, Pepa, Antonia, Rosalie, Nuri, Pedro, Nando, all in the service of Sebastiano. A priest. Place, the Pyrenees and the valley of Catalonia. First production, Prague, 1903.

PROLOGUE: A rocky fastness in the Pyrenees. The shepherd Pedro, as long as he can remember, has lived among the hills, which he loves. (Pedro: "Wonderful 'tis to me.") He seldom sees any one except his fellow-shepherd, Nando, and women almost not at all, but he dreams that the Mother of God will some day send him a wife. (Pedro: "Nay, do not laugh, I mean it.") He is satisfied with his free life (Pedro: "Glorious 'tis to me") and thankfully repeats the Paternoster. His employer, the rich Sebastiano, has forced the beautiful Martha to accede to his desires, installing her as manager of the mill. He now wishes her to marry (Sebastiano: "Have no fear") and to take Pedro for her husband. He has brought her to the hills with this end in view, trusting to Pedro's ignorant simplicity and obedience for the rest. Pedro, of course, thinks the long-wished-for wife has been sent to him, and willingly consents to go to the Lowlands and live with Martha in the mill. Martha is less willing and will not look at Pedro. She departs with Sebastiano, and Pedro tells Nando of his good fortune. (Pedro: "Joy comes to me!")

ACT I. The interior of the mill. Sebastiano's servants know that he is Martha's lover, but that their master must make a rich marriage to maintain his position. They discuss the matter, and little Nuri innocently tells them of a conversation she has overheard between Sebastiano and Martha. (Nuri: "If I walk, and walk, and walk"; " 'Twas eventide.") The maidservants scorn Pedro, who, unaware of the situation, is betrothed to Martha ("This great fool knows less than nothing"), and joke broadly with Martha over her coming nuptials. She drives them away, bitterly complaining of her loneliness. (Martha: "No one have I to help me in my need.") Nuri tries to make her smile, but her innocent questions only hurt, and Martha sends her away. (Martha: "His, body and soul.") Moruccio tells old Tommaso the real state of affairs, and they quarrel. The villagers are hilarious over the deception of Pedro. (Pedro: "I thank you all.") The marriage takes place, and it is Sebastiano's intention to return at night and visit Martha as usual. (Sebastiano: "Martha, you know.") She, wishing to avoid him, does not enter her chamber, nor does she accompany Pedro, although she is now convinced that the simple shepherd has acted in good faith and knows nothing of her relations with Sebastiano. (Pedro: "You mean that

I have earned this without working.") Poor Pedro is
puzzled by her strange conduct and tears, and knows not
what to do. (Pedro: "Now what to do I scarcely know.")
A light appears suddenly in Martha's room—Sebastiano's
signal—which adds to the mystery.

ACT II. Same scene, at dawn. Nuri is heard singing
outside. (Nuri: "The stars are going to sleep.") She
enters, knitting industriously, and tells Pedro she is making
him a fine new jersey. He replies that he is going away.
(Pedro: "Yes, far away from Martha.") Martha's love is
turning toward her husband, and she becomes jealous of
Nuri, driving her from the house. Pedro goes with her,
and Martha, running after them, half distraught, meets
old Tommaso. She confides in him, explaining that her
old rascal of a stepfather had sold her to Sebastiano.
Tommaso advises her to tell Pedro all. (Tommaso: "Every
one laughs, and Pedro knows not why"; Martha: "Think of
your own dear daughter.") She feels that Pedro really
loves her. (Martha: "Let him despise me, then! He loves
me.") The old man leaves her with his blessing. (Tommaso: "In God's strong arms I leave you.") The chattering women drive Pedro to return. He shakes one of them
in exasperation, then entering the house, tells Martha he
must go back to his solitude in the hills. She asks him to
take her with him, and he answers her with bitterness.
(Martha: "Ah! thou art right. With my beloved.") She
laughs hysterically, and Pedro advances with a knife to kill
her. (Martha: "Only a weariness is life to me!" Pedro:
"I sought to kill the woman whom I love!") He suffers remorse, and they determine to fly together. (Duet: "There
shall we go, high up in the hills!") They are intercepted by
the villagers, who enter with Sebastiano to congratulate
them. Sebastiano, with effrontery, thrums on a guitar for
Martha to dance as of old. (Sebastiano: "Wind round
your form the seductive mantilla.") He strikes Pedro, who
rushes at him furiously, but is overpowered by the villagers
and dragged away.

ACT III.   The same scene.   The news of Sebastiano's conduct has caused the rich heiress to reject him.   With increasing passion he desires Martha, but she loves Pedro. (Sebastiano: "Little sweetheart, you are mad.")   He defies God.   ("Heaven has no ears for you.")   Martha scornfully refuses to listen to him.   ("No longer am I weak and helpless.")   She calls to Pedro.   He has escaped and bounds into the room like some savage animal, drawing a knife. ("Sneak away, wouldst thou, coward dog!")   Seeing Sebastiano is unarmed, he throws down his weapon and they fight with their bare hands.   Sebastiano tries to pick up the knife.   Pedro puts his foot on it, and flies at his enemy's throat.   Silently they wrestle, until Pedro throws Sebastiano aside as if he were a rat and calls the people in to witness his work.   Scornfully he asks them, as they stand dumb with amazement, why they do not laugh now.   (Pedro: "Well, good friends, why don't you laugh?")   Then, bearing Martha in his strong young arms, he escapes with her to freedom among the mountains.   (Pedro: "Far up, far up in the mountains!   To sunshine and freedom and light.")

THE TWO GUARDSMEN

Opera in three acts by Lortzing (first produced under the title "The Two Knapsacks").   Libretto by the composer, from the French vaudeville "Les deux grenadiers."

CAST: Wall, bailiff—Basso.   Caroline, his daughter—Soprano.   William, his son, soldier in the First Battalion of the Guards, under the name of Wilhelm Stark—Baritone. Peter, his cousin—Tenor Buffo.   Busch, innkeeper—Basso. Süschen, his daughter—Soprano.   Gustav, his son, soldier in the Third Battalion of the Guards—Tenor.   Dame Lieblich, housekeeper—Mezzo-soprano.   Schwarzbart, dragoon —Basso Buffo.   Barsch, corporal—Baritone.   Place, a small town.

ACT I.   Busch, the innkeeper, after a long time of waiting, expects the arrival of his son from the army. The peasants join in his joy. He invites the bailiff to be his guest through Dame Lieblich. Wilhelm, the long-forgotten son of Wall, the bailiff, appears in soldier's dress and frightens Caroline and Süschen. As he opens his knapsack, in order to take out a lottery ticket which has won the capital prize he and his friend Schwarzbart discover that the knapsack and a pocketbook therein are not his own, but have been changed by mistake. From this the comic action of the opera develops, as the pocketbook contains the papers of Gustav, the son of Busch. Wilhelm resolves to take his name and station.

ACT II. Wilhelm has fallen in love with Süschen, who is supposed to be his sister, and has beaten his cousin Peter for his stupidity when the real Gustav appears. The latter attempts to greet his own father and is believed by all to be insane, especially as by the papers in his knapsack it appears his name is Wilhelm Stark. As the prison is not serviceable, Gustav is confined in the arbour outside the inn.

ACT III. Bailiff Wall, having read the documents in the knapsack, now believes that Gustav is his son Wilhelm. Schwarzbart and Wilhelm quickly take action in the affair, and, aided by Caroline, who loves Gustav, they try to force the stupid Peter to free the prisoner.

Change of scene: A room in the summer-house. Gustav is alone in the dark when Caroline comes to assist in his deliverance. She conceals herself on the arrival of Wilhelm, who has arranged a meeting in the arbour with Süschen. She is late, and the two men, being found together, are separated by the invalid corporal Barsch, who fears a conspiracy for Gustav's release. In the darkness Barsch takes off Gustav by mistake, so that Wilhelm remains. Wilhelm strikes a light and in his turn finds Caroline in the arbour. As Süschen comes near, Caroline blows out the light at the sound of her footsteps. They are all groping about when Peter, Dame Lieblich, Schwarzbart and Gustav arrive on the scene, and a merry play begins in the darkness. All are

at cross-purposes, but at last, as the other personages of
the drama come upon the scene, lights are brought in and
the whole mystery is made plain to the general satisfaction
of all.

TRISTAN AND ISOLDE

Musical drama in three acts by Wagner.

CAST: King Mark—Basso. Isolde—Soprano. Tristan—
Tenor. Kurwenal—Baritone. Melot—Baritone. Brangäne—Mezzo-soprano. A steersman—Tenor. A shepherd—Tenor. Place, Act I., on board a ship. Act II., in
Cornwall, at the castles of King Mark. Act III., in Brittany, at Tristan's castle. First production, Munich, 1865.
In the principal parts of this opera Wagner has followed
the romance of Gottfried of Strasburg and in the musical
portion has perhaps reached the highest summits of his art.

ACT I. A vessel. Tristan has been sent to bring Isolde,
the intended bride of King Mark, from Ireland to Cornwall.
Isolde and her companion, Brangäne, are seated amidships
of the vessel, which is divided by a curtain for privacy.
The princess has recognised in Tristan a wounded knight
whom she has nursed when wounded, but who has slain her
betrothed Marold in combat. She wavers between love and
hate, but finally resolves to kill Tristan, and commands
Brangäne to prepare a poisoned potion. Isolde's mother,
who was versed in sorcery, has given Brangäne several
magic drugs, and by mistake Tristan and Isolde both drink
a love potion. They gaze upon each other in wonder, and
under the influence of the draught they finally sink into
each other's arms in an ecstasy of love.

ACT II. King Mark's castle. The king is hunting, and
Tristan and Isolde plan to meet in secret. Brangäne warns
Isolde against the traitorous and jealous Melot, but Isolde
gives the signal to Tristan to draw nigh. A beautiful love
duet follows, probably the longest ever written for any
opera. The faithful Kurwenal comes to warn Tristan, but

It is too late, for he is closely followed by Melot, bringing King Mark and his attendants. The chivalrous Mark, however, despises Melot for his treachery. Tristan draws his sword upon the traitor, but is defeated in the combat and sorely wounded.

ACT III. Tristan's castle in Brittany. Kurwenal has brought the wounded Tristan to the castle. He grows rapidly worse and Kurwenal sends for Isolde to heal him. A shepherd stands on the ramparts to watch for her ship, the coming of which he announces by a strain on his pipe. When she approaches, Tristan tears the bandages from his wounds in an effort to go to her, and after recognising her by name, dies in her arms. Mark has followed Isolde to unite her to Tristan. Kurwenal, who thinks he has come with evil intent, slays the false Melot and is himself slain. Isolde dies of grief by the side of Tristan, and in sorrow Mark remains in prayer beside the dead.

THE TRUMPETER OF SÄCKINGEN

Opera in three acts by E. Kaiser. Text founded upon the work of Scheffel.

CAST: The baron—Basso. Margarete, his daughter— Soprano. The bailiff of Säckingen—Basso. Gertrud, his housekeeper—Alto. Junker von Wildenstein—Tenor. Werner Kirchhof—Baritone. Carlo, an Italian boy— Soprano. Place, Säckingen and Rome. Time, after the Thirty Years' War. First production, Olmütz, 1882.

ACT I. Market-place in Säckingen. Festival and appearance of Werner as the trumpeter. He tells the bailiff that he has been compelled to fly from Heidelberg, where he was a student, on account of his love for the Countess of the Pfulz, and had become trumpeter of the regiment. The baron joins in the festivities, is pleased with Werner and invites him to be his guest.

ACT II. Courtyard of the castle of the baron. Margarete has been selected by the baron to become the wife of Junker Kuno von Wildenstein, who has defended the castle against the rebelling citizens and peasants. But Margarete loves Werner and they are discovered by the baron during a love scene. Werner is ordered to depart, and when from the distance his trumpet is heard in the song of farewell ("God guard thee, love, it was too fair a dream") Margarete sinks to the ground in a swoon.

Act III. A square in Rome. The baron, with Margarete and his housekeeper, Gertrud, is residing at Rome. Margarete meets Werner, who is now a celebrated papal Capellmeister, and both renew their vows of eternal love. Werner resigns his position, and the Pope, for services rendered, confers on him the title of Marquis of Composanto, and the baron consents to the union, not, as he says, because Werner has become a nobleman, but because he has elevated German music and art.

THE TRUMPETER OF SÄCKINGEN

Opera in three acts and a prologue by Neszler. Text founded upon the work of Scheffel by R. Bunge.

Cast of the Prologue: Werner Kirchhofer—Baritone. Konradin, foot soldier—Basso. Majordomo—Baritone. The rector—Basso. Place, the courtyard at Heidelberg.

Cast of the Opera: Baron von Schönau—Basso. Maria, his daughter—Soprano. Count von Wildenstein—Basso. The countess, his divorced wife and sister-in-law of the baron—Alto. Damian, son of the count by his second wife—Tenor. Werner—Baritone. Konradin—Basso. Place, in and near Säckingen. Time, after the Thirty Years' War. First production, Leipsic, 1884.

Prologue: Courtyard of the castle at Heidelberg. At one side students, at the other foot soldiers, drinking and singing. When the majordomo of the princess demands quiet, the tumult increases. Werner climbs upon a table

and plays a love song upon the trumpet of the rider Konradin. The rector of the university chides the students,
whereupon Werner and his comrades join the soldiers.
Singing a merry song, they march away.

ACT I. Square before the Fridolin church at Säckingen.
Konradin has entered the service of the city, and the citizens
are engaged in festivities. Werner, arriving on horseback
as a trumpeter, is warmly welcomed by Konradin, and protects Countess von Wildenstein and her niece from the re-
bellious peasants.

Change of scene: A room in the castle of the baron. He
is drinking wine and cursing the gout with which he is
afflicted. He is informed that he is about to receive a visit
from his brother-in-law, the Count von Wildenstein, and
is delighted with the proposal to marry Maria to his son
Damian. Maria and the countess return, and the baron is
enraged at the news of the attack of the peasants. A
trumpet is heard before the castle and Werner is admitted,
and to the joy of Maria is appointed trumpeter.

ACT II. The garden of the castle and terrace. Konradin visits Werner and is informed by him of his love for
Maria. The countess surprises Werner and Maria making
love to each other, and the baron angrily orders her to
marry Damian. Count von Wildenstein arrives with his
son and a festival is held in their honour. (Intermezzo, the
grand ballet of the May festival.) Werner is ordered to
leave. (Werner's song with the refrain: "God guard thee,
love, it was too fair a dream.") Werner departs and once
more sends forth his farewell song. Maria, in tears, sinks
to the ground.

ACT III. The courtyard of the castle, its walls protected
by cannon. The peasants beleaguer the castle. Damian
proves himself a coward when the peasants storm the walls,
but the courageous Werner places himself at the head of
the besieged and drives the assailants off. He is wounded,
and in binding up his wounds they discover a mark by which
he is recognised as the son of the Count and Countess von

Wildenstein, who as a child had been stolen by gipsies. The baron is reconciled with his divorced wife and Werner receives Maria as his betrothed.

IL TROVATORE

Opera in four acts by Verdi. Text by Cammerano.

CAST: Count di Luna—Baritone. Countess Leonora—Soprano. Azucena, a gipsy—Alto. Manrico—Tenor. Ferrando, Luna's vassal—Basso. Inez, Leonora's confidante—Soprano. Ruiz, friend of Manrico—Tenor. An old gipsy—Basso. A messenger—Tenor. Place, Biscay and Aragon. Time, the fifteenth century. First production, Rome, 1853.

ACT I. The guard room in the castle of Luna. Ferrando, an old and trusted vassal of the count, orders the guards to keep watch while Di Luna wanders restlessly beneath the windows of Leonora, whom he loves. Luna's heart is torn with jealousy against his fortunate rival, the troubadour Manrico. In order to keep awake, Ferrando narrates the history of the count to the guard. (Ferrando: "Once upon a time a father of two sons lived happily.") It appears that a gipsy of dreadful aspect had once exercised her magic arts upon the little brother of the count, making the child weak and ill, and for this had been burnt alive as a witch. Dying, she had commanded her daughter Azucena to avenge her, which vengeance had been partially accomplished by the carrying off of the child. Although no news had been heard of him, the father refused to believe in his son's death, and dying, commanded his son, Count di Luna, to seek for the gipsy.

Change of scene: Garden in the palace of the princess. Leonora confesses her love for Manrico to her confidante, Inez. ("The stars shone.") When they have gone, Count Luna hears the voice of his rival. (Manrico, behind the scenes: "Alone and forsaken am I.") Leonora in the dark-

ness mistakes the count for her lover, when Manrico himself
enters the garden, and she rushes to his arms. The count
recognises Manrico as his enemy, who has been condemned
to death, and endeavours to compel him to fight. When
they cross swords Leonora intervenes.

Act II.   Camp of the gipsies.   Manrico at the bedside
of his mother, Azucena.   (Chorus: "See the clouds in
heaven's vault.")   Azucena is the daughter of the gipsy
burnt by the count.   She is old, but still nurses her vengeance.   (Aria: "Flames rise to heaven.")   The gipsies
break up camp while Azucena confesses to Manrico that
after stealing him she had intended to burn the count's little
son, but had thrown her own child into the flames instead.
Manrico realises that he is not the son of Azucena, but
loves her as if she were indeed his mother, as she has always
been faithful and loving to him.   A messenger arrives and
reports that Leonora, who believes Manrico dead, is about
to take the veil.   Manrico rushes away to prevent her from
following out this purpose.

Change of scene: Before the convent.   Luna and his attendants intend to abduct Leonora.   (Aria: "Her eyes'
heavenly light.")   Leonora and the nuns appear in procession, but Manrico prevents Luna from carrying out his
plans.

Act III.   Luna's camp.   (Chorus: "In the midst of conflict.")   Ferrando brings in the captured Azucena.   She is
recognised by Luna and sentenced to be burnt.

Change of scene: Chamber in the castle, which is besieged
by Manrico.   Leonora and Manrico live only for each
other.   (Aria, Manrico: "For you, my dear one, would I
willingly die.")   Ruiz, Manrico's comrade, reports that
Azucena is to be executed.   Manrico flies to her aid.
(Stretta: "I see the flames to heaven reach.")

Act IV.   Before the dungeon keep.   Leonora attempts to
free Manrico, who has been captured by Luna.   (Miserere
of the prisoners and aria of Manrico in the turret: "The
death hour is near.")   Leonora begs Luna for mercy and

offers herself in place of her lover. She promises to give herself to the count, but intends to take poison before the marriage.

Change of scene: Manrico and Azucena. Manrico attempts to soothe Azucena, whose mind wanders. (Duet: "Home to our mountains.") At last the gipsy slumbers. Leonora comes to Manrico and tells him that he is saved. When he discovers she cannot accompany him, he refuses to leave his prison. He believes Leonora to be a traitress until he hears that she has taken poison to remain true to him. As she dies in agony the count enters and orders Manrico to be led to execution. Azucena arises from her couch and when Luna, dragging her to a window, shows her the dying Manrico, she cries in triumph: "He was your brother. Now are you avenged, mother!" and falls dead at his feet.

UNDINE

Fairy opera in four acts by Lortzing. Text founded on Fouqué's tale by the composer.

Cast: Bertalda, daughter of Duke Heinrich—Soprano. Hugo of Ringstetten—Tenor. Kühleborn, a mighty water spirit—Baritone. Tobias, an old fisherman—Basso. Martha, his wife—Alto. Undine, her foster daughter— Soprano. Father Heilman—Basso. Veit, Hugo's shield-bearer—Tenor. Hans, cellarer—Basso. Place, Act I., a fishing village; Act II., Reichstadt; Act III., castle of Ringstetten. First production, Hamburg, 1845.

Act I. A fisherman's hut. Bertalda is the supposed daughter of Duke Heinrich and has sent the Knight Hugo of Ringstetten, one of her suitors, into the magic wood to seek adventure. Hugo forms the acquaintance of Undine in a fishing village. She is the reputed daughter of the fisherman Tobias, and Hugo marries her. (Chorus and quintet, Undine, Tobias, Father Heilman, Hugo and Martha: "What joy, what rapture." Romance of Hugo:

"I rode to the lists." Chorus and duet, Kühleborn, Veit:
"The capital is well known to us." Scene, chorus and song
of Veit: "Many handsome gifts," with refrain: "What
may that be?—It is wine!" Finale.) Kühleborn now
appears as Father Heilmann, but is repulsed by Undine,
who recognises him. (Undine is a child of the sea and a
daughter of Kühleborn, a mighty water spirit. He brought
Undine, who is soulless, as are all water sprites, to Tobias
and Martha in her childhood, and allowed the fishermaiden
Bertalda to be found by the duke, who brought her up as
his own daughter. Kühleborn played this trick in order
to ascertain in what degree men with souls are superior
to the soulless water sprites.)

ACT II. Hall in garden with vases of flowers. Hugo
and Undine repair to the court of the duke, and the jealous
Bertalda now wishes to become the wife of the King of
Naples. But when they open the casket which was found
with her it is discovered that she is but a foundling. Kühleborn, who is at court in the guise of ambassador from
Naples, introduces the fisherman and his wife as the parents
of Bertalda. Bertalda repudiates them and they attack
Kühleborn, who acknowledges that he is the mighty water
spirit. (Duet, Hans and Veit: "What do I see, are you
here again?" Recitative and aria of Undine: "Know there
are beings like you in all elements." Kühleborn's aria composed by Gumbert: "Naples' ambassador approaches the
city." Recitative and quartet, Hugo, Undine, Bertalda,
Kühleborn: "Attacked with fright." Ballet. Scene and
romance of Kühleborn: "There lives on the shore of the
sea." Finale: "Miscreant, how dare you.")

ACT III. The sea and castle of Ringstetten. Bertalda
has been compelled to leave the court, but is received by
Undine and gains Hugo's love. Having ascertained the
origin of Undine, he thrusts her from him and celebrates
his marriage with Bertalda. Undine in distress returns to
the water spirits. (Chorus: "Up, drink merrily." Song of
Veit: "Father, mother, sisters, brothers have I none."

Finale, Hugo and Bertalda: "I will not leave thee." Then Undine: "What do I see?") When Undine is alone, the water spirits arise from the sea and Kühleborn approaches. (Kühleborn: "It is performed, return to your home.") Undine sinks beneath the sea.

Act IV. Court of the castle. Veit and Hans lift the stone that covers the well. Hugo has placed it there to prevent the reappearance of Undine. Undine appears. (Love duet between Hans and Veit: "In my young days," with the refrain: "Only in wine is truth.")

Change of scene: Festal chamber in the castle. Marriage feast of Hugo and Bertalda. When Undine appears, Hugo's love is rekindled and he falls at her feet. A flood of water rushes into the castle and the palace of the prince of the sea arises from the waves. Kühleborn is appeased and greets Hugo, who is to remain united with Undine. (Finale, Hugo, Bertalda and chorus: "Fill the beakers.") The clock strikes twelve, the lights go out, and in a blue mist Undine stands before Hugo. He rushes to her arms to die, the waves of the sea enter, the people flee. Kühleborn appears. "You have sinned against her pure heart," he declares "Hear, ye soulless ones, who scorn us, this is the vengeance of the soulless."

THE VAMPIRE

Romantic opera in four acts by Marschner. Text by Wohlbrück.

Cast: Sir Humphry—Basso. Malvina, his daughter— Soprano. Edgar Aubrey, a relative—Tenor. Lord Ruthven—Baritone. Sir Berkley—Basso. Ianthe, his daughter—Soprano. George Dibdin, in the service of Humphry—Tenor. John Perth, bailiff of the earl of Marsden. Emmy, his daughter—Soprano. Gadshill, Blunt, Scrope and Green, countrymen—Small singing parts. Suse, wife of Blunt—Alto. Place, Scotland. First production, Leipsic, 1828. The opera has four scenes and is sometimes produced in two acts, when the second and fourth acts are changes of scene.

ACT I. Rocks and cavern. Lord Ruthven, through his crimes, is forfeit to the spirits and is brought forward to suffer his doom. He asks for a respite, and three years are granted him on condition that each year he shall bring a pure maiden as his bride to the sacrifice. Ruthven takes the oath and the spirits disappear with the warning that the first victim is approaching. (Recitative and aria of Ruthven: "Ha! what joy! from lovely eyes.") Ruthven is a vampire, who lives on the heart's blood of his victims. Ianthe appears. (Love duet: "The pride of dear parents.") Ruthven drags her to the cavern, where Berkley and his companions find her dead, with the marks of the teeth of a vampire. Berkley stabs Ruthven all but mortally. The vampire is dragged by Aubrey to a hiding place among the rocks, where he is healed by the rays of the moon. Aubrey is compelled to take a dreadful oath to remain silent.

ACT II. (or change of scene). A chamber in Sir Humphry's castle. (Aria of Malvina, who awaits Aubrey: "The morning sun of spring.") Aubrey arrives. (Duet: " 'Tis you, 'tis no dream.") Sir Humphry has selected the Earl of Marsden to be Malvina's husband. (Terzett: "What, father! Woe is me! I am lost!") Aubrey recognises, to his horror, the earl as the vampire, but is prevented by his oath from exposing him.

ACT III. A square. Drinking and dancing. (Chorus: "Merrily drink," and "Do you hear the fiddle?") Emmy, the daughter of the bailiff, is about to marry George Dibdin, but as the bridegroom is tardy, she entertains the guests. (Aria: "There on the rocks," and ballad of the vampire: "See, mother, the pale man.") Ruthven endeavours to captivate Emmy. George listens. (Terzett: "You only desire to shame me.") Aubrey tells Ruthven that he will expose him, but to his horror learns that if he did so he would himself become a vampire. (Aria of Aubrey: "Ha! what dreadful picture.") Ruthven succeeds in deluding Emmy (Duet: "Come to yonder arbour") and she follows him. The countrymen make merry (Quartet: "In the fall we must drink"; Quintet: "At last, old man, I find you"), but the festivities are interrupted by finding Emmy dead.

ACT IV. (or change of scene). Chamber at Sir Humphry's. The marriage of Ruthven is about to be celebrated. Aubrey is desperate and desires to prevent the ceremony, and Malvina also refuses to wed Ruthven. Humphry threatens to curse them, and Malvina is about to comply when Aubrey exclaims, pointing to Ruthven: "That horror is a vampire." At this moment Ruthven is struck by lightning. Humphry consents to the union of Aubrey and Malvina.

THE VILLAGE BARBER

Opera in two acts by Johann Schenk. Libretto by Weidemann.

CAST: Lux, a village barber—Baritone. Maid Süschen, his ward—Soprano. Rund, the schoolmaster—Basso. Joseph, son of a farmer—Tenor. Adam, a barber's apprentice—Tenor. Frau Marguerete, widow—Mezzo-soprano. Peter, a tailor—Basso. Philip and Thomas, peasants and conspirators—Basso. Place, the barber shop of Lux. Time, in the time of the queue. First production, Vienna, 1796.

Joseph and Süschen are in love. But as the village barber and quack Lux himself wants to marry his ward, the lovers plan a comedy. The girl pretends to abhor the sight of the youth, and he declares he has taken poison in despair at her heartlessness. Lux, out of charity, allows the seemingly dying man to be married to Süschen on his death-bed. When this has been done, Joseph develops a fine appetite, devours a large portion of ham, and to the astonishment of the barber regains his health.

ACT I. Introduction: "It is true and certain, blessed is this year for doctor and barber"; Aria of Lux: "Anger, jealousy and vengeance"; Couplet of Adam, with the refrain: "And that was good"; Süschen's aria: "Who would not be touched by my woes"; Duet between Lux and Süschen: "I am admired and respected"; Finale: "God greet you in honour."

ACT II. Terzett, Joseph, Süschen and Rund: "Soon the torment will end"; Adam's aria: "The devil take the business"; Lux's aria: "The head is my pride"; Süschen's aria: "Maidens are easily deceived"; Joseph's aria: "Desperate is my state"; Duet between Lux and Joseph: "Death sits already on his brow"; Rund's aria: "Think, oh man, you are from dust"; Closing chorus: "Long live Lux, the miracle worker."

THE VIOLIN MAKER OF CREMONA

Opera in two acts by Jenö Hubay. Text by François Coppée and Henry Beauclair. German by Max Kalbeck.

CAST: Taddeo Ferrari. His scholars, Filippo, Sandro. Giannina, his daughter. The burgomaster. Place, Cremona. Time, 1750.

ACT I. Workshop of Ferrari. After an introductory chorus Ferrari enters and announces that the council of the city has resolved to reward the maker of the best violin with a golden chain. He adds that he will also give to the victor his daughter in marriage and his house as a dowry. Giannina, who loves Sandro, but is doubtful of his success in the contest, in vain tries to dissuade her father from his project. After a love scene between Giannina and Sandro, Filippo rushes in. On account of his deformed stature he has been annoyed by street urchins. He is passionately in love with Giannina, who does not return his love, but tells him of her grief. Filippo secretly exchanges violins with his rival to give him the victory. Sandro, however, desires to defraud Filippo and again exchanges the instruments so that he obtains his own inferior one. Suffering from remorse he confesses to Filippo what he has done, and begs for his forgiveness.

ACT II. The principal square in Cremona. The burgo-master declares Filippo the victor, but the hunchback hands Giannina the chain as a wedding gift and relinquishes her in favour of Sandro.

THE WATER CARRIER

(Les deux Journées)

Opera comique in three acts by Cherubini. Text by Bouilly. CAST: Count Armand—Tenor. Costanza, his wife—So-prano. Michele, Savoyard water-carrier—Basso. Daniel, his father—Basso. Anton, his grandchild—Tenor. Mar-celline, his sister—Soprano. Semos, a rich countryman. Angelina, his daughter. A captain of Italian troops. A lieutenant—Tenor. A sergeant. A corporal. A girl—Soprano. Place, in and near Paris. Time, the seventeenth century. First production, Paris, 1800.

The text is founded upon an actual occurrence, the savoy-ard having carried Count Armand out of Paris in a water butt, when pursued by Mazarin, thus saving his life.

ACT I. Dwelling of the water-carrier Michele. Anton narrates to his friends that he had once as a lad been saved from death through cold and hunger by a stranger. ("Poor little Savoyard.") Michele ascertains that Mazarin has been pursuing his benefactor, Count Armand and his wife, Costanza. He desires to save them. (Aria: "Heavens! let my plan succeed.") When he has brought them safely to his dwelling (Terzett, Armand, Costanza, Michele: "Come to my heart"; and duet, Costanza, Armand: "To part from my husband"), Anton recognises in Armand the saviour of his life. (Finale: "Oh God, whom do I behold?") Michele now insists that the count and his wife shall be carried to safety out of Paris. He has a pass made out in the name of his daughter, Marcelline, and Anton is to take her through the gates.

Act II. The gates and guard house. The watch retains Anton and Costanza. (Terzett, Costanza, Anton, lieutenant: "Oh my brother, can you allow.") The countess plays the part of sister so naturally that they allow her to pass, while Anton is detained. Michele now arrives with a large water butt. He seemingly betrays the whereabouts of the count in order to get rid of the soldiers, and they depart eager to earn the price set by Mazarin upon his head. (Finale: "March! away! let us not tarry.") While the watch is preparing to leave, Michele cautiously opens the cask; Count Armand slips through the gate and disappears.

Act III. A square in a village near Paris. Anton's arrival is expected to celebrate his marriage with Angelina, but he does not appear. The soldiers, who have followed the count to the village, enter. The countess arrives dressed as a peasant in order to bring food to her husband. (Aria: "Could I but suffer death.") When the soldiers threaten the countess the count rushes to her rescue and his name escapes her lips. About to be arrested, the honest Michele appears and brings the pardon of the king. (Closing song of Michele: "Friends, let us be merry.")

WERTHER

Lyric drama in three acts by Massenet. Text founded on Goethe's novel by Blair, Milliet and Hartmann. German by Max Kalbeck.

Cast: Werther—Tenor. Albert—Baritone. The bailiff —Basso. Schmidt and Yohann, his friends—Basso and Tenor. Lotte, his daughter—Soprano. Sophie, her sis-

ter—Mezzo-soprano. Bühlmann—Baritone. Käthchen—
Mezzo-soprano. Six younger children of the bailiff. Place,
in the vicinity of Wetzlar. Time, 1772.

ACT I.   A terrace before the house of the bailiff. He is
practising a Christmas carol with his six young children—
"Holy night." They are inattentive and sing incorrectly,
and he thinks they will do better with Lotte. Yohann and
Schmidt join him and enjoy the music; upon their inquiry
for Lotte, Sophie answers that she is arranging her costume for the ball. It appears that Werther is also to be
at the ball, although he is usually quiet and depressed, car-
ing little for gaiety. The two friends repair to the inn
and invite the bailiff to follow them. Albert, Lotte's intended husband, is expected; they all praise him as an honest and capable man. Werther approaches the house unperceived ("How sweet to dwell here") ; the songs of the
children are heard, and with emotion he thinks of his childhood. Lotte appears in ball dress, surrounded by the noisy
children, and gives them their supper. The bailiff, per-
ceiving Werther, calls him and presents him to his daughter; Werther is impressed by her appearance. Other ball
guests, among them Bühlmann and Käthchen, deeply in
love with each other, assemble and leave the house with
Lotte and Werther; Sophie remains with her father and
persuades him to follow the stranger to the inn. When
he has gone, Albert returns from a long journey. He inquires for Lotte; he is glad that she has thought of him
and retires to surprise her in the morning. It is night;
Lotte and Werther approach arm in arm. He has taken
her home, but cannot tear himself away, and makes her a
violent declaration of love. ("Joy must be expressed.")
She refuses modestly, but at last becomes confused. She
thinks of her mother, whose last wish was the union of her
eldest daughter with Albert, and is frightened at having
broken her oath for the sake of Werther. Werther leaves
in despair.

ACT II.   Square before the inn. Yohann and Schmidt

are drinking and pay no attention to the choral, which is heard from the church. Lotte and Albert, who have been married three months, appear; they enter the church. Werther has watched them from a distance and falls to the ground in despair. ("Another is her husband.") Albert steps to his side and tells him that he understands and forgives everything. Werther thanks him and asks for his friendship. Sophie arrives with a bouquet of flowers (Song: "At early morn"); her cheerfulness only causes Werther to be more despondent, and Albert's hints to Werther to court Sophie remain unregarded. Lotte convinces Werther that she is true to her husband, and invites him to the Christmas festivities. Werther tries to conquer his love ("I will be a man"), but neglects Sophie at the dance. Lotte and Albert find her weeping.

ACT III. A room in Albert's house. Lotte is sitting at her work table. She now knows that she loves Werther and reads his letters with a mixture of joy and dread, especially as he hints at a tragic end. Albert is on a journey, and she is invited to visit her father's house, but expects Werther. When alone she sinks half fainting to the ground ("Air, I am stifling") just as Werther, pale and distraught, appears at the door. They have a long explanation (Song: "Am I awake?"); he becomes more and more passionate; she can hardly resist. She does not deny that she loves him, but at last conquers her sentiments and flees. Werther rushes away in despair. Albert returns; he notices something has occurred, and Lotte cannot conceal her emotion. He receives a letter, in which Werther asks the loan of his pistols, as he is about to travel. Lotte guesses his purpose, but does not dare to speak; Albert forces her to give the pistols personally to the messenger and departs in anger. Lotte also hurriedly leaves the house to prevent Werther from killing himself.

Change of scene: Werther's room. He lies mortally wounded upon the floor; Lotte rushes in and kneels by his side in anguish. With words of love she brings him back to consciousness, and reproaches herself bitterly for being the cause of his death. For the first and last time they can give themselves up to each other. (Duet: "Away with dread and fear.") The children's Christmas carol is heard, and with the last tones of the music in his ears Werther expires in Lotte's arms.

WILLIAM TELL

Opera in three acts by Rossini. Text by Bis and Jouy.
CAST: Gessler—Basso. Rudolf de Harras—Tenor. William Tell—Baritone. Walter Fürst—Basso. Melchthal—Basso. Arnold, his son—Tenor. Leuthold—Tenor. Mathilde, daughter of Gessler—Soprano. Hedwig, Tell's wife—Soprano. Jemmy, Tell's son—Soprano. Ruodi, a fisherman—Tenor. Place, Switzerland. Time, the thirteenth century. First production, Paris, 1829.

The shore of Lake Lucerne with Tell's house. (Chorus: "Mildly shines the sun of May"; Quartet, Ruodi, Tell, Hedwig, Jemmy and chorus: "Oh come, my love.") The venerable Melchthal comes thither to take part in the festival of the shepherds. His son, Arnold, has fallen in love with Mathilde, the daughter of the tyrant Gessler. (Scene and departure of the shepherds.) Arnold hates Gessler and the oppressors of his country, but his love for Mathilde, whose life he has saved, causes him to espouse the enemy's cause. In a spirited scene between Arnold and Tell (Duet: "Whither goest thou? Speak, why hasten?") Arnold confesses his love (Arnold: "Oh Mathilde, thou angel"), and Tell endeavours to win him back to the cause of the people. The entrance of the shepherds interrupts them. (Chorus and dance: "Day of joy.") Leuthold rushes in, declaring passionately that a soldier was about to rob him of his only daughter, and that he had split his head with an axe; that he is even now pursued. He prays for refuge, but the fisherman Ruodi does not dare to carry him over the lake in the storm which is raging. Tell steps into the boat with him as the pursuers appear. Finale. (Chorus: "God of mercy.") Rudolf, who leads the soldiers, plunders and sets fire to the fishermen's huts. (Ensemble: "Let the flames rage.") He drags Melchthal away as a hostage, charging him with stirring up the people.

ACT II. A wood. (Chorus of huntsmen: "Let the horns sound," answered by a distant chorus of shepherds: "The sun sinks into the waters"; Romance, Mathilde: "Thou quiet wood.") Arnold joins her (Duet: "Mathilde, forgive my love"), and she acknowledges that she reciprocates his passion. This avowal separates him once more from his native land, but when Tell and Walter Fürst inform him that his father Melchthal has been murdered by the tyrants, revenge takes him back to patriotism. (Terzett: "Thy fatherland lies in chains.")

Change of scene: (Ruodi, Tell, Arnold, Walter and chorus of Swiss patriots: "The fatherland calls"; Chorus, Swiss patriots: "Our burden is heavy"; and "Hail, hail to our country.") The citizens of each canton assemble to take the oath, and prepare for the combat.

ACT III. Open country. (Arnold's aria: "The hut of my fathers.") He places himself at the head of a band of armed Swiss. (This scene is often omitted.)

Change of scene: The market place of Altdorf, where Gessler has erected a pole surmounted by a hat, to which all bow. (March and chorus: "Hail to thee, lord.") Gessler enters. A Tyrolean dance follows. Tell, for refusing to make obeisance, is arrested by Rudolf and brought before Gessler. (Quartet: "Bitterly shall you rue it.") The tyrant orders Tell to shoot an apple from his son's head. (Finale: "I bless you, my dear child.") Tell shoots and splits the apple, and upon being asked by Gessler what he intended to do with a second arrow, which he had in his doublet, answers that had he failed he would have pierced the tyrant's heart with it. Notwithstanding the prayer of Mathilde Tell is bound and led away.

Act IV.   Scene as in the first act.   Hedwig, Tell's wife, is grieving over her lost husband, when the boy Jemmy is brought to her by Mathilde.   (Terzett: "I give you back your son.")   Tell enters, having escaped; he awaits Gessler and pierces him to the heart with an arrow.   Arnold approaches with his band and proclaims a victory for the Swiss patriots.   ("Hail, the burgs are no more.")   With a prayer and invocation to freedom the opera ends.

SUPPLEMENT

APHRODITE

Music drama in five acts and seven scenes. Music by Camille Erlanger. Text by Louis de Gramont, after the romance of Pierre Louys.

CAST: Demetrios—Tenor. Timon—Baritone. Philodemos—Second Tenor. The High Priest—Lyric Bass. Callides—Lyric Bass. The Jailer—Bass. Chrysis—Dramatic Soprano. Bacchis—Mezzo-Soprano. Myrto—Soprano. Rhodis—Mezzo-Soprano. Chimairis—Mezzo-Soprano. Young men, courtesans, philosophers, sailors, temple-guards, dancers, merchants. Time, Greek occupation of Alexandria. Place, Alexandria. First performance, Opéra Comique, Paris, 1906.

After a short prelude, suggesting the sea and its mystery, the certain rises upon the quay at Alexandria. It is twilight; a crowd comes and goes: made up of marketmen, merchants, beggars, rich young men, courtesans, sailors, and philosophers, all talking together in groups, or plying their various trades. Some have stopped to listen to Rhodis and Myrto, two flute-players, who accompany with their instruments the posture dances of Theano, sister of Rhodis. Women's voices are heard calling (Chorus: "Eros! Eros!"), and the musicians take up the song (Duet, Rhodis, Myrto: "Eros, pallid Eros"), to the delight of the crowd. Theano speaks softly to Myrto, while Rhodis collects coins from the bystanders. The courtesans discuss the banquet to be given in the house of Bacchis, during the festival of Aphrodite. Myrto and Rhodis depart with arms interlaced. There is a stir in the crowd, as the rich sculptor Demetrios enters with an air of boredom. Several women try to engage him in conversation, but he pointedly ignores them. The courtesans gossip about Queen Berenice, said to be the model

for his statue of Aphrodite.   Demetrios passes to the end
of the quay, dreamily looking out over the sea.   Chimairis,
a withered old fortune-teller, comes forward, and is quickly
surrounded by customers.   She looks at several palms, complaining that all say the same thing, pleasure, garlands,
jewels, feasting, handsome young lovers, or rich old ones.
They laugh, telling her this is her "bad-tempered day,"
and run off gaily.   Chimairis shrugs her shoulders, and
Demetrios asks her to read his future.   She hesitates, then
tells him that all his happiness is in the past; his hand
is filled with blood, that of two women, and at last, his
own.   He scoffs at this, and sings musingly of his statue,
which is his life, his world (Demetrios: "Since I modeled
the divine Aphrodite").   Receiving money from him,
Chimairis goes out.   Chrysis is seen in the distance.
With the eye of an artist, Demetrios notes her grace and
suppleness as she comes toward him, passing by without
looking at him, to the end of the quay.   She stands a moment in deep thought, then turns back.   Demetrios addresses her, asking her name.   Is she seeking her husband, he asks.   She laughs oddly.   "I have no husband,"
she says; then tells him she is called Chrysis, because of
her golden hair.   She coquettes with him (Chrysis:
"Thinkest thou that thou art in Aphrodite's garden?")
by turns leading him on and drawing back, until he becomes infatuated, and seizes her violently.   She tells him
she is not to be won by force.   He declares that he is
weary of love, and she replies that she is equally weary
of gold.   Only three things does she desire: a mirror, a
comb, a necklace.   "That is simple enough," Demetrios
says eagerly.   Possibly, but will he swear that he will
get them for her, by an oath that cannot be broken.
Rashly, he swears by Aphrodite.   She then tells him that
the mirror belongs to Bacchis, the courtesan; it is said
that Sappho has looked into it.   Bacchis has an odd hiding
place for it, near the altar in the temple of Aphrodite.
(Chrysis: "Bacchis, the courtesan has a silver mirror.")

Demetrios must steal it. "What! Steal for you?" he cries indignantly. Chrysis continues imperturbably, "The wife of the high priest has an ivory comb. I desire it. You must kill her." Demetrios is appalled. "And the necklace?" he says sarcastically. "It adorns the neck of Aphrodite's statue," is the calm reply. Demetrios is enraged by these extraordinary demands, and refuses them, but Chrysis quietly assures him she will surely have these little presents. (Chrysis: "Speak not thus! The three gifts are mine.") She inflames his ardor with every possible seduction, eluding him when he tries to embrace her, but when he promises her the necklace, she offers her lips, then quickly leaves him, looking back to remind him of his promises.

Act II. The temple of Aphrodite. A colossal statue of the goddess is adorned with a magnificent necklace of pearls. Staircases are on each side of the altar. The curtain rises on an empty stage. It is moonlight. The temple-guards, eunuchs, enter with torches, searching for possible marauders. As their departing footsteps die away, Demetrios enters by a secret entrance, looking wildly about him. (Demetrios: "Chrysis! Chrysis! This woman's name.") He declares that the very audacity of the girl's requests had made him consider them. The first two crimes are accomplished; now he will attempt the third. The moonlight seems to caress the statue. (Demetrios: "Aphrodite, 'tis thou!") He begs forgiveness of the goddess, saying that his love is hers alone, and cursing his insane passion for Chrysis. He kneels before the statue, and rising, caresses it.

Day dawns, and with it comes the sound of voices chanting. The festival of Aphrodite has begun. (Chorus off stage.) Demetrios hastily conceals himself as a procession headed by the high priest, followed by courtesans and dancers carrying garlands, doves, and jewels, enters the temple. (Chorus: "Hail to thee, Aphrodite divine.") They group themselves before the altar, prostrating themselves one by one, and leave their offerings on the altar steps, or in baskets held out by the priestesses. Myrto and Rhodis come forward hand in hand, bearing twin turtle doves, and at last Chrysis herself appears. The other courtesans assert that as a stranger she has no right there, but the high priest rebukes them. Chrysis sings of the symbolic rites of Aphrodite, and dedicates to her her mirror, and her comb of copper, and, after a pause, her necklace. (Chrysis: "To the goddess of night.") "What askest thou in return?" says the high priest. "Nothing," replies the girl, retiring with a low obeisance. The priest prostrates himself before the altar, and the procession slowly moves toward the gardens, the doors of the temple closing behind it. Demetrios comes from his hiding place (Demetrios: "I, who thought myself cured,'), saying that the sight of Chrysis has made him long for her love more than ever. Seizing the necklace, he hides it under his robe and flees.

ACT III. The house of Bacchis. A marvellous banquet is in progress. Bacchis is attended by her favorite slave Corinna. Dancers and musicians enliven the scene. (Chorus: "Bacchis! To Bacchis!") Timon is trying to arouse Chrysis from a pensive mood! (Timon: "How sweet it is to recline"), but she shakes her head listlessly. The banqueters drink to their hostess. (Chrysis: "I am distrait.") Six mulatto women enter, with a flamingo held high on a dish. The guests acclaim Bacchis, who laughingly tells them that Corinna is their real hostess; the banquet is given for her. Her six sisters stand apart grumbling. (Sextette: "Yes, our sister, always petted.") The banquet becomes an orgy. Theano is seen in a dagger dance (Bacchis: "Here is the little dancer") to a flute accompaniment, removing her garments as she proceeds. The guests applaud loudly. At last, in a frenzy of exhaustion, Theano throws herself on a couch. Mousarion plies her with wine, the others guests holding her by the hands and feet, and forcing it down, with shrieks of laughter. Bacchis demands her mirror, which cannot be found. (Chrysis: "Rhodope's mirror.") Chrysis narrowly watches as Selene, the maid, returns without it. Bacchis is furious, and the six sisters volubly accuse Corinna of the theft. (Sextette: "Yes, 'tis Corinna.") The young slave falls fainting at the feet of Bacchis, who sentences her to be crucified. The mulatto women procure hammer and nails, and Corinna is dragged forth. Timon and Callides protest, but Bacchis is relentless, and drives the nails herself. Chrysis standing apart triumphs. (Chrysis: "O triumph! O joy unspeakable!") Corinna dies in agony; Timon covers her face, closing the staring eyes. Day dawns. Curtain.

Act IV. Studio of Demetrios, with statues in groups. A broad couch, magnificent hangings. It is dawn. The prelude expresses the longing of Demetrios, his remorse, and the coming of day. Demetrios, at work on a statue is completely absorbed. In the street people are shouting that Aphrodite's necklace has been stolen, and the wife of the high priest murdered. (Demetrios: "These rumors, this excitement in the city.") Demetrios is overcome with shame (Demetrios: "Ah, vainly I labor.") He can think only of Chrysis, whose promise he has not yet claimed. Quietly, she enters. He tells her he has done her bidding. "That I know!" is her reply. (Chrysis: "This night at Bacchis' house I knew.") She has come to give herself to him, not, she tells him, with the wiles of a courtesan, but in the purity and innocence of her girlhood. She throws aside her mantle. Demetrios extols her beauty (Demetrios: "O delicate loveliness"), giving her the mirror, the comb, and the necklace. There is a long embrace (Demetrios: "The joys of passion"; Chrysis: "I am the Rose of Sharon"), and they sink into each other's arms. The increasing tumult of the crowd comes to them from without. (Chrysis: "Oh, my Demetrios.") Demetrios now begins to realise the full extent of his infamy (Demetrios: "I am no longer the haughty

sculptor"), and beseeches Chrysis to leave him.   (Chrysis:
"What, must I go?")   Becoming more and more excited
he pushes her out of the room, declaring he hates her for
what she has made of him.   Chrysis laughs gaily (Chrysis:
"Nay, do not lie"), saying that since he has committed
these crimes for her it is now her turn for a sacrifice, swearing first by Aphrodite, and then by Jehovah, that she will
do whatever he asks.   In a sort of exaltation, he demands
that she show herself in public, wearing the necklace of
Aphrodite, carrying the mirror, and with the ivory comb
in her hair.   He points implacably to the door.   Gazing
at him fixedly, she takes her mantle, and goes quickly out.
As she disappears, Demetrios bursts into a wild fit of
laughter, and throws himself on the couch.

ACT V.   The Pharos of Alexandria.   It is surrounded
by a vast crowd, all talking of the sensations of the preceding day and night; the crucifixion of Corinna, the murder of Touni, the high priestess, the sacrilege in the temple.   Chrysis appears, arrayed in a scarlet mantle.
Talking half to herself, she tells Myrto and Rhodis they
will soon see a sight they have never dreamed of.   Observing their amazement she puts her finger on her lip, to
ensure their secrecy.   The two girls look at one another
in perplexity.   A clamor is heard in the distance, as of
people running with shouts of anger.   Chrysis enters the
Pharos, closing the door after her.   The temple-guards
and the priestesses of Aphrodite rush in, dishevelled and
covered with dust.   (Chorus: "Abomination!   The temple is profaned.")   Chrysis appears on the outer gallery
of the Pharos, clad in a tunic.   She has the mirror in her
hand, the ivory comb in her hair, and the necklace clasped
around her neck.   Slowly she mounts the circular way
around the tower, as the people supplicate the goddess for
forgiveness.   (Chorus: "Grace, O goddess.")   A storm
arises, and in the glare of the lightning Chrysis is still
seen mounting to the summit of the tower.   The crowd
believes that a miracle has taken place, and that Aphro-

dite herself stands before them.   At the summit Chrysis
stands motionless.   (Chrysis: "I am the immortal goddess;"
Chorus: "Glory to thee.")   Presently the crowd gazing
intently recognise Chrysis.   Filled with furious anger at
her temerity, they storm the bronze doors of the Pharos.
(Chorus: "Death! Death!")   They force them, and rush
in with shouts of vengeance.   As the leaders appear on
the gallery Chrysis is seen still standing immovable, and
as they approach to take her the curtain falls.

Change of scene.   A prison, with a barred window and
door.   Through the latter a hall is seen.   Chrysis is
seated on the bed in an attitude of dejection, awaiting
Demetrios, who has promised to visit her.   He comes not,
and the jailer appears with a draught, which he tells her
is hemlock, bidding her drink it and pass into oblivion.
She is fortunate, he says, to have so easy a death, instead
of crucifixion, or being torn by wild bulls, or with hooks,
or by the hands of the crowd.   She calmly swallows the
draught, the jailer instructing her that when her limbs
grow heavy, she must lie down upon the couch, and all
will soon be over.   He leaves her, wishing her a brave end.
The plaintive voices of Rhodis and Myrto are heard singing (Duet; Rhodis, Myrto: "When for thee comes the
final test.")   Chrysis, hearing their voices stands on the
couch, and gazes through the window, bidding them
adieu.   She falls back, with a last cry, "Demetrios!"
Her lover enters with the jailer, who, seeing his agitation,
goes out.   Demetrios gazes sadly at her, remembering
Chimairis's prediction.   He sees before him a vision of the
enraged goddess, and falls to the ground, dead.   (Demetrios: "I brought thee love; death was my greeting").
Curtain.

Change of scene.   The garden of Hermanubis.   A
ruined temple in the morning light.   Sombre evergreen
trees stand like sentinels before an open sepulchre.   After
a strange funereal prelude, Myrto and Rhodis carry in the
body of Chrysis (Duet, Myrto, Rhodis: "With neither

torch nor funeral car"), laying it down beside the tomb
for a moment. Then they lay it within the sepulchre,
which is filled with flowers, and the curtain slowly falls.

ARIANE ET BARBE BLEUE

(Ariana and Bluebeard)

Fairy tale in three acts. Music by Paul Dukas. Text
by Maurice Maeterlinck, based upon the old fairy tale of
Bluebeard.

CAST: Barbe Bleue (Bluebeard)—Bass. Ariane—Mezzo-
Soprano. The Nurse—Contralto. Selysette—Mezzo-
Soprano. Ygraine — Soprano. Mélisande — Soprano.
Bellangère—Soprano. Alladine—Dumb rôle. An old
peasant—Bass. Second and third peasants—Tenor and
Bass. Chorus of peasants, and negroes. Place and time,
legendary. First performance, Opéra Comique, Paris,
May, 1907.

ACT I. After a short and mysterious prelude, the great
hall of Bluebeard's castle is disclosed. It has a wide door
at the rear, flanked by smaller doors, and a staircase in
the centre. A semi-circular gallery, lighted by high windows runs around the hall. It is evening, with lights
burning and windows open. Outside is heard the murmur
of an excited crowd, at times almost menacing, and finally
breaking into a shout of "Death to him!" The peasants
are talking among themselves of the coming of Ariane,
Barbe Bleue's new wife, commenting upon her beautiful
sad face, and sweet smile. Must she be allowed to disappear mysteriously, like the giant's other wives? They fear
to storm the castle, lest death lurk within. They plan to
burn it down—perhaps; but courage fails. As they gaze
affrighted, the windows close, and Ariane enters the hall,
with her nurse, through a side door. They hear the
ominous murmurs of the crowd. "Listen!" says the nurse,
"The peasants wish to save us. Let us open the door,
now we are alone. It appears this wicked man has already

killed five wives." "They are not dead," replies Ariane,
dreamily. "There is some mystery, and since Barbe Bleue
loves me, I shall be able to find it out. The first step is
to disobey him, since he has threatened us. He has given
me these keys to unlock his jewel vaults. The six silver
ones, I can use, but the gold one is forbidden. That is
the only important one! I shall throw the others away."
As she speaks, she flings them, clattering, to the marble
floor. The nurse reminds her that the jewels may be
worth seeing. "Look at them, if you choose," cries
Ariane, "I am more concerned with the forbidden door;
the others will tell us naught of the mystery."

After much fumbling, the nurse opens the first door, and
a stream of amethysts, fashioned into all sorts of jewelry,
rushes forth. The nurse, trembling with excitement, tries
to pick them up. Ariane looks on indifferently, and commands her to open the second door, which discloses a rain
of sapphires. The music expresses the sound of the falling jewels, which the nurse, babbling with delight, gathers
into her mantle. The third door brings forth pearls, the
fourth emeralds, the fifth rubies, which the nurse cries out
fearfully are like blood, and the sixth door glittering
diamonds.

Ariane, enchanted, decks herself with these (Ariane:
"Oh, my brilliant diamonds"), declaring that they are like
light. She rushes to the window, and as she eagerly gazes
out, the rain, which has been falling, suddenly ceases, and
she beholds a beautiful rainbow. "Now for the seventh
door," she cries, exultingly, while the terrified nurse begs
her to pause and reflect. "Hide yourself, then," says
Ariane, "I shall open the seventh door!" She turns the
key with decision, and as the door swings open, from
within comes a hollow chant, in muffled women's voices.
Ariane pauses a moment, listening. (Subterranean
chant: "The five daughters of Orlamonde.") "Oh!" cries
the nurse, "It is the other women." The song swells in
volume, as the nurse pleads in vain with Ariane to close

the door.   They try to close the other six doors, but without success.

The nurse, now beside herself with terror, spreads her mantle over her face to keep out the sound of the chant. "I hear footsteps," cries Ariane, and Barbe Bleue enters. He silently contemplates the two women. "You, too," he says bitterly. "I above all," is Ariane's brave reply. "I thought you were stronger and wiser than the others," he continues. "How long have they been there?" she demands. "Some a few days, some a few months, the first a year." Barbe Bleue goes on to say that Ariane has now irrevocably lost the happiness which might have been hers, but he will pardon her if she goes no further. "I will perhaps pardon *you* when I know all," is her reply.

Barbe Bleue seizes her roughly by the arm, and as she shrieks loudly, the crowd without throw stones through the windows. The nurse, hastening to the great door, removes the bars, and the furious peasants rush in. Barbe Bleue draws his sword, but Ariane fearlessly advances towards the peasants. "What do you desire?" she asks calmly. "He has done me no harm." They retire abashed, and having closed the door behind them Ariane slowly comes toward her husband, who gazes silently at his sword point, as the curtain falls.

Act II. Prelude. A dark subterranean cavern, with heavy pillars supporting the roof, and a long narrow hallway at one side. Ariane and the nurse come cautiously down a staircase at the back of the hallway. The clanging of a door is heard behind them. The nurse is utterly despairing. "Onward, onward," cries Ariane. "He is beaten, and knows it not. We shall now penetrate the mystery."

Bearing a lamp, she leads the way, peering eagerly into the darkness. "Come, nurse," she says, "let us see what is here, and if the others are still living." There is a timid stir in the darkness. "Who are you?" demands Ariane. Advancing, she perceives the indistinct forms of

five women. "Oh, they are here," she calls back, exultingly, and the nurse hastens forward. The women are
trembling. Ariane runs to them and embraces them
warmly, while the nurse looks on with apprehension.
"Oh, they are alive, and so sweet," declares the girl.
(Ariane: "Ah, I have found you.") She looks anxiously
at them, to see if they have been harmed in any way.
"No," they assure her, "but we are afraid." "Oh, how
lovely I shall make you look, when we get to the light,"
Ariane continues.

The nurse brings the lamp and the five women are found
to be dishevelled and in rags, blinking pitifully as the
light strikes them. Ariane is filled with compassion.
They regard her silently at first, but answer when she
asks their names, and how long they have been in the
cavern. Selysette, it appears, has been there for more
than a year, the others for shorter periods, so Barbe
Bleue has told the truth. The poor prisoners look with
admiration at their deliverer, and tell her mournfully how
they have prayed and sung, and wept, waiting, waiting
forever, it seemed to them. "Why did you not try to get
out?" asks Ariane. "It was forbidden," they reply, surprised. They repeat their names in order. The long-
haired one is Mélisande, the one with the great eyes, Bellangère, the little one hiding behind the pillar is Alladine,
who speaks no tongue known to them. Alladine runs sobbing to Ariane, who is plainly astonished that the women
have made no effort to free themselves. (Ariane: "Do
you mean to live always in terror?")

She sings to them of light and of a beautiful garden,
with birds singing in the glorious spring-time; of the
great sea with its mighty waves. As she ends, the water
dripping from the roof extinguishes her lamp. The
nurse shrieks with terror, and even Ariane is disconcerted.
The five prisoners reassure her, pointing out that at the
back of the cavern it is lighter. "Where does the light
come from?" cries Ariane. She hurries forward to recon-

noitre, and finds that above the rocks in the rear are
great shutters. "Yes, but behind them is the sea. We
have heard it beating against them," say the others in
terror. Ariane declares it is light instead, and tries to
open the shutters. She finds behind them glass which has
been painted black, and calling for a stone she breaks
through it. Eagerly gazing through, the women see a
wondrous star. Ariane, overcome with joy continues to
break the glass (Ariane: "See! This pane, and then
that"), still singing triumphantly of the light. Trembling with emotion, the women crowd around her, mounting the rocks to look out. The light of day floods the
cavern, the sea is heard booming without, the birds are
carolling, and a flock of sheep go by, their bells jangling
softly. Gazing eagerly forth, the women see different
things: one the sea, another the sky, a third the trees
alone. Filled with delighted curiosity they observe a
peasant at whom Selysette excitedly waves her long hair.
He piously crosses himself. The village clock strikes
noon. The women look at each other in compassion, no-
ticing their rags and dishevelled hair; they comfort Alladine, who has begun to cry.

Ariane urges instant departure, before they are discovered. She forces her way through the aperture she
has made, and, mounting a staircase disappears. The
others follow, singing their strange chant. They emerge
in a beautiful garden, flooded with sunshine and bright
with flowers, and express their joy and relief in graceful
gestures as the lovely music surges about them and the
curtain falls.

Act III. A short prelude, expressive of a new order of
things. Scene, the same as in Act I. The jewels are still
scattered about; it is night, and the room is softly lighted.
Great chests, filled with costly raiment and ornaments
stand about. The five women are posing before mirrors,
arraying themselves in splendor, and arranging their hair,
while Ariane advises and suggests. The music is now

gay and happy.   All are willing to remain for the present
in the castle, for Barbe Bleue has departed, they know not
where.   They cannot depart in any case, for the moats
are filled with water, and the bridges are gone.   The
peasants are standing guard.

Ariane amuses the five women with bright chatter, admiring their charms, and showing them how to accentuate
them.   Alladine's love for bright colours of discordant
shades is gently checked.   In a charming scene, each of
the women chooses appropriate jewels for her adornment.
(Ariane: "How will you use these lovely gems?")

The nurse hurries in, proclaiming Barbe Bleue's approach.   (Nurse: "He has returned, he is here.")   She
mounts the staircase, to see what is happening without.
The five women rush about shrieking, in search of a hiding
place, gathering at last at a window in the gallery to
gaze forth.   Barbe Bleue advances, surrounded by huge
blacks, with drawn swords.   Terrified, all crowd around
Ariane.   The peasants charge the blacks, and drive them
back, seizing Barbe Bleue, who is wounded and falls unconscious.   They bind him hand and foot and bring him
into the castle, as the five women wail in chorus that the
peasants are drunk, and as much to be feared as the giant.
Ariane opens the door, however (Chorus: "Open, open"),
and the peasants stand on the threshold, in uncertainty.
Their clothes are torn and disordered from the combat;
they are impressed by Ariane's majesty of demeanor.
The oncoming crowd, at first inclined to disrespect, become silent when they behold her, and the leader, an old
peasant, removing his cap, humbly asks if they may enter.

Barbe Bleue is laid on a couch, and delivered to Ariane.
She thanks the peasants for their fealty, and enquires if
any have been wounded; then, bidding them farewell, she
shuts the door.   The other women have fallen on their
knees in abject terror, during the colloquy with the peasants.   Ariane examines Barbe Bleue's wounds, which are
trifling; the others rise, and crowding around him pity-

ingly busy themselves with his comfort. Alladine kneels beside him, weeping. They find his bonds too tight, so Ariane cuts them with a dagger, despite the protestations of the nurse. Barbe Bleue sits up, stretches himself, and looks about him in silence. He rises to his feet, gazing at his wounded hand. Ariane gently kisses him on the forehead, bidding him adieu. He tries to detain her, but she steadily moves forward, followed by the nurse. Selysette asks her whither she is going. "Far from here," is the firm response. She asks each of the women in turn to accompany her, but all refuse, preferring their servitude. (Ariane: "The moon stars shine upon our way.") Alladine runs to her and throws herself into her arms, with tears. Ariane bids them all farewell, wishing them happiness, and departs, with the nurse. Barbe Bleue, desiring the unattainable, gazes wistfully after her as do the others, and the curtain falls.

CENDRILLON

(Cinderella)

Fairy tale in four acts. Music by Massenet. Text by Henry Cain, after Perrault's story.

CAST: Cendrillon (Cinderella)—Soprano. Madame de la Haltière—Mezzo-soprano, or Contralto. Prince Charming—Falcon. The Fairy—Light Soprano. Noëmia— Soprano. Dorothea—Mezzo-soprano. Pandolphe—Bass, or Baritone. The King—Baritone. The Dean of the Faculty—Tenor. The Master of Ceremonies—Baritone. The Prime Minister—Bass, or Baritone. Six sprites, servants, courtiers, ballet of fairies, the king's herald. Place and time legendary; about the eighteenth century. First performance, Opéra Comique, Paris, 1899.

ACT I. Short prelude, descriptive of legendary times. The house of Madame de la Haltière. A great room with a fireplace, servants running to and fro, trying to carry

out conflicting orders. "Heavens, what a woman!" is
their cry, but they stop short, dismayed, as Pandolphe
enters. He smiles, ruefully (Pandolphe: "Go on, it's only
I"), telling them not to trouble. They inform him that
their master suits them, but their mistress, "La, la!" quite
another story. Pandolphe is amused. "Why," he says
to himself, "did I marry the creature?" (Pandolphe:
"To the husband should the power belong!") "The new
wife has turned my house upside down, and ill-treats my
beloved daughter. And her airs, good heavens! But
some day I will be master!" As he speaks, the servants
announce their mistress, who enters with her two proud
daughters. (Mme. de la Haltière: "Make yourselves
beautiful to-night.") She tells them they are to see the
king to-night, and instructs them as to their behaviour.
"A ball is like a battlefield," she declares. "Hold yourselves straight, and don't fidget!" She puts them
through the minuet, with great ceremony. (Mme. de la
H: "Take a graceful attitude.") The servants, who are
still rushing about, bring in dressmakers, tailors, and
hairdressers, who gorgeously array the two girls, and
then depart. In the midst of their toilette, their mother
starts convulsively, looking so strange that all gaze apprehensively at her. Pandolphe appears, handsomely attired; the three women make scornful comments upon his
promptness. "And has he nothing to say about our
fine raiment?" angrily demands his wife. "Certainly she
is mad," he says gleefully to himself. "She will have to
be shut up somewhere before long. How delightful!"
They hurry off to the ball (Pandolphe: "My poor Lucette, I go!"), chattering about their approaching triumphs, while the servants comment on their ugly faces.

Enter Cinderella sadly. (Cinderella: "How happy are
my sisters!") Her sisters go to balls, and enjoy themselves in idleness, while she must always work. She is the
little cricket, she supposes, whose place is by the hearth;
they are butterflies fluttering in the sunshine. Sitting be-

side the fire, she falls asleep. The music grows soft and sweet, and the fairy godmother enters. (The Fairy: "Dear little child.") She calls on the goblins, sprites, and will-o'-the-wisps to appear. (The six sprites: "What is your will?") She tells them to make Cendrillon always happy and beautiful. (The Fairy: "Make her a robe of magic tissue." (Chorus of fairies: "All the little birds.") She appoints one to be her coachman, another hostler, another to make a love philtre, another to act as page, the rest to be postilions. When all is ready, she awakens Cendrillon, and informs her that she is to go to the ball. "But how can I in this dress?" asks the puzzled girl. "Look at it!" cries the fairy, and with delight Cendrillon sees her lovely robe. Overjoyed, she dances about, and admires the pretty little fairies and her fine carriage. The fairy godmother warns her to leave the ballroom exactly at midnight, and gives her a magic glass slipper, so that her stepmother and stepsister will not recognise her. In wild excitement, with all the fairies dancing around her, Cendrillon hurries away.

Act II. The king's palace. The ballroom and the palace gardens are brilliantly illuminated. There is a short prelude, and at the rising of the curtain Prince Charming, the king's only son, is listening to the music of the lute, which does not amuse him. The master of ceremonies, followed by the courtiers, advances, uttering empty compliments and bowing obsequiously. The prince does not even notice them, and there is a murmur of disappointment, as the courtiers depart. A company of learned men now approach, but the pursuit of culture has no interest for the prince; he will not even listen. A group of statesmen receive the same treatment. Shrugging their shoulders, they leave the royal presence. Sighing, the prince deplores his unhappy lot. (Prince Charming: "Go, leave me to my boredom.") He longs to find a woman whom he can love with all his heart, but none pleases him. The King enters in pomp, with his court

(The King: "My son, you must obey"), and announces
that the daughters of the greatest nobles of his kingdom
are to pass in procession before the prince, and from
among them he must choose his bride. They enter, richly
arrayed (Chorus: "Make a choice! Take thy bride!"),
and with great ceremony bow before the prince. At the
end of the procession Madame de la Haltière appears,
with her two daughters, accompanied by the dean of the
faculty, the master of ceremonies and the prime minister.
The wretched Pandolphe stands apart. (Septette: "We
are in his presence.") Madame and her daughters dance a
stately minuet with the three officials. The two girls are
nervous and frightened, and forget their steps. In the
midst of the confusion, Cendrillon appears. The prince
regards her with delight, and there is a general stir in the
ballroom. (Chorus: "Behold the wondrous beauty!")
The stepmother and her daughters are furious, but thanks
to the magic slipper do not recognise Cendrillon. All
bow before her as to the future queen. Pandolphe is lost
in admiration. The prince addresses Cendrillon with rapture (Prince: "O lovely dream, which comes to me alone"),
asking her name. Cendrillon replies modestly, "To you
I am the Unknown." (Cendrillon: "You have said I am
a dream"; Duet, Cendrillon, the Prince: "I should lose
thee.") The prince, more and more enamoured, declares
his passion, and Cendrillon's shy glances show that it is
returned. In the height of their ecstatic happiness the
clock strikes twelve. Cinderella hastily departs, leaving
the prince bewildered, but the ball continues as the curtain
falls.

Act III. Same as Act I. Enter Cendrillon, out of
breath, and excited. (Cendrillon: "At last I have arrived!") She tells of her hurried flight through the palace gardens, the terror she felt as she passed the ghostly
marble statues in the moonlight, and how at last she had
lost the precious glass slipper. Piteously, she calls upon
her fairy godmother to help her, for indeed, indeed, she

avows, she has done her best.   The carillon sounds.   Cendrillon is reassured, and laughs aloud at her fears; then,
observing her familiar surroundings, contrasts this miserable state with her triumph at the ball.   Hearing her parents approaching, she hides within the bedroom.

The four enter quarrelling.   Pandolphe insists that the
Fair Unknown is beautiful; the others can see nothing in
her.   (Quartette: " 'Tis true, 'tis true!")   The stepmother, indeed, is quite abusive, and declares the prince
was quite right to send the baggage about her business.
Pandolphe tries to protest, but is quelled when his wife
begins to boast of her ancestry.   (Mme. de la H.: "When
one has more than twenty quarterings.")   The daughters
uphold her, but Pandolphe says dolefully he would not
mind obscurity, if it brought peace.   Cendrillon enters.
"What is the matter, dear father," she asks gently.   Her
calm enrages the excited women, who all tell the story of
the ball at once.   (Terzette: "An unknown, an *intrig-
ante.*")   Pandolphe cannot get in a single word.   Cendrillon inquires what the prince said when the Unknown suddenly vanished.   "He said that his eyes must have deceived him at first; the Unknown was ugly enough to be
hung," is the glib reply.   Cendrillon turns pale, and
swoons.   Pandolphe orders the three women out.   They
retort with insults, and in wild hysterics rush from the
room.   Pandolphe tries to soothe his child (Pandolphe,
Recitative: "My poor beloved child"; Duet, Pandolphe,
Cendrillon: "Come, let us leave this town"), saying that
they will go away to the country, and be happy once more.
Cendrillon is enchanted.   They will gather flowers, and
listen to the nightingale, and all sorrow will be forgotten!
Kissing her tenderly, Pandolphe departs.   Cendrillon,
alone, muses upon all that has happened (Cendrillon:
"Alone I will depart, dear father"), mourning over the
prince's doubt of her.   She has dreamt of love, but now
awakening, she bids farewell to all she is leaving behind:
her turtle-doves, the palm branch blessed by the priest,

the big armchair, in which as a child, she sat on her mother's knee. Weeping, she calls upon her mother. Thunder and lightning now begin, and Cendrillon departs through the storm.

The scene changes to the home of the fairies, a beautiful meadow, full of flowers; the sea in the distance. It is night. (Chorus of sprites: "Ah, fugitive shapes!") Enter three sprites in haste (Terzette: "But yonder, back there in the darkness!"); they tell the others they have seen a mortal child. The fairy godmother, who is perched in the oak-tree, adds to their news that there is another mortal also, a beautiful youth; that the two are lovers, but cannot see each other. (The Fairy: "Let them not see each other.") Prince Charming and Cendrillon wander side by side, in the meadow, separated only by a hedge of flowers, each invisible to the other; nor can they see the fairies. They kneel before the oak. (Duet, the Prince, Cendrillon: "A poor soul in deep distress": "You who can see all.") The prince tells of his lost happiness, and Cendrillon begs the fairy to restore it to him. While they are pleading, they recognise each other's voices, but still are invisible as before. The fairy, appearing to them, amid the oak branches, waves her wand, and the ban is removed. Fairies surround them, singing, and lulled by their voices, they fall into a magic slumber (Chorus of sprites: "Sleep, dream").

ACT IV. Cendrillon's terrace. Short prelude, telling of peace and contentment. Pandolphe is bending over Cendrillon, who sleeps. He had found her beside a brook, insensible, and since then she has been in a deep stupor. Suddenly she awakens, bewildered. Her father reassures her, saying that she has talked in her long sleep of the ball and of Prince Charming, and of an enchanted oak and a glass slipper. "Then I have been dreaming all these things?" says the girl in wonder. "Undoubtedly, my child, for they never happened!" is the reply. Voices of young girls are heard in the distance (Chorus: "Open thy door and thy window"), greeting the spring. Joyously they call to Cendrillon, who answers (Cendrillon: "Spring returns!"). Passing by, the girls go off, singing. The stepmother approaches, and seizing Cendrillon's hand, Pandolphe takes to flight. Madame de la Haltière, as usual, rushes in tumultously, followed by a rabble of servants (Mme. de la H.: "Come here; go back"). She announces that the king has sent to all lands for princesses of high degree to please Prince Charming (Mme. de la H.: "Learn, that to-day the order of our king"), but that after he has seen them all, she and her daughters will appear, and one of them will surely capture his fancy. As the king's herald is heard approaching, she makes a deep curtsey, then hurries out, pushing the poor servants to right and left in her haste.

The herald announces that the prince will receive that day the princesses, who are to try on a glass slipper which the Fair Unknown had dropped in her flight.

Change of scene: the Court of Honour, high noon. (Chorus: "Hurrah, Hurrah, the cortège advances.") The princesses appear in procession and pass before the prince (Chorus: "All hail! All hail!"). The prince is sad and distrait (The prince: "Placed in its case, on a cushion of flowers"); his eyes are fixed upon the glass slipper, or else closed in indifference. The fairy's voice is heard without. (Chorus: "Enchantment, Oh wonder.") She bids the prince look up, and lo! and behold Cendrillon stands before him. She speaks to him gently, and the fairy puts her hand in his. The fairy slipper fits her alone. Pandolphe joyfully embraces his daughter, and her stepmother, not to be outdone, greets her effusively, as "My daughter, my adored Lucette!" Pandolphe, addressing the crowd declares that all is now happily ended, and asks their congratulations. (Chorus: "The play is ended!")

DER ROSENCAVALIER

(The Knight of the Rose)

Lyric drama in three acts. Music by Richard Strauss. Text by Hugo von Hoffmansthal.

Cast. The Princess von Werdenberg—Soprano. Octavian, a youth familiarly known as "Quin-Quin"—Mezzo-Soprano. Sophie — Soprano. Marianne — Soprano. Annina—Contralto. Baron von Lerchenau—Bass. Herr von Faninal—Baritone. Valzacchi—Tenor. Time, the eighteenth century, under Maria Theresa. Place, Vienna. First performance, Dresden, January, 1911.

Act I. The bedroom of the Princess von Werdenberg. Her husband, the Field-Marshal, being absent she is entertaining Octavian, a youth of seventeen. They have just rung for breakfast, which is brought in by a little negro boy. They sing a love duet, and to waltz measure Octavian contrasts the privations of a soldier on the field with their luxurious surroundings. He would not change for all the honours of a Field-Marshal! Baron von Lerchenau, a cousin of the Princess, is now announced. He is a middle-aged roué, with an evil tongue, and it would never do for him to see Octavian. The latter hides behind a screen, and dresses himself as a chambermaid, emerging demurely, to the great appreciation of the Baron, who almost forgets what he is saying to the Princess. His mission is to find some relative who will be the bearer of the silver rose, his betrothal token, to the fair Sophie von Faninal. She is the daughter of an army sutler, who has been made a noble. The Baron thinks marriage with her a descent in the social scale. Still, she has money, and that is the main thing. The Princess, the Baron, and Octavian as the chambermaid, join in a merry terzette on the subject of the approaching marriage.

The Princess now receives callers; and protegés, who ask for alms. The dressmaker presents herself, asking

questions incessantly. Valzacchi and Annina, two scandal-
mongers, who gather news for their disreputable news-
paper, "The Black Times," manage to gain admittance.
While the Princess is in the hands of the hairdresser, she
is amused by a flute-player and a singer. The Baron's
attendants, a scoundrelly lot, come in, with the notary, to
make the final money arrangements for the betrothal.
The Baron quarrels hotly with the notary, and the singer
to drown their angry voices sings louder and louder, until
he almost bursts. The two scandal-mongers impudently
assure the Baron that they will take excellent care of
Sophie in the "Black Times."

The Baron having departed in a fury, the Princess plaintively sings of her unhappy fate, married to an old man,
whom she does not love. Octavian assures her of his undying affection, but she cynically speaks of the passing of
time. "To-day, or to-morrow or the next day, he will forget." And since it is only a matter of time, why not send
the boy with the silver rose to Sophie? She has read often
in legends of the results of sending handsome messengers
on a love-errand, but nevertheless, he shall go! She bids
him farewell. Curtain.

Act II. The house of Herr von Faninal. Like all "beggars on horseback," he is greatly set up by his new honours. Languidly, he awaits the coming of the messenger
with the silver rose. Sophie and Marianne, beautifully
dressed, are with him. Octavian, to his amusement, is preceded by a flourish of trumpets, and a regiment of foot-
men. He sings of the silver rose, which he gracefully
presents to Sophie. She is unspoiled by all her grandeur,
and replies simply. The Baron bustles in, and seeing that
Sophie is charming vulgarly embraces her, to Octavian's
dismay, and breaks into a charming waltz song, with rather
questionable words, which make the women blush. His
attendants suddenly appear, preceded by a crowd of
frightened maid-servants, to whom, following their master's
example, they have been making rude advances. As the

Baron and Sophie's father depart to arrange the details
of the marriage contract, Sophie lingers with Octavian,
who tells her he loves her, and cannot bear to think that
she is to marry the Baron.   He says he will think of some
plan to break off the match, but the ever present scandal-
mongers overhear him, and inform the Baron.   A quarrel
follows, and the Baron is unable to see why any girl should
not be charmed to marry him.   It takes a sword thrust
from Octavian to convince him to the contrary.   The
Baron shouts for help, and all the servants rush in.   Sophie's father is determined to have the match take place,
as it will complete his aggrandisement, he thinks; and Octavian sorrowfully departs.   The Baron now soothes his
wounded feelings in wine, and becomes as brave as a
lion.   He drunkenly sings the "Leiblied," with variations,
and his joy is complete when he receives a letter from
the Princess's supposed chambermaid, saying she will
meet him the following night.   This gives him an excuse
to encore himself in the "Leiblied."

ACT III.   A questionable hotel.   Supper for two is laid
on a table decorated lavishly with candles.   Valzacchi and
Annina are bustling about, making preparations.   Their
plan is to station spies everywhere so that everything the
Baron says or does can be heard and seen.   Octavian
has been helping them, but goes out, presently returning
with the Baron.   He looks very attractive in his maid's
costume, and the Baron is delighted.   When the latter enters the room he makes a dash for the table and extinguishes most of the candles.   "Such extravagance!" he
declares.   Octavian is not responsive to his overtures at
first, and when the Baron tries to embrace him, a head
appears from a trap door in the floor.   The Baron is
mystified by this and also by the fact that Octavian
seems to him to resemble the youth who bore the silver
rose to Sophie.   Yet he is sure he is not drunk—not yet,
at least.   The mystery increases when Annina appears,
how he cannot determine, as a deserted wife.   She points

to her four children who crowd around the Baron, calling him "Papa." The Baron tries to make his escape, but is intercepted by the chief of police, who asks him to explain his presence in a bedroom with a young woman. He declares it is perfectly proper; the girl is his betrothed. Faninal enters just in time to hear an uncomplimentary remark of the exasperated Baron, who finds he has lost his wig. Faninal falls in a swoon, and the Baron hopes he can escape, but Octavian, after a whispered conversation with the chief of police is divesting himself of the chambermaid disguise behind the bed-curtains, and handing the articles of apparel, one by one to that functionary, who receives them with due solemnity.

The Princess now makes her appearance, and takes in the whole situation. The Baron declares he has done nothing to prevent his marriage with Sophie, and is indignant because Faninal, now his natural self, does not agree with him. The Princess tells him a few home truths, and to add to his discomfiture, servants bring in huge bills for the expense incurred by the inn on his account, including an impossible number of candles. He hurries away, lest any further misfortune befall him, and the Princess, in a charming scene, joins the hands of the young pair, who, singing an ecstatic love duet, depart with her. Sophie has forgotten her handkerchief, and the little negro page comes back to find it. The curtain falls.

ELEKTRA

Tragedy in one act. Music by Richard Strauss. Text by Hugo von Hoffsmansthal.

Cast. Clytemnestra—Mezzo-Soprano. Elektra—Soprano. Chrysothemis—Soprano. Aegisthus—Tenor. Orestes—Baritone. The Foster-father of Orestes—Bass. The Confidant—Soprano. The Train-bearer—Soprano Two servants—Tenor and Bass. The Housekeeper—

Soprano. Five Servants—Two Sopranos, Two Mezzo-Sopranos, and an Alto. Men and Women servants. Time, shortly after the Trojan War. Place, the King's Palace at Mycene. First performance, Dresden, 1909.

Act I. The inner court, back of the palace of Clytemnestra, near the servants' quarters. Servants gossiping at the well, as they draw water. One of them asks: "Where is Elektra?" "This is the hour in which she mourns for her father," is the reply. Elektra, as they speak is creeping along by the wall. As they go up to her she shrinks back, like a frightened wild beast, into the shadow of the wall, her arm held before her for protection. The maids nudge each other. "Did you see that?" says one. "Yes, she is nothing but an animal. Now, she will lie there and groan." "Better not go near her." They tell each other the strange things the girl says, and how when they remonstrate with her, her only answer is to howl like an animal. Once she had cried out "A vulture is tearing my breast!" Why the Queen should permit such a creature to roam about unchecked, they cannot see. She should be shut up, and would be if they had any say in the matter. Some of the younger servants pity her, saying that she has had a terrible sorrow, and see how she is treated, fed from a bowl, like a dog, and beaten so cruelly. "She is a king's daughter," says one little maid, excitedly. "I would serve her if I could. I would bathe her poor torn feet, and wipe them with my hair." "Stuff and nonsense!" says the Housekeeper. "Go in, to your work!" "All the same," persists the girl, "if she is mad, no one can look her in the eyes, without fear. She is royal, after all, and I, for one long for the day when she will be avenged."

"Go in, I tell you," says the Housekeeper. "Do you think we will have this mad creature at table with us when she spits in our faces, and calls us everything she can think of that is horrible."

The others continue to talk of Elektra's constant prayer

that the blood of her father shall be wiped from the floor,
and that the foul blot upon his name be wiped out also.
Even the children born in the palace are tainted with
blood, she continually declares. "Was not that what she
kept saying?" asks the Housekeeper, and all the servants
in chorus, cry out "Yes, Yes! That and more." "Oh, oh,
they are killing me," cries the little maid, who is being
whipped for her defence of the unfortunate princess.
Elektra herself now appears (Elektra: "Alone, ah, all
alone!") wildly lamenting the murder of her father Agamemnon by his wife Clytemnestra, and her paramour,
Aegisthus. She shrieks aloud: "Agamemnon! Agamemnon!" imploring him to return to her. "This is the hour,"
she says, "when they struck thee in thy bath, and the blood,
the blood, gushed forth! But thou shalt return, and
avenge thyself! Thou wilt return in kingly strength, not
as the pale shadow that I have seen in the twilight. All
those that loved thee shall give thee their strength, thy
horses and dogs, that went with thee to the chase, and thy
three children, thy son Orestes, and thy two daughters. I
shall skip and dance like a shadow, for all the world to see,
that men may say 'This was a king!' Agamemnon! Agamemnon!" She has worked herself into a frenzy of hatred,
and desire for revenge, when Chrysothemis, her younger
sister calls softly "Elektra!" She starts, then asks
her what she desires. Let her say it quickly, and depart.
Chrysothemis is frightened, and shields herself with her
hands. "What do you desire, daughter of Clytemnestra?" cries Elektra going up to her. "They are plotting,"
says the girl trembling. "Those two?" contemptuously.
"Yes, to shut you up in a tower, ne'er more to see the
light of day." Elektra laughs horribly. "Yes, I heard
them," persists the girl; "I listened at the door." "There
is no need of that," declares Elektra. "The very walls
speak of carnage! But sit down by my side and implore
the gods with me for the death of these wretches."
"Nay," says Chrysothemis, "I am not like you. I can-

not remain quiet, but must wander here and there, hearing voices call me, but seeing nothing. My eyes are blinded with tears and my voice fails me. Oh, my sister!" "Yes?" sharply. "It is you who bring this torment," goes on Chrysothemis. "But for you they might let us go free. I am a woman, I desire to live and to love; to hold a child in my arms, and shield it with my body. Canst thou not see?" "Always the body," says Elektra, but Chrysothemis does not heed. "Mercy!" she cries. "Let these things rest! Our brother comes not; there is no word from him. We shall grow old, as other women do without having lived. I am a woman, I desire the life of a woman." She bursts into tears. "Howl, then," is Elektra's contemptuous answer. "I hear running. Something evil is afoot." "Clytemnestra has dreamed," cries Chrysothemis, "and her dream was of Orestes. She shrieked in her sleep. Fear has made her an evil thing. Go, or she will kill thee!" "I will speak to her to-day," declares Elektra, quietly.

A torchlight procession is seen, with overdriven animals, and every sign of cruelty. Clytemnestra appears in the window, pallid, and bloated of countenance, and wearing a purple robe which ill becomes her. She is supported by her confidant, and leans upon an ivory cane, set with jewels. Her trainbearer, dark-skinned, and dressed in yellow, with thin lips and a sinuous motion, like a serpent, stands close behind. The Queen wears many jewels and amulets, which clank as she moves. Her eyelids are so thick and heavy, that she can scarcely hold them up. Elektra stands proudly before her. "What do you desire?" shrieks the queen. "Oh, why are you free to torment me? You would blast me with your glance. Why must I suffer you? Tell me, O gods?" Elektra craftily flatters her. "Art not thou among the gods, being thyself a goddess?" she says. Clytemnestra suspects a ruse, and turns to her maids. "She mocks you!" is their verdict. "She reads my thoughts," says the queen, "but

hers are always a mystery." Elektra speaks in her ear:
"This vermin hanging to thee keeps thee from thinking."
"I will speak with her alone," cries the perplexed Clytemnestra. She comes with her maid to the door. They try
to keep her from going to Elektra, but she becomes furious (Clytemnestra: "You two, be silent!"), telling them
they are sucking her blood like vampires, and are creatures
of Aegisthus. She desires the truth alone, but where shall
she seek it. "I will speak with my daughter. Leave me
with her," she commands. The two women slowly go in.
It is dark in the court.

"What shall I do to keep me from evil dreams,"
says the wretched queen. "Do you dream, then?"
"Yes, even in waking. These amulets are worn to
keep away evil dreams. Canst thou, too, help me in
this?" "I, my mother?" says Elektra, evenly. "Yes,
thou art wise; speak a few words. I toss restlessly at
night upon my bed, and am in terror. Or else I dream of
horrors, and wake to find that night still lingers, and the
torches burn beside me. But this must end, when blood
flows again—*the right blood.*" "How strange," says
Elektra monotonously. "The right blood," the queen
continues, "When it flows, I shall sleep." Elektra, with
her eyes fixed on her mother, slowly repeats her last words,
with deep meaning. "But what blood is this?" asks the
queen. "What beast shall furnish it?" Elektra laughs.
"An impure beast," she declares. "Then, a prisoner?"
"No." "And what drugs must be used?" says the queen.
"Very powerful ones," Elektra intimates, covertly smiling.

Playing upon Clytemnestra's credulity, Elektra tells her
that the victim is to be a woman, "one who has mated,"
and the slayer a man who belongs to their house. The
time and place she knows not, nor does it matter. She
suddenly accuses her mother of having plotted Orestes'
death lest he should kill her. She sees fear in her eyes;
by this she knows Orestes lives. Clytemnestra denies
everything and hysterically threatens Elektra, because,

knowing the remedy for her sleeplessness, she will not disclose it.   (Clytemnestra: "Of those without I have no
fear") Elektra, who has been standing in the shadow,
springs toward the queen, speaking in a sort of trance.
(Elektra: "Who must bleed? Thine own throat!") She
graphically describes the queen's death, which she sees
before her as in a vision; always gazing steadily at her
mother, who stands panting with terror. Lights shine
into the court, and the confidant, hurrying in, whispers
in the queen's ear. She listens dully at first, then with
excitement. Servants crowd into the Court, and the light
falls upon their interested and excited faces. Clytemnestra looks threateningly toward Elektra, then almost
runs into the house, the servants hastening after her.
"What is this news?" muses Elektra. "Oh, why does
nothing tell me what gave this woman such joy!" Chrysothemis rushes in, crying "Orestes is dead!" Elektra, deep
in thought, waves her aside. She repeats her words, saying it is known to all but his sisters. "It is not true,"
declares Elektra, quietly, and Chrysothemis falls on the
ground, in despair. "Do not believe this," says Elektra,
roughly shaking her sister. "Well, I saw the men who
brought the tidings." "It is not true," her sister continues to repeat. "Oh, he is dead," Chrysothemis laments, "dragged by his horses, which trampled him to
death." The two girls fall down upon the doorsill, and
are almost stumbled over by a servant, who orders a horse
to be saddled immediately. A message is to be sent in
haste to Aegisthus. "*We* must do it then," says Elektra.
"I?" asks Chrysothemis, timidly. "Yes, we two."
"When?" "To-day; or better still, to-night." "What
must we do, sister?" "That which our brother would
have done; since he cannot be here to do it." "Oh, what
is it?" cries Chrysothemis. "You and I," says Elektra
slowly, "must kill this man and this woman." "Our
mother?" asks Chrysothemis, trembling. "Yes, and that
other. And we must not fail. How shall we do it?"

"How can we with these weak hands?" "*I* can accomplish
it," declares Elektra, calmly. "The axe, with which our
father." "It is you who have kept it," the cowardly
Chrysothemis quickly reminds her. "Yes, for our
brother. But now we must do it." "Sister, will you kill
Aegisthus?" inquires the younger girl, in terror. "Either
one first. What does it matter?" "I am afraid!" cries
Chrysothemis. "No one watches at the door. I will go
alone," Elektra plans quietly. "If I need thee—" Chrysothemis protests, not wishing to be implicated in the deed.
Elektra seizes her and by sheer force of will endeavours
to inflame her sister's more sluggish intelligence. She
flatters her, working upon her physical emotions. (Elektra: "So strong art thou.") She describes her strong
supple body, so full of life and beauty, and the vigour of
womanhood. She will be a sister to her more than ever
before, and prepare her for her bridal, and for the coming
of a child. Chrysothemis cries out in anguish, and Elektra reminds her that first she must help her with her
purpose. She embraces her sister, who weakly says:
"Count not upon it," and flees in terror of Elektra. "I
hate thee!" calls Elektra after her. "I will go alone."
She crawls along by the wall of the palace, keeping in
shadow, and listening. She stops, then resumes her
progress.

Orestes appears, and his outline is seen in the dim
light. He comes forward; Elektra sees him, and his
eyes rest upon her. "What seekest thou, O stranger,"
she says. "I perform a task. Leave me alone!" "I am
waiting," declares Orestes. "Are you a servant here?"
"Yes, *I serve*," answers Elektra, significantly. "Begone!"
"I have an errand, and await a signal," declares Orestes.
"The Master is not here," persists Elektra. "Why should
she want you?" "My errand is with the Queen," the
young man continues. "I bring her proofs of the death
of Orestes." Elektra, almost distraught by this news, denounces him. Why should he live, she cries passionately,

when one so much more needed is gone? "Speak not of him," is Orestes' reply and he asks her who she is. In the same exaltation, she tells him she is of the blood of Agamemnon and Orestes; she is Elektra. He cannot believe it, and bitterly laments over her changed looks, wildly calling her by name. She is terrible to behold, he cries out. "Yes," she says, "but my sister Chrysothemis within is fair to look upon, and awaits a lover." He whispers in her ear, "Orestes lives." She looks at him in excitement. He swears it by the body of his father. "Who, then are you?" demands the girl. The old servant interrupts them, kneeling with others who follow him, before Orestes and kissing his robe. Elektra trembles violently. "Who are you?" she says again. "The dogs knew me," answers Orestes, softly, "but my sister knows me not!" The girl pronounces his name in a sort of muffled shriek, and falls into a frenzy of joy, as she examines him feature by feature, hungrily. He embraces her, but she draws back in shame. This is not the Elektra he knew, beautiful and desirable, but the shadow of his sister, a creature consecrate to hate, and lost to all that means womanliness. Why does he tremble? she asks. "Because of the path I must take," he declares; "but the gods will strengthen me." "Ah," she tells him, "action is the rest of the soul, a soft couch bringing relief. Happy a thousand times will he be who brings this relief about, and those who see his work, or have a part in it." The foster-father of Orestes comes to call him, cautioning silence. Orestes arises, and goes in.

Elektra hides within the shadow waiting, with the impatience of an animal. All she regrets is that she has not given Orestes the axe. A faint cry is heard within. "Strike, strike," shrieks Elektra, in a demoniac joy. A louder cry is heard in the palace, and a crowd of women servants rush out, with Chrysothemis, saying apprehensively that strangers are in the palace, the door is locked, and the queen is screaming horribly. "Assassins," cries

one, in terror. "There is Elektra," says another.
"Speak, speak, Elektra!" "No, no, we must seek aid."
"Open the door, Elektra." The girl stands before it,
and will allow no one to pass. "Here is Aegisthus," calls
a maid, and the frightened servants run to hide themselves.
Aegisthus calls loudly for torches, but no one responds.

Elektra takes the torch from before the door and runs
forward to meet him, bowing almost to the ground. She
joyfully leads the way. Aegisthus asks her if Orestes
is really dead. "The proofs are sure," she answers la-
conically. "And you, why do you hold the torch so unsteadily, why does your voice tremble?" "Because," says
Elektra, "I am wise, and go with the majority now."
She dances about him, then bows again. Aegisthus wonders at the darkness, but Elektra keeps his attention, and
he enters the house. There is a sudden tumult within, and
he appears at a window, tearing aside the curtain, and
calling for help. "Agamemnon hears thee," cries Elektra,
joyfully. He is dragged away, but again struggles to
the window; then disappears. Elektra's face expresses
exultant hate; she can hardly breathe. The servants
pour out of the house pell-mell, Chrysothemis crying out
that Orestes has delivered them. All call his name aloud,
and the cry is taken up within the palace also. (Chrysothemis: "Come, he is in the hall.") Chrysothemis describes the scene within and the frightful wounds
of the slain. There is a tumult throughout the palace.
"Hearest thou? Hearest thou?" cries Chrysothemis.
"Do I not," says Elektra. "All that thou hearest comes
from within me. I must lead them in the dance, yet I am
rooted to this spot." She rises, with an effort. "We are
in the hands of the gods," she says solemnly. The two
sisters rejoice each according to her nature. Chrysothemis's thoughts are upon love and freedom; Elektra's
upon the fulfilment of a great purpose, which had its
roots in the eternal justice. "Yes, love kills," she declares, "but we cannot live without it." In the peculiar ex-

altation, which always characterises her, Elektra begins to
dance, with strange steps. Chrysothemis calls to her,
but she bids her be silent. The servants come curiously to
behold her. "I bear the burden of happiness," she cries,
exultant, then suddenly falls to the ground. "Orestes!
Orestes!" calls Chrysothemis, wildly beating upon the
door. There is a silence, and the curtain falls.

THE GIRL OF THE GOLDEN WEST

(La Fanciulla del West)

Opera in three acts. Music by Giacomo Puccini. Italian
text by Guelfo Civinini and Carlo Zangarini from the
drama by David Belasco. English text by R. H. Elkin.
   CAST. Minnie—Soprano. Jack Rance, Sheriff—Baritone. Dick Johnson (Ramerrez)—Tenor. Nick, Bartender—Tenor. Ashby, Express Agent—Bass. Sonora
—Baritone. Trin, Sid, Handsome, Harry, Joe, Happy,
Larkens, all Miners—Three Baritones, Three Tenors and
a Bass. Billy Jackrabbit, an Indian—Bass. Wowkle, his
Squaw—Mezzo-Soprano. Jake Wallace, a travelling minstrel—Baritone. Jose Castro, a Mexican—Bass. Postilion—Tenor. Miners, etc.
   Time, Gold Fever Era, 1849-50. Place, California,
near the Cloudy Mountains. First production, Metropolitan Opera House, New York, 1910.
   ACT I. Scene, "The Polka", a miner's saloon and dance-
hall. Through a door at the rear there is a view of the
mountains. It is sunset, but dark indoors. In the gloom,
Jack Rance, the Sheriff, sits smoking. A mournful song
arises from the camp. Nick, the bartender, appears, and
lights the lamps and candles. The scene immediately becomes more lively. Miners troop in, calling for drinks.
With rude horse-play they sing and dance together, to the
tune of "Dooda - dooda - day." A game of cards is begun.
Other miners enter, and, throwing down their saddles in

a corner, crowd around the card table or call for food and
drink.   They look with rough sympathy at Larkens, who
is wretchedly homesick, a feeling they themselves understand.   Rance asks for Minnie.   Trin, soon "cleaned out"
at the faro table, throws down his cards, and leaves.
Billy Jackrabbit craftily filches some cigars from the
bar.   Nick tells each of the miners that Minnie likes him
best, to their great joy.   In the distance Jake Wallace is
heard singing a song of home (Jake: "I am thinking of
my folks"), to a banjo accompaniment.   The miners applaud, and join in the song with their rough voices, the
chorus increasing in volume as more and more come in to
listen.   Larkens, completely overcome, begins to sob
(Larkens: "I've had enough").   Sonora takes up a col-
lection for Larkens among the boys, and he departs joyfully for home.   The faro game continues; Sid, found
cheating, is threatened with hanging, but Rance suggests
that a worse punishment will be to placard him with a card,
and turn him loose, hanging him if he takes it off.   This
is done, and the cheat is kicked out of the "The Polka" by
the miners.   Ashby, the Wells Fargo Express Agent, enters,
calling for whiskey, and tells Rance he will soon catch the
road agent Ramerrez, being hot on his trail.   The miners
drink a toast to Minnie.   "Soon to be Mrs. Rance," declares the Sheriff.   Sonora scoffs at this, calling Rance
a "yellow-faced old Chinaman."   Rance accuses him of
being drunk, and draws his pistol.   After a scuffle, Sonora
fires on the Sheriff, but Minnie, entering, seizes the pistol.
The miners greet her warmly.   She affectionately scolds
Sonora; the others stand up for him.   Joe brings a bunch
of flowers, and all the others some little gift.   As she
greets the Sheriff, Sonora pays his account in gold-dust;
Ashby commenting on the folly of keeping so much gold
at "The Polka," with road agents abroad.

Minnie quietly takes a Bible from the counter, and the
men gather around her.   She asks them questions, and
they in return ask the meaning of certain words, some-

times with facetious comments, which she overlooks, speaking with simple sincerity of goodness and love.   Billy sidles in, and drinks the heeltaps of the liquor in the glasses. He is already half drunk.   Minnie inquires if he has married Wowkle, and he replies, "No, it is too late; got 'um baby!"   She feels in his pockets, and finds the cigars, which she restores, and sends the Indian off.   The mail carrier arrives.   Ashby asks him if he knows a certain Nina Micheltorena.   Minnie interposes, declaring that Nina is a hussy.   Ashby tells Rance she is the betrayer of Ramerrez.

The miners have gradually been leaving, and at last Rance and Minnie are alone.   Rance begins to make love to her, but she repulses him, drawing her pistol.   He tells her he loves her, and will have her although he is married. (Rance, Minnie: "When I left my little home"; Minnie: "Down home in Soledad")   She replies that she will love no one until she is sure she has found the right man.   Nick comes in, saying a man outside wants whiskey and water. "Tell him we drink our whiskey straight at 'The Polka' but will curl his hair for him," returns Minnie.   Nick brings in the stranger, who is annoyed by this retort. When Minnie sees him she treats him with marked politeness and favour.   He says he is Dick Johnson of Sacramento.   Rance, becoming jealous, insults him.   Minnie talks with him apart, recalling a former meeting when he had offered her a spray of jasmine.   Rance angrily calls in the miners to make Johnson explain his business.   Minnie vouches for him.   Johnson invites Minnie to dance. She is shy, but finally accepts.   The miners cheer them, and mark time by stamping their feet and clapping their hands.   Castro, a Greaser, is brought in bound, and is about to be strung up, when he offers to show the men Ramerrez's hiding place.   He manages to get in a word with Johnson, concerning a certain signal, and the miners all join in the hunt, leaving Minnie with Johnson, and Nick, who is closing up the place.

'As they talk together, Johnson speaks of a kiss, and the girl says simply that she has yet to give the first kiss of love to any man. She lives alone in a little hillside cabin, and is happy. It is strange, she goes on naïvely, but in Johnson she finds something that helps her and makes her happy. He explains her feeling as love, and assures her that his feeling toward her is the same. She comments on the fact that the miners' gold is in her keeping, and she would give her life to protect that for which they have worked and struggled so hard! Many of them are toiling for the comfort of the families they have left at home, and they are often desperately homesick. Johnson suddenly declares he must go, and Minnie invites him to come and see her later at her cabin. She speaks sadly of her ignorance and her desire to learn, calling herself in disgust "a good-for-nothing." Johnson replies impulsively that she has the face of an angel. He hastily departs, and Minnie stands dreamily in the middle of the room, repeating: "He said—the face of an angel!" Curtain.

Act II. Minnie's cabin, one hour later. Wowkle, the squaw, sits on the floor with her pappoose, which she is singing to sleep. (Wowkle: "Grant, O Sun-God, grant thy protection!") Billy enters, and squatting beside her announces that Minnie says they must marry; he bargains with her as to the price. Minnie comes in wearing a red cloak. The table is set for one, but Minnie tells the squaw to put on another place. Wowkle is greatly surprised, and still more so when the girl puts roses in her hair, and with great difficulty struggles into a pair of tight white slippers. To this magnificence she adds scent on her handkerchief, and a pair of gloves, anxiously asking the squaw if this is too much dress. Johnson knocks, and is about to embrace Minnie as he enters, when he sees the squaw. He apologises, but at intervals repeats the attempt, but Minnie repulses him each time. She tells him of her life (Minnie: "You've no notion how exciting"), of her rides among the mountains, and how she teaches, the miners; "her boys," she calls them. She offers him food, and he promises to send her some books. She likes love-stories she declares, but does not understand them altogether. He tries to embrace her again, but she escapes, warning him. She sends Wowkle home. As the squaw opens the door, it is seen that a heavy snow-storm has begun. The wind rises in great gusts. Johnson again begs a kiss, and Minnie with a sudden impulse throws herself into his arms. As the storm increases the door blows open and snow drifts in. Johnson gazes out, and gives a start. She tells him all her simple heart, and he bids her a hurried farewell. The snow has drifted against the door and he cannot leave. "It is Destiny," asserts Minnie. (Duet, Minnie and Johnson: "Ah, how good to live and die.") He declares passionately that he will never leave her. She gives him her bed, and after undressing lies down before the fire herself, first saying her prayers. As she bids him good night, a call is heard: the miners coming to warn her of Ramerrez. She hides Johnson behind the bed curtains as the miners come in. Rance tells her that Johnson, whom she danced with, is the road agent, Ramerrez, but she cannot believe it. They have tracked him to her cabin. "Who told you he is Ramerrez?" asks Minnie. "Nina Micheltorena, who gave us this picture of her lover," replies Rance. "He is not here!" cries the girl, and they bid her good night.

Contemptuously, she orders Johnson to come out. He tells her the men are right, but asks her pity (Johnson: "Let me just say one word"), declaring that it had been his purpose to begin life anew, having been awakened to good by her love. Weeping, she tells him he has betrayed her trust, and robbed her of her first kiss. "Go!" she says sternly, and he obeys. A pistol shot follows, and the sound of a fall. Minnie opens the door and helps Johnson in. He resists (Johnson: "Don't shut the door"). She drags him up a ladder into the garret chamber. As she returns, loud knocking is heard, and she admits Rance, who

has come to arrest Johnson as Ramerrez. She denies that
he is there, and tells him to look thoroughly to convince
himself. He seizes her in his arms, and she threatens him
with a bottle. As he stands underneath the loft a drop
of blood falls on his hand. Minnie hastily says she must
have scratched him, but he looks up and another drop is
seen.

Overjoyed, Rance starts toward the ladder, but Johnson comes down, half fainting. Rance sneeringly asks him
if he is still anxious for that game of poker. Johnson
faints, and Minnie declares she will play instead. "We are
three of a kind," she alleges, "one no better than another." The stakes are to be her freedom and Johnson's,
against her marriage with Rance, and Johnson's surrender. They begin to play with feverish haste, deciding
upon the best two hands out of three. Minnie wheedles
Rance, and pretends she is faint. While he is looking for
whiskey to revive her, she stacks the cards, from her
stocking, and thus wins the game. Rance, in a rage gets
up and goes out. Minnie, laughing wildly, throws her
arms around her lover. Curtain.

ACT III. The Great California Forest, at early dawn.
Rance is seated in a clearing, near the fire. He is pale
and his clothes are torn. Nick and Ashby, accompany
him, and Nick says he wishes none of them had ever seen
Johnson. "And to think she is nursing him," adds
Rance, "while we sit here in the cold." Men are heard
shouting, and Ashby dashes off on horseback. A band of
miners come running in, yelling with the indescribable excitement of a man hunt. Hurrying across the stage they
disappear, and Rance gloats over the coming capture
(Rance: " 'Tis your turn now!"), which means his revenge.
Other miners come hurrying in. A savage yell of triumph is heard in the distance. "Come on, boys," shout
the miners. Sonora arrives on horseback, and all crowd
around him for news. He tells them the bandit when
taken was like a wolf set upon by dogs. Billy appears with

a rope, for which he is trying to find a convenient branch. "Billy is the best at a noose," declare the miners, laughing triumphantly. (Chorus: "The very finest hanging."). Nick gives Billy money not to make the noose until he gives the sign.

Johnson is brought in by a troop of horsemen, pale and scratched, with torn and disordered dress; one shoulder is bare. The horses are methodically tied and the men fall into groups; six with drawn pistols are stationed on each side of Johnson, who stands in the centre, bound. Rance puffs cigar smoke in his face, with bitter insults. Johnson stands motionless, but defiant, as the miners close in around him with insulting epithets, making their accusations, which he denies, one by one. He has been a thief, he says, but not a murderer. They tell him they know he was planning to rob "The Polka," and take their hard-earned gold. Instead, he had robbed them of Minnie, whom they loved. Now, they will teach him to dance! They hustle him roughly to the tree picked out by Billy. (Johnson: "At least spare me your mocking.") He asks to be allowed to speak. "What cheek!" is their answer, "Let him speak from the branch." Sonora overrules them, saying this is not fair. Johnson begs that Minnie shall not know how he met his death. (Johnson: "Let her believe that I have gained my freedom.") Rance, at this, strikes him in the face; but the miners demur. Johnson advances quietly to the tree, where Billy waits with the noose. Rance stands apart with folded arms.

A cry is heard and the sound of a galloping horse. All quickly turn, crying: "It's Minnie!" Rance rushes forward, demanding that the hanging proceed at once. Minnie appears on horseback, with hair flying in the wind, and a pistol held between her teeth. Dismounting, she runs swiftly toward the group of men surrounding Johnson. Rance, in a rage, repeats his order. Minnie throws herself before Johnson, protecting him with her pistol. Rance commands the miners to drag her away, but no one stirs. (Rance: "Drag her away from there.") The crowd presses round them in excitement. "Let's hang him." "Stop it," is the cry. Sonora calls upon two men who have seized Minnie to let her go. All draw back; Rance, pale, and with set teeth, sits down beside the fire. Minnie pleads with her boys for Johnson's life (Minnie: "Was ever one of you that said 'Stop it!' "), reminding them of her loving care when they were sick. She claims Johnson's life and freedom as a guerdon for all she has done. She will be answerable for him, she says. Sonora asserts that they are heart-broken, because Johnson has robbed them of her. He relents, but the others are obdurate. She coaxes them, reminding each of some past benefit. At last all are cajoled into forgiveness, and Minnie throws down her pistol. The miners are almost in tears, and fear they will be ridiculed for letting Johnson go when they return to camp. Johnson kneels before Minnie, kissing the hem of her dress. Sonora, speaking for the others, bids her farewell. (Sonora: "Oh, girl, your words must come from God.") She goes off with her lover, leaving the miners dejected and sorrowful. (Minnie: "Good-bye, beloved country; good-bye, my California!"; Chorus: "You'll never come again.") Curtain.

GRISELIDIS

(Patient Griselda)

Lyric drama in three acts, with a prologue. Music by Massenet. Poem by Armand Silvestre and Eugène Morand, based upon an old story.

CAST: Grisélidis—Lyric soprano. Fiamina—Soprano. Bertrada—Soprano. Loys, a little child, son of Grisélidis. The Devil—Baritone. Alain—Tenor. The Prior—Baritone. The Marquis—Baritone. Gondebaud—Baritone or Bass. Men-at-arms, spirits, voices of the night.

angelic voices, servants, etc.   Time, the fourteenth century.   Place, Provence.

PROLOGUE.   A short prelude, describing the peace of the forest and the song of birds.   Scene, a forest in Provence.   It is evening.   The shepherd Alain, lost in thought, is seated on the ground.   He is in an ecstasy of joy over his love for Grisélidis.   (Alain: "Open before me, O gates of Paradise.")   The prior and Gondebaud, a retainer of the Marquis, enter, talking earnestly.   They ask Alain if he has seen the Marquis, who has gone hunting.   "No," he answers, "but he must surely pass this way."   They decide to wait and during their conversation say what a pity it is that the Marquis does not marry. "He has not seen the right woman," declares Gondebaud.   "If he were to see Grisélidis, he would surely marry her," says the lovesick Alain, impulsively, desirous of praising his beauteous lady-love.   He describes her in glowing words.   (Alain: "To see Grisélidis is to know.")   Blue eyes and golden hair, fair as a lily, and best of all, with the charm and sweetness of a pure and gentle heart.   The Marquis is seen coming towards them, but looking far into the depths of the forest, as if he saw a vision.   (Marquis: "Behold, an angel passes by.") Grisélidis emerges from the wood, her golden locks touched by the sunset light.   "She looks like Saint Genevieve," exclaims the prior.   The Marquis, half believing it to be a miracle, falls on his knees, (Marquis: "Thou who bearest heaven's peace"), and as she approaches, asks if she will be his bride.   Grisélidis, with great simplicity accepts him, saying that since his will is one with the will of God, it must be right for her to do so.   (Grisélidis: "Since heaven's will with thine accords.")   The Marquis kisses her reverently, saying the Prior will lead her to the castle the next day.   The Prior takes her away, and Alain, heartbroken, sings a song of farewell.   (Alain: "Close before mine eyes, oh, gates of Heaven.")   Curtain.

'ACT I. The oratory of Grisélidis. Bertrada, her serving woman sits alone, spinning (Bertrada: "In Avignon, the land of love"). Gondebaud comes in, reproving her for singing love songs, when there is so much else to be thought of. (Gondebaud: "Hush, these songs of love have had their day.") The Marquis, it appears, is going to a far country to fight the Saracens. He enters, bidding Bertrada take the news to her mistress. He commends Grisélidis and her babe to the Prior's care. The latter declares she shall not even leave the castle during his absence. (Marquis: "Wouldst thou make a prisoner of Grisélidis?") "No," cries the Marquis," she shall be free to go whither she will, and to do what pleases her." The Prior asserts that to trust a woman thus is to tempt God, but the Marquis is confident of her purity, faithfulness and obedience. "Still, there *is* a devil," persists the Prior. "Certainly, but were he here, I would repeat my words!" "He *is* here," cries the Devil, suddenly appearing. The Prior is terrified, but the Marquis asks the new comer if he is indeed the Foul Fiend. "Yes," he replies, "but such a nice devil!" (Devil: "I've played the devil upon the earth.") How he does enjoy stirring up a pretty little scandal, and then, there are always husbands to be deceived! "Not all of them," says the Marquis. "Yes, *all*," insists the Devil, blandly. "You have invoked me, and now I shall make you lose that wager I heard you making." He mockingly repeats the Marquis's confident boasts, in the very tone he had used. "Begone!" cries the Marquis, exasperated. "You are beginning to doubt, already," jeers the Fiend, with a grin. "But give me a pledge of some kind." The Marquis solemnly gives him his signet ring, and laughing derisively at their defiance (Marquis, Prior: "We defy your power.") the Devil leaps out of the window.

Dismissing the Prior, the Marquis sits alone (Marquis: "A brave soldier thinks naught") thinking of his coming separation from his wife and little son. "Will she indeed

be true, this beauteous Grisélidis?" Looking up, he sees
her by his side. (Grisélidis: "Pardon, my lord and my
master.") The Marquis speaks tenderly of his love for
her. She is free, he says, to go where she will during his
absence. She assures him that life will mean little without him, and to reassure himself, he bids her repeat her
conjugal vows. (Grisélidis: "Before the sun of heaven.")
She declares her undying love, and promises obedience.
The trumpet sounds a warning. Bertrada brings the
child to take leave of his father (Marquis: "The sweetness of kisses"). He bids Grisélidis farewell, as Gondebaud comes to summon him, and they depart for the war.
(Flourish of trumpets.) Grisélidis at the window,
watches the cavalcade out of sight. Bertrada begins to
read the story of Ulysses and the faithful Penelope, and
the curtain falls.

ACT II. After a graceful and idyllic entr'acte, the terrace of the castle comes into view, a blue sea in the distance. The Devil stands waiting with a bouquet.
(Devil: "Far from one's wife, what peace there is.")
He gets on very well with himself he declares, whereas
near one's wife there is always quarrelling and jealousy.
"Yes, when the cat's away—" "But she is *not* away,"
declares Fiamina, appearing. "And what may you be doing?" "Thinking of you, dearest wife," says the Devil.
"And dancing around like that? Stuff! You are planning mischief." "Oh, no, not I," he asserts. "Yes, you
are, I saw your nose quiver!" They call each other
names, and finally come to blows. (Fiamina, the Devil:
"You scoundrel! You wanton!") At last he acknowledges that he really has some work on hand, as the supply
of souls is running short. He is to tempt a certain Marquise. "What? Then I'll help you!" cries Fiamina, joyfully. They kiss and make up (Fiamina, Devil: "My
heart! My soul!"), then hide as Grisélidis comes sadly
from the castle (Grisélidis: "The sea") mourning her
husband's absence. (Angelus) Bertrada brings in Loys,

whom his mother teaches to pray for his father's safety
(Grisélidis: "Dear Lord, I pray thee"). The women
sing within the castle (Chorus: "Hail Mary, full of
grace").

Bertrada returns, announcing that two strangers wish
to see Grisélidis. "Let them enter," she says, and Bertrada departs with Loys. The scene is full of peace and
beauty, soon to be disturbed, alas! "Be clever," whispers the Devil to Fiamina. "Of course!" she answers.
Grisélidis greets them courteously, and they respond
(Fiamina, Devil: "Thanks for the courtesy"). They tell
her they have travelled far and seen many countries. The
Devil says that he is in sooth a slave-dealer, and bears a
message from the Marquis. "Have you a token from
him?" asks Grisélidis. "Naturally! Here is his signet
ring." They show the ring which the Marquis gave to
the Devil as a pledge. They go on to say that he has
bought Fiamina, as his slave, and is so enamoured of her
that he now wishes Grisélidis to obey her, and to give her
the wedding ring, and whatever else she desires in the
castle (Fiamina, Devil: "When we saw the Marquis").
When he returns, Fiamina will be his bride. Grisélidis is
indignant at first, but remembering that she promised to
obey gives up the ring, and goes in search of her son.
The two devils talk the conversation over, saying that
perhaps they had better go with what they have, since
the ring will fetch a good price, and surely Grisélidis will
not be so simple as to fall into their trap altogether.
"Better wait and see," concludes the Devil. "Besides,
she must be tempted further. With love this time. I
have it! Alain the Shepherd. He is quite a poet."
They plan that Fiamina shall take her place as Marquise,
and dance together, laughing uproariously. Fiamina
runs off.

Night has now fallen, and the Devil, making cabal-
istic signs in the air, calls around him the voices of
the night (Voices. "From woodland depths"). Spirits

appear, whom he orders to spread abroad evil fancies and
amorous thoughts (Devil: "You, who within you bear").
Brought thither by the spirits, Alain appears in the
garden. The moon rises, giving an air of fantasy to
the scene. (Alain: "Behold a bird that the cold breath
of winter.") Grisélidis, led by strange influences descends the staircase. (Grisélidis: "Sleep has deserted
me.") Alain speaks pathetically of his sorrow at losing
her, and she tries to comfort him (Grisélidis: "With
happiness again I see thee"), saying she will always remember him. He had sworn, he declares, never to see
her more, and bids her farewell. "Stay!" she cries. He
looks at her dumbly (Alain, Grisélidis: "List to my
words"), then speaks of his lost faith, in his disappointment at losing her. "Had you loved me truly, faith
would not have fled," she replies. "You know that I am
now a wife and must maintain my husband's honour."
He tries to embrace her, but she moves away, then, half
fainting falls into his arms. (Duet, Alain, Grisélidis:
"In all my being.") The Devil stands near, gloating;
but Alain, coming to himself, rushes away. Grisélidis
calls to him, and the Devil suddenly snatches the child
who has toddled in, from beside her, and vanishes.
Grisélidis calls wildly for assistance, then prays to God
to bring back the boy. Servants come forth with torches,
calling "Loys! Loys!" The Devil is heard far off laughing derisively. Curtain.

Act III. Oratory of Grisélidis. She is anxiously leaning from the window (Voices: "Loys! Loys!"), having
prayed all night for the return of the child. (Grisélidis:
"Mine eyelids burn with tears.") She now prays fervently to St. Agnes for his recovery. Opening the triptych, she finds it empty. The image has disappeared.
Bertrada hurries in, saying that an old man is waiting
without, who declares that he knows who has the child.
"And I know he is the Devil," she asserts bluntly. The
Devil enters in the guise of an old man, and offers to tell

Grisélidis who the thief is. "Speak," she commands.
"He is an admirer of the lovely eyes of the Marquise."
"Oh! Oh!" wails Grisélidis in anguish, and the Devil
smiles gleefully. "The Eves are not all dead yet!" he
chuckles to himself. "He will return the child for a kiss;
just an airy trifle!" he goes on. Grisélidis is in agony,
but the Devil says that since her husband has deserted
her for another she can now retaliate. "God will know!"
answers Grisélidis piously. "The old excuse," says the
Devil to himself with a grin. "It often spoils my plans."
Aloud he replies indifferently, "Of course the man may
prefer to carry him off, or even string him up to the mast
of his ship." He laughs. "But hurry, hurry!" Grisélidis takes a dagger from the case of arms on the wall,
and sprinkles herself with holy water. The Devil winces,
as if touched by flame. "Oh, oh!" he cries. "How that
stings and burns!" Grisélidis after praying in an ecstasy
of faith departs. "She will go!" declares the Fiend sa-
gaciously. "But I must say, my Lady Grisélidis has
given me more trouble than any other woman I ever
tempted!"

As he makes this reflection, the Marquis enters,
unarmed and bareheaded. "Ah, the Marquis! More
trouble!" grumbles the Devil. "How still it is here,"
says the Marquis. "No one will speak to me. Where
are my wife and child? Holà!" he shouts. "Sir,
I greet you," answers the Devil politely, "though we
have never met. Whom are you seeking?" "The Marquise." "Oh, then you are a friend of the late Marquis.
Poor man, since he is dead the Marquise has every excuse for—" "You lie!" declares the Marquis. "Oh, no,
not at all. Look out of the window. There she goes
to meet her lover!" "Oh, shameful," groans the Marquis. "Yes, quite so, but it is true! Why not kill her
with this?" He hands a dagger to the Marquis, who,
as he takes it sees his own signet ring on the hand of
the stranger. "It is the Devil!" he exclaims. "Kill them

both!" suggests the Fiend, cajolingly, and departs. "He lies!" cries the Marquis. "And yet, should I not go? No, no! The guilt is mine. (Marquis: "In the fate which overcomes thee.") I invoked the fiend through a foolish boast, and brought about this sorrow." (Marquis: "And my heart forever faithful.") Grisélidis approaches. "Grisélidis! Grisélidis!" he cries in anguish. She stands motionless on the threshold. "Am I still your wife?" she asks. "That rests with you!" answers the Marquis. "What prompts the question?" "Thou hast sent another woman to take my place," she informs him. "It is a lie," he asserts, astonished, "I swear that I have never desired any but thee for my wife. In return, he tells her what the Devil has charged against her, and she swears also that she has been true. He kneels before her, confessing that he had invoked the Devil, before his departure, and that the Fiend's lies have brought sorrow upon them. Grisélidis throws herself into his arms. (Grisélidis: "Oh, my master"; Marquis: "As on the river's bank.")

The Devil enters, regarding them with interest. "Here is the Fiend," cries the Marquis. "Know, Sirrah, that my wife still has my heart." "Ask her where the child is," says the Devil, quietly. "He is stolen," Grisélidis confesses. "Oh, God!" exclaims the Marquis, and the Devil, with a triumphant laugh, wishes them happiness, and vanishes. (Duet, Grisélidis, Marquis: "Ah, cruel hour, alas!") The Marquis calls for his arms, but they have disappeared from the wall. He implores the aid of God, and kneels with his wife before the altar. (Duet: "Oh, Holy Cross, Immortal Flame.") The cross above it is transformed into a sword of flame. The Marquis seizes it in exaltation. (Marquis: "Now, by this cross.") He swears that he will recover his son, and Grisélidis calls once more upon St. Agnes. Amid thunder-claps and lightning, the candles on the altar suddenly flame forth. A strange light fills the chapel, and as the doors of the triptych slowly open, St. Agnes is seen within, with Loys by her side. The servants and retainers stand spell-bound upon the threshold of the chapel. (Chorus: *"Magnificat anima mea"*.) The Marquis with gratitude takes the child, giving him to his mother who embraces him tenderly. "The Evil Spirit is vanquished!" they cry in thankfulness and exultation. Curtain.

KONIGSKINDER

(Children of Kings)

A Fairy Opera in three acts. Music by Engelbert Humperdinck. Text by Ernst Rosmer.

CAST: The King's Son—Tenor. The Goose-girl—Soprano. The Fiddler—Baritone. The Witch—Contralto. The Wood-cutter—Bass. The Broom-Maker—Tenor. Two Children—Sopranos. The Councillor—Baritone. The Inn-keeper—Bass. The Inn-keeper's Daughter— Mezzo-Soprano. The Tailor—Tenor. The Stable-Maid—Contralto. Two Gate-keepers—Baritones. Citizens, Councillors and their wives, Burghers and their wives, craftsmen, musicians, youths, maidens and children. Time, the days of legend. Place, Hellabrunn, and the forest in its vicinity. First performance, Metropolitan Opera House, New York, 1910.

ACT I. A forest glade, with a mountain seen in the distance. The Witch's Hut to the left, with a yellow cat sunning itself, and a raven hopping about. There is an overgrown garden; and a drinking fountain, made from a tree trunk, has formed a little pool, wherein geese are paddling. The marks of their feet are in the soft mud. To the right is a great linden tree, beneath which lies the Goose-girl. She wears a ragged brown dress, and a red kerchief over her hair, a few golden locks of which fall over her forehead. She has hung a wreath of flowers on a branch, and is singing to herself. The Witch shouts to her out of the window, asking where she has left her geese. The girl laughs, calling to them, and the Witch sharply bids her come in and bake. "It is so dark in there, grandmother," says the girl. "You will never be a real witch's child," the old woman grumbles, "loving the sun and air as you do!" The Goose-girl, mourning that her lily which she loves is drooping, slowly enters the hut, and returns with a large copper kettle and a key. She bends down, looking at herself in the fountain, and smiling at her reflection. The Witch angrily orders her to get to work. She scours the kettle with sand. (Goose-Girl: "Grandmother, how long have I lived, out here in the wood with you?") She questions the Witch about herself. (Witch: "Were you not so stupid"), and is crossly told that while she is making the bread she must not talk or sing, for magic is afoot. The Goose-Girl mixes the bread, and kneads it, putting a mysterious powder into the dough. Then she asks the Witch what is to be seen out in the great world. She will go herself to see, she thinks. The Witch informs her that she has placed spells all about to keep her from leaving, so she had better be careful. The maiden swings the bread three times around her head saying: "Who eats of this shall the loveliest see, As he desires them, things shall be." The Witch warns her that the bread she has made will kill anyone who eats it. The Goose-Girl begs her not to harm anyone, and she goes in, muttering. (Goose-Girl: "Linden beloved.") Soon the Witch comes out with a basket and goes to gather herbs for her magic arts.

The Goose-girl, happy in being alone, feeds the birds, and puts the flower wreath on her head; then stops up the trough, so that she can see herself in the water. "Oh, I am pretty! Oh, I am pretty!" she cries joyfully, calling the geese to come and look at her. As they surround her, a branch is heard snapping in the forest. The Goose-Girl is frightened. (Goose-Girl: "The wind blew in the trees.") She steals a glance at her reflection, and the King's Son comes behind her, smiling. He wears hunting dress and has great, burning eyes; he carries a bundle tied to a stick, and a sword by his side. "I bid thee good day!" he says, politely. The girl is more frightened than ever, and jumps off the trough. "Have you no word of cheer for me?" cries the youth. "Is this a man?" asks the girl, shyly. "From head to foot," is the firm reply. "I have never seen one before. What ought I to say?" she stammers. The King's Son tells her she has red lips, but he fears the truth does not fall from them (King's Son: "Maiden, how came thy lips so red?"). She assures him that no one has ever come there but the sun in summer and the snow in winter (Goose-Girl: "No one comes to the magic wood"). He answers that he has not come from the wood, but from the mountain, and is tired and hungry. "Is that a sword?" she asks, curiously. "Yes, but as yet untried," is the response. "Are you then a mighty one?" demands the girl. "Why, that is what my mother said, a great lady! You are only a beggar-maid, but," as she looks into his eyes, "oh, how lovely?" He stares at her with mute admiration, then asks her for a drink from the fountain. She shows him how to get one, and they drink alternately. "It tastes much better so," declares the King's Son simply. The Goose-Girl is dazed as if in a dream. She asks him to rest beneath the linden-tree, and he insists that she must sit beside him. (The King's Son: "Is this a riddle that I read?") He tells her of his home across the river where he has served a great king. "And what is a King?" "Why, that is hard to tell you! Wait though, what do you do for your geese?" "I watch over them to keep them from danger, and sometimes I have to beat them." "That is what a king does, only with people instead of geese," declares the youth. "Then, are you the king?" asks the girl naïvely. He explains as well as he can, the office of a king, how in spite of his power and luxury he is hedged about with bonds that he cannot break, and his only freedom is in the hunt. He knows, for he is a King's son. (The King's Son: "As kings, young boys are only useless.") With the wind blowing against his cheek, happiness comes to him. "King's child!" he cries impetuously, "Can you understand a fool like this." "I would go with him," says the Goose-Girl. "And without fear?" "No, for I love you," she says simply. He takes her in his arms. "Then you will be my little may-blossom?" he asks with deep tenderness. (The King's Son: "Wilt thou my little may-blossom be?")

He kisses her, and her heart thrills with joy. Clasped in each other's embrace they are silent. The Goose-Girl's wreath falls upon the ground and he picks it up. She tries to take it from him, but it breaks. The Goose-Girl is filled with shame, but the King's Son puts the broken wreath into his tunic. He takes from his bundle a crown of gold, but the Goose-Girl refuses to wear it (Goose-Girl: "I have no wish thy crown to wear"), saying it seems like a chain to her. The King's Son throws it down upon the grass (The King's Son: "There mayst thou rest"), once more begging her to go with him. She gives him her hand, and they run toward the wood. A wind blows in strong gusts. The geese crowd around the Goose-Girl in terror. "What makes thine eyes open so wide?" demands the youth. "The magic wood," breathes the Goose-Girl. "It would keep me here." "That must be magic!" says her lover. "But if thou fail'st me I will never return!" (The King's Son: "Fear is but weakness.") He upbraids her. (The King's Son: "King's blood and beggar's blood.") The poor girl tells him it is plain he no longer loves her, and with a last wild outburst he rushes into the wood.

The Goose-Girl flings herself upon the ground, weeping, and pushing away the geese, which crowd around her. (Goose-Girl: "Go, from me you have him taken.") "Oh, were I only a King's child!" she cries miserably. The

Witch is heard calling. "The crown! she will beat me if
she finds it," gasps the Goose-Girl. She hangs it around
the grey goose's neck, bidding her hide it. The goose
runs off, and the girl hastily bathes her eyes. The Witch
enters with her basket. "What have you been doing?"
she says severely, "And why do you hold your hand before your eyes. And why are your cheeks so white and
your lips so red?" "I am afraid, grandmother," says
the girl in a low voice, "and I have been eating fruit."
The Witch catching hold of her feels her heart beating
fast. "Grandmother, I have seen a man," she confesses.
"What!" cries the Witch. "Whence came he?" "Down
from the mountain," answers the Goose-Girl. "No man
has ever climbed it before, declares the Witch. "You must
be locked up after this!" "No, no," the girl sobs passionately. "Let me go away!" "Go, indeed," storms
her grandmother, "Want to be married, do you? Well,
you'll stay here instead!" The Fiddler is heard singing
behind the scenes (Fiddler: "A fool went forth one day").
"More people," angrily cries the Witch. "Go in at once."
She pushes the Goose-Girl in, and following her, closes
the door behind her with a bang. The Fiddler appears,
with his fiddle over his shoulder. "Come on, Brother
Woodcutter and Brother Broom-maker," he shouts.
"Here is the Witch's den!" "The devil take it and you!"
is the Woodcutter's uncivil reply. "Not so much noise,"
cautions the Broom-maker. "Let's wake the Witch up,"
suggests the Fiddler. "What, the wood-wife, the wise
woman!" cry the others. "All hail to the hell-hag," says
the Fiddler defiantly, but the Broom-maker knocks softly
on the door, and asks if those within will buy a broom.
They knock more loudly but no one answers. "Witch-
woman!" calls the Fiddler. With a bang the old Witch
opens the door, and stands leaning on her crutch, sur-
veying them maliciously. All take to flight but the Fiddler, who addresses her with derision. (Fiddler: "Thy
lovely red eyes.") "You think you are wondrous witty,"

responds the Witch. "Come, speak up," calls the Fiddler
to the Woodcutter and the Broom-maker. "I have
opened the way."

Clearing their throats they endeavour to inform the
Witch that they have been sent by the Councillors
of Hellabrunn to consult her on an important matter.
They stammer and stutter over their story, and the Witch,
growing impatient, appeals to the Fiddler, who can at
least speak out. "The truth is, the burghers desire a
king to rule over them," he replies. "One of the most
royal blood, a real king's child." The Goose-Girl looks
eagerly out of the window, and the Fiddler stares curiously at her. She puts her finger on her lip. He runs
off behind the hut. "What does he mean?" demands the
Witch, "You really want chains, then? "It must be
settled, somehow," says the Woodcutter. "Very well,
then," the Witch announces. "To-morrow, when you are
all arrayed in your best, the first person that enters the
town gate, after the clock strikes noon, be he dressed
richly or poorly, will be your king." She goes in and
slams the door.

The three men quarrel fiercely over the money they
are to receive from the burghers; the Fiddler drives
the others off, and begins to walk up and down in front
of the hut. "Well, why don't you go back to Hellabrunn?" cries the Witch looking out of the window. "I
am setting a trap for a golden bird," he replies. She
shakes her fist, and goes in. "Hey, traderaray!" sings
the Fiddler, as she drags the Goose-Girl out, speaking
kindly enough, but giving her sly cuffs. "You peeped
out the window," she says beneath her breath. "Why
should not she reign over a kingdom?" asks the Fiddler.
"She is pretty enough! Who are you?" he continues.
"Only the Goose-Girl," she says trembling. "Where is
your mother?" "I have only a grandmother, and there
she stands!" The Fiddler looks from one to the other,
and laughs loudly. "She cannot hold you here," he de-

clares. The Goose-Girl, sobbing, tells her pitiful little
story. The King's Son had come to that very meadow, and
had spoken of maying, and now he is gone. (Goose-Girl:
"I cannot go.")   "Let us seek him!" says the Fiddler. At
these words the Witch flies into a passion. "Yes, a fine
couple," she shrieks. "The King's Son and the beggar-
girl. Your father and mother were food for the hangman. A fine bride you will make!" The Fiddler protects the Goose-Girl, saying that in spite of the Witch's
words, he knows that "the Child of Kings is the Beggar-
Maid."

The Girl bids the grey goose bring back her crown
(Goose-Girl: "Thou grey one, thou wise one"). She
rushes at the Witch. "Release me!" she demands.
"Never!" shrieks the Witch. "To prove thyself of the
royal race, the Witch's wiles alone thou must face," chants
the Fiddler. The Goose-Girl seizes the crown from the
goose, and takes it to the Fiddler. "Dare everything!"
he advises. The Goose-Girl puts the crown on her head,
first removing her kerchief. Her beautiful golden hair
falls about her like a robe. Kneeling down, she lifts the
crown toward the sky. (Goose-Girl: "Father, Mother,
here will I kneel!")   A star falls from the heavens, and
touching the drooping lily, causes it to open. The Goose-
Girl, with a cry of joy, puts on the crown, and stands on
her feet. "I am free! I am free!" she declares, and
rushes into the wood, followed by the geese. (Fiddler:
"Hey, Traderaray.")   He follows the Goose-Girl, and
the Witch shakes her fist after them, and then breaks
the beautiful lily. Curtain.

Act II. A square in Hellabrunn. Inn, with tables and
benches outside, on the right. An orator's pulpit on the
left, and in the background the town-gate; closed, and
guarded by two Gate-keepers. The Innkeeper's daughter
is seated in the foreground, making a wreath. Music in
the distance. The stable-maid enters. "Gay is the life of
a town," she says, "such excitement is seldom seen." "Yes,

you have been hob-nobbing with the men, I suppose,"
replies the Innkeeper's daughter. "Well, no great harm
in that," declares the girl. "Men who have been drinking are none too shy." The other girl throws a handful
of fir-cones in her face, and she goes off whimpering.
"Stuck-up, painted thing," she grumbles to the Bar-maid.
The King's Son enters, and stands before the gate, as if
listening. "You are going to welcome his Majesty, I
daresay," says the Stable-maid, impudently. "Why not?"
is the reply of the Innkeeper's daughter. "With a kiss?"
"Go back to your low friends. What is rude in them is
not a sin for a King." "Well said!" chimes in the King's
Son. The Innkeeper's daughter looks at him scornfully.
"Who is this fellow?" she whispers to the Stable-maid.
"One who slept with the pigs last night," she replies.
"He's not bad looking," admits the Innkeeper's daughter.
"Get me some yarn!" "You like him, don't you," mutters
the Stable-maid, departing. The King's Son sits down
beside the Innkeeper's daughter, who orders food for him.
He declines, but says he would like some bread and water.
"Such food is only for poor people," she asserts. "And
are you highly born?" he asks simply. "Well, we have
always worn good clothes," she declares. The Bar-maid
brings the food, but the King's Son cannot eat the greasy
pork. He tastes the wine, and likes it even less. "That's
what one gets for feeding gutter cats!" the girl says indignantly, then relenting takes him to a secluded bench,
under the linden tree. She makes love to him, but his
thoughts are on the Goose-Girl, and he is distrait. In a
fury, she boxes his ears, driving him away. The Stable-
maid maliciously offers her the yarn, which she throws in
the face of the King's Son. "Take that and choke!" she
cries angrily, and rushes into the house. The King's Son
ruefully rubs his cheek, and the Stable-maid laughs with
the Bar-maid over the incident. (The King's Son: "Ah
me, it's hard to beg for bread.") He decides to leave
Hellabrunn, but a doubt springs up in his heart. He feels

in his doublet, and finds the wreath, as if fresh picked.   It
seems to say to him "Stay." (The King's Son: "Must
these tender flowers say it?")   "I was a craven to think
of going," he muses. "Poverty brings fear. I must
conquer it." As he runs toward the inn, he hears the
murmur of a crowd.   The gate-keepers are with difficulty
keeping the people back with their spears. They make
gruff comments upon the crowd's unmannerliness.

"A dance! A dance!" cry the young people, gaily.
The pipes sound merrily, as the dance begins.   The maids
grumble at the extra work, and the constant watching of
the innkeeper.   The King's Son applies to the latter for
work, but is only offered the place of swineherd. He hesitates, but finally accepts.   (The King's Son: "I have made
a complete mistake.") He sits beneath the linden-tree.
(King's Son: "Let the dew-drops from thy branches"),
and falls into a deep reverie.   The people cheer the Woodcutter and the Broom-maker.   The last-named has thirteen
children who trail behind him like steps of stairs, each with
a broom.   (Children: "Ra, Ra Roach, we travel in a
coach.")   The Broom-maker bids them keep their eyes
open, so that when the King comes they can each sell him
a broom.   (Broom-maker: "When the bells are striking
noon"; Children: "Buy a broom!")   The Innkeeper calls
the Woodcutter, and the Broom-maker.   The former
throws down gold on the table to settle an old score.   The
Innkeeper waves him aside, and while his back is turned
to order wine the Woodcutter pockets the coin. Soon a
merry party are drinking. The Innkeeper's daughter
joins the group.   The Broom-maker's little girl comes to
speak to the King's Son, asking him to buy a broom. He
tells her he has no money, and kisses the little girl.   "Will
you play with me?" she says innocently. "What shall
we play?" "Why, ring-a-round-a-rosy!" She instructs
him in the childish game.   (Child: "Ring-a-round-a-rosy.
A pocket full of posies.")   "The Council! The Council!"
cry the people. They cheer loudly. The Senior Council-

lor begins a long, tiresome speech, but is rudely interrupted. They call for the Woodcutter, who tells a thrill-
ing tale of his adventures in the magic wood. The King's
Son contradicts him, being surprised at his lack of
truthfulness, but the gist of his story is that the King
may be expected at noonday. (Children: "Ri ra ray, Let
all be blithe and gay.") He will no doubt be clad in gorgeous robes, with a gold chain around his neck. "What
if he were in rags?" cries the King's Son. "How, then,
should we know him?" ask the people, scoffingly. They
plan his manner of reigning. He will do thus and so,
and no other way, they are sure. "But what if a real king
should appear?" suggests the King's Son. "Why, he
would agree with the Council," of course. "Ye know not
what a King may be," declares the youth, sadly. "You
are no wiser, yourself," retort the people. "You shall rise
with him to Heaven, if indeed he is a King!" he continues
fervently. (King's Son: "Towering castles shall you be
building.") "Fool! Fool!" cry the people, in mockery,
and the Innkeeper shakes with laughter. He demands
money of the King's Son, for the meal provided that morning by his daughter. The youth shows that his pockets
are empty, and is set upon by the crowd, but drives them
back. He is drawing his sword when the clock strikes the
first stroke of noon. The people hasten toward the gate,
thinking they hear the King's horses approaching. They
jostle each other in their desire to see everything. (The
King's Son: "Will she appear?") At the eleventh stroke
the gates are thrown open. The sun shines on the golden
hair of the Goose-Girl, who enters, followed by her geese,
and attended by the Fiddler. She addresses the King's
Son, who has sprung toward her with a cry of joy.
(Goose-Girl: "My dearest Boy, I come to thee.") He
kneels before her, calling her his Queen. The crowd laughs
derisively. "The Goose-Maid and the Beggar-Man," is
the cry of all. The Fiddler tries to turn the tide, but it
is useless. The people crowd around the young pair, de-

riding them with coarse insults. Only the Broom-maker's
little daughter calls out shrilly: "Long live the King!"
She is pushed aside by the Woodcutter. "So ends the
great day," is the ultimatum of the Council. "But the
Royal Children?" "Down with them," is the prompt retort. The Children of Kings are driven through the
gates, and beaten with sticks; some of the townspeople
even throw stones at them. "Away with them!" cry the
mob. The Broom-maker's little daughter throws herself
down and weeps bitterly. "What is the matter, my
child," asks the Senior Councillor," as he passes. "Have
you lost your broom?" "No, no, but the King and Queen
are gone for ever!" He shakes his head slowly, and lays
his wrinkled hand on her shoulder to comfort her. Curtain.

Act III. The forest glade in winter. The Witch's
hut. No glass is in the windows. The water-trough is
frozen, and the linden tree has no leaves. Snow falls
softly. A dove flies down for its supper. (Fiddler: "My
little grey dove.") The Fiddler feeds it, and others come
to seek food also. He asks the doves if they have seen the
King's Children. The Woodcutter and the Broom-maker
hurry in; the latter has his little daughter by the hand,
and the others follow. (Fiddler: "Thou alone of all these
shall always welcome be.") He greets the child; then
speaks of his imprisonment, and the burning of the wicked
witch. They tell him his offences will all be forgiven, if
he will only come back and sing them a song. The children coax and beg. "No," he says firmly, "I have left
Hellabrunn for ever." The little girl has a wonderful
secret; she and all the children want the King and Queen
to return. The Fiddler says that but for his lame leg,
he would have sought them long ago, but when the spring
comes he will go. (Fiddler: "Oh, thou dear innocent.")
The visitors go through the hovel but find nothing. The
Fiddler declares that only the children are welcome in his
hut. He goes out and they sneak after him.

He is heard singing. (Fiddler: "Oh whither hast thou

wandered, O royal maiden mine?") The snow is falling
heavily now, and the wind begins to blow. The King's
Son enters from the hill, bearing the Goose-Girl in his
arms. She looks about her. (Goose-Girl: "Thou dear
one! Leave me!"; King's Son: "Thou'rt light as snow-
flakes.") He lays her down. They recognise the water-
trough and the linden-tree, now covered with snow. They
knock at the door, and the Woodcutter repulses them.
"Dog!" cries the King's Son. "Let us rest here," cries
the Goose-Girl. "Would that we had stayed in our cavern." "There was naught to eat there," said the King's
Son sadly. "And the way toward home is still to seek."
He has lost heart, and she cheers him with thoughts of
summer. "Dost thou not remember our mossy nest," she
cries. "Day's darling," murmurs the King's Son. "No
more shall I be weary," she says exultantly. "I love thee,
dear!" She croons a little song, then falls backward.
The King's Son utters a groan, and kneels beside her.
"Awaken! Awaken!" he cries, lifting her up. "I love
thee, dear," she repeats, with a last effort, and falls again.
The King's Son wraps her in his cloak, crying out "King,
forsooth. A Martyr's throne is mine." He resolves to
sell the crown for food. "Do not sell the crown," calls the
Goose-Girl, over and over again. He exchanges it with
the Woodcutter for a pasty, but is refused shelter. The
two starving young creatures ravenously devour the pasty,
which is the poisoned cake of the Witch. They dream of
spring, and the beautiful warm days to come. Then wrapt
in each other's arms, with a last kiss lie down to sleep beneath the linden-tree, where their love began. The Fiddler, returning is shown the crown by the others, and knows
who has sold it for bread. He hurries out into the snow
to search for them and led by the little grey pigeon finds
them dead.

The Broom-maker's children creep out of the wood,
and gather around. The Woodcutter and Broom-
maker, shamefacedly return to the hut. The sunset glow

reddens the whiteness all about them. "Starved! Done to death!" says the Fiddler, sadly. (Fiddler: "Children, they are found and lost.") The children kneel on the snow, the sunset light on their faces. "Your fathers have shamefully treated them," he continues, "and you must bury them like the King and Queen they were." The Woodcutter and Broom-maker, who have made a bier of branches, bring it in, and the children lay the Children of Kings upon it. The Fiddler covers them with a cloak, and lays the broken crown thereon. "A kingly grave above valley and stream," he says dreamily, "I will sing them their last song, and play the last melody on my fiddle. Then I will break it in two, that all may remember their story. So, though they are dead they will live for ever in your hearts." The Woodcutter and the Broom-maker kneel, with bared heads, as the children depart, carrying the bodies of the Royal Children. "Children of Kings," they chant, "Children of Kings." The Fiddler slowly follows them, as the sun sets. "Children of Kings" sounds faintly from the distance. The curtain slowly falls.

LA HABANERA

Lyric drama in three acts. Music and text by Raoul Laparra.

CAST: Pilar—Soprano. A betrothed girl—Soprano. A little girl—Contralto. Ramon—Bass. Pedro—Tenor. An old man—Bass. Blind men, gossips, servants, neighbours. Time, the present. Place, a town in Spain. First performance, Paris, 1908.

ACT I. The great hall of a ruined palace, now inhabited by peasants. It is a fête day. A high window opens on a square, where comes the murmur of a gay, animated crowd, and the sound of bells. Tables stand here and there, with dishes and remains of food. Near the window four men are seated drinking, and teasing a girl, who runs away, with shrill screams. They are half drunk already, and are making gross comments upon the passersby. Near the staircase, which leads to the street sits Ramon, leaning on a table in a dejected attitude. He is drinking heavily, and from time to time looks toward the staircase, or taps his foot on the floor, as if waiting for someone. The four boon companions sing a ribald song (Quartette: "Thirty-one others to love"). One of them goes out on the balcony, and seeing someone he knows, calls out "Pilar! Pilar!" At the name Ramon starts. A girl's voice answers saucily. "Pretty girl that," the fellow declares, and his friends agree, talking in their familiar way of Pilar's attractions. They envy Pedro, who has that day married the girl. "Lucky fellow, eh," they agree, winking and nudging each other. They would give all they have to be in his place. As the wine flows freely their comments become free also. At last they rise unsteadily, and lurch down the stairs into the street. As the last of the four passes Ramon, he rallies him on his low spirits. "Cheer up, my boy," he says thickly. "Sing and be gay while you are young." He staggers down the stairway, humming "Thirty-one others to love." Left alone, Ramon closes the window with a bang, and bursts into a passion of grief (Ramon: "They say to me, sing"), saying that all joy is gone from him, for his brother Pedro has married Pilar, the woman he loves. He would far rather die than suffer the pangs of a living death. He draws his knife (Ramon: "Farewell, my home"), but overcome with horror at his thought lays it on the table, and goes to the window. Hearing the merry crowd outside, he takes heart. Pilar's voice calls "Ramon! Ramon!"

She enters gaily, in the dress of a rustic bride. "Ramon, I am going to dance the Habanera with my dear bridegroom," she says. "You, too, must find a partner." "I have one," says Ramon grimly, glancing at the knife. Surprised, she throws her arms around his neck, calling out merrily: "Ramon has a sweetheart." Ramon strains her tightly to him, stifling her protests with kisses. "You will kill me," she cries. "Be still," he mutters. Pedro is coming up the stairs, full of joy over his new found happiness. He is almost boastful. "Ramon has a bride," says Pilar, to cover her agitation. "Who is she?" asks Pedro, happily. "She is named Flesh and Blood, and Mine," returns Ramon, in excitement. (Ramon: "Her name is Flesh.") "And you love her?" "Yes, yes, more than you have ever loved." "No, not more than Pedro loves me," interrupts Pilar. Pedro, amused, puts all sorts of questions to Ramon about this wonderful love of his, and Ramon says he loves her more than dancing or a horse race, or even than his redemption, and hope of salvation. Unable to look upon the happiness of his brother and Pilar, he goes halfway downstairs, then returns, drawn and haggard, and flings himself on a bench, like a hurt animal. Pedro sings tenderly of his love for Pilar. (Pedro: "I know that I love her.") A band (The Rondalla) is heard outside. "Let us stay here," says Pedro, coaxingly. "No," cries Pilar merrily, "we must first dance the Habanera." She runs out, laughing coquettishly. Pedro is about to follow her, when Ramon bars his way. From the street, Pilar calls "Pedro! Pedro!" amid the shouts of the crowd. (Chorus: "Habanera! Habanera!") Pedro thinks his brother must be drunk, and becomes exasperated. They struggle fiercely, and at last Pedro escapes, but as he descends the staircase, Ramon strikes at him in the back with his knife. He falls in a heap on the stairs, and Ramon starts back in horror, but Pedro raises himself up, and reaching the room confronts Ramon. Pilar, without, complains of Pedro's neglect. The four boon companions comment upon her beauty, and Pedro suddenly realises why Ramon has stabbed him. He is about to die. (Pedro: "Ramon, Pilar, know ye that in a year I shall return.") He dies. Ramon takes to flight. Pilar returns to find her bridegroom lying dead. (Chorus without: "What happiness.") She shrieks loudly for help, and falls upon the body, embracing it. The crowd enters, and the old father of Pedro and Ramon, who is almost blind, is led in by a little girl. He is incredulous, until he has felt Pedro's wound and the wet blood stains his hands. The neighbours crowd around in morbid curiosity. Ramon comes in, supported by two men, and apparently heart-broken. The music is hushed, and all fall upon their knees. (Chorus: *"Ora pro nobis."*) The little girl screams shrilly. The father calls upon Ramon to avenge the crime. (Duet; The Father, Pilar: "Ramon, if thou art indeed my son.") He stretches out his hand, stained with Pedro's blood. Ramon swears that he will find the murderer. Curtain.

Act II. After an entr'acte, indicating Ramon's sorrow and remorse, the scene changes to the court of an ancient dwelling. It is surrounded by two tiers of galleries, on which people are sitting. It is moonlight. Pilar, Ramon and the old father are together, the father sleeping, the others sad and distrait. On an upper gallery, a betrothed pair are courting. Ramon silently recalls Pedro's promise that he would return in a year. The anniversary is to-morrow. "No, to-day," says the old man. (The Father: "Alas, my son, and Pedro has not been avenged.") Ramon declares he cannot sleep for thinking of it. (Ramon: "Speak not, my father.") To-morrow, he suggests, he and Pilar will go and place flowers on Pedro's grave. Beggars are singing in weird chorus outside. (Chorus of blind men: "My hand is not white. Beware! Beware!") Loud knocking is heard and a demand for alms. To Ramon's horror, he hears the voice of Pedro, calling: "Ramon! Ramon." The blind men are heard, plaintively weeping. "Do not open the door!" cries Ramon, pressing against it. Pedro calls again. "It is an owl hooting," says Pilar. "No, it is he," replies Ramon, desperately. He stands back, and a servant opens the door, and reports that three blind men stand outside. They enter, wearing long black capes, and clinging together uncertainly. The servant leads them across the court to procure food. Ramon is somewhat reassured, but as he turns toward the door, he sees Pedro's spirit, and starts back in terror. He wears the same garb as the three blind men, and like them carries a guitar under his arm.

"Do you see him?" says Ramon, in a choked voice to Pilar. "He went through the closed door." The ghost follows the blind men to the gallery, and leans against a pillar. "How many men do you see there?" Ramon carelessly asks a child. "One, two, three," she says, counting, and runs off frightened by Ramon's face. "He is making an X with his hands," shrieks Ramon. The neighbours, who have gathered round, squabble as to the meaning of this sign, which in different provinces, has a different signification. The father at last suggests that it is the Habanera. Pedro's ghost smiles, Ramon tells them. The music strikes up. "Oh, not that tune," cries Ramon in agony, for it is the one played the night of the murder. "How he loved him!" murmur the neighbours. Pedro, heard only by Ramon, says sternly: "Before you desecrate my tomb to-morrow, you must tell Pilar all." The dance begins. Pilar whispers to Ramon of her love for him, and the betrothed pair make soft eyes at each other, the maiden coquettishly reproving the audacious speeches of her lover. Ramon makes false steps in his agitation and dismay. Pedro speaks again: "If you do not tell her," he says grimly, "I will take Pilar into the grave with me." Ramon stops dancing. "Jesus!" he exclaims. The music takes a weird note. "What is wrong with the blind men?" asks Pilar. "God knows," says the miserable Ramon, in despair, and the curtain falls.

ACT III. There have been two entr'actes, the second of which describes the night of horror spent by Ramon after the visit of the ghost. Ramon and Pilar are now in a cemetery, surrounded by galleries containing tombs. In the centre are graves of the humbler class. Mourners, dimly seen in the gloom, are praying among the graves. It is autumn, just before sunset, and the leaves are changing color. Ramon and Pilar are seated beside the grave of Pedro, at the head of which is a wooden cross, bearing his name in red letters. Pilar is placing flowers upon the grave, on which flares a lighted candle. (Pilar: "When we are old, dear shade.") A funeral procession winds through the cemetery. (Chorus, sung softly throughout the act: "*Ego sum resurrectionem.*") Ramon resolves to tell Pilar at once (Ramon: "This night, he has told me"), following Pedro's mandate. Pilar thinks his mind is un-hinged, and soothes him with gentle words, as he becomes more and more agitated and despairing. (Pilar: "Stay, I can console thee by my tenderness.") She says to cheer him, that in no time at all he will be in good spirits once more, and they will dance the Habanera again together. Ramon tries to make her understand by every means he can think of. In dismay he sees that the sun is setting in a crimson glare, and hears the voice of Pedro, humming the Habanera. Looking at Pilar, he sees that she has sunk upon the grave, as if sleeping. Ramon tries to rouse her, but she only says, "I must sleep." He shrieks in her ear. "It is I! It is I who am the murderer," but she makes no reply. A storm rises, great clouds cover the sky, and the wind begins to blow. The lights on the graves flicker, and go out one by one, and a flame seems to envelope Pilar. Suddenly all is dark; no light anywhere. Ramon has covered his face with his hands. When he looks up he sees Pilar lying motionless upon the grave. He shakes her violently, calling her name aloud, then tries to raise her up but cannot lift her. Shivering with fear, he envelopes himself in his mantle to shut out the sight, and stands trembling. His reason has fled. "No one will ever know," he says in a strange voice. Taking his guitar, he plays a few bars of the fateful Habanera, then throws down the guitar, which breaks, and rushes away into the darkness. The gate of the cemetery clangs behind him. Curtain.

LA PRINCESSE D'AUBERGE

(Queen of the Inn)

Lyric drama in three acts and four scenes.   Music by Jan Blockx.   Text by Gustave Lagye.

CAST: Bluts, an Innkeeper—Bass.   Rita, his daughter—Soprano.   Katelyne, Bourgeoise of Brussels—Contralto. Merlyn, her son—Tenor.   Reinhilde, adopted daughter of Katelyne—Mezzo-Soprano.   Marcus, a friend of Merlyn—Baritone.   Rabo, a Smith—Baritone.   Three sisters of Rita, two friends of Bluts, an old peasant, a young peasant, a *bourgeois*, a singer, a neighbour.   Townspeople, peasants, artists, boon companions, maskers, soldiers, populace.   Time, about 1750, under the Austrian rule.   Place, Brussels.   First performance, Brussels, October, 1896.

ACT I.   A cross-road, near the great square of Brussels. Rita's inn at the right.   Autumn, just before dawn. Rabo, a brawny smith, slumbers upon the inn doorstep. Peasants pass by, driving carts filled with vegetables, and drawn by donkeys, horses or dogs.   (Chorus of peasants: "The night is gone, the day returns.")   They are hastening to the market.   One young peasant points to Rabo, asking if he is dead.   "No, only asleep!" is the reply. "But is not that the house of Rita?"   "Yes, plague take the sorceress!   Come away quickly, lest she ensnare you. Hers is a devil's beauty!"   He drags away the curious youth, who would fain stop and stare.

Rabo awakens, with a huge yawn, and looks about him, astonished.   He must have been very drunk the night before.   He remembers that he tried to get into the inn, but knock as he might was not admitted.   "Strange, that!" he smiles at the recollection.   A young bourgeois comes out, his face concealed in a mantle; stumbling over the smith, who attacks him.   The inn door shuts with a bang.   Rabo accuses his adversary of having visited Rita, and the bourgeois tries to pacify him with gold, which he refuses.   Rabo furiously pounds on the door (Rabo: "Ho,

Rita! It is I, Rabo!"). Receiving no reply, he curses her roundly, and departs.

Reinhilde enters, bearing a prayer book (Reinhilde: "Oh, dark and sombre dream"); she denounces the wicked Rita, who she believes has stolen her betrothed, Merlyn. Marcus joins her, declaring his hopeless passion. (Marcus: "Reinhilde here, always dreaming.") She avows her undying love for his friend, but Marcus declares that his own love for her is the greater, since Merlyn looks upon her only as a sister. (Marcus: "Love alone is earthly law.") Reinhilde tells him he is a false friend. (Reinhilde: "My heart cannot change its love.") As the Angelus rings, she begs him to leave her, but he follows her into the church. (Chorus behind scenes: "Joyous song! Hail to the lovely Rita.") A crowd of young men enter, painters, musicians and poets, followed by a curious crowd of townspeople. They noisily acclaim the beauty of Rita, the pearl of Brussels, and celebrate the joys of youth. A lad sings, accompanying himself on the guitar (Solo: "Rita, the sun of ravished hearts"), begging her to awaken and come forth that they may gaze upon her beauty. The crowd throws flowers upon her balcony.

The window opens, and Rita appears half clad, followed by her three sisters. (Carillon) She picks up the flowers, kissing them. (Rita: "A fête, a fête indeed.") The crowd joins in the song, (Rita: "Ring out, O carillon!") She invites the crowd to drink at the inn, saying that since to-day is her birthday wine shall flow freely. The crowd goes into the inn pell mell, by doors and windows. Day dawns. The drunken Bluts and his boon companions are heard singing behind the scenes. (Bluts: "Rub-a-dub-dub; we drink to the morning.") They enter unsteadily, holding each other up. Bluts is astonished to see the inn door open, and a crowd of merry-makers within. He straightens up with dignity, telling the people what an excellent father he is. With this boast he stumbles, pull

ing the others down, and the three are passed into the inn
through the window by the laughing crowd.   Enter Merlyn and Marcus (Marcus: "Love calls thee in vain").
The latter tries to entice Merlyn into the inn, but the
youth shakes his head (Merlyn: "No, a higher art appears").   Marcus still persists (Marcus: "I know of other
victories"), singing of the wondrous flame of love.   Merlyn, only half understanding, looks at his friend with an
expression almost of fear.

The gay throng come out of the inn, drinking cups held
high above their heads, and last of all come Rita and
her sisters, bearing more wine.   The crowd eagerly surrounds the young girls (Chorus: "The glass resounds").
The passers-by stop to look at the strange scene, and the
townspeople, rudely awakened, open their windows, and in
night attire peer angrily forth.   (Rita: "Long live the
follies of youth"; Chorus of protesting citizens: "Foolish
and shameless girls.")   Marcus, eulogizing Rita's beauty,
takes Merlyn by the hand, and leads him to her, saying
lightly, "Here is the Puritan!"   She salutes him ironically, as the crowd presses about them.   Rita feigns shy-
ness at first, but soon approaches Merlyn with an alluring air.   (Rita: "I am the child of liberty.")   He draws
back and his lofty bearing impresses the crowd.   Rita's
face darkens, but she soon resumes her song, smiling
coquettishly (Rita: "What, do I frighten you?")   As
she draws nearer, he steps back.   (Rita: "Stay, what
poet has not sung?")   Still smiling, she invites him to
drink from her glass, throwing one arm around his neck.
He stands mute, and embarrassed, then suddenly succumbs to her allurement (Merlyn: "I am like a child"),
embracing her passionately.   All drink to the loves of
the young pair.   Enter Rabo, threatening.   Bluts and
his friends come to the window, unsteadily.   The scan-
dalised bourgeois protest, as the chorus swells louder
and louder, and Marcus exults over his success.   Rabo
frantically denounces Rita.   The three sisters sing of

love and wine. (The three sisters: "Pour the wine.")
Curtain.

ACT II. A room in Katelyne's house, with a large bay
window, looking on the square; a harpsichord; a table
with books and papers. After a prelude, Katelyne deplores the downfall of Merlyn (Katelyne: "Noon sounds
from the tower"), who now passes all his time in carousing.
With Reinhilde, who enters, she discusses the unhappy
state of affairs, declaring that her son has certainly gone
mad, and is breaking both their hearts. Reinhilde says
she will make one last plea to him. A carnival chorus is
heard behind the scenes (Chorus: "Holà Holà! Traderi,
Traderi, Tradera!"). Reinhilde sits down quietly with a
book; Katelyne has departed. Enter Merlyn, dishevelled,
and with disordered hair. Without seeing Reinhilde, he
seats himself at the table, restlessly moving the papers
about. Nothing but bills, it appears! (Merlyn: "No
more money, nothing more.") He regrets his wasted
time and strength, aimlessly trying to write. Reinhilde
sings softly of their love in the old days, now gone (Reinhilde: "Little mother, loved by all"). Merlyn rises, and
goes toward her. She bursts into tears, and Merlyn,
realising that she has been repeating one of his own
poems, gently asks her why she weeps. She begs him to
return to the old days (Reinhilde: "Merlyn, thy mother
lives beside thee"). In a passionate outburst she bids
him remember his great gift of genius, and forget his
unworthy dream of passion. Much moved, Merlyn embraces her (Merlyn: "Evil was sleeping within me"), telling her that his true self turns always to her. The crowd
without sing gaily of pleasure. Merlyn opens the window, and with Reinhilde gazes out at the throng of
masques in the square. He assures her that he will stay
at home that day, and departing, she throws him a kiss.
Bluts, half drunk, enters the room, and Rabo is seen at the
window in the rear. Reinhilde frowns, and Merlyn is
uncertain what to do. (Bluts: "Door open. No in-

trusion? Here I am.") He demands money for a gambling debt of Merlyn's. Reinhilde, producing the money,
tries to make him leave, and failing goes sorrowfully to
church. Merlyn, in a passion, turns the two men out
(Merlyn: "Leave the house, you two").

Left alone, he is melancholy and remorseful (Merlyn:
"Oh, shame, how low have I fallen!"), resting his head on
his hands. (Merlyn: "O thou bright day.") Once more
the carnival music is heard (Chorus: "Carnival returns
again.") Marcus appears, regarding Merlyn with mockery, and slily asking if his purse is empty. Merlyn
seizes him by the arm (Merlyn: "Marcus, thou hast
taught me life"), and tells him of his new emotions.
Marcus craftily arouses his jealousy by declaring that
Rita has a new lover (Marcus: "For you, too delicate a
morsel is Rita"). Merlyn seizes him by the throat, and
stung by his taunts cries out that Rita may go where she
will, to the devil if she likes! Rita, dressed as Flora enters with her sisters and their friends in carnival guise.
They kiss their hands to Merlyn, who starts back in surprise (Rita and chorus: "Upon this day all laugh at
love"), and with gay mockery beg him to come with them.
Rita says that since she is Flora, he must be Zephyrus, her
lover. She suddenly throws over his shoulders a blue
mantle, and crowns him with a wreath of violets; then
stands back in pretended rapture at his beauty. He succumbs once more to her enchantment, recklessly breaking
into a mad love song (Merlyn: "O potent bonds of ardent
love.") Rita carries him off in triumph, as Katelyne and
Reinhilde return. The two women weep sadly, and Reinhilde, going to the window looks out sorrowfully at the
gay, pleasure-mad town (Reinhilde: "O God of pity, still
I live"), denouncing Merlyn for his broken faith.
Marcus enters unobserved. He points out Merlyn's un-
worthiness, and offers her his whole heart, but once more
she refuses. (Marcus: "Merlyn, too late; the mire has
stifled thee!")

Change of scene. Square with a joyous crowd singing and dancing; some are masked. (Chorus: "Holà! Holà! Traderi, Traderi, Tradera!") Boys and girls march ahead of the procession, which is announced by heralds. Merlyn and Rita recline in a chariot, covered with flowers. (Rita, Merlyn, Chorus: "Hymn to Love.") Rabo shakes his fist at them from the street. The crowd cheer them wildly, and the curtain falls.

ACT III. A room in Rita's inn, richly furnished in the Flemish style. Enter Rita, complaining that although it is three o'clock, no one has come to drink at the inn that day; probably they are all asleep after the orgy of the night before. Rabo enters, reproaching Rita for her inconstancy, and swearing vengeance, as usual. She laughs scornfully, yawning in his face. "That's all very well now," cries the smith, "but there was a time when you were very glad of the money I foolishly wasted on you. Now I am ruined, so good-bye is the word." She orders him out, saying hotly that nobody wants a wild tiger for a lover. He declares that she has instead made a dog of him, and dogs can bite. The three sisters, who have been listening to this quarrel, come into the room to make a diversion, and Rabo goes off in a rage. The girls inform Rita that she is a fool to make an enemy of an ill-tempered wretch like Rabo; let him hang on and spend his money, if he has any. But no, she must rule everybody of course; that is her way! She tells them to mind their own affairs; she knows what she is doing. And anyway, who is the real queen of the inn, and the moneymaker for all? The girls leave the room in high dudgeon, unable to answer this statement. Rita laughs triumphantly, as Katelyne enters with Reinhilde. She introduces herself as Merlyn's mother (Katelyne: "I am the mother of Merlyn"), asking if Rita knows where he is. "So lovely a face," she asserts, "must surely mean kindness and sympathy!" Rita answers her with careless insolence, saying, "Anyone is free to come in here." She

is not accountable for all the guests that come and go.
How should she know where Merlyn is? Reinhilde denounces the heartless girl. (Reinhilde: "No, more, my
mother.") Rita is highly amused at this, and laughs
merrily as the women hurry away from the inn. (Rita:
"Poor thing, she's mad!")

Shutting the door after them, she pours herself a glass of
wine, and turning sees Merlyn standing beside her, heavy-
eyed and with an air of dissipation (Merlyn: "Hullo, you
little rascal"). He greets her familiarly. Rita smiles
at him (Rita: "Love unties all bonds"). Five artists file
in, and Merlyn calls for wine. (Merlyn: "A bumper for
every good fellow.") They drink Rita's health. Enter
Marcus, who, deriding Merlyn, ironically begs Rita to
sing a song Merlyn had composed for her (Rita: "The
birdling sings to his mate a song"), which she does amid
loud applause. Merlyn calls loudly for more wine, saying
he will pay to-morrow. "Yes, when you win the prize,"
cries Marcus, mockingly. Bluts, behind the scenes, trolls
forth an old Flemish song (Bluts: "In autumn, after a
shower, the streams grow high"), accompanied by six
wandering musicians. He looks in on the revellers, but
is hurried off to bed by the old servant, with scant ceremony. The young people plan a dance; the old servant
seizes an unwilling partner. There are not enough girls
to go round, so the men dance together.

Rabo appears with five companions, rough men like himself. They lean on the bar, and call for wine, Rabo
jealously watching Rita, who is dancing with Merlyn.
Not being served immediately they pound on the table
with their drinking cups, and becoming angry break everything within reach, cursing the dancers meanwhile. As
Rabo rises shouting: "We'll do the dancing now," the
music stops. Merlyn and his friends advance toward the
intruders, armed with chairs and tables. Rabo and his
companions draw knives. The women try uselessly te
make peace. Rita orders all to leave the inn, saying im-

periously: "I am the mistress here." Rabo insults her
(Rabo: "You were mine for long!") and glaring savagely
at Merlyn calls him a coward.   He throws down his knife
at Merlyn's feet (Rabo: "Defiance and death"), seizing
another for himself from one of his companions.   Rita
tries to interpose, but the crowd votes for the fight.   The
two men brandish their knives.   Merlyn wounds Rabo in
the arm, and with a savage cry, the smith, leaning forward
stabs him in the breast.   Merlyn totters and falls.   Rita
rushes at Rabo, and violently pushes him back.   Merlyn's
friends lay him on the floor, and the girls bring a pillow
for his head.   Rabo, cursing Rita, threatens to kill her
too.   Marcus hurries out to summon help.   The guard
arrives, and as Rabo surrenders himself joyous acclama-
tions are heard in the street.   Merlyn's poem has won the
prize.   Katelyne and Reinhilde enter seeking the victor.
His friends crowd around him trying to hide him from his
mother.   Rita veils her face.   But it is too late; the
women have seen all.   (Katelyne, Reinhilde: "Thou, thou,
wounded and bleeding.")   The townspeople enter with
palms and bouquets for the victorious poet.   Merlyn, dying, looks wildly around him for Rita, who is overcome
with grief and remorse.   His mother and Reinhilde are
bending over him (Merlyn: "You, dear angels.")   Katelyne kisses his forehead in farewell.   Reinhilde bitterly
denounces Rita (Reinhilde: "Sorrow to thee, accursed
one!"), and advances as if to kill her.   On a last chorus
of horror and dismay, the curtain falls.

LA WALLY

Lyric Opera in four acts.   Music by Catalani.   Text by
Luigi Illica, based upon a novel by Wilhelmine Von Hil-
lern.
CAST: Wally — Soprano.   Walter — Mezzo-soprano.
Hagenbach—Tenor.   Gellner—Baritone.   Stromminger

—Bass.   Afra — Mezzo-soprano.   Maidens, Guides,
Hunters, Villagers. Time, early 19th century. Place,
Switzerland. First performance, Turin, 1892.

Act I. A square in Hochstoff. Stromminger's house
to the left; to the right the peasant's cottages. A bridge
in the background, connecting two high cliffs, between
which flows the river Ach. Mountains in the distance.
Stromminger is celebrating his birthday; and his friends
drink his health. A target shows the prowess of Gellner,
Stromminger's old friend. Girls and hunters are dancing
together, while the older people look on. Stromminger
is in a jolly mood, having drunk deeply. He congratulates Gellner on making a good shot, and the crowd applaud. "They say," says Stromminger, "that at Sölden,
there is a boastful fellow, who declares that our targets
are too easy." "Ah, Hagenbach!" replies Gellner. "Yes,
the same. I knew his father," continues Stromminger,
becoming silent as he sees that Gellner does not fancy the
subject. "But to the devil with him! Your health,
friend Gellner!" They drink. Walter, a zither-player,
enters looking about him. "You are seeking someone?"
asks the curious Stromminger. "Yes, your Wally."
"Who can tell where she is?" laughs Stromminger. "On
the mountain, or by the stream, or perhaps swinging on
the branch of a tree. Why seek her?" "We sing together," says the boy earnestly. "A lovely song about
the Edelweiss. It has yodling in it." "Sing it, Walter,"
coax the girls, and he complies. (Walter: "One day, toward Mount Murzoll.") It is the story of a beautiful
maiden, who climbed the mountain, because she had always loved it. But when she reached the summit, and
asked that she herself might have the alluring beauty
of the mountain, pale phantoms appeared to her, and
engulphed her in an avalanche. But amid the snow, she
is still seen in the guise of a flower—the beautiful Edelweiss.

"How beautiful, but how sad!" cry the people, impressed.

"Wally composed it," says Walter, triumphantly. "So sorrowful a song?" asks her father in surprise, but Gellner mutters, "I knew it! I knew it! She herself is as cold as the snow." The hunters' horns resound cheerily, and a band of hunters come into view, headed by a youth with bold eyes, who carries a bear-skin wound round his gun. This is the famous Hagenbach. (Hunters: "Hunter, return.") Crossing the bridge, they approach the village. Hagenbach shows his trophy in triumph. "Only one shot!" he cries. "You will get the prize," shout the villagers, "Twenty-five golden florins." He boastfully relates the story of the hunt to an admiring audience (Hagenbach: " 'Tis not the gold"), telling of the terrific strength of the bear, and how he had overcome him, after a fierce struggle. (Hagenbach: "Oh, thou brown king, why to the forest dark.") They cheer him lustily. Stromminger begins to grumble in an undertone. "What did you say?" asks Hagenbach, sharply. "That other men beside you do things, but do not talk about them." "Who, for example?" says the hunter. "I, Stromminger," shouts the old man, striking an attitude, and the hunters laugh uproariously. The old man is infuriated. "Your father," he says hotly, "knows all about Stromminger." "You lie," declares Hagenbach, angrily. Stromminger rushes toward him, but is overcome.

The people come to Stromminger's defence, and the hunters protect Hagenbach, who shouts loudly, "I *will* be the first." At this moment a girl, fancifully dressed, and wearing an edelweiss wreath, pushes her way through the crowd. She has dark, fiery eyes, and walking up to Hagenbach, takes him by the shoulder, "Who dares to harm my father?" she demands. Hagenbach turns to confront her, but is abashed when he sees a girl standing before him. "He was the offender!" he asserts. She looks tenderly into his eyes, recognising him. "Get out, braggart," storms her father. Hagenbach gazes curiously at Wally, but is dragged away by the hunters, who are offended. Stromminger jeers at them. Hagenbach curses him, but Wally interposes. (Wally: "Do not speak so!") The villagers among themselves whisper that Stromminger is drunk. Wally looks after the hunters, while her father and Gellner talk together. Gellner declares that Wally loves Hagenbach. "Can this be true?" muses the old man. "Yes, I saw that she looked strangely at him." Gellner voices his despair. "Be not afraid! He shall not have her," answers Stromminger, lightly. "Ah," seeing Gellner's face, "you love her!" Going to the door he calls, "Wally!" and when she comes tells her that Gellner loves her, and she will be his bride within a month. He goes out, leaving them together, and the girl begs Gellner to release her, but he cannot give her up (Gellner: "Love, like a wave.") She speaks to him sharply, and he weeps. "I will never love you, never," she cries, with determination. (Wally: "Never! Never! I am free as the light.") Stromminger returns to give them his blessing, but hearing his daughter's words, exchanges it for a curse, declaring that he will drive her from her home, if she does not obey. (Stromminger: "Do you see? Now wanes the day.") The Ave Maria tolls. Wally is still defiant. (Wally: "Well, then, I will go.") "Forward!" she cries bravely. She meets the villagers on their way to church. "Where are you going, Wally?" they call to her, gaily. "My father has driven me from home," says the girl proudly, "I would not marry Gellner." "But where can you go?" "To the mountains," she answers. (Wally: "I want to go with the setting sun.") Walter joins her, and they mount the mountain-side together, as the villagers bid them farewell. They sing the Edelweiss Song, as they climb, but are soon lost to sight in the darkness. Curtain.

Act II. A square at Sölden. In the rear a church, to which a stairway leads. The square is prepared for a dance, and decorated with flowers for a festival, that of

Corpus Domini. The crowd is gaily dressed in the Tyro-
lese costume. Soldiers are drinking before the inn, and
joking with Afra, the Innkeeper. Gellner stands gloomily apart. It is a year since Wally's departure. (Chorus:
"In the midst of the crowd.") The girls are laughing
and flirting with the young men of the town. "See, there
is Walter!" calls a soldier. They scoff at him, asking if
his mistress gave him these fine clothes. He answers
angrily. Hagenbach sits down at a table, and Afra
greets him joyfully. "Is Wally coming?" ask the young
men. "Yes, she is enjoying herself, now poor old Stromminger is dead," declares a soldier. Gellner looks at Hagenbach. "Wretched woman. She is only coming for
him," he mutters. "I do not want her," says Hagenbach
indifferently. "People say she has never been kissed,"
continues the soldier. "I might dance with her," replies
Hagenbach. Afra comes close to him, smiling. (Afra:
"No, you must not jest with love.") "I am not to be
caught," boasts the hunter. Walter says proudly, "And
neither is Wally." The crowd are enjoying the festival,
when Wally appears, in fine clothes, and wearing a beautiful pearl necklace. "What a beauty!" whisper the people.

She and her friends speak to Walter, and are welcomed
by the crowd. Wally, who is about to take a glass of
wine, puts down the cup when she sees Hagenbach. The
young men crowd around her. "I will dance with all
of you for the fun of dancing," is her answer. "Even
the dance of the kiss?" asks a soldier, impudently. "He
who tries to kiss me will find it no easy task!" the girl
declares. (Wally: "So far I have been kissed by none.")
She falls into a reverie; but seeing Afra whispering to
Hagenbach, her face darkens. "How could anyone help
trying?" she says, sarcastically. "And if there were such
a man?" asks the soldier. "He is the man for me!" is
the laughing reply. She strolls off with Walter, looking archly at Hagenbach, and then giving him the same

penetrating look, as when she saw him the year before.
"Come on, friends," says the soldier, "we all have a
chance."

The organ in the church sounds forth, and the villagers flock to Mass. Afra and Hagenbach separate.
He goes into the church, "That strange look once more!"
he says to himself. Wally and Walter are about to enter
also, when Gellner steps in front of them. "You?" exclaims Wally. "Yes, I." "When my father died you
did not come to me, and through you I was driven from
his roof. Now, I bid you leave me," says the girl.
"What should I want from you?" sneers Gellner, then
suddenly cries out: "I love you! I love you!" "Thus it
is in life," declares Wally, "we hate those who love us!
Sometimes it is the other way, but always in love tears and
laughter are close together." (Wally: "My grandmother
sang a song to me.") She laughs mockingly. "I am
happy to-day," she declares. "Once you were wild and
loved to be among the mountains. Now you dress grandly,
and are seen at the festivals," says Gellner. "You are running after love." "No, no!" the girl interrupts. "You
lie," he asserts. "I know your heart." He informs he
that he himself had told her father that she loved Hagenbach. Wally fiercely curses him. "To torture you shall
be my pleasure," she cries savagely. Gellner foolishly
continues to entreat. (Gellner: "Slave of your lovely
eyes.") She confesses her love for Hagenbach, and Gellner tells her his wedding day with Afra is set. He laughs
as she turns pale. "Ask Afra," he suggests. Wally is
overcome, remembering Afra's look as she stood beside
Hagenbach, and tries to choke back a sob. Gellner hums
the song she has sung to him (Gellner: "My grandmother
sang a song to me.") "They are not married yet," she
cries angrily, striking the table with her hand. Afra
hurries toward her, asking if she desires anything. She
throws the wine pitcher on the ground spilling the wine
on her clothes. "Such swash is only fit for your lovers,"

she shrieks, beside herself. Afra begins to cry. The people crowd around them, asking what has happened. "Nothing!" says Wally contemptuously. "Don't cry. I know how to make a maidservant stop weeping." She throws a coin upon the ground. Someone passes quickly in front of her, and picking up the money, throws it to some travelling musicians. "The heiress of Hochstoff desires a lively tune," he declares. "Long live Hagenbach!" cry the people. "Gellner was right," comments Wally ruefully, for Hagenbach now comforts Afra. "Come, let's dance!" suggest the young men. "Yes," answers Hagenbach, "but first let me wager that I will kiss Wally." "Done with you!" they shout joyously. The square now becomes a ballroom, and the musicians climb nimbly upon the tables. The older people seat themselves on benches, commenting upon everything. Hagenbach takes the feather from his hat and puts it on the other side, as a token that he need not keep his promise unless he chooses. Gellner observes this. Hagenbach asks Wally to dance. She accepts, and while they are dancing tells her he wishes to dance the famous Kiss Dance with her also. He asks her if she hates him. "How strange a fancy?" she answers. "I want to contend with you, and be conquered," he goes on. "Still more strange!" she says smiling. "Do you fear me?" he asks looking into her eyes. He hurries her off to the dance. (Song of the peasants: "Now the passionate song rushes through the air.") The excitement of the forced kisses gives zest to the dance. Walter is successful with his partner amid loud applause. Soon most of the dancers have stopped, but Wally and Hagenbach continue to dance. They seem unconscious of their surroundings and as they talk to each other, everyone is watching. "What, what!" says Hagenbach. "Tell me what you said." "To lean upon your breast, forget the world and God," murmurs Wally, as if under a spell. "Your heart is a Paradise," answers Hagenbach, astonished, "and I thought it empty and cold." "They said you hated me," confesses the girl. "No, no!" cries Hagenbach, "That has never been true. I swear it!" He tries to return to the dance, but turns pale, and cannot go on. Wally leads him on. "Stop!" he implores. "You have conquered me." "Why then did you say you would kiss me?" whispers Wally. "Why? Why? Because you are beautiful." (Hagenbach: "Why, you ask?") The soldier has told everybody about the bet, and there is a general interest in the outcome. The two now seem to be quarrelling, and at last Wally tells him she hears he is betrothed. "You are laughing at me!" declares Hagenbach. "Oh, no, no!" says Wally, almost crying. He suddenly kisses her passionately. "Wally. Wally, you are mine," he cries. She falls into his arms and he kisses her upon the lips. The crowd applauds; some laugh loudly. "Afra is avenged," they triumph. But Hagenbach had entirely forgotten the wager. "Why do they laugh?" asks Wally, anxiously, as the young men take Hagenbach off to the Inn. "You see?" sneers Gellner. "Was it only for revenge?" gasps Wally, staring ahead of her unseeing. But Hagenbach has turned his back, and her cup of sorrow is complete when the women of Sölden surround her jeering. "Let us go," says Gellner, pointing to Hagenbach, who is drinking heavily. "Nothing is better than a brimming flagon," shouts the soldier. "Health to Hagenbach." The others join in the toast. Wally gazes fixedly at Hagenbach, then lays her hand on Gellner's arm. "Do you still want me?" she says in a strained voice. "Always," he replies. She looks toward Hagenbach once more, and declares with bitter emphasis, "I want him dead!" Curtain.

Act III. The town of Hochstoff. The stage is divided in the centre. On the right is Wally's dwelling, showing the interior of her bedchamber. On the left is a road, with houses straggling along it. Wally is led into her room by Walter, who lights a lamp, then tells

her to keep up her courage. "You haven't seen Gellner?"
she asks. She takes off her necklace and lets down her
hair. Walter shakes his head sorrowfully. Gellner
comes from the darkness of the street, crosses it and
enters a house. The Soldier goes by singing drunkenly.
"Shall I stay?" says Walter. "No, dear Walter, I would
rather be alone!" He kisses her and goes out. Wally
sits listening, and trying to pray. At last she begins to
weep, and falls on her knees beside the bed. Gellner
comes out of the house, and passes the drunken soldier
(Soldier: "Always gay.") Waiting stealthily beside the
path, he speaks to him. "Well?" he asks eagerly. "I
stayed there a long time," the Soldier says thickly, "but
Hagenbach got away." Wally, within the house suddenly
gets up and begins to take off her clothes, feeling her
cheek, as if surprised that it is wet with tears. "Peace
nevermore," she murmurs. "Go on," says Gellner outside.
"I saw a man take the path beside the river," continues
the Soldier. "Hagenbach?" asks Gellner. "Yes, it was
he." "Hush! and then—" "He is no coward," declares
the Soldier, "to come to Hochstoff, when everyone desires
to avenge Wally." Gellner laughs. "What foolishness!
But who can say how things will turn?" He gives the
Soldier money. "Better not fall asleep here," he advises.
"No fear," laughs the drunken man. He goes off trying
to whistle.

"Hagenbach cannot be in Hochstoff," mutters Gellner. "The Soldier is drunk!" "But if—" he looks
about him fearfully, "if an accident—Wally is in
danger!" he cries out suddenly. He hurries down the
path, listening at every step. He crouches down as he
crosses the bridge, looking cautiously about him. He
puts out the lamp above the crucifix. The wind is blowing fiercely. Gellner waits silently in the darkness.
Hagenbach is seen stepping upon the bridge, walking uncertainly in the unfamiliar path. "The lamp is out," he
says, "but my love will guide me straight to Wally."

He is half way over the bridge, when Gellner leaps out of
the darkness, and hurls him into the river. He gives a
loud cry as he falls, and Gellner flees in terror. He is
about to enter his house, when he sees the light in Wally's
window, and runs lightly toward her house, knocking on
the window. Wally has been struggling with her love,
almost deciding to tell Gellner she had been mad.   (Wally:
"Youth with its amorous dreams.")   She herself will
warn Hagenbach. She looks out into the darkness and
sees that the lamp over the crucifix has gone out. She
has become calm, and is beginning to undress when she
hears the knocking. "It is Gellner," she says, terror-
stricken, and runs out. "He is dead!" whispers Gellner.
"Come and see for yourself."   "No, no!" gasps Wally, in
an agony. "Yes, it is true. I hurled him over the
bridge!"

Wally now flies at his throat, and drags him toward
the scene of his crime. Her purpose is to throw herself
and Gellner after Hagenbach, and thus avenge him.
They have nearly reached the bridge when a faint cry
is heard from below. Wally listens; the cry is repeated.
Pushing Gellner aside, she hurries down into the street,
knocking loudly at several doors. Windows and doors
are opened, and men and women half-dressed, and carrying torches peer forth curiously. "Help! There is a
man in the river," cries the girl, and armed with ropes
and ladders, the villagers crowd to the river bank. The
people of Sölden have also been aroused, and are seen
hurrying to the spot; Afra is among them. "Hasten!"
says Wally. As the party moves forward they are intercepted by the people of Sölden, who ask where Hagenbach is. No one answers. "He is murdered," wails
Afra, in tears. "No!" says Wally firmly. "He will be
restored to you!" Wally runs down the steep river bank
by a winding path, while the men hold torches. The
women fall on their knees in prayer. Wally shouts back
that Hagenbach is still alive. She attaches his body to

a rope that has been let down, then ties herself to the rope and they are slowly drawn up.   The ropes are untied, and Wally stands on the cliff beside Afra.   She is in a state of exaltation from the tension she has been through.   "He is saved, Afra," she cries aloud.   "Through the mercy of God, by my hand.   He is yours and I give you also my house and lands, for ever !"   She kneels beside Hagenbach, kissing him, in farewell, then says to the crowd, "I have given back the kiss he took in the dance."   The crowd applaud.   Curtain.

Act IV.   On the mountain.   Wally is seated on one of the highest peaks of the mountain, surrounded by snow and ice.   Walter is seen coming up the path, which is very steep and dangerous.   "Let us return, Wally," says the boy, "there is danger here."   He tries to cheer her, with talk of Christmas and a home-coming, but she will not listen.   She bids him leave her to her solitude, without home or friends.   She gives him her pearl necklace as a remembrance, and gently pushing him down the path despite his protests bids him farewell.   (Wally: "Ever my heart's deep sorrow pierces the snow with tears.")   She sings of her departed youth and joy.   Walter half way down the mountain sings the song of the Edelweiss.   (Walter: "From faraway came the wind.")   Wally takes up the strain in answer, saying first, "Oh, might I only be like the girl in the song, and meet so beautiful a death !"   (Wally: "Oh, snow, white daughter of God.")   She ends with a yodle of great beauty.   "Wally! Wally!" cries a voice far off in the distance.   The call comes nearer.   "Whose voice is that?" she asks in alarm.   She listens, but all is still.   "Wally!"   "It is the ice children!" she says, now terrified.   She puts her hands before her face to shut out the sight of their pallid faces and glassy eyes.   (Wally: "Already the dread cortège seems to advance.")   She falls to the ground, trembling.   Hagenbach mounts the path, using his iron-pointed stick.   He gently calls to Wally.   "Holy Virgin, 'tis he!" gasps the girl.   "Why

have you come?" "Can you ask?" he says simply.
(Hagenbach: "Far from you how long were the days.")
"Can I bear the music of his voice?" says the girl
brokenly. "I love you, Wally!" cries Hagenbach. He
tells her how he had mourned her, but now is happy, having found her again. The kiss in the dance, which she
thought an insult, had really declared his undying love.
(Hagenbach: "When you tormented me at Sölden.")   He
believes, he says, that God punished his sin by hurling him
into the abyss. "God!" answers Wally, hoarsely. "Not
God, but a man. He was told, I told him—'I wish to see
him dead.'" She is shaking with apprehension. "Can
you love me, even so?" she demands, then stands before
him with bowed head, awaiting her doom. "I love you!"
says Hagenbach tenderly. The lovers embrace, whispering happily to each other. Clouds gather, and a thick
mist envelopes them. The wind blows in increasing fury.
The lovers, completely engrossed dream of fair meadows.
and gardens full of flowers. Wally, suddenly looking up
sees that it is growing dark. "Oh, look!" she cries.
"The black storm is upon us," says Hagenbach, moving
off. "Leave me not!" cries Wally. He is groping his
way among the rocks. "I am trying to find the path," he
shouts back.

The wind blows more and more furiously, and strange
rumblings are heard. "I see him not," says Wally, but
he calls her name "Wally!" "I hate you," she shouts
back. "Have no fear," the voice says distinctly. "The
path leads over the rocks, and you—The Avalanche!" in
terrified accents, and a horrible crash is heard. Wally is
hurled aside, shrieking. She crawls weakly to the brink
of the precipice, formed by the avalanche, calling "Giuseppe! Do you hate me?" The silence seems to mock
her. "Death is there!" she declares weeping, and lies
motionless with horror, her hands before her eyes. Suddenly she springs to her feet, and standing beside the
abyss raises her arms to heaven. (Wally: "Oh, snow, fate

of glorious whiteness.") Then she throws herself over the precipice, and is lost to view. Curtain.

LE CHEMINEAU
(The Wayfarer)

Lyric drama in four acts. Music by Xavier Leroux. Poem by Jean Richepin.

CAST: Toinette—Dramatic Soprano. Aline, Maître Pierre's daughter—Soprano. Catherine—Soprano. The Wayfarer—Baritone. Toinet, son of Toinette—Tenor. François, husband of Toinette—Baritone. Maître Pierre —Bass. Martin—Tenor. Thomas, an Innkeeper, husband of Catherine—Baritone. Harvesters, peasants, children. Place, a small village in France. Time, the present. First performance, Opéra Comique, Paris, 1907.

ACT I. No overture. Scene, a forest glade, near the harvest field. The reapers are cutting the grain, aided by the rhythmic song of the Wayfarer. Toinette prepares the noonday meal for the men, over a fire laid on a heap of stones, near a great oak tree. In the background are seen fields, ripe with grain, vineyards, and a village in the distance. Far away is heard the voice of the Wayfarer (Wayfarer: "Jeannette goes forth to the fields"), in a quaint folksong. Toinette listens with a tender smile as he approaches. "He is the soul of the harvest," she declares. "Can it be that he really loves me?" François enters wearily, followed by the other reapers, who throw themselves on the ground, calling loudly for dinner; they eat with huge appetites, and quickly fall asleep. The music plays a soft slumber song.

Toinette speaks proudly to François of the Wayfarer's strength and prowess. "Yes," he replies drily, "when a sluggard gets to work, he always works well." She pouts, and he warns her to take little notice of the man; vagabonds like him are poor companions for young girls. He asks her to marry him; she shakes her head. "Because I am too old?" he demands, bitterly, "or because of this fly-by-night?" "It is true, I love him," says Toinette, impulsively. "It is but a fancy," declares François, "once married, you would soon forget him."

As they talk, the insistent music comes nearer, with its burden of the sad fate of a too trusting maiden. François returns to his work, with the prophecy, "That is what will happen to you!" Toinette is terror stricken. The Wayfarer enters with a light step, joking about the tired reapers, who have left him to drink alone, and steal a kiss, perhaps, from a pretty girl. He eagerly quaffs a drink, which Toinette offers, saying his throat must be dry. "Oh, no!" he says merrily. "Like the birds, I am used to singing." Maître Pierre, a rich and crafty farmer, enters with a hospitable greeting. François summons the men to work. The Wayfarer hastily snatches a crust of bread, and Toinette goes out. The farmer slily inquires how he had cured the white bull. The Wayfarer only laughs. "And my sheep, also?" "That is my business!" is the reply. He will not tell the tricks of his trade, but begins to whistle and sing. "Are you then a sorcerer, with secrets for sale?" persists Maître Pierre. "No, for I will give them freely to those I love." "Why not stay with me as head farmer!" cries the rich man, "I will pay you well." "Let me talk to Toinette, first," says the Wayfarer, laughing. Maître Pierre goes out muttering that she perhaps may be the twig to lime his bird on. The Wayfarer tries to kiss Toinette, but she says she has something grave to tell him. "Kiss me first!" "Ah," she cries, "like the wind, you will take my kisses, and go swiftly away. What I should choose is the peace of a home nest!" "Wild birds cannot settle down," he declares, "ask me anything but that." (Wayfarer: "I see myself with hobbled feet, like an old horse.") Toinette asks his pardon, saying she will go with him instead. (Toinette: "But lead me by the hand.") "My life is not the one for you," he cries, "weary days and nights with-

out rest; no bed to sleep on." "Ah, but the sweet spring
breeze in our faces," says the girl in ecstasy. The Wayfarer, fearing that he will give in, hurries back to his
work, crying out that he is late. Toinette happily makes
her plans to leave that night, and when Maître Pierre asks
if she is to wed her lover, proudly says, "Yes, indeed."
"We shall grow rich with his help," says the avaricious
farmer.

François presently returns, grumbling that the Wayfarer has not done all he agreed to do. "There he goes
now, sneaking off with his knapsack!" he says, pointing.
Toinette, heartbroken, attempts to follow, but is held
back by François. Beside herself, she cries aloud that
she has given herself to him. (Toinette: "I love him
guiltily, and without shame.") All believe her to be mad,
and restrain her. The curtain falls on the struggle, with
the Wayfarer's song echoing in the distance. Curtain.

ACT II. Interior of a poor and humble cottage. François, now Toinette's husband, reclines in an invalid's chair.
Toinette is busily ironing. A door looks into a courtyard.
The prelude indicates a quiet domestic scene, but with a
background of sorrow and unrest. (Toinette: "Always
with bowed head"; François: "At my age there is no more
hope.") François has lost heart because he can no longer
work. Toinette, to encourage him, reminds him that
Toinet, their son can do the work of two, and will help
them to keep the home which François has earned for
them, by his industry and thrift. François, cheered by
her words, goes on to say that he is troubled also on
Toinet's account. Once gay, he is now always sad; his
mother, too, he thinks, has a look of sorrow. "The reason? Something grave, no doubt!" Aline here enters,
weeping, and throws herself into Toinette's arms. François is surprised; Maître Pierre is his enemy. (Aline:
"Oh, pardon, but so much I suffer!") Her father, it
seems will not allow her to marry Toinet. François
grieves that they have kept things from him; he was ig-

norant that Toinet loved Aline. (Duet; Toinette, Aline:
"Why seek, my good husband.") Toinet enters unobserved, in deep distress, crying out that Maître Pierre has
insulted him, and has declared he would rather see Aline
dead than married to him. "Tell that to your parents,
above all to your mother," he had said. Toinette, terrified, is about to speak, when François stops her. "I alone
have the right to talk to this man," he announces. He
bids Aline tell her father he must explain his statement,
either in his own house, or that of François. They must
face each other, that is certain. Toinet and Aline go out
slowly, looking back from the threshold in farewell.
(Duet, Toinet, Aline: "Alas, our poor love, with broken
wings.") Aline throws her lover a kiss; he responds, and
they hurry away. Toinette cajolingly begs François to
avoid a quarrel; she will go to Maître Pierre. (Toinette:
"You must not do too much.") But the farmer is already on their threshold. "What have you to say?" he
demands brusquely. "Why are you so angry?" asks
François, quietly. "Thus one speaks to robbers." "You
have tried to steal my daughter," roars the farmer, "but
I will prevent it. I will tell all—all—do you hear, unless you leave the neighbourhood. François, overcome with
anger, orders Maître Pierre out, declaring that his son is
quite as good as the farmer's daughter. "Your son, indeed," cries the farmer, "you are far behind on town
talk." François, now suffering, informs him that Toinet
is indeed his beloved son. "I myself will tell him the
truth—that he is a bastard. Yes, a bastard!" shrieks the
farmer. François hangs his head, then makes an attempt
to reach his tormentor, and falls senseless. Maître
Pierre, now alarmed, runs out, and as Toinette screams
loudly for help, the curtain falls.

ACT III. Scene, an inn, with a hanging sign; table and
chairs outside. A cross-roads, with a sign-post. Fields
and a village in the distance. After a long prelude,
Martin and Thomas, the innkeeper, are discovered drink-

ing a friendly glass, served by Catherine. They speak of
the strange illness of François, and of Toinet's drunken
habits. Toinet enters, reeling; scarcely conscious where
he is. Catherine kindly bids him come in and rest; it will
be like home. He declares sadly that happiness has left
their roof (Toinet: "There, all is misery"), his father
in a living death, his mother always weeping, and he himself a wretched drunkard. Catherine leads him away, and
the two men surreptitiously wipe their eyes on their
sleeves, singing a jovial song to disguise their feelings.
(Martin, Thomas: "Thou art no longer gay.") Far
away is heard the Wayfarer's song. (Wayfarer: "Sing
my lad, and lass reply!") Thomas brightens up, and
calls to Catherine to bring wine. She is holding the
pitcher ready to pour, when the Wayfarer walks in; she
sees, however, by his dress that her pains are all for nothing. No money there! Thomas hails him, and he turns
his pockets inside out. The three turn their backs, but
undaunted, he sits down at the table, asking gaily, "How
much for the wine, and how much more for a kiss from the
hostess?"

Thomas is furious, but the vagabond mischievously
seizes the pitcher, and runs off with it. When Catherine hotly pursues, he seizes her around the waist, and
makes her dance. Martin, at a sign from him does the
same with Thomas. (Wayfarer; "Gather, oh gather, the
strawberry and the raspberry.") Embracing Catherine,
the Wayfarer returns the pitcher. All are now merry,
and Thomas is delighted to treat the Wayfarer, who has
brought his own good cheer. He drinks a long draught,
and Martin, suddenly recognizing him, nudges Thomas,
whispering in his ear. They remind him that twenty
years ago he had sung there with the reapers. He cannot
recall it, there are so many places, until Toinette's name
is spoken. He starts. "Ah, I remember now! There
was no girl like her." He springs to his feet, looking over
the country; then sinks into a reverie. (Wayfarer: "Oh,

how clear her image.") Being questioned, he replies gaily, but grows serious as he asks if Toinette is well and happy. They tell him of her marriage to François, whom he remembers, and of her son, Toinet. He is startled, but Catherine calls them to dinner. Catherine alone, looks in to see how Toinet is. (Catherine: "He sleepeth still, may God be praised!") Toinette comes running in, wildly calling "Toinet! Toinet!" Catherine kisses her, leading her to where the boy lies asleep on the floor. (Toinette: "Asleep upon the ground.") She sits down beside him; Catherine goes out sadly. The men appear, and the Wayfarer seats himself with a sombre air. The others whisper that he wishes to see Toinet. Catherine tells him of their troubles, but he replies at random. "Will he take counsel with the boy's mother?" she asks. He answers shortly "No." Telling him where the boy is, she leaves him to his reflections. In a few moments the Wayfarer goes hastily toward the door, but dreads to enter. (Wayfarer: "I am afraid to see him.") He picks up his hat and knapsack, which he has hung on the sign-post, and sets off rapidly, saying, "Wayfarer, onward!" but turns back.

With a whimsical look, he takes himself by the collar, and forcing himself toward the door opens it quickly. Toinette stands before him, frightened; she thinks she sees a ghost. He assures her he desires only to repair the misery he has wrought. (Toinette: "Ah, for this word so brave.") She grants her forgiveness, and hand in hand they approach their son. The Wayfarer says that since his rôle in life is to be always gay, and make others so, he will cheer his own boy. Half choked with sobs, he sings a joyous song. Toinet awakens, bewildered. Between laughter and tears, he embraces the boy. (Wayfarer: "Ah, what a fine fellow!") His absurd antics finally make Toinet laugh heartily. Delighted, he drags him off, followed by Toinette. (Wayfarer: "Sing, my lad, and lass reply.") Curtain.

Act IV. Scene as in Act II. Toinet, Aline, and
Toinette seat themselves at table, happy and united.
Toinette rises to arrange François's pillows, and Aline
asks who will watch over him during the midnight mass.
"I, to be sure," gaily cries the Wayfarer, entering, covered with snow. He sings of the joys of "the open road."
(Wayfarer: "Yes, but the snow falling is beautiful.")
Martin raps at the door, with the neighbours. All are
on their way to mass. (Chorus: "What is this?") The
young people begin to get ready, and quickly depart,
Toinette going last, with the lantern. She and the Wayfarer gaze lovingly after the young couple, and she reproaches him for his thought of leaving them. (Carillon.)
He muses over her words. (Wayfarer: "Alas, I feel that
she is right.") The lugnots (children of the poor) are
heard singing softly outside (Chorus: "Lugnots, lugnots, the wards of God"), asking for alms. The Wayfarer recalls his own sordid childhood ("Ah, through the
village go the little lugnots"); he, the homeless one, cannot become a bird in a cage. And yet—. He is interrupted by Maître Pierre, who has overheard. "Not if
your nest be soft?" he asks insinuatingly. The Wayfarer rises, indignantly. "Naturally enough, all the
neighbours speak of you and Toinette," continues the
farmer, but midnight strikes, and he has to go without
finishing his sentence. The Wayfarer is troubled. "They
say this!" he cries in anguish, "No Judas bread for me!"
At a feeble call from François, he hurries away to rebuild
the fire, talking brightly with the sick man. François,
begging him to sit beside him, says gently that he understands all. The Wayfarer should have a reward for his
sympathy and kindness. (François: "Without appearing
to, I know all.") Weeping, he takes from his finger his
espousal ring and gives it to the Wayfarer, who breaks
down completely. The lugnots are now before the door.
The Wayfarer gives them bread and meat. They come
into the house, and sing sweetly for the sick man. With

the few remaining sous of the Wayfarer, they depart, rejoicing. During this scene, the church music, and even the bells struck during the mass are plainly heard. The Wayfarer is deeply moved. He gazes at François, who is sleeping peacefully, and is near his end. (Wayfarer: "For thee, a happy Christmas.") No such death for a vagabond like himself! His passing will be lonely, with naught but the wind for a covering. (Carillon.) He opens the door, and sees the villagers coming from church. Bidding François adieu (Wayfarer: "Farewell, old friend!") calling with bitter sorrow upon Toinette and his son, he goes out into the snow, and with a last brave cry, "Wayfarer, onward!" takes up his lonely road. Curtain.

LE ROI D'YS

Opera in three acts and five scenes, by Edward Lalo. Text by Edouard Blau, founded on a Breton legend.

CAST: Mylio—Tenor. Karnac—Baritone. The King —Lyric Bass. Saint Corentin—Bass or Baritone. Jahel—Baritone, or Second Tenor. Margared—Mezzosoprano, or Falcom. Rozenn—Soprano. Noblemen, soldiers, pontiffs, pages, squires, ladies, retainers, populace. Time, the Middle Ages. Place, the town of Ys. First production, Opéra Comique, Paris, May, 1888.

ACT I. A terrace in the palace of the Kings of Ys. Gardens at the left; at the right the entrance to the palace, to which leads a magnificent staircase. The sea in the distance. The populace are gathered to celebrate the feast of Noël. (Chorus: "Noël, Noël, Noël.") Jahel, a trusted retainer, announces that this day the king intends to give the crown to his son-in-law to celebrate his marriage with the lovely princess Margared, the pearl of Brittany. He calls upon St. Corentin, the patron saint of the country, to grant protection to all. (Chorus: "The wars are ended.") All are joyously anticipating

the return of the troops. A trumpet sounds far away.
Jahel calls upon the people to rejoice. They hasten in
the direction of the trumpet call, singing and laughing
as they go.

The princesses Rozenn and Margared, who are sisters,
come slowly down the palace staircase. Margared is sad,
and Rozenn questions her. Taking her hand, she finds it
burning. Margared turns away, protesting that there is
nothing wrong. Why should she not be happy, since she
is to be a queen? If she appears sad, it is perhaps because she is a little awed by her coming splendour. Rozenn, undeceived shakes her head, and begs her sister to
keep silent no longer. She herself may know a way to
cure her sorrow. (Duet, Rozenn and Margared: "Oh, my
sister, why dost thou suffer so?") Together they sing,
Rozenn entreating, Margared protesting. Rozenn asks
if she feels that she has been sacrificed to the good of the
realm. Margared replies that her grief can never be
healed, for she loves someone, not the prince, and that the
ship that bore away Mylio, their childhood's friend, had
borne away her heart. Margared's maids come to attend
her to her chamber, to be arrayed for her marriage. Rozenn tries to shield her sister from their curious eyes.
(Chorus of women: "Come, the hour is at hand.") Bitterly deploring her lot, Margared is led away.

Rozenn, now alone reveals her love for Mylio (Rozenn:
"Vainly I spoke of absence without end"), saying that
since she still lives, she knows he is not dead, as has been
reported. She calls his name aloud, and he suddenly appears before her. She stands staring at him, but his
voice reassures her, and she throws herself into his arms.
(Duet, Rozenn, Mylio: "Yes, I, the one thou lovest.")
He tells her he and his companions had been taken prisoners, but had escaped, and having defeated their enemies,
were now returning as conquerors. Rozenn, though overjoyed, trembles, as the trumpets sound once more. "It is
the prince who comes," she cries, "my sister's promised hus-

band." Mylio hurries away to his companions, declaring
he will return "To-night! To-morrow! Forever!" Rozenn gazes after him dreamily, and departs. The King
descends the staircase with Margared in bridal array, and
the courtiers, sumptuously attired. Karnac and his warriors, and the people of Ys come forward to meet them.
All is excitement and anticipation. Karnac salutes the
King, assuring him that through this happy event the
war will end. The King solemnly adjures the people to
obey their new king. (Recitative. The King: "In my
rival I find a son"; Chorus: "Here will we promise them
future obedience.") They accept Karnac as their ruler,
and the King presents him to his subjects. Rozenn approaches Margared, to tell her that Mylio still lives.
Margared's low exclamation of surprise, and her abrupt
declaration that if that is true she will break her troth
with Karnac is overheard by the court ladies, who begin
to gossip about it. Margared defiantly repeats her words
aloud. (Ensemble: "Oh, wicked madness.") The news
travels swiftly; all fear that Karnac will wreak some terrible vengeance upon the city, but Margared continues to
assert that she will never marry him. This rash vow
comes to his ears, and he revokes the treaty of peace,
throwing down his gauntlet as a challenge to mortal combat. Mylio accepts the challenge, acclaimed by all.
Karnac scornfully asks if he is courting death. "Not I,
but thou!" is the reply. A combat seems impending, for
the adherents of each hero take sides, but the King declares that the forces are too unequal. Karnac departs
in anger, swearing vengeance.

Act II. Scene 1. The great hall in the palace of Ys.
Trumpet calls in the distance. Margared stands by a
window, looking out over the country. She sees Karnac's
forces gathering from far and near to attack her people.
(Margared: "Oh, Mylio, if the struggle be near.") She
sings passionately of her own struggle within, and of her
knowledge that it is Rozenn whom Mylio loves. As the

King enters with Mylio and Rozenn, she conceals herself behind a pillar. The King speaks of the approaching combat. Rozenn is fearful, but Mylio assures her that Saint Corentin will surely carry their arms to victory. (Mylio: "Yes, I feel it, I know it!") Margared, still listening, softly joins in as they declare their confidence in the outcome of the battle. (Quartette: "Heaven will bless our cause.") The King takes heart anew, and Rozenn tenderly asks Mylio to be of good courage, since he is to be her husband. He departs filled with hope, and Margared, in her hiding-place is transfixed with grief. Rozenn gives expression to her happiness, but Margared, in a passionate outburst declares that she, too, loves Mylio. (Margared: "I have struggled too long.") Rozenn, overcome, tries to soothe her, but she wildly cries out that she hopes he will never return. Rozenn, now believing her to be mad (Rozenn: "Margared, be silent"), gently rebukes her in a charming avowal of her love for Mylio. Margared, defying her and the power of St. Corentin, departs in a transport of furious rage.

Scene 2. A great plain. The town of Ys in the distance. An ancient chapel to the right. As the curtain rises, Mylio is surrounded by his soldiers, some with drawn swords, others bearing flags and arms taken from the enemy. They have been victorious, and are acclaimed by the people. (Chorus: "Victory! Honour to Mylio!") Mylio points to the chapel, saying that to St. Corentin the real honour is due. The soldiers, advancing, reverently place the flags within the chapel. Mylio, the soldiers, and the populace march in procession past the chapel, falling on their knees, as they pass the door. When all have departed, Karnac enters slowly, with disordered dress, mourning over his defeat. Margared suddenly appears, clad in sombre garments, and listens. Karnac says: "These people have called the saints to their aid and have been answered; but hell answers me not!" Margared, coming forward answers: "Hell indeed hears

thee." Starting back, Karnac accuses her of insulting
him once more, but she replies that her hope is to avenge
him. She has been betrayed by all, and now will join
forces with him. "What can we do?" he asks despairingly, "I am defeated, and without adherents." "You
have one powerful ally," is her answer, "the Ocean!"
She explains that the city of Ys is protected from the in-
roads of the sea by a dyke. If the gates should be
opened, all would perish.

Karnac listens eagerly, and they hasten away, Margared
stopping before the chapel for a moment, and derisively
calling upon St. Corentin to work a miracle for his people,
if indeed he is able. The sky becomes overcast; all is
dark. Margared shrieks with terror as she sees that the
statue is moving. The saint curses her. Karnac, with a
desperate effort defies the saint (Corentin: "Misfortune
be upon your heads"), who enumerates his sins, and warns
him to repent. He returns again to Margared, who implores pity. A celestial chorus demands their repentance,
and the saint disappears.

ACT III. Scene 1. A gallery in the palace of Ys; to
the right Rozenn's apartment. Young girls and youths
in merry combat stand before the doorway, according to
the old Breton custom. Jahel enters, and explains this
ancient marriage ceremony, by which the bridegroom's
friends come to the door of the bride's room to seek her,
but are driven back by the young maidens. (Chorus:
"Open the door of the bride.") All persuasions having
failed, Mylio himself appears and tells of his great love
(Mylio, Chorus of Women: "Vainly, my beloved"), declaring he will die if she refuses to come forth. Rozenn in
bride's dress appears on the threshold, and is saluted by
her friends. (Rozenn; Chorus: "Why struggle against
fate.") She tells her lover it is no use to deny him, since
she loves him truly. She places her hand in his, and all
depart in procession toward the chapel, from which comes
the sound of a Te Deum. Karnac and Margared enter.

They advance toward the chapel, then pause in fright.
Karnac demands from Margared the fulfillment of her
promise to show him how to open the dyke. She firmly
refuses to commit the crime. (Karnac: "Go forth no
more in weakness.") He depicts to her graphically the
marriage scene, her lover wedded to her sister while she
is sad and lonely. (Karnac: "See thy lover, handsome and
glad!") She repeatedly begs him to be silent, but he persists, torturing her more and more, with his description of
the love and happiness of the newly wedded pair. At last,
inflamed with disappointed love, she calls aloud for vengeance. (Margared, Karnac: "Let them perish!")

The marriage procession comes from the chapel.
(Chorus: "Health to the happy pair.") Rozenn looks
shyly at her husband (Rozenn: "God has been good to
us; Mylio: Gladly I went to the altar"), and they exult
in their happiness. The King slowly advances, with a
look of sadness. Rozenn motions to Mylio to leave them
alone. She assures her father that she will soon return,
and Margared will repent of her madness. (Trio: Rozenn, Margared, The King: "That in the chosen path.")
Margared has entered unobserved; sounds of terror are
heard without. The King demands the reason, and turning sees Margared pale and distraught. Rozenn runs to
embrace her. "Fly," cries the girl, "these sounds are
the voice of death!" (Margared "These confused noises,
this heavy rumbling.") She confesses her sin; Mylio enters, and Rozenn throws herself into his arms. (Chorus:
"Away, away.") Mylio carries off Rozenn, and the King
tries to take Margared, who refuses to go. A crowd enters, mad with terror, as the flood seems about to engulf
them.

Scene 2. A hill near the sea, on which the people have
taken refuge. The waves are dark and threatening. On
the rocks, a group of men are watching the progress of
the disaster. The people kneel in prayer. (Chorus: "O
Infinite Power.") As the flood increases, Margared ad-

vances, and declares that the sea will rise until it has received its prey, and will then recede. The King asks who is to be the victim? Margared replies: "It is I, the guilty one!" In the hearing of all she confesses her wicked plot, and her defiance of the saint. (Chorus: "Death to the wicked one!") Rozenn pleads for her sister.

The water still rises, and there is a clap of thunder. All are terrified, and in the confusion Margared escapes from those who are holding her. Rushing to the highest point of the rocks, and pleading piteously to God for the safety of the people, she leaps into the sea. As Mylio and Rozenn follow, in the hope of saving her, St. Corentin appears before them and bars the way. They fall on their knees, and the people also kneel in prayer, as the water recedes. (Chorus: "Oh Justice, O Terror.") Curtain.

NATOMA

Opera in three acts. Music by Victor Herbert. Text by Joseph D. Redding.

CAST: Don Francisco de la Guerra—Bass. Father Peralta—Bass. Juan Battista Alvarado, a young Spaniard—Baritone. José Castro, a half breed—Baritone. Pico and Kagama, bravos, friends of Castro—Tenor and Bass. Paul Merrill, Lieutenant on the U. S. Brig. *Liberty*—Tenor. Barbara, daughter of Don Francisco— Soprano. Natoma, an Indian girl—Soprano. Officers, innkeeper, dancing girls, ladies, dignitaries, nuns, sailors, *vaqueros*, populace. Place, California. Time, 1820; under the Spanish régime. First performance, Philadelphia, 1911.

ACT I. Hacienda of Don Francisco, on Santa Cruz Island. Don Francisco, standing on the hill-top, looks out across the water, musing. He is expecting his daughter Barbara, who has just finished her education in Santa Barbara. (Recitative, Don Francisco: "Alas, impatient father that I am"; Song, id: "Oh, child of love.") Alvarado, a young Spaniard, a suitor for Barbara's hand, approaches, with Castro, the half breed, and two vaqueros, pretending to have come on a hunting trip. They are received with Spanish ceremony. Natoma, an Indian girl, foster sister of Barbara brings in the American lieutenant, Paul Merrill, naïvely leading him by the hand, and expressing a childish admiration of his beauty. (Paul: "Gentle maiden, tell me.") He asks her to tell him of her people and their legends, and of the lovely Barbara. She recounts the story of the amulet she wears (Natoma: "Would you ask me of my people?"), and the history of her tribe. Paul, much impressed, salutes her as a princess, but she smiles sadly, telling him that those days are in the past, and "Now the stranger comes as chieftain."

To change her mood, he asks about Barbara, and she describes her wonderful beauty (Natoma: "Barbara, my Barbara"), declaring that he will surely love her when he sees her. Then realising that he will no longer care for poor Natoma, she wildly begs him to receive her as his slave, to beat her or even kill her, but not to forget her, and, overcome with emotion, falls at his feet. Far off music gaily announces the coming of Barbara and her young friends from the convent. She is greeted by the island folk, who have crowded to the shore, and appears with Father Peralta. Her first thought is of Natoma, then she greets her father, and her friends and the padre are welcomed in Spanish fashion. Natoma brings forward the young lieutenant, who has been gazing at Barbara, during the interchange of greetings. They are at once in love, and Natoma is forgotten. (Chorus: "While shadows darken.") The Indian girl is in a reverie, still thinking of Paul, when Castro appears, bitterly taunting her with her servile condition (Scene: Natoma: "Oh, the wonder of his speaking!"; Castro: "Can I believe my eyes?"), and trying to arouse her to independence. Together, he declares, he and she could restore the glories of the tribe. She tells him he is no Indian, and he, angrily accusing her of love for Paul, asserts that the lieutenant will never wed her but Barbara instead.

The hunters return, and Castro tells them of the young officer and his sudden infatuation for Barbara, then hides in the arbour as Alvarado begins a serenade. (Alvarado: "When the sunlight dies.") Barbara appears on the veranda to greet him with laughing coquetry. His song will fit any girl, she asserts, and she is sure he has used it for more than one. As the convivial song of the merry-makers is heard in the distance (Chorus: "To him who drinks the wine of Spain"), Alvarado impetuously assures Barbara of his undying affection, and finally asks her to marry him. (Alvarado: "Fair one, listen to my vow of love.") Her friends call her from within, but Alvarado attempts to detain her, angrily declaring that her heart has already been given away. She tears herself from him, and now furious, and unaware that Natoma is listening, he threatens the "Americano." With Castro, he plans the abduction of Barbara. Natoma, bearing a pitcher on her shoulder, slowly passes across the stage, and behind the hacienda.

Barbara and her friends have been enjoying to the full their freedom from school tasks (Chorus: "The hour has come for us to sever"), but the time for farewells has come, and the guests depart. Barbara sits with her father on the veranda, and they wave their last greetings to their friends who row away in their boats. Don Francisco lovingly embraces his child and then retires to rest. Barbara begs for a few moments alone in the moonlight. (Barbara: "Oh, wondrous night!") She confesses aloud her love for Paul, and he returning hears her avowal (Paul: "Let come what will"), and impulsively declares his own passion (Paul, Barbara: "I love thee"). A passionate love scene follows. The young pair ardently embrace, but as a light appears in the window, Barbara reluctantly tears herself away, and quickly enters the house. Natoma is seen at the window, holding a lighted candle.

ACT II. Plaza before the Mission Church, Santa Barbara. Roadway. Mountains in the distance. An inn with a fountain. Booths with articles for sale. Raised benches for the spectators at the *fiesta*. Natoma enters, looking about her. She goes to the church, as if for holy water, but turns back, softly singing of her love for Barbara and Paul (Natoma: "Within an hour the morning sun"), with fanciful imagery, and listening sadly to the revelry and music. As the church bell sounds, she speaks of the padre's counsel to embrace the Christian faith, if she wishes to escape eternal death, and with superb disdain invokes the Indian deity (Natoma: "Great Manitou, the spirit of the hills"). As she departs, village sounds are heard: a shepherd's pipe, the steps of a boy who performs some homely errand and goes off whistling, the tramp of soldiers bearing a flag for the church, which is raised by the friars. The townspeople come in and enter the booths to make purchases, while the soldiers complacently eye the pretty girls. (Chorus: "Come buy, step up!") The sound of guitars and mandolins strikes the ear; there is much laughter and jesting. Whips are heard cracking loudly (Song, Pico: "Who dares the bronco?"; Chorus: "*Vaqueros*, devils to dare"), and a troop of vaqueros and rancheros appear. Carpenters are finishing their work upon the benches, with loud knocking of hammers. Enter Alvarado and his companions. He calls the innkeeper, and tells him to keep open house at his expense all day. Dancing girls come forward and dance the Habanera. Kagama announces the arrival of Don Francisco and Barbara, with their party.

The plot has been subtly arranged, and all is ready, as Paul approaches from his ship, with a band of sailors. The Alcalde and the town officers come forward. The crowd pushes and jostles to see better. The church bell sounds, as the convent girls begin to sing. (Chorus of convent girls: "Happy day that bids us to attend.") Don Francisco and Barbara are on horseback, Natoma.

walking beside Barbara's horse. They take their seats
on the benches. Don Francisco greets the people. (Don
Francisco: "Good friends, retainers, trusty servants all";
Chorus, "Around thy radiant brow.") Barbara also addresses them with affection. (Barbara: "Dear father,
friends of my girlhood"; Song: "Rule thou by love.")
She asks all to be merry for her sake, breaking gaily into
a love song (Barbara: "I list the thrill in golden throat").
Alvarado asks her to dance the minuet with him, but the
stately measures are broken into by the sound of saluting
cannon. The sailors from the brig *Liberty* approach
headed by Paul. (Chorus: "Blow, Boreas, blow.") Paul
greets Don Francisco, and shows himself to be a patriot.
(Paul: "No country can my own outvie.") Approved
by Don Francisco, he takes his seat. The interrupted
minuet proceeds, followed by the *Panuelo*, or Handkerchief
dance, in which Barbara refuses Don Alvarado as her gallant, by throwing his hat on the ground. The crowd
murmurs at this, but Don Francisco tactfully declares it
to be a jest. Throughout this scene Natoma sits silent
and watchful, until Castro elbows his way through the
crowd, sneering at the dances he has just seen, and daring
someone to be his partner in the ancient dagger dance.
Sinuously, he makes his way about the arena, but no one
accepts his challenge until Natoma suddenly throws down
her dagger, when the dance begins, gaining in wild fury
as it proceeds. (Dagger Dance: "Those mincing steps.")
So engrossed is the crowd that no one notices Alvarado
and Kagama, who are making preparations to abduct
Barbara, by throwing a serape over her head, and carrying her off unobserved. Natoma, apparently absorbed,
lunges at Castro with her dagger, and, as he counters slips
by him and stabs Alvarado to the heart. He falls, and
Don Francisco seizes Barbara; Natoma remaining unmoved. The people, headed by Castro, are about to attack
the Indian girl, when Paul, drawing his sword, and calling the sailors to his aid, forces the crowd back. All is

uproar and confusion, but Father Peralta stills the tumult
by bringing the crucifix from the church, and holding it
up before their eyes. (Solo, Peralta: "Vengeance is
mine.") They fall on their knees, and the padre signs to
Natoma that the protection of the church will be hers.
The dagger falls from her hand, and she slowly walks
toward the chapel, kneeling before the priest.

Act III. Inside the church Natoma is alone on the altar
steps, crooning an Indian lullaby ("Beware the hawk, my
baby.") She sings of her love, and calls on Manitou to
aid her, deploring the passing of her race (Natoma:
"Lonely am I.") The padre rebukes her for thus dese-
crating the chapel. (Scene, Peralta: "Peace in the house
of God.") Natoma is defiant at first, but the gentleness
of the priest disarms her. She listens quietly as he speaks
of the Blessed Virgin, and of Natoma's love for Barbara.
Deeply touched, she consents to receive the Christian
faith. The priest summons the people to mass, and the
choir chants softly. Paul enters alone, then Don Francisco and Barbara. Natoma stands motionless on the altar steps, facing the congregation. (Chorus of nuns
without: "*Sanctus Dominus Deus Sabaoth.*") The nuns
enter the church; Natoma slowly passes down the aisle to
where Paul and Barbara are seated. She turns toward the
altar. Paul and Barbara step into the aisle, and with
clasped hands kneel in prayer in front of the Indian girl.
Natoma gives them her amulet, in token of complete submission, then facing the congregation passes between the
kneeling nuns to the door of the convent garden. The
nuns rise and follow her, going before her, however, into
the garden. Natoma, sobbing bitterly, pauses a moment,
then passes into the garden, and the gates are shut (Chor-
ale: *Te lucis ante omnium*). Curtain.

THE SECRET MARRIAGE

Opera in two acts by Cimarosa. Text by Bertati.

CAST: Count Tiefenthal (Conte)—Baritone. Roms, a rich miser (Geronimo)—Basso. Beatrix (Fidalma)—Mezzo-soprano. Lisette (Lisetta)—Soprano. Caroline (Karolina) — Soprano. Sander (Paolino) — Tenor. Paul, Peter, Jacob, Martin, and Anton, servants in Roms' house. Place, in Roms' house. Time, the 18th century. First production, Vienna, 1792.

ACT I. Sander and Karoline are secretly married. (Duet: "Dear one, doubt not.") Roms wishes to unite Lisette and Count Tiefenthal (Aria: "Hear every one"). The Count arrives, but meeting Lisette feels only coldness for her while he loves Karoline. (Quartette: "I feel but hate.") When Tiefenthal confesses the state of his mind to Sander, whom he already knows, the latter is indignant, as he believes that the Count is only attracted by Roms' riches. Karoline also refuses him (Aria: "Dear Count, pardon me"), and when he continues his attentions, he is surprised by the jealous Lisette who rouses the house with her cries. (Finale: "What, the Count is not satisfied.")

ACT II. The Count declares he will remit 50,000 guilders of the dowry if Roms will give him Karoline instead of Lisette, and the penurious Roms agrees. (Duet: "You must agree.") Sander now resolves to elope with Karoline. (Aria: "Before the morn appears.") The Count attempts to induce Lisette to release him by claiming to possess all the vices, but she refuses. (Duet: "I am silly, fond of fashion.") Beatrix and Lisette induce Roms to send Karoline to a convent and she is in despair. Lisette rejoices. (Aria: "Oh what pleasure.") When the Count ascertains that Sander and Karoline have been secretly married for over two months, he assuages the wrath of the irate father and declares he will marry Lisette.

QUO VADIS

("Whither goest thou?")

Opera in five acts and six scenes. Music by Jean Nouguès. Text by Henry Cain, after the romance by Henry Sienkiewicz.

CAST: Lygia—Dramatic Soprano. Eunice, slave of Petronius—Soprano. Poppæa, wife of Nero—Contralto. Iras, slave of Petronius—Soprano. Miriam—Mezzo-soprano. Nazaire, son of Miriam—Tenor. Lilith, Ethiopian attendant of Poppæa. Psyllia, wife of Sporus. Vinicius—Tenor. Petronius—Baritone. Chilon—Baritone. Peter the Apostle—Bass. Nero—Tenor. Sporus, an Innkeeper—Baritone. A young Christian—Tenor. Tigellin, Vitellinus, Vatinius—Baritone, and Bassos. A Sailor—Tenor. Two centurions—Tenor and Bass. Ursus, servant, Croton, gladiator, Theocles, physician—Silent parts. Patricians, plebeians, flute and cithara players, vestals, gladiators, soldiers of the Prætorian Guard, slaves. Time, the Roman Empire under Nero. Place, Rome.

ACT I. The kiss of Eunice. The inner court of Petronius's house, beautifully adorned with frescoes; a statue of Petronius; a fountain and the altar of Venus Genetrix. It is the eve of the festival of that goddess. Soft music precedes the rising of the curtain. Eunice and Iras are decking the atrium and the little altar with garlands. (Duet: Eunice, Iras: "Love to-morrow!") Chilon limps in, miserably clad, and listens with derisive pantomine. They jestingly ask if he has come to gossip, or to sell them an amulet. He shows them one, which he solemnly declares has strange powers, but Eunice tells him she has given all she has to Venus, without avail. (Eunice: "I have given her all.") "But who is the lucky man?" cries Chilon, always curious. "Ah, that is a secret!" says the girl, but Chilon's face shows he has made a shrewd guess. Petronius and Vinicius appear in the garden, and the girls resume their song (Duet, Eunice, Iras: "The gentle spring resumes love's tender sway"), hastening away to fill their baskets anew. Vinicius is in love, and Petronius tells him no one can resist him long, for is he not rich, and brave and great? Vinicius shakes his head (Vinicius: "Honour

and power would not avail"), declaring that these things
mean little to the woman he loves. He knows her not, but
one day, unperceived, has seen her bathing in a garden.
"Who is this wonder?" asks Petronius. "They call her
Lygia." "A slave? Then buy her! Or stay, I will give
you one of my slaves." He designates Eunice, who stands
trembling and dismayed, but Vinicius refuses the gift almost with violence. Petronius insists, and Eunice kneels
before him, humbly imploring mercy. "Have you a lover,
then?" he asks kindly. She hangs her head in shame, and
blushing, kisses the hem of his garment, saying: "A fortune-teller has promised me happiness." Vinicius desires
to consult him, and Chilon is brought in. They ask him
his business, and he tells them that he is a bit of a philosopher, and also a collector of news. (Chilon: "A philosopher, misunderstood!") "Indeed? He knows then what
they have been talking about?" "Of course! About a
certain Lygia, daughter of a barbarian King, who is always guarded by a giant called Ursus." "That is true,"
cries Vinicius, "I saw him bearing the water for her flowers. When I spoke to her, she listened, and then pointing
downward traced something upon the sand. As I approached, she fled." "What did she trace?" asked Petronius, with interest. "A fish!" "A well-known sign,
that," puts in Chilon, importantly. "Of what?" demands
Petronius, suddenly. "Of—of—" stammers the charlatan,
"of what I know not yet, but I will soon discover." With
a promise of gold if he succeeds, he hurries away. The two
friends talk of the coming feast of Nero, where, ever hungry for flattery, he is to read his verses. (Petronius:
"Wander across the sea.") They go out, still talking
earnestly. Eunice watches them out of sight, then standing up on a marble seat passionately kisses the lips of the
statue of Petronius over and over again. This is her secret. She loves her master with an undying and absorb-
ing love, which has no hope of return. The curtain slowly
falls.

ACT II. Terraces on the Palatine Hills, overlooking

Rome.   Music and the sound of revelry within the palace
of Nero.   The jealous Empress, Poppæa is hiding among
the trees, to see what is happening at the feast.   An Ethiopian slave comes from the banquet hall, and kneels before
her.   She reports that Petronius, the "Arbiter of Elegance," has brought to the feast a beautiful barbarian.
Poppæa sends for him, just as the revellers come trooping
joyously into the gardens.   (Chorus: "With perfumes
rare, flowers and caresses.")   Petronius appears before the
irate empress, who reproaches him.   (Poppæa: "At the
side of Nero another woman sits.")   Petronius explains
that she has been brought for Vinicius (Petronius:
"Divine one, behold for thyself") ; he will swear it.   With
a courtier's grace, he sings rapturously of Poppæa's
charms (Petronius: "See, the moon herself a silver aureole
gives !")   Poppæa, on the shoulders of her slave, preceded by torch-bearers goes into the hall.   The courtiers
follow, acclaiming her.   Vinicius and Lygia are alone in
the garden.   (Vinicius, Lygia: "Ah, stay within the azure
shade.")   He ardently declares his passion, but Lygia reminds him that her God is not his (Lygia: "There is a
God who rules the earth"), and she can serve no other.
Overwhelmed with desire, he seizes her, and is about to
embrace her when the giant Ursus breaks through the
hedge, and taking the girl in his huge arms carries her
off.   The revellers come forth once more, dancing and
singing.   (Chorus: "Io! Io! Io!")   Dawn appears, and
in the sky a flame is seen.   "Rome is burning!" cry the
revellers, startled.   Nero breaks into an exultant song
(Nero: "Arise! Arise! O ardent flame"), and the ready
courtiers acclaim him.   A clamour is heard without; it is
the populace menacing their emperor.   Nero, overcome
with terror, tries to put the blame upon his friends, who
refuse to accept it.   A centurion enters with the news
that his men have been slain by the people.   The patricians flee, shrieking with ignoble fear.   Petronius, offering to pacify the mob, goes out, and the orgy proceeds,

with drinking, dancing and revelry. The fire is at its
height as the curtain falls.

ACT III. QUO VADIS? ("Whither goest thou?")
The banks of the Tiber, with shops, taverns, and small
houses of plebeians, that of Demas, and Sporus's inn
being the most prominent. A number of gladiators and
circus attendants are seated at tables outside the inn,
drinking. Chilon walks about, listening to everything.
He is almost dead with fatigue, and sinks upon a bench
(Chilon: "I can do no more"), grumbling that he can discover nothing about the sign of the fish. While gossiping with Sporus, he absently traces the sign on the
ground. Sporus has no news, and Chilon tells him he
is looking for a virgin, and also for a giant. "What,
here?" cries the innkeeper, incredulously. "I have no
virgins here, but I have a giant!" He calls the huge
gladiator Croton, who comes lazily to the window, surrounded by admiring women and men. They stare curiously out. Chilon shakes his head; this is not Ursus.
"Well, then," he continues, pointing to the ground,
"What does this sign mean?" Sporus shrugs his shoulders, and everyone laughs. Sporus goes inside to settle
a dispute, and the Christian Demas approaches Chilon,
telling him that he has observed the sign, and wishes him
to know that the Lord has appeared unto Peter. Chilon
informs him of his quest, and Demas says that those he
seeks are in his house. Chilon is overjoyed, but controls
himself until Demas has departed. He calls Sporus, and
giving him gold asks the attendance of Croton for a piece
of work he has on hand. The night watch passes by.
Miriam, a Christian, comes with Lygia and Nazaire from
the house of Demas. Christians gather silently in
groups, talking in low tones of their faith. Some are inclined to doubt the news of the Lord's appearance, but
Demas reassures them. The apostle Peter approaches in
a boat. (Lygia: "He appears to us as did the Lord
Jesus.") He steps on shore, addressing the awed assem-

blage (Peter: "It was at dawn"), and recounting his vision of the Saviour. (Chorus: "O wonder untold.") The other Christians depart one by one, but Lygia kneels before the apostle, confessing her unconquerable love for Vinicius, and asking his protection (Lygia: "Father, I will tell thee of all my sorrow"; Peter: "Remember poor Mary Magdalen.") Gravely he counsels her, and they enter the house. Chilon appears, then Vinicius and Croton, who go into the house of Demas. Chilon is exulting over his success (Chilon: "None can resist Croton"), when a cry is heard within, and after peering in, Chilon flattens himself against the wall, in deadly fear. Ursus emerges, with Croton's body in his arms. He throws it into the river, and reënters the house, cautiously barring the door behind him. Chilon curses him (Chilon: "May hell swallow him up!"), and flees in terror as the curtain falls.

ACT IV. The Martyrs. A huge crypt in the Coliseum, lighted by a single lamp, a trap door forming the entrance. The Christians, trembling and wounded, are clinging to two pillars. Miriam and Demas are among them, and Lygia lies asleep, watched over by Ursus. A centurion and his soldiers walk about among them. Miriam is holding the dead body of her son, Nazaire, which the soldiers roughly take from her. The Christians relate their terrible sufferings. Their daughters have been outraged, their children tortured, their parents cruelly slain. (Chorus: "Have pity on us, O Lord.") Peter appears in their midst (Peter: "Why pity you yourselves?") reassuring them. Vinicius enters, with a plan to save Lygia from the terrible fate which awaits her. Peter bids him call upon the Master for aid. Lygia awakens (Lygia: "Who weeps in the darkness?"; Duet, Lygia, Vinicius: "He who gave me the happiness of love"), and talks with Vinicius of their love and a possible future. A clamour is heard, and Petronius appears with a centurion, to warn Vinicius that the games are beginning, and Lygia is to suffer martyrdom at once. The martyrs are heard chanting as they approach their doom. (Chorus: "O Lord, be glorified.") "Who are those who sing?" asks Petronius, in wonder. "The Christians, going to meet death," he is told. "And singing?" he exclaims in surprise. Lygia bids her lover farewell, and he boldly declares himself a Christian. The chorus swells triumphantly, and Lygia, torn from the arms of her lover, points to heaven. Curtain.

After an interlude of turmoil, ending with crashing chords, trumpets are heard, and the noise of the crowd in the circus. The curtain rises on the familiar scene of a gladiatorial contest, between Calendio and Lanio. The latter is vanquished, and Lanio appeals to the people. The thumbs of the spectators are all turned down, and Calendio dispatches his fallen foe. The body is being removed, when the courtiers attending Nero and Poppæa enter the circus, and seat themselves in the imperial enclosure. The people acclaim them. (Chorus of children and vestals: "Thrice our Cæsar.") Nero, addressing them announces that a giant barbarian is to meet in single combat a huge bull, to whose back is to be tied a beautiful Christian. She will be naked. Ursus appears in the arena, dazzled by the light. Chilon is trembling with fear. The trumpets sound. Petronius covers the face of Vinicius with his mantle. After a scene of breathless suspense, Ursus overthrows the bull, and holds up the senseless body of Lygia before the emperor for mercy. Vinicius makes an impassioned appeal to Nero, who at last makes a sign of assent. Vinicius, rushing into the arena covers the senseless girl with his cloak, and bearing her away, leaves the circus amid the shouts of the populace. Nero, seized with sudden anger, orders a general massacre of all the Christians in the crypt, young and old. They are driven out with whips, like animals. Chilon becomes more and more horror struck at the scene (Funeral March. Chilon: "All this blood"), and at last, in a frenzy denounces Nero, and is thrown to the lions.

With a last effort, he calls upon the Romans to repent.
(Chilon: "Roman people, you are deceived.") His tongue
is torn out, by order of the emperor. The people, weary
of carnage, hiss Nero, calling out the detested name
"Ahenobarbus!" and bitterly cursing him. They hurl
at him projectiles of all kinds, but through the interven-
tion of the Prætorian guard he and Poppæa escape.
Curtain.

ACT V. The death of Petronius. Scene, the villa of
Petronius, near Antium. A garden with a terrace, at
twilight. Distant view of the sea. Flute players and
cithara players with their instruments; singers voicing
soft harmonies. A banquet is spread for Vinicius, Lygia,
and other guests of Petronius. After a beautiful and expressive prelude, Petronius is seen reading to his friends
a letter of farewell to Nero, in which he takes leave of
a life no longer sweet, since all that made it so is now
but a memory. The guests are astounded. Continuing,
he declares that he no longer wishes to blush with shame
for the Cæsar, once his friend, whose cruelty and turpi-
tude have become the scorn of the world. If he must
burn and slay, let him at least spare imperial Rome.
This, he announces, is the last counsel of the "Arbiter of
Elegance." A hush falls upon the assemblage as Petronius places the missive in a coffer, held by a slave, and
bids him bear it to Nero.

As the women crowd around him dismayed, Petronius
gently thanks them for their beauty, giving them rich
jewels. Vinicius and Lygia try to speak, but Petronius
restrains them, saying his time has come to depart. They
beg him to fly with them, but he assures them that while
their young lives are about to begin anew, his is now at
an end. Vinicius and Lygia continue to entreat (Vinicius,
Lygia: "Come with us, Petronius"; Petronius: "No, No!
It is too late.") As they cling to him, weeping, he gently
puts them aside, and they depart in tears. Petronius, returning to the banquet, calls upon Eunice to bring him

wine. (Chorus, old men, young men and maidens: "It is
evening, arise.") The sound of music and singing is
heard, and the dancers, in rhythmic poses circle about
the table. Petronius calls for Theocles, his physician, and
Eunice knowing the end is at hand falls sobbing at his
feet. He bids her farewell, granting her freedom, and
the gift of all his possessions. She frantically begs to
be allowed to die with him (Duet, Petronius, Eunice:
"With one last word"), declaring that he alone has her
love. He draws her to him, saying that he dies happy,
knowing himself beloved (Petronius: "Gather the roses in
this cup"), and drinks the poisoned wine, refusing it to
Eunice. As he tenderly kisses her (Eunice: "Oh, gather
from my lips"), the wine cup falls from his hand and
breaks. Petronius stretches out his arm to the physician,
who is about to sever the artery when Eunice pleads to be
allowed to die first. Theocles fulfils his part and with a
last kiss, Petronius and Eunice pass into the realm of
shades, just as the Prætorian Guard advances to seize
them. Soft music attends their passing. The moonlight
falls gently upon them, and upon the spears of the soldiers
who appear through the trees. (Chorus: "Star of evening, pure and radiant.") Curtain.

THE SECRET OF SUZANNE

An Intermezzo in one act by Ermanno Wolf-Ferrari.

Cast: Countess Suzanne—Soprano. Count Gil—Tenor.
Sante, a servant—silent rôle. Time, the present. First
performance, Munich, December, 1909.

The story is a very slight one, but gives rise to many
amusing complications. Count Gil and Countess Suzanne
have recently been married, and the youthful bride has not
dared to tell her husband that she smokes cigarettes for
fear that he will disapprove, and perhaps scold her. So
she is obliged to take a puff at a cigarette when he is away,

or whenever a good opportunity offers. Gil observes the odour of tobacco about the house, and his jealousy is at once aroused. Not dreaming that his wife is the culprit, he fears that she has a lover, whom she is secreting. His accusations drive her to all sorts of absurd excuses, which seem to confirm his suspicions. A game of cross-purposes results, in which she is frightened and mystified, and he is enraged, and the stupidity of the servant adds to the confusion. At last, Count Gil feels that he must know the truth, even at the cost of his happiness. He follows the supposed lover from room to room of the house, sniffing the fresh tobacco smoke as he goes. At last be believes he has entrapped him, but suddenly finds out that his pretty little wife is the smoker. She looks so charming when engaged in her pet vice, and he is so relieved to find that she still loves only her husband that he is enraptured, and peace is restored.

VERSIEGELT

(Sealed up!)

Comic Opera in one act, after Rauppach. Music by Leo Blech. Text by Richard Batka.

CAST. Braun, the Burgomaster—Baritone. Else, his daughter—Soprano. Frau Gertrud Schramm, a young widow—Mezzo-soprano. Frau Willmer, a neighbour—Contralto. Bertel, her son—Tenor. Lampe, the factotum of the Burgomaster—Bass. Neighbour Knote—Bass. The Champion shot—speaking part. Place, a small village in Germany. Time, 1830.

Scene, the sitting room of Frau Gertrud. In the rear, a broad window; to the left, an alcove; to the right, a bay window, and a door leading to the street. In this room, which is comfortably furnished, sits Frau Gertrud, in a colored apron, sewing. Frau Willmer rushes in breathlessly from the street, making signs that she is in great trouble. "What is the matter, neighbour?" asks the

widow, kindly. "Oh, help me, help me!" gasps Frau Willmer, "I know your good heart." "But, tell me, what is
it?" "Such trouble, such trouble!" "Your son is drafted
as a soldier, perhaps?" "No, no, thank God! It is the
heirloom," cries the good frau, rambling off into irrevelant
details, that explain nothing. "A question of money,
then," says the widow. "No, no, not money either!" She
finally falls exhausted into a chair, and explains that the
Burgomaster for a long time had let her taxes go on, without troubling her, but now he had come down upon her,
and everything she had was to be sold at auction. "And
my wardrobe, my wardrobe!" she wails. "They will sell
that too." "Well, I have bought it," says the widow
calmly. "To be sure I have very little room here, but it
is a fine piece of furniture." "A thousand thanks!" cries
Frau Willmer. "You quite understand me. I will get
Neighbour Knote and his son to bring it here at once."
She hurries off, joyfully, and Frau Gertrud muses upon
her lonely state, which she thinks she can easily change by
marrying the Burgomaster.

The great wardrobe is brought in by the two men, with
Frau Willmer in attendance to see that no harm comes to
it. They set it in place, and go out. Frau Willmer
speaks of the love of her son Bertel for Else, the Burgomaster's daughter. A knock is heard at the door, and the
young pair enter. The Burgomaster, it appears, will not
hear of their marriage. "Never," he has declared to
Bertel, "shall my daughter be your wife." Else takes this
terrible mandate lightly. "I shall let him grumble," she
laughs, "and then do as I choose." "Well, who will plead
my cause with him?" asks Bertel. "Not I!" exclaims his
mother in terror. Frau Gertrud offers herself as go-be-
tween, reproving the young people for disrespect (Frau
Gertrud: "You malign the Burgomaster, I fear"). These
things are not to be decided hastily, she informs them;
marriage is a serious matter. And how does the Burgomaster know that this youthful love will endure? "Shall

I always be dear to you Bertel?" asks Else impulsively, and the two older women discreetly turn aside, and begin to discuss household matters. (Duet, Else, Bertel: "Thee, only thee do I love.") The lovers are completely engrossed in their plans, and continue to implore Frau Gertrud to speak for them to the stern parent. "If you only knew," declares Else, "how my father praises and admires you." "Such flattery!" laughs the widow, pleased, nevertheless. They coax her, and all sing, hand in hand, a song of victory. (Quartette: Else, Gertrud, Frau Willmer, Bertel: "Love will win.")

The young pair go out gaily, dragging the mother off with them, and calling out joyous reminders to the widow, quickly to fulfil her mission. She sits down and lays plans for the subjugation of the Burgomaster (Gertrud: "So, so, so, so! What talk would make in the town"). She laughingly rehearses the scene. It would be "Frau Burgomaster here, Frau Burgomaster there!" with everyone bowing and scraping, much to her secret merriment. Once more a knock at the door; Frau Gertrud screams loudly. This time Lampe enters, with a roll of papers under his arm, and carrying a huge red umbrella. He is self-important, and extremely talkative. "Yes, Lampe goes everywhere," he declares, "bringing joy to some and sorrow to others. But not to you, Frau Gertrud," he adds, politely. "Poor Frau Willmer, with that son of hers who has managed, God alone knows how, to get into the Burgomaster's office, and now is making eyes at his daughter is the one to suffer this time." "Ah, you are jealous of the boy," says the widow lightly. (Duet, Gertrud, Lampe: "That, it seems, awakens your envy.") She flatters him a little, saying that his clever brain must find a way to solve the young pair's difficulties (Lampe: "My wisdom to prove and demonstrate"). "Oh, yes, I don't deny that I am clever," he tells her. "Very little escapes me. Nothing happens in the town that I am not concerned in, in one way or another." He goes on boasting interminably, and at last Gertrud becomes impatient, and interrupts him repeatedly, which does not stop the clacking of his tongue. She busies herself with household tasks, but he still goes on talking, until finally she is obliged to shake him violently. "Why don't you deliver your message?" she asks, sharply, "What are you here for?" "A most important mission," replies the lackey. "The Burgomaster himself has sent me to greet the lovely widow Schramm." "Oh, what an honour!" exclaims the widow, hastily giving him a gold piece. "But poor Frau Willmer!" Lampe, suddenly looking up sees the famous wardrobe, and changes countenance. "What is the matter?" asks Frau Gertrud, innocently, but he is suspicious, and goes to Frau Willmer's house to investigate, the widow calling after him to get out quickly, and return, as she has something more to say. "Oh, I am undoubtedly the ablest man in the town!" he chuckles, as he departs.

Gertrud, now alone, repeats the compliment unctuously, *"The lovely Widow Schramm!* But oh," remembering, "poor Frau Willmer and the wardrobe!" A knock is heard at the door. "Oh, how sick I am of people," cries the widow, stamping her foot. "Let them knock!" The knocking grows louder and louder, and at last she is forced to open the door. The Burgomaster stands before her, bowing low. She makes a sweeping curtsey and invites him in. (Duet, Gertrud, Burgomaster: "Oh, excuse that I detain you.") They sit down, and begin to talk (Duet, Gertrud, Burgomaster: "Good Burgomaster, 'tis difficult to fathom"). He tells her that the bringing up of a pretty daughter is simple enough until she falls in love, and then a father can do nothing with her. She counsels leniency. "For my part," she declares, with an unconscious air, *"My* heart is not of stone!" He quickly suggests that she prove it by showing a little affection. "We were speaking of your daughter, were we not?" asks the widow. Taking her hand, he replies ardently, "True, but now we will speak of *your* happiness." Pretending not to

understand, she leads him on skilfully to an avowal of love,
and a suggestion that a little kiss would not be very
wicked. (Duet: "A kiss with discretion.") He is about
to steal one from her fair lips when Lampe's raucous voice
is heard without, arguing with Frau Willmer. The
Burgomaster wishes to conceal himself from these prying
eyes, and hides in the wardrobe. Gertrud locks him in,
then admits Lampe and his companion. To her dismay,
Lampe, pointing to the wardrobe demands of Frau Willmer if it is hers. She is obliged to admit her ownership,
and the factotum, puffed up with his own cleverness, asks
for the key, which is missing. To keep it from being
opened, he seals it up elaborately, and then, to determine
its contents, pokes his umbrella viciously through the
crevices of the carving. Something alive in there, he is
convinced! "A cat, perhaps?" suggests Gertrud. "No,
for it does not mew!" "A mouse, then?" says the widow,
somewhat annoyed by his persistence. Frau Gertrud's
answers to his questions lead him to think she is concealing a lover (Trio, Gertrud, Frau Willmer, Lampe: "Not
a single word is to be obtained"; Lampe: "Within this
wardrobe, a lover's sealed up"). Well pleased, Lampe
hurries off to tell the Burgomaster. "Thank heaven, he's
gone!" cry the women relieved, as Else and Bertel enter.
Putting their heads together, the four concoct a scheme
for the undoing of the obdurate parent (Quartette: "How
to use this great good fortune, let us now begin to
ponder").

In a most absurd scene, the lovers ardently woo each other
in an extravagant manner, and roundly abuse the Burgomaster for his hardheartedness. (Else, Bertel: "Adal-
bert, my loved one, I am thine, thine, thine!") Else
tells Bertel she will give him one hundred kisses, and then
bid him a long, an everlasting farewell! This is too much
for her father's patience, and he calls to them. They look
about, as if puzzled to know where the voice comes from,
and pretend to be amazed, when he tells them he is in the

wardrobe. He begs them to let him out, but they remind him of Lampe's seals. He implores, and they bargain that he shall give Else to Bertel, as the price of his
freedom. Impatient, and almost suffocated, he agrees to
this, but the naughty Else will not free the poor man, until
he promises to sign a contract giving her as dowry a house
and garden, five hundred thalers, and everything else that
her fertile brain can conceive at the moment. Bertel,
meanwhile, is copying the contract in his best clerky style.
At last, they begin fumbling with the lock, to the exasperation of the unhappy prisoner, who is finally released.
At this moment the watchman comes blundering down the
street with his lantern (Watchman: "Listen, good people,
while I tell ye"), and the three hide precipitately. The
Burgomaster, frantically declaring that he will somehow
get even locks and seals the wardrobe, as before.

Gertrud enters, calling "Else! Bertel!" Behind her are
a company of merry villagers, who have just returned
from a shooting contest. The champion shot gallantly
accompanies the widow. (Chorus: "Burgomaster! Burgomaster! Within a wardrobe why dost thou hide?") They
laugh uproariously, and dance around the wardrobe, making rude jests at the official's expense. At last Gertrud,
who has managed to secure the key, opens the wardrobe,
and behold! it is empty. The Burgomaster, stepping from
his hiding place in the room, while all are crowding round
the wardrobe suddenly appears before them. Gertrud is
really mystified this time, and the Champion, disappointed,
accuses her of having made up a fine tale, as a practical
joke. She declares she only told the truth, and appeals
to the others, who all stick to their stories. Lampe bustles
in with a rumour that the Burgomaster has disappeared,
and not only he but Else and Bertel also. "The Burgomaster is dead!" says the Burgomaster himself, solemnly,
and all the people shout with laughter. "Then, who *was*
in the wardrobe?" demands Lampe, anxiously, and he never
finds out. All declare that he is drunk, and hurry him

out protesting volubly. (Quartette: "I fear that soon the whole affair will surely come to light.")

The Burgomaster, to end the matter, orders that the wardrobe be removed by the accommodating Neighbour Knote and his son. The young people are blissfully happy, and the Burgomaster, turning to Gertrud at last, asks her to be his wife. He kisses her ardently, then, looking up they perceive that Else and Bertel are following their example. "Another seal!" cries the Burgomaster, happily, and with hand clapping, laughter and cheers from the crowd, the curtain falls.

GERMANIA

Lyric drama in a prologue, two acts and an epilogue. Music by Baron Alberto Franchetti. Text by Luigi Illica.

CAST: John Philip Palm—Bass. Frederick Loewe—Tenor. Carl Worms—Baritone. Crisogonus—Baritone. Ricke—Soprano. Jane, her little sister—Mezzo-soprano. Lena Aimuth, an old beggar—Mezzo-soprano. Jebbel, her grandson—Soprano. Pastor Stapps—Bass. Karl Theodor Körner, a poet—Tenor. Lützow—Bass. Lady Hedwig, Loewe's mother—Mezzo-soprano. The Chief of Police—Bass. A lady, really Queen Louise of Prussia—Contralto. Historical personages, students, soldiers, members of secret societies, police. Time, during the Napoleonic invasion of Germany. Place, Nüremberg. First performance, La Scala Theatre, Milan, March, 1902.

Prologue. Scene, an old mill on the Pegnitz river, which is crossed by a bridge near by. Near the mill are the dwellings of peasants, among them that of Lena Aimuth, an old beggar, who lives there with her grandson, Jebbel. The lower floor of the mill is filled with sacks of grain, etc.; a staircase leads to the upper story. Here, John Philip Palm, a patriot printer has been preparing literature against Napoleon, which has secured for him the Emper-

or's enmity. A band of students, disgused as millers, and
headed by Carl Worms as master miller are reading and
sorting out correspondence, or setting type at printing
presses, so arranged that they can quickly be concealed,
if the police appear. Palm, having been proscribed, is in
hiding in Lena's hut. Crisogonus, a daredevil student,
and a crack swordsman is providing entertainment for the
crowd, by his caustic comments. The students talk in a
curious slang of their own. All have nicknames; Worms
being "the mossy oak," and Crisogonus "fox heart." For
patriotic reasons, and to facilitate organization, they are
hoping to consolidate the secret societies of which all are
members, into one central society, which will issue general
orders, but the aims of the individual societies are still to
be maintained. Frederick Loewe, one of their leaders, now
absent at the war, has been chosen to arrange this. He is
betrothed to Ricke, Palm's daughter, whom Carl Worms
has seduced, during his absence. Old Lena, seated on the
doorsill of her hut, is teaching little Jebbel a popular song,
to bring alms from the passers-by. (Lena, Jebbel: "So
many stars are shining.") Crisogonus, within the mill,
is lightly humming a love song (Crisogonus: "Lili, fair
mistress"), when he breaks off with an oath. The students crowd around him. (Chorus: "What is it? What
has happened?") A letter has told him that Napoleon
is now Germany's Protector. All are dismayed, and Carl,
beside himself, bursts into bitter invective, ending with
"Have patience! Justice will have its way!" In derision he begins to sing "Gaudeamus igitur," but the students shake their heads. The news is too disquieting.
Worms then sings wildly of a great destiny, which has
been but a dream, and intimates that Palm had gone too
far, and had caused its failure. Defiantly, he sings
"Gaudeamus igitur," and with a bitter laugh departs.
The students in silence return to their work. Crisogonus
hastily destroys the letters. Ricke, entering, asks him if
he has written to her brother and Loewe. "No," he tells

her. She makes a despairing gesture. "The road of
patriotism is a weary one," he says kindly, "but peace be
to you, Ricke!" "You speak of peace to me?" says the
girl sadly. With bent head she goes out. Crisogonus
cannot understand her melancholy. "Some man!" is his
shrewd conjecture. The students, under Carl's direction
have been loading the sacks of papers on the backs of
mules, to be carried away. A letter from Loewe brings
the news that the Tugenbund, so long hoped for, is estab-
lished. The students cheer, and Crisogonus gaily shouts
the news to Ricke, who turns pale. "How contrary are
women!" he sighs, as he joins his friends. Carl has returned to the mill, and Ricke implores him to make some
plan for her future. Frederick must be told, she says.
Carl declares that for many reasons this must not be.
She must lie, and lie convincingly. She refuses, cursing
him, but gives in just as Frederick's voice is heard in the
distance. "Germania!" he shouts. Entering, he embraces Worms. Lena, Palm, and Ricke's little sister Jane
come hurrying in, Palm anxiously inquiring for his son.
The students crowd around, and in a hurried aside to
Ricke, Frederick tells her that her brother has been killed
in battle, and that his last words were for her, giving her
to Frederick. He gives her a letter confirming this.
(Frederick: "Listen, O students, old friends and new.")
He addresses the students, presenting to them a group of
men, who have accompanied him, and who are representing
the other Universities in the matter of the Tugenbund. All
bear names now well known in history, and are acclaimed.
As the composer Weber is introduced, the students, led
by little Jane break into the Huntsman's Chorus, from
"Der Freischutz" with wild enthusiasm, but are interrupted by the arrival of the police. All set to work to
hide Palm, and the evidences of their work, so that the
mill shall seem to be running as usual. Worms begins to
sing (Worms: "Around, around in whirling motion, the
water ever comes and goes"). The French soldiers, en-

tering, search the mill, headed by the chief of police, and a French spy, Otto, Minister to Monaco. Worms, as head miller, denies all knowledge of Palm, but he is discovered and arrested. Jane rushes forward to bid him farewell, and amid a scene of consternation the curtain falls.

ACT I. A hut in the Black Forest. Before it sits Crisogonus, smoking a huge pipe, and talking with Lady Hedwig, Loewe's mother. Frederick and Ricke are close by, and Jane is playing in the forest. All are awaiting the arrival of Pastor Stapps to marry Frederick and Ricke. Hedwig breaks the news of Carl's supposed death (Hedwig: "United to the end.") Within the hut Ricke talks to little Jane who has followed her in, and innocently asks why her eyes are red. "Do not speak of it!" commands her sister. (Duet, Ricke, Jane: "The sister who seems like my mother.") Peters, a woodsman, leads in Pastor Stapps. Frederick explains the circumstances (Frederick: "I am like many another.") Other woodsmen have decorated the hut, and the wedding is performed. (Stapps: "Not from the Book of Books.") As all crowd around the pastor, bidding him adieu, Crisogonus packs his knapsack, and departs hurriedly; he cannot stand a parson. With a ringing "Gaudeamus," he strides through the forest. Frederick and Ricke, left alone, sing of their love (Frederick: "No, no close those eyes"; Ricke: "I tremble with the menace of a coming sorrow"). Frederick speaks lovingly of "Those eyes that never lie." At this moment the voice of Worms is heard in the "Huntsman's Chorus." Entering, he relates that he has been taken prisoner, but has escaped. (Worms: "All is lost, but the one boon of liberty.") Frederick asks him to share in their joy, for Ricke is now his wife. Worms sternly commands his friend to follow him, in the name of the Tugenbund. They go out together, leaving Ricke standing motionless and horror-stricken, now fully realizing what she has done. The moonlight falls upon her agonised face. With arms upraised, she reviles the Almighty

(Ricke: "What ardent longing, already my heart awoke"), and bemoans her sorrowful fate. What can she do? Sitting down she hastily writes a few lines to her husband. A storm is rising, so she wraps herself in a mantle and bidding farewell to her home departs. Frederick, returning, sees her hurrying through the forest (Frederick: " 'Twas his wish to go"), and catching sight of the letter, reads as follows: "For thee, for mamma, for all I am no more." He is thunderstruck. (Frederick: "A terrible storm seizes my soul in fury.") He hears Carl singing in the distance, and it comes to him that he is the cause of Ricke's departure. Jane enters, weeping, and her innocent answers to his questions confirm his suspicions. Ricke always called Carl "the accursed one," she informs him. (Jane: "Always she wept, and muttered to herself.") She is astonished when Frederick springs to his feet, with a burst of grief, swearing vengeance, and declaring that hereafter his country shall be his only love. The tempest is not stilled, and Jane, trying to pacify Frederick, sings childishly of Ricke's return (Jane: "See the moon again in splendour").

Act II. The headquarters of the Louise-Bund at Königsberg, a subterranean retreat decorated with symbolic devices, portraits, and a stand of arms in case of surprise by the police. Crisogonus is responsible for these decorations, of which he is very proud. Worms is in charge, and sits wearily at a table. Voices are heard, far off, calling "Germania! Germania." Crisogonus hands Worms a mantle and mask, in which to receive the "companions," who enter, repeating the password. Some are masked. Worms asks if there is any news of Frederick. Crisogonus shakes his head. Crisogonus beats on the table with a rapier to ensure silence, and calls the roll. All are then put through the catechism of the order, in which they declare that Germania is their mother, their love, their life, and there is nothing they would not do for her. Worms tells them of the wrongs their beloved country has suffered

at the hands of Napoleon. These must be avenged.
Crisogonus leads forward the pale and terrified Jebbel,
who confesses that he was the betrayer of Palm, but had
kept silence until the death of his aged grandmother. He
throws on the table the money he received for this wicked
deed. All are silent, then break into maledictions, but
Lützow declares that he will be responsible for the boy,
and their anger is appeased (Chorus: "Long live Lützow"). Pastor Stapps rises, holding out a little box
(Stapps: "He was a son to me, born to this destiny") telling of Frederick's death, (Chorus: "Proud, oh, old man, be
thy grief"). All sing of the honour due to those who die
for their country, but a voice interrupts, saying "Oh, vile
words, oh, false faith." Amid general excitement, the unknown, who is masked, denounces Worms. (The Unknown: "Victory ever is holy and pure.") There is a
tumult, and all demand the name of the intruder. (The
Unknown: "Sun of Glory.") He advances towards
Worms with an accusing gesture. The latter tearing off
his mask discloses Frederick Loewe. All are silent as
Frederick challenges his friend to mortal combat. Ra-
piers are quickly secured, but Worms at first will not fight.
The crowd murmurs (Chorus: "We do not desire a fratri-
cide"). Frederick's eyes, burning with revenge, are fixed
on his opponent, who stepping forward, declares he is
ready. (Worms: "Hear ye! I will die.") He bids farewell to Crisogonus and the others, and the duel is about
to begin when a lady suddenly appears, leading a little
boy. It is Queen Louise with her son (Chorus: "It is our
queen"). All bow before her and break into cheers. She
stops the combat, and makes peace between Frederick and
Carl.

Epilogue. After an intermezzo, describing the battle of
Leipsic, in which the heroes of the past greet their brethren
of the present, soon to join them in glory (Chorus: "Glory,
O coming heroes"), the curtain rises on the battlefield.
The scene is one of devastation and carnage, the battle

having lasted three days. Everywhere, dead men and
horses are piled in heaps. Two pallid creatures wander
over the silent place, Ricke and Jebbel, both dishonoured
and forlorn. Through them Frederick and Carlo have really
come to their death. The lamentations of the wounded rise
in plaintive chorus. Jebbel, standing on a little hill overlooking the scene, sings of the sure advance of liberty, even
though her adherents are destroyed. (Jebbel: "No, come
what may, Liberty forever advances.") Ricke stops a
moment beside the body of Thorberg, and closes his eyes.
They hear a groan; it is Frederick, still living, but at the
point of death. Running to him they revive him with
brandy, and he opens his eyes. (Frederick: "O thou who
aidest me!") He gasps out a few words, trying to speak
the word "Germania!" which Ricke pronounces for him,
weeping bitterly. He recognises her, and she flings herself down beside him. (Ricke: "Drink, 'twill bring life";
Frederick: "I know the infinitely desolate story of thy sorrow.") He tells her all has been made known to him. She
implores him not to die but he falls back with a groan. In
a frenzy of grief, she curses Worms, but Frederick rebukes
her, saying that he has need rather of her prayers. Re-
pentantly she seeks out his body and lays over it the flag
which he had carried in the battle, then returns to Frederick, and raises him, that he may see the sky. The sun is
setting, and its last rays are red as blood. Frederick sees
before him the vision of an army in retreat, above which fly
many eagles, with wings outspread. At the head of this
army, Napoleon rides on a horse splashed with blood. The
Emperor's head is sunk upon his breast, but he is alone in
his sorrow as in his glory. Behind him ride his generals,
and soldiers bearing arms and banners. Frederick gasps
out "Oh, free Germa—Ah," and dies. Ricke piously com-
poses the poor, worn body, and falls across it herself, in
death. The sun sets in red splendour. Curtain.

MONA

Opera in Three Acts.   Music by Horatio Parker.   Poem by Brian Hooker.

CAST: Mona, princess of Britain—Mezzo. Enya, her foster-mother—Soprano. Arth, a Briton, husband of Enya—Bass. Gloom, their son, a Druid—Baritone. Nial, a changeling—Tenor. Caradoc, chief bard of Britain—Baritone. The Roman Governor of Britain—Baritone. Quintus, his son, known to the Britons as Gwynn—Tenor. Roman soldiers, Druids, Bards and Britons, both men and women. Place, Southwestern Britain. Time, End of first century A. D.

This opera won the prize offered by the Metropolitan Opera Company for the best grand opera, written in English and composed by an American.

ACT I. Morning in midsummer. Arth's hut: a primitive and rather sombre interior of rough wood and stone, lighted only from the doorway to the rear above which appears the Druidic sign of the Unspeakable Name ———— and from the opening in the roof to the right through which the smoke of the fire ascends. Enya busy about the house, Nial lying by the fire, Mona and Gwynn in the foreground. Gwynn pleads with Mona to fulfil her troth to him, long since pledged. She answers that in his absence her old dreams of war and the Roman oppressor hurled back into the sea and of some great part for herself in the freeing of Britain have pressed closer, driving the thought of him away. Against Enya's protest she shows him on her breast the sign of the Name wherewith she was born; declaring herself set apart by that sign for some great destiny above womanhood. Gwynn urges that her fancies are mere loneliness, and that whatever her destiny may be they can fulfil it better together; while Nial asks innocently if God's name is written upon those who may not love. Mona relates a dream of walk-

ing between a storm darkened forest and a raging sea:
she had a naked sword wherewith she drove back the
billows that poised to plunge down upon her; but there
came a veiled white figure with no face and tried to take
the sword away; and when she slew him therewith the
waves broke and the forest fell and overwhelmed her.
This dream neither Gwynn nor Enya can interpret.
Arth, entering, hurls at Mona's feet the sword of a Roman
soldier whom he has encountered and slain; and Mona
recognises the sword of her dream. Gwynn censures Arth
for wanton folly in breaking the peace; Arth retorts
with a furious tirade against Rome, in which the women
hysterically join; but Gwynn prevails, and sends Arth
out to bury the body. Gwynn illustrates the use of the
sword with unconscious enthusiasm. Enya grows suspicious and Mona, crying out that he looks like a Roman
soldier, snatches it from him and in so doing wounds his
arm. As they stand aghast at the omen, Gloom enters
and confirms it; prophesying that Gwynn shall die by that
same blade. He sends away the women and ushers in
Arth and Caradoc, who proposes a solemn oath of secrecy
and union. Gwynn, suspecting conspiracy, is unwilling to
swear himself blindly into their fellowship; but lest the
secret of his own birth be suspected and he lose Mona
and all his influence for peace, is constrained to yield.
Caradoc administers the oath with Druidic ritual; then
tells Gwynn that Britain is ripe for a universal uprising,
and that Mona by her descent from Boadicea and by
signs and prophecies is ordained to be their leader. Gwynn
furiously protests but is overruled by Caradoc and Gloom.
Mona is brought in to choose between her love and her
mission. Caradoc formally recognises her as the predestined leader. Gwynn does his utmost to hold her; but
Gloom artfully playing upon her dream and sneering at
her love as a trifle, is too strong for him. She flies into
an ecstasy, waving her sword and calling down ruin upon
Rome. Gwynn is driven away and banished. As he dis-

appears into the forest, Mona suddenly drops the sword, crying out his name, and breaks into tears.

ACT II. A month later. Evening. The Cromlech in the forest: A huge oak tree in the centre; at its foot an altar graven with the Sign of the Name; behind that, a crumbling stone wall in the form of a semicircle; and behind this, deep forest, through which appear the great standing stones of the outer circle. Nial alone, dancing with his shadow. In monologue he declares himself happier, being a changeling with no soul, brother to all the wild things of the earth, than his wise friends whose souls torment them. The Governor, entering at the head of a scouting party, captures him and questions him as to the evident signs of a recent gathering there; but Nial, fearless through sheer ignorance of harm, refuses to answer. As he is about to be tortured, Gwynn suddenly appears and interposes. The Governor questions him about the reported rebellion, adding that Gwynn is freely accused of treason in siding with the Britons. Gwynn, refusing to break his oath by revealing their plans, yet claims as his own work the peace of the past years, and promises that through Mona and his own influence as a Bard the threatened uprising shall be averted. The Governor is for crushing the conspiracy by immediate force; but is at length brought to refrain on condition that Gwynn shall hold the tribes from any overt act of war. On this Gwynn stakes everything and sets out to guide his father back to the Roman town. After a momentary soliloquy by Nial in the gathering darkness, Mona and Gloom enter together. They have been going about the country preparing universal rebellion; and on that night they themselves are to lead the attack upon the Roman town whose flames will be the signal for a general uprising. Mona, inspired with the ecstasy of her mission, yet dreads their own opening battle upon which all depends. In the enthusiasm of his reassurance, Gloom throws off the mask of priesthood and brotherliness, avowing open-

love of her.   She silences him by turning against him his
own teaching that she is not woman but a sword.   After
a short colloquy with Arth and Enya in which Mona relates her triumphant progress among the tribes the others
go to prepare for the sacrifice which is to initiate the
battle, leaving Mona praying alone in the moonlight before the altar.   Gwynn, entering, brushes aside the frozen
holiness with which she had crushed Gloom, by defying her
to call in the Druids and have him put to death; and catching her in his arms, so prevails upon her by the sheer reality of their love that she is for the moment utterly his own,
wishing only to forget all else.   In premature triumph, he
tells her that their union shall unite Britain and Rome,
and goes on to reveal the secret of his birth.   But she,
understanding merely that he is a Roman, without waiting to hear the rest, cries out for help.   Gloom and Arth
rush in, followed by Bards and Druids and a frantic horde
of Britons.   Gwynn is about to be torn in pieces when
Mona, unable to see him slain, checks herself in the very
word of denouncing him as a spy, and reminds them that
he is a Bard whose person is sacred; then, bidding them
make him prisoner unhurt, she hurries on the preparations
for the attack.   Men and women bring torches, weapons,
and materials of war.   The Bards and Druids gather
about the altar, where Mona, Gloom and Caradoc, to the
music of a barbaric chant, perform the ceremony of
blessing and distributing the swords.   As they receive
their weapons the priests rush out to lead the onslaught,
followed by the tribesmen; until the stage is left empty
and dark but for Enya who throws herself sobbing at the
foot of the altar as the sound of the singing dies away in
the forest.

ACT III.   The same night, just before dawn, A plateau
on the edge of the forest; across a valley, the Roman
Town in the distance.   Enya and Nial come to watch and
wait for tidings of the attack.   Her agony of suspense
and foreboding contrasts with his innocent unconcern.

Instead of the expected beacon-signals of victory, scattered fugitives rush past; and from one of these Enya learns that the attack is crushed.   Nial, with unconscious irony, protests that the news must be false, since God had promised them victory.   Mona, stunned with shame and exhaustion, is dragged in by Gloom, who is himself mortally wounded.   He confirms the tidings of defeat: the Roman garrison, swelled to an overwhelming force, was awaiting them under arms; Arth is dead; it is all over but paying the price.   Mona despairs over her people who have trusted her vainly through her own vain trust in her mission; and searches her conscience for some fault or failure of her own that has ruined all.   But Gloom, with savage cynicism, retorts that they have only dressed their own desires in fine names like everyone else: Mona was moved by a girl's vanity of greatness, himself by lust of power and rivalry with Gwynn; the rest was self-deception.   And Mona, shocked and shaken, fixes upon her love for Gwynn as the weakness that has destroyed her work: she has saved his life knowing him to be a Roman spy and a traitor to her people.   The appearance of Gwynn, who has escaped from his guards, confirms her belief that it was he who warned the Romans.   Gwynn tells them that he is the son of the Governor with authority to speak for Rome, and tries to induce her to aid him in preventing further bloodshed.   But it is too late for the truth: Gloom receives it with mere derision; and Mona, taking it for the keystone upon an arch of lies, works herself into a vengeful holiness as she listens to his protestations.   At last she pretends to yield, and as he catches her in his arms, stabs him with her Roman sword. In the pause that follows, Nial sees through the grey twilight of dawn the soul of Gwynn floating like a bright shadow above him and seeming to listen and to wait.   The sound of an approaching army is heard in the distance and presently the Governor enters at the head of his legions. Discovering Gwynn's body, he tells them furiously that in slaying his son, the one Roman who befriended them and who had wasted himself to save them from their own folly, they have destroyed their last hope of mercy. Mona avows her deed and he promises her full time in which to pay. She, at length understanding all Gwynn's truth and her own error, takes farewell of him laying the sword across his breast: saying that in seeking great deeds beyond love and above beauty she has done only what she must have done being herself; that the ordinary happiness through which she might have accomplished her mission was too small and too near; and regretting most that she cannot follow Gwynn to an honourable death. She bends down and kisses him on the forehead, then, rising, stands among the soldiers while they bind her hands, bidding them take their will of her; and adding, as the curtain falls, "I have had great dreams—only great dreams. . . . A woman would have won."

SUPPLEMENT NO. 2

BORIS GODOUNOFF

An opera in four acts and eight scenes by Moussorgsky, text founded on the drama of the same name by Pushkin. First produced in Petrograde in 1874.

CAST: Boris Godounoff—Baritone. Feodor—Mezzo-soprano. Xenia—Soprano. The Old Nurse—Contralto. Prince Shouisky—Tenor. Andrey Stchelakov, clerk of the Douma—Baritone. Pimen, monk and chronicler—Bass. The Pretender Dimitri, called Gregory—Tenor. Marina—Soprano. Rangoni, a Jesuit in disguise—Bass. Varlaam—Bass. Missail—Tenor. The Hostess—Mezzo-soprano. Nikitin (Michael) constable. Place, Russia. Time, 1598-1605.

ACT I. Scene I is laid in front of the Novodievitchi Convent and the populace, sufficiently inspired by a Police Officer, are demanding that the Tzar reassume the sceptre of Russia. The secretary of the Douma comes out of the convent, and informs the crowd that the Tzar still refuses. The crowd again renews its appeal. Scene II is laid in a cell within the convent. Gregory awakes from a horrible dream. He bemoans the fate of the murdered Tzarevitch. Scene III is in the great Square between the two Cathedrals of the Assumption and the Archangels. The populace are awaiting the coming of the Tzar. He appears amid cries of joy, addresses the people, and then enters the Cathedral of the Assumption.

ACT II. Scene I is in an inn. Gregory and two monks who have escaped from the convent with him, enter. Shortly afterwards a guard appears in search of a fugitive whose description tallies with that of Gregory. He rushes from the room with the guard in pursuit. Scene II is in the Tzar's apartments in the Kremlin. Word is brought to the Tzar that Dimitri who was murdered (impersonated by Gregory) has reappeared and is rousing the people. The Tzar betrays great agony of mind.

Act III. Scene I is in a garden before the Polish Castle of Mniscek. In a love scene between the False Dimitri and Marina, she spurs him on to lead the attack against Moscow so that he may seize the throne and make her queen. Scene II is in the Forest of Kromy where Dimitri's army disperses a crowd of vagrants and rescues some of his adherents. Scene III is before the Kremlin. A session is being held, presided over by the Tzar to decide what judgment shall be meted out to the false Dimitri. An old peasant tells the Tzar how he was cured of blindness when praying at the tomb of the dead Tzarevitch, and the Tzar deeply impressed after counselling his son to reign wisely, prays that his great crimes may be forgiven him and falls dead.

THE CANTERBURY PILGRIMS

An American opera in four acts by Reginald de Koven. Text by Percy Mackaye. First produced at the Metropolitan Opera House, March 8, 1917.

Cast: Geoffrey Chaucer, First Poet Laureate of England. Knight. Squire, his son. Friar, Miller, Cook, Shipman, Summoner, Pardoner—Alisoun's Swains. Host. Man of Law. Joannes, the Prioress' Servitor. Richard II, King of England. The Wife of Bath (Alison) The Prioress (Madame Eglantine) Johanna. Pilgrims, Nobles, Choir-boys, Prelates, Nuns, Brooch-girls, Serving-maids, etc. Place, England. Time, 1387.

Act I. Scenes. The Tabard Inn, at Southwark, near London.

ACT II. Garden of the One-Nine-Pin Inn, at the little hamlet of Bob-up-and-down, en route to Canterbury.

ACT III. The Hall of the Inn.

ACT IV. Before the west Front of Canterbury Cathedral.

The story has to do with the merry schemes of the Wife of Bath who has fallen in love with Chaucer, who in his turn loves the Prioress, and of her winning of a bet to gain possession of a certain brooch which carries with it Chaucer's promise of marriage. He is finally rescued by Richard II who decides that the Wife may marry a sixth time only on condition that she marry a miller. A devoted miller joyfully accepts the opportunity and the Proiress and Chaucer are reconciled.

CLEOPATRA'S NIGHT

(Une Nuit de Cléopâtre)

An American Opera in two acts. Music by Henry Hadley. (Op. 90). Text by Alice Leal Pollock, based on a story by Théophile Gautier.

CAST: Cleopatra, Queen of Egypt—Dramatic Soprano. Meïamoun, a young Egyptian—Tenor. Mark Anthony—Baritone. Mardion, the favourite maid to the Queen—Mezzo-soprano. Diomedes, Chief of Cleopatra's rowers. The Distiller of Poisons. Iras, a maiden—Mezzo-soprano. A Eunuch—Baritone. Anthony's Chief Officer—Baritone. A Guest—Tenor. A Hungry Guest—Bass. A Female Guest—Mezzo-soprano. Place, Egypt. Time, midsummer. First produced, January 31, 1920, at the Metropolitan Opera House.

ACT I. It is a hot and oppressive day in midsummer; and Mardion, who is in love with Meïamoun, tells Iras of her unrequitted love for him and of Cleopatra's many amours as they wait for the Queen to come for her bath. Cleopatra arrives with her retinue and her lament about the loneliness of queens is cut short by an arrow which suddenly falls beside her bearing the message "I love you." The head of Meïamoun appears in the water, and the guards are about to kill him, when Cleopatra, upon learning of his love for herself, offers to give him a night of happiness if he will be willing to die at sunrise. He consents and Mardion kills herself in despair and her body is thrown to the crocodiles.

Act II. The Queen keeps her guests waiting at the banquet on the terraces of the palace while she lingers with Meïamoun. When she does enter with him there is a scene of unlicensed passion. Finally the guests and the dancing-girls stroll off into the garden. The dawn is breaking, and Cleopatra longs to save her lover from his fate. But even she may not reverse an order once given. He drinks the poison prepared for him and falls dead at her feet. The arrival of Mark Anthony is announced; and with a parting kiss on the lips of her dead lover, she goes to meet the Roman.

CONCHITA

An opera in four acts by Riccardo Zandonai. Text by Vaucaire and Zangarini, based on Lierre Louy's "La Femme et le Pantin." First produced in Milan in 1911.

Cast: Conchita—Soprano. Mateo—Tenor. Conchita's mother—Mezzo-soprano. Rufina—Mezzo-soprano. Estella—Mezzo-soprano. The Superintendent—Mezzo-soprano. Garcia, Dance Hall Proprietor—Bass. Tonio, a waiter—Bass. Various characters in dance hall, factory and street. Place, Seville. Time, present.

Act I. In a cigar factory. Mateo, a wealthy Spaniard, comes to visit the factory and Conchita recognizes him as the man who rescued her from the unwelcome attentions of a policeman. She invites him to her home, and unseen by her, he gives her mother some money to make some purchases. When she discovers it, she thinks he has tried to buy her love, and refusing to have anything more to do with him, she leaves home.

Act II. In a dance hall, Conchita is supporting herself by executing some very daring dances. Mateo, after a search, finds her and begs her to give up this life and go and live in a little house he owns. She finally consents.

Act III. A street in Seville. Instead of letting him in when Mateo arrives at midnight, as agreed, Conchita talks with him out of the window and arouses his jealousy by turning and calling as if to a male companion within. Mateo tries to break into the house without success; Conchita taunts him, and he staggers off.

Act IV. Conchita comes to Mateo's house and tells him she had expected that he would at least kill himself for love of her. He suddenly seizes and beats her. She tries to stab him, and then confesses her love for him. He takes her in his arms.

CYRANO

An American opera in four acts. Music by Walter Damrosch. Text by W. J. Henderson, after the drama by Edmond Rostand. First production, Metropolitan Opera House, February 27, 1913.

Cast: Cyrano de Bergerac—Baritone. Roxane—Soprano. Duenna—Alto. Lise—Soprano. A Flower-Girl —Soprano. Christian—Tenor. Ragueneau—Tenor. De Guiche—Bass. Le Bret—Bass. A Tall Musketeer— Bass. Montfleury—Tenor. First Cavalier—Bass. Second Cavalier—Tenor. Third Cavalier—Bass. A Cadet —Tenor. Chorus of Precieuses, Pages, Nuns, Cavaliers, Gascony Cadets, Marquises, etc. Place, France. Time, Reign of Louis XIII.

Act I. In the Hotel de Bourgogne, in Paris, a coterie of literary ladies, whose leader is the witty Roxane, and their admirers are waiting for a play to begin. Christian, who has recently joined the Gascony Cadets, tells Le Bret, who is also a member, that he is hopelessly in love with Roxane. He learns from Le Bret that she is the cousin of Cyrano, who has a nose that "None may speak of it, save under breath: it is the very nose of death." When the audience is assembled and Montfleury begins to sing, Cyrano forces him to retire. De Guiche makes a cutting remark about Cyrano's nose; and Cyrano after showing him how much more witty he could have made this remark, challenges him to a duel, and wounds him. All leave the hotel except Cyrano who tells Le Bret that he himself dares to love Roxane. As he is about to leave, De Guiche returns with a hundred bravos and Cyrano joyously fights his way out.

Act II. Into the pastry-shop of Ragueneau comes Cyrano and begins to write verses to Roxane. When she appears, he drives all the other occupants of the shop out into the street. Roxane, relying on his brotherly affection for her, tells Cyrano that she loves Christian and asks him to watch over him. Cyrano, suppressing his own grief and love, consents; and Roxane leaves. The "Gascony Cadets" enter and congratulate Cyrano on his defeat of De Guiche and his bravos; and Cyrano recounts the circumstances to them. Christian, wishing to prove his bravery, twits Cyrano on his nose from time to time, during the story. Cyrano orders the others out of the room, and explains to Christian that he is Roxane's "brother," that she loves him [Christian] and that he desires to help him woo her. Christian gladly agrees. A musketeer presuming upon the fact that Christian was not punished for mentioning Cyrano's nose, speaks of it and is knocked down.

Act III. De Guiche comes to tell Roxane, who is reclining in the moonlight before her house, that he has been placed in command of the Gascony Cadets and can now revenge himself on Cyrano. She suggests that his greatest revenge would be to leave the Cadets behind when he starts for Arras. He agrees and then declares his love for her. He leaves and she goes into her house. Cyrano and Christian appear. Cyrano impersonates Christian and enchants Roxane, who appears on her balcony. A monk arrives with a letter from De Guiche who says he will be there shortly, but which Roxane interprets to the monk as a command to marry her at once to Christian. They go into the house while Cyrano remains without to detain De Guiche. He arrives and Cyrano detains him with a fanciful tale until the lovers reappear and he realises he has been outwitted. He at once orders Cyrano and Christian to Arras.

Act IV. Scene I. Cyrano has been writing love letters to Roxane in Christian's name. She suddenly appears upon the scene, and tells him she would love him even if he were ugly. Christian becomes jealous and demands that Cyrano tell her whose the letters are that she admires so much. He then rushes off into the battle. Soon his dead body is brought in and Roxane finds Cyrano's letter upon it. Cyrano himself is wounded, and Roxane is borne off fainting by Ragueneau.

Scene II. Roxane seeks shelter at a convent where Cyrano has already been carried. They meet before the convent and Roxane discovers that it is he and not Christian she has learned to love through the letters. Le Bret and Ragueneau enter hastily in search of Cyrano, and discover that his wound has reopened in his excitement and that he is bleeding to death. He dies with the words, "My soldier's snow-white plume," and Roxane leaning over him.

DON CARLOS

An opera in four acts by Giuseppe Verdi. Text by Méry and du Locle, after the tragedy of the same title. First produced in Paris in 1867.

CAST: Philip II, King of Spain. Don Carlos, "Infant" of Spain. Rodrigo, Marquis of Posa. Grand Inquisitor, aged 90, blind. A Friar. Elizabeth of Valois. The Princess Eboli. Theobald, Elizabeth's page. The Countess of Aremberg. The Count of Lerna. A Royal Herald. Flemish Ladies, Inquisitors, Gentlemen, and Ladies of the Courts of France and Spain. Members of the Populace, Pages, Guards, Familiars of the Holy Office, Soldiers, Magistrates, Deputies from the various provinces constituting the Spanish Empire, etc. Time, about 1560.

ACT I. Forest of Fontainbleau. Don Carlos, son of Phillip II and Crown Prince of Spain, is the affianced lover of the beautiful Elizabeth of Valois, daughter of Henry II. Don Carlos and Elizabeth meet for the first time, and Don Carlos pretends that he is only a messenger from the "Infant" with a gift for her. He tells her of Don Carlos's admiration for her. She opens the package and finds a miniature of Don Carlos, and at once recognises him as the original. They fall deeply and passionately in love with each other. A messenger arrives with the news that she is to marry, for reasons of state, Phillip II, not his son, Don Carlos. The lovers are in despair.

ACT II. The royal marriage is duly solemnised; but Don Carlos can not overcome his love for Elizabeth. His friend, Rodrigo, advises him to go to Flanders, to forget his passion; and Don Carlos asks Elizabeth to gain the requisite permission from the King. Their interview serves to re-awaken the intensity of their love; and Don Carlos clasps her in his arms forgetful of all else, and then flees from the scene.

ACT III. Part I. The Queen's Garden. During a carnival Don Carlos meets the Princess Eboli, and mistaking her for Elizabeth, tells her of his love. The Princess loves him herself, and she joyously removes her mask. When she learns of her mistake, filled with jealousy, she threatens to reveal Don Carlos's love for Elizabeth to the King. Part II. A large square before Nostra Donna d'Atocha, with a funeral pile. The bells are ringing joyously. The Court and the Queen, and later the King, enter, as for a holiday. Don Carlos appears at the head of a delegation of Flemings and begs for mercy for them. The King refuses, and Don Carlos, drawing his sword, vows to be their savior. The King orders him disarmed, but everyone is afraid to attempt it until Rodrigo asks him for his sword and Don Carlos yields. The funeral pile is lighted and the joyous song of the Inquisitors is heard.

Act IV. Part I. In the King's Library. The Grand Inquisitor convinces the king that Don Carlos must be imprisoned. The Princess Eboli arouses his jealousy by telling him of the love between his son and his wife. Part II. The prison of Don Carlos. Rodrigo comes to visit his friend and is shot by unknown men, by order of the Inquisition which fear his enlightened spirit. Part III. The Cloisters of the Convent of St. Just. Don Carlos has been freed at the demand of the populace and hastens to the Convent for a last farewell with Elizabeth. Elizabeth is exhorting him to help Flanders, and so distract his mind from his own sorrows, when the King suddenly arrives, having heard of their clandestine meeting, and delivers his son over to the Inquisition.

FRANCESCA DA RIMINI

Opera in four acts by Riccardo Zandonai. Text by T. Riccardi, founded on the drama by Gabriele d'Annunzio. First produced at Turin, Italy, February 1, 1914.

Cast: Giovanni, the lame—Baritone. Paolo, the beautiful—Tenor, Malatestino, the one-eyed—Tenor, sons of Malatesta da Verrucchio. Ostasio, son of Guido

Minore da Polenta—Baritone. Ser Toldo Berardengo, a
Notary—Tenor. A Jester—Bass. A Bowman—Tenor.
Tower Warden—Baritone. Francesca, daughter of
Guido and sister of Ostasio—Soprano. Samaritana, a
sister of Francesca and Ostasio—Soprano. Biancofiore,
Garsenda, Altichiara, women of Francesca, Smaradi, a
slave. Bowman, archers, and musicians. Place, Ravenna
and Rimini.

Act I. The court of the house of the Plentani. For
reasons of state it is necessary that Francesca marry
Giovanni, the Lamester, or Gianciotto as he is called; but
as she would surely refuse to comply, a plot is laid whereby
she is made to think that Paolo, his handsome brother,
is the destined bridegroom. She falls deeply in love with
him, and he with her, though they are not allowed to
exchange a word.

Act II. A platform of the tower of the Malatesti. A
fight is in progress between the Guelfs and the Ghibellines.
Francesca, now married to Gianciotto, meets Paolo for
the first time and reproaches him for his deception of her.
He protests that he knew nothing of it, and declares his
love for her. Word is brought of his election as Captain
of the People and the Commune of Florence and he sets
out for Florence.

Act III. The beautiful apartments of Francesca. She
is reading to her women from an ancient tome, the story
of *Lancelot and Guenevere*. At a whispered word from
her slave she dismisses them, and Paolo sick for love of
her, enters. He has returned from Florence to see
her. Together they continue reading the story; and
as the passion in the ancient tale increases so their passion for each other increased until they give kiss for
kiss.

Act IV. Malatestino, the youngest brother of Gianciotto, who himself loves Francesca, betrays the secret
meeting of Francesca and Paolo of which he has learned,
by chance, to the husband. Gianciotto determines to learn

the truth for himself.   He lies in wait for them; **finds**
them together, and slays them in the early dawn.

GIANNI SCHICCHI

Opera in one act by Puccini.   Text by G. Forzano.
Cast: Gianni Schicchi.   Lauretta.   Zita, Rinuccio,
Gherardo, Nella Gherardino, Betto, Simone, Marco, La
Ciesca—all relatives of Buoso Donati.   Master Spinel-
loccio, physician.   Amantio Di Nicolao, notary.   Pinel-
lino, shoemaker.   Guccio, a dyer.   Place, Florence.
Time, 1299.   First produced at Metropolitan Opera
House, New York, December 14, 1918.
The scene is laid in the bed-chamber of Buoso Donati.
Donati has been dead two hours and his relatives are reading the will.   They find he has left all to charity.   Gianni
Schicchi is called in and consulted.   So far only those in
the room know Donati is dead.   Schicchi hides the corpse,
with the consent of the others, gets into bed, and when
the doctor calls, imitates Donati's voice and pretends he
wants to sleep.   The lawyer is sent for, and Schicchi dictates a new will in favour of himself, as sole heir, to the
consternation and of the anger of the others, who dare
not interfere.

GOYESCAS OR THE RIVAL LOVERS

An opera in three Tableaux.   Music by Enrique Granados.
Text by Fernando Periquet.
Cast: Rosario, a high-born lady, 25 years of age.
Pepa, a popular *maja* of Madrid, 25 years of age.   Fernando, Captain of the Royal Spanish Guard, 25 years
of age.   Paquiro, a toreador, 25 years of age.   *Majos*
and *Majas*.   Place, Madrid.   Time, 1800.   First produced at the Metropolitan Opera House, January 28, 1916.

The characters and settings were suggested by the paintings of Goya.

The opera opens with a crowd of *majos* and *majas*, enjoying a holiday on the outskirts of Madrid. Some of them are tossing a *pelele* (a man of straw) in a blanket, a popular pastime. Pepa, the present sweetheart of Paquiro, drives up in her dog-cart; shortly afterwards the great lady, Rosario arrives in her sedan-chair to keep a rendezvous with her lover, Fernando, the captain of the Royal Guard. Paquiro arouses Fernando's jealousy by reminding Rosario of a *baile de candil* she once attended, and invites her to go again. Fernando accepts the invitation both for himself and Rosario. Pepa, in a rage, swears to best Rosario.

Fernando brings Rosario to the ball. His haughty words and bearing offend the *majos* and *majas*. Pepa taunts Fernando to madness, and in the excitement Rosario faints. Fernando and Paquiro exchange challenges for a duel.

Later there is a passionate love scene in Rosario's garden between her and Fernando which is terminated by Paquiro reminding Fernando it is time for the duel. The duel is fought, and Fernando is mortally wounded and dies in Rosario's arms.

HERODIAS

An opera in five acts. Music by Massenet. Text by M. M. Milliet, H. Gremont and A. Zanardini. First produced at the Théâtre de la Monnaie, 1881.

CAST: Salome. Herod. Herodias. Phanuel. John the Baptist. Vitellius. The High Priest. Desert Chiefs, Merchants, Slaves, Dancers, Citizens, Jewish priests, Sadducees and Pharisees, Arabian envoys, Nobles, Romans. Place, Jerusalem. Time, about 30 A.D.

ACT I. The great court of Herod's Palace. Salome

arrives at the palace with a caravan bringing gifts to
Herod. She was mysteriously separated from Herodias
in childhood, and does not know she is her daughter.
Herod is attracted toward her; but her one desire is to
return to the Prophet in the wilderness who was kind to
her. Herodias enters, demanding John's head as he has
publically insulted her by calling her Jezebel. Herod refuses. John enters and continues his denunciations. The
king and Herodias flee from him. Salome throws herself
at his feet, and confesses her love for him, but he demands
that she turn her thought to the ideal love of the new faith
in which he believes.

Act II. Herod is unable to break himself of his infatuation for Salome and endangers the safety of his
kingdom by conspiring against the Romans.

Act III. Herodias consults Phanuel, an astrologer,
who tells her that Salome is her daughter. She sees
Salome entering the Temple, recognises her as her rival,
in Herod's affections, and repudiates her. Within the
Temple Salome prays to God to save John who has been
thrown into prison. Herod tells Salome of his love and
she repulses him with: "I love another who is mightier
than Cæsar, stronger than any hero." In a fury, he condemns them both to death.

Act IV. Salome implores Herodias to save John, who,
unknown to her, has already been executed. When she
learns of his death she attempts to kill Herodias.
Herodias cries, "Have mercy, I am your mother."
"Then take back your blood and my life," and Salome
stabs herself instead.

IL TABORRO

(The Cloak)

Opera in one act by Puccini. Text by G. Adami after "La
Houppelande," by Didier Gold.

CAST: Michele, a skipper. Luigi, a longshoreman. Tinca, a longshoreman. Talpa, a longshoreman. Giorgetta, Michele's wife. Frugola, wife of Talpa. Longshoremen, a Song Peddler, Midinettes, an Organ Grinder, Two Lovers. Place, Seine River. First produced at the Metropolitan Opera House, December 14, 1918.

The scene is laid on a barge, just at sunset. The day's work is done and the two bargemen leave. Luigi lingers in the cabin and arranges with Giorgetta to strike a match when it is safe for him to return. He then departs. Michele, the husband, enters; and though he suspects his wife, reminds her of their early love and how he used to shelter her under his cloak. Giorgetta receives these reminiscences coldly, and retires to the cabin on the plea of weariness. The husband lights his pipe; and Luigi, thinking it is the signal, clambers on board and is choked to death by Michele, who covers the body with his cloak and resumes his smoking. Giorgetta, hearing the struggle, returns to the deck and is relieved to find her husband so composed. She in her turn tries to recall their former love-making; and in answer he suddenly flings back his coat and reveals the dead body. He then throws his wife violently upon it.

I. PURITANI

An opera in three acts, by Bellini. Text by Count Pepoli. First produced in Paris, January 25, 1835.

CAST: Lord Gautier Walton of the Puritans—Bass. Sir George Walton, his brother—Bass. Lord Arthur Talbot of the Cavaliers—Tenor. Sir Richard Forth of the Puritans—Baritone. Sir Benno Robertson, of the Puritans—Tenor. Henrietta, of France, widow of Charles I.—Soprano. Elvira, daughter of Lord Walton—Soprano. Puritans, Soldiers of the Commonwealth, Men-At-Arms, Women, Pages, etc. Place, near Plymouth,

England. Time, during the Wars between Cromwell and the Stuarts.

ACT I. A fortress near Plymouth, commanded by Lord Walton. His daughter, Elvira, has been promised in marriage to Sir Richard Forth by Lord Walton; but when he finds she is in love with Lord Arthur Talbot, a cavalier, he relents and arranges for her marriage with him. Upon his arrival, Talbot finds that Queen Henrietta is imprisoned in the fortress and assists her to escape, wrapped in Elvira's bridal veil. On the way they encounter Forth; and when he discovers that the woman with Talbot is not Elvira, he is content to let them pass. When the escape is discovered, Elvira believes herself deserted and loses her reason.

ACT II. Another part of the fortress. It concerns itself chiefly with exhibitions of Elvira's madness.

ACT III. A grove near the fortress. Talbot, who is proscribed, returns to see Elvira. The meeting temporarily restores her reason. Even when he hears the men in pursuit of him, Talbot refuses to leave her and is captured. He is about to be executed when word is brought of the pardoning of all prisoners; and this shock of joy permanently restores Elvira's reason.

JACQUERIE

(The Peasants' Revolt)

An opera in three acts by Gino Marinuzzi. Text by A. Donaudy. First produced by the Chicago Opera Co., 1920.

CAST: Isaura. Mazurec, her husband. William, her father. The Viscount Corrado. Glorianda, his betrothed. Notary. The Giacomi. Peasants. Landlords. Minstrel. Voices, etc. Time, the Middle Ages. Place, near little city of Nointel. Before the marital home of Isaura.

Act I. Isaura and Mazurec are celebrating their marriage when they discover that Viscount Corrado has placed a gleaming unsheathed sword above their door to signify his intention of exercising his ancient right of taking "the Virgins on their marriage night." When the Viscount appears, Mazurec pleads with him to forego his privilege, but to no avail, and the father, William, attacks the Viscount and is arrested.

Act II. In the great-room of the castle. The Viscount and Glorianda are celebrating their betrothal. It is a day of pardon and William is released. Isaura, too, is returned to Mazurec, and becomes delirious in his arms, then dies, from her sufferings.

Act III. Mazurec has become deformed and almost unrecognizable from his grief and is living alone in the woods. He with William joins Giacomi in an attack upon the castle. The peasants and even the servants in the castle have revolted. They are successful, and Glorianda is given to Mazurec to treat as the Viscount treated Isaura. But as he takes her in his arms, he sees a vision of his Isaura in the same plight and helps Glorianda escape through the woods. The castle goes up in flames and the hymn of the enslaved, breaking their century old chains, rings out,—"Let there be annihilation of the oppressors!"

THE JEWELS OF THE MADONNA

(I Giojelli Della Madonna)

An opera in three acts by Wolf-Ferrari; plot by the composer and the verse by C. Zangarini and E. Golisciani. First produced in Berlin, December 23, 1911.

Cast: Gennaro, in love with Maliella—Tenor. Maliella, in love with Rafaele—Soprano. Rafaele, leader of the Camorrists—Baritone. Carmela, Gennaro's mother—Mezzo-soprano. Biaiso—Tenor. Cicillo—Tenor. Stella

—Soprano.   Concetta—Soprano.   Serena—Soprano.
Rocco—Bass. Grazia, a dancer. Totonno, Venders,
Monks, Populace. Place, Naples. Time, the present.

Act I. A small square in Naples in which stand the
houses of Carmela, Gennaro, and Biaso. It is the festival
of the Madonna and the square is crowded. Maliella, a
potential Carmen, had been adopted when a baby by Carmela to fulfil a vow made for the recovery of her son
from a childish illness. She had been a foundling. Maliella runs out of the house in a wild holiday mood and down
to the sea. She soon returns pursued by Rafaele and his
band of Camorrists; he catches and kisses her, and
she stabs his hand with a dagger-like hat-pin. While
hymns to the Virgin are chanted, Rafaele pours out his
passion to Maliella and says he would even rob the sacred
image of its jewels to bedeck her in their glory. The
superstitious girl is horrified; but after the procession
which appears has passed, she picks up the flower Rafaele
has tossed her and runs indoors.

Act. II The garden of Carmela's house in the late evening. Gennaro detains Maliella when she starts to leave
the house with her bundle. In answer to his pleading she
tells him that Rafaele has offered to steal the jewels of the
Madonna. He locks the gate upon her and she goes back
to her room resentfully. He then takes several skeleton
keys and some files, wraps them in a piece of leather and
goes out. Rafaele appears at the gate with his band;
and he and Maliella have a love duel. It is scarcely finished when a signal is given that some one approaches, and
he leaves, but not before she has promised to join him on
the morrow. Gennaro enters and spreads before her the
jewels of the Madonna. She yields herself to his embrace
in an ecstasy, half mystic, half sensual.

Act III. A haunt of the Camorrist. The Camorrists, men and women, are gathered together; and Rafaele
tells them that the charm to him of Maliella, is that he
will be the first man to whom she has yielded herself. Mali-

ella rushes in; and in an agony confesses that she confused
Gennaro with him the night before, and has yielded herself
to him.   Furiously Rafaele flings her to the ground; and
the jewels of the Madonna fall from her cloak.   Gennaro,
half mad, has followed her in.   The crowd, as superstitious
as it is criminal, recoils from both intruders.   Rafaele
curses her, and she rushes out to drown herself.   Gennaro
finds a knife among the débris and stabs himself.

JULIEN

(Or a Poet's Life)

In a prologue, four acts, and eight tableaux, by Gustave
Charpentier.   The sequel to Louise.   First produced in
Paris, June 4, 1913.

CAST: Julien—Tenor.   The High Priest, The Peasant,
The Showman—Baritones.   The Officiant—Tenor.   Voice
from the Abyss—Tenor.   The Bell-ringer—Tenor.   The
Acolyte—Tenor.   A Woodcutter.   A Gypsy.   Four Com-
rades.   A Stonebreaker.   Voice from the Abyss.   Labour-
ers.   A Rowdy.   Waiters in the Cabaret.   A Student.
A Citizen.   Louise, Beauty, The Young Girl, The Grand-
mother, The Grisette—Sopranos.   The Peasant Woman
—Contralto.   The Dream-maidens.   The Chimeras.
Fairies.   A Citizen's Wife.   A Girl.   Two Grisettes.
Levites, Augurs, Sages, Worshippers of Beauty, Muses,
Lovers, Chosen Poets, Hapless Poets, Woodcutters,
Ditchers, Peasant Men and Women, Gipsies, Breton
Women, Carnival Crowd, Sacred Dancers, Carnival
Dancers.

The story is allegorical and might be called the Dream
of a Poet's Life.   The Prologue is laid in Julien's Villa
Medici in Rome.   Louise and he are together and finally
overcome by his emotions he flings himself into a chair
and falls asleep.

ACT I.   *Enthusiasm.*   Various dream-forms pass by him

in his search for supreme beauty, some encouraging him, some representing the cavilling doubts of ordinary mortals. Louise suddenly appears as the incarnation of Supreme Beauty; and he prostrates himself before her altar and receives her benediction.

Act II. *Doubt.* Julien, wearied by his failure to convert the world to a love of beauty, meets a peasant who advises him to "stay close to the good earth." A Young Girl also urges him to stay. The Peasant invites him into the warmth of his cottage but Julien curtly refuses, and is left alone with mysterious voices.

Act III. *Impotence.* Julien addresses the pitiless heavens and the derisive Voices of the Tempest answer him. The Grandmother, the fond memory of his youth, comes to him, and tries to win him back to faith and hopeful resignation. There is a prolonged struggle between her and the choir of the Hapless Poets for the possession of his soul.

Act IV. *Intoxication.* He seeks forgetfulness of his despair at the fruitlessness of his search in a travesty of the Temple of Beauty, surrounded by fays, sirens and rabble. In the midst of the scene of ribald revelry, a majestic phantom vision of the Temple of Beauty appears. He turns to the Grisette, who has usurped Louise's place. She heartlessly derides him; the vision vanishes; and he falls dead at her feet.

The Grisette, the Young Girl, the Grandmother are none other than Louise whose love responds to his changing state.

LA FORZA DEL DESTINO

(The Force of Destiny)

A Lyric drama in four acts. Music by Giuseppe Verdi. Libretto by Francesco Maria Piave, founded on a drama of the Duke of Rivas, called "Don Alvaro o la Fuerzer del Sino."

CAST: Marquis of Calatrava. Donna Leonora, Don Carlo of Vargas, his children. Don Alvaro. Preziosilla, gipsy girl. Abbot of the Franciscan friars. Militone, a friar. Curra, Leonora's maid. Trabucco, muleteer, afterwards a peddler. A Spanish military surgeon. An Alcade. Muleteer, Spanish, and Italian peasants and soldiers, Friars of the Order of St. Francis, etc. Place, Spain. Time, 18th Century. First produced at the Imperial Theatre of St. Petersburg and at Madrid.

ACT I. Don Alvaro is a young nobleman from India who has settled in Seville, where, however, he is not very well thought of. He falls in love with Donna Leonora, the daughter of the Marquis of Calatrava, who, notwithstanding his love for his daughter, is determined that she shall marry only a man of the highest origin. Leonora, knowing her father's aversion, and deeply in love with Alvaro, determines to elope with him, aided by her confidante, Curra. On the point of departure with him, she suddenly desires to see her father for a last time. Her father unexpectedly enters and discovers Alvaro; he threatens him with death, and Alvaro in order to remove any suspicion as to Leonora's purity, offers to surrender himself to the Marquis. He flings down his pistol which goes off and mortally wounds the Marquis who dies cursing his daughter.

ACT II. The Alcade, several peasant muleteers, and Don Carlo of Vargas, the brother of Donna Leonora, are gathered in the kitchen of an inn in the village of Hornachuelos. Don Carlo is searching for Don Alvaro to avenge the death of his father and is disguised as a student of Salamanca, under the fictitious name of Pereda. Leonora, in male attire arrives. During the supper, Preziosilla, a young gipsy, tells the young men's fortunes and exhorts them to enlist in the war for Italy's freedom, which all agree to do. In a very beautiful solo, Don Carlo tells them of his father's death. Leonora overhears his song and barely escapes discovery by him. She takes refuge in a monastery where she tells the abbot her true name and that she intends to spend the remainder of her life in a hermitage. After the abbot has recounted the trials she will have to undergo, she departs for her cave.

Act III. Meanwhile Don Alvaro has joined the Spanish army under the name of Don Federico Herreros. One night he saves the life of Don Carlo who is serving in the same army under the name of Don Felix Bornos. They become close friends and go into battle side by side. In one of these engagements Don Alvaro is, as he supposes, mortally wounded, and confides to Don Carlo's care a valise containing a bundle of letters which he is to destroy as soon as Don Alvaro dies. Don Carlo has sworn not to look at the contents of the letters; but he becomes suspicious of his friend, opens the valise and finds his sister's picture. At that moment a surgeon brings word that Don Alvaro may recover. Don Carlo is overjoyed at the idea of revenging his father's death. The scene changes to a camp near Velletri (Italy) where Don Carlo and Don Alvaro fight a duel, in which Don Alvaro thinks he has killed his opponent. In expiation, Don Alvaro vows to enter a monastery.

Act IV. Don Alvaro has entered the monastery at Hornachuelos, near which is Leonora's cave, under the name of Father Raphael. Don Carlo arrives cured of his wound and forces him to fight. They chose the ground before Leonora's cave; and Don Carlo is mortally wounded. Alvaro calls for help, and Leonora recognizing his voice rushes out, and seeing her brother dying, stoops over him; he thereupon stabs her to the heart. Don Alvaro flings himself to death from some rocks, before the monks arrive singing the *Miserere*.

LA NAVARRAISE

A lyric episode in two acts. Music by J. Massenet. Text by Jules Claretie and H. Cain. First produced at Covent Garden, June 24, 1894.

CAST: Garrido, General of the Royalist troops. Remigio, a farmer. Araquil, his son, Sergeant in the Biscayan Regiment. Ramon, Lieutenant in the same. Bustamente, Sergeant in the same. Anita, a girl of Navarre, betrothed to Araquil. Officers, Soldiers, Villagers, Military Chaplain, and Surgeon. Place, Spain. Time, during the Carlist war.

General Garrido of the Royalist troops has been vainly trying to take a Basque village from the Carlist enemy, Zuccaraga. Araquil is madly in love with Anita, but his father opposes their union as she has no dowry. Anita overhears Garrido offer a fortune to any one who will take Zuccaraga. To Anita this offer means, Araquil, marriage, happiness. She tells Garrido of her intention, and goes to Zuccaraga's camp. When Araquil learns where she has gone and knowing that Zuccaraga loves pretty women, he is frantic and follows her. Shots are heard and Anita returns and claims her reward from Garrido. She is caressing her gold when Araquil appears, desperately wounded. She says she can marry him now; but he does not believe her story of what she has done. Then suddenly the bell announcing Zuccaraga's death begins to toll, and Araquil realizes that she has told him the truth. He dies horrified at her crime. Anita first tries to kill herself and then goes mad with grief.

LA REINE FIAMMETTE

An opera in four acts and two scenes by Xavier Leroux, with a libretto adapted from his play by Catulle Mendés.

First produced in America at the Metropolitan Opera House, January 24, 1919.

CAST: Orlanda. Danielo. Giorgio d'Ast. Cardinal Sforza. Pantasille. Mother Agramente. Violette. Violine. Viola. Pomone. Michela. Angioletta. Chiarina. Two boys. Luc Agnolo. Castiglione. Cortez. Cesano. Vasari. Prosecutor. Two Novices. Place, in the imaginary Kingdom of Bologna, Italy. Time, 16th century.

ACT I. The court yard of an inn near Bologna. The young Queen, Orlanda, affectionately called "the little flame," has shown some sympathy with the teachings of Luther; and the Pope's nephew, Cardinal Cesar Sforza, decides she must expiate her heresy with her life. He incites her Consort, Giorgio of Ast, an ambitious adventurer who is humiliated by his own lack of authority, to consent to her death by promising him her kingdom. They arrange to incite Danielo, whose brother had been put to death by the Queen's order, to be the assassin. The Queen is at the time at a convent in Assisi and they must await her return.

ACT II. Scene I. Convent at Assisi. Danielo has fallen in love with a beautiful yet unknown woman at the Convent at Assisi, and goes to take final leave of her. In a passionate love scene he confesses to her (she is really Orlanda) that he has been selected to carry out a dreadful plan and that death awaits him. Overcoming his scruples she induces him to become her lover, and carries him off to one of her castles. Scene II. At the Castle. It is the fatal day on which Danielo is to kill the Queen. The lovers awake in each other's arms in the castle. He falls asleep again, and a gipsy warns Orlanda of the plot against her life. She awakes Danielo and tells him she has had a dream in which she saw him attacking her with a knife. She then sends him to the city to perform his deed and gives him her own stiletto.

ACT III. Scene I. The royal garden at Bologna. The Queen is watching the dancers. Danielo creeps in and has raised his hand to strike before he recognises her. She treats his act as a jest and throws him a kiss. Scene II is laid in the same place a few minutes later. Danielo has been seized by the Cardinal's orders. Giorgio offers to save Danielo's life if the Queen will abdicate. Finally, amid tears, she consents and distributes the pearls from her crown to passing gipsies. The Cardinal then turns her over to the Mother Superior of the Convent at Assisi.

ACT IV. In the chapel of the convent. Orlanda has been sentenced to death. Left alone after her sentence is read, Danielo enters and demands that she make her last confession to him. She finally yields; and he learns that she is innocent of his brother's murder. When the Cardinal and his suite enter for the execution of Orlanda, Danielo attacks him. He is overcome and the Cardinal sentences the lovers to die together. They stand clasped in each other's arms by the block as the curtain descends.

LE COQ D'OR

(The Golden Cock)

An opera in three acts by N. Rimsky-Korsakov. Text by V. Bielsky, based on Pushkin's "Golden Cock."

CAST: King Dodon—Baritone. Prince Guidon—Tenor. Prince Afron—Baritone. Voevoda Polkan, the general— Baritone. Amelfa, the royal housekeeper—Contralto. The Astrologer—Tenor. The Queen of Shemakhan— Soprano. The Golden Cock—Soprano.

ACT I. A great hall in the palace of King Dodon. He is a gluttonous man, much oppressed by the cares of state, and harassed by warlike neighbours. During a meeting of his Boyards, he asks the advice of his two sons, but the wise old general Voevoda Polkan disagrees with the suggestions of both of them. The entire assembly becomes in an uproar; and in the midst of it, an astrologer

offers the king a golden cock which has the power to foretell events and give warnings of approaching danger.
The bird is placed on the spiral of the capital to send the
citizens rushing for their weapons or back to their peace-
ful occupations as its prophecies vary. Then the bird
suddenly sounds the alarm of great danger approaching, and Didon and his warriors set out to journey to
the land of the enemy.

Act II. The moonlight of the narrow pass reveals the
dead bodies of Didon's two sons. As the dawn breaks he
sees a tent which he thinks belongs to the victorious commander of the enemy, but from which, to his surprise,
emerges a beautiful woman. She lures him on, makes him
dance, and finally agrees to become his bride.

Act III. Before Didon's palace. The populace are
awaiting the King and his bride in vague alarm. The King
and the Queen enter, followed by a grotesque train of
giants and dwarfs. Soon the Queen becomes bored. The
astrologer appears and claims as the reward which had
been promised him, for his magic bird, the Queen. Didon
kills him with a blow from his sceptre and the bird flies
at him and kills him with its beak. There is a clap of
thunder and the Queen and the bird disappear together.
In the epilogue the head of the astrologer appears, and
he says that he and the Queen alone were real, all the
others are merely a dream.

THE LEGEND

A lyric tragedy in one act. Music by Joseph Breil.
Text in English by Jaques Byrne. First produced at
the Metropolitan Opera House, New York, March 12,
1919. Place, Muscovadia, a mythical country in the
Balkans.

Cast: Count Stackareff, an impoverished nobleman, by
night the bandit Black Lorenzo. Carmelita, his daughter.

Stephen Pauloff, her lover. Marta, an old servant.
Soldiers.

No one but his daughter knows the double life Count
Stackareff is leading. He tells her that he has captured
a rich merchant and is awaiting the return of a messenger with his ransom. Marta tells her that Stephen,
whom she has met in Vienna and loves, is on his way to
see his sweetheart. This is the night of the Evil One,
according to legend. Marta tells Carmelita's fortune, and
the death card, the ace of spades, is present at every
cutting. Stephen arrives, and after a love scene Carmelita
learns that Stephen has been sent to capture the bandit
Black Lorenzo, dead or alive. She prepares to elope
with him. Her father enters and when Stephen tells him
of his mission, he escapes through the door shouting that
he himself is the bandit. Carmelita tries to prevent
Stephen from pursuing him; and when she fails, stabs
him. Two soldiers bring in the dead body of her father,
and when they see Stephen dead, they shoot Carmelita.

L'ITALIANA IN ALGERI

A comic drama in three acts. Music by Rossini. Text
by Angelo Anelli.

Cast: Mustafa, Bey of Algeria. Elvira, his wife. Zulma,
confidential slave to Elvira. Haly, Captain of Algerian
Corsari. Lindoro, young Italian, favourite slave of
Mustafa. Isabella, Italian Lady. Taddeo, companion
of Isabella. Eunuchs of the Harem, Algerian Corsari,
Italian slaves, Pappataci, Women of the Harem, European
Slaves, Sailors. Place, Algeria. Produced at Metro-
politan Opera House, December 5, 1919.

Act I. Scene I. In the palace of Mustafa. He has
tired of his favourite wife and has decided to give her in
marriage to an Italian slave, Lindoro, despite her lamentations. He commands his vizier and Haly to abduct

some beautiful Italian lady to take her place in his affections. He then tells Lindoro of his plan for him and overcomes his objects. Lindoro is still lamenting a sweetheart in Italy.

Scene II. On the seashore. Haly finds a wrecked vessel on which is Isabella, the beautiful sweetheart of Lindoro, and an importunate suitor, Taddeo. When they are captured, they arrange for him to pose as her uncle. They learn they are to be taken to the Bey, to become part of his household. Isabella at once begins to scheme for their escape.

Act II. Apartments of the Bey. Mustafa is at once smitten with Isabella, and for her sake saves the life of Taddeo who is condemned to die because he refuses to work. Elvira and Lindoro enter; and he and Isabella at once recognise each other. She demands that the Bey give up his plan of forcing him to marry Elvira; and there is general consternation at her boldness.

Act III. The same room as Act I. Mustafa boasts of his ultimate success with Isabella; but as soon as he goes out, Lindoro and Isabella plan their escape. Mustafa, believing Taddeo to be Isabella's uncle, rewards him by making him "Kaimakan," whose distasteful duty it is to bring Isabella to the Bey when he sends for her.

Scene II. Isabella is summoned to the apartment of the Bey; and she and others whom she had taken into her confidence, hide themselves about the apartment. When Mustafa enters, Isabella calls Elvira into the room and they tell the Bey that they belong to a secret Society, "Pappataci," whose members lead a life of gluttony and sensuality. He is delighted to join; and they initiate him by a series of stupid ceremonies, of which he is made the butte. He sits mumbling and eating while Isabella, Lindoro, and Taddeo make their escape. When he discovers the deception it is too late to recapture them; and he decides to take Elvira back into his favour.

LODOLETTA

Opera in three acts by Mascagni.   Text by G. Forzano,
founded on Ouida's novel, "Two Little Shoes."   First
produced in Rome, April 30, 1917.

Cast: Lodoletta—Soprano.   Flammen—Tenor.   Franz
—Bass.   Gianetto—Baritone.   Antonio—Bass.   A Mad
Woman — Mezzo-soprano.   Vannard — Mezzo-soprano.
Maud—Soprano.   A Voice—Tenor.   A letter carrier, an
old violinist.   Place, a Dutch village and in Paris.   Time,
Second Empire.

Act I.   It is Lodoletta's bithday and the village is making merry and decorating her cottage.   Antonio, her
foster-father, wants to buy her some red "shoon" but is
too poor.   Her lover Gianetto brings her a handsome
present.   Flammen and a party of his Parisian friends
arrive, and he offers a gold piece to be allowed to
copy a picture of the Madonna he admires.   Antonio
consents in order to get the money for his present.   During the merrymaking which greets Lodoletta upon her
return from the flower-market, old Antonio falls from a
tree and dies.   She is inconsolable and refuses to go to
her lover's home with him.   He departs; and Flammen
unaware of the catastrophe, returns, finds her crying and
comforts her.

Act II is laid in the autumn in the same village.   Flammen is painting Lodoletta's picture.   The village mis-
interprets their relations, and shuns her.   Gianetto again
offers her his heart and hand; she refuses while denying
his imputation of evil and defending the painter.   The
painter, returning after an interval, finds her in tears, and
declares his love for her.   But her purity and innocence
triumph, she will not accept the kind of love he offers and
runs away.

Act III is laid in the garden and in the villa of Flammen in Paris on New Year's Eve.   Flammen is entertain-

ing his friends. He can enjoy nothing, for her thoughts
are always with Lodoletta. Soon after he returns to the
villa, Lodoletta enters the garden, worn out and in rags;
she has come to offer him her love. When she sees the
lights and the beautifully dressed women, she realizes he
is not for her and dies, with the illusion that his lips are
pressed on hers. After the party breaks up, Flammen
stumbles over her shoes, finds her dead body, and flings
himself upon it crying that he will die for love of
her.

L'OISEAU BLEU

(The Blue Bird)

A lyric comedy in four acts and eight scenes. Music
by Albert Wolff. Text by Maurice Maeterlinck. First
produced at Metropolitan Opera House, New York, December 27, 1919.

CAST: Tyltyl. Mytyl. Mummy Tyl. Daddy Tyl.
Granny Tyl. Gaffer Tyl. The Maternal Love. The
Joy of Understanding. Light. Father Time. Bread.
The Little Girl. The Little Lovers. The Joy of Being
Just. The Joy of Seeing What is Beautiful. The Fairy.
The Night. The Cat. The Dog. Neighbour Berlingot.
Happiness. A Child. Milk. Water. Sugar. Fire.
Children. Time, Christmas Eve.

ACT I. *Tableau I.* On Christmas Eve, Tyltyl and
Mytyl, the two children of a woodcutter, are awakened
from their sleep by a bright light shining in their
room. They run to the window and watch the Christmas celebration of their rich neighbours. The door of
their own house opens, and the fairy Berylune enters
and bids the children go to seek the Blue Bird of Happiness for her little daughter who is ill. She gives Tyltyl
a green cap with a diamond in it which will trans-

form things when he turned. Tyltyl turns the diamond
and everything is altered. The furniture takes life and
becomes resplendent; the door of the clock opens and
the Hours dance out. The souls of Bread, Sugar,
Water, Fire, etc., together with Light appear. The Cat
and the Dog become persons with animal heads. In the
midst of the enchantment, a loud knock from Daddy Tyl
is heard, and Tyltyl turns the diamond so briskly that
all of the souls can not return to their original elements.
Those so prevented, with the two children, go out through
the window, Bread carrying the cage in which to put the
Blue Bird. Daddy and Mummy Tyl enter to find the children, as they think, quietly sleeping.

Tableau II. The Land of Memory. The two children
see their Grandmother and Grandfather sitting before a peasant's hut as the mists gradually rise. Their
little dead brothers and sisters run out of the house to
greet them. After a visit with them, they start back
with a bird which, when they examine it closely, turns out
to be black not blue, and which they release as they leave.

Act II. *Tableau III.* The Palace of the Night. Light
leads the children to the Palace and then leaves them.
When Tyltyl claims the Blue Bird from Night, she gives
him the keys to the caverns where the plagues and evils
are imprisoned, and which he insists upon opening one
by one. When he opens the forbidden door of Destiny,
he finds a beautiful garden filled with birds that die when
the children catch them. They go into a forest where the
spirit of the Oak wants to kill them for seeking the Blue
Bird.

Tableau IV. The Palace of Happiness. The great luxuries are having a banquet and try to make the children
join them; but Tyltyl turns his diamond and the palace
radiates an ethereal brightness. The Luxuries take
refuge in the Cave of Miseries and the children meet the
various Happinesses and Joys.

Act III. *Tableau V.* The Cemetery. It is midnight

and at a turn of Tyltyl's diamond the place loses its horror and becomes beautful.

Tableau VI. The Kingdom of the Future. Everywhere are crowds of Unborn Children in azure garments. Mytyl and Tyltyl watch Father Time sending the children down to earth to be born. Light tells Tyltyl that she has the Blue Bird. He turns his diamond.

Act IV. *Tableau VII.* Before Tyltyl's house at daybreak. Light and the other souls take leave of the children. The clock strikes and the children enter their home without the Blue Bird.

Tableau VIII. The Awakening. Christmas Morning. Mummy Tyl comes in to awaken the sleeping children. They try to tell her all that has happened to them, but she fears they are sick. Their neighbour, Mme. Beringot, comes in to ask Tyltyl for his bird for her little sick daughter. He gives it to her gladly; and shortly afterwards the little girl enters well and happy with the cage in her hand. The children play with it and the bird escapes. Tyltyl addresses the audience, "If any of you should find him, would you be so very kind as to give him back to us? We need him for our happiness, later on."

L'ORACOLO

(The Oracle)

A musical drama in one act, based on the "Cat and the Cherub" of C. B. Fernald. Text by Camillo Zanoni. Music by Franco Leoni. Place, the Chinese Quarter in San Francisco. Time, the present. First produced at Covent Garden, June 28, 1905.

Cast: Win-Shee, a learned doctor. Chim-Fen, a proprietor of an opium den. Hoo-Tsin, a wealthy merchant. Win-San-Luy, Win-Shee's son. Hoo-Chee, Hoo-Tsin's little son. Ah-Yoe, Hoo-Tsin's niece. Hua-Quee, Hoo-

Chee's nurse. A policeman, an opium maniac, a fortune-teller, Chinese men, women and children.

It is the Chinese New Year, and the devout are going to the House of Prayer, and the late revellers returning from opium dens. Chem-Fen, the proprietor of one of these dens, pretends to love the nurse, Hua-Quee, in order to gain access to the house of Hoo-Tsin, whose niece, Ah-Yoe, is the real object of his ambitions. Ah-Yoe is in love with Win-San-Luy, however. Chim-Fen overhears Hoo-Tsin consulting the father of Win-San-Luy, a learned astrologer, as to the future of his beloved little son, and determines to use the predictions of evil fortune that are to befall the child, for purposes of his own. He kidnaps the child. The frantic father offers the hand of his niece as a reward to whomever can find him. Win-San-Luy suspects Chim-Fen, forces his way into the opium den and rescues the child. Chim-Fen pursues him, kills him with a hatchet, and pushes the child down a trap-door. Ah-Yoe goes mad, and Win-Shee, Win-San-Luy's father, determines to discover his murderer.

After an interval the scene opens on the second night. Win-Shee hears the child cry and rescues him. He then lies in wait for Chim-Fen and strangles him with his own que so cleverly that a passing policeman sees only two Chinamen quietly talking.

THE LOVE OF THREE KINGS

(L'Amore Dei Tre Re)

An opera in three acts by Italo Montemezzi. Text by Sem Benelli, from his tragic poem of the same title. First produced in Milan, April 10, 1913.

CAST: Archibaldo, King of Altura—Bass. Manfredo, son of Archibaldo—Baritone. Avito, a former prince of Altura—Tenor. Flaminio, a castle guard—Tenor. Fiora, wife of Manfredo—Soprano. A Youth, a Boy Child, a Voice behind the scenes, a Handmaiden, an Old Woman, People of Altrua. Place, a remote castle in Italy, forty years after a barbarian invasion, led by Archibaldo. Time, the Middle Ages.

Act I. A spacious hall, opening on a terrace and lighted by a lantern, used as a signal lantern. The old blind king, Archibaldo, enters with Flaminio, and they talk of Avito, to whom Flaminio is secretly attached, and who was betrothed to Fiora when Archibaldo forced her to marry his son, Manfredo, as part of the terms of peace. As his son, whose arrival he is awaiting, comes not, he orders the lantern extinguished and goes out with his companion. But before he goes, he intimates that he is doubtful of Fiora's fealty. After their departure, Fiora and Avito come out of her chamber; and he notices that the lantern no longer burns and fears that they are discovered. She reassures him, and he goes out. The old blind Archibaldo returns and she tells him she has come out to watch for the arrival of her husband. The husband who has forsaken the siege of an enemy's stronghold, to return to his wife, enters; and they all retire to their chambers.

Act II. The terrace of the castle in the afternoon. Manfredo and Fiora enter; and Fiora promises to wave her scarf to her husband, who is returning to the siege, as long as she can see his marching men. He, too, goes out; and while she is waving to him, Avito appears to bid her farewell. She drops the scarf and they kiss as if dying of love. Old Archibaldo enters and in his blindness senses what has happened. Avito wants to kill him but Flaminio prevents him, and advises him to depart. The old man hears his retreating footsteps and becomes more suspicious. Suddenly it is seen that Manfredo is returning, and Flaminio is sent to learn the reason. Old Archibaldo accuses Fiora of having a lover; and when she admits it, though refusing to divulge his name, the old man strangles her. When Manfredo arrives she is dead. His father pours out the tale to him; but even then he can not bring himself to hate her.

ACT III. The crypt of the castle with Fiora lying on her bier. A crowd of her fellow countrymen come to view the body. After their departure, Avito appears and laments beside it. In an ecstasy of love he presses his lips upon hers, which old Archibaldo has caused to be touched with poison. Manfredo enters and finds him there beside his wife and yet he feels no hate for the man who loved her, even as he did, rather a sense of comrade‑ship. Avito dies; and Manfredo presses his lips to those of Fiora and draws in the remaining poison. Here the old king finds them both dead beside the woman they loved.

MADAME SANS GÊNE

An opera in four acts by Umberto Giordano. Text by Renato Simoni after the play by Victorien Sardon and E. Moreau. First produced at the Metropolitan Opera House, New York, January 25, 1915.

CAST: Napoleon Bonaparte—Baritone. Lefebvre, a ser‑geant of the National Guard, later a Marshal of France and Duke of Danzig—Tenor. Fouche, officer of the Na‑tional Guards, later Minister of Police—Baritone. Count de Neipperg—Tenor. Vinaigre, drummer boy—Tenor. Despréaux, dancing master—Tenor. Gelsomino, page—Baritone. Leroy, tailor—Baritone. De Brigode, cham‑berlain—Baritone. Roustan, head of the Mamelukes—Baritone. Catherine Huebscher, "Madame Sans Gêne," laundress, later Duchess of Danzig—Soprano. Toinette, Julia, La Rossa, laundresses—Sopranos. Queen Caro‑line, Princess Elisa, sisters of Napoleon—Sopranos. Mme. de Bulow, matron of honour to the Empress—Soprano. Maturio, Constant, valet to Napoleon. The voice of the Empress, Citizens, Shopkeepers, Villagers, Soldier, Ladies of the Court Officials, Diplomatists, Academicians, Hunt‑

ers, Pages and two Mamelukes. Place, Paris. Time, August 10, 1792, and September, 1811.

ACT I is laid in the stormy days of the Revolution and during the scene constant cannon shots are heard. Catherine, "Madame Sans Gêne," has met with a rough adventure with some soldiers, and she is giving a humorous account of it to the laundresses in her employ. She tells of her romantic engagement to her childhood friend, Lefebvre. Left alone for a moment, she is surprised to have a wounded Austrian officer, Neipperg, stumble in and ask refuge. She hides him in her own room; and shortly afterward the pursuit, led by her lover, enters and searches the place. Lefebvre finds the officer in her room, but does not tell the others. He makes a feint to learn her real feelings toward the man by telling her he is dead; and as she shows no emotion, his own jealousy is stilled. He promises to arrange for the flight of the man that night.

ACT II is laid in the château of Compiègne, nineteen years later. Lefebvre, Duke of Danzig, is the trusted general of Napoleon, now at the height of his power, and is married to Catherine. Catherine who has remained a woman of the people, scandalises the Court by her many breaches of etiquette. Napoleon has even suggested that Lefebvre divorce her, but he is far too much in love with her. Neipperg, now Austrian ambassador, is said to be in love with the Empress. The two sisters of Napoleon come to visit Catherine, and in a most amusing scene she so offends them by her manners that they depart vowing vengeance. Shortly afterward she is summoned to the Cabinet of Napoleon.

ACT III. Cabinet of Napoleon. Napoleon hears the report of Neipperg's feigned departure, but is jealous and suspicious of him. Catherine enters, and in response to Napoleon's accusation that she covers his court with ridicule, she first defies him, then so wins his heart by her recitals of her experiences as a lowly vivandiere, and her reminding him that he still owes her a laundry bill, he contracted as a young lieutenant, that he kisses her and all is forgiven. Roustan tells Napoleon that the secret door of the Empress's apartments is ajar; the lights are turned out; and as they wait, Neipperg, with Mme. de Bulow enters, and approachs the Empress's door. Napoleon has him arrested in spite of Catherine's assertions of his innocence.

Act IV is laid in the same scene. Napoleon tries to make Catherine admit she knows of the guilt of the Empress; then as she refuses, he commands her to announce to the Empress the arrival of Neipperg. She reluctantly complies and receives a package from the Empress, which, when Napoleon opens it, proves to be a letter to her father, the Emperor of Austria, asking him to recall the count. Napoleoen, delighted that his suspicions are unfounded, extols Catherine's loyalty before the whole court.

MÂROUF, THE COBBLER OF CAIRO

A comedy-opera in five acts by Henry Rabaud. Text by Lucien Népoty. First produced in America at the Metropolitan Opera House, December 19, 1917.

Cast: Princess Saamcheddine. Fattoumah, the Killjoy. Mârouf. The Sultan. The Vizier. Ali. A fellah, Ahmad, the pastry-cook. First Merchant. Second Merchant. A Donkey-driver. A Sea Captain. First Muezzin Second Muezzin. First Policeman. Second Policeman. Mamelukes, Caravaneers, Slaves, Ladies of the Harem. Populace.

Act I. In Cairo. Mârouf's wife demands a cake made of honey; and when he can only provide her with one made of sugar, she makes such an outcry that two policemen think he has beaten her, and give him a hundred strokes with their staves. Whereupon he runs away with some passing sailors.

ACT II. In the market-place of Khaïtân. Mârouf, who has been shipwrecked, is rescued by Ali an old school-friend. Ali is the richest man in Khaïtân, and he determines to dress Mârouf sumptuously, and pass him off as the richest man in the world. His scheme works so well that the Sultan hears of this wonderful personage, and invites him to dinner at his palace.

ACT III. The Sultan has been so much impressed with the story of this fabulously rich man that he forces his daughter upon him in marriage. Mârouf is so delighted, when he finds the princess is beautiful and not homely like his wife, that he faints away, though not before he has betrayed to her the true state of affairs as to his pennilessness. She, however, loves him and protects him.

ACT IV. The Sultan becomes suspicious of the non-arrival of the much heralded caravans of Mârouf and tries to find out the truth, but his daughter fools him to the top of her bent. Later, when Mârouf comes in, the princess questions him and he gaily admits the fraud. She in turn joins in his mirth. But fearing that her father may not view it in the same amusing light, they decide to elope together.

ACT V. A plain near Khaïtân. The pair find a fellah ploughing and ask food from him. While he is absent preparing it, the princess begins to plough; her shaft dislodges a ring that has been attached to a great stone that seem to hide a treasure. Mârouf struggles to move the stone and the ring comes off in his hand; it is engraved with mystic characters. The princess polishes it in order to see the lettering, and the fellah suddenly appears, turned into a Genie, and creates wealth for them such as Mârouf had claimed. When the Sultan arrives in pursuit of the runaways he sees the vast caravans that have magically appeared and is overjoyed.

MIREILLE

An opera in three acts, music by Charles Gounod, founded on a poem of Frederick Mistral by Michel Carré.

CAST: Mireille, the daughter of Ramon. Vincent, her lover. Vincenette, the sister of Vincent. Ramon, a wealthy farmer. Ambroise, the father of Vincent. Taven, a fortune-teller. Ourrias, the rival of Vincent. Andreloun, a shepherd boy. Clemence, a peasant girl. A passerby. Place, the Province of Maillaine.

ACT I is laid in a mulberry plantation where Mireille is surrounded by the neighbouring village girls who, after singing a pastoral chorus, tease her about her affection for Vincent, the handsome but poor basketmaker. Mireille admits she loves him, and Taven, a reputed witch, warns her to be careful as her father will bitterly oppose such a match. Vincent arrives and the two young people express their undying love for each other.

ACT II. In the Arena of Arles, after a chorus and a dance by a crowd of citizens and peasants, Mireille and Vincent meet again for a few miuutes. They separate; and Ourrias, a wild herdsman who has gained her father's consent to his suite, approaches Mireille and she repulses his advances. He reports her refusal to her father; and when Ambroise (the father of Vincent) asks Ramon's consent to the union of the lovers, he meets with a stern refusal. Whereupon Mireille vows she will marry no one else. Ramon casts off his daughter, and Ourrias vows vengeance. The two lovers, however, renew their vows.

ACT III. A harvest festival is being celebrated at Ramon's house. A shepherd boy sings and plays on a bagpipe. Mireille, unable to shake off her despondency, retires to her room, attended by Vincenette, who tells her that Vincent has been wounded by Ourrias with an iron trident, but that he will recover. Mireille determines to make a pilgrimage to the Church of Sainte Marie in behalf of her lover.

ACT IV. A crowd of pilgrims enter the Church of Sainte Marie singing a religious march. Vincent enters and Mireille, who does not recognise him, falls unconscious in his arms. During the chant of the pilgrims her sanity returns; and recognising him, she declares she sees Heaven opening and that they will be forever united. Her father, Ramon (now repentant), Vincenette and the pilgrims witness their reunion.

MONNA VANNA

A lyric drama in four acts and five tableaux. Music by Henry Février. Text by Maurice Maeterlinck. First produced in Paris, January 13, 1909.

CAST: Guido Colonna, Commander of the Pisan Garrison. Marco Colonna, Guido's father. Prinzivalle, General in the pay of Florence. Trivulzio, Commissioner of the Florentine Republic. Borso and Torello, Guido's Lieutenants. Vedio, Prinzivalle's Secretary. Giovanna (Monna Vanna) Guido's wife. Nobles, soldiers, peasants, etc. Place, Pisa and vicinity. Time, end of the 15th Century.

ACT I. Great Hall of Guido Colonna's palace. Besieged by the Florentines, Pisa is in the last extremity. All envoys have failed. Finally Marco Colonna, the father of Guido, is sent and returns with the message that Pirnzivalle will raise the siege if Monna Vanna will spend the night in his tent, clad only in her cloak. In spite of her husband's almost violently jealous objections, she says she is willing to make the sacrifice to save the people of the city from death.

ACT II. In Prinzivalle's tent. Prinzivalle disarms and arrests the commissioner of the Florentines, sent to spy upon him. Monna Vanna enters; and in return Prinzi-

valle sends the promised food to Pisa. He pours out his
love for her, which he tells her began when they were
children and played in a garden together. She remains
outwardly firm in her devotion to her husband, though
inwardly moved by his generosity. Word is brought that
the Florentine commissioners are coming to arrest him
and that he must fly. Monna Vanna persuades him to
return with her to Pisa where he shall be an honoured
guest, and he consents.

ACT III. The Great Hall of Guido's palace. Guido is
almost beside himself with jealousy. The acclamation of
the citizens who are greeting Monna Vanna as their
saviour, only adds to his sufferings. Monna Vanna enters
with Prinzivalle and in spite of all her assertions that
Prinzivalle treated her with the utmost respect he could
show to a sister and that she still loves her husband,
Guido will not believe her. He orders Prinzivalle cast into
prison; and Monna Vanna, suddenly feigning an ecstasy
of cruel triumph, insists that he did wrong her after all,
and that she desires to be his jailer so that she may revenge herself. Guido believes her and gives her the key
to the dungeon in which Prinzivalle is confined.

ACT IV. The Prison. Monna Vanna enters and leads
Prinzivalle out to freedom. Her love for him, awakened
by the contrast between his generous treatment of her
and her husband's insane jealousy, she goes with him out
into the sunlight.

PRINCE IGOR

An opera in four acts and a prologue by Borodin. Produced at Metropolitan Opera House, New York, December 30, 1915.

CAST: Prince Igor. Skoula. Eroshka. Prince Galitsky.
Yaroslavna, the wife of Igor. Kontchakovna, the daugh-

ter of Khan Kontchak, Vladimir, son of Igor. Ovlour. Khan Kontchak. Khan Gzak. Peasants, soldiers, citizens, etc.

The Prologue. Prince Igor, who is about to start on a campaign against the Khan of the Polovsy, refuses to heed the warnings of his wife and his people who interpret a recent eclipse into a bad omen. Prince Galitsky bribes Skoula and Eroshka to encourage Prince Igor in his determination to depart as he himself wants to usurp Igor's place. Igor, unsuspectingly entrusts his wife to his care.

Act I. Scene I is laid in the court-yard of Galitsky's house, where the people are welcoming him as their prince. A group of young women beg the prince to restore one of their friends whom he has carried off; but he frightens them away. Scene II. The young women appeal to Yaroslavna, who is lamenting Igor's absence, and while they are relating the story, Galitsky enters. Yaroslavna questions him as to the truth of their story and he only laughs. Word is brought that Igor and his son have been taken captive, and that an attack upon them is eminent.

Act II. The Polovtsy Camp. Vladimir has fallen in love with Kontchakovna. She is sure her father will consent to the marriage, but Vladimir is doubtful if his father, Prince Igor, will. Kontchak offers Igor freedom if he will promise not to wage war on him again, but he refuses.

Act II. Igor learns that an attack is to be made on his city. He escapes. He tries to persuade his son to accompany him but Kontchakovna clings to him, and the father leaves alone. When the Khan learns of Igor's escape, he refuses to pursue, retains Vladimir as a hostage, and marries him to his daughter.

Act IV. Igor arrives safely at the Kremlin, and is welcomed with great rejoicing.

RIP VAN WINKLE

An American folk-opera in three acts. Music by Reginald De Koven. Text by Percy Mackaye. The first opera that was written in America as a commission by producers of opera.

CAST: Rip Van Winkle. Hendrick Hudson. Dirck Spuytenduyvil. Derrick Van Bummel. Hans Van Bummel (Mute). Peterkee Vedder, Katrina Vedder. Goose Girl. Old Dutchmen of the Tavern. Women at the Fountain. Children of the Village. Crew of the "Half Moon." Fairies of the Mountain. Place, in the Catskill Mountains. Time, middle of 18th century.

This version of Rip Van Winkle differs quite widely from the version played for so many years by Joseph Jefferson. In the first act, Rip is a young man about to be married to Katrina. He forgets his wedding, and goes off fishing with some children. With little Peterkee, Katrina's sister beside him, he tells the children of the legend of Hendrick Hudson's reappearance in his ghostly ship every twenty years. He and Peterkee suddenly see Hudson who offers them a magic flask, if they will come to the hills at midnight. They go; and Hudson plots to marry Rip to Peterkee instead of Katrina. They send the child back to the world and keep Rip in the hills by a magic draught. Twenty years later, Rip, as an old, white bearded man, returns to the village to find Peterkee on the point of marrying; he has come to claim his promised bride. In the midst of the mockery that greets his claim, Hudson and his men appear and Rip's youth is magically restored to him.

SEMIRAMIDE

A tragic opera in three acts by Gioachino Antonio Rossini. Text by Rossi, founded on the tragedy of Voltaire,

"Semiramis." First produced in Venice, February 3, 1823.

CAST: Semiramide, Queen of Babylon—Soprano. Arsaces, commander in the Assyrian army, afterwards the son of Ninus and heir to the throne—Contralto. The Ghost of Ninus—Bass. Oroe, chief of the Magi—Bass. Assur, a Prince of the Royal Blood—Bass. Azema, Princess of the Royal Blood—Soprano. Idrenus of the royal household—Tenor. Mitranes, of the royal household—Baritone. Magi, Guards, Satraps, Slaves. Place, Babylon.

Semiramide, assisted by her lover Assur, has murdered her husband, King Ninus. She becomes enamoured of a comely youth, Arsaces, the victorious leader of her army, thought to be a Scythian but who is in reality her own son, a fact known only to Oroe, the chief priest. Arsaces is himself in love with the royal princess Azema.

At a gathering in the temple, the Ghost of King Ninus announces Arsaces as his successor and summons him to come at midnight to his tomb, there to learn how he was assassinated. Assur hides in the tomb intending to kill Arsaces; but Semiramide, who has learned he is her son, arrives in time to save him and to receive the death wound intended for him. Arsaces then kills Assur, ascends the throne and marries Azema.

SHANEWIS

(The Robin Woman)

An American opera in two parts. Music by Charles Wakefield Cadman. Text by Nelle Richmond Eberhart. First produced at the Metropolitan Opera House, March 23, 1918.

CAST: Shanewis. Mrs. Everton. Amy Everton. Lionel. Philip.

Shanewis is a beautiful Indian girl who has been given a musical education by the wealthy Mrs. Everton. Lionel is engaged to Amy Everton, but he falls in love with Shanewis and follows her to the Indian reservation. There he witnesses a pow-wow and becomes even more madly infatuated with her. Mrs. Everton tries to recall him to his duty to his race without success. He is finally killed by a former lover of Shanewis who has a morbid hatred of the white race. Amy and Shanewis kneel beside him as he dies.

SOEUR ANGELICA

(Sister Angelica)

Opera in one act by Puccini. Text by G. Forzano. First produced at Metropolitan Opera House, New York, December 14, 1918.

CAST: Sister Angelica. The Princess, her aunt. The Abbess. The Sister Monitor. The Mistresses of the Novices. Sister Genevieve. Sister Osmina. Sister Dolcina. The Sick Nurse Sister. The Questuants. The Novices. The Postulants. Place, a convent. Time, latter part of the 17th Century.

Sister Angelica has retired to the convent to expiate an unfortunate past, and her first contact with the outside world is through her aunt who comes to have a document signed. Sister Angelica asks about the child that she abandoned, and the aunt responds harshly that it is dead. Sister Angelica in remorse puts an end to her life; but before she dies she prays for pardon and the doors of the church open and the Virgin is seen on the threshold surrounded by angels.

THE SPANISH HOUR

(L'Heure Espagnole)

Opera in one act by Maurice Ravel. Text by Franc Nohain. First produced in Paris in 1911. Place, Toledo. Time, 18th Century.

Cast: Torquemada, an absent-minded clockmaker. Concepcion, his wife. Ramiro, a muleteer. Gonzalve, her lover. Inigo, a banker. A gallant.

The scene is laid in Torquemada's shop. Since this is his day to regulate the public clocks, he asks Ramiro who arrives to have his watch fixed, to await his return. Concepcion desires to get rid of the waiting Ramiro in order to receive her lover; he, upon his side, is embarrassed in her presence. He offers to carry to her room a heavy clock which her husband said was too heavy for him to lift. While he is gone, Gonzalve arrives and is hidden in a large grandfather's clock. The muleteer returns and carries Gonzalve in the clock into Concepcion's room. Inigo, a banker and another gallant enter, and Inigo, too, is hidden in a clock. Meanwhile, the prowess of the muleteer so wins Concepcion's admiration, that she begins a flirtation with him. While they are in another room, the husband returns and finds the two rejected philanderers hidden in his clocks. He does not seem to object in the least; and the opera ends in a sparkling quintet.

STRADELLA

An opera in three acts by F. von Flotow.

Cast: Stradella. Bassi. Barbarino. Malvolio. Leonora. Place, Venice and Rome.

Act I. A small piazza overlooking the canal. Stradella, a famous singer, falls in love with Leonora, whose guardian, Bassi, wishes to marry her. He comes to woo her in his gondola, and tries to persuade her to escape with him; but she insists she is too carefully guarded to attempt it. Then a band of carnival masqueraders appear and with their assistance the lovers are able to flee.

Act II and Act III.   Stradella's house near Rome. Stradella and Leonora are about to be married; and Stradella spends his time singing and making love to her. Bassi has sent two cut-throats, Barbarino and Malvolio, after them to murder Stradella; but they are so charmed by his songs that they refuse to perform their mission. Even Bassi when he arrives is conquered by the wonder of his music, and all ends happily.

THE TEMPLE DANCER

Opera in one act by John Adam Hugo. Text in English by Jutta Bell-Ranske. First produced at the Metropolitan Opera House, March 12, 1919.

Cast: Temple Dancer—Soprano. Guard—Tenor. Yoga —Bass. Priests.

The leading dancer of the Temple of Mahadeo, which is supported by selling the beauty of its dancers to passers-by, falls in love with a youth not of her faith. After a ceremony in the Temple, she pleads for a sign from the god as to what she shall do, and as she receives none, she threatens the temple. The temple guard, returning, hears her, and threatens to kill her. She begs to be allowed to do a dance-prayer before the god, before being slain, and with a snake wound around her, so fascinates the temple-guard that he promises to protect her. In a love-scene between them, she drops a letter telling of her plan to steal the jewels of the god. He determines to torture her. She begs for water; and when he gives it to her poisons it and cajoles the guard into drinking it. As he falls dead at her feet, she curses the temple. A thunder-storm comes as if in answer; and a bolt of lightning strikes her dead as she attempts to grasp the jewels.

ZAZÀ

A lyric comedy in four acts. Music and text by Ruggiero Leoncavallo, after the play by P. Berton and Ch. Simon. First produced in Milan, 1900.

CAST: Zazà. Anaide, her mother. Floriana, Concert Hall singer. Natalia, Zazà's maid. Mme. Dufresne. Milio Dufresne. Cascart, Concert Hall singer. Bussy, journalist. Marlardot, proprietor of a Concert Hall. Lartigon, monologist. Duclou, stage managre. Michelin, journalist, habitue of the Concert Hall. Marco, butler in Dufresne's house. Totò. Singers, Dancers, Scene Shifters, Firemen, Property men, etc. Place, Paris. Time, present.

ACT I. Zazà, a Music Hall favourite, favours most among her many admirers Milio Dufresne, who is apparently indifferent to her. She makes a wager with Bussy, who has written a Musical Review for her, that she can overcome his coldness; and she finally succeeds.

ACT II. Zazà falls deeply in love with Dufresne, and he spends most of his time with her. He is called away on business and she goes to the station to see him off. Meanwhile her mother and her singing partner Cascart, who disapprove of her infatuation, plan to bring it to naught. When Zazà returns, Cascart tells her that he has seen Dufresne in Paris with another woman. Thinking it is another sweetheart, she, at once jealous, follows him to Paris.

ACT IV. Dufresne is leaving to return to Zazà, and his wife has accompanied him to the station when Zazà and her maid arrive at his home. The butler mistaking them for some one whom Mme. Dufresne expects, admits them and Zazà discovers that Dufresne is married and meets his little child. Though she had intended to betray to his wife her relations with him, the meeting with the child makes her depart without creating a scene, or divulging their relations.

Act V. Zazà comes home broken-hearted, though she still has a faint hope that Dufresne's love for her is genuine. Dufresne returns and tries to continue the old deception; but she tells him that she has seen Totò. He is furious, and she tells him in retaliating anger that she told his wife everything. Then, when she finds that his love for his wife is real, and his attraction toward her has been merely a passing fancy, she relents, tells him the truth, and sends him back to his family.

ALKESTIS

A choral drama by Rutland Boughton. English Rhyming Verse by Gilbert Murray from Euripides. First produced August 22, 1922, at Glastonbury by the Glastonbury Players. Then by British National Opera Co. at Covent Garden, January 11, 1924.

Cast. Admetus, King of Pherae—Tenor; Alkestis, his wife—Contralto; Pheres, his father—Bass; First Child —Soprano; Second Child—Soprano; The Handmaid— Soprano; Youth—Soprano; Chief Citizen—Tenor; The God Apollo—Tenor; The Hero Herakles—Baritone; Thanatos (Death)—Bass. Chorus of Elders of Pherae, etc.

Scene. Outside the ancient Castle of Admetus near Pherae, in Thessaly.

Admetus, King of Pherae, in Thessaly, had obtained from the Gods as a special gift that, when his time came to die, he might live if someone who loved him would die in his stead. When the time came, his own parents refused to die for him, but his wife, Alkestis, offered herself and died.

Just after the funeral, the hero Hercules, on his wander-

ings through Thessaly, came to Admetus's house asking
hospitality. Admetus, already bitterly ashamed of his
selfishness, determined at least to be true to the Laws of
Hospitality. So he concealed his wife's death, and entertained Hercules. Hercules discovered the truth from a
slave, whom he found weeping for his mistress, and
amazed at the sacrifice which Alkestis had made for her
husband, went forth into the night to wrestle with Death
for the life of Alkestis.

In due course Hercules returned, bringing with him an
unknown woman, deeply shrouded and unable to speak.
He compelled the heart-broken Admetus, against his will,
to take the unknown woman into his house, and, lifting
her veil, revealed Alkestis returned from the dead.

COUNT BLUEBEARD'S CASTLE

Opera in one act, by Béla Bartók. Hungarian text by
Béla Balázs.

CAST: Count Bluebeard—Baritone; Judith—Mezzo-
soprano; The Other Wives.

SCENE: A Hall in Bluebeard's Castle.

A Bard first appears and cries to the spirits to begin
their story. Bluebeard's Hall is then revealed, a dark
rocky cave filled with gloom. Bluebeard and Judith are
conversing. Judith freely consents to leave her family
and follow him forever; for she is deeply in love with
Bluebeard, who has a most attractive personality. He
tests her strength of will; but she tells him that if he
sends her away she will lie forever on his doorstep. He
now closes the door. It becomes gradually lighter and
now seven large doors are revealed leading out of the
room. He asks Judith if she knows the curse on his
stronghold. It is no wonder that no light ever shines
through and that it is always silence in the Castle. She

examines the place and cries to him to open the seven
doors and finally demands that they shall be opened. He
knocks on one and she is affrighted by the sighs which
echo and re-echo; but still she asks for the key, and
caresses him in order to obtain it. A door opens slightly
and a blood-red streak appears. She sees chains and
implements. Bluebeard tells her it is his torture chamber,
and asks if she is afraid. Judith shudders but answers
"No." She tells him that already the sun has come in
and all the doors shall open and the wind shall enter the
place. She says she will do this because she loves him.
She opens the second door. Another streak of light joins
the first. She sees a thousand terrible things. He tells
her that it is his armoury. Still she is unafraid. In the
third door are seen jewels. Judith is now stained with
the blood-red light. The fourth door shows flower gardens
but only adds to the sinister light. The fifth reveals
wide landscapes—still washed in gory light; the sixth
has naught but a pool of silent, dead waters. "Tears
they are, Judith," he tells her. A long and passionate
scene follows when Judith begs for the key of the seventh
door which reveals his other wives. "See all my earlier
wives," Bluebeard says, "they are still living." The wives
pass proudly before her, pallid visions, but splendid in
their regal robes. Judith declares she is but as a beggar
beside them, and is still willing to be his. Bluebeard
fetches crown, mantle and jewels and puts them on her.
As he places a sombre cloak on her, she shrinks and cries
and at last breaks down and follows the other wives
through the seventh door. The light has gradually disappeared and Bluebeard cries out that with him it remains
night forever and disappears from view.

HUGH THE DROVER

Or Love in the Stocks

A romantic ballad-opera in two acts, by R. Vaughan
Williams. Words by Harold Child. First produced at
Royal College of Music, London, July 4, 1924; then by
the British National Opera Co., at His Majesty's Theatre,
London, on July 14, 1924.

Cast: (In order of entrance) A Cheap Jack—Bari-
tone; A Shell-Fish Seller—Bass; A Primrose Seller—
Contralto; A Showman—High Baritone; A Ballad Seller
—Tenor; Susan—Soprana; Nancy—Contralto; Wil-
liam—Tenor; Robert—Bass; Mary (the Constable's
daughter)—Soprano; Aunt Jane (the Constable's sister)
—Contralto; The Turnkey—Tenor; The Constable—
Bass; John the Butcher—Bass Baritone; A Fool, a
member of the chorus—Baritone; Hugh the Drover—
Tenor; An Innkeeper, (a member of the chorus)—Bass;
A Sergeant—High Baritone; Chorus: Inhabitants of the
town, Toy-lamb sellers, Primrose sellers, Village Boys,
Soldiers. Non-singing Characters: Stall-keepers, Showman's troupe, Bugler, Drummer.

Place: A small town in the Cotswolds. Period:
Early years of the nineteenth century (about 1812).
Time: Act I., about 11 a.m. on Monday, April 30th.
Act II., 4 a.m. on Tuesday, May 1st.

Act I. A fair in an open field near the town. Stalls
and booths with sellers and buyers. A party of men and
women enters and gathers round a showman. Susan,
Nancy, William and Robert crowd round a ballad-singer,
looking at his ballads. He sings one, "On Tuesday morning the bells they shall ring." At the end of it, Mary
bursts into tears. Her father, the Constable, enters and
asks for the reason of the tears—Hasn't he, like a good
father, picked her a fine fellow for a husband in John
the butcher? John, who is the village bully, asks whether

he is not good enough. Let them show her a richer and a stronger man in all the town. But Mary refuses to take his arm. The entry of the Morris-men makes a diversion. At length, Aunt Jane and Mary are left on the stage by themselves. Mary confesses she does not love the butcher. Hugh the Drover, wandering in, overhears the end of the conversation. He sings a song to the linnet, and then another about his own wild business. Mary falls under his spell; but their love-making is broken into by the return of Aunt Jane who has brought Mary's father to stop these goings-on. The Showman's return, followed by a crowd of holiday-makers, eager for a show-fight, affords the Drover the opportunity of a fight with John the Butcher, for a prize of twenty pounds. The Drover, taunted with poverty, produces a bag of fifty pounds as his pledge. When the Butcher says it is to be a fight to the death, the Drover declares the stake too low, and says he will fight John for the prize of Mary, his bethrothed. The ring is arranged and Hugh and John have a sparring match on the stage. The fight is stopped once by a foul blow. At last, John falls and is counted out. The Drover has won. Mary goes to Hugh; but John presently brings the Constable back and charges Hugh with being in Napoleon's pay as a spy. Hugh is surrounded and put in the stocks.

ACT II. The market place in the town. It is dark (4 a.m.). Lights shine from the windows of the inn, where singing is heard. Hugh is sitting in the stocks motionless. John wanders across drunk and insults Hugh, striking him. Mary comes out of the Constable's house secretly; she has obtained the key of the stocks. Hugh is free, but they dally with love-making, and the Constable is heard calling for his boots and raising the town. Hugh gets back into the stocks again. Mary crouches beside him. The cloak covers them both. They say the spy has escaped but they find him safe in the stocks. The villagers are sent back to bed. The Turn-

key sleeps. Hugh and Mary begin to creep away quietly.
Horns are heard; people are coming. Back the two go
to the stocks. This time, Mary puts her feet in too; but
she has dropped a shoe and cannot find it. Dawn is
approaching. The May Song is heard, and a procession
enters, singing and greeting May Day. John batters on
Jane's window, calling for Mary, whose disappearance is
now discovered. A commotion ensues and Mary's shoe
is found. It is not long before they notice the four feet
in the stocks and Mary herself is discovered. She refuses
to leave Hugh. The Constable, her father, then disowns
her, and tells the butcher he can have the drab, but not
a penny will he give with her. John abandons his claim.
There is a fight between the supporters of John and those
of Hugh. John is dragged to the stocks. A bugle and
drum are heard. A sergeant and a small company of
soldiers enter to arrest the spy. The sergeant, however,
recognizes in Hugh his friend and boon companion, a loyal
servant to the King. However, he insists on some prize,
and so claims John the Butcher and takes him away for
the army. So the Drover gets his bride, at last, with her
father's blessing.

THE IMMORTAL HOUR

Music drama by Rutland Boughton. Libretto adapted
from the play of William Sharp (Fiona Macleod). First
produced in August, 1914, at Glastonbury, England.

CAST: Dalua, a shadow-god—Baritone; Etain, a lost
faery maiden—Soprano; Eochaidh, King of Ireland—
Baritone; A Spirit Voice—Mezzo-Soprano; Manus, a
peasant—Bass; Maive, his wife—Contralto; Midir, a
prince of faery—Tenor; An Old Bard—Bass. Choruses
of Tree Spirits, Faeries, Druids, Warriors and Court
Women.

Act I.   Dalua, the Shadow that lies behind Life, is derided in the woods by ghostly voices.   The tree-spirits
dance amongst the trees, mocking at him.   To him comes
Etain, a girl of the faery-folk, who is lost and has forgotten all but her name in her wanderings; and later there
comes the dreamer, Eochaidh, King of Ireland.   The
scene changes to the peasant hut of Manus and Maive.
Etain has sheltered there from the storm.   Eochaidh follows in search of his heart's desire.   It seems as though
he might find it, but the call of the faery-folk lingers in
Etain's mind.

Act II.   A festival in honor of the completed year of
Etain's marriage with Eochaidh.   Both are oppressed, in
different ways, by a presentiment of unearthly happen-
ings.   Eochaidh has been visited by strange dreams.
Etain withdraws in a strange manner.   A stranger, Midir,
a prince of the faery-folk enters, and asks a boon of the
King, who accedes it without knowing what it is he grants.
Midir sings of legends of love, and demands as his boon
that he may kiss Etain's hand.   Etain reappears, and
hearing Midir's song of "the lordly ones who dwell in the
hills," she falls under his spell, and, deaf to the pleadings
of Eochaidh, she follows Midir, as in a trance, back to
the Land of Heart's Desire.   Dalua (who represents
Oblivion) enters, and at his touch, Eochaidh falls to the
ground lifeless.

NERO ("NERONE")

Tragedy in four acts.   Music and text by Arrigo Boïto.
Left unfinished at his death in 1918.   Completed and first
produced under Arturo Toscanini, May 1, 1924, at La
Scala, Milan.

Cast: Nerone—Tenor; Simon Magus, Nero's agent—
Baritone; Fanuel, leader of the Christians—Baritone;

Asteria, a snake-charmer—Soprano; Rubria, a Vestal
Virgin—Mezzo-Soprano; Tigellino—Bass; Dositeo—
Baritone; Perside—Soprano; Cerinto—Contralto; Il
Tempiere—Tenor; Primo Viandante—Tenor; Secondo
Viandante—Baritone; Lo Schiavo Ammonitore—Baritone; Terpnos—Announcer. Groups of Ambibarii,
Gaditanean girls, Augustinian cavalry, trumpeters, free-
men, charioteers of the Green faction and of the Blue
faction, the mob, slaves, senators, a company of Dionysian
actors, three companies of the foreign legion, priests,
matrons, students, pretorians, Christians. Non-singing
parts: A Spanish girl, the Arcigallo, an idol-seller, a
flamen, the successful charioteer, a gladiator-trainer,
zither-players, sistrum-players, merchants, etc.

Act I. On the Appian Way near Rome. Nero has
foully murdered his mother Agrippina. Simon Magus
(the agent of Nero's terrible cruelties) is digging the
grave for her ashes. Suddenly a wild cry of "Nero,
matricide" rings out, and Nero rushes on in terror, hug-
ging the cinerary urn under his toga. Urged by Simon
to carry out the funeral expiatory rites, he is about to
comply, when there arises from one of the tombs a figure
which Nero takes to be one of the Eumenides. It is really
Asteria, but he flies before the accusing apparition.
Rubria, a Vestal Virgin, converted to Christianity, enters
and makes her prayers among the tombs. Simon begs
Fanuel, the Christian leader, to reveal to him the secret
of his divine power, and uses both persuasion and menace
to wring it from him. The crowd comes to fetch Nero
back in triumph to Rome. Banishing his terror, he
mounts the triumphal car and drives in gorgeous procession toward the city.

Act II. In the Temple of the sorcerer. Simon Magus
arranges his obscene rites, and uses Asteria to impose on
Nero, who discovers the fraud, and breaks down altar and
shrine in ungovernable rage. He even flings a burning

torch into the mouth of the oracle, and calls on his Pretorian guards to wreck the temple.

Act III. The Christians conduct their simple worship in an olive orchard on the Pincian Hill, near Rome. Fanuel, their leader, is betrayed and condemned to death in the Arena.

Act IV. Part of the city near the Maximillian Arena. Chariots pass across the stage. Crowds of Roman people and strange Orientals fill the city and throng round the Emperor. One of the many street incidents is a dance by an Oriental girl to double-flute and castanets. A string of Christians is led to martyrdom in the arena. But the holiday-making is turned into dire confusion by the outbreak of the Great Fire. Flames burst out from the Amphitheatre. The populace fly hither and thither.

The second scene is in the crypt beneath. Fanuel searches for Rubria, who has paid the price of her effort to save the Christians. He finds her, still breathing, amongst the falling ruins. The opera ends with her farewell message, as she dies in the Christian faith.

THE PERFECT FOOL

Opera in one act, by Gustav Holst. Libretto by the composer. First produced May 14, 1923, by the British National Opera Co., at Covent Garden.

Cast: The Fool—Speaking Part; His Mother—Contralto; The Wizard—Baritone, also speaks; The Princess —Soprano; The Troubadour—Tenor; The Traveller— Bass; A Peasant—Speaking Part; Three Girls— Soprano; The Troubadour's Retainers—Bass. Chorus of Courtiers and Subjects of the Princess. Ballet of Spirits of Earth, Spirits of Water, and Spirits of Fire.

It is night. The Wizard is performing a magic rite. He calls upon the Spirits of the Earth to bring him a

cup for working magic. Then he invokes the Spirits of
Water to bring the sweetest essence of Love. Finally, he
calls up the Spirits of Fire. The spell cast, the Wizard
settles down to sleep. The Mother enters dragging The
Fool after her. She utters mysteriously the prophecy
made at his birth.

He wins a bride with the glance of his eye.
With a look he kills a foe.
He achieves where others fail,
With one word.

The Fool sleeps. The Wizard wakens and curses. He
tells the Mother about the potion which he has not yet
drunk; and also about the Princess he will woo, about
whom there is a legend.

She shall marry the man, who does
The deed no other can do.

He is sanguine. As the dawn advances, the Mother
strives to hide her half-witted son. The Wizard rehearses
his Wooing Song on the Mother; but she does not play
the Princess's part well enough, and so he settles down
to sleep, telling the Mother to wake him when the Princess
comes. Maidens enter bearing pitchers. The Mother
cunningly snatches up the Wizard's magic cup and holding her son's head back by the hair, pours the potion
down his throat. She refills the cup with water. The
Princess enters, heralded by trumpeters and followed by
her suite who sing her wedding-day song. The Wizard
wakes in a hurry, drinks from the cup, and offers himself
as husband to the Prinecss. Greeted with derision, he
rushes away angrily to summon fresh magic for the
destruction of these scoffers.

A Troubadour enters, with a group of retainers, who
group themselves stiffly round him, while he sings an air
in the donizetti style. He breaks down on the top-notes
and is helped out by the Princess. She dismisses him,
telling him to learn to sing better. A third suiter enters
in the form of a traveller, accompanied by Wotan-like

(Wagnerian) themes on the orchestra. He also is unsuccessful; in a general frenzy, he stumbles over The Fool and awakens him. Gazing ahead, the Fool's glance falls straight on the Princess. The spell of the potion works. The Princess loves him.

Presently, news comes that the Wizard and his fiery imps are devastating the country, but the Mother induces the Fool to hold his ground and so he fulfils the second part of the prophecy. This danger averted, the Fool succeeds in resisting the Princess's charms, for when she asks him the question, "Do you love me?" he answers her with one word, "No"—the only word which comes from him throughout the whole work. Then, just as he is about to be crowned, he falls asleep again.

THE DEAD CITY

Music by Erich Wolfgang Korngold; libretto by Paul Schott. First produced simultaneously at Hamburg and Cologne, Dec. 4th, 1920. CAST. Marietta (soprano); Brigitta (contralto); Paul (tenor); Frank (baritone).

The Dead City is Bruges, and the story is taken from Georges Rodenbach's novel "Bruges la morte." Time, end of nineteenth century. Paul cherishes the memory of his dead wife, by living a secluded life. Amongst a troupe of actors which visits the city there is a dancer, Mariette, with so marvelous a likeness to his lost love that he fancies he sees his wife reincarnated, and gives her his affection. He invites Mariette to visit him, and her song on the discarded lute convinces him of his wife's return. But disillusionment awaits him. In Act I Paul dreams that Mariette is casting a spell over him and then mocking at his fidelity to his dead wife's memory. Finally Paul can stand Mariette's trials and taunts no longer, and angered

beyond measure he attempts to strangle her. This climax
puts an end to his vision and Mariette enters, just as he
awakens. But he no longer responds to her smiles, for
he knows now that the dead do not return. A friend
arrives and he goes out with him to face the battle of life
again.

KITESH

An opera in 4 acts by N. Rimsky-Korsakof. Text by
W. I. Bielsky. First produced in St. Petersburg in 1907.
Revived by Albert Coates in Madrid 1926. Performed
under Coates in concert version, Covent Garden, London,
for the British Broadcasting Company in 1926. CAST:—
Fevronia, soprano; Sirin, soprano; A Youth, Otrok,
mezzo-soprano; Alkonost, contralto; Grisha, tenor;
Prince Vsevolod, tenor; Bear-leader, tenor; Poyarok,
baritone; Bedyai, Tartar Chief, bass; Burundai, Tartar
Chief, bass; King Yury, bass; A Dulcimer-player, bass;
Chorus of Hunstmen, Warriors, Townsfolk, Tartars and
Angels.

Act I. In the Forest. The maid Fevronia was brought
up piously in the solitude of a deep forest by a wandering
monk in the worship of God and Mother Earth. A
young man, when hunting, discovered her and secured
her promise of marriage, without revealing his identity.
She learns later that he is none other than the Prince
Vsevolod, son of King Yury and joint-ruler of the Sacred
City of Great Kitesh and its domains. Act II. The
bridal procession, winding its way through Little Kitesh,
is interrupted by the derision and curses of the village
drunkard Grisha, but the bride addresses him kindly. A
more serious interruption takes place when a horde of
Tartars suddenly sweeps into the village, slaying hundreds
of the people and carrying off Fevronia alive. Grisha,

the drunkard, is also taken and made to act as the Tartars' guide to Great Kitesh.

Act III is in the Sacred City with all the inhabitants assembled before the Cathedral, the saintly King Yury standing at the summit of the steps in the Great Doorway. Comes to him his Chief Huntsman, who tells him how he has been blinded by the cruel enemy, and how Fevronia has turned traitor and is leading the enemy hither. The old king exhorts the people to prayer; whereupon a great miracle happens. A lovely golden mist descends, covers the great city and carries it up to Paradise, leaving only a great flaming cross of light to mark the place where once the city stood. In the second scene of Act III, the Tartars are camped by the side of a lake and the two Chiefs are fighting for the possession of the captive, Fevronia. Grisha the drunkard hears the Bells of Great Kitesh, and the sounds work on his conscience so much, that he confesses to Fevronia how he has played her false. She forgives him. He rushes away to the vanished city, dragging Fevronia off with him through the forest.

Act IV, Scene I. In the Forest, there is a weird scene of dancing goblins and devils. Fevronia has sunk down tired out, and her companion witnesses the magic dance with terror. Suddenly, however, flowers of Paradise spring up all round the maiden and birds of Paradise sing of eternal bliss. The Spirit of the Prince, her betrothed, approaches her and leads her gently into the Sacred City; and in the Final Scene, in the Heavenly City itself, King Yury and his people are seen welcoming the Prince and his Bride.

PALESTRINA

Music and words by Hans Pfitzner. Written at Strasburg between 1912 and 1915. Produced in Munich 1919.

This opera contains no female rôles at all. The book is a free treatment of the well-known story of how Palestrina the great composer is supposed to have saved Church music from wholesale condemnation at the Council of Trent.

Act I finds Palestrina in great despair at the death of his wife. Cardinal Borromeo comes to tell him how the Council of Trent are about to forbid all music but plainsong, on account of the insincerity of the florid style of *a cappella* music in vogue. The Cardinal tries in vain to induce Palestrina to write such a Mass as will turn the minds of the Council and prove to them that sincerity and idealism are compatible with the contrapuntal style. The Cardinal leaves disappointed; but soon Palestrina is visited by the spirits of nine departed composers who persuade him again to take up his pen. Angels appear, first one by one, and then in hosts, singing passages from Palestrina's since-famous Mass of Pope Marcello. Palestrina writes it down as it were from their dictation.

Act II represents the Council of Trent in sitting, with the Archbishop in the chair. The scene is a satire on the futility of such Councils and an exposure of the materialism which prevails at such gatherings. The Bishop of Budoja is facetious over the musical questions, and the name of Palestrina is too much for the venerable Patriarch of Abysinnia who stumbles over it. An adjournment is soon made for refreshment. The servants quarrel and soldiers are sent in to clear the chamber.

Act III takes us back to Palestrina's house in Rome. The new Mass has been shown to the Pope who comes in person to give the composer his blessing. Cardinal Borromeo is reconciled to Palestrina, and the opera ends with the composer playing his chamber-organ whilst the crowds outside hail him as the saviour of Church music.

TURANDOT

BY GIACOMO PUCCINI. LIBRETTO BY RENATO SIMONI AND
GUISEPPE ADAMI

The opera was left unfinished by Puccini at his death,
and completed by Franco Alfano. First performed at
La Scala, Milan, April 25th, 1926.

CAST:—Turandot (soprano); Liu (soprano); Calaf
(tenor); Ping (baritone).

The story is founded on one of the theatrical fables of
Carlo Gozzi, the well-known eighteenth-century playwright
of Venice, the rival of Goldini. It is a story of a Chinese
Princess whose hand is to be given to the suitor who
solves three riddles put to him, failure to be punished by
death. Three unlucky wooers have already been put to
death by the cruel Princess, when Calif comes and guesses
all three answers successfully. But his generous nature
refuses to take the prize on such terms, and he declares
he will follow the other suitors to the block if the Princess
can guess his name. His father and a loving hand-maiden
come seeking him, and are tortured unsuccessfully by the
Princess's command in order to extort the youth's name.
However, his generosity does not lead to a tragic end;
for his wooing melts the ice in the Princess's heart and
she surrenders to him, who chose the word "Love" for
his name.

THE WOMAN WITHOUT A SHADOW

Music by Richard Strauss, book by Hugo von Hofmann-
sthal. First produced at Vienna in 1919.

CAST:—Princess, soprano; Barak's Wife, mezzo;
Nurse, contralto; Barak, baritone; his brother, bass.

A symbolical fairy-story. Act I. A fairy Princess
married to an Eastern Emperor finds herself a stranger

to both fairy and mortal worlds. She has no shadow; she is childless. It is decreed by the spirit-world that if she cannot find a shadow, the Emperor will turn into stone. The Princess's Nurse takes her disguised to the house of a poor dyer, Barak, who has just married a young wife and longs for children of his own. The Nurse tempts the dyer's poor wife to part with her "shadow," the endowment of possible children, in return for gold and jewels. Barak returns home to find his wife refusing his caresses, and the room is surrounded by the wailing of their unborn children.

Act II shews us the Empress and the Nurse, both still disguised, continuing their temptation of the poor dyer's wife. The Nurse calls up the phantom of a handsome youth who attracts the dyer's wife. The Emperor's heart, we learn, has already become stone. The poor distraught woman confesses to her husband Barak, more than she has really committed. He and her brothers find to their horror that she now casts no shadow. Barak seizes a sword to kill his wife; but the remorseful Empress cries out now that she will not have the shadow. The house collapses and a river flows in from the back, separating Barak and his wife, the Empress escaping in a boat.

Act III. Scene I. Barak and his wife are enclosed in separate caverns; but a spirit-messenger sends them searching for one another.

Scene 2. A flight of steps, leading up to a temple. A river at the foot. A boat comes carrying the Empress who lands and walks up the steps to her judgment. The voices of Barak and his wife are constantly heard, searching for one another.

Scene 3. The interior of the temple. The Empress stands before a fountain, behind which is a curtain. Mysterious voices bid her drink of the water and so obtain the shadow of Barak's wife. But she cannot bring herself to do it. The curtain becomes transparent and she sees through it the Emperor now nearly congealed into stone. She will not however gain her happiness at the cost of the peace of others. The Emperor completely turns to stone; the Princess cries out "I will not drink" and a sudden shaft of light shews her that at last she has a shadow. The spirit-world has rewarded her unselfishness.